Mathematics of Computational Finance

Mathematics of Computational Finance

Andrzej Palczewski
University of Warsaw, Poland

World Scientific

NEW JERSEY • LONDON • SINGAPORE • BEIJING • SHANGHAI • HONG KONG • TAIPEI • CHENNAI • TOKYO

Published by

World Scientific Publishing Co. Pte. Ltd.

5 Toh Tuck Link, Singapore 596224

USA office: 27 Warren Street, Suite 401-402, Hackensack, NJ 07601

UK office: 57 Shelton Street, Covent Garden, London WC2H 9HE

Library of Congress Control Number: 2025020925

British Library Cataloguing-in-Publication Data
A catalogue record for this book is available from the British Library.

MATHEMATICS OF COMPUTATIONAL FINANCE

ISBN 978-981-98-1511-1 (hardcover)
ISBN 978-981-98-1577-7 (paperback)
ISBN 978-981-98-1512-8 (ebook for institutions)
ISBN 978-981-98-1513-5 (ebook for individuals)

For any available supplementary material, please visit
https://www.worldscientific.com/worldscibooks/10.1142/14365#t=suppl

Desk Editors: Nambirajan Karuppiah/Angeline Husni

Typeset by Stallion Press
Email: enquiries@stallionpress.com

Preface

The goal of this book is to provide a relatively short (but sufficiently rigorous and hopefully readable) account of basic numerical methods used in pricing derivative financial products — one of the essential problems of financial mathematics. Rigorous pricing methods started in the 1970s with the celebrated Black–Scholes model (also called the Black–Scholes–Merton model) and became the basis for the pricing of thousands of complex financial products. Many excellent books deal with the numerical implementations of these pricing methods. However, the majority is only focused on the numerical algorithms used in pricing. This book originated from a course given to mathematics students at the University of Warsaw. This audience obliged the lecturer to speak not only about algorithms but also about the mathematical foundations behind these algorithms: convergence, stability, and error estimates. The main body of the text concentrates on theoretical material. Numerous examples illustrate the introduced theoretical concepts using simple financial models. In contrast to this theoretical analysis, the problem sections at the end of each chapter are very practical. The exercises at the end of each chapter deal with many more advanced financial models and numerical algorithms applied to them. Some problems analyze the theoretical aspects of the described algorithms, but many require computer implementations and analysis of the obtained results. Several exercises extend the material of the corresponding chapter by presenting additional (less frequently used) algorithms or supplementary material. It can be said that the main body of the book teaches the reader how to analyze numerical algorithms, and the problem sections serve to improve their computational skills.

In writing this book, I assumed that the reader possesses a broad knowledge of continuous finance and its mathematical models. Thus, there are no introductory chapters on quantitative finance. The introductory material in some chapters establishes the terminology used in the book and cannot be treated by the reader as a source of knowledge on quantitative finance. All the described numerical methods begin with a presentation of the analytical problem described as a system of stochastic or partial differential equations without discussing their financial motivation. The described numerical methods are quite general, and the experienced reader can recognize that they cover not only the Black–Scholes model but also some advanced local and stochastic volatility models. On the other hand, the reader whose acquaintance with quantitative finance is limited to the Black–Scholes model can ignore the multidimensional approach because the results are also valid for simple models.

The fundamental principle of numerical analysis is that one can compute only solutions that do exist. Following this principle, I have included in the book theorems that guarantee the existence (and possibly uniqueness) of solutions to equations that are the subject of subsequent numerical analysis. This goal is easy to achieve for financial models formulated in probabilistic terms (random variables, stochastic processes, stochastic differential equations) because they are standard tools used in continuous finance. In addition, the most advanced result I use is the existence and properties of solutions for the stochastic differential equation of the Itô type, the results belonging to the usual prerequisites for any course of quantitative finance. The situation is completely different for financial models described by partial differential equations (PDEs). First, a course in PDE theory is rarely required as a prerequisite for financial courses. Second, to formulate a theorem on the existence of solutions for a PDE model, we need advanced tools: weak derivatives, Sobolev's spaces, weak solutions, etc. Therefore, I have decided to give a thorough introduction to PDEs together with the Feynman–Kac theorem, which gives a rigorous passage from the stochastic to the PDE formulation of financial models. Finally, presenting proofs of existence for PDEs has some didactic aspects, as these proofs are, in many cases, prototypes for the design of numerical methods and their proofs of convergence.

Hence, before passing to operations with multiple indices of a numerical algorithm, the reader can see the proof idea in a clean Banach's space formulation.

Since the book is written mainly for students of mathematics or mathematically oriented students of economics or natural sciences who study quantitative finance for academic or professional purposes, the presentation is quite advanced, taking for granted a broad knowledge of analysis, probability, and statistics with some orientation in stochastic processes. The entire presentation is restricted to pricing derivative instruments in a financial model described by the Itô SDE and the corresponding parabolic PDE. This simplification makes it easier to achieve the main goal of presenting complete proofs. These complete proofs are compilations from many sources, sometimes with my original additions. References to these sources in the body of the text are rather limited. They usually indicate the paper or book that inspired my writing and/or give the reader a broader account of the discussed topic. Of course, I could not succeed in writing the proofs of all the theorems. There are many theorems without proof. For such theorems, I usually quote the reference in which the proof can be found. Essentially, I omit proofs that do not belong to the area of numerical analysis, and the reason for skipping them is twofold: first, some proofs belong to the field of mathematics, which is very distant from the topic of the book, and presenting them will require a significant amount of auxiliary material (this is particularly the case of the chapter on American options); second, some proofs need advanced tools far beyond the knowledge that I can expect from the reader. In some places, I have made a compromise by just quoting a result necessary in the proof without mentioning where such a result comes from. The theorems are formulated in full generality with possibly weak assumptions. However, the presented proofs are written for the most elementary cases: one-dimensional, with constant coefficients, smooth data, etc. The reason for such an approach is purely didactic: I intend to present to the reader the main idea that remains behind the proof, which can be lost in multiple indices, splittings into subdomains, smoothing of data and coefficients, etc., required for the proof of the sharp version.

The interest of this book lies in the computation of derivative prices. Because financial models rely on stochastic differential equations, applying Monte Carlo methods to derivative pricing is very natural. Similarly, tree methods are very intuitive and fast. Applying the Feynman–Kac theorem, we can replace probabilistic methods of derivative pricing with solutions of partial differential equations, which gives rise to a large class of numerical methods for PDEs. All of these computational approaches are described in the book. However, the presentation is far from complete. After all, this is just a textbook and not a monograph, and the author has selected the most popular methods and algorithms for presentation. Of course, the selection is biased by the author's experience in computational finance. The algorithms and methods of this book have been practically tested by myself and my students during many years of teaching computational finance. The experienced reader can ask why the book is limited to models in which randomness is described by Wiener processes and there are no models with jumps and Lévy processes. The reasons are numerous. One of these is that including Lévy processes will require writing a thorough monograph instead of a medium-sized textbook. Such a monograph is beyond the aspirations of the author.

The book is organized as follows. After the introductory Chapter 1, in which binomial and trinomial trees are presented, Chapter 2 addresses the generation of pseudo-random numbers. This chapter explains how samples from a given distribution can be generated using pseudo-random numbers. Algorithms for generating normal deviates receive particular attention in this chapter. Chapter 3 begins with crude Monte Carlo. Then the variance reduction technique is presented. The chapter concludes with the computation of Greeks, i.e., the sensitivities of prices to model parameters. In Chapter 4, numerical solutions of stochastic differential equations are discussed with proofs of convergence for the Euler and Milstein schemes and error estimates. A large part of the book is devoted to numerical solutions of partial differential equations that arise in finance. As an introduction to the topic, Chapter 5 collects fundamental facts from the theory of weak solutions of PDEs in Sobolev's spaces. Chapter 6 focuses on finite difference methods for partial differential equations of the parabolic type. The most popular finite difference schemes are described, and their accuracy (order of approximation) and stability are proved. Finite element methods are discussed in Chapter 7 for both elliptic and parabolic problems. This chapter proves that finite element approximations converge to the corresponding solutions of differential problems. Chapter 8 is devoted to American options. Both Monte Carlo and PDE methods of pricing are presented. The Monte Carlo approach is limited to the description of the well-known algorithm of Longstaff and Schwartz. Then a careful analysis of its convergence is provided. In the final part of this chapter, the variational approach to pricing American options is discussed. After a short introduction to variational inequalities related to American options, the presentation focuses on two popular numerical methods: the projected SOR and the penalty method. For both of these methods, the proofs of stability and convergence are given. As I have mentioned before, this book originated from a course in computational finance. However, the scope of the book is too broad to fit into a single course. A reasonable selection of material from Chapters 2–6 can be lectured in one course. On the other hand, the chapter on American options, supplemented by more information on optimal stopping problems and variational inequalities in continuous time, can be sufficient for a special course.

I would like to express my gratitude to several people who have influenced my writing of this book. I owe a particular debt to Piotr Kowalczyk, with whom I have been lecturing computational finance to several cohorts of students at the University of Warsaw. I gained much from my colleagues in the Department of Mathematics at the University of Warsaw, whose broad knowledge and competence helped me navigate the corners of this project. I would also like to acknowledge the students who, during the courses given in the past years, have helped to improve the quality of the book through their questions, comments, and feedback. Finally, many thanks to my wife Iwona and son Jan for their encouragement and support, and to Iwona for her tolerance and patience in allowing me to complete the project.

About the Author

Andrzej Palczewski is currently a Professor Emeritus at the University of Warsaw. He earned his MS from the Chemistry Department of the University of Warsaw and his Ph.D. and Habilitation doctorate from the Mathematics Department of the University of Warsaw. In 1993, he was awarded the title of professor by the President of the Polish Republic. From 1968 to 1970, he was a staff member of the Institute of Nuclear Research, and from 1973 to 1975, he was at the Institute of Mathematics, Warsaw Technical University. In 1975, he moved to the University of Warsaw, where he was employed until 2018 as a Professor of Mathematics.

Professor Palczewski's current research interests are primarily in the mathematical modeling of financial markets, with an emphasis on the computational aspects of the considered models. For a long time, his research concentrated on problems related to equations in mathematical physics, including quantum mechanics, statistical physics, and fluid mechanics. He has authored over 60 research papers and many educational articles, co-authored two monographs, and authored two textbooks.

Professor Palczewski was Deputy Dean of the Faculty of Mathematics, Informatics and Mechanics at the University of Warsaw from 1984 to 1986, and he served as Director of the Institute of Applied

Mathematics and Mechanics at the University of Warsaw from 1993 to 1999. He was a member of the editorial boards of several mathematical journals, a member of the Council of the European Consortium for Mathematics in Industry from 1998 to 2008, and from 2011 to 2017, the head of the IFIP TC 7 Working Group "Modeling and Simulation".

Contents

Chapter 1

Introduction

1.1 Financial Market

This book deals with computational finance problems with a focus on the analysis of numerical algorithms for pricing financial derivatives. There are two broad groups of numerical methods for derivative pricing: stochastic methods using random simulations and deterministic methods based on numerical solutions to partial differential equations of the Kolmogorov type. We cover both approaches in this book, emphasizing the mathematical backgrounds of the discussed algorithms.

We begin this chapter by reviewing basic information about the mathematical models of financial markets. This is a collection of definitions and facts. The purpose of this introductory part is to establish the terminology used in the book, and it cannot be considered a survey of mathematical modeling in finance. Readers interested in deeper insights into the mathematical modeling of financial markets should consult books by Eberlein and Kallsen [24], Hull [40], Jeanblanc, Yor and Chesney [45], Karatzas and Shreve [49], Lamberton and Lapeyre [55], Shiryaev [81], or Shreve [82].

We consider a financial market in continuous time. When modeling a real market, we typically assume that the *time horizon* is finite. However, the probabilistic model is valid for any time interval. Thus, in this collection of facts and definitions, we assume that time t belongs to an interval $\mathbb{T}$, where $\mathbb{T} = [0, \infty)$ or $\mathbb{T} = [0, T]$ with $T < \infty$. Uncertainty in the market is modeled by a probability space $(\Omega, \mathcal{F}, \mathbb{P})$. The probability space is assumed to be complete: if $B \subset A$

with $A \in \mathcal{F}$ and $\mathbb{P}(A) = 0$, then $B \in \mathcal{F}$. The space $(\Omega, \mathcal{F}, \mathbb{P})$ is equipped with a filtration $\mathbb{F} = (\mathcal{F}_t)_{t \in \mathbb{T}}$, a family of σ-algebras which are monotonic with respect to t: $\mathcal{F}_s \subseteq \mathcal{F}_t \subseteq \mathcal{F}$, for $s \leq t$, satisfying the *usual conditions*: (i) completeness ($\mathcal{F}_0$ contains all sets of $\mathbb{P}$-measure zero) and (ii) right continuity ($\mathcal{F}_t = \mathcal{F}_{t+} = \bigcap_{s>t} \mathcal{F}_s$). The σ-algebra $\mathcal{F}_t$ represents the information available in the market up to time t. In addition, we assume that the σ-field $\mathcal{F}_0$ is trivial, i.e., for every $A \in \mathcal{F}_0$ either $\mathbb{P}(A) = 0$ or $\mathbb{P}(A) = 1$.

Prices of *financial securities* in the market are modeled by stochastic processes in continuous time.

Definition 1.1. A stochastic process $X = (X_t)_{t \in \mathbb{T}}$ is a family of random variables defined on a probability space $(\Omega, \mathcal{F}, \mathbb{P})$ and parameterized by time variable t. Process X is *adapted* to the filtration $\mathbb{F}$ if X_t is $\mathcal{F}_t$-measurable for $t \in \mathbb{T}$. For X, we can define filtration $\mathbb{F}^X = (\mathcal{F}_t^X)_{t \in \mathbb{T}}$, where $\mathcal{F}_t^X$ is a completion of $\sigma(X_s\colon s \leq t)$. This filtration is called the *natural filtration* for X.

Definition 1.2. The following classes of stochastic processes are essential for modeling financial markets:

(1) A process X is a Markov process if $\mathbb{E}\big(f(X_s)|\mathcal{F}_t\big) = \mathbb{E}\big(f(X_s)|X_t\big)$ for any bounded Borel function f and $s \geq t$.
(2) A process X is a martingale if: (i) X is $\mathbb{F}$-adapted; (ii) $\mathbb{E}(|X_t|) < \infty$ for all t; (iii) $\mathbb{E}(X_s|\mathcal{F}_t) = X_t$ for $s \geq t$.
(3) A process X is a submartingale if: (i) X is $\mathbb{F}$-adapted; (ii) $\mathbb{E}(|X_t|) < \infty$ for all t; (iii) $\mathbb{E}(X_s|\mathcal{F}_t) \geq X_t$ for $s \geq t$.
(4) A process X is a supermartingale if: (i) X is $\mathbb{F}$-adapted; (ii) $\mathbb{E}(|X_t|) < \infty$ for all t; (iii) $\mathbb{E}(X_s|\mathcal{F}_t) \leq X_t$ for $s \geq t$.

The most widely used process for describing the uncertainty of financial markets is a *Wiener process* (also called *Brownian motion*).

Definition 1.3. A (*standard, one-dimensional*) *Wiener process* with respect to filtration $\mathbb{F} = (\mathcal{F}_t)_{t \geq 0}$ is a continuous, adapted process $W = (W_t)_{t \geq 0}$ defined on a probability space $(\Omega, \mathcal{F}, \mathbb{P})$, with the following properties: (i) $W_0 = 0$ a.s.; (ii) the increments $W_t - W_s$ are independent of $\mathcal{F}_s$, for $0 \leq s < t$; (iii) the increment $W_t - W_s$ is normally distributed with mean zero and variance $t - s$.

Although the sample paths of a Wiener process are continuous, their behavior is very irregular. The following theorem summarizes the important properties of a Wiener process (for its proof see the book by Karatzas and Shreve [48]).

Theorem 1.4. *Let W be a Wiener process on probability space $(\Omega, \mathcal{F}, \mathbb{P})$ and adapted to filtration $\mathbb{F}$.*

(1) *$\mathbb{P}$-almost all paths of W_t are nowhere differentiable as functions of t.*
(2) *$\mathbb{P}$-almost all paths of W_t have unbounded variation.*
(3) *W is an $\mathbb{F}$-martingale.*

When investing in a financial market, we often decide to close a certain position provided a particular phenomenon occurs. We are then interested in the moment of time $\tau(\omega)$, $\omega \in \Omega$, at which the phenomenon occurs for the first time. Therefore, we are interested in detecting random events $\{\omega\colon\ \tau(\omega) \le t\}$ informing if the phenomenon occurred before time t. These considerations can be formalized in the notion of *stopping time.*

Definition 1.5. Let $(\Omega, \mathcal{F})$ be a measurable space equipped with filtration $(\mathcal{F}_t)_{t\ge 0}$. A random time τ is a *stopping time* of the filtration, if the event $\{\tau \le t\}$ belongs to the σ-field $\mathcal{F}_t$, for every $t \ge 0$.

The following theorem describes the decomposition of supermartingales (of class D) as the difference between a martingale and an increasing process. An analogous result is also valid for submartingales (the difference is replaced by sum). The proof of this theorem can be found in Karatzas and Shreve [48].

Theorem 1.6 (Doob–Meyer Decomposition). *If X_t is a supermartingale of class D, it admits the decomposition*

$$X_t = M_t - A_t,$$

where M_t is a uniformly integrable martingale, and A_t is an integrable, increasing process.

A process X_t is of class D if the family $(X_\tau)_{\tau\in\mathcal{S}}$ is uniformly integrable, where $\mathcal{S}$ is the set of all stopping times such that $\mathbb{P}(\tau < +\infty) = 1$.

The uniform integrability *of a family of random variables $Y = (Y_t)_{t\in I}$ means that*

$$\lim_{K\to\infty} \sup_{t\in I} \mathbb{E}\big(|Y_t| \mathbb{1}_{\{|Y_t|>K\}}\big) = 0.$$

Using the Doob–Meyer decomposition, we can define the *quadratic variation* of a continuous martingale.

Definition 1.7. Let $X = (X_t)_{t\geq 0}$ be a continuous martingale. Let X be *square integrable*, i.e., $\mathbb{E}(X_t^2) < \infty$ for all $t \geq 0$. Then X^2 is a submartingale with the Doob–Meyer decomposition

$$X_t^2 = M_t + A_t,$$

where M is a continuous martingale, and $A = (A_t)_{t\geq 0}$ an increasing process. The process A is called the *quadratic variation* of X and denoted $\langle X\rangle_t = A_t$.

We are now in a position to define a class of stochastic processes that model the prices of financial instruments.

Definition 1.8. A *continuous semimartingale* $X = (X_t)_{t\geq 0}$ in a probability space $(\Omega, \mathcal{F}, \mathbb{P})$ with filtration $\mathbb{F}$ is an adapted process with decomposition

$$X_t = X_0 + M_t + B_t, \quad \mathbb{P}\text{-a.s.}, \quad t \geq 0,$$

where M is a local martingale and B is the difference ($B_t = A_t^+ - A_t^-$) of two continuous, nondecreasing, adapted processes A^+ and A^-.

A continuous process $M = (M_t)_{t\geq 0}$ is a *local martingale* if there exists a sequence of stopping times $(\tau_n)_{n=1}^{\infty}$ such that $X_{t\wedge\tau_n}$ is a martingale for each $n \geq 1$ and $\mathbb{P}(\lim_{n\to\infty} \tau_n = \infty) = 1$.

We now define a mathematical model of a continuous-time financial market in probability space $(\Omega, \mathcal{F}, \mathbb{P})$ with filtration $\mathbb{F}$. We assume a finite time horizon $[0, T]$, $T < \infty$, and consistency of the σ-field $\mathcal{F}$ with filtration: $\mathcal{F}_T = \mathcal{F}$. The market contains $d + 1$ basic traded assets, called *underlying securities*, whose prices are given by stochastic processes $X_t^0, X_t^1, \ldots, X_t^d$ for $t \in [0, T]$. We assume that these processes are adapted to filtration $\mathbb{F}$, positive semimartingales that are right-continuous with left limits. This last property is usually called *càdlàg* (from French “continue à droite avec des limités à gauche”). To account for the time value of money, we introduce a discount process — a *numéraire*.

Definition 1.9. A *numéraire* is a stochastic process X_t almost surely strictly positive for each $t \in [0, T]$.

In the following, we assume that X_t^0 is a nondividend paying asset that is almost surely strictly positive for each $t \in [0, T]$, and we use it as numéraire. We will also use the *discount process* $\beta_t = (X_t^0)^{-1}$.

Remark 1.10. Usually, the money banking account $B_t = e^{\int_0^t r(s)ds}$ with deterministic $r(t)$ (say $r(t) = r$, a constant interest rate) plays the role of numéraire.

If $B(t,T)$ is the value at $t \leq T$ of an asset, called the *zero-coupon bond*, paying one currency unit at time T, then $B(t,T) = e^{-\int_t^T r(s)ds} = B_t B_T^{-1}$.

Hence, the financial market consists of d price processes $X_t = (X_t^1, \ldots, X_t^d)$, which we call risky assets and the numéraire X_t^0, all defined on the probability space $(\Omega, \mathcal{F}, \mathbb{P})$. The dynamics of X_t is given by a system of stochastic differential equations

$$dX_t = b(t, X_t)dt + \sigma(t, X_t)dW_t, \quad X_0 = x, \tag{1.1}$$

where b is a d-dimensional vector, σ a matrix of dimension $d \times m$, and W_t is an m-dimensional Wiener process.

In the components of vector X equation (1.1) reads

$$dX_t^i = b_i(t, X_t)dt + \sum_{j=1}^{m} \sigma_i^j(t, X_t)dW_t^j, \quad X_0^i = x_i, \quad i = 1, \ldots, d.$$

We assume that the coefficients of equation (1.1) fulfill conditions that guarantee the existence and uniqueness of solutions (these conditions are discussed in detail in Chapter 4).

In the above-introduced financial market, we consider the valuation of contingent claims defined by payoffs $g(X_T)$, depending on the value of the underlying securities X_T at expiration time T. Such instruments are called *European contingent claims.* We also analyze computational methods for *American instruments* that give the holder the right (but not the obligation) to buy or sell the underlying at any time $t \in (0, T]$. On a limited scale, we consider instruments with prices that depend on the entire trajectory of the process $(X_t)_{0 \leq t \leq T}$ (*exotic instruments*).

The pricing problem will be analyzed in an idealized market that fulfills the following conditions:

(1) The market is frictionless: there are no transaction costs, no taxes, costs of borrowing and lending are equal, and there are

no liquidity restrictions — all assets are accessible in unlimited quantity.

(2) Market participants are price takers and are rational: they prefer more to less.

(3) The market is arbitrage-free (see Definition 1.11).

To valuate contingent claim $g(X_T)$, we introduce the notion of a *trading strategy.*

Definition 1.11. An $\mathbb{R}^{d+1}$-valued, predictable, left-continuous process

$$\varphi_t = (\varphi_t^0, \varphi_t^1, \dots, \varphi_t^d), \quad t \in [0, T]$$

such that

$$\int_0^T \mathbb{E}(\varphi_t^0)dt < \infty, \quad \sum_{i=1}^d \int_0^T \mathbb{E}(|\varphi_t^i|^2)dt < \infty$$

is called a *trading strategy.* Here, φ_t^i is understood as the number of shares of asset i in the portfolio. (A trading strategy is also called a *portfolio process* and φ itself is often called a *portfolio.*)

Process X_t is predictable ($\mathbb{F}$-predictable) if mapping $(t, \omega) \to X_t(\omega)$ is $\mathcal{P}$-measurable, where $\mathcal{P}$ is the smallest σ-field such that all continuous, $\mathbb{F}$-adapted processes are $\mathcal{P}$-measurable.

The value of the portfolio φ at time t is given by the expression

$$\mathcal{V}_\varphi(t) = \sum_{i=0}^d \varphi_t^i X_t^i, \quad t \in [0, T].$$

The process $\mathcal{V}_\varphi(t)$ is called the *value process* of the trading strategy φ.

The *gain process* $G_\varphi(t)$ is defined as follows

$$G_\varphi(t) = \sum_{i=0}^d \int_0^t \varphi_s^i dX_s^i.$$

A trading strategy φ is called *self-financing* if the wealth process $\mathcal{V}_\varphi(t)$ satisfies the equality

$$\mathcal{V}_\varphi(t) = \mathcal{V}_\varphi(0) + G_\varphi(t), \quad t \in [0, T].$$

The *market is arbitrage-free* if there is no *arbitrage opportunity,* where an arbitrage opportunity is a self-financing trading strategy φ

such that the wealth process $\mathcal{V}_\varphi(t)$ satisfies the conditions

$$\mathcal{V}_\varphi(0) = 0, \quad \mathbb{P}\big(\mathcal{V}_\varphi(T) \geq 0\big) = 1, \quad \mathbb{P}\big(\mathcal{V}_\varphi(T) > 0\big) > 0.$$

Definition 1.12. Assume now that on $(\Omega, \mathcal{F})$ there exists a measure $\mathbb{P}^*$ equivalent to $\mathbb{P}$ such that the discounted price process $\beta_t X_t$ is a $\mathbb{P}^*$-martingale. The measure $\mathbb{P}^*$ is called a strong *martingale measure*, or a *risk-neutral measure*.

A self-financing trading strategy φ is called $\mathbb{P}^*$*-admissible* if the discounted gain process $\beta_t G_\varphi(t)$ is a $\mathbb{P}^*$-martingale.

A contingent claim $g(X_T)$ is called *attainable* if there exists an admissible trading strategy φ such that

$$\mathcal{V}_\varphi(T) = g(X_T).$$

The trading strategy φ is then called a *replicating strategy* for $g(X_T)$.

Because of the no-arbitrage condition, the value of the replicating strategy φ_t defines the price $V(t)$ of the attainable contingent claim $g(X_T)$ at time t

$$V(t) = \mathcal{V}_\varphi(t).$$

For attainable contingent claims, we can use a more convenient pricing method called the *risk-neutral pricing*.

Theorem 1.13. *Assume that on $(\Omega, \mathcal{F})$ there is a risk-neutral measure $\mathbb{P}^*$. The price of the $\mathbb{P}^*$-attainable contingent claim $g(X_T)$ at time $t \in [0, T]$ is*

$$V(t) = \beta_t^{-1} \mathbb{E}^* \big(\beta_T g(X_T) \big| \mathcal{F}_t\big),$$

where $\mathbb{E}^*$ denotes the expectation with respect to $\mathbb{P}^*$.

Remark 1.14. To simplify notation, we assume that the measure $\mathbb{P}$ from the definition of the probability space $(\Omega, \mathcal{F}, \mathbb{P})$ is already a strong martingale measure, and the discount process is constant $\beta_t = 1$. Under these simplifications, valuation is reduced to the computation

$$V(0) = \mathbb{E}\big(g(X_T)\big).$$

In some special cases, we will consider variable β_t — a market *risk-free* discount factor (typically a deterministic function of time).

Remark 1.15. When the strong martingale measure $\mathbb{P}^*$ is unique, the market is called *complete*. Then every contingent claim is attainable, and its price is uniquely defined.

There are many equivalent martingale measures in incomplete markets, and nonattainable contingent claims have no uniquely defined prices. Prices that do not generate arbitrage opportunities usually cover a certain interval. To compute prices in that interval, particularly to find the endpoints of this interval, we can still use the formula from Theorem 1.13. The problem does not exist for attainable contingent claims in an incomplete market. If a claim is attainable in one equivalent martingale measure, it is attainable in all equivalent martingale measures and has the same price under all measures.

Black–Scholes model. The Black–Scholes model is a simple, complete market model. There is only one risky asset in this model with a price process S_t. The discounting process is defined by a banking account with a constant interest rate r. Since the market is complete, there is a unique martingale measure $\mathbb{P}$. The dynamics of asset prices in this martingale measure are given by the one-dimensional equation, which is a special case of equation (1.1)

$$dS_t = rS_t dt + \sigma S_t dW_t,$$

where r and σ are positive constants, and W_t is a standard one-dimensional $\mathbb{P}$-Wiener process.

In this model, the prices of European call and put options with strike K and maturity T are given by the celebrated *Black–Scholes formula*

$$V(t) = \kappa S_t \Phi(\kappa d_1) - \kappa K e^{-r(T-t)} \Phi(\kappa d_2), \tag{1.2}$$

where $\kappa = 1$ corresponds to a call option, $\kappa = -1$, to a put option, and

$$d_1 = \frac{\ln(S_t/K) + (r + \sigma^2/2)(T-t)}{\sigma\sqrt{T-t}}, \quad d_2 = d_1 - \sigma\sqrt{T-t}.$$

In the Black–Scholes model, closed-form formulas exist not only for call and put options and their combinations but also for several types of exotic options: binary options, barrier options, compound options, and others. These closed-form formulas are very useful in computational finance because they serve as benchmarks for numerical algorithms.

Local volatility models: In the Black–Scholes formula, the only unobservable parameter is the volatility σ. Since the formula can be inverted numerically, volatility can be computed from the option prices observed in the market. The volatility computed in this manner is called the *implied volatility*. Under the assumptions of the Black–Scholes model, implied volatility should be a constant function. In reality, we observe the *volatility smile*, a U-shaped function of the strike price K that additionally varies with time to maturity T. The existence of the volatility smile indicates that the assumptions of the Black–Scholes model should be relaxed. The simplest extension of the model is to assume that asset prices follow a one-dimensional diffusion process, however, with a deterministic volatility function depending on asset price and time. Such models are called *local volatility models*, and the price process in these models follows the following dynamics

$$dS_t = b(t, S_t)dt + \sigma(t, S_t)dW_t. \tag{1.3}$$

This equation is a one-dimensional version of equation (1.1) and requires similar assumptions on its coefficients as (1.1) to guarantee the existence of a unique solution. Unfortunately, in several popular local volatility models as the Constant Elasticity of Variance (CEV) model ($\sigma(t, S) = \sigma_0 S^\beta$ with $0 < \beta \leq 1$ and σ_0 a positive constant), quadratic model ($\sigma(t, S) = \sigma_0 S^2$ with σ_0 a positive constant), or "limited" CEV (LCEV) model ($\sigma(t, S) = \sigma_0 S \min(S^{\beta-1}, \varepsilon^{\beta-1})$ with $0 < \beta \leq 1$ and σ_0, ε positive constants), the volatility function does not fulfill standard assumptions, and proof of the existence of solutions to equation (1.3) requires special approach (see Chapter 4 for details).

Stochastic volatility models: Although local volatility models are easy to calibrate to market data and, in many cases, give closed-form expressions for option prices, their dynamics are not realistic. In particular, the dynamics are not time-invariant. To obtain more realistic dynamics, local volatility models were expanded to *stochastic volatility models*. In these models, volatility is assumed to be a stochastic process that is dependent on further exogenous parameters. We consider stochastic volatility models, which are defined as a set of two correlated one-dimensional diffusion processes:

$$\begin{aligned} dS_t &= b(t, S_t)dt + \sigma(Y_t)C(S_t)dW_t^S, \\ dY_t &= m(t, Y_t)dt + \nu(t, Y_t)dW_t^Y, \\ d\langle W^S, W^Y\rangle_t &= \rho dt. \end{aligned} \tag{1.4}$$

Formally, this model does not fit the market model described at the beginning of this section as the volatility process Y_t is not a traded asset. Thus, the market is incomplete, and there is no unique risk-neutral measure. On the other hand, the structure of system (1.4) is the same as equation (1.1) (if necessary after de-correlation of the Wiener processes W^S and W^Y). As a result, a similar numerical technique can be used. However, similarly to local volatility models, there are stochastic volatility models with coefficients that do not fulfill standard assumptions. Proof of the existence of solutions to such models requires individual analysis.

The risk-neutral option pricing described above can be easily approximated using stochastic or deterministic numerical methods. The easiest stochastics are realized by binomial and trinomial trees, which can be considered as stochastic simulations in a probability space with two or three states of the world. The advantage of trees is that they can be easily implemented and, in many cases, provide quite accurate results. The far more popular stochastic method is a Monte Carlo simulation realized on a finite probability space with a huge number of states. Thanks to the Feynman–Kac formula, the search for a solution to a stochastic differential equation similar to equation (1.1) can be reformulated as a solution problem for partial differential equations. This reformulation has an obvious advantage — one replaces the random error in stochastic approximation with the deterministic error in PDE algorithms. In subsequent chapters, we analyze the theoretical and computational aspects of these methods.

1.2 Trees

We begin this section by applying binomial trees to pricing European- and American-style contingent claims written on a single risky asset whose dynamics in a risk-neutral measure is given by the Black–Scholes model

$$dS(t) = rS(t)dt + \sigma S(t)dW_t, \quad S(0) = S_0, \quad 0 \le t \le T. \tag{1.5}$$

We discretize the time interval $[0, T]$ and process $S(t)$ as follows

$$\delta t = \frac{T}{N}, \quad t_n = n\delta t, \quad S_n = S(t_n), \quad n = 0, 1, \ldots, N.$$

The dynamics of S_n is given by the equation

$$S_{n+1} = Z_{n+1} S_n,$$

where Z_n is a sequence of independent random variables that can take for each n only two states (we assume $u > d$)

$$Z_n = \begin{cases} u, & \text{with probability } p, \\ d, & \text{with probability } 1 - p. \end{cases}$$

We assume a constant risk-free interest rate r that gives the money banking account

$$B_n = e^{r\, n\delta t}.$$

This assumption implies the following relation in the risk-neutral measure

$$\mathbb{E}(S_{n+1}|S_n) = e^{r\delta t} S_n. \tag{1.6}$$

The above expression, written in terms of the random variables Z_n, leads to the equation

$$pu + (1 - p)d = e^{r\delta t}$$

which defines the risk-neutral probability

$$p = \frac{e^{r\delta t} - d}{u - d}. \tag{1.7}$$

Condition $0 < p < 1$ is equivalent to

$$d < e^{r\delta t} < u, \tag{1.8}$$

and guarantees the existence of a unique risk-neutral measure for the binomial model. The first few nodes in the binomial tree are shown in Fig. 1.1.

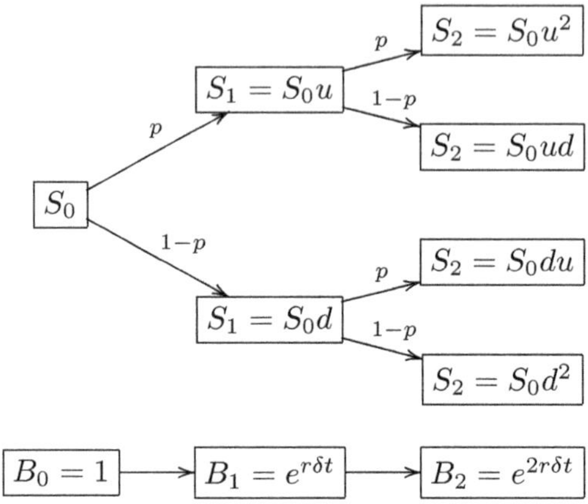

Fig. 1.1. Binomial tree.

The pricing process of a European option with payoff $g(S(T))$ can be described by the following steps:

(1) Fix the input parameters: u, d, r, T, and the number of time steps N.
(2) Compute the risk-neutral probability p.
(3) Compute the payoff $g(S)$ for each node in period N.
(4) For each n, starting from $N-1$ to 0, compute the payoff in each node using formula (1.6), the payoffs of the previous step, and the value of p.
(5) The value at the root of the tree is the option price.

The above algorithm has a very large computational complexity because the number of nodes increases exponentially with the number of time steps. This algorithm can only be run with a small number of time steps, which can result in inaccurate pricing. To reduce computational complexity, we limit the algorithm to the so-called *recombining binomial trees*, where we glue identical nodes into one node. A recombining binomial tree is shown in Fig. 1.2.

Recombining trees can be used to compute the prices of European and American contingent claims, however, not for pricing path-dependent(exotic) instruments.

Let $S_{j,n}$ denote the price after n time steps, where j is the number of up moves. Since we deal with a recombining tree, we obtain

$$S_{j,n} = S_0 u^j d^{n-j}.$$

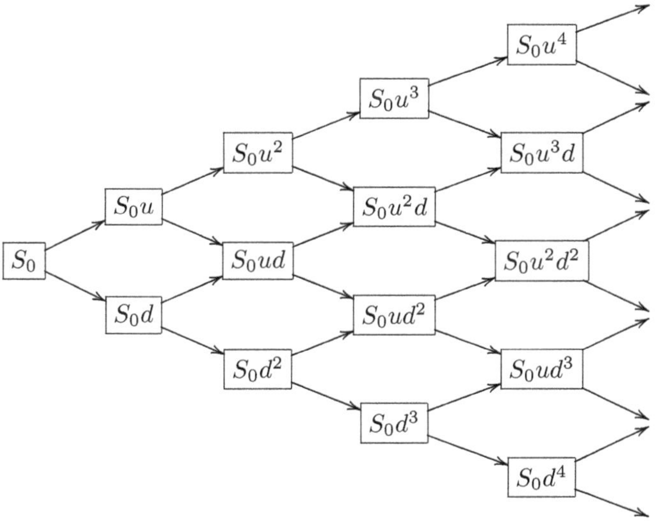

Fig. 1.2. Recombining binomial tree.

In the risk-neutral measure, we have

$$S_{j,n} = e^{-r\delta t}\left(pS_{j+1,n+1} + (1-p)S_{j,n+1}\right).$$

For a European option with payoff function $g(S(t))$, the price is obtained from the iterative computations of the option price at each node in the tree as follows:

$$\begin{aligned} V_{j,N} &= g(S_{j,N}), \quad j = 0, 1, \ldots, N, \\ V_{j,n} &= e^{-r\delta t}\left(pV_{j+1,n+1} + (1-p)V_{j,n+1}\right), \quad n < N. \end{aligned}$$

The procedure is more complicated for American options. First, we compute the option value in each node as the discounted prices at higher nodes (similarly to a European option). Then the option value is compared with the option payoff at this node, and the decision is made whether to exercise the option (choose the payoff) or continue the option (choose the option value). Hence, the price of an American option can be obtained from the sequence of iterations as follows:

$$\begin{aligned} V_{j,N} &= g(S_{j,N}), \quad j = 0, 1, \ldots, N, \\ V_{j,n} &= \max\left(g(S_{j,n}), e^{-r\delta t}\left(pV_{j+1,n+1} + (1-p)V_{j,n+1}\right)\right), \quad n < N. \end{aligned}$$

To use this algorithm in practical computations, we must calibrate the model to the market. Parameters r and S_0 are observed in the market. Parameters u and d are model idealizations that cannot be directly determined by the observation of the market data. We now turn to the Black–Scholes model (1.5) in which we know asset prices

$$S(t) = S_0 e^{(r-\sigma^2/2)t+\sigma W_t}, \quad S_0 > 0.$$

Hence, the expected value of $S(t+\delta t)$ conditional on $S(t)$ is

$$\mathbb{E}\big(S(t+\delta t)|S(t)\big) = S(t)e^{r\delta t},$$

and the conditional variance

$$\mathrm{Var}\big(S(t+\delta t)|S(t)\big) = S(t)^2 e^{2r\delta t}\left(e^{\sigma^2\delta t} - 1\right).$$

In the binomial tree the corresponding values are as follows:

$$\begin{aligned}\mathbb{E}\big(S(t+\delta t)|S(t)\big) &= S(t)\big(pu + (1-p)d\big),\\ \mathrm{Var}\big(S(t+\delta t)|S(t)\big) &= \mathbb{E}\big(S^2(t+\delta t)|S(t)\big) - \big(\mathbb{E}\big(S(t+\delta t)|S(t)\big)\big)^2\\ &= p(S(t)u)^2 + (1-p)(S(t)d)^2\\ &\quad - \big(S(t)\big)^2\big(pu + (1-p)d\big)^2.\end{aligned}$$

Comparing the right-hand sides of the relevant equations, we get

$$\begin{aligned}&S(t)\big(pu + (1-p)d\big) = S(t)e^{r\delta t},\\ &p(S(t)u)^2 + (1-p)(S(t)d)^2 - \big(S(t)\big)^2\big(pu + (1-p)d\big)^2\\ &\quad = \big(S(t)\big)^2 e^{2r\delta t}\left(e^{\sigma^2\delta t} - 1\right).\end{aligned}$$

After simplifications, we have

$$\begin{aligned}pu + (1-p)d &= e^{r\delta t},\\ pu^2 + (1-p)d^2 &= e^{2r\delta t+\sigma^2\delta t}.\end{aligned} \tag{1.9}$$

The first equation (1.9) gives the known expression of the risk-neutral probability

$$p = \frac{e^{r\delta t} - d}{u - d},$$

the second equation is not sufficient to compute parameters u and d. We need an additional relation. The choice of this relation gives rise to different binomial models. Here are some examples:

- the Cox–Ross–Rubinstein model (CRR) [18] in which we set $ud = 1$; this model is the industry standard,
- the Jarrow–Rudd model [44] in which $p = (1 - p) = 1/2$.

However, many other possibilities can be used in practice.

We will analyze more carefully the Cox–Ross–Rubinstein model.

Theorem 1.16. *Consider the CRR model for fixed N with arbitrary u and d fulfilling conditions* (1.8) *and $ud = 1$, with p given by formula* (1.7). *The price at time $t_n = n\delta t$ of a European call option with maturity T and strike K is*

$$V_N(t_n) = e^{-r(N-n)\delta t} \sum_{j=0}^{N-n} \binom{N-n}{j} p^j (1-p)^{N-n-j} \times \left(S(t_n) u^j d^{N-n-j} - K\right)^+,$$

where the subscript N indicates the price computed in the model with N time steps.

Proof. Since $S(t_n) = S_0 \prod_{j=1}^{n} Z_j$, then using Theorem 1.13, we obtain

$$\begin{aligned}
V_N(t_n) &= e^{-r(T-t_n)} \mathbb{E}\left((S_T - K)^+ | \mathcal{F}_{t_n}\right) \\
&= e^{-r(T-t_n)} \mathbb{E}\left(\left(S(t_n) \prod_{j=n+1}^{N} Z_j - K\right)^+ \middle| \mathcal{F}_{t_n}\right) \\
&= e^{-r(T-t_n)} \mathbb{E}\left(\left(S(t_n) \prod_{j=n+1}^{N} Z_j - K\right)^+\right) \\
&= e^{-r(N-n)\delta t} \sum_{j=0}^{N-n} \binom{N-n}{j} p^j (1-p)^{N-n-j} \\
&\quad \times \left(S(t_n) u^j d^{N-n-j} - K\right)^+.
\end{aligned}$$

The above equalities follow from: (i) the independence of Z_j of $\mathcal{F}_{t_n}$ for $j > n$, (ii) the $\mathcal{F}_{t_n}$-measurability of $S(t_n)$, and (iii) the nonnegativity of $(x-K)^+$. $\square$

Calibrating u and d in the Cox–Ross–Rubinstein model to the Black–Scholes model, we obtain

$$u = \beta + \sqrt{\beta^2 - 1},$$
$$d = \beta - \sqrt{\beta^2 - 1},$$

where

$$\beta = \frac{1}{2}\left(e^{-r\delta t} + e^{(r+\sigma^2)\delta t}\right).$$

In practice, there is a tendency to use the simplified version of the CRR model

$$u = e^{\sigma\sqrt{\delta t}}, \quad d = e^{-\sigma\sqrt{\delta t}}.$$

The simulations for the full and simplified models are close to each other for large N due to the convergence of the CRR model to the Black–Scholes model.

Theorem 1.17. *Consider a sequence of CRR models starting from the same S_0 with N increasing to infinity. Let $\delta_N = \frac{T}{N}$. Define*

$$u_N = e^{\sigma\sqrt{\delta_N}}, \quad d_N = e^{-\sigma\sqrt{\delta_N}}, \quad p_N = \frac{e^{r\delta_N} - e^{-\sigma\sqrt{\delta_N}}}{e^{\sigma\sqrt{\delta_N}} - e^{-\sigma\sqrt{\delta_N}}}.$$

Let $V_N(0)$ denote the price at time $t = 0$ of a European call option with maturity T, strike K, and parameters u_N, d_N, and p_N defined above.

If $V_{BS}(t)$ denotes the Black–Scholes price of that option at time t, then

$$\lim_{N\to\infty} V_N(0) = V_{BS}(0).$$

Proof. Let $S_n^N = S(n\delta_N)$ denote the asset prices in the model for fixed N. Denote $Z_n^N = \frac{S_n^N}{S_{n-1}^N}$, then

$$S_n^N = S_0 \prod_{j=1}^{n} Z_j^N.$$

Since $\mathbb{P}(Z_j^N = u_N) = p_N$, $\mathbb{P}(Z_j^N = d_N) = 1 - p_N$, and $N\delta_N = T$, we obtain

$$S_N^N = S^N(T) = S_0 \exp\left(\sigma\sqrt{\delta_N}\sum_{j=1}^{N} R_j^N\right),$$

where $R_j^N = \frac{\ln Z_j^N}{\sigma\sqrt{\delta_N}}$.

R_j^N are independent (because Z_j^N are independent) and with the identical distribution

$$\mathbb{P}(R_j^N = 1) = p_N, \quad \mathbb{P}(R_j^N = -1) = 1 - p_N, \text{ for } j = 1, \ldots, N.$$

Expanding p_N into Taylor's series, we obtain

$$p_N = \frac{1}{2} + \frac{r - \sigma^2/2}{2\sigma}\sqrt{\delta_N} + O(N^{-1}).$$

Then for each j

$$\mathbb{E}\left(\sigma\sqrt{\delta_N}R_j^N\right) = \left(r - \sigma^2/2\right)\frac{T}{N} + o(N^{-1})$$

and

$$\mathrm{Var}\left(\sigma\sqrt{\delta_N}R_j^N\right) = \sigma^2\frac{T}{N} + o(N^{-1}).$$

Hence, by the central limit theorem, we obtain

$$\sigma\sqrt{\frac{T}{N}}\sum_{j=1}^{N} R_j^N \to \mathcal{N}\big((r - \sigma^2/2)T, \sigma^2 T\big) \text{ in distribution as } N \to \infty$$

and

$$S^N(T) \to S_0 \exp\big((r - \sigma^2/2)T + \sigma\sqrt{T}Z\big) \text{ in distribution as } N \to \infty,$$

where $Z \sim \mathcal{N}(0, 1)$.

Since

$$V_N(0) = e^{-rT}\mathbb{E}\big((S^N(T) - K)^+\big),$$

$V_N(0)$ converges to

$$V(0) = e^{-rT}\mathbb{E}\left(\left(S_0 \exp\left((r-\sigma^2/2)T + \sigma\sqrt{T}Z\right) - K\right)^+\right)$$
$$= \frac{1}{\sqrt{2\pi}}\int_{-\infty}^{\infty}\left(S_0 \exp\left(-\sigma^2 T/2 + \sigma\sqrt{T}x\right) - e^{-rT}K\right)^+ e^{-x^2/2}dx.$$

Let

$$\gamma = \frac{\ln(K/S_0) + (\sigma^2/2 - r)T}{\sigma\sqrt{T}}.$$

The integrand is nonzero only in the interval (γ, ∞) since

$$\sigma\sqrt{T}x - \sigma^2 T/2 > \ln(K/S_0) - rT$$

only in this interval. Then we have

$$V(0) = \frac{1}{\sqrt{2\pi}}S_0\int_{\gamma}^{\infty} e^{-\sigma^2 T/2}e^{\sigma\sqrt{T}x - x^2/2}dx - Ke^{-rT}\big(1-\Phi(\gamma)\big)$$
$$= \frac{1}{\sqrt{2\pi}}S_0\int_{\gamma}^{\infty} e^{-1/2(x-\sigma\sqrt{T})^2}dx - Ke^{-rT}\big(1-\Phi(\gamma)\big)$$
$$= S_0\big(1-\Phi(\gamma-\sigma\sqrt{T})\big) - Ke^{-rT}\big(1-\Phi(\gamma)\big),$$

where Φ is the cumulative distribution function of a standard normal distribution.

By symmetry $\big(1-\Phi(\gamma)\big) = \Phi(-\gamma)$, we obtain

$$-\gamma + \sigma\sqrt{T} = \frac{\ln(S_0/K) + (r + \sigma^2/2)T}{\sigma\sqrt{T}} \equiv d_+,$$
$$-\gamma = \frac{\ln(S_0/K) + (r - \sigma^2/2)T}{\sigma\sqrt{T}} \equiv d_-.$$

Hence,

$$V(0) = S_0\Phi(d_+) - e^{-rT}K\Phi(d_-)$$

which is the Black–Scholes formula for call options. □

In the Jarrow–Rudd model, we have

$$u = e^{r\delta t}\left(1 + \sqrt{e^{\sigma^2\delta t} - 1}\right),$$

$$d = e^{r\delta t}\left(1 - \sqrt{e^{\sigma^2\delta t} - 1}\right).$$

The following simplified version of these parameters is frequently used:

$$u = e^{(r-\sigma^2/2)\delta t + \sigma\sqrt{\delta t}},$$

$$d = e^{(r-\sigma^2/2)\delta t - \sigma\sqrt{\delta t}}.$$

For a general binomial model, we can assume without loss of generality

$$ud = e^{2\nu\delta t},$$

for a scalar parameter ν. This leads to the simplified version of parameters u and d (the exact expressions are very complicated):

$$u = e^{\nu\delta t + \sigma\sqrt{\delta t}},$$

$$d = e^{\nu\delta t - \sigma\sqrt{\delta t}},$$

$$p = \frac{1}{2} + \frac{1}{2}\left(\frac{\mu - \nu}{\sigma}\right)\sqrt{\delta t}, \quad \text{where } \mu = r - \sigma^2/2.$$

The value $\nu = 0$ corresponds to the CRR model (the tree is symmetric). Choosing $\nu = \mu$ we obtain the Jarrow–Rudd model (there is a deterministic drift $e^{\mu\delta t}$).

Binomial models are the simplest lattice models used in financial computations. However, trees with a larger number of states are also in use. We present an implementation of trinomial trees. We assume, as for binomial trees, that

$$S_{n+1} = Z_{n+1}S_n.$$

For trinomial trees, Z_n is a sequence of independent random variables which, for each n, take three states

$$Z_n = \begin{cases} u, & \text{with probability } p_u, \\ m, & \text{with probability } p_m, \\ d, & \text{with probability } p_d. \end{cases}$$

Our goal is to find p_u, p_m, and p_d, which define a risk-neutral measure. Here, we have the obvious condition $p_u + p_m + p_d = 1$. In addition, to obtain a recombining tree, we require $ud = m^2$, where we assume $u > m > d$. Computing $\mathbb{E}(S_{n+1}|S_n)$ in risk-neutral measure, we obtain

$$p_u u + p_m m + p_d d = e^{r\delta t}.$$

The above three equations are not sufficient to uniquely determine a risk-neutral measure. Hence, there are many risk-neutral measures for trinomial trees, and the market is incomplete. This means that not all contingent claims can be uniquely priced in this model. (Note the difference with binomial models where risk-neutral measure is uniquely defined by (1.7) independently from the model specification.)

The calibration process for trinomial trees is similar to the process for binomial trees. The comparison of conditional expectations and variances between the trinomial model and the Black–Scholes model gives

$$\begin{aligned} p_u u + p_m m + p_d d &= e^{r\delta t}, \\ p_u u^2 + p_m m^2 + p_d d^2 &= e^{(2r+\sigma^2)\delta t}. \end{aligned} \tag{1.10}$$

Together with equations $p_u + p_m + p_d = 1$ and $ud = m^2$ we have four equations for six unknowns. To make the problem solvable, we assume

$$Z_n = \begin{cases} e^{\mu\delta t + \lambda\sigma\sqrt{\delta t}}, & \text{with probability } p_u, \\ e^{\mu\delta t}, & \text{with probability } p_m, \\ e^{\mu\delta t - \lambda\sigma\sqrt{\delta t}}, & \text{with probability } p_d. \end{cases}$$

Computing u, m, and d by this approximation and inserting $p_m = 1 - p_u - p_d$ in (1.10), we obtain

$$\begin{aligned} p_u(U-1) + p_d(D-1) &= F - 1, \\ p_u(U^2-1) + p_d(D^2-1) &= H - 1, \end{aligned}$$

where $U = e^{\lambda\sigma\sqrt{\delta t}}$, $D = e^{-\lambda\sigma\sqrt{\delta t}}$, $F = e^{(r-\mu)\delta t}$ and $H = e^{(2r+\sigma^2-2\mu)\delta t}$. Solving the above equations yields

$$
\begin{aligned}
p_u &= \frac{H - (D+1)F + D}{(U-D)(U-1)}, \\
p_m &= \frac{-H + (U+D)F - UD}{(1-D)(U-1)}, \\
p_d &= \frac{H - (U+1)F + U}{(U-D)(1-D)}.
\end{aligned}
\tag{1.11}
$$

This model has a built-in deterministic drift $e^{\mu\delta t}$. To obtain a symmetric trinomial tree, we assume $\mu = 0$. The symmetric model with

$$
Z_n = \begin{cases} e^{\lambda\sigma\sqrt{\delta t}}, & \text{with probability } p_u, \\ 1, & \text{with probability } p_m, \\ e^{-\lambda\sigma\sqrt{\delta t}}, & \text{with probability } p_d. \end{cases}
\tag{1.12}
$$

can be considered a trinomial version of the CRR model. Expanding all terms in equations (1.11) in power series of $\sqrt{\delta t}$ we obtain, after tedious computations, the following expressions in the first-order approximation

$$
\begin{aligned}
p_u &= \frac{1}{2\lambda^2} + \frac{(r - \sigma^2/2)\sqrt{\delta t}}{2\lambda\sigma}, \\
p_m &= 1 - \frac{1}{\lambda^2}, \\
p_d &= \frac{1}{2\lambda^2} - \frac{(r - \sigma^2/2)\sqrt{\delta t}}{2\lambda\sigma}.
\end{aligned}
\tag{1.13}
$$

Kamrad and Ritchken [47] have obtained a similar result under the additional assumptions that $\mathbb{E}(\ln Z_n) = (r - \sigma^2/2)\delta t$ and $\operatorname{Var}(\ln Z_n) = \sigma^2\delta t$ which corresponds to a discrete version of Black Scholes. These assumptions greatly simplify the computation, giving the following match of the first two moments of $\ln Z_n$

$$
\begin{aligned}
\lambda\sigma\sqrt{\delta t}(p_u - p_d) &= (r - \sigma^2/2)\delta t, \\
\lambda^2\sigma^2\delta t(p_u + p_d) &= \sigma^2\delta t.
\end{aligned}
$$

Solving that system of equations, we obtain (1.13) as exact solutions.

Thus, for the symmetric trinomial tree, we know the model parameters as functions of λ. Let us note that to obtain nonnegative probabilities, we must take $\lambda \geq 1$. On the other hand, there is the stability problem of the model. $\lambda = 1$ is on the edge of the stability region. To obtain a stable model, we must choose λ substantially greater than 1. The choice of λ influences the rate of convergence of model prices to Black–Scholes prices. Kamrad and Ritchken demonstrated that the value of λ that produces the best convergence rate is

$$\lambda = \sqrt{3/2}.$$

1.3 Implied Trees

It is clear from market observations that the prices of the underlying asset do not exactly follow the model of Black and Scholes, with prices given by a geometric Brownian motion. In this model, all options for a single underlying must have the same Black–Scholes implied volatility, whereas volatility implied by market prices demonstrates a volatility smile. There are various proposed extensions of the Black–Scholes model to account for the volatility smile. One such extension mentioned in this chapter is a local volatility model. On the level of binomial trees, local volatility models correspond to so-called *implied volatility trees* or just *implied trees.*

Here, we present implied trees by Derman and Kani [21], and later the modifications proposed by Barle and Cakici [6]. These models assume that stock prices are generated by a modified random walk, where the underlying asset has variable volatility that depends on both stock price and time. The model uses observed market option prices to estimate implied volatilities.

We recursively build an implied tree from a node at time level 0 to a node at time level N. At each time step, nodes and their corresponding transition probabilities are chosen in such a way that a European call/put option is priced consistently with the market, and the expected stock price is equal to its forward price. Assume that the tree is already constructed up to the nth time step. Since only two time levels n and $(n+1)$ are considered, we apply the simplified notation denoting by s_i stock prices $S_{i,n}$ at level n, S_j stock prices $S_{j,n+1}$ at level $(n+1)$, and F_i the forward price of $S_{i,n}$ at level $(n+1)$. The probability that stock price s_i at level n will increase to S_{i+1} at level $(n+1)$ is denoted by p_i, whereas the probability that stock price will decrease to S_i at level $(n+1)$ is given by $1 - p_i$. The forward price of s_i at lattice level $(n+1)$ is given by $F_i = s_i \exp(r\delta t)$, where we assume a constant risk-free interest rate r and a constant distance δt between subsequent time levels. To assure risk neutrality in the tree, the forward price must satisfy the following condition

$$F_i = p_i S_{i+1} + (1 - p_i) S_i, \quad i = 0, 1 \ldots, n. \tag{1.14}$$

Let $C(K, t_{n+1})$ and $P(K, t_{n+1})$ be the time t_0 prices of European call and put options on a stock with initial price S_0, strike K and maturity t_{n+1} corresponding to lattice level $(n+1)$. These prices can be obtained from known market prices. On the other hand, these prices can also be computed by the Black–Scholes formula using the binomial lattice values. For the call option, we have the following formula

$$C(K, t_{n+1}) = \sum_{i=0}^{n+1} \lambda_{n+1,i} \max(S_i - K, 0),$$

where $\lambda_{n+1,i}$ is the *Arrow–Debreu price* at node i of the $(n+1)$th time level.

The concept of Arrow–Debreu securities (and Arrow–Debreu prices as prices of these securities) is the building block for analyzing economic equilibrium under uncertainty. In this approach, the price of a financial security is equal to the expected net present value of its future payoffs calculated under an equivalent martingale measure. The Arrow–Debreu price at a lattice node is the value of a security that pays a unit of currency if the stock price reaches that node and zero otherwise. The value of $\lambda_{n,i}$ corresponding to node i at time level n is computed as the sum, over all paths from the root (time level 0) to node i at time level n, of the product of the discounted transition probabilities along each path connecting these nodes. An efficient method of calculating the Arrow–Debreu prices is an iterative method in which prices at level $(n+1)$ are computed from the known Arrow–Debreu prices at level n. Assuming $\lambda_{0,0} = 1$, the Arrow–Debreu prices are given by

$$\lambda_{n+1,i} = e^{-r\delta t} \begin{cases} (1 - p_0)\lambda_{n,0}, & \text{for } i = 0, \\ p_{i-1}\lambda_{n,i-1} + (1 - p_i)\lambda_{n,i}, & \text{for } 1 \le i \le n, \\ p_n \lambda_{n,n}, & \text{for } i = n + 1. \end{cases} \tag{1.15}$$

In Derman and Kani approach the strike K in $C(K, t_{n+1})$ and $P(K, t_{n+1})$ is taken equal to s_i. Using (1.15), we obtain

$$\begin{aligned} C(s_i, t_{n+1}) &= \sum_{j=0}^{n+1} \lambda_{n+1,j} \max(S_j - s_i, 0) \\ &= e^{-r\delta t} \sum_{j=0}^{n} \lambda_{n,j} \big(p_j \max(S_{j+1} - s_i, 0) + (1 - p_j) \max(S_j - s_i, 0)\big). \end{aligned}$$

Because $S_j \le s_i$ for $j \le i$, only terms with $j > i$ differ from zero in the above sum. For $j = i$, only $\max(S_{i+1} - s_i, 0)$ differs from zero because $S_{i+1} > s_i$. Then the above expression can be rewritten as

$$\begin{aligned} C(s_i, t_{n+1}) = e^{-r\delta t} \Bigg(& \lambda_{n,i} p_i (S_{i+1} - s_i) \\ & + \sum_{j=i+1}^{n} \lambda_{n,j} \big(p_j (S_{j+1} - s_i) + (1 - p_j)(S_j - s_i)\big) \Bigg). \end{aligned}$$

Subtracting s_i from both sides of equation (1.14)

$$F_j - s_i = p_j (S_{j+1} - s_i) + (1 - p_j)(S_j - s_i),$$

and inserting this identity into the formula for $C(s_i, t_{n+1})$, we obtain

$$C(s_i, t_{n+1}) = e^{-r\delta t} \left(p_i \lambda_{n,i} (S_{i+1} - s_i) + \sum_{j=i+1}^{n} \lambda_{n,j} (F_j - s_i) \right). \tag{1.16}$$

Equation (1.14) can also be used to find the transition probabilities

$$p_i = \frac{F_i - S_i}{S_{i+1} - S_i}. \tag{1.17}$$

Inserting this expression into equation (1.16), we find

$$S_{i+1} = \frac{S_i \delta C_i - \lambda_{n,i} s_i (F_i - S_i)}{\delta C_i - \lambda_{n,i}(F_i - S_i)}, \tag{1.18}$$

where

$$\delta C_i = e^{r\delta t} C(s_i, t_{n+1}) - \sum_{j=i+1}^{n} \lambda_{n,j}(F_j - s_i).$$

Expressions (1.18) and (1.17) can now be used to find stock prices and the corresponding transition probabilities above the center of the tree for time level $(n+1)$. Similarly, prices and transition probabilities below the center of the tree can be derived using put options instead of call options. The formula for transition probabilities is unchanged, and the formula for stock prices is as follows

$$S_i = \frac{S_{i+1} \delta P_i + \lambda_{n,i} s_i (F_i - S_{i+1})}{\delta P_i + \lambda_{n,i}(F_i - S_{i+1})}, \tag{1.19}$$

with

$$\delta P_i = e^{r\delta t} P(s_i, t_{n+1}) - \sum_{j=0}^{i-1} \lambda_{n,j}(s_i - F_j).$$

Here, the summation is performed only over nodes below node i.

To apply formulas (1.18) and (1.19) and find the entire set of prices and probabilities at time level $(n+1)$, we must know the value of S_i at the center of this level. When $(n+1)$ is even, then there is the middle node $(n+1)/2$ (nodes are numbered from 0 to $n+1$) and $S_{(n+1)/2} = S$, where $S = S_{0,0}$ is the stock price at the central node of the lattice. When $(n+1)$ is odd (thus n is even), there are two central nodes at time level $(n+1)$. Derman and Kani chose these two central stock prices to satisfy

$$S_{1+n/2} S_{n/2} = s_{n/2}^2, \tag{1.20}$$

which corresponds to the logarithmic CRR centering condition. From this relation, we obtain

$$S_{1+n/2} = \frac{s_{n/2}\delta C_{n/2} + \lambda_{n,n/2}s_{n/2}^2}{\lambda_{n,n/2}F_{n/2} - \delta C_{n/2}}, \tag{1.21}$$

and $S_{n/2} = s_{n/2}^2/S_{1+n/2}$.

To guarantee nonnegative values for transition probabilities p_i, the following relation must hold

$$F_i \leq S_{i+1} \leq F_{i+1}.$$

In the Derman–Kani model, the violation of the above relation is possible, and negative probabilities can occur. The authors suggest in their paper how to replace bad probabilities with "good" values. However, a better result can be obtained by applying the method proposed by Barle and Cakici.

Barle and Cakici retain the formula (1.17) for transition probabilities but postulated using forward price F_i as strike price K in the computation of option prices $C(K, t_{n+1})$ and $P(K, t_{n+1})$. This leads to a change in the formula for S_{i+1} in the upper part of the lattice, namely

$$S_{i+1} = \frac{S_i\delta C_i - \lambda_{n,i}F_i\big(F_i - S_i\big)}{\delta C_i - \lambda_{n,i}\big(F_i - S_i\big)}, \tag{1.22}$$

where

$$\delta C_i = e^{r\delta t}C(F_i, t_{n+1}) - \sum_{j=i+1}^{n} \lambda_{n,j}\big(F_j - F_i\big).$$

Changes in the S_i formula in the lower part of the lattice are analogous

$$S_i = \frac{S_{i+1}\delta P_i + \lambda_{n,i}F_i\big(F_i - S_{i+1}\big)}{\delta P_i + \lambda_{n,i}\big(F_i - S_{i+1}\big)}, \tag{1.23}$$

where

$$\delta P_i = e^{r\delta t}P(F_i, t_{n+1}) - \sum_{j=0}^{i-1} \lambda_{n,j}\big(F_i - F_j\big).$$

The second modification proposed by Barle and Cakici involves a new method for computing values for the central node(s)

$$\begin{aligned} S_{(n+1)/2} &= e^{rt_{n+1}} S_{0,0}, \quad \text{for } n+1 \text{ even}, \\ S_{n/2} S_{1+n/2} &= F_{n/2}^2, \quad \text{for } n+1 \text{ odd}. \end{aligned} \tag{1.24}$$

Then Barle and Cakici set

$$S_{1+n/2} = \frac{F_{n/2}\delta C_{n/2} + \lambda_{n,n/2} F_{n/2}^2}{\lambda_{n,n/2} F_{n/2} - \delta C_{n/2}}, \tag{1.25}$$

and $S_{n/2} = F_{n/2}^2 / S_{1+n/2}$.

If Barle and Cakici encounter a problem with negative probabilities, the algorithm uses the average of F_i and F_{i+1} as the re-estimation of S_{i+1}.

Example 1.18 (Implied trees computations). This example is adapted from the paper by Barle and Cakici, however, with different numerical values. The underlying asset is a stock with a current spot price $S_0 = 100$. The annual risk-free interest rate is 10%. The volatility smile is defined by the formula $\sigma(K) = 0.1 - 0.001(S_0 - K)$. We consider a 2-year tree with $\delta t = 0.5$ year. Since we have assumed a constant riskless interest of 10%, the forward price F_i of any node is 1.05 times the node's stock price s_i.

The stock price at node $(0, 0)$ in the implied tree is 100, and the corresponding initial Arrow–Debreu price $\lambda_{0,0} = 1.0$. We now find the stock price at node $(1, 1)$. Since at level 1, we have two central nodes, we apply formula (1.25). For strike $K = F_0 = 105$, the call price at level 1 is equal $C(F_0, t_1) = 2.68$. Since above node $(1, 1)$ there are no higher nodes, then $\delta C = 1.05 * C(F_0, t_1)$. Applying (1.25), we obtain $S_{1,1} = 110.91$. Using (1.24) one gets $S_{1,0} = 99.65$. The transition probability $p_{0,0} = 0.487$ is obtained from equation (1.17) and the implied Arrow–Debreu prices given by equation (1.15) are $\lambda_{1,1} = 0.463$ and $\lambda_{1,0} = 0.488$.

On level 2, we have a central node with price $S_{2,1} = 110.52$ computed from relation (1.24). To obtain the price at upper node $(2, 2)$, we compute forward price $F_{1,1} = 1.05 * S_{1,1}$ and call price $C(F_{1,1}, t_2) = 1.35$. The price for the upper node is computed from (1.22) giving $S_{2,2} = 122.77$. Similarly, we compute $F_{1,0} = 1.05 * S_{1,0}$ and the price of the put option $C(F_{1,0}, t_2) = 1.66$. Then equation

(1.23) gives $S_{2,0} = 95.32$. The corresponding transition probabilities are $p_{1,1} = 0.496$ and $p_{1,0} = 0.621$. Then we can compute the Arrow–Debreu prices $\lambda_{2,2} = 0.218$, $\lambda_{2,1} = 0.510$, and $\lambda_{2,0} = 0.176$.

On level 3, we again have two central nodes $(3,2)$ and $(3,1)$. In node $(3,2)$, we easily obtain $F_{2,1} = 1.05 * S_{2,1}$ and the call price $C(F_{2,1}, t_3) = 4.09$; however, when computing δC, we must take into account that there is node $(3,3)$ above node $(3,2)$. Then in computing δC, we must subtract from $e^{r\delta t}C(F_{2,1}, t_3)$ the sum $\sum_{j=i+1}^{n} \lambda_{n,j}(F_j - F_i)$, which in our case contains only one term $\lambda_{2,2}(F_{2,2} - F_{2,1})$. Applying formula (1.25), we find $S_{3,2} = 122.17$. From formula (1.24), we get $S_{3,1} = 110.49$. To obtain the stock price in node $(3,3)$, we compute the call price $C(F_{2,2}, t_3) = 0.50$ and get $S_{3,3} = 132.79$. The stock price in node $(3,0)$ is computed from the put price $P(F_{2,0}, t_3) = 0.62$ to give $S_{3,0} = 94.38$. Then formula (1.17) gives the transition probabilities $p_{2,2}$, $p_{2,1}$, and $p_{2,0}$. The Arrow–Debreu prices $\lambda_{3,3}$, $\lambda_{3,2}$, $\lambda_{3,1}$, and $\lambda_{3,0}$ can be now easily computed from formula (1.15).

We can similarly continue the computations, reaching level 4, which is the last level of the tree. The complete tree of the computed stock prices and transition probabilities is presented in Fig. 1.3, and the Arrow–Debreu prices are presented in Fig. 1.4.

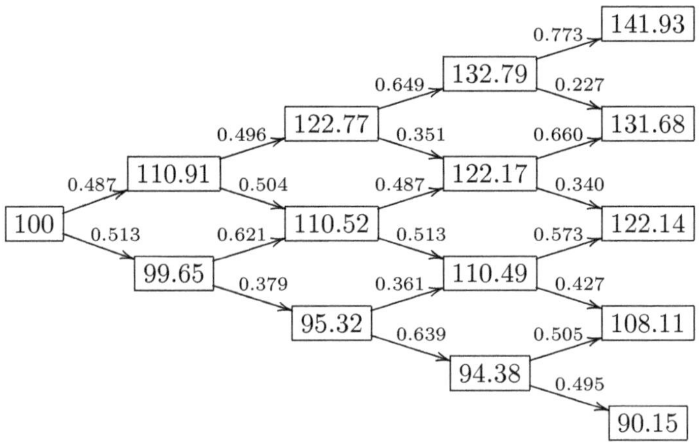

Fig. 1.3. The stock prices and the transition probabilities of Example 1.18.

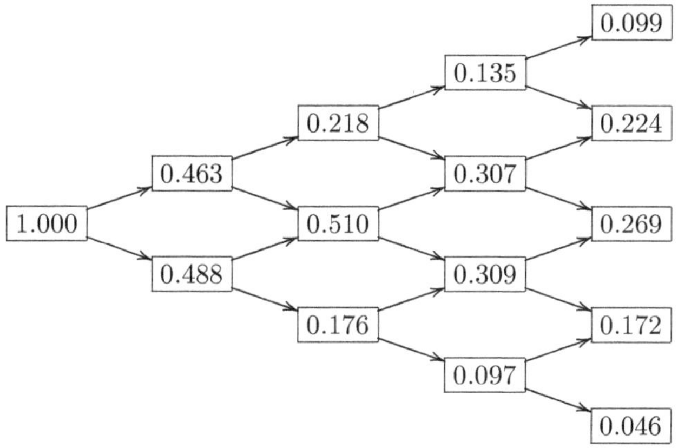

Fig. 1.4. The Arrow–Debreu prices of Example 1.18.

1.4 Exercises

Exercise 1.1. The contingent claim X, attainable with an investment strategy φ, can be bought at some time $t \in [0, T]$ at a price cheaper than $V(t) = \mathcal{V}_\varphi(t)$. Prove that there exists an arbitrage opportunity in this market.

Exercise 1.2. Prove that in the binomial model the condition

$$d < e^{r\delta t} < u$$

is necessary and sufficient for the absence of arbitrage.

Exercise 1.3. (Farkas' Lemma). Consider a one-period market with $(d+1)$ assets and k states of the world. $S = (S^0, S^1, \dots, S^d)^\top$ is a vector of asset prices at time $t = 0$. By u_j^i, we denote the price at time $t = 1$ of asset S^i in state j. A portfolio (investment strategy) $(\varphi^0, \varphi^1, \dots, \varphi^d)^\top$ is made up of φ^i stocks of type i. Its value at time $t = 0$ is $S^\top \varphi = \sum_{i=0}^d \varphi^i S^i$, and its value at time $t = 1$ is $\sum_{i=0}^d u_j^i \varphi^i$ if the world is in state j. Denote by U the matrix with components u_j^i. Prove that the implication $U\varphi \geq 0 \Rightarrow S^\top \varphi \geq 0$ holds if and only if there exists a sequence $(\beta_j)_{j=1}^k$ of nonnegative numbers such that $S^i = \sum_{j=1}^k u_j^i \beta_j$, $i = 0, \dots, d$.

Hint: If $S \neq U^\top \beta$ then $S \notin V = \{x \in \mathbb{R}^{d+1} : x = U^\top \beta,\ \beta \geq 0\}$. Using the hyperplane separation theorem, prove that the inequalities $U\varphi \geq 0$ and $S^\top \varphi \geq 0$ cannot be valid simultaneously.

Exercise 1.4. Consider a one-step market model with two states of the world and two assets: one riskless (with interest rate r) and the other risky stock with prices either S_1^u or S_1^d at time 1. The risky asset has at time $t = 0$ a purchase price S_0 and a selling price $S_0' \leq S_0$. Denote by φ^+ the amount of bought stock, by φ^- the amount of stock sold, and by φ^0 the amount of riskless assets held. The cost of this portfolio at time $t = 0$ is then $\varphi^0 + \varphi^+ S_0 - \varphi^- S_0'$, and it pays at time $t = 1$

$$(1+r)\varphi^0 + (\varphi^+ - \varphi^-)S_1^u \quad \text{in the high state (after the up-move)},$$

$$(1+r)\varphi^0 + (\varphi^+ - \varphi^-)S_1^d \quad \text{in the low state (after the down-move)}.$$

Using Farkas' lemma, show that there is no arbitrage opportunity if and only if there exists at least one probability p such that

$$S_0' \leq \frac{S_1^u p}{1+r} + \frac{S_1^d(1-p)}{1+r} \leq S_0.$$

Exercise 1.5. A one-step market model has two bonds, called B and B', with associated interest rates $r = B_1/B_0 - 1$ and $r' = B_1'/B_0' - 1$. Investors may take long or short positions in as many of these bonds as they wish. Show that if $r \neq r'$, then the model allows arbitrage. This result explains why increasing the number of risk-free assets is redundant.

Exercise 1.6. Consider a one-period model with $\Omega = \{\omega_1, \omega_2, \omega_3\}$, with final stock price $S_1(\omega_1) = 230$, $S_1(\omega_2) = 210$, $S_1(\omega_3) = 190$, and initial stock price $S_0 = 220$. Prove that this model has infinitely many risk-neutral probability measures given by

$$Q_\lambda = (\lambda, 3/2 - 2\lambda, \lambda - 1/2)$$

for $\lambda \in (1/2, 3/4)$.

Exercise 1.7. Consider a recombining binomial model with N time steps, where N is even, and with parameters u, d, p. The model is calibrated to the Black–Scholes model, assuming the equality of the first two moments and the additional relation between parameters

$$S_0 u^{N/2} d^{N/2} = K.$$

This relation asserts that at time step N the central node takes value K.

(a) Prove that there exists a constant $\gamma = ud$ such that

$$u = \beta + \sqrt{\beta^2 - \gamma}, \quad d = \beta - \sqrt{\beta^2 - \gamma}, \quad \text{where}$$
$$\beta = \frac{1}{2}(\gamma e^{-r\delta t} + e^{(r+\sigma^2)\delta t}).$$

Compute the value of γ.

(b) Prove that $d < e^{r\delta t} < u$.

Exercise 1.8. Consider the Tian binomial model [89] in which parameters u, d, and p are computed by matching the first three moments to those of the Black–Scholes model:

$$\begin{aligned} pu + (1-p)d &= R, \\ pu^2 + (1-p)d^2 &= R^2 Q, \\ pu^3 + (1-p)d^3 &= R^3 Q^3, \end{aligned}$$

with $R = e^{r\delta t}$, $Q = e^{\sigma^2 \delta t}$.

(a) Prove that

$$\begin{aligned} u &= \frac{RQ}{2}\left(1 + Q + \sqrt{Q^2 + 2Q - 3}\right), \\ d &= \frac{RQ}{2}\left(1 + Q - \sqrt{Q^2 + 2Q - 3}\right). \end{aligned}$$

Hint: $ud = R^2 Q^2$.

(b) Prove that up to $O\big((\delta t)^{3/2}\big)$ the model parameters are given by the expressions:

$$p = \frac{1}{2} - \frac{3}{4}\sigma\sqrt{\delta t}, \quad u = e^{(r+\sigma^2)\delta t + \sigma\sqrt{\delta t}}, \quad d = e^{(r+\sigma^2)\delta t - \sigma\sqrt{\delta t}}.$$

Exercise 1.9. Consider the Jarrow–Rudd model with the simplified version of parameters u and d:

$$u = e^{(r-\sigma^2/2)\delta t + \sigma\sqrt{\delta t}},$$
$$d = e^{(r-\sigma^2/2)\delta t - \sigma\sqrt{\delta t}}.$$

(a) Show that

$$u = 1+\sigma\sqrt{\delta t}+r\delta t+O\big((\delta t)^{3/2}\big), \quad d = 1-\sigma\sqrt{\delta t}+r\delta t+O\big((\delta t)^{3/2}\big).$$

(b) Take the full version of the parameters:

$$u = e^{r\delta t}\left(1 + \sqrt{e^{\sigma^2\delta t} - 1}\right),$$
$$d = e^{r\delta t}\left(1 - \sqrt{e^{\sigma^2\delta t} - 1}\right),$$

and demonstrate that the above parameters have the same expansions up to $O\big((\delta t)^{3/2}\big)$.

Exercise 1.10. Consider a binomial model with a riskless asset with rate of interest r and a risky asset paying a continuous dividend at rate q. The equations for u, d, and p are modified as follows

$$pu + (1-p)d = e^{(r-q)\delta t},$$
$$pu^2 + (1-p)d^2 = e^{2(r-q)\delta t}e^{\sigma^2\delta t}.$$

Compute parameters u and d assuming $ud = 1$.

Exercise 1.11. In the CRR model, consider a binary call option with strike K, for which the payoff at time T is

$$V^B(T)(\omega) = \begin{cases} 1 & \text{if } S_T(\omega) > K, \\ 0 & \text{if } S_T(\omega) \le K. \end{cases}$$

To derive a formula for option price $V^B(0)$ at time $t = 0$, define

$$A = \min\{a \in \mathbb{N}\colon\ S_0 u^a d^{N-a} > K\}.$$

(a) Note that if $K > S_0 u^N$ then $A > N$. Therefore, the payoff $V^B(T) = 0$ and the option price is zero.

(b) For $A \le N$, apply Theorem 1.13 to obtain the pricing formula

$$V^B(0) = e^{-rN\delta t} \sum_{j=A}^{N} \binom{N}{j} p^j (1-p)^{N-j}.$$

Exercise 1.12. In the CRR model, consider the pricing of the down-and-in barrier call option with barrier $H < K$, i.e., a call option that pays its premium $(S_T - K)^+$ only if the stock price $S(t) < H$ at some time $t \in [0, T]$. Assume $H < S_0$ for, otherwise, the option is identical to a vanilla call option.

To simplify computations, define a, the smallest nonnegative integer such that $S_0 u^a d^{N-a} > K$. The value of a is the ceil (the smallest integer, greater than the specified real number) of the following expression

$$\frac{\ln(K/(S_0 d^N))}{\ln(u/d)}.$$

Similarly, define h as the largest nonnegative integer such that $S_0 u^h d^{N-h} < H$. Taking the logarithm of both sides, obtain h as the floor (the greatest integer, smaller than the specified real number) of the expression

$$\frac{\ln(H/(S_0 d^N))}{\ln(u/d)}.$$

The expression $S_0 u^h d^{N-h}$ defines the effective barrier $\tilde{H}$.

(a) Consider the path starting from S_0 with terminal value $S_0 u^j d^{N-j}$. Prove that there is $\binom{N}{j}$ of such paths each reaching the effective barrier $\tilde{H}$ with probability $\binom{N}{N-2h+j} p^j (1-p)^{N-j}$.
(b) Conclude from the above that the price of the down-and-in call is

$$V(0) = e^{-rN\delta t} \sum_{j=a}^{2h} \binom{N}{N-2h+j} p^j (1-p)^{N-j} \left(S_0 u^j d^{N-j} - K\right).$$

Exercise 1.13. Following the approach for the down-and-in barrier call option, derive pricing formulas for the other three barrier options: down-and-out, up-and-in, and up-and-out.

Exercise 1.14. Consider a sequence of CRR models starting from the same S_0 with the number of time steps $N \to \infty$. Following the approach of Theorem 1.17, prove that the price of the down-and-in call option from Exercise 1.12 converges to the Black–Scholes price given by

$$S_0\left(\frac{H}{S_0}\right)^{2\lambda}\Phi(x) - Ke^{-rT}\left(\frac{H}{S_0}\right)^{2\lambda-2}\Phi(x-\sigma\sqrt{T}),$$

where $x = \frac{\ln(H^2/(KS_0))+(r+\sigma^2/2)T}{\sigma\sqrt{T}}$ and $\lambda = \frac{r+\sigma^2/2}{\sigma^2}$.
Hint: Prove that

$$\left(\frac{up}{d(1-p)}\right)^{2h-N} \to \left(\frac{H}{S_0}\right)^{2\lambda}.$$

Exercise 1.15. Consider the trinomial Hull–White model [41]

$$S_{t+\delta t} = \begin{cases} uS_t, & \text{with probability } p_u, \\ mS_t, & \text{with probability } p_m, \\ dS_t, & \text{with probability } p_d, \end{cases}$$

with

$$m = 1, \quad u = e^{\sigma\sqrt{3\delta t}}, \quad d = u^{-1}.$$

Probabilities p_u, p_m, and p_d are computed assuming

$$p_u + p_m + p_d = 1$$

and matching the first two moments to the corresponding moments of the Black–Scholes model

$$p_u u + p_m m + p_d d = R,$$
$$p_u u^2 + p_m m^2 + p_d d^2 = R^2 Q,$$

where $R = e^{r\delta t}$, $Q = e^{\sigma^2\delta t}$.

(a) Compute p_u, p_m, and p_d as functions of r, σ, and δt.
(b) Compute approximate values of p_u, p_m, and p_d neglecting terms of order higher than $O(\sqrt{\delta t})$.

Exercise 1.16. Consider the trinomial version of the CRR model

$$\ln(Z_n) = \begin{cases} v, & \text{with probability } p_u, \\ 0, & \text{with probability } p_m, \\ -v, & \text{with probability } p_d, \end{cases}$$

with $p_m = 0$ and $p_u = 1 - p_d = p$. By matching the mean and variance of $\ln(Z_n)$ with the parameters of the Black–Scholes model and applying the Kamrad–Ritchken simplification $\mathbb{E}(\ln Z_n) = (r - \sigma^2/2)\delta t$ and $\mathrm{Var}(\ln Z_n) = \sigma^2 \delta t$, one obtains

$$\mathbb{E}\big(\ln(Z_n)\big) = 2pv - v = \left(r - \sigma^2/2\right)\delta t,$$
$$\mathrm{Var}\big(\ln(Z_n)\big) = v^2 - \mathbb{E}\big(\ln(Z_n)\big)^2 = \sigma^2 \delta t.$$

Show that the parameters v and p obtained by solving the above equations are

$$v = \sqrt{\left(r - \sigma^2/2\right)^2 (\delta t)^2 + \sigma^2 \delta t},$$
$$p = \frac{1}{2}\left(1 + \frac{\left(r - \sigma^2/2\right)\delta t}{\sqrt{\left(r - \sigma^2/2\right)^2 (\delta t)^2 + \sigma^2 \delta t}}\right).$$

Exercise 1.17. Consider a binomial model in which, for each up move, the stock price increases by 10, and for each down move, the price decreases by 10. Let $S_0 = 80$ and interest rate $r = 0$. Compute the price of a call option with strike $K = 80$ in the model with five time steps.

Exercise 1.18. Consider a binomial model with $N = 3$, $S_0 = 100$, $u = 1.1$, $d = 0.9$, and $r = 0$.

(a) Show that the model is arbitrage-free and find an equivalent martingale measure.
(b) Compute in this model the price of an up-and-in call option with barrier $B = 110$ and strike $K = 100$, whose payoff at time step N is

$$V(\omega) = \begin{cases} (S_3(\omega) - K)^+ & \text{if } S_n(\omega) \geq B \text{ for some } n \leq 3, \\ 0 & \text{if } S_n(\omega) < B \text{ for all } n. \end{cases}$$

Exercise 1.19. Compute the price of an American call option with strike $K = 50$ in a binomial model with parameters $N = 3$, $r = 0$, $S_0 = 100$, $u = 1.2$, $d = 0.6$.

Exercise 1.20. Consider a binomial model with $N = 2$, $S_0 = 100$, $S_1^u = 110$, $S_1^d = 95$, $S_2^{uu} = 150$, $S_2^{ud} = 80$, $S_2^{du} = 100$, and $S_2^{dd} = 90$. The banking account at time 0 is $B_0 = 1$, and the interest rate for one period $r = 5\%$.

(a) Construct an equivalent martingale measure for this model.
(b) Compute in this model the price at time $t = 0$ of an American call option with strike 95. Verify that this price is the same as the price of a European call option with the same strike.
(c) Compute the prices at time $t = 0$ of American and European put options, both with strike 110.

Exercise 1.21. We know from Theorem 1.17 that the option price in the CRR model converges to the Black–Scholes price. The rate of this convergence is $O(\frac{1}{N})$ but the convergence is not monotone. To see how convergence looks, we compute the value of a European call option with parameters $S_0 = 2$, $K = 1$, $r = 5\%$, $\sigma = 25\%$, and $T = 3$ years.

(a) Compute the option price for the above parameters taking N from 100 to 1000 in step 100. Compare the computed price V_N with the Black–Scholes price $V_{BS} = 1.1447$ drawing the computational error $\varepsilon_N = |V_N - V_{BS}|$ as a function of N. Compare the obtained curve with the graph of function $1/N$.
(b) Perform the computations for N between 100 and 200 in step 1 and similarly for N between 900 and 1000 again in step 1. Observe a "saw-tooth" pattern to the sequence of approximations as N increases. Notice that, despite nonmonotonic convergence, the error for N around 1000 is, on average, one order of magnitude smaller than that for N close to 100.

Exercise 1.22. (Greeks in binomial models). To compute the Greeks, i.e., option price sensitivities with respect to parameters, one can easily apply a finite difference approximation. Let $V(\theta)$ be an option price computed in a binomial model that depends on a parameter θ. Then

$$\frac{\partial V}{\partial \theta} \approx \frac{V(\theta + \delta\theta) - V(\theta - \delta\theta)}{2\delta\theta}.$$

By this formula, Theta, Vega, and Rho can be obtained by computing the changes in option prices for small changes in time-to-maturity, volatility, and risk-free rate. The formula is not appropriate for computing Delta and Gamma since, for suitably small δS, the finite difference of option prices (which in the binomial model is a ladder-like function of S) will not correctly approximate the derivative. Thus, Delta and Gamma should be computed from the option values in the tree

$$\begin{aligned} \Delta &= \frac{\partial V}{\partial S} \approx \frac{V_{1,1} - V_{0,1}}{S_{1,1} - S_{0,1}}, \\ \Gamma &= \frac{\partial^2 V}{\partial S^2} \approx \frac{\frac{V_{2,2}-V_{1,2}}{S_{2,2}-S_{1,2}} - \frac{V_{1,2}-V_{0,2}}{S_{1,2}-S_{0,2}}}{(S_{2,2} - S_{0,2})/2}. \end{aligned} \tag{1.26}$$

(a) For a European put option with parameters $S_0 = 50$, $K = 50$, $r = 5\%$, $\sigma = 30\%$, and $T = 0.5$ year compute Delta in the CRR model by the above formula taking the number of time steps $N = 1000$. Compare the obtained result with the value computed by finite differences with the same number of time steps and $\delta S = 0.25$. Perform the same comparison for Gamma.

(b) Delta and Gamma computed by formula (1.26) are computed at time δ_N and $2\delta_N$, respectively. For $N \to \infty$, both of these time moments converge to zero. However, for finite N it increases computational error. To avoid this error, it is recommended to compute Delta and Gamma in the binomial tree starting two periods earlier, as shown in Fig. 1.5.

In the extended binomial tree Delta and Gamma are computed by the formula:

$$\begin{aligned} \Delta &= \frac{\partial V}{\partial S} \approx \frac{V_{1,0} - V_{-1,0}}{S_{1,0} - S_{-1,0}}, \\ \Gamma &= \frac{\partial^2 V}{\partial S^2} \approx \frac{\frac{V_{1,0}-V_{0,0}}{S_{1,0}-S_{0,0}} - \frac{V_{0,0}-V_{-1,0}}{S_{0,0}-S_{-1,0}}}{(S_{1,0} - S_{-1,0})/2}. \end{aligned}$$

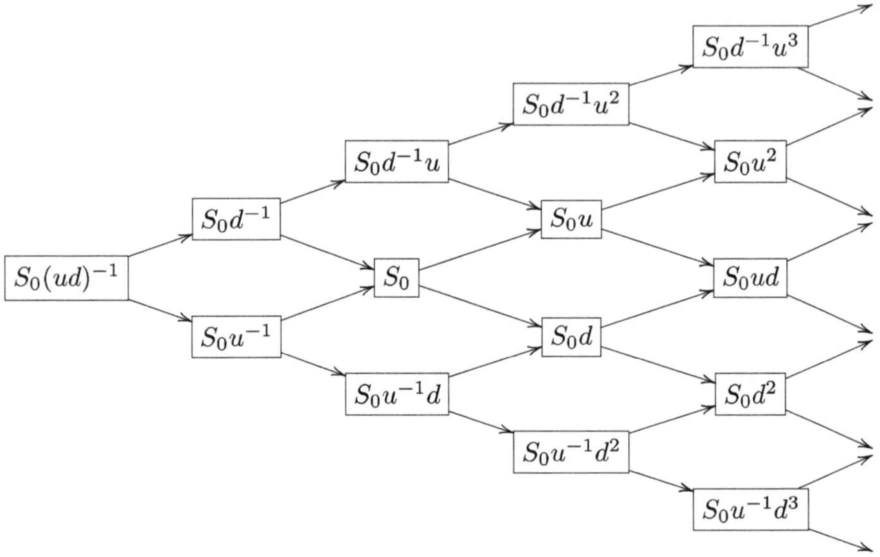

Fig. 1.5. Extended binomial tree.

For the put option defined above, compare Delta and Gamma computed by the formula (1.26) with values obtained on the extended tree of Fig. 1.5.

(c) To analyze the dependence of the finite-difference approximation on $\delta\theta$, perform the computations for such a number of time steps N, which makes the computational error of the option price an order of magnitude smaller than the error of the finite-difference approximation. Compute Rho for the above European put option with $N = 100000$ and δr in the range $0.00001 \div 0.001$ with step 0.00001. Compare the results of these computations with the Black–Scholes Rho.

Hint: The algorithm presented in Section 1.2 has a computational complexity that is too high to perform the computations with $N = 100000$. For a computer system with vectorized computations, several efficient simplifications of this algorithm have been presented in the paper by Higham [37].

Exercise 1.23. (Accelerating binomial convergence for American options). The convergence of prices for American options on a binomial tree faces similar problems as those faced for

European options. As the number of time steps N increases, the binomial price converges to its true value (by the central limit theorem), but the convergence is slow and nonmonotone. Consider the pricing of an American out-of-the-money put option with parameters $S_0 = 50$, $K = 50$, $r = 5\%$, $\sigma = 30\%$, and $T = 0.5$ year.

(a) Compute the price of the above American option in the CRR model for N from 50 to 300 in step 1. Observe price oscillations.

(b) To improve the accuracy of the binomial model, Broadie and Detemple [14] modify the model as follows: (i) the Black–Scholes formula is used to value the option at the penultimate time step, and (ii) two-point Richardson extrapolation is used to reduce the error.

If the option is not exercised at time step $N-1$ (i.e., one step from the expiry), then since there are no further opportunities for early exercise, the American option at step $N-1$ is equivalent to the European option, and its value is given by the Black–Scholes formula. Therefore, the option value at time step $N-1$ can be improved by replacing the value obtained from the tree with the value computed by the Black–Scholes formula. This is known as the *Binomial–Black–Scholes* (BBS) method.

The BBS method is combined with *Richardson extrapolation.* Richardson extrapolation is a method that can improve the efficiency of any algorithm by "extrapolating to the limit". In the case of a binomial model, the idea is to extrapolate values calculated for different numbers of periods (different N) to estimate the value for $N = \infty$. Suppose that errors decline inversely with N (this is true for European options and is expected to be valid also for American options), then

$$V_{N_1} \approx V + \frac{C}{N_1}, \quad V_{N_2} \approx V + \frac{C}{N_2},$$

where V is the (unknown) true value, and V_{N_1} and V_{N_2} are estimates with the number of time steps N_1 and N_2, respectively. Solving for V gives

$$V \approx \frac{N_2 V_{N_2} - N_1 V_{N_1}}{N_2 - N_1}.$$

There are many possibilities to choose N_1 and N_2. A common approach is to take $N_1 = N/2$ and $N_2 = N$. This gives

$$V = 2V_N^{\mathrm{BBS}} - V_{N/2}^{\mathrm{BBS}}.$$

Compute the price in the BBS model with Richardson extrapolation for N from 50 to 300 in step 1. Compare the result with the computations for the plain binomial tree of point (a).

Exercise 1.24. Following the approach used in the derivation of formula (1.18), derive equations (1.21) and (1.25).

Exercise 1.25. Construct a four-step Barle and Cakici implied volatility tree ($N = 4$) with the following inputs: initial stock price $S_0 = 100$, annual risk-free interest rate $r = 10\%$, $\delta t = 1/2$ year and time-independent implied volatility function

$$\sigma(K) = 0.1 + 0.05\left(1 - \frac{K}{100}\right)^2.$$

Check that with a multiplication factor 0.1 instead of 0.05, one obtains negative probabilities at level 4. Improve the algorithm to avoid such negative probabilities.

Chapter 2

Random Number Generators

To run Monte Carlo simulations, we require random numbers with a specified distribution. To generate truly random numbers, we must use a physical device with random behavior. Such generators are not used in modern digital computers (there are some exceptions such as generating seeds for pseudo-random generators). "Random numbers" generated by digital computers are obtained using deterministic algorithms. We only require that a sequence of generated numbers sufficiently accurately mimic the statistical properties of true random numbers. To indicate the deterministic character of the generated sequences, we call them *pseudo-random* numbers. Most of the generators used in practice are those with uniform deviates on $[0, 1]$. The generators of other distributions can be obtained using a suitable transformation of uniform distributions.

2.1 Generators of Uniform Deviates

Linear congruential generators are the simplest generators of pseudo-random numbers.

Definition 2.1. A linear congruential generator is a recurrence of the form:

(1) Choose x_0 (seed).
(2) Compute $x_i = (ax_{i-1} + b) \bmod M$ for some integers a, b, and M.
(3) Compute $u_i = x_i/M$.

Corollary 2.2. *Sequences generated by linear congruential generators have the following properties:*

(1) $x_i \in \{0, 1, \ldots, M-1\}$.
(2) *The sequence x_i is periodic with period not greater than M.*

However, an incorrect choice of a, b, or M can result in a period that is much smaller than M!

Linear congruential generators should generate independent samples $\{u_i\}$ of a random variable with uniform distribution. This independence can be investigated by analyzing n-tuples $(u_i, u_{i+1}, \ldots, u_{i+n-1})$.

Example 2.3. Let us consider two-dimensional vectors (u_{i-1}, u_i). For the congruential generator, we have

$$x_i = (ax_{i-1} + b) \bmod M = ax_{i-1} + b - kM,$$
$$\text{for } kM \leq ax_{i-1} + b < (k+1)M.$$

For arbitrary z_0 and z_1, we obtain

$$\begin{aligned} z_0 x_{i-1} + z_1 x_i &= z_0 x_{i-1} + z_1(ax_{i-1} + b - kM) \\ &= x_{i-1}(z_0 + az_1) + z_1 b - z_1 kM \\ &= M\left(x_{i-1}\frac{z_0 + az_1}{M} - z_1 k\right) + z_1 b. \end{aligned}$$

Denoting the quantity in parentheses by c, we obtain the equation

$$z_0 u_{i-1} + z_1 u_i = c + z_1 b M^{-1}. \tag{2.1}$$

This is the straight-line equation. Choosing integers z_0 and z_1 and requiring $z_0 + az_1 = 0 \bmod M$, we obtain an integer c. This observation will be used in the subsequent analysis. The straight line given by equation (2.1) depends on i since c is a function of x_{i-1}. We expect sufficiently many such lines to densely cover the square $[0, 1)^2$. This expectation appears to be wrong in many practical situations. For many a and M, points (u_{i-1}, u_i) lie along very few straight lines. For example, consider the linear congruential generator with $a = 1229$, $b = 1$, $M = 2048$, and $x_0 = 1$. By choosing $z_0 = -1$ and $z_1 = 5$, we obtain $-1 + 1229 \cdot 5 = 6144 = 3 \cdot 2048 = 0 \bmod 2048$, which gives an integer c. By equation (2.1) and inequality $0 \leq u_i < 1$, the value of

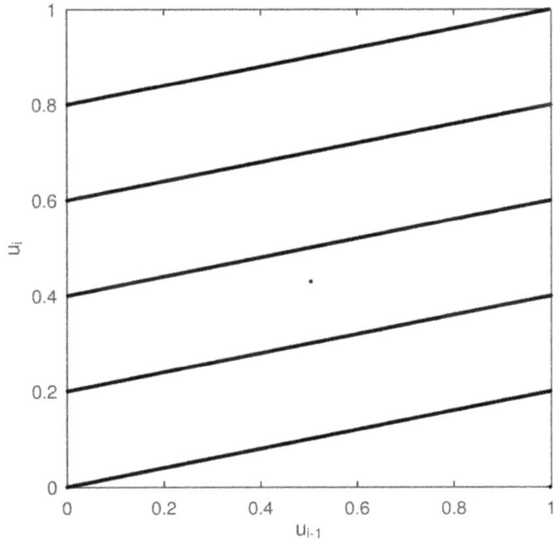

Fig. 2.1. The points (u_{i-1}, u_i) for $a = 1229$, $b = 1$, $M = 2048$.

c can only be a number in the set $\{-1, 0, 1, 2, 3, 4\}$. Hence, there are only six straight lines on which vectors (u_{i-1}, u_i) lie. Figure 2.1 shows the picture of such vectors for 5000 simulations. In that picture, we observe only five lines. The explanation comes from the fact that $c = -1$ corresponds to the straight line, which is in the lower right corner of the figure and is not visible.

A better choice of a, b, and M yields a better picture. Taking $a = 2^{16} + 3$, $b = 0$, and $M = 2^{31}$, we obtain the picture shown in Fig. 2.2. This picture suggests a deceptively good congruential generator.

This positive impression breaks down with three-dimensional vectors (u_{i-2}, u_{i-1}, u_i). Figure 2.3 shows that three-dimensional vectors are concentrated on a small number of planes in the three-dimensional cube $[0, 1)^3$ (analysis similar to the previous generator reveals that there are 15 such planes).

The poor behavior of linear congruential generators observed in the above example is not exceptional. The following theorem due to Marsaglia [61] explains that this behavior is typical.

Theorem 2.4. *For each linear congruential generator, there exists an $n \ll M$ such that n-tuples $(u_i, u_{i+1}, \ldots, u_{i+n-1})$ lie on a relatively low number of hyperplanes in $\mathbb{R}^n$.*

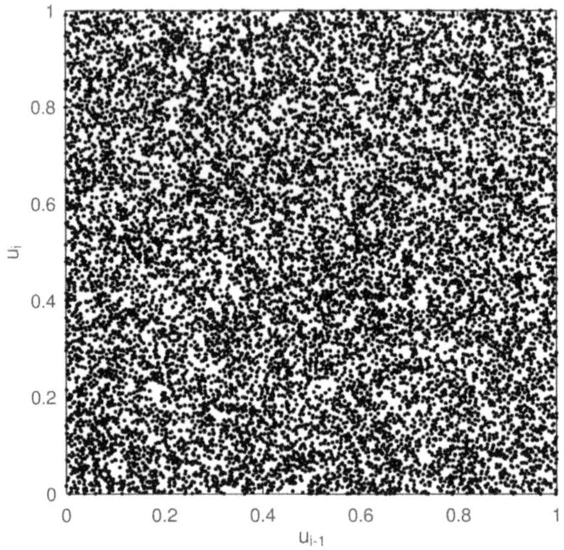

Fig. 2.2. The points (u_{i-1}, u_i) for $a = 2^{16} + 3$, $b = 0$, $M = 2^{31}$.

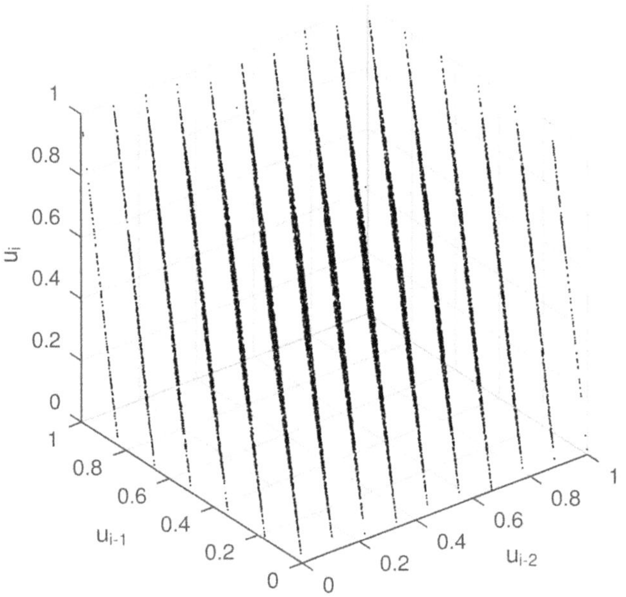

Fig. 2.3. The points (u_{i-2}, u_{i-1}, u_i) for $a = 2^{16} + 3$, $b = 0$, and $M = 2^{31}$.

To avoid the described above effect of correlation, more sophisticated generators are used, for example, generalized congruential generators

$$x_i = (a_1 x_{i-1} + \cdots + a_k x_{i-k}) \bmod M.$$

L'Ecuyer [56] recommends designing mixed generators from several generalized congruential generators. Taking J generalized generators,

$$x_{j,i} = (a_{j,1} x_{j,i-1} + \cdots + a_{j,k} x_{j,i-k}) \bmod M_j, \quad j = 1, \ldots, J,$$

we can construct the mixed generator

$$z_i = (b_1 x_{1,i} + \cdots + b_J x_{J,i}) \bmod M,$$

where $b_1, \ldots, b_J$ are integers, and M is the largest of all M_j. It appears that sequences generated by such a generator are equivalent to sequences generated by a single generalized congruential generator with M, which is the product of M_j. The advantage of mixed generators is that the sequences generated by these generators have better statistical properties than those generated by the corresponding generalized generator.

As mixed generators, we can also use the Fibonacci generators

$$x_i = x_{i-n} \odot x_{i-k} \bmod M \text{ for some } n \text{ and } k,$$

where $\odot$ denotes addition, subtraction, or multiplication. To guarantee the "good" properties of such generators, a long seed is required, which must be generated by another generator.

Currently, a widely used random number generator in Monte Carlo simulations is the 32-bit Mersenne Twister generator MT19937 developed by Matsumoto and Nishimura [63]. This generator has a fast and efficient implementation with a very long period ($2^{19937} - 1$), and no correlation was observed for vectors to dimension 623. The generator is implemented in many computer packages and is freely available from various sources. The above advantages of this generator are mitigated by the fact that it fails in some tests in the commonly used *TestU01* suite [57] and exhibits the poor diffusion property: it can take a long time from the generator initialization before generating outputs meet the randomness tests. In subsequent years, the generator has been updated to 64-bit word length, its initialization has been improved, and a graphics processing unit version has been implemented.

In the 2000s, several generators better than MT19937 were designed (they usually pass TestU01). We can mention WELL ("Well Equidistributed Long-period Linear") generator by Panneton *et al.* [72], Marsaglia's Xorshift generators [62], or SFMT generator by Saito and Matsumoto [77]. A thorough analysis of generators available up to 2015 can be found in a review paper by Fog [30]. In recent years, new, faster, and/or with better statistical properties algorithms have been announced, and studies on new, better generators for Monte Carlo simulations are still ongoing. We can expect that the coming years will bring about nonnegligible changes.

2.2 Nonuniform Variates

As mentioned previously, pseudo-random number generators usually produce samples from a uniform distribution $\mathcal{U}(0,1)$. Samples from other distributions are obtained by transforming a uniform distribution.

Discrete distribution

To obtain a sample from discrete distribution X

$$\mathbb{P}(X = a_i) = p_i, \quad i = 1, \ldots, n,$$

we apply the following algorithm:

(1) Compute $c_k = \sum_{i=1}^{k} p_i$, $k = 1, \ldots, n$.
(2) Generate $u \sim \mathcal{U}(0,1)$.
(3) Find the smallest k such that $u \leq c_k$.
(4) Put $Z = a_k$.

Then Z is a sample from the distribution of X.

Inversion

Theorem 2.5. *Let a random variable X possess a continuous, strictly increasing cumulative distribution function F_X. If $u \sim \mathcal{U}(0,1)$, then $F_X^{-1}(u)$ is a sample of X.*

Proof. The condition $u \sim \mathcal{U}(0,1)$ means $\mathbb{P}_{\mathcal{U}}(u \le \xi) = \xi$ for $\xi \in [0,1)$. Hence, $\mathbb{P}_{\mathcal{U}}(F_X^{-1}(u) \le x) = \mathbb{P}_{\mathcal{U}}(u \le F_X(x)) = F_X(x)$. □

Example 2.6 (Cauchy distribution). The Cauchy distribution *Cauchy*(x_0, γ) with location parameter x_0 and scale parameter γ has the probability density

$$f(x) = \frac{1}{\pi} \frac{\gamma}{\gamma^2 + (x - x_0)^2}.$$

Its cumulative distribution function is

$$F(x) = \frac{1}{\pi} \arctan\left(\frac{x - x_0}{\gamma}\right) + \frac{1}{2}.$$

Since $F(x)$ is easily invertible, a sample x from the Cauchy distribution can be generated by the formula

$$x = \gamma \tan(\pi(u - 1/2)) + x_0, \quad \text{where } u \sim \mathcal{U}(0,1).$$

Acceptance–rejection method

Let X be a random variable with density $f(x)$. Although the density is known, sampling from this density is complicated (large computational complexity). Assume there is another random variable Y with density $g(x)$ that can be easily simulated. If $f(x) \le C\,g(x)$ for a constant $C < +\infty$, we can use Y to generate samples of X ($Cg(x)$ is then called a *majorizing density* of $f(x)$ or an *envelope* of $f(x)$).

The sampling algorithm of X is as follows:

(1) Generate $x \sim Y$ and $u \sim \mathcal{U}(0,1)$.
(2) If $u \le \frac{f(x)}{C\,g(x)}$, accept x as a sample X. Otherwise, return to p. (1).

Theorem 2.7. *The above algorithm generates a sample of X.*

Proof. Let

$$A = \left\{\omega \colon \mathcal{U}(\omega) \le \frac{f(Y(\omega))}{C\,g(Y(\omega))}\right\}.$$

Then

$$\mathbb{P}(Y \in dx|A) = \frac{\mathbb{P}(A \cap \{Y \in dx\})}{\mathbb{P}(A)} = \frac{g(x)\frac{f(x)}{C\,g(x)}dx}{\int_{\mathbb{R}} g(y)\frac{f(y)}{C\,g(y)}dy}$$

$$= \frac{f(x)dx}{\int_{\mathbb{R}} f(y)dy} = f(x)dx = \mathbb{P}(X \in dx),$$

where the value of $\mathbb{P}(A)$ is obtained by the following computation

$$\mathbb{P}(A) = \mathbb{P}\left(\mathcal{U} \leq \frac{f(Y)}{C\,g(Y)}\right) = \mathbb{E}\left(\mathbb{P}\left(\mathcal{U} \leq \frac{f(Y)}{C\,g(Y)}\middle| Y\right)\right)$$

$$= \mathbb{E}\left(\frac{f(Y)}{C\,g(Y)}\right) = \int_{\mathbb{R}} \frac{f(y)}{C\,g(y)} g(y)dy = \frac{1}{C}\int_{\mathbb{R}} f(y)dy. \qquad \square$$

Example 2.8 (Gamma distribution). The gamma distribution $\Gamma(\alpha, \lambda)$ with shape parameter α and scale parameter λ has the density

$$f(x) = \frac{\lambda^{\alpha} x^{\alpha-1} e^{-\lambda x}}{\Gamma(\alpha)}, \quad x \in (0, \infty),$$

where $\Gamma(\alpha)$ is the gamma function.

There are several reasons for the search for an efficient generator from a gamma distribution: exponential and chi-squared distributions are special cases of a gamma distribution, and some other distributions, such as beta distribution, can also be generated from samples of a gamma distribution.

Using the scaling property of the gamma distribution $X \sim \Gamma(\alpha, \lambda) \Rightarrow cX \sim \Gamma(\alpha, c\lambda)$, we can limit considerations to the generation of $\Gamma(\alpha, 1)$-distributed random variables.

The algorithm due to Chang [15] generates a sample from the distribution $\Gamma(\alpha, 1)$ with density proportional to $f(x) = x^{\alpha-1}e^{-x}$, $x \geq 0$. The acceptance–rejection method is used with the majorizing density

$$g(x) = \frac{Kx^{\nu-1}}{(\mu + x^{\nu})^2},$$

where

$$\mu = \alpha^{\nu}, \quad K = 4\alpha^{\alpha+\nu}e^{-\alpha}, \quad \nu = \begin{cases} \sqrt{2\alpha - 1}, & \text{for } \alpha \geq 1, \\ \alpha, & \text{for } \alpha < 1. \end{cases}$$

The cumulative distribution function corresponding to $g(x)$ is

$$G(x) = \frac{x^\nu}{\mu + x^\nu}.$$

A sample from the distribution $G(x)$ can be generated by the inverse transform $G^{-1}(u) = \left(\frac{\mu u}{1-u}\right)^{1/\nu}$, where $u \sim \mathcal{U}(0,1)$.

Then the algorithm for generating a sample from density $f(x)$ is as follows:

(1) Generate $u_1, u_2 \sim \mathcal{U}(0,1)$.

(2) Compute ν and $x = \alpha\left(\frac{1-u_1}{u_1}\right)^{1/\nu}$.

(3) Accept x if

$$u_2 < \frac{f(x)}{g(x)} = \left(\frac{x}{\alpha}\right)^{\alpha-\nu} e^{\alpha-x} \left(\frac{1+(x/\alpha)^\nu}{2}\right)^2$$

or equivalently if

$$\ln(4u_1^2 u_2) < (\alpha - \nu)\ln\left(\frac{x}{\alpha}\right) + \alpha - x.$$

Unfortunately, for $\alpha < 1$, the Chang method is rather slow. Thus, many more efficient methods are used to generate samples from the gamma distribution. Readers interested in other methods should refer to the book by Gentle [33].

Transformation of random variables

The following theorem easily follows from the change of variables theorem.

Theorem 2.9. *Let X be a random variable in $\mathbb{R}^d$ with a positive density ϕ supported on a domain S. Assume that a transformation $g\colon S \to B$, where B is a subset of $\mathbb{R}^d$, is invertible and that the inverse is continuously differentiable on B. Then $Y = g(X)$ has the density*

$$\phi(g^{-1}(y)) \left|\frac{\partial(x_1,\ldots,x_d)}{\partial(y_1,\ldots,y_d)}\right|, \quad y \in B,$$

where $x = g^{-1}(y)$ and $\frac{\partial(x_1,\ldots,x_d)}{\partial(y_1,\ldots,y_d)}$ denotes the Jacobian matrix of g^{-1}.

We can apply this transformation method to generate samples from a normal distribution.

Example 2.10 (Box–Muller algorithm). Let us define the transformation

$$y_1 = \sqrt{-2\ln x_1}\cos 2\pi x_2 = g_1(x_1, x_2),$$
$$y_2 = \sqrt{-2\ln x_1}\sin 2\pi x_2 = g_2(x_1, x_2),$$

for $(x_1, x_2) \in [0, 1]^2$.

The inverse transformation is given by

$$x_1 = \exp\left(-\frac{y_1^2 + y_2^2}{2}\right),$$
$$x_2 = \frac{1}{2\pi}\arctan\frac{y_2}{y_1}.$$

The Jacobian matrix is given by

$$\det\begin{pmatrix} \frac{\partial x_1}{\partial y_1} & \frac{\partial x_1}{\partial y_2} \\ \frac{\partial x_2}{\partial y_1} & \frac{\partial x_2}{\partial y_2} \end{pmatrix} = \frac{1}{2\pi}\exp\left(-\frac{y_1^2 + y_2^2}{2}\right)$$
$$\times\left(-y_1\frac{1}{1+\frac{y_2^2}{y_1^2}}\frac{1}{y_1} - y_2\frac{1}{1+\frac{y_2^2}{y_1^2}}\frac{y_2}{y_1^2}\right)$$
$$= -\frac{1}{2\pi}\exp\left(-\frac{y_1^2 + y_2^2}{2}\right).$$

The above computations show that $|\det(\frac{\partial(x_1,x_2)}{\partial(y_1,y_2)})|$ is the density of a two-dimensional standard normal variable.

When $X \sim \mathcal{U}(0,1)^2$, then $Y = (Y_1, Y_2) = (g_1(X), g_2(X))$ is a two-dimensional standard normal variable, and Y_1, Y_2 are i.i.d.

Remark 2.11 (Neave effect). In 1973, Neave [66] discovered a surprising result when applying the Box–Muller algorithm to a sample obtained from a linear congruential generator. Since the density of normal distribution is supported on the whole $\mathbb{R}$, we can expect that pairs (Y_1, Y_2) will cover the whole $\mathbb{R}^2$. Contrary to this expectation, the generated pairs fall into a small range (rectangle) around

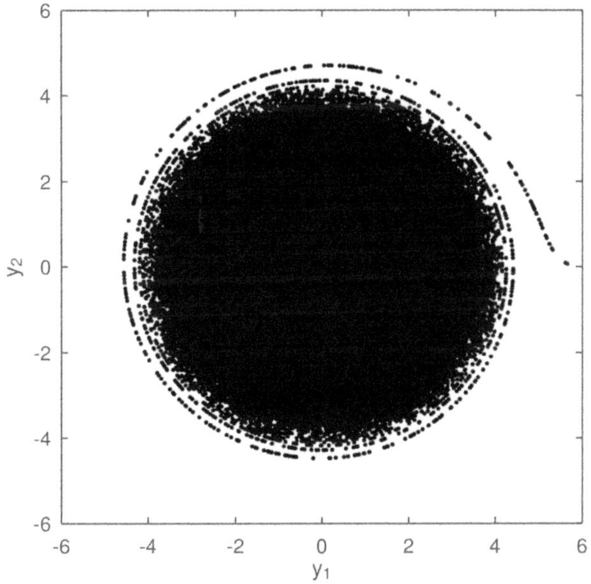

Fig. 2.4. The Neave effect for the Box–Muller algorithm.

zero. This surprising behavior is illustrated in Fig. 2.4 obtained for 10^7 simulations. The Neave effect was observed for the Box–Muller algorithm and other uniform generators. It is suspected that this effect can also occur for other random number generators.

Example 2.12 (Marsaglia's polar method). The Box–Muller algorithm was improved by Marsaglia to avoid the use of trigonometric functions. This modification is important since the computation of trigonometric functions is time-consuming. Marsaglia's algorithm replaces the evaluation of trigonometric functions in the Box–Muller algorithm with the acceptance–rejection method:

(1) Generate $u_1, u_2 \sim \mathcal{U}(0,1)$.
(2) Perform transformation $v_1 = 2u_1 - 1$, $v_2 = 2u_2 - 1$. Then $v_1, v_2 \sim \mathcal{U}(-1,1)$.
(3) Accept a pair (v_1, v_2), when $v_1^2 + v_2^2 \leq 1$. Such pairs are uniformly distributed on $D = \{(v_1, v_2)\colon\ v_1^2 + v_2^2 \leq 1\}$.
(4) Every pair $(v_1, v_2) \in D$ can be considered as defined by the polar coordinates (z, θ):

$$v_1 = z\cos\theta, \quad v_2 = z\sin\theta.$$

The variates $w = z^2$ and θ are independent: $w \sim \mathcal{U}(0,1)$, $\theta \sim \mathcal{U}(0,2\pi)$.

(5) The variables

$$y_1 = \sqrt{-\frac{\ln w}{w}}v_1, \quad y_2 = \sqrt{-\frac{\ln w}{w}}v_2$$

are normally distributed and independent.

The pair y_1, y_2 is normally distributed by the Box–Muller algorithm. Since $\theta = \arctan \frac{v_2}{v_1}$, then taking $x_1 = v_1^2 + v_2^2 \equiv w$ and $x_2 = \frac{1}{2\pi}\theta$, we obtain $x_1, x_2 \sim \mathcal{U}(0,1)$, where $\cos(2\pi x_2) = \frac{v_1}{\sqrt{w}}$ and $\sin(2\pi x_2) = \frac{v_2}{\sqrt{w}}$. These transformations reduce the Marsaglia algorithm to the Box–Muller algorithm.

Example 2.13. The Box–Muller and Marsaglia algorithms are not sufficiently accurate for financial applications. Many algorithms use inversion to provide more accurate normal distributions. As an example, we present a modification by Moro [64] of the Beasley–Springer algorithm [7] with accuracy 3×10^{-9}. However, there are algorithms with higher accuracy and compatible computational complexity (cf. [80]). For $0.5 \le y < 0.92$, the Beasley–Springer–Moro algorithm uses the formula

$$F^{-1}(y) \approx \frac{\sum_{n=0}^{3} a_n (y-0.5)^{2n+1}}{1 + \sum_{n=0}^{3} b_n (y-0.5)^{2n+2}},$$

and for $y \ge 0.92$, the formula

$$F^{-1}(y) \approx \sum_{n=0}^{8} c_n (\ln(-\ln(1-y)))^n.$$

The case $0 \le y \le 0.5$ is handled by symmetry.

The constants for the Beasley–Springer–Moro algorithm are given in Table 2.1.

Example 2.14 (Chi-squared distribution). The chi-squared distribution χ_ν^2 with ν degrees of freedom has the density

$$f(x) = \frac{x^{\nu/2-1}e^{-x/2}}{2^{\nu/2}\Gamma(\nu/2)}, \quad x \in [0,\infty).$$

The chi-squared distribution is the gamma distribution $\Gamma(\nu/2, 1/2)$. Then to generate samples from χ_ν^2, we can use a gamma distribution

Table 2.1. Constants for the Beasley–Springer–Moro algorithm.

a0 = 2.50662823884	b0 = –8.47351093090
a1 = –18.61500062529	b1 = 23.08336743743
a2 = 41.39119773534	b2 = –21.06224101826
a3 = –25.44106049637	b3 = 3.13082909833
c0 = 0.3374754822726147	c5 = 0.0003951896511919
c1 = 0.9761690190917186	c6 = 0.0000321767881768
c2 = 0.1607979714918209	c7 = 0.0000002888167364
c3 = 0.0276438810333863	c8 = 0.0000003960315187
c4 = 0.0038405729373609	

generator. When ν is an even integer, we can obtain the chi-squared deviate x from $\nu/2$ independent uniforms deviates u_i by the formula

$$x = -2\ln\left(\prod_{i=1}^{\nu/2} u_i\right).$$

Example 2.15 (Student's t distribution). The Student's $t(\nu)$ distribution with ν degrees of freedom has the density

$$f(x) = \frac{\Gamma\left(\frac{\nu+1}{2}\right)}{\Gamma\left(\frac{\nu}{2}\right)\sqrt{\nu\pi}}\left(1+\frac{x^2}{\nu}\right)^{-(\nu+1)/2}, \quad x \in \mathbb{R}.$$

The standard representation of the $t(\nu)$ distribution is obtained by dividing a standard normal variable by the square root of a chi-squared variable with ν degrees of freedom

$$t(\nu) \sim \frac{Z}{\sqrt{\chi^2_\nu/\nu}} \quad Z \sim \mathcal{N}(0,1).$$

This relation can be used to generate t deviates; however, this method is not efficient. More efficient is the Bailey polar method [4]:

(1) Generate $u_1, u_2 \sim \mathcal{U}(0,1)$.
(2) Perform transformation $v_1 = 2u_1 - 1$, $v_2 = 2u_2 - 1$. Then $v_1, v_2 \sim \mathcal{U}(-1,1)$.
(3) Accept a pair (v_1, v_2), when $v_1^2 + v_2^2 \leq 1$.
(4) For the accepted pair, compute $w = v_1^2 + v_2^2$.
(5) Compute $c = v_1/\sqrt{w}$, $r^2 = \nu\big(w^{-2/\nu} - 1\big)$, and $x = cr$.
(6) x is a sample from the $t(\nu)$ distribution with ν degrees of freedom.

2.3 Multivariate Random Variables

Multivariate distributions are typically obtained from one-dimensional distributions. Only in very particular situations can multivariate distributions be obtained as the Cartesian product of univariate distributions.

Uniform distribution

A multidimensional uniform distribution can be obtained as a tuple of independent one-dimensional distributions $(U_1, \ldots, U_d)$, where $U_i \sim \mathcal{U}(0, 1)$.

Normal variates

A standard d-dimensional normal distribution $\mathcal{N}_d(0, I_d)$, where I_d is the d-dimensional identity matrix, can be obtained from one-dimensional normal distributions

$$X \sim \mathcal{N}_d(0, I_d) \iff X = (X_1, \ldots, X_d),$$
$$\text{where } X_i \sim \mathcal{N}(0,1), \;\; X_i \text{ are i.i.d.}$$

This is due to the form of density of the d-dimensional normal distribution $\mathcal{N}_d(\mu, \Sigma)$

$$\phi(x) = \frac{1}{(2\pi)^{d/2}} \frac{1}{(\det \Sigma)^{1/2}} \exp\left(-\frac{1}{2}(x-\mu)^\top \Sigma^{-1}(x-\mu) \right).$$

For $\mu = 0$ and $\Sigma = I_d$, this density is the product of the standard one-dimensional densities. Knowing the density of a correlated normal distribution, we can transform a standard normal distribution $\mathcal{N}_d(0, I_d)$ to generate samples from the correlated distribution.

Lemma 2.16. *Let $Z \sim \mathcal{N}_d(0, I_d)$ and A be a nonsingular matrix of dimension $d \times d$. Then $AZ \sim \mathcal{N}_d(0, AA^\top)$ and $\mu + AZ \sim \mathcal{N}_d(\mu, AA^\top)$.*

Proof. Let $X = AZ$ and $\phi(z)$ be the density of Z. Substituting $x = Az$, we obtain

$$\exp\left(-\frac{1}{2}z^\top z\right) = \exp\Big(-\frac{1}{2}(A^{-1}x)^\top (A^{-1}x)\Big)$$
$$= \exp\Big(-\frac{1}{2}x^\top (A^{-1})^\top A^{-1}x\Big).$$

Changing variables, we obtain

$$\int_{\mathbb{R}^d} \phi(z)dz = \int_{\mathbb{R}^d} \phi(x)|\det A|^{-1}dx$$
$$= \int_{\mathbb{R}^d} \frac{1}{|\det A|}\frac{1}{(2\pi)^{d/2}} \exp\left(-\frac{1}{2}x^\top \left(AA^\top\right)^{-1}x\right)dx.$$

Hence,

$$\frac{1}{|\det A|}\frac{1}{(2\pi)^{d/2}} \exp\left(-\frac{1}{2}x^\top \left(AA^\top\right)^{-1}x\right)$$

is the density of $\mathcal{N}_d(0, AA^\top)$. □

To generate samples from $\mathcal{N}_d(\mu, \Sigma)$, we must find a matrix A such that $\Sigma = AA^\top$. The covariance matrix Σ is symmetric and positive definite. Hence, we find A by the Cholesky decomposition of Σ.

Remark 2.17. To generate samples from $\mathcal{N}_d(\mu, \Sigma)$, we can also use spectral decomposition of Σ. Since Σ is a symmetric, positive definite matrix, it has d positive eigenvalues and d eigenvectors that span $\mathbb{R}^d$. Then $\Sigma = \Gamma\Lambda\Gamma^\top$, where Λ is the diagonal matrix of eigenvalues and Γ is the matrix of eigenvectors. If $Z \sim \mathcal{N}_d(0, I_d)$, then $\mu + \Gamma\Lambda^{1/2}Z \sim \mathcal{N}_d(\mu, \Sigma)$. Let us observe that $\Lambda^{1/2}$ is well-defined due to the positivity of the eigenvalues.

Remark 2.18. In general, the Cholesky decomposition and the spectral decomposition construction do not yield the same results. Indeed,

since

$$\Sigma = AA^\top = \Gamma\Lambda\Gamma^\top = \Gamma\Lambda^{1/2}\Lambda^{1/2}\Gamma^\top,$$

then

$$\Sigma(A^\top)^{-1} = A = \Gamma\Lambda^{1/2}\Lambda^{1/2}\Gamma^\top(A^\top)^{-1}.$$

Noting that

$$\Lambda^{1/2}\Gamma^\top(A^\top)^{-1} \neq I_d,$$

we have

$$AZ \neq \Gamma\Lambda^{1/2}Z,$$

although both methods generate samples from $\mathcal{N}_d(\mu, \Sigma)$.

In implementations, Cholesky decomposition is more effective. In the Cholesky factorization, matrix A is lower triangular. It makes the computations of AZ particularly convenient because it reduces the computational complexity by a factor of 2 compared to the multiplication of Z by the full matrix $\Gamma\Lambda^{1/2}$. In addition, the error propagates more slowly in the Cholesky factorization. However, there are situations in which using spectral decomposition offers some advantages. The eigenvalues and eigenvectors of the covariance matrix have a statistical interpretation that is sometimes useful. They can also be explored in some variance reduction methods.

Generating sample paths of a Wiener process

Consider a standard Wiener process W_t in probability space $(\Omega, \mathcal{F}, \mathbb{P})$. Let $(t_0, t_1, \ldots, t_N)$ be an increasing sequence of time moments $0 = t_0 < t_1 < \cdots < t_N$. Our goal is to simulate discrete sample paths of process W_t in moments t_n, $n = 0, \ldots, N$. The sequence of values $(W_{t_0}, W_{t_1}, \ldots, W_{t_N})$ is often called the *random walk*. Since the Wiener process has independent normally distributed increments, the simulation of the random walk is straightforward. Let $Z_1, \ldots, Z_N$ be independent, standard normal random variables.

For a standard Wiener process, $W_0 = 0$. The subsequent values are computed as follows:

$$W_{t_n} = W_{t_{n-1}} + \sqrt{t_n - t_{n-1}}\, Z_n, \quad n = 1, \ldots, N.$$

For a Wiener process X_t with drift μ and variance σ^2, a random walk simulation is obtained by the formula

$$X_{t_n} = X_{t_{n-1}} + \mu(t_n - t_{n-1}) + \sigma\sqrt{t_n - t_{n-1}}\, Z_n, \quad n = 1, \ldots, N.$$

The vector $(W_{t_1}, \ldots, W_{t_N})$ is a linear transformation of the vector of increments $(W_{t_1} - W_{t_0}, \ldots, W_{t_N} - W_{t_{N-1}})$. Since the increments are independent and normally distributed, then $(W_{t_1}, \ldots, W_{t_N})$ has a multivariate normal distribution.

Noting that $\mathrm{Cov}(W_s, W_t) = \min(s,t)$, we define the covariance matrix C of $(W_{t_1}, \ldots, W_{t_N})$ as the matrix with entries $C_{n,m} = \min(t_n, t_m)$. Then the vector $(W_{t_1}, \ldots, W_{t_N})$ has the distribution $\mathcal{N}(0, C)$. To simulate a sample from this distribution, we apply the Cholesky decomposition $C = AA^\top$. Then the simulation is obtained using the following vector operation

$$\begin{pmatrix} W_{t_1} \\ W_{t_2} \\ \vdots \\ W_{t_N} \end{pmatrix} = A \begin{pmatrix} Z_1 \\ Z_2 \\ \vdots \\ Z_N \end{pmatrix},$$

where matrix $A = \left(\sqrt{t_m - t_{m-1}}\mathbb{1}_{\{n \geq m\}}\right)_{1 \leq n,m \leq N}$. This method of generating sample paths is particularly efficient in computer systems with implemented vector operations.

To simulate a random walk for an m-dimensional standard Wiener process $W_t = (W_t^1, \ldots, W_t^m)$ with continuous sample paths and independent increments $W_t - W_s \sim \mathcal{N}(0, (t-s)I)$, where I is the $m \times m$ identity matrix, consider N random vectors $Z_1, \ldots, Z_N$ in $\mathbb{R}^m$ sampled from the distribution $\mathcal{N}(0, I)$. The simulation of discrete sample paths is analogous to the one-dimensional case. We take an increasing sequence of time moments $0 = t_0 < t_1 < \cdots < t_N$. Then setting $W_0 = 0$, we obtain

$$W_{t_n} = W_{t_{n-1}} + \sqrt{t_n - t_{n-1}}\, Z_n, \quad n = 1, \ldots, N.$$

For a Wiener process X_t with drift μ and covariance matrix Σ, we must perform the Cholesky decomposition of the covariance matrix

$\Sigma = AA^\top$. Then assuming $W_0 = 0$, we obtain

$$X_{t_n} = X_{t_{n-1}} + \mu(t_n - t_{n-1}) + \sqrt{t_n - t_{n-1}}\, AZ_n, \quad n = 1, \ldots, N.$$

Other multidimensional distributions

Uniform or normal distributions give exceptional examples of designing multivariate distributions as the Cartesian products of one-dimensional distributions. In most cases, generating samples from multivariate distributions requires special algorithms.

A good example is an algorithm for sampling from a d-dimensional Student's distribution $t_d(\nu, \mu, \Sigma)$, with ν degrees of freedom, location vector μ, and dispersion matrix Σ. To generate samples from this distribution, we can use the formula

$$t_d(\nu, \mu, \Sigma) \sim \frac{\mathcal{N}_d(\mu, \Sigma)}{\sqrt{\chi^2_\nu/\nu}},$$

where χ^2_ν denotes an independent of $\mathcal{N}_d(\mu, \Sigma)$ chi-squared distribution with ν degrees of freedom. Using the above relation to generate a sample from $t_d(\nu, \mu, \Sigma)$, we must generate two independent samples: one from $\mathcal{N}_d(\mu, \Sigma)$ and another from χ^2_ν.

A similar algorithm works for a d-dimensional asymmetric Laplace distribution $AL_d(m, \Sigma)$. This class of distributions is suitable for modeling heavy-tailed multivariate data that retain the moments' finiteness. To obtain samples from $Y \sim AL_d(m, \Sigma)$, we generate a sample from $\mathcal{N}_d(0, \Sigma)$ and an independent sample from a standard exponential distribution $Ex(1)$. Then for an asymmetric Laplace distribution, we have

$$AL_d(m, \Sigma) \sim mEx(1) + \sqrt{Ex(1)}\mathcal{N}_d(0, \Sigma).$$

2.4 Low-Discrepancy Sequences

Consider the computation of a definite integral $\int_0^1 f(x)dx$. When function $f(x)$ is complicated, we approximate the value of this integral by a numerical procedure. To this end, we can use the Monte Carlo method, which gives the approximation error $O(N^{-1/2})$ (see Chapter 3). On the other hand, we can apply a deterministic quadrature dividing interval $[0, 1]$ into N subintervals of equal length and using trapezoidal approximation. The error of such an approximation is $O(N^{-1})$, which is much smaller than the Monte Carlo error (in addition, this error is deterministic contrary to the Monte Carlo error, which is of statistical nature).

On the other hand, the error estimate obtained in advance of computations gives only the order of magnitude of the error. The exact value can be reasonably approximated only after computations. If the computed error exceeds the assumed accuracy, the computation must be repeated with larger N. For the trapezoidal method, this requires the repetition of all computations for the new N. The Monte Carlo method is much more flexible: we draw additional samples and perform computations only for these additional samples, preserving the previously computed values. The idea of low-discrepancy sequences is a compromise between numerical quadratures giving deterministic error and the advantages of Monte Carlo, which enables the free placing of sample points until the desired accuracy is met. The most important advantage of low-discrepancy sequences is the improvement of error estimates to $O(N^{-(1-\varepsilon)})$ independently of the problem dimension, which is significantly better than that of Monte Carlo methods (in fact, the constant in the error estimate depends on the dimension; hence, the picture is not as good as the expression $O(N^{-(1-\varepsilon)})$ can suggest).

Definition 2.19. Let $\{u_n\}_{n\geq 1}$ be a sequence of points in $[0, 1]^d$. This point set is called *uniformly distributed* in $[0, 1]^d$ if, for each cube $Q_y = \{x \in [0, 1]^d\colon\ 0 \leq x_i \leq y_i, i = 1, \ldots, d\}$ defined by $y \in [0, 1]^d$, holds the equality

$$\lim_{N\to\infty} \frac{1}{N} \sum_{n=1}^{N} \chi_{Q_y}(u_n) = vol(Q_y),$$

where χ_A denotes the characteristic function of set A.

Definition 2.20. For a sequence $u = \{u_1, \ldots, u_N\}$ of points in $[0, 1]^d$, we define the *star discrepancy*

$$D_N^*(u) = \sup_{y\in[0,1]^d} |F(y) - F_N^u(y)|,$$

where

$$F(y) = vol(Q_y), \quad F_N^u(y) = \frac{1}{N}\sum_{n=1}^{N} \chi_{Q_y}(u_n).$$

Remark 2.21. By the definition of discrepancy if $u = \{u_1, \ldots, u_N\}$ is a subsequence of a uniformly distributed sequence $\{u_n\}_{n\geq 1}$, then $\lim_{N\to\infty} D_N^*(u) = 0$.

Theorem 2.22 (Koksma–Hlawka inequality). *Let $f\colon [0,1]^d \to \mathbb{R}$ be a function of bounded variation. For each sequence $u = \{u_1, \ldots, u_N\}$ in $[0,1]^d$*

$$\left| \int_{[0,1]^d} f(x)dx - \frac{1}{N}\sum_{n=1}^{N} f(u_n) \right| \leq V(f) D_N^*(u),$$

where $V(f)$ is the variation of f (in a multidimensional case, this is the multidimensional Hardy–Krause variation).

Proof. For simplicity, we consider only a one-dimensional case assuming, in addition, that f is of class $C^1([0,1])$ (for a more complete proof see [22]). Then the variation of f is the total variation which for $f \in C^1([0,1])$ is equal $V(f) = \int_0^1 |f'(x)|dx$.

Let $u = \{u_1, \ldots, u_N\}$ be a sequence of points in $[0,1]$. Using identity $f(x) = f(1) - \int_x^1 f'(y)dy$, we obtain

$$\begin{aligned}
\int_0^1 f(x)dx - \frac{1}{N}\sum_{n=1}^{N} f(u_n) &= \frac{1}{N}\sum_{n=1}^{N}\int_{u_n}^1 f'(y)dy - \int_0^1\int_x^1 f'(y)dy\,dx \\
&= \int_0^1 \frac{1}{N}\sum_{n=1}^{N} \mathbb{1}_{(u_n,1]}(y) f'(y)dy \\
&\quad - \int_0^1\int_0^y f'(y)dx\,dy \\
&= \int_0^1 f'(y)\left(\frac{1}{N}\sum_{n=1}^{N} \mathbb{1}_{(u_n,1]}(y) - y\right)dy.
\end{aligned}$$

Let us observe that for a given y

$$\frac{1}{N}\sum_{n=1}^{N} \mathbb{1}_{(u_n,1]}(y) = \frac{1}{N}\sum_{n=1}^{N} \mathbb{1}_{[0,y)}(u_n).$$

The right-hand side of this equality is $F_N^u(y)$ by Definition 2.20. Since in one dimension $F(y) = y$, we obtain

$$\int_0^1 f(x)dx - \frac{1}{N}\sum_{n=1}^N f(u_n) = \int_0^1 f'(y)\big(F_N^u(y) - F(y)\big)dy.$$

Hence,

$$\left|\int_0^1 f(x)dx - \frac{1}{N}\sum_{n=1}^N f(u_n)\right| \leq \int_0^1 |f'(y)|\big|(F_N^u(y) - F(y)\big|dy$$

$$\leq \sup_{y\in[0,1]} \big|(F_N^u(y) - F(y)\big| \int_0^1 |f'(y)|dy = V(f)D_N^*(u).$$

□

Definition 2.23. A sequence $u = \{u_1, \ldots, u_N\}$ in $[0,1]^d$ is called the *low-discrepancy sequence*, if

$$D_N^*(u) = O\left(\frac{(\ln N)^d}{N}\right).$$

Remark 2.24. One can prove that if $(U_n)_{n\geq 1}$ is a sequence of independent random variables with uniform distribution on $[0,1]^d$, then samples from this sequence are uniformly distributed on $[0,1]^d$. For the discrepancy of such samples, we obtain the estimate

$$\mathbb{E}\big(D_N^*(U)\big) = \frac{C_d}{\sqrt{N}}, \quad \text{where } C_d = O(\ln\ln N),$$

which indicates that the discrepancy of a sequence of random variables is of order $N^{-1/2}$.

Example 2.25 (Halton sequences). This is an example of easily computable sequences of low discrepancy.

Let $b \geq 2$ be a prime number. As is well known, each integer n can be expanded in base b

$$n = a_0 + a_1 b + \cdots + a_k b^k, \quad \text{where } a_i \in \{0, 1, \ldots, b-1\}.$$

For n with the above expansion, we define the *radical-inverse function*

$$\Psi_b(n) = \frac{a_0}{b} + \frac{a_1}{b^2} + \cdots + \frac{a_k}{b^{k+1}}.$$

Then the b-adic *Van der Corput sequence* is defined as the one-dimensional sequence $\{\Psi_b(n)\}_{n\in\mathbb{N}}$.

Van der Corput sequences are used as ingredients in the construction of Halton sequences. The *Halton sequence* [36] of dimension d is a sequence $u = \{u_i\}$ in $[0,1]^d$ defined for $b_1, \ldots, b_d$, pairwise prime numbers, as the sequence of vectors

$$u_i = \big(\Psi_{b_1}(i), \Psi_{b_2}(i), \ldots, \Psi_{b_d}(i)\big).$$

One can prove (but the proof is not easy, see [22]) that the Halton sequence is a sequence of low discrepancy

$$D_N^*(u) \le C\frac{(\ln N)^d}{N}, \quad \text{for a constant } C > 0.$$

Example 2.26 (Sobol sequences). The construction of a *Sobol sequence* [83] of points in $[0,1)^d$ starts with a selection of $P_1, \ldots, P_d$ *primitive polynomials* in base 2 (modulo 2) ordered according to their degree

$$P_i(x) = x^{s_i} + a_{1,i}x^{s_i-1} + a_{2,i}x^{s_i-2} + \cdots + a_{s_i-1,i}x + 1$$

with binary coefficients $a_{k,i} \in \{0,1\}$.

A polynomial $P(x)$ of positive degree q is called *primitive modulo M* if: (i) is irreducible modulo M, i.e., there are no other two polynomials $Q(x)$ and $R(x)$ such that $P(x) = Q(x)R(x) \bmod M$; (ii) the smallest power p for which the polynomial $P(x)$ divides x^p+1 is $p = M^q - 1$.

We choose odd natural numbers $1 \le m_{1,i}, \ldots, m_{s_i,i}$ such that $m_{k,i} < 2^k$ for $1 \le k \le s_i$. Let us note that not all admissible choices are equivalent, and many authors have proposed different initializations of these numbers. The interested reader should consult [46]. For $k > s_i$, we define $m_{k,i}$ recursively,

$$m_{k,i} = 2a_{1,i}m_{k-1,i} \oplus \cdots \oplus 2^{s_i-1}a_{s_i-1}m_{k-s_i+1,i} \oplus 2^{s_i}m_{k-s_i,i} \oplus m_{k-s_i,i},$$

where $\oplus$ is the bit-by-bit exclusive-or operator.

The so-called *direction numbers* $\{v_{1,i}, v_{2,i}, \ldots\}$ are defined by

$$v_{k,i} = \frac{m_{k,i}}{2^k}.$$

We expand a natural number n in base 2 writing $n = n_0 + 2n_1 + \cdots + 2^{r-1}n_{r-1}$. Then we define

$$x_{n,i} = n_0v_{1,i} \oplus n_1v_{2,i} \cdots \oplus n_{r-1}v_{r,i},$$

The Sobol sequence is then the sequence of points $(x_n)_{n\geq 1}$ in $[0,1)^d$, where $x_n = (x_{n,1}, x_{n,2}, \ldots, x_{n,d})$.

The Sobol sequences remain unrivaled among practitioners and are massively used in quantitative finance.

Although the Halton sequence is a sequence with low discrepancy, it is not recommended for the computation of high-dimensional integrals because in pairs of the Van der Corput numbers for large bases, cycles with decreasing periods occur. The Halton sequence is a good choice for moderate dimensions where the bases of the Van der Corput sequences are not too large. For higher dimensions, one can use the Sobol sequences as well as the sequences proposed by Faure or Niederreiter, which are obtained by permuting terms in the Van der Corput sequences for small bases. The construction of these sequences is rather involved, and their detailed description is beyond the scope of this book. The interested reader can consult the book by Glasserman [34] and the references cited herein.

The computational method that uses low-discrepancy sequences as nodes of approximation is called the *Quasi Monte Carlo* method. From the Koksma–Hlawka inequality and the definition of low-discrepancy sequences, we obtain an error estimate for this method $O(N^{-(1-\varepsilon)})$. Hence, the estimation is better than that of the Monte Carlo method, which uses pseudo-random nodes.

2.5 Exercises

Exercise 2.1. Consider a linear congruential generator

$$x_{i+1} = ax_i \bmod M.$$

The generator is called *the multiplicative prime modulus generator* if M is prime and a is the primitive root of M i.e., $M \nmid (a^{(M-1)/q} - 1)$ for every prime factor q of $(M-1)$. Show that over the entire cycle

$$\mathbb{E}(x_i) = \frac{M}{2},$$

$$\mathrm{Var}(x_i) = \frac{M(M-2)}{12}.$$

Hint: Show that if $u_i = x_i/M$ then $\mathbb{E}(u_i) = 1/2$ and $\mathrm{Var}(u_i) \to 1/12$ for $M \to \infty$.

Exercise 2.2. Let U and V be independently distributed uniform random variables in $[0, 1]$. Show that $(U + V) \bmod 1$ is also $\mathcal{U}(0, 1)$.

Exercise 2.3. Derive an acceptance–rejection procedure for sampling variates from the density proportional to

$$f(x) = \frac{\exp(-x^2/2)}{1 + |x|}, \qquad x \in \mathbb{R}.$$

Exercise 2.4. Let f be any nonnegative, L^1 function. Consider the set $B = \{(u, v)\colon\ 0 < u \leq \sqrt{f(v/u)}\}$. Prove that if the pair (U, V) is uniformly distributed over B then the *ratio of uniform variates* $X = V/U$ has the probability density function $f(x)/\|f\|_{L^1(\mathbb{R})}$.

Exercise 2.5. Devise an algorithm for sampling from a density proportional to $f(x) = x^2(1 - x)$ on interval $(0, 1)$ using the ratio of uniform variates. Calculate the acceptance probability.

Exercise 2.6. Let U_1 and U_2 be two $\mathcal{U}(-1, 1)$ independently distributed random variates. Show that U_2/U_1, subject to $U_1^2 + U_2^2 < 1$, has the standard Cauchy distribution with density

$$f(x) = \frac{1}{\pi(1 + x^2)}.$$

Exercise 2.7. Let (U, V) be uniformly distributed over the unit circle $D = \{(u, v) : u^2 + v^2 \leq 1\}$. Consider the random variables $Y = U^2 + V^2$ and $\theta = \tan^{-1}(V/U)$. Find the joint density of Y and θ. Show that these two random variables are independent.

Exercise 2.8. Let Y be a random variable with a density proportional to

$$h(y) = y^{\alpha-1}(1 + \rho y)^{-\alpha-\beta}, \qquad y \in [0, \infty),$$

where $\alpha > 0$, $\beta > 0$, and $\rho = \alpha/\beta$.

Prove that random variable $X = \rho Y/(1 + \rho Y)$ has the density of beta distribution with parameters α and β.
Hint: The density of beta distribution with parameters (α, β) is

$$f(x) = \frac{\Gamma(\alpha + \beta)x^{(\alpha-1)}(1 - x)^{(\beta-1)}}{\Gamma(\alpha)\Gamma(\beta)}.$$

Exercise 2.9. Consider $X = WY$ where W and Y are independent random variables. W has exponential density $w(x) = e^{-x}$, and Y has the beta density with parameters $(\alpha, 1-\alpha)$, $\alpha \in (0,1)$. Prove that $X \sim \Gamma(\alpha, 1)$.

Exercise 2.10. Let Y be a random variable with uniform distribution $\mathcal{U}(0,1)$. Taking a nonzero integer k, and a real constant c define

$$X = (kY + c) \bmod 1.$$

Show that $X \sim \mathcal{U}(0,1)$.

Exercise 2.11. Prove that if X is a random variable uniform on the integers $\{0, 1, \ldots, M-1\}$ and Y is any integer-valued random variable independent of X, then the random variable $W = (X+Y) \bmod M$ is uniform on the integers $\{0, 1, \ldots, M-1\}$.

Exercise 2.12. Implement a linear congruential generator with $a = 17$, $c = 0$, and $M = 2^{13} - 1$. Generate 1000 numbers $u_i = x_i/M$. Plot the pairs of successive numbers u_{i+1} and u_i. Compute their sample correlation. Note the number of lines on which pairs (u_i, u_{i+1}) lie.

Exercise 2.13. Consider the acceptance–rejection method for generating a sample of a random variable X with density $f(x)$ using the random variable Y with density $g(x)$. Let T be the number of loops through steps 1 and 2 of the acceptance–rejection algorithm until a single sample of X is delivered. Determine the mean and variance of T in terms of $f(x)$ and $g(x)$.

Exercise 2.14. Let X_1 and X_2 be independent standard normal random variables. Represent the pair in polar coordinates

$$X_1 = R\cos\theta,$$
$$X_2 = R\sin\theta.$$

Show that R and θ are independent, $\theta \sim \mathcal{U}(0, 2\pi)$, and R^2 has an exponential distribution with parameter $1/2$.

Exercise 2.15. Consider the sampling algorithm

(1) Generate $u \sim \mathcal{U}(0,1)$.
(2) Take $x = -\ln(u)/\lambda$.

Prove that the algorithm generates samples from an exponential distribution

$$f(x) = \lambda e^{-\lambda x}, \quad x \in [0, \infty).$$

Exercise 2.16. Prove that if U is a uniform random variable on $(0,1)$, then the cumulative distribution function of $V(U) = \inf\{x\colon F(x) \geq U\}$ is F.

Exercise 2.17. Generate an i.i.d. sample $X_1, X_2, \ldots$ of an exponential random variable with density $f(x) = \lambda e^{-\lambda x}$, one at a time, until the sum exceeds 1. Let in the i-turn of the procedure N_i be such that $X_1 + \cdots + X_{N_i} < 1 < X_1 + \cdots + X_{N_i+1}$. Prove that the distribution of successive numbers N_i is the distribution of a Poisson random variable X with rate λ, i.e., $\mathbb{P}(X = n) = e^{-\lambda}\lambda^n/n!$.

Exercise 2.18. Generate a sample from the distribution of $X = |Z|$, where Z is a standard normal random variable. Apply the acceptance–rejection method using a random variable Y with a standard exponential density $g(x) = e^{-x}$. Find a constant C such that $f(x)/g(x) \leq C$.
Hint: Prove that the density of X is $f(x) = \sqrt{2/\pi}e^{-x^2/2}$.

Exercise 2.19. The inverse Gaussian distribution $ING(c, \xi)$ with mean c/ξ and variance c/ξ^3 has the density

$$f(x) = \frac{c}{x^{3/2}\sqrt{2\pi}} \exp\left(c\xi - \frac{1}{2}\left(\frac{c^2}{x} + x\xi^2\right)\right), \quad x > 0.$$

Derive an algorithm to generate a sample of random variable $X = ING(1,1)$ using the acceptance–rejection method.

Exercise 2.20. Prove that $X = (X_1, X_2)$ is a two-dimensional normal variable with mean $\mathbb{E}X = 0$, variances $\operatorname{Var} X_i = \sigma_i^2$, and correlation $\operatorname{Corr}(X_1, X_2) = \rho$ if

$$X_1 = \sigma_1\Big(\sqrt{1 - |\rho|}Y_1 + \sqrt{|\rho|}Y_3\Big),$$

$$X_2 = \sigma_2\Big(\sqrt{1 - |\rho|}Y_1 + \operatorname{sgn}\, \rho\sqrt{|\rho|}Y_3\Big)$$

where Y_1, Y_2, and Y_3 are independent standard normal variables $\mathcal{N}(0,1)$.

Exercise 2.21 ([3]). Write a code to generate the Halton sequence of dimension $d = 16$ choosing as bases $b_1, \ldots, b_d$ first d prime numbers. With this generator, generate $n = 1000$ of 16-dimensional vectors.

(a) To analyze the uniformity of the obtained quasi-random numbers, draw pictures for components (x_1, x_2) and (x_1, x_4).
(b) To investigate the behavior of the Halton sequences at higher dimensions, draw pictures for components (x_1, x_{16}), (x_4, x_{16}), and (x_8, x_{16}). Observe that points are more concentrated on bands. This is an empirical indication that the Halton sequences are not appropriate for high-dimensional computations.

Exercise 2.22. The discrepancy D_N (without star) is defined for a sequence $u = \{u_1, \ldots, u_N\}$ of points from $[0,1]^d$ by the expression

$$D_N(u) = \sup_{Q \subset [0,1]^d} \left| \frac{1}{N} \sum_{n=1}^{N} \chi_Q(u_n) - vol(Q) \right|$$

where the cubes Q are the Cartesian products of arbitrary intervals in $[0,1]$. Verify the inequality

$$D_N^* \leq D_N \leq 2^d D_N^*.$$

Hint: Each cube in the definition of D_N can be obtained as the difference of a finite number of cubes Q_y with one edge at the origin.

Chapter 3

Monte Carlo Methods

The history of Monte Carlo methods goes back to Stanislaw Ulam, who, working on the Manhattan Project, suggested to John von Neumann that the newly developed ENIAC computer would give them the means to carry out computations based on statistical sampling.

The term "the Monte Carlo method" is attributed to their coworker Nicholas Metropolis, who was partly inspired by Ulam's anecdotes about his gambling uncle who "just had to go to Monte Carlo". The term has appeared in print for the first time in the paper by N. Metropolis and S. Ulam. The Monte Carlo method, *Journal of American Statistical Association*, 44 (1949). Phelim Boyle [11] was the first who, in 1977, used Monte Carlo methods in quantitative finance to compute option prices.

3.1 Monte Carlo Integration

Consider the Monte Carlo (MC) computation of the expected value $\mathbb{E}(X)$ of a random variable X with a known distribution. The simplest algorithm, the so-called *crude Monte Carlo*, can be summarized as follows:

(1) Generate a sample $X_1, \ldots, X_N$ from the distribution of X.

(2) Compute the sample average $\hat{X}_N$ (subscript N indicates the estimator computed from an N-element sample)

$$\hat{X}_N = \frac{1}{N} \sum_{i=1}^{N} X_i.$$

(3) Approximate the exact mean value by the estimator

$$\mathbb{E}(X) \simeq \hat{X}_N.$$

The Monte Carlo method is based on two fundamental results: the strong law of large numbers and the central limit theorem.

Theorem 3.1 (Strong Law of Large Numbers). *Let $X_1, X_2, \ldots$ be a sequence of square-integrable, identically distributed, independent random variables with $\mathbb{E}(X_i) = \mu < \infty$. Let*

$$Y_n = \frac{X_1 + X_2 + \cdots + X_n}{n}, \quad n = 1, 2, \ldots.$$

Then

$$\lim_{n\to\infty} Y_n = \mu, \ \ a.s.$$

The following theorem, implied by the strong law of large numbers, gives detailed information on the estimators obtained from MC simulations.

Theorem 3.2. *Let $X_1, \ldots, X_N$ be an i.i.d. sample from the distribution of X, where $\mathbb{E}(X) = \mu$, $\mathrm{Cov}(X) = \Sigma$. Let $\hat{X}_N$ denote the sample mean value and $\hat{\Sigma}_N$, the sample covariance matrix. Then:*

(1) $\mathbb{E}(\hat{X}_N) = \mu$.
(2) $\mathbb{E}(\hat{\Sigma}_N) = \Sigma$.
(3) $\lim_{N\to\infty} \hat{X}_N = \mu$, *a.s.*
(4) $\lim_{N\to\infty} \hat{\Sigma}_N = \Sigma$, *a.s.*

Theorem 3.3 (Central Limit Theorem). *Let $X_1, X_2, \ldots$ be a sequence of square-integrable, identically distributed, independent random variables with expectations $\mathbb{E}(X_i) = \mu < \infty$ and variances $\mathrm{Var}(X_i) = \sigma^2$. Define the sequence*

$$Z_n = \frac{(X_1 - \mu) + (X_2 - \mu) + \cdots + (X_n - \mu)}{\sqrt{n}}.$$

Then

$$Z_n \to \mathcal{N}(0, \sigma^2) \text{ in distribution.}$$

The central limit theorem implies that if X_i, $i = 1, \ldots, N$, is a sample drawn independently from the distribution of X, then the estimator $\hat{X}_N$ converges in distribution to $\mathcal{N}(\mu, \frac{\sigma^2}{N})$. This gives the error estimate $\mathrm{Var}(\hat{X}_N) = O(N^{-1})$.

The central limit theorem gives the following corollary.

Corollary 3.4. *If X is one-dimensional, then*

$$\sqrt{N}(\hat{X}_N - \mathbb{E}(X)) \to \mathcal{N}(0, \sigma^2) \text{ in distribution.}$$

Therefore, if z_α denotes α-quantile of a standard normal distribution, then

$$\frac{\sigma z_{\alpha/2}}{\sqrt{N}} < \hat{X}_N - \mathbb{E}(X) < \frac{\sigma z_{1-\alpha/2}}{\sqrt{N}}.$$

Definition 3.5. The confidence interval with a confidence level α for $\hat{X}_N$ is

$$\left(\hat{X}_N - \frac{\sigma z_{1-\alpha/2}}{\sqrt{N}}, \hat{X}_N - \frac{\sigma z_{\alpha/2}}{\sqrt{N}}\right).$$

Since $z_{1-\alpha/2} = -z_{\alpha/2}$, this confidence interval can be written as

$$\left(\hat{X}_N - \frac{\sigma z_{1-\alpha/2}}{\sqrt{N}}, \hat{X}_N + \frac{\sigma z_{1-\alpha/2}}{\sqrt{N}}\right).$$

Remark 3.6. In real simulations, we do not know the true value of variance σ^2, and we replace that value with the sample variance

$$\hat{\sigma}^2 = \frac{1}{N-1}\sum_{j=1}^{N}(X_j - \hat{X})^2 = \frac{1}{N-1}\sum_{i=j}^{N} X_j^2 - \frac{N}{N-1}\hat{X}^2.$$

Let Φ be the cumulative distribution function of a standard normal variable. Then we have the identity

$$\Phi(z_{1-\alpha/2}) - \Phi(z_{\alpha/2}) = (1 - \alpha/2) - \alpha/2 = 1 - \alpha.$$

Hence, if I_α is the confidence interval with a confidence level α, then $\mathbb{P}(\mathbb{E}(X) \in I_\alpha) = 1 - \alpha$, i.e., the confidence interval I_α contains the true value of $\mathbb{E}(X)$ with probability $(1 - \alpha)$.

MC simulations of $\mathbb{E}(g(X))$

Consider the MC computation of $\mathbb{E}(g(X))$, where X is a random variable with a known density $\phi_X(x)$

$$\mathbb{E}(g(X)) = \int_{\mathbb{R}^d} g(x)\phi_X(x)dx = \int_{[0,1]^d} f(x)dx,$$

where $f(x)$ is obtained by changing variables $\mathbb{R}^d \to [0,1]^d$. The last integral can be treated as the mean value $\mathbb{E}(f(Y))$ of a random variable Y with uniform distribution on $[0,1]^d$. The simulation algorithm of crude Monte Carlo is then:

(1) Generate a sample $Y_1, \ldots, Y_N$ from the uniform distribution of Y on $[0,1]^d$.
(2) Compute the average $\hat{f} = \frac{1}{N}\sum_{j=1}^{N} f(Y_j)$ which approximates the integral.

This algorithm is similar to a deterministic quadrature. The difference lies in the error estimates: a deterministic quadrature of order k approximates the integral with the error $O(N^{-k/d})$ and the Monte Carlo approximation, using randomly sampled points, gives the error of order $O(N^{-1/2})$ independent of dimension d. The exact estimate of the Monte Carlo error is given by the following theorem.

Theorem 3.7. *Let* $f \in L^2([0,1]^d)$ *and*

$$V^2(f) = \int_{[0,1]^d} f^2(x)dx - \left(\int_{[0,1]^d} f(x)dx\right)^2 < \infty.$$

The estimator $\hat{f}$ *computed by the crude Monte Carlo algorithm has the following properties:*

(1) $\hat{f} \to \mathbb{E}(f(Y))$ *for* $N \to \infty$, *a.s.*
(2) *Let* $\hat{\delta} = \mathbb{E}(f(Y)) - \hat{f} = \int_{[0,1]^d} f(x)dx - \hat{f}$, *then* $\operatorname{Var}(\hat{\delta}) = \frac{V^2(f)}{N}$.

Proof. If $Y_1, \ldots, Y_N$ are i.i.d., then $f(Y_1), \ldots, f(Y_N)$ are i.i.d. too, since $f \in L^2$ can be approximated by simple functions. The convergence $\hat{f} \to \mathbb{E}(f(Y))$ follows from the strong law of large numbers.

To compute $\mathrm{Var}(\hat{\delta})$, we observe that $\mathbb{E}(\hat{\delta}) = 0$ which follows from the equality $\mathbb{E}(\hat{f}) = \mathbb{E}(f(Y))$ valid by the i.i.d. property of $Y_1, \ldots, Y_N$. Then we get

$$\mathrm{Var}(\hat{\delta}) = \mathbb{E}(\hat{\delta}^2) = \mathbb{E}\left(\int_{[0,1]^d} f(x)dx - \frac{1}{N}\sum_{j=1}^{N} f(Y_j)\right)^2.$$

Let $v(x) := \int_{[0,1]^d} f(x)dx - f(x)$. Then

$$\mathrm{Var}(\hat{\delta}) = \mathbb{E}\left(\frac{1}{N^2}\left(\sum_{j=1}^{N} v(Y_j)\right)^2\right),$$

due to the equality $\int_{[0,1]^d} f(x)dx = \frac{1}{N}\sum_{j=1}^{N}\int_{[0,1]^d} f(x)dx$.

Since $v(Y_j)$ are i.i.d., we have $\mathbb{E}\big(v(Y_i)v(Y_j)\big) = 0$ for $i \neq j$. These equalities supplemented with $\mathbb{E}(v(Y_j)) = 0$ yield

$$\mathrm{Var}(\hat{\delta}) = \frac{1}{N^2}\sum_{j=1}^{N}\mathbb{E}\big(v^2(Y_j)\big) = \frac{1}{N}\mathrm{Var}\big(v(Y)\big) = \frac{1}{N}\int_{[0,1]^d} v^2(x)dx.$$

On the other hand, $\mathrm{Var}\big(v(Y)\big) = V^2(f)$ because

$$\mathrm{Var}\big(v(Y)\big) = \int_{[0,1]^d} v^2(x)dx = \int_{[0,1]^d} f^2(x)dx - \left(\int_{[0,1]^d} f(x)dx\right)^2.$$

□

3.2 Variance Reduction Methods

We have observed that the size of the confidence interval is determined by the value of $\sqrt{\mathrm{Var}(X)}/\sqrt{N}$. We would like to decrease the size of this interval without increasing the sample size N, which is usually very costly (computational complexity is, in the majority of cases, a linear function of N). These methods are called *variance reduction* methods. We describe a number of these methods, illustrating the effects of their application with examples from quantitative finance. A more complete analysis of the variance reduction technique can be found in the monographs by Asmussen and Glynn [3], Glasserman [34], Jäckel [42], or Pagès [70].

3.2.1 *Importance sampling*

The concept of importance sampling in computing $x = \mathbb{E}(X)$ is to modify the distribution of X so that most sampling is performed on regions that contribute the most to x. This requires a change of the initial distribution $\mathbb{P}(d\omega)$ of X to an importance sampling distribution $\tilde{\mathbb{P}}(d\omega)$ such that $x = \mathbb{E}(X) = \tilde{\mathbb{E}}(LX)$, where $L = \frac{d\mathbb{P}}{d\tilde{\mathbb{P}}}$ is the Radon–Nikodym derivative. The problem is to make an efficient choice of the modified distribution $\tilde{\mathbb{P}}(d\omega)$.

Theorem 3.8. *Let X be a random variable with distribution $\mathbb{P}$. Define $\mathbb{P}^*$ by the Radon–Nikodym derivative*

$$\frac{d\mathbb{P}}{d\mathbb{P}^*} = \frac{\mathbb{E}|X|}{|X|} = L^*, \quad i.e., \quad \mathbb{P}^*(d\omega) = \frac{1}{L^*}\mathbb{P}(d\omega).$$

The importance sampling estimator of the expectation of X under measure $\mathbb{P}^*$ has a smaller variance than any other estimator obtained by a change of measure. If $X \geq 0$ a.s., then the $\mathbb{P}^*$-variance of the importance sampling estimator is equal 0.

Proof. Let $X_1, \ldots, X_N$ be an i.i.d. sample of X. The importance sampling estimator under measure $\mathbb{P}^*$ is

$$\hat{x}^* = \frac{1}{N}\sum_{j=1}^{N} X_j L^*(X_j).$$

Its variance is

$$\mathrm{Var}^*(\hat{x}^*) = \mathrm{Var}^*(XL^*).$$

We have by the definition of L^*

$$\mathbb{E}^*\big((XL^*)^2\big) = \mathbb{E}^*\big(|X|^2(L^*)^2\big) = \mathbb{E}^*\big((\mathbb{E}|X|)^2\big) = \big(\mathbb{E}|X|\big)^2.$$

If $\tilde{\mathbb{P}}$ is another measure with the Radon–Nikodym derivative $\tilde{L}$ such that $\mathbb{E}(X) = \tilde{\mathbb{E}}(X\tilde{L})$, then

$$\big(\mathbb{E}|X|\big)^2 = \big(\tilde{\mathbb{E}}(|X|\tilde{L})\big)^2 \leq \tilde{\mathbb{E}}\big((X\tilde{L})^2\big).$$

Hence,

$$\mathbb{E}^*\big((XL^*)^2\big) \leq \tilde{\mathbb{E}}\big((X\tilde{L})^2\big).$$

Since $\mathbb{E}(X) = \mathbb{E}^*(XL^*) = \tilde{\mathbb{E}}(X\tilde{L})$, we obtain $\mathrm{Var}^*(XL^*) \leq \widetilde{\mathrm{Var}}(X\tilde{L})$.

If $X \geq 0$, then

$$\mathrm{Var}^*(XL^*) = \mathbb{E}^*\big((XL^*)^2\big) - \Big(\mathbb{E}^*(XL^*)\Big)^2 = \big(\mathbb{E}(X)\big)^2 - \big(\mathbb{E}(X)\big)^2 = 0.$$

□

Remark 3.9. The choice of measure suggested by Theorem 3.8 can never be implemented in practice since to obtain L^*, we must know $\mathbb{E}|X|$, and this is the value we seek to estimate. Nevertheless, Theorem 3.8 suggests that variance reduction can be achieved by sampling in proportion to $|X(\omega)|$.

Example 3.10. Consider the Monte Carlo estimation of

$$I = \mathbb{E}\big(g(X)\big),$$

where X denotes a random variable with density $\phi(x)$ and $g \geq 0$. Importance sampling after changing $\phi(x)$ to $f(x)$ gives

$$\begin{aligned}\mathbb{E}\big(g(X)\big) &= \int_{\mathbb{R}^d} g(x)\phi(x)dx = \int_{\mathbb{R}^d} \frac{g(x)\phi(x)}{f(x)} f(x)dx \\ &= \mathbb{E}_f\left(\frac{g(X)\phi(X)}{f(X)}\right).\end{aligned}$$

Theorem 3.8 implies that

$$f(x) = \frac{g(x)\phi(x)}{\int_{\mathbb{R}^d} g(x)\phi(x)dx}$$

defines an estimator with zero variance. Since the denominator in the above expression is the searched quantity, this change of distribution is not achievable in practice.

This problem can be overcome by searching for $f(x)$ in a given family of distributions $f(x,\theta)$ parameterized on θ, and minimizing with respect to θ the function

$$\mathrm{Var}_f\left(\frac{g(X)\phi(X)}{f(X,\theta)}\right) = \int_{\mathbb{R}^d} \frac{g^2(x)\phi^2(x)}{f(x,\theta)} dx - I^2.$$

The upper bound of the variance can be estimated by

$$\mathrm{Var}_f\left(\frac{g(X)\phi(X)}{f(X,\theta)}\right) \leq IJ(\theta) - I^2,$$

where

$$J(\theta) = \sup_{x \in \mathbb{R}^d} \frac{g(x)\phi(x)}{f(x,\theta)}.$$

Thus, we seek f that minimizes $J(\theta)$ with respect to θ. The resulting f is presumably not the best importance sampling density, but that f is providing a good fit to $g(x)\phi(x)$.

We test this approach by evaluating the integral

$$I_a = \int_a^{\infty} x^{\alpha-1} e^{-x} dx$$

with $\alpha > 1$ and $a > 0$, using the Monte Carlo method with the importance sampling density sought in the form

$$f(x,\theta) = \theta \exp\bigl(-\theta(x-a)\bigr),$$

where θ must be determined.

Since f is a shifted exponential density, we can simulate samples from density f taking $X_n = a - \theta^{-1} \ln u_n$, where $u_n \sim \mathcal{U}(0,1)$. The importance sampling estimator of I_a is then

$$\hat{I}_a = \frac{1}{N} \sum_{n=1}^{N} \frac{X_n^{\alpha-1} e^{-X_n}}{\theta \exp\bigl(-\theta(X_n - a)\bigr)}.$$

Following the aforementioned approach, we can minimize variance of $\hat{I}_a$ by minimizing $J(\theta)$

$$\min_{0 \le \theta \le 1} \max_{x > a} \frac{x^{\alpha-1} e^{-x}}{\theta \exp\bigl(-\theta(x-a)\bigr)}.$$

Let $(\hat{x}, \hat{\theta})$ be a saddle point of this minimax problem. Simple computations provide the easily solvable system of equations

$$\frac{\alpha - 1}{\hat{x}} + \hat{\theta} = 1,$$

$$\hat{x} - 1/\hat{\theta} = a.$$

Then with $\hat{\theta}$ that solves this system of equations, we can perform the importance sampling estimation of I_a.

Example 3.11. Consider the computation of $z = \mathbb{P}(X \in A)$, where X is a d-dimensional Gaussian random vector with mean 0 and covariance matrix Σ. Theorem 3.8 suggests sampling in proportion to $\phi_X(x)\mathbb{1}_{\{x\in A\}}$, where ϕ_X is the density of X. The rapid decay of $\phi_X(x)$ for large x suggests sampling in the vicinity of point x^*, where ϕ_X has a maximum over A. Hence, the distribution $\tilde{\mathbb{P}}(d\omega)$ can be obtained by a shift of $\mathbb{P}(d\omega)$, with mean 0, to $\tilde{\mathbb{P}}(d\omega)$, with mean x^*. This gives $L = \frac{\phi_X}{\tilde{\phi}_X}$, where $\tilde{\phi}_X$ is the density with mean x^*. Knowing the Gaussian distribution formula, we obtain

$$L = \exp\Big(-(x^*)^\top \Sigma^{-1} X + \frac{1}{2}(x^*)^\top \Sigma^{-1} x^* \Big).$$

Example 3.12. A special case of the previous example is the computation of VaR of an investment portfolio. Let us recall that

$$\mathrm{VaR}_\alpha(X) = \inf_z \big\{ \mathbb{P}(-X \le z) \ge 1 - \alpha \big\}.$$

Usually, VaR is estimated by computing $\mathbb{P}(-X > z)$ for a sequence of different z and selecting z corresponding to the prescribed confidence level α. These computations can be improved using importance sampling.

Consider an investment portfolio $X = w^\top S$ of d assets with prices $S = (S_1, \ldots, S_d)$, where w are the weights of assets in the portfolio.

As in the previous example, assume that $S \sim \mathcal{N}(0, \Sigma)$. To implement the importance sampling technique to compute $\mathbb{P}(-X > z) = \mathbb{P}(-w^\top S > z)$, we must know $x^* \in \mathbb{R}^d$, a point at which the distribution of S has the maximum over $\{-w^\top S > z\}$. This leads to the following optimization problem

$$\begin{cases} \max\limits_x \exp\big(-\frac{1}{2} x^\top \Sigma^{-1} x\big), \\ -w^\top x > z. \end{cases}$$

This problem is equivalent to

$$\begin{cases} \max\limits_x -\frac{1}{2} x^\top \Sigma^{-1} x, \\ -w^\top x > z, \end{cases}$$

which can be solved by Lagrange multipliers giving

$$x^* = -\frac{z}{w^\top \Sigma w} \Sigma w.$$

Inserting that x^* into the formula from the previous example, we obtain the importance sampling change of measure in the MC simulations for $\mathrm{VaR}_\alpha(X)$.

Remark 3.13. In practice, we are interested in computing VaR of losses over a certain time interval. Let the loss be given by $-X = V(t_0+\delta t) - V(t_0) = \delta V$, where V is the portfolio value. By a first-order approximation, we get $\delta V \simeq \partial V/\partial t\, \delta t + \partial V/\partial S\, \delta S$. Assuming that δS has a multivariate normal distribution, we obtain

$$\mathbb{P}(-X > z) \simeq \mathbb{P}\left(\frac{\partial V}{\partial S}\delta S > z - \frac{\partial V}{\partial t}\delta t\right).$$

Thus, the problem is reduced to the problem analyzed in the last example.

Example 3.14 (Exponential change of measure). The change of measure described in Example 3.11 is a special case of a more general procedure called *exponential twisting* (Glasserman [34]). If X is a d-dimensional random variable such that $\mathbb{E}\big(\exp(\theta^\top X)\big) < +\infty$, for $\theta \in \mathbb{R}^d$, then the exponentially twisted measure is defined as

$$\frac{d\mathbb{P}_\theta}{d\mathbb{P}} = \frac{\exp(\theta^\top X)}{\mathbb{E}\big(\exp(\theta^\top X)\big)}.$$

We apply exponential twisting to the computation of VaR in the so-called *delta–gamma approximation*. To this end, we consider losses over time interval δt of portfolio $V(t) = w^\top S_t$, where $S_t = (S_t^1, \ldots, S_t^d)$ is a vector of asset prices and w, a vector of asset weights. We approximate the change in portfolio value $\delta V = V(t+\delta t) - V(t)$ over time interval δt up to second order as $\delta V = \partial V/\partial t\ \delta t + \partial V/\partial S\, \delta S + 1/2\, \delta S^\top \Gamma \delta S$. Assuming that δS has a multivariate normal distribution $\delta S \sim \mathcal{N}(0, \Sigma)$ and defining losses $X = -\delta V$ one gets

$$\mathbb{P}(-X > z) = \mathbb{P}(\Delta^\top \delta S + 1/2\, \delta S^\top \Gamma \delta S > a),$$

where $a = z - \partial V/\partial t\ \delta t$, $\Delta = \partial V/\partial S$ is the portfolio Delta, and Γ is the matrix of the portfolio Gamma with $\Gamma_{ij} = \partial^2 V/\partial S_i \partial S_j$.

The bilinear form $\Delta^\top \delta S + 1/2\, \delta S^\top \Gamma \delta S$ can be transformed into $Q = b^\top Z + Z^\top \Lambda Z$, where $Z \sim \mathcal{N}(0, I)$ and Λ is a diagonal matrix.

For this transformation, it is sufficient to take A such that $AA^\top = \Sigma$ and $1/2\, A^\top \Gamma A = \Lambda$. Then we can draw samples from the distribution of δS taking $\delta S = AZ$, where $Z \sim \mathcal{N}(0, I)$. Finally, we obtain

$$\mathbb{P}(\Delta^\top \delta S + 1/2\, \delta S^\top \Gamma \delta S > a) = \mathbb{P}(Q > a),$$

with $Q = b^\top Z + Z^\top \Lambda Z$, where b is a vector with components b_j and Λ is a diagonal matrix with diagonal entries λ_j, $j = 1, \ldots, d$.

Applying exponential twisting, we perform the change of measure

$$\frac{d\mathbb{P}_\theta}{d\mathbb{P}} = \exp\big(\theta Q - C(\theta)\big)$$

with $C(\theta) = \ln \mathbb{E}\big(\exp(\theta Q)\big)$, the *cumulant generating function* of Q. Then

$$\mathbb{P}(Q > a) = \mathbb{E}_\theta \left(\exp(-\theta Q + C(\theta))\,\mathbb{1}_{\{Q>a\}}\right),$$

which shows that to estimate $\mathbb{P}(Q > a)$ it is sufficient to estimate the expectation of $\exp\big(-\theta Q + C(\theta)\big)\mathbb{1}_{\{Q>a\}}$ on samples Z generated from a $\mathbb{P}_\theta$-normal distribution.

To perform these estimates, let us compute $C(\theta)$. For $Z = (Z_1, \ldots, Z_d)$ a random variable with $\mathbb{P}$-distribution $\mathcal{N}(0, I)$, where I is the $d \times d$ identity matrix, the loss function can be written as

$$Q = \sum_{j=1}^{d} (b_j Z_j + \lambda_j Z_j^2) = \sum_{j=1}^{d} \left(\lambda_j \left(Z_j + \frac{b_j}{2\lambda_j} \right)^2 - \frac{b_j^2}{4\lambda_j} \right). \tag{3.1}$$

Then using the identity

$$\mathbb{E}\big(\exp\big(u(Z + a)^2\big)\big) = (1 - 2u)^{-1/2} \exp\left(\frac{a^2 u}{1 - 2u} \right), \tag{3.2}$$

valid for $Z \sim \mathcal{N}(0, 1)$ and $a < 1/2$, we obtain

$$C(\theta) = \ln \mathbb{E}\big(\exp(\theta Q)\big) = \frac{1}{2} \sum_{j=1}^{d} \left(\frac{\theta^2 b_j^2}{1 - 2\theta\lambda_j} - \ln(1 - 2\theta\lambda_j) \right). \tag{3.3}$$

To generate samples from a $\mathbb{P}_\theta$-normal distribution, we take Z with $\mathbb{P}$-distribution $\mathcal{N}(0, I)$. Then the $\mathbb{P}_\theta$-distribution of Z is normal

$Z \sim \mathcal{N}(\mu(\theta), \Sigma(\theta))$, where

$$\mu_j(\theta) = \frac{\theta b_j}{1 - 2\theta\lambda_j}$$

and $\Sigma(\theta)$ is a diagonal matrix with diagonal elements

$$\sigma_j^2(\theta) = \frac{1}{1 - 2\theta\lambda_j}.$$

Indeed, using the formula for the densities of $\mathcal{N}(\mu, \Sigma)$ and $\mathcal{N}(0, I)$, we obtain

$$\frac{d\mathbb{P}_\theta}{d\mathbb{P}} = \frac{|\Sigma|^{-1/2} \exp\big(-1/2(Z-\mu)^\top \Sigma^{-1}(Z-\mu)\big)}{\exp\big(-1/2 Z^\top Z\big)}.$$

Then inserting into this formula the expressions for μ_j and σ_j, we obtain

$$\frac{d\mathbb{P}_\theta}{d\mathbb{P}} = \exp\big(\theta Q - C(\theta)\big)$$

with Q and $C(\theta)$ given by equations (3.1) and (3.3), respectively, which proves the desired $\mathbb{P}_\theta$-distribution of Z.

Hence, to estimate $\mathbb{P}(Q > a)$, we simulate $\exp\big(-\theta Q + C(\theta)\big)\mathbb{1}_{\{Q>a\}}$ with Z from the above described normal distribution $\mathcal{N}(\mu(\theta), \Sigma(\theta))$.

3.2.2 *Stratified sampling*

Consider the estimation of the expectation of a random variable X. Assume that there is another random variable Y, called a *stratification variable*, which takes finitely many values $\{y_1, \ldots, y_R\}$ with known probabilities $p_i = \mathbb{P}(Y = y_i)$. If the conditional expectation $\mathbb{E}(X|Y = y_i)$ can be easily simulated, we can stratify the sample space Ω into R disjoint *strata* $\{\Omega_i,\ i = 1, \ldots, R\}$ determined by $Y = y_i$.

Then one can compute

$$\mathbb{E}(X) = \sum_{i=1}^{R} \mathbb{E}(X|Y = y_i)\mathbb{P}(Y = y_i).$$

If probabilities $p_i = \mathbb{P}(Y = y_i)$ are known, then an estimator of $\mathbb{E}(X)$ is obtained by simulating only the R different conditional expectations.

We simulate a sample of N independent copies of X with N_i copies $X_j^{(i)}$, $j = 1, \ldots, N_i$ in the ith stratum, where μ_i, σ_i^2 the ith stratum mean and variance, respectively,

$$\mu_i = \mathbb{E}(X|Y = y_i) \quad \sigma_i^2 = \mathrm{Var}(X|Y = y_i), \quad i = 1, \ldots, R.$$

The stratified estimator of x is

$$\hat{x}_{ST} = \sum_{i=1}^{R} p_i \frac{1}{N_i} \sum_{j=1}^{N_i} X_j^{(i)}.$$

Since $\mathbb{E}\big(X_j^{(i)}\big) = \mathbb{E}(X|Y = y_i)$, the stratified estimator is unbiased. Since the samples $X_j^{(i)}$ are i.i.d., the variance of the stratified estimator is

$$\mathrm{Var}(\hat{x}_{ST}) = \sum_{i=1}^{R} p_i^2 \frac{1}{N_i^2} \sum_{j=1}^{N_i} \mathrm{Var}\big(X_j^{(i)}\big) = \sum_{i=1}^{R} p_i^2 \frac{1}{N_i} \sigma_i^2.$$

A common scheme is *proportional stratified sampling*, where $N_i = Np_i$. Then

$$\mathrm{Var}(\hat{x}_{ST}) = \sum_{i=1}^{R} p_i^2 \frac{\sigma_i^2}{N_i} = \frac{1}{N} \sum_{i=1}^{R} p_i \sigma_i^2.$$

By the relations

$$\sigma^2 = \mathrm{Var}(X) = \mathbb{E}\big(\mathrm{Var}(X|Y)\big) + \mathrm{Var}\big(\mathbb{E}(X|Y)\big) \geq \mathbb{E}\big(\mathrm{Var}(X|Y)\big),$$

$$\mathbb{E}\big(\mathrm{Var}(X|Y)\big) = \sum_{i=1}^{R} \mathrm{Var}(X|Y = y_i)\mathbb{P}(Y = y_i) = \sum_{i=1}^{R} p_i \sigma_i^2,$$

one can show that the variance of the crude MC estimator $\hat{x}_C$

$$\mathrm{Var}(\hat{x}_C) = \frac{\sigma^2}{N} \geq \frac{1}{N} \sum_{i=1}^{R} p_i \sigma_i^2 = \mathrm{Var}(\hat{x}_{ST})$$

is greater than the variance of the stratified estimator $\hat{x}_{ST}$ with proportional sampling.

Example 3.15. We have shown above that stratified sampling with proportional sampling reduces the estimator variance compared to the crude MC estimator. It is, however, important to find the optimal strata allocation. A very natural choice is to choose strata with minimal variance of the estimator.

By selecting strata of arbitrary sizes N_i such that $N_1+\cdots+N_R = N$, we obtain

$$\mathrm{Var}(\hat{x}_{ST}) = \sum_{i=1}^{R} p_i^2 \frac{\sigma_i^2}{N_i}.$$

To find the minimal value of this expression, we apply the method of Lagrange multipliers

$$\min_{N_i} \sum_{i=1}^{R} p_i^2 \frac{\sigma_i^2}{N_i} + \lambda \left(\sum_{i=1}^{R} N_i - N \right).$$

Then the Kuhn–Tucker theorem gives

$$N_j = \frac{p_j \sigma_j}{\sum_{i=1}^{R} p_i \sigma_i}.$$

In practice, since σ_i are unknown, pilot samples are used to obtain estimates for σ_i. Then using these pilot variances, the final sample allocations are computed.

3.2.3 *Antithetic variates*

To implement antithetic variates, we generate N i.i.d. random pairs

$$(X_1, X_2), (X_3, X_4), \ldots, (X_{2N-1}, X_{2N}).$$

We assume that variables X_{2j-1} and X_{2j} have identical variances and negative correlations for $j = 1, \ldots, N$.

Then

$$\mathrm{Var}\left(\frac{1}{2N}\sum_{i=1}^{2N} X_i\right) = \frac{1}{N}\mathrm{Var}\left(\frac{X_1 + X_2}{2}\right) = \frac{1}{4N}\left(2\sigma^2(X_1) + 2\sigma^2(X_1)\rho\right)$$
$$= \frac{1}{2N}\sigma^2(X_1)(1+\rho),$$

where ρ is the correlation of X_1 and X_2.

Hence, we must choose X_{2j-1}, X_{2j} to make ρ possibly close to -1. There is no simple method for such a choice. The following theorem is a further step toward identifying a suitable candidate.

Theorem 3.16. *Let X be a one-dimensional random variable with a symmetric density $\phi(x)$, i.e., X and $-X$ have the same density. If g is a monotonic function and $\mathbb{E}\big(g(X)\big) < +\infty$, then*

$$\operatorname{Corr}\big(g(X), g(-X)\big) \leq 0.$$

The above inequality is sharp if g is strictly monotonic over a set of positive $\mathbb{P}$-measure, where $\mathbb{P}$ is implied by the distribution of X.

Proof. Let $m = \mathbb{E}\big(g(X)\big) < +\infty$, $c = \inf\{y \in \mathbb{R}\colon\ g(y) \geq m\}$. Then we get

$$\begin{aligned}
&\int_{\mathbb{R}} \big(g(x) - m\big)\big(g(-x) - m\big)\phi(x)dx \\
&\quad = \int_{\mathbb{R}} \big(g(x) - m\big)\big(g(-x) - g(-c)\big)\phi(x)dx \\
&\qquad + \big(g(-c) - m\big) \int_{\mathbb{R}} \big(g(x) - m\big)\phi(x)dx.
\end{aligned}$$

Since

$$\big(g(x) - m\big)\big(g(-x) - g(-c)\big) \leq 0$$

and by definition $\int_{\mathbb{R}} \big(g(x) - m\big)\phi(x)dx = 0$, then

$$\operatorname{Cov}\big(g(X), g(-X)\big) = \int_{\mathbb{R}} \big(g(x) - m\big)\big(g(-x) - m\big)\phi(x)dx \leq 0.$$

If $g(x)$ is strictly monotonic over $\phi(x) > 0$, then

$$\big(g(x) - m\big)\big(g(-x) - g(-c)\big) < 0, \text{ a.s.,}$$

and the integral is strictly less than zero. □

Example 3.17. The standard example of antithetic variates appears in the computation of option prices in the Black–Scholes model. Since the price of the underlying is

$$S_T = S_0 \exp\big((r - \sigma^2/2)T + \sigma W_T\big),$$

we use as an antithetic variate

$$S_T^- = S_0 \exp\big((r - \sigma^2/2)T - \sigma W_T\big),$$

thus, W_T is replaced by $-W_T$.

Since W_T has a symmetric density, for a monotonic $g(X_T)$ the function $f(W_T) = g(S_T)$ is monotonic as the superposition of a monotonic function g with a strictly increasing exponential function. Hence, for monotonic g, the use of antithetic variates in the Black–Scholes model always reduces the variance.

3.2.4 *Control variates*

The idea behind the control variates is as follows. Suppose that our goal is to estimate the expectation $x = \mathbb{E}(X)$ and we can somehow find another random variable Y close to X, in some sense, and with known expectation $y = \mathbb{E}(Y)$.

Let $\hat{x}$, $\hat{y}$ be estimators of x and y, respectively. Then the control variate estimator is

$$\hat{x}_{cv} = \hat{x} + \alpha(\hat{y} - y).$$

The optimal choice of α should minimize the variance of the control variate estimator

$$\mathrm{Var}(\hat{x}_{cv}) = \mathrm{Var}(\hat{x}) + \alpha^2 \mathrm{Var}(\hat{y}) + 2\alpha \mathrm{Cov}(\hat{x}, \hat{y}).$$

The right-hand side is minimal for

$$\alpha = -\frac{\mathrm{Cov}(\hat{x}, \hat{y})}{\mathrm{Var}(\hat{y})}.$$

Then

$$\mathrm{Var}(\hat{x}_{cv}) = \mathrm{Var}(\hat{x}) - \frac{\big(\mathrm{Cov}(\hat{x}, \hat{y})\big)^2}{\mathrm{Var}(\hat{y})} = \mathrm{Var}(\hat{x})(1 - \rho^2),$$

where ρ is the correlation of $\hat{x}$ and $\hat{y}$.

This shows that we must look for Y with $|\rho|$ possibly close to 1. The precise value of α is not known but can be estimated from the simulations used to estimate $\hat{x}_{cv}$. This estimator of α is, of course, biased. Fortunately, the bias is $O(1/N)$ and vanishes for a large sample. The problem is that not knowing α, we cannot decide the number of simulations required to obtain the desired level of variance. A remedy to this problem is to use an initial run with fewer iterations to estimate an approximate value of α and then use this α to evaluate the number of iterations in a production run.

Example 3.18 (Underlying asset as a control variate). Assume we are pricing in the Black–Scholes model a European option with payoff $Y = g(S_T)$ and maturity T. Note that in this model, if S_t is an asset price, then $\tilde{S}_t = \exp(-rt)S_t$ is a martingale. To estimate S_T we perform N simulations S^j, $j = 1, \ldots, N$, and compute $Y^j = g(S^j)$. The control variate estimator is

$$\frac{1}{N}\sum_{j=1}^{N}\left(Y^j - \left(S^j - \exp(rT)S_0\right)\right).$$

Example 3.19 (Hedge control variates). Since the payoff of a hedged portfolio has a lower standard deviation than the payoff of an unhedged portfolio, hedges can reduce portfolio volatility. Let $V(t) = g(S_t)$ denote an option price at time t. The delta hedge consists of holding $\Delta = \partial V/\partial S$ shares of the underlying asset that are rebalanced at discrete time intervals. At time T, the hedge consists of the savings account and the asset, and closely replicates the payoff of the option. If $\tilde{V}(t)$ is the discounted price, then

$$\tilde{V}(T) = \tilde{V}(t_0) + \int_{t_0}^{T}\frac{\partial \tilde{V}}{\partial \tilde{S}}d\tilde{S}.$$

We write a discrete approximation to the above formula dividing $[t_0, T]$ into n subintervals with endpoints t_i, $i = 0, \ldots, n$, and replacing the integral with a discrete sum. In addition, we discount all terms to time T. Then we can write

$$V(T) = V(t_0)e^{r(T-t_0)} + \sum_{i=0}^{n-1}\frac{\partial V(t_i)}{\partial S}\left(S_{t_{i+1}} - S_{t_i}e^{r(t_{i+1}-t_i)}\right)e^{r(T-t_{i+1})}.$$

Let us note that

$$\mathrm{CV} = \sum_{i=0}^{n-1}\frac{\partial V(t_i)}{\partial S}\left(S_{t_{i+1}} - S_{t_i}e^{r(t_{i+1}-t_i)}\right)e^{r(T-t_{i+1})}$$

is an approximation of a martingale with expectation zero (a stochastic integral). We use this expression as the control variate. To this end, we simulate M trajectories $S^j_{t_i}$, $j = 1, \dots, M$. On each trajectory we compute the option price $V^j(T) = g\big(S^j_{t_n}\big)$ and the control variate

$$\mathrm{CV}^j = \sum_{i=0}^{n-1} \frac{\partial V^j(t_i)}{\partial S} \left(S^j_{t_{i+1}} - S^j_{t_i} e^{r(t_{i+1}-t_i)} \right) e^{r(T-t_{i+1})}.$$

Then we obtain the control variate estimator

$$V(t_0)e^{r(T-t_0)} = \frac{1}{M}\sum_{j=1}^{M}\big(V^j(T) - \mathrm{CV}^j\big).$$

Example 3.20 (Asian option in the Black–Scholes model). Asian options are options with payoffs that depend on the average price of the underlying asset on $[0,T]$

$$S_{ar} = \frac{1}{T}\int_0^T S_t dt.$$

Even in the most elementary Black–Scholes model, there is no analytic expression for the price of a call or put option on that underlying. On the other hand, for the corresponding geometric average Asian option

$$S_{gm} = \exp\left(\frac{1}{T}\int_0^T \ln S_t dt\right)$$

there exists an analytic formula similar to the Black–Scholes formula.

To derive this formula, we take $S_t = S_0 \exp((r - \sigma/2)t + \sigma W_t)$. Assuming $S_0 = 1$, computing $\ln S_t$ and integrating, we obtain

$$\frac{1}{T}\int_0^T \ln S_t \, dt = (r - \sigma^2/2)\frac{T}{2} + \frac{\sigma}{T}\int_0^T W_t dt.$$

To evaluate integral $\int_0^T W_t dt$, we observe that this random variable is normally distributed. Thus, it is sufficient to compute the mean and variance of $X := \frac{\sigma}{T}\int_0^T W_t dt$. It is easy to see that $\mathbb{E}(X) = 0$

due to $\mathbb{E}(W_t) = 0$. To evaluate the variance of X, we compute only

$$\mathbb{E}(X^2) = \frac{\sigma^2}{T^2}\mathbb{E}\left(\int_0^T W_t dt\right)^2.$$

Integrating by parts, we obtain $\int_0^T W_t dt = \int_0^T (T-t)dW_t$. Then

$$\mathbb{E}\left(\int_0^T W_t dt\right)^2 = \mathbb{E}\left(\int_0^T (T-t)dW_t\right)^2 = \int_0^T (T-t)^2 dt = \frac{1}{3}T^3.$$

This gives the distribution of $\sigma/T \int_0^T W_t dt \sim \mathcal{N}(0, \sigma^2 T/3)$ and also

$$\frac{1}{T}\int_0^T \ln S_t dt \sim \mathcal{N}\big((r - \sigma^2/2)T/2, \sigma^2 T/3\big). \tag{3.4}$$

Hence, the geometric Asian option can be priced using the Black–Scholes formula.

Let us recall that in the Black–Scholes model for a stock paying a continuous dividend with rate r_d, we have

$$\ln S_t \sim \mathcal{N}\left(\left(r - r_d - v^2/2\right)t, v^2 t\right), \tag{3.5}$$

where v is the stock volatility.

The call price in this model is given by the formula

$$V_t = e^{-r_d(T-t)} S_t \Phi\big(d_1(S_t, T-t)\big) - K e^{-r(T-t)} \Phi\big(d_2(S_t, T-t)\big), \tag{3.6}$$

where

$$d_1(S_t, T-t) = \frac{\ln(S_t/K) + (r - r_d + v^2/2)(T-t)}{v\sqrt{T-t}}$$

$$d_2(S_t, T-t) = d_1(S_t, T-t) - v\sqrt{T-t}.$$

Comparing the distribution given by (3.4) with the distribution of $\ln S_T$ from (3.5), we see that, by making in the Black–Scholes formula (3.6) the substitutions

$$v = \frac{\sigma}{\sqrt{3}}, \quad r_d = \frac{r}{2} + \frac{\sigma^2}{12}, \quad r - r_d - \frac{1}{2}v^2 = \frac{r}{2} - \frac{\sigma^2}{4},$$

we arrive at the price of the geometric average Asian call option

$$V_0 = e^{-1/2(r+\sigma^2/6)T} S_0 \Phi(b_1) - e^{-rT} K \Phi(b_2),$$

where

$$b_1 = \frac{\ln(S_0/K) + (r + \sigma^2/6)T/2}{\sigma\sqrt{T}/\sqrt{3}}, \qquad b_2 = b_1 - \frac{\sigma}{\sqrt{3}}\sqrt{T}.$$

Kemna and Vorst [50] propose the following algorithm for the pricing of the arithmetic average Asian call option with the geometric average option as a control variate: discretize the time interval $[0, T]$ with points t_i, $i = 1, \ldots, n$, simulate M price trajectories $(S^j_{t_i})_{1 \le i \le n}$, $j = 1 \ldots, M$, and on each trajectory compute the estimators of the arithmetic and geometric average Asian option

$$A^j = \exp(-rT) \left(\frac{1}{n} \sum_{i=1}^{n} S^j_{t_i} - K \right)^+,$$

$$G^j = \exp(-rT) \left(\left(\prod_{i=1}^{n} S^j_{t_i} \right)^{\frac{1}{n}} - K \right)^+.$$

The price estimator of the arithmetic average Asian call option is then

$$\hat{X} = \frac{1}{M} \sum_{j=1}^{M} X^j,$$

where

$$X^j = A^j - (G^j - V_0).$$

Remark 3.21. The estimator in the last example is biased. This bias can be explained by the fact that in the MC simulation, we use discrete geometric averaging, and the analytic price was computed for the continuous geometric average. Fortunately, we can derive (computations are a bit more complicated) an analytic formula for the discrete geometric average call option. Discretizing the time interval

$[0,T]$ into n subintervals of equal length, we obtain the following price of the discrete geometric average Asian call option

$$V_D = \exp\Big(-rT + \frac{n+1}{2n}(r-\sigma^2/2)T + \frac{(n+1)(2n+1)}{12n^2}\sigma^2 T\Big) S_0\Phi(\hat{b}_1) \\ - e^{-rT} K\Phi(\hat{b}_2),$$

where

$$\hat{b}_1 = \frac{\log\frac{S_0}{K} + \frac{n+1}{2n}(r-\sigma^2/2)T + \frac{(n+1)(2n+1)}{6n^2}\sigma^2 T}{\sigma\sqrt{\frac{T(n+1)(2n+1)}{6n^2}}},$$

$$\hat{b}_2 = \hat{b}_1 - \sigma\sqrt{\frac{T(n+1)(2n+1)}{6n^2}}.$$

Using V_D rather than V_0 removes the bias.

3.3 Greeks

In this section, we describe the methods of estimation sensitivities, i.e., derivatives with respect to parameters of the expectations of certain random variables. In the case where these expectations are contingent claim prices, sensitivities are called *Greeks*. We now discuss how to compute Greeks by finite differences, pathwise differentiation, and the likelihood method. The application of the Malliavin calculus to the computation of Greeks is not discussed since this method is beyond the scope of this book (see [52] or [70] for details of this method).

3.3.1 *Finite differences*

Consider contingent claim $Y(\theta)$ depending on parameter θ. Our goal is to compute the derivative with respect to θ of the expectation $y(\theta) = \mathbb{E}(Y(\theta))$. We can approximate this derivative by finite differences. To understand existing possibilities, we take a function $f(\theta)$ of class C^3. The derivative can be approximated in at least two ways:

$$f'(\theta) \approx h^{-1}\big(f(\theta+h) - f(\theta)\big), \quad \text{forward difference,}$$

$$f'(\theta) \approx (2h)^{-1}\big(f(\theta+h) - f(\theta-h)\big), \quad \text{central difference.}$$

Each of these methods yields a different error

$$\left|\frac{f(\theta+h)-f(\theta)}{h}-f'(\theta)\right|=O(h),$$

$$\left|\frac{f(\theta+h)-f(\theta-h)}{2h}-f'(\theta)\right|=O(h^2).$$

Consider N simulations $Y_j(\theta)$, $j = 1,\dots,N$. Let $\hat{y}(\theta) = \frac{1}{N}\sum_{j=1}^{N} Y_j(\theta)$ be the estimator of $y(\theta)$. We can estimate $y'(\theta)$ using forward or central differences

$$\hat{y}'_F(\theta)=\frac{1}{N}\sum_{j=1}^{N} h^{-1}\big(Y_j(\theta+h)-Y_j(\theta)\big),$$

$$\hat{y}'_C(\theta)=\frac{1}{N}\sum_{j=1}^{N}(2h)^{-1}\big(Y_j(\theta+h)-Y_j(\theta-h)\big).$$

We also have a choice in selecting pseudo-random numbers in the simulation of $Y(\theta)$: (i) we can simulate $Y(\theta+h)$ and $Y(\theta)$ ($Y(\theta+h)$ and $Y(\theta-h)$, respectively) independently or (ii) simulate both random variables $Y(\theta+h)$ and $Y(\theta)$ ($Y(\theta+h)$ and $Y(\theta-h)$, respectively) using a common sequence of pseudo-random numbers. Hence, we have, in fact, four estimators: $\hat{y}'_{F,i}$, $\hat{y}'_{F,ii}$, $\hat{y}'_{C,i}$ and $\hat{y}'_{C,ii}$.

To determine which of these estimators can be applied in computation, we analyze the bias for the two derivative approximation methods:

$$\text{Bias}(\hat{y}'_F)=\mathbb{E}(\hat{y}'_F-y'(\theta))=O(h),$$

$$\text{Bias}(\hat{y}'_C)=\mathbb{E}(\hat{y}'_C-y'(\theta))=O(h^2).$$

The above formulas suggest that the smaller h, the better the accuracy. This conclusion is premature. The impact on bias must be mitigated by the impact on variance. Let us compute the variances for the aforementioned methods of simulation $Y(\theta+h)$ and $Y(\theta)$

($Y(\theta+h)$ and $Y(\theta-h)$, respectively). When the sequence $Y_j(\theta+h)$ is generated independently from the sequence $Y_j(\theta)$, then

$$\begin{aligned}\operatorname{Var}&\left(\frac{1}{N}\sum_{j=1}^{N}\frac{Y_j(\theta+h)-Y_j(\theta)}{h}\right)\\ &=\frac{1}{h^2}\frac{1}{N^2}\sum_{j=1}^{N}\big(\operatorname{Var}\big(Y_j(\theta+h)\big)+\operatorname{Var}\big(Y_j(\theta)\big)\big)\\ &\simeq\frac{1}{h^2}\left(\frac{\operatorname{Var}(Y(\theta+h))}{N}+\frac{\operatorname{Var}(Y(\theta))}{N}\right)\to\frac{2}{h^2N}\operatorname{Var}(Y(\theta)).\end{aligned}$$

Hence, $\operatorname{Var}(\hat{y}'_{F,i})=O(N^{-1}h^{-2})$.

Similar computations for $Y(\theta+h)$ and $Y(\theta)$ ($Y(\theta+h)$ and $Y(\theta-h)$, respectively), when both sequences are simulated using common pseudo-random numbers, and $Y(\theta)$ fulfills the assumptions of Lemma 3.23 (see the next section), give

$$\begin{aligned}\operatorname{Var}&\left(\frac{1}{N}\sum_{j=1}^{N}\frac{Y_j(\theta+h)-Y_j(\theta)}{h}\right)\\ &\simeq\frac{1}{N}\operatorname{Var}\left(\frac{Y(\theta+h)-Y(\theta)}{h}\right)\to\frac{1}{N}\operatorname{Var}\big(Y'(\theta)\big).\end{aligned}$$

Hence, $\operatorname{Var}(\hat{y}'_{F,ii})=O(N^{-1})$.

If the assumptions of Lemma 3.23 are not fulfilled, we can only expect that $\operatorname{Var}\big(Y(\theta+h)-Y(\theta)\big)\to 0$ for $h\to 0$. There are no rigorous results concerning the convergence rate. Numerical experience indicates that the typical rate is $\operatorname{Var}(\hat{y}'_{F,ii})=O(N^{-1}h^{-1})$. The results for the estimators $\hat{y}'_{C,i}$ and $\hat{y}'_{C,ii}$ are similar. Thus, variance increases with $h\to 0$. The best choice of step size h must be a compromise between a small h that decreases $\operatorname{Bias}(\hat{y}')$ and a large h, which decreases the variance of the estimator.

Example 3.22. Let us compute the value of Delta for an option with payoff $g(S_T)$ in the Black–Scholes model. As

$$S_T^x=x\exp\big((r-\sigma^2/2)\,T+\sigma W_T\big),$$

we have

$$\Delta = \frac{1}{2hN}\sum_{j=1}^{N}\Big(g\Big((x+h)\exp\Big((r-\sigma^2/2)T+\sigma\sqrt{T}\xi_j\Big)\Big) \\ - g\Big((x-h)\exp\Big((r-\sigma^2/2)T+\sigma\sqrt{T}\xi_j\Big)\Big)\Big),$$

where we have applied central differences and a common sequence of normal variables ξ_j to simulate the Wiener process.

3.3.2 *Pathwise differentiation*

The proposed method is based on the equality

$$\frac{d}{d\theta}y(\theta) = \frac{d}{d\theta}\mathbb{E}(Y(\theta)) = \mathbb{E}\left(\frac{dY}{d\theta}\right). \tag{3.7}$$

The conditions for the validity of (3.7) are given by the following lemma.

Lemma 3.23. *Assume that $Y(\theta)$ is differentiable a.s. at θ_0 and satisfies a.s. the Lipschitz condition*

$$\big|Y(\theta_1) - Y(\theta_2)\big| \le M|\theta_1 - \theta_2|,$$

for θ_1, θ_2 in a nonrandom neighborhood of θ_0, and $\mathbb{E}(M) < +\infty$. Then (3.7) is satisfied at $\theta = \theta_0$.

Proof. Let $y(\theta) = \mathbb{E}(Y(\theta))$. Then

$$y'(\theta_0) = \lim_{h\to 0}\frac{y(\theta_0+h)-y(\theta_0)}{h} = \lim_{h\to 0}\mathbb{E}\left(\frac{Y(\theta_0+h)-Y(\theta_0)}{h}\right). \tag{3.8}$$

Since $\big(Y(\theta_0+h)-Y(\theta_0)\big)/h \le M$, this quotient converges to $Y'(\theta_0)$. By the theorem of dominated convergence, the right-hand side of (3.8) converges to $\mathbb{E}(Y'(\theta_0))$. □

Example 3.24. As previously, we compute Delta of a call option in the Black–Scholes model

$$\mathbb{E}\big(g(S_T^x)\big) = \exp(-rT)\mathbb{E}\left(\left(S_T^x - K\right)^+\right),$$

where

$$S_T^x = x \exp\Big(\big(r - \sigma^2/2\big)\, T + \sigma\sqrt{T}\xi\Big), \quad \xi \sim \mathcal{N}(0,1).$$

Then

$$\Delta = \mathbb{E}\left(\frac{dg}{dx}\right) = \mathbb{E}\left(\frac{dg}{dS_T^x}\frac{dS_T^x}{dx}\right).$$

By simple computations, we get:

$$\frac{dS_T^x}{dx} = \frac{S_T^x}{x}, \quad \frac{dg}{dS_T^x} = e^{-rT}\frac{d}{dS_T^x}\big(S_T^x - K\big)^+ = e^{-rT}\begin{cases} 0, & \text{for } S_T^x < K, \\ 1, & \text{for } S_T^x > K. \end{cases}$$

To compute Delta, we ignore the fact that the derivative in the last equality does not exist for $S_T^x = K$ since this is an event with probability 0.

Eventually, we obtain

$$\Delta = \mathbb{E}\left(\frac{dg}{dx}\right) = e^{-rT}\mathbb{E}\left(\frac{S_T^x}{x}\mathbb{1}_{\{S_T^x > K\}}\right).$$

Gamma cannot be computed by this approach, even for the Black–Scholes model, since the payoff function is not twice differentiable.

3.3.3 *The likelihood ratio method*

The most generally applicable method for computing Greeks is the likelihood ratio method. Suppose we compute the derivative of $\mathbb{E}(Y(\theta))$ with respect to θ. The key feature is that the dependence on θ is restricted to the measure $\mathbb{P}_\theta(d\omega)$, i.e.,

$$y(\theta) = \mathbb{E}(Y(\theta)) = \int_\Omega Y(\omega)\mathbb{P}_\theta(d\omega).$$

The conditions for the interchange of differentiation and integration are given in the following lemma.

Lemma 3.25. *Let $\big(\phi_\theta(x)\big)_{\theta\in\Theta}$ be a family of densities on $\mathbb{R}$ such that $\phi_\theta(x)$ is continuously differentiable with respect to θ a.e. $x \in \mathbb{R}$. Then*

$$\frac{d}{d\theta}\int_{\mathbb{R}} g(x)\phi_\theta(x)dx = \int_{\mathbb{R}} g(x)\frac{d\phi_\theta}{d\theta}(x)dx$$

for θ in an open interval $\Theta_0 \subset \Theta$, if and only if $g \in L^q$ and $\big|\frac{d\phi_\theta}{d\theta}(x)\big| \le M(x)$ x-a.s., for each $\theta \in \Theta_0$, and $M \in L^p$, where $1/p + 1/q = 1$.

Proof. Assuming that $(\theta-\varepsilon,\theta+\varepsilon)\subset\Theta_0$ and $|h|<\varepsilon$, we have

$$\begin{aligned}&\frac{1}{h}\left(\int_{\mathbb{R}}g(x)\phi_{\theta+h}(x)dx-\int_{\mathbb{R}}g(x)\phi_{\theta}(x)dx\right)\\&=\int_{\mathbb{R}}g(x)\frac{\phi_{\theta+h}(x)-\phi_{\theta}(x)}{h}dx=\int_{\mathbb{R}}g(x)\phi'_{\theta^*}(x)dx,\end{aligned}\tag{3.9}$$

where $\theta^*\in(\theta-|h|,\theta+|h|)$.

By the theorem assumptions $|\phi'_{\theta^*}(x)|\le M(x)$ and

$$\left|\int_{\mathbb{R}}g(x)\phi'_{\theta^*}(x)dx\right|\le\int_{\mathbb{R}}|g(x)M(x)|dx\le\|g\|_{L^q}\|M\|_{L^p}<+\infty.$$

Hence, the left-hand side of (3.9) is bounded from above, and we can pass to the limit for $h\to0$ by the dominated convergence theorem.

□

Example 3.26. We illustrate the method by computing Delta and Gamma in the Black–Scholes model, i.e., we compute the x-derivatives of $\mathbb{E}(g(S_T^x))$.

Let us assume that we know the transition density from x to S_T^x: $\phi(S_T^x)=\phi(x,S_T^x)$. This function is, in fact, the density of S_T^x. Then we have

$$\mathbb{E}\big(g(S_T^x)\big)=\int_{\mathbb{R}}g(S_T^x)\phi(x,S_T^x)dS_T^x=\int_{\mathbb{R}}g(S)\phi(x,S)dS.$$

We formally differentiate under the integral sign to obtain Delta

$$\begin{aligned}\Delta=&\frac{\partial}{\partial x}\mathbb{E}\big(g(S_T^x)\big)=\int_{\mathbb{R}}g(S)\frac{\partial}{\partial x}\phi(x,S)dS\\=&\int_{\mathbb{R}}g(S)\frac{\partial\ln\phi}{\partial x}\phi(x,S)dS=\mathbb{E}\left(g(S)\frac{\partial\ln\phi}{\partial x}\right).\end{aligned}$$

The second derivative gives Gamma (in the Black–Scholes model ϕ is a smooth function)

$$\begin{aligned}\Gamma&=\frac{\partial^2}{\partial x^2}\mathbb{E}\big(g(S_T^x)\big)=\int_{\mathbb{R}}g(S)\left(\frac{\partial^2\ln\phi}{\partial x^2}\phi(x,S)+\frac{\partial\ln\phi}{\partial x}\frac{\partial\phi}{\partial x}\right)dS\\&=\int_{\mathbb{R}}g(S)\left(\frac{\partial^2\ln\phi}{\partial x^2}+\left(\frac{\partial\ln\phi}{\partial x}\right)^2\right)\phi(x,S)dS\end{aligned}$$

$$= \mathbb{E}\left(g(S)\left(\frac{\partial^2 \ln\phi}{\partial x^2} + \left(\frac{\partial \ln\phi}{\partial x}\right)^2\right)\right).$$

Using the density of S_T^x in the Black–Scholes model

$$\phi(x,S) = \frac{1}{\sqrt{2\pi\sigma^2 T}S}\exp\left(-\frac{\left(\ln S/x - (r-\sigma^2/2)T\right)^2}{2\sigma^2 T}\right)$$

we obtain

$$\frac{\partial \ln\phi}{\partial x} = \frac{\ln S/x - (r-\sigma^2/2)T}{x\sigma^2 T},$$
$$\frac{\partial^2 \ln\phi}{\partial x^2} = -\frac{1 + \ln S/x - (r-\sigma^2/2)T}{x^2\sigma^2 T}.$$

Remark 3.27. The likelihood ratio method can be used for the computation of other Greeks provided we know $\phi(x,S)$, i.e., for many European options.

3.4 Exercises

Exercise 3.1. The stock price follows the Black–Scholes model

$$dS_t = rS_t dt + \sigma S_t dW_t.$$

Consider a European put option with the payoff

$$g(X) = \begin{cases} (K_1 - S_T)^+, & \text{if } S_{T/2} < H \\ (K_2 - S_T)^+, & \text{otherwise,} \end{cases}$$

where $X = (S_{T/2}, S_T)$.

(a) Compute the Monte Carlo price of this option assuming $S_0 = 100$, $T = 1$ year, risk-free rate $r = 3\%$, volatility $\sigma = 30\%$, $K_1 = 110$, $K_2 = 120$, and $H = 105$.

(b) Suggest a method to estimate the price of this option using just one normal random variable per path.

Exercise 3.2. To estimate $\mathbb{E}(Z'Z'')$, simulate N replications $Z'_1, \ldots, Z'_N$ of Z' and independently N replications $Z''_1, \ldots, Z''_N$ of Z'' . Using the observation that for independent random variables $\mathbb{E}(Z'Z'') = \mathbb{E}(Z')\mathbb{E}(Z'')$, consider the following two estimators:

$$\left(\frac{1}{N}\sum_{n=1}^{N} Z'_n\right)\left(\frac{1}{N}\sum_{n=1}^{N} Z''_n\right) \quad \text{and} \quad \frac{1}{N}\sum_{n=1}^{N} Z'_n Z''_n.$$

Prove that the first estimator has a smaller variance.

Exercise 3.3. Let X_t be a stationary process. To estimate its time average

$$\bar{X}_T = \frac{1}{T}\int_0^T X_t dt,$$

simulate kN values $X_1, \ldots, X_{kN}$ from X. Together with the sample mean $\hat{X}_{kN}$ consider the alternative estimator $\hat{X}^{(k)}_{kN} = (X_k + X_{2k} + \cdots + X_{Nk})/N$. One can expect that the spacing will reduce dependence and, thus, the overall variance. Show that this is not the case, i.e., that $\operatorname{Var}(\hat{X}_{kN}) \leq \operatorname{Var}(\hat{X}^{(k)}_{kN})$.

Exercise 3.4. In Monte Carlo simulations, the goal is to compute $\hat{X}$ to a desired level of accuracy ε. To obtain absolute precision ε, one should choose the sample size N such that the half-width of the confidence interval is approximately equal to ε. That gives

$$N \approx \frac{z^2_{1-\alpha/2}\sigma^2}{\varepsilon^2},$$

where z_α denotes the α-quantile of a standard normal distribution.

This rule for selecting N cannot usually be implemented directly since σ is unknown. The standard approach is a two-stage procedure. Generating first a small number of *trial runs* to estimate sample variance $\hat{\sigma}^2$, then use the estimated $\hat{\sigma}^2$ to determine N for *production runs* in which desired accuracy can be achieved.

Analyze the effectiveness of the two-stage procedure by simulating samples of a random variable $X_u = \mathbb{1}_{\{U>u\}}$, where $U \sim \mathcal{U}(0,1)$. Produce M = 10,000 95% confidence intervals using the two-stage method with 10, 100, and 1,000 trial runs and ε = 0.05. For

$u = 0, 0.5, 0.9, 0.95, 0.99$, compare the fraction of confidence intervals in which the mean $x = \mathbb{E}(X_u)$ is inside the interval ($x \in \hat{x} \pm 1.96\hat{\sigma}/\sqrt{N}$, where $\hat{\sigma}^2$ is the sample variance and N is the number of production runs).

Exercise 3.5 (Hit-or-miss Monte Carlo simulations). In the early days of Monte Carlo, the "hit-or-miss" method was a common approach to estimating definite integrals. To describe the method, we consider the computation of the integral

$$I = \int_0^1 f(x)dx$$

for a function $0 \leq f(x) \leq 1$.

The estimate of the above integral is obtained by generating N pairs (x_i, y_i), where x_i, y_i are independent samples from a uniform distribution over $[0, 1]$, and counting the pairs for which $y_i \leq f(x_i)$. Let N_1 be the number of such pairs. This means sampling N points in the unit square and counting those below the curve $y = f(x)$. Then the estimator of I is

$$\hat{I} = \frac{N_1}{N}.$$

(a) Compute the variance of the hit-or-miss estimator of I.
(b) Compare the variance of the hit-or-miss estimator with the variance of the crude MC estimator of I.

Exercise 3.6. In Example 3.11, take $d = 2$, $A = \{(x, y) : x \geq 8, y \geq 8\}$ and

$$\Sigma = \begin{pmatrix} 4 & -1 \\ -1 & 4 \end{pmatrix}.$$

Find the point $x^* \in A$ that maximizes the $\mathcal{N}(0, \Sigma)$ density and perform simulations with the importance distribution $\mathcal{N}(x^*, \Sigma)$. Compute the sample variances for sample sizes $n = 10000$, 20000, 30000. Compare the obtained variances with the sample variances in the crude Monte Carlo simulations.

Exercise 3.7. Consider the problem of estimating

$$x = \mathbb{P}(X > 6),$$

where $X \sim \mathcal{N}(0, 1)$.

(a) Estimate x by crude Monte Carlo.
(b) Estimate x applying importance sampling with a new random variable $Y \sim \mathcal{N}(\mu, 1)$ with an appropriate choice of μ.

Exercise 3.8. Following the approach of Example 3.10, estimate the integral

$$I = \int_1^\infty x^{\alpha-1} e^{-x} dx$$

with $\alpha > 1$ applying Monte Carlo simulations with the importance sampling density

$$f(x, \theta) = \theta \exp\big(-\theta(x - a)\big).$$

Find $(\hat{x}, \hat{\theta})$ that approximately minimizes the variance of the Monte Carlo estimator.

Perform importance sampling simulations with $\alpha = 2$ for the found value of $\hat{\theta}$ with sample sizes $n = 10000, 20000, 30000$. Compute the sample variances of these simulations and compare them with the variances of crude Monte Carlo for the same sample sizes. Compute the variance reduction ratio.

Exercise 3.9. Let S_t be the price of a risky asset. S_t is a geometric Brownian motion with stochastic volatility σ_t, that is a Markov chain with two states $\sigma^+ = 0.25$ and $\sigma^- = 0.75$, and switching intensities $\lambda^+ = 1$ for transitions $\sigma^+ \to \sigma^-$ and $\lambda^- = 3$ for transitions $\sigma^- \to \sigma^+$.

After the change of variables $X_t = \log S_t$, the dynamics of X_t is described in a risk-neutral measure by the equation

$$dX_t = \left(r - \sigma_t^2/2\right) dt + \sigma_t dW_t,$$

where W_t is a standard Wiener process. To estimate the price of a European call option on that asset, apply importance sampling using a change of drift in the Wiener process W_t from 0 to μ^*, choosing μ^* to satisfy

$$S_0 \exp\big((r - \sigma^2/2)T + \mathbb{E}_{\mu^*} W_T\big) \approx K.$$

Carry on the simulations for $S_0 = 100$, maturity $T = 3$ years, $K = 150$, and risk-free interest rate $r = 4\%$. Compare the variance of the importance sampling estimator with that of the crude Monte Carlo estimator.

Exercise 3.10. (Out-of-the-money option). Consider the Black–Scholes model with the underlying asset price S_t given in a risk-neutral measure by the expression

$$S_t = S_0 \exp\big((r - \sigma^2/2)t + \sigma W_t\big)$$

with $S_0 = 100$, risk-free rate $r = 4\%$, and volatility $\sigma = 30\%$. The goal is to price a "deep-out-of-the-money" call option with payoff $X = (S_T - K)^+$ where $T = 2$ years and $K = 200$.

(a) Compute the option price by crude Monte Carlo with $n = 10000$, 30000, 60000, 100000 simulations. Compare the obtained result with the exact value given by the Black–Scholes formula.

(b) The accuracy of the crude MC simulations is not impressive since K substantially exceeds the typical range of S_t. Improve the result by increasing the likelihood of large values of X by implementing importance sampling. This can be achieved by shifting the distribution of S_T so that its maximum is close to K. To this end, use the change of measure

$$\frac{d\tilde{\mathbb{P}}}{d\mathbb{P}} = L = \exp\big(\lambda W_T - \kappa(\lambda)\big),$$

where $\kappa(\lambda)$ is such that $\mathbb{E}(L) = 1$.
Since W_t is a standard Wiener process, then

$$\kappa(\lambda) = T\lambda^2/2.$$

W_t under $\tilde{\mathbb{P}}$ is again a Wiener process but now with drift λt. Look for λ such that

$$\tilde{\mathbb{E}}\left(S_0 \exp\big((r - \sigma^2/2)T + \sigma W_T\big)\right) \approx K.$$

Find λ that fulfills this approximate equality, perform the corresponding change of measure, and run simulations in the new measure with the same number of samples as for the crude MC. Compute the obtained variance reduction factor.

Exercise 3.11. Derive the price of the discrete geometric Asian call option given in Remark 3.21.

Exercise 3.12. Consider a European call option on an asset with price S_t that follows the Black–Scholes model

$$dS_t = rS_t dt + \sigma S_t dW_t,$$

with risk-free rate $r = 4\%$, volatility $\sigma = 35\%$, and $S_0 = 100$. The option maturity is $T = 2$ years.

Compute Monte Carlo estimates of the option price for $K = 50$, 100, 150 using the control variates

$$S_T,\ Y_T,\ Y_T^2,\ \exp(Y_T),\ \big(S_0 \exp(Y_T) - K\big)^+,$$

where Y_t is given by the equation

$$dY_t = (r - \sigma^2/2)dt + \sigma dW_t$$

with $Y_0 = 0$ (the Wiener process W_t is the same in both equations). Compute the sample variance for each control variate and compare the efficiency of these control variates for different strikes.

Exercise 3.13. Assume the stock price is given by a geometric Brownian motion

$$S_t = S_0 \exp\big((r - \sigma^2/2)\,t + \sigma W_t\big),$$

with positive constants r and σ.

(a) Design a stratified sampling scheme to estimate the price of a call option with maturity T and strike price K.
(b) Perform simulations with $S_0 = 100$, strike $K = 90$, risk-free rate $r = 4\%$, volatility $\sigma = 30\%$, and time to maturity $T = 1$ year. In Monte Carlo simulations, make $M = 10000$ simulations. Test performance as a function of strata number. Consider no more than 50 of strata.

Exercise 3.14. Assume that our goal is to estimate the integral

$$I = \int_0^1 f(x)dx$$

using stratified sampling with proportional strata

$$\Omega_i = \{\omega\colon\ (i-1)/R \le U(\omega) \le i/R\},$$

where U is a uniform distribution over $[0, 1]$. Show that if f is sufficiently smooth, then $\mathrm{Var}(\hat{x}_{ST})$ is of order $O(R^{-2})$.

Exercise 3.15 (Conditional Monte Carlo). Consider for a given random variable X the estimation of $\mathbb{E}(X)$ by Monte Carlo simulations. Clearly, X can be replaced by $Y = \mathbb{E}(X|Z)$ for some random variable Z which gives $\mathbb{E}(Y) = \mathbb{E}\big(\mathbb{E}(X|Z)\big) = \mathbb{E}(X)$. On the other hand

$$\mathrm{Var}(X) = \mathrm{Var}\big(\mathbb{E}(X|Z)\big) + \mathbb{E}\big(\mathrm{Var}(X|Z)\big) \geq \mathrm{Var}\big(\mathbb{E}(X|Z)\big) = \mathrm{Var}(Y).$$

Hence, conditional Monte Carlo always gives variance reduction.

To see the advantage of conditional Monte Carlo, compute the price and variance of a forward starting option with a strike set at some future time t_1 as a percentage of the stock price at that time. Assume the option maturity T, starting time $t_1 > 0$, strike $K = \lambda S_{t_1}$, and stock initial price S_0. The stock price dynamics is given by the Black–Scholes model with volatility σ and risk-free rate r.

(a) Take $T = 5$ years, $t_1 = 0.2T$, $\lambda = 80\%$, $\sigma = 30\%$, and $r = 5\%$. Compute the price of the forward starting call option and its variance by conditional Monte Carlo simulating the stock price from $t = 0$ to t_1 and at t_1 using the Black–Scholes formula for pricing the option with maturity T and already known strike $K = \lambda S_{t_1}$ (remember to discount the price to time $t = 0$).

(b) Compare the obtained result with the crude Monte Carlo simulations where the stock price is first simulated in time interval $[0, t_1]$ and then the simulations are extended on interval $[t_1, T]$ and used to compute the option price.

Exercise 3.16. Consider a financial instrument with payoff $(X - K)^+$, where $K = 100$ and $X \sim \mathcal{N}(\mu, \sigma^2)$ with parameters being independent random variables $\mu \sim \mathcal{N}(100, 25)$ and $\sigma \sim Ex(4)$ ($Ex(\lambda)$ denotes an exponential distribution with parameter λ).

Compute the expected value of this instrument using conditional Monte Carlo. Compare the sample variance of this procedure with the sample variance of crude Monte Carlo and compute the variance reduction ratio.

Hint: In conditional Monte Carlo, use the analytical formula

$$\mathbb{E}\big((X - K)^+\big) = \sigma\phi\left(\frac{K - \mu}{\sigma}\right) + (\mu - K)\Phi\left(\frac{\mu - K}{\sigma}\right),$$

which holds for $X \sim \mathcal{N}(\mu, \sigma^2)$. Here, ϕ denotes the normal probability distribution function and Φ, the normal cumulative distribution function.

Exercise 3.17. A financial institution has sold a European call option with maturity T and strike K, for an underlying with dynamics given by the equation

$$dX_t = \mu X_t dt + \sigma X_t dW_t,$$

where drift μ and volatility σ are positive constants, and the initial price X_0 is deterministic.

The market risk-free interest rate is r and is, in general, different from μ. After selling the option, the institution uses the following form of discrete hedging: at time $t = 0$ it purchases $\Delta(0)$ shares for borrowed $\Delta(0)X_0$ units of currency and at time $t = T$ it purchases additional $(1 - \Delta(0))$ shares ($\Delta(t)$ denotes the delta sensitivity of the option at time t). Let C denote the total cost of writing the option and hedging it. Prove that if Delta is computed from the corresponding Black–Scholes formula for continuous hedging, then

$$\begin{aligned}\mathbb{E}(C) =& V_{BS} + X_0 e^{(\mu-r)T}\left(\Phi(d_\mu) - \Phi(d)\right)\\ &+ Ke^{-rT}\left(\Phi\left(d - \sigma\sqrt{T}\right) - \Phi\left(d_\mu - \sigma\sqrt{T}\right)\right)\end{aligned}$$

where Φ denotes the normal cumulative distribution function, V_{BS} is the Black–Scholes price of the option at time zero,

$$d_\mu = \frac{(\mu + \sigma^2/2)T + \ln(X_0/K)}{\sigma\sqrt{T}}$$

and

$$d = \frac{(r + \sigma^2/2)T + \ln(X_0/K)}{\sigma\sqrt{T}}.$$

Exercise 3.18. Consider a random variable $Y(\theta)$ with expectation $y(\theta)$. Approximate the derivative of this expectation by the central difference estimator

$$\hat{y}'(\theta) = \frac{1}{N}\sum_{n=1}^{N}\frac{Y_n(\theta + h/2) - Y_n(\theta - h/2)}{h}$$

with independent sampling of $Y_n(\theta + h/2)$ and $Y_n(\theta - h/2)$. Prove that the mean-square error $\mathbb{E}\big((\hat{y}'(\theta) - y'(\theta))^2\big)$ is asymptotically minimized by

$$h = \frac{1}{N^{1/6}}\frac{\big(576\mathrm{Var}(Y(\theta))\big)^{1/6}}{\big(y'''(\theta)\big)^{1/3}}.$$

Exercise 3.19. Consider two independent random variables X_1 and X_2 with finite expectations $\mathbb{E}(X_1) < \mathbb{E}(X_2) < +\infty$. Show that for $Y(\theta) = \mathbb{1}_{\{\theta X_2 > X_1\}}$, $0 \le \theta \le 1$, identity (3.7) does not hold.

Exercise 3.20. Consider a European option in the Black–Scholes model. Prove that the Vega of this option can be computed by the sample path differentiation given by (3.7).
Hint: Vega is the option price sensitivity with respect to changes in volatility.

Exercise 3.21. Consider a weekly sampled arithmetic Asian option in the Black–Scholes model with risk-free rate $r = 4\%$ and volatility $\sigma = 30\%$. The option has maturity $T = 1$ year, strike $K = 110$, and initial stock price $S_0 = 100$.

(a) Compute the option price $V(\theta)$, its Delta $V'(\theta)$, and associated variances, where parameter θ is the initial stock price S_0.
(b) To improve efficiency, apply antithetic variates and compare the change in variances of both estimators.

Chapter 4

Integration of Stochastic Differential Equations

The computation of $\mathbb{E}(X)$ from a known distribution of X is a rare event. A more common situation is where X is the value at time T of a stochastic process X_t, and the dynamics of X_t is given by a stochastic differential equation. MC simulations can be used to solve this equation and obtain an approximate distribution of X. In the following, we restrict our presentation to stochastic equations in $\mathbb{R}^d$

$$dX_t = b(t, X_t)dt + \sigma(t, X_t)dW_t, \quad t > 0, \quad X_0 = \xi, \tag{4.1}$$

where W_t is an m-dimensional standard Wiener process.

4.1 Introduction to Itô Stochastic Calculus

Let us note that equation (4.1) cannot be understood as a typical differential equation. Since Wiener paths are nowhere differentiable, the equation is not well defined even pathwise. To provide a mathematical meaning to this equation, we must introduce some elements of *stochastic calculus*. This section presents a quick introduction to stochastic calculus, including stochastic integrals, Itô formula, and Itô stochastic differential equations. Similarly to Chapter 1, we present a collection of basic definitions and facts. The rigorous treatment of stochastic calculus can be found in advanced textbooks by Karatzas and Shreve [48], Krylov [53], or Øksendal [69].

We begin with transforming differential equation (4.1) into the integral equation

$$X_t = X_0 + \int_0^t b(s, X_s)ds + \int_0^t \sigma(s, X_s)dW_s. \tag{4.2}$$

The situation seems to be not much better as the integral

$$\int_0^t \sigma(s, X_s)dW_s$$

cannot be defined even as a pathwise Lebesgue–Stieltjes integral due to the infinite variation of Wiener paths.

4.1.1 *Stochastic integral*

A meaningful definition of the integral with respect to a Wiener process W_t can be given in a framework of *stochastic calculus* developed by Kiyoshi Itô. This theory is called *Itô stochastic calculus* and the defined integral *Itô stochastic integral* or just *Itô integral.* We begin by defining the class of *simple processes* and their Itô integrals. The simple process is a process with paths defined by step functions where the jump times are all fixed, but the jump heights are random.

Definition 4.1. Let $(W_t)_{t\in[0,T]}$ be a one-dimensional Wiener process adapted to filtration $\mathbb{F} = (\mathcal{F}_t)_{t\in[0,T]}$ on a probability space $(\Omega, \mathcal{F}, \mathbb{P})$.

(1) A stochastic process $(X_t)_{t\in[0,T]}$ is called a *simple process* if for a partition $0 = t_0 < t_1 < \cdots < t_N = T$ of interval $[0, T]$ there exist bounded random variables $\phi_n\colon \Omega \to \mathbb{R}$, $n = 1, \ldots, N$, such that ϕ_n is $\mathcal{F}_{t_{n-1}}$-measurable, and for each $\omega \in \Omega$ process X_t has the representation

$$X_t(\omega) = \sum_{n=1}^{N} \phi_n(\omega)\mathbb{1}_{(t_{n-1},t_n]}(t).$$

(2) The stochastic integral of a simple process X_t is the continuous process $\big(I_t(X)\big)_{t\in[0,T]}$ defined for any $t \in (t_k, t_{k+1}]$ as

$$I_t(X) := \int_0^t X_s dW_s = \sum_{n=1}^{k} \phi_n(W_{t_n} - W_{t_{n-1}}) + \phi_{k+1}(W_t - W_{t_k}).$$

After defining the stochastic integral for simple processes, we extend it to a larger class of adapted processes

$$\mathbb{L}^2[0,T] = \left\{ (X_t)_{t\in[0,T]} \colon X_t \text{ is } \mathcal{F}_t\text{-adapted}, \quad \mathbb{E}\left(\int_0^T X_s^2 ds \right) < \infty \right\}.$$

Definition 4.2. For any square-integrable, adapted process $(X_t)_{t\in[0,T]}$, with continuous sample paths, one can easily prove that there exists a sequence of simple processes X_t^i approximating X_t in $\mathbb{L}^2[0,T]$

$$\lim_{i\to\infty} \mathbb{E}\left(\int_0^T \left| X_t - X_t^i \right|^2 dt \right) = 0.$$

The Itô integral of X_t is defined as follows

$$\int_0^T X_t dW_t = \lim_{i\to\infty} \int_0^T X_t^i dW_t,$$

where the limit exists in $L^2(\Omega)$.

The following theorem summarizes the fundamental properties of the Itô integral.

Theorem 4.3. *If $(X_t)_{t\in[0,T]}$ is a square-integrable, adapted process, then:*

(1) *$(\int_0^t X_s dW_s)_{t\in[0,T]}$ is a continuous $\mathbb{F}$-martingale.*
(2) *(Itô isometry) $\mathbb{E}((\int_0^t X_s dW_s)^2) = \mathbb{E}(\int_0^t X_s^2 ds)$.*

Example 4.4. Let $f(t)$ be a deterministic, square-integrable function. Consider the stochastic integral

$$\int_0^T f(t) dW_t.$$

Defining a partition $0 = t_0 < t_1 \cdots < t_N = T$, we approximate this integral by the sum

$$S_N = \sum_{n=1}^{N} f(t_{n-1}) \left(W_{t_n} - W_{t_{n-1}} \right).$$

It is easy to see that S_N is normally distributed with mean 0 and variance

$$\mathrm{Var}(S_N) = \sum_{n=1}^{N} f^2(t_{n-1})(t_n - t_{n-1}).$$

Since

$$\int_0^T f(t)dW_t = \lim_{N\to\infty} S_N$$

and

$$\mathrm{Var}(S_N) \to \int_0^T f^2(t)dt,$$

then $\int_0^T f(t)dW_t$ is normally distributed with mean 0 and variance $\int_0^T f^2(t)dt$.

Example 4.5. To illustrate the difference between the stochastic integral and the Riemann integral, we compute the integral

$$\int_0^T W_t dW_t.$$

By partitioning the interval $[0, T]$ into N equal subintervals $0 = t_0 < t_1 \cdots < t_N = T$ with $t_n = nT/N$, we define a sequence of random variables

$$Z_n = \frac{W_{t_n} - W_{t_{n-1}}}{\sqrt{T/N}}, \qquad n = 1, \ldots, N.$$

$Z_1, \ldots, Z_N$ are independent, standard normal random variables. Approximating the stochastic integral by simple processes and using the properties of Wiener processes, we obtain (the limit is in the $L^2(\Omega)$ sense)

$$\begin{aligned}
2\int_0^T W_t dW_t &= \lim_{N\to\infty} \sum_{n=1}^{N} 2W_{t_{n-1}}\left(W_{t_n} - W_{t_{n-1}}\right) \\
&= W_T^2 - \lim_{N\to\infty} \sum_{n=1}^{N} \left(W_{t_n} - W_{t_{n-1}}\right)^2
\end{aligned}$$

$$= W_T^2 - \lim_{N\to\infty} \frac{T}{N} \sum_{n=1}^{N} Z_n^2 = W_T^2 - T.$$

Observe the difference with respect to the Riemann integral, which is due to the nonzero quadratic variation of a Wiener process (for Riemann integral quadratic variation is 0 !)

$$\lim_{N\to\infty} \sum_{n=1}^{N} \left(W_{t_n} - W_{t_{n-1}}\right)^2 = T.$$

The following two theorems form the core of Itô stochastic calculus.

Theorem 4.6 (Martingale Representation Theorem). *Let $(W_t)_{t\geq 0}$ be a Wiener process on a probability space $(\Omega, \mathcal{F}, \mathbb{P})$ with filtration $\mathbb{F} = (\mathcal{F}_t)_{t\geq 0}$ generated by W_t. For any square-integrable martingale X_t, adapted to $\mathcal{F}_t$, there exists an adapted, square-integrable process ψ_t such that*

$$X_t = \mathbb{E}(X_t) + \int_0^t \psi_s dW_s, \quad t \geq 0.$$

Theorem 4.7 (Itô's formula). *Let $X_t = (X_t^1, \ldots, X_t^d)$ be a d-dimensional semimartingale given by the formula*

$$X_r = X_s + \int_s^r F dt + \int_s^r G dW_t,$$

where W_t is an m-dimensional Wiener process. It is also said that X_t has the stochastic differential

$$dX_t = F dt + G dW_t, \quad t \in [0, T].$$

Let $f\colon [0,\infty) \times \mathbb{R}^d \to \mathbb{R}$ be a $C^{1,2}$-function, i.e., f is once continuously differentiable with respect to the first variable (time) and twice continuously differentiable with respect to the last d variables (space). Set

$$Y_t = f(t, X_t).$$

Then

$$Y_t = Y_0 + \int_0^t \frac{\partial f}{\partial t}(s, X_s)ds + \sum_{i=1}^{d} \int_0^t \frac{\partial f}{\partial x_i}(s, X_s)dX_s^i$$
$$+ \frac{1}{2}\sum_{i,j=1}^{d} \int_0^t \frac{\partial^2 f}{\partial x_i \partial x_j}(s, X_s)d\langle X^i, X^j\rangle_s.$$

The above equality is often written in differential form, meaning that Y has the stochastic differential

$$dY_t = \frac{\partial f}{\partial t}dt + \sum_{i=1}^{d} \frac{\partial f}{\partial x_i}dX_t^i + \frac{1}{2}\sum_{i,j=1}^{d} \frac{\partial^2 f}{\partial x_i \partial x_j}d\langle X^i, X^j\rangle_t$$
$$= \left(\frac{\partial f}{\partial t} + F\nabla f + 1/2\, GG^\top \nabla\nabla^\top f\right) dt + G\nabla f dW_t.$$

The above formula is the "chain rule" of stochastic calculus.

Itô's formula has numerous applications in computing stochastic integrals and solving stochastic differential equations. Here, we show some examples of such applications.

Example 4.8. Let X_t be a standard Wiener process W_t and $f(x) = x^m$. Then $dX_t = dW_t$ and Itô's formula gives

$$d(W_t^m) = mW_t^{m-1}dW_t + \frac{1}{2}m(m-1)W_t^{m-2}dt.$$

In particular, for $m = 2$, we have

$$d(W_t^2) = 2W_t dW_t + dt.$$

Integrating this identity, we obtain the formula

$$2\int_0^T W_t dW_t = W_T^2 - T,$$

established earlier from the definition of stochastic integral.

Example 4.9. Let $X_t = W_t$ and $f(t,x) = \exp(\sigma x - \sigma^2 t/2)$. Then by Itô's formula,

$$d\left(\exp\left(\sigma W_t - \frac{\sigma^2 t}{2}\right)\right)$$
$$= \left(-\frac{\sigma^2}{2}\exp\left(\sigma W_t - \frac{\sigma^2 t}{2}\right) + \frac{\sigma^2}{2}\exp\left(\sigma W_t - \frac{\sigma^2 t}{2}\right)\right) dt$$
$$+ \sigma \exp\left(\sigma W_t - \frac{\sigma^2 t}{2}\right) dW_t.$$

Thus, $Y_t = f(t, W_t)$ fulfills the stochastic differential equation, which is a special case of the Black–Scholes model

$$dY_t = \sigma Y_t dW_t, \quad Y_0 = 1.$$

Example 4.10. Take again $X_t = W_t$. For a continuous function $\sigma(t)$ define

$$M_t = \exp\left(\int_0^t \sigma(s) dW_s - \frac{1}{2}\int_0^t \sigma^2(s) ds\right).$$

To compute differential dM_t, we introduce the auxiliary process

$$Q_t = \int_0^t \sigma(s) dW_s - \frac{1}{2}\int_0^t \sigma^2(s) ds.$$

By Itô's formula, we obtain

$$dQ_t = \sigma(t) dW_t - \frac{1}{2}\sigma^2(t) dt, \quad d\langle Q^2 \rangle_t = \sigma^2(t) dt.$$

Then for $M_t = e^{Q_t}$, we have

$$dM_t = e^{Q_t} dQ_t + \frac{1}{2} e^{Q_t} d\langle Q^2 \rangle_t = \sigma(t) M_t dW_t.$$

4.1.2 *Stochastic differential equations*

We have mentioned already in Chapter 1 that stochastic differential equations are used to model financial markets. At the beginning of this chapter, we indicated that to give a clear mathematical meaning to these equations, we must consider their integral form

$$X_t = X_0 + \int_0^t b(s, X_s)ds + \int_0^t \sigma(s, X_s)dW_s,$$

where the stochastic integral on the right-hand side of the equation is understood as Itô stochastic integral.

We begin the analysis of stochastic differential equations by establishing the concept of *strong solution* of the equation.

Definition 4.11. A *strong solution* of the stochastic differential equation (4.1) on the given probability space $(\Omega, \mathcal{F}, \mathbb{P})$ with respect to the fixed Wiener process W_t with Wiener filtration $\mathbb{F}$ and initial condition ξ is a process $(X_t)_{t \geq 0}$ with continuous sample paths and the properties:

(1) X is adapted to filtration $\mathbb{F}$.
(2) $\mathbb{P}(X_0 = \xi) = 1$.
(3) $\mathbb{P}\big(\int_0^t (|b_i(s, X_s)| + |\sigma_i^j(s, X_s)|^2)ds < \infty\big) = 1$ holds for $1 \leq i \leq d$, $1 \leq j \leq m$, and $t \geq 0$.
(4) The integral version (4.2) of equation (4.1) holds almost surely.

Remark 4.12. Let us note that the strong solution is a stochastic process that exists in a given probability space and with a fixed Wiener process in this space. This is the difference comparing to *weak solutions* (that we are not going to discuss), where a solution process X_t is constructed together with a probability space and a Wiener process.

The following theorem provides sufficient conditions that guarantee the existence of strong solutions. The theorem also summarizes the important properties of these solutions. According to the author's knowledge, there is no single source where the proof of this theorem can be found. The interested reader can find partial results in the books by Friedman [32], Karatzas and Shreve [48], Krylov [53], and Kunita [54].

Theorem 4.13. *Let the coefficients in equation* (4.1) *be such that:*

(A1) $|b(t, x) - b(t, y)| + |\sigma(t, x) - \sigma(t, y)| \leq K|x - y|$;
(A2) $|b(t, x)| + |\sigma(t, x)| \leq K(1 + |x|)$;

for $x, y \in \mathbb{R}^d$ and $t \in [0,T]$, where $|\cdot|$ denotes the Euclidean norm in $\mathbb{R}^d$ and K is a finite, positive constant.

If ξ is a square-integrable random variable ($\mathbb{E}(|\xi|^2) < \infty$) independent of W_t, then:

(1) *The sequence of iterates*

$$X_t^{(0)} = \xi, \quad X_t^{(n+1)} = \xi + \int_0^t b(s, X_s^{(n)})ds + \int_0^t \sigma(s, X_s^{(n)})dW_s$$

converges to X_t.

(2) *X_t is a unique strong solution of the stochastic differential equation*

$$X_t = \xi + \int_0^t b(s, X_s)ds + \int_0^t \sigma(s, X_s)dW_s.$$

(3) *The process X_t is square-integrable and for each $T > 0$ there exists a constant C such that*

$$\mathbb{E}(|X_t|^2) \le C\,(1 + \mathbb{E}(|\xi|^2))\,e^{Ct}, \quad 0 \le t \le T.$$

(4) *If $\mathbb{E}(|\xi|^k) < \infty$ for some $k \ge 2$, then*

$$\mathbb{E}\left(\sup_{0\le s\le t} |X_s|^k\right) \le C\left(1 + \mathbb{E}(|\xi|^k)\right), \quad 0 \le t \le T.$$

(5) *If $\mathbb{E}(|\xi|^k) < \infty$ for some $k \ge 2$, then*

$$\mathbb{E}(|X_t - X_s|^k) \le C\left(1 + \mathbb{E}(|\xi|^k)\right)|t-s|^{k/2}, \quad |t-s| \le 1, t, s \in [0,T].$$

(6) *Let $X_t^{s_1,x_1}$ and $X_t^{s_2,x_2}$ denote solutions of equation (4.1) with initial conditions $X_{s_1} = x_1$ and $X_{s_2} = x_2$, respectively. Let x_1 and x_2 be deterministic. Then for any $k \ge 2$, there exists a positive constant C such that*

$$\mathbb{E}\left(|X_t^{s_1,x_1} - X_t^{s_2,x_2}|^k\right)$$
$$\le C\left(|x_1 - x_2|^k + |s_1 - s_2|^{k/2}\right), s_1, s_2 \in [0,T].$$

The above theorem guarantees that if coefficients $b(t,x)$ and $\sigma(t,x)$ are globally Lipschitz-continuous in x, then there is a unique strong solution of (4.1). The assumption of global Lipschitz continuity is very restrictive. In several popular financial models, for example, local volatility models, the volatility function is not globally Lipschitz-continuous.

It appears that the existence of solutions for equation (4.1) can be obtained under local Lipschitz continuity.

Theorem 4.14. *Consider the d-dimensional stochastic differential equation*

$$dX_t^i = b_i(t, X_t)dt + \sum_{j=1}^{m} \sigma_i^j(t, X_t)dW_t^j, \quad i = 1, \ldots, d. \tag{4.3}$$

Assume that the coefficients of equation (4.3) *are locally Lipschitz-continuous*

$$|b_i(t,x) - b_i(t,y)| + |\sigma_i^j(t,x) - \sigma_i^j(t,y)| \le K_n|x-y|, \quad |x|, |y| < n,$$

for $x, y \in D$, an open subset of $\mathbb{R}^d$, and $t \in [0,T]$. Then equation (4.3) *possesses a unique, strong solution up to an explosion time.*

If the coefficients of (4.3) *fulfill the linear growth condition*

$$|b_i(t,x)| + |\sigma_i^j(t,x)| \le K(1+|x|),$$

then the solution does not explode in finite time.

From the above theorem, we conclude that for the quadratic and LCEV models of local volatility, there exist unique local solutions, as these models satisfy the local Lipschitz condition. However, in the CEV model for $0 < \beta < 1$, the function $\sigma(t,s)$ is not locally Lipschitz continuous. For this model, the state $s = 0$ is absorbing, and a unique solution exists only for $1/2 \le \beta \le 1$ (cf. Andersen and Andreasen [2]).

The existence of explicit solutions to stochastic differential equations is a rare event. Nevertheless, several important equations admit explicit solutions. In finding these solutions, Itô's formula and changes of variables can often be helpful.

Example 4.15. Consider the Black–Scholes model of financial market

$$dS_t = rS_t dt + \sigma S_t dW_t, \quad S(0) = S_0,$$

where r and σ are positive constants.

Defining process $Y_t = e^{-rt}S_t$, we obtain

$$dY_t = -re^{-rt}S_t dt + e^{-rt}dS_t = \sigma Y_t dW_t.$$

Applying the results of Example 4.10, we get

$$Y_t = \exp\left(\sigma \int_0^t dW_s - \sigma^2/2 \int_0^t ds\right) = \exp\left(\sigma W_t - \sigma^2 t/2\right).$$

This gives the solution of the Black–Scholes model

$$S_t = S_0 \exp\left(\left(r - \sigma^2/2\right) t + \sigma W_t\right).$$

Example 4.16 (Ornstein–Uhlenbeck process). Consider a particle moving with velocity V_t through a fluid. The particle exerts a frictional drag proportional to its velocity and random perturbations resulting from the bombardment by the molecules of the surrounding fluid. The equation that describes the velocity of the particle is the so-called *Langevin equation*

$$dV_t = -\kappa V_t dt + \sigma dW_t, \quad V(0) = V_0.$$

By substituting $X_t = e^{\kappa t}V_t$, we obtain

$$dX_t = \sigma e^{\kappa t} dW_t.$$

Then we can easily obtain the *Ornstein–Uhlenbeck process*, which solves Langevin's equation

$$V_t = e^{-\kappa t}V_0 + \sigma \int_0^t e^{-\kappa(t-s)} dW_s.$$

Note that the mean value of V_t is $\mathbb{E}(V_t) = e^{-\kappa t}\mathbb{E}(V_0)$. To obtain the variance of this process, we recall the standard assumption that V_0 is independent of the Wiener process $(W_t)_{t\geq 0}$. Then

$$\begin{aligned}\mathbb{E}(V_t^2) &= \mathbb{E}\left(e^{-2\kappa t}V_0^2 + \sigma^2 \left(\int_0^t e^{-\kappa(t-s)} dW_s\right)^2\right.\\ &\qquad \left. + 2\sigma e^{-\kappa t}V_0 \int_0^t e^{-\kappa(t-s)} dW_s\right)\\ &= e^{-2\kappa t}\mathbb{E}\left(V_0^2\right) + \sigma^2 \int_0^t e^{-2\kappa(t-s)} ds\\ &= e^{-2\kappa t}\mathbb{E}\left(V_0^2\right) + \frac{\sigma^2}{2\kappa}\left(1 - e^{-2\kappa t}\right).\end{aligned}$$

Thus, the variance of V_t is

$$\mathrm{Var}(V_t) = e^{-2\kappa t}\mathrm{Var}\big(V_0\big) + \frac{\sigma^2}{2\kappa}\big(1 - e^{-2\kappa t}\big).$$

Assume that $\mathbb{E}(V_0) < \infty$ and $\mathrm{Var}(V_0) < \infty$. Then for $t \to \infty$

$$\mathbb{E}(V_t) \to 0, \quad \mathrm{Var}(V_t) \to \frac{\sigma^2}{2\kappa}.$$

This shows that as $t \to \infty$ the distribution of V_t approaches normal distribution $\mathcal{N}\big(0, \sigma^2/(2\kappa)\big)$ independently of the initial distribution of V_0.

A time-reverting version of Langevin's equation is also considered

$$dV_t = \kappa\big(\theta - V_t\big)dt + \sigma dW_t, \quad V(0) = V_0.$$

Then the asymptotic distribution of V_t is $\mathcal{N}\big(\theta, \sigma^2/(2\kappa)\big)$.

Example 4.17 (Brownian bridge). The one-dimensional *Brownian bridge* process on $[0, T]$ is a process that starts in a at time $t = 0$ and ends in b at time T. This process solves the following stochastic equation

$$dX_t = \frac{b - X_t}{T - t}dt + dW_t, \quad X_0 = a, \quad t \in [0, T),$$

where W_t is a standard Wiener process in probability space $(\Omega, \mathcal{F}, \mathbb{P})$.

This linear equation can be solved explicitly to give

$$X_t = a\left(1 - \frac{t}{T}\right) + b\frac{t}{T} + (T - t)\int_0^t \frac{dW_s}{T - s}, \quad t \in [0, T). \tag{4.4}$$

A more convenient form of expressing the Brownian bridge process is the formula

$$X_t = a\left(1 - \frac{t}{T}\right) + b\frac{t}{T} + \left(W_t - \frac{t}{T}W_T\right). \tag{4.5}$$

To demonstrate that both expressions represent the same process, we analyze the process

$$Y_t = \begin{cases} (T - t)\int_0^t \frac{dW_s}{T - s}, & t \in [0, T), \\ 0, & t = T. \end{cases}$$

We show that Y_t, for $t < T$, is a continuous, Gaussian process with covariance function

$$\rho(s,t) = s \wedge t - \frac{st}{T}, \quad 0 \le s,t \le T. \tag{4.6}$$

Indeed, Y_t is Gaussian since the integrand is square integrable for $t < T$. Simple computations for $s \le t$ give

$$\begin{aligned}
\mathbb{E}\big(Y_s Y_t\big) &= (T-t)(T-s)\mathbb{E}\left(\int_0^s \frac{dW_u}{T-u} \int_0^t \frac{dW_v}{T-v}\right) \\
&= (T-t)(T-s)\int_0^s \frac{du}{(T-u)^2} \\
&= (T-t)(T-s)\left(\frac{1}{T-s} - \frac{1}{T}\right) = s - \frac{st}{T}.
\end{aligned}$$

This proves that the covariance function of Y_t is given by equation (4.6). The proof that $\lim_{t\to T^-} T_t = 0$ is complicated, and we skip its presentation (for that proof, see [48]).

Comparing equations (4.4) and (4.5), we see that the expectation of process X_t in both equations is the same. It is also clear that the process X_t given by equation (4.5) is Gaussian. Computing $\mathbb{E}\big(X_s X_t\big)$ for processes X_s and X_t given by equation (4.5), we obtain formula (4.6) similarly as for processes defined by equation (4.4). This proves that equations (4.4) and (4.5) define the same process.

4.2 Numerical Schemes for Stochastic Differential Equations

The numerical integration of equation (4.2) means, in fact, a numerical approximation of the corresponding integrals. The main difficulty is the approximation of the Itô integral. We begin our analysis by demonstrating how to approximate the one-dimensional Wiener process W_t. To approximate W_t in interval $[0,T]$, we divide this interval into N equal subintervals of length $h = T/N$ with the grid points

$$t_n = nh = n\frac{T}{N}, \quad n = 0,\ldots,N.$$

The Wiener process W_t can be approximated in points t_n by the expression

$$W_{t_{n+1}} = W_{t_n} + \delta W_n, \quad W_{t_0} = W_0 = 0,$$

where δW_n are i.i.d. variables with distribution $\mathcal{N}(0,h)$.

Lemma 4.18. *Let W_t^h take values W_{t_n} at points t_n and be linearly interpolated between these points. Then*

$$\mathbb{E}\left(\int_0^T |W_t^h - W_t| dt\right) = CN^{-1/2}.$$

Proof. Let $Z_t^T = W_t - t/T\, W_T$ denote the Brownian bridge in the interval $[0,T]$. Then the process

$$\int_0^T |W_t^h - W_t| dt$$

has the same distribution as the sum of N copies of

$$\int_0^{T/N} |Z_t^{T/N}| dt.$$

Let us note that $\{Z_{tT}^T\}_{0\le t\le 1}$ has the same distribution as $\{\sqrt{T} Z_t^1\}_{0\le t\le 1}$ by the scaling property of Wiener process. Further, $Z_t^1 \sim \mathcal{N}(0, t(1-t))$ since $\mathbb{E} Z_t^1 = 0$ and $\mathbb{E}\left((Z_t^1)^2\right) = \mathbb{E}(W_t^2 - 2tW_tW_1 + t^2W_1^2) = t - t^2$.

Hence,

$$\begin{aligned}
&\mathbb{E}\left(\int_0^T |W_t^h - W_t| dt\right) \\
&\quad = N\,\mathbb{E}\left(\int_0^{T/N} |Z_t^{T/N}| dt\right) = T\,\mathbb{E}\left(\int_0^1 |Z_{sT/N}^{T/N}| ds\right) \\
&\quad = \frac{T^{3/2}}{N^{1/2}}\,\mathbb{E}\left(\int_0^1 |Z_s^1| ds\right) = \frac{T^{3/2}}{N^{1/2}} \int_0^1 \sqrt{\frac{2s(1-s)}{\pi}} ds = CN^{-1/2}.
\end{aligned}$$

The second equality above is obtained by substitution $t \mapsto s\frac{T}{N}$; the fourth, follows from the formula $\mathbb{E}|\xi| = \sqrt{2\sigma^2/\pi}$ for $\xi \sim \mathcal{N}(0,\sigma^2)$, and the distribution of Z_t^1. □

Numerical schemes for the integration of SDEs can be easily obtained by expanding coefficients of the equation in Taylor's series combined with Itô's formula and truncating the expansion at an appropriate level. That procedure, called the *Itô–Taylor expansion*, can be applied to stochastic differential equations of any finite dimension.

Consider the multi-dimensional equation

$$X_t = X_{t_0} + \int_{t_0}^{t} b(s, X_s)ds + \int_{t_0}^{t} \sigma(s, X_s)dW_s, \tag{4.7}$$

where X and b are d-dimensional vectors, σ is a matrix with dimension $d \times m$, and W_t is an m-dimensional Wiener process. Applying Itô's formula to the coefficients b and σ, we obtain

$$\begin{aligned} b(s, X_s) = b(t_0, X_{t_0}) &+ \int_{t_0}^{s} \frac{\partial b(v, X_v)}{\partial v} dv + \int_{t_0}^{s} \sum_{i=1}^{d} \frac{\partial b(v, X_v)}{\partial x_i} b_i(v, X_v)dv \\ &+ \frac{1}{2} \int_{t_0}^{s} \sum_{i,j=1}^{d} \frac{\partial^2 b(v, X_v)}{\partial x_i \partial x_j} \left(\sum_{k,l=1}^{m} \sigma_i^k(v, X_v) Q_{kl} \sigma_j^l(v, X_v) \right) dv \\ &+ \int_{t_0}^{s} \sum_{i=1}^{d} \frac{\partial b(v, X_v)}{\partial x_i} \left(\sum_{j=1}^{m} \sigma_i^j(v, X_v) dW_v^j \right), \end{aligned}$$

and

$$\begin{aligned} \sigma(s, X_s) = \sigma(t_0, X_{t_0}) &+ \int_{t_0}^{s} \frac{\partial \sigma(v, X_v)}{\partial v} dv \\ &+ \int_{t_0}^{s} \sum_{i=1}^{d} \frac{\partial \sigma(v, X_v)}{\partial x_i} b_i(v, X_v)dv \\ &+ \frac{1}{2} \int_{t_0}^{s} \sum_{i,j=1}^{d} \frac{\partial^2 \sigma(v, X_v)}{\partial x_i \partial x_j} \left(\sum_{k,l=1}^{m} \sigma_i^k(v, X_v) Q_{kl} \sigma_j^l(v, X_v) \right) dv \\ &+ \int_{t_0}^{s} \sum_{i=1}^{d} \frac{\partial \sigma(v, X_v)}{\partial x_i} \left(\sum_{j=1}^{m} \sigma_i^j(v, X_v) dW_v^j \right), \end{aligned}$$

where Q denotes the covariance matrix of W_t.

Defining the operators

$$L^0 f = \frac{\partial f}{\partial t} + \sum_{i=1}^{d} \frac{\partial f}{\partial x_i} b_i + \frac{1}{2} \sum_{i,j=1}^{d} \frac{\partial^2 f}{\partial x_i \partial x_j} \left(\sum_{k,l=1}^{m} \sigma_i^k Q_{kl} \sigma_j^l \right),$$

$$L^j f = \sum_{i=1}^{d} \frac{\partial f}{\partial x_i} \sigma_i^j, \quad j = 1, \ldots, m,$$

we can write

$$b(s, X_s) = b(t_0, X_{t_0}) + \int_{t_0}^{s} L^0 b(v, X_v) dv + \sum_{j=1}^{m} \int_{t_0}^{s} L^j b(v, X_v) dW_v^j,$$

$$\sigma(s, X_s) = \sigma(t_0, X_{t_0}) + \int_{t_0}^{s} L^0 \sigma(v, X_v) dv + \sum_{j=1}^{m} \int_{t_0}^{s} L^j \sigma(v, X_v) dW_v^j.$$

Inserting these expansions into (4.7), we get

$$X_t = X_{t_0} + b(t_0, X_{t_0})(t - t_0) + \sigma(t_0, X_{t_0})(W_t - W_{t_0}) + r(t), \quad (4.8)$$

where the remainder is

$$\begin{aligned} r(t) = &\int_{t_0}^{t} \int_{t_0}^{s} L^0 b(v, X_v) dv ds + \sum_{j=1}^{m} \int_{t_0}^{t} \int_{t_0}^{s} L^j b(v, X_v) dW_v^j ds \\ &+ \int_{t_0}^{t} \int_{t_0}^{s} L^0 \sigma(v, X_v) dv dW_s + \sum_{j=1}^{m} \int_{t_0}^{t} \int_{t_0}^{s} L^j \sigma(v, X_v) dW_v^j dW_s. \end{aligned} \quad (4.9)$$

By discarding the remainder, we obtain the first-order approximation

$$X_t \approx X_{t_0} + b(t_0, X_{t_0})(t - t_0) + \sigma(t_0, X_{t_0})(W_t - W_{t_0})$$

which is called the *Euler–Maruyama scheme*. In one dimension, the algorithm of the Euler–Maruyama scheme has the form:

$$\begin{aligned} X_0 &= x, \\ X_{n+1} &= X_n + b(t_n, X_n) h + \sigma(t_n, X_n) \delta W_n, \end{aligned}$$

where $\delta W_n = W_{t_{n+1}} - W_{t_n}$.

To obtain a better approximation, we can expand terms $L^j\sigma(t, X_t)$ using Itô's formula

$$L^{j_0}\sigma(t, X_t) = L^{j_0}\sigma(t_0, X_{t_0}) + \int_{t_0}^{t} L^0 L^{j_0}\sigma(v, X_v)dv + \sum_{j=1}^{m}\int_{t_0}^{t} L^j L^{j_0}\sigma(v, X_v)dW_v^j.$$

Substituting these expansions into $r(t)$, we obtain the following expression for X_t

$$X_t = X_{t_0} + b(t_0, X_{t_0})(t - t_0) + \sigma(t_0, X_{t_0})(W_t - W_{t_0}) + \sum_{j=1}^{m} L^j\sigma(t_0, X_{t_0})\int_{t_0}^{t}\int_{t_0}^{s} dW_v^j dW_s + r_1(t), \tag{4.10}$$

where the new remainder is

$$\begin{aligned} r_1(t) = {} & \int_{t_0}^{t}\int_{t_0}^{s} L^0 b(v, X_v)dvds + \sum_{j=1}^{m}\int_{t_0}^{t}\int_{t_0}^{s} L^j b(v, X_v)dW_v^j ds \\ & + \int_{t_0}^{t}\int_{t_0}^{s} L^0\sigma(v, X_v)dvdW_s \\ & + \sum_{j=1}^{m}\int_{t_0}^{t}\int_{t_0}^{s_1}\int_{t_0}^{s_2} L^0 L^j\sigma(v, X_v)dvdW_{s_2}^j dW_{s_1} \\ & + \sum_{j_1, j_2=1}^{m}\int_{t_0}^{t}\int_{t_0}^{s_1}\int_{t_0}^{s_2} L^{j_1}L^{j_2}\sigma(v, X_v)dW_v^{j_2}dW_{s_2}^{j_1}dW_{s_1}. \end{aligned}$$

Discarding $r_1(t)$, we obtain the *multi-dimensional Milstein scheme.* To implement this scheme effectively, we must compute the iterated Itô integrals

$$\int_{t_0}^{t}\int_{t_0}^{s} dW_v^j dW_s,$$

which is a highly nontrivial operation. Hence, we limit our considerations to a one-dimensional case, where the integral can be easily computed

$$\int_{t_0}^{t}\int_{t_0}^{s} dW_v dW_s = \int_{t_0}^{t}(W_s - W_{t_0})dW_s = \frac{1}{2}\big((W_t - W_{t_0})^2 - (t - t_0)\big).$$

Then we obtain the one-dimensional Milstein scheme:

$$\begin{aligned} X_0 &= x, \\ X_{n+1} &= X_n + b(t_n, X_n)h + \sigma(t_n, X_n)\delta W_n \\ &\quad + \frac{1}{2}\frac{\partial \sigma}{\partial x}(t_n, X_n)\sigma(t_n, X_n)\big((\delta W_n)^2 - h\big). \end{aligned}$$

Here, we focus on one-dimensional schemes. To investigate the convergence of numerical schemes, we must compare the stochastic process X_t with its numerical approximation. The problem is that numerical schemes generate only a sequence of random variables X_n. Hence, we extend this sequence to a process defined for all t either by the linear interpolation

$$\tilde{X}_t^h = X_n + \frac{t - t_n}{t_{n+1} - t_n}(X_{n+1} - X_n) \quad \text{for } t \in [t_n, t_{n+1})$$

or the piecewise constant interpolation

$$\tilde{X}_t^h = X_n \quad \text{for } t \in [t_n, t_{n+1}),$$

where the superscript h indicates the dependence on the time increment h.

Despite the difference in these approximations, one obtains the same limits for $N \to \infty$.

Definition 4.19. A numerical scheme is strongly convergent of order γ, if for each $h < h_0$

$$\mathbb{E}\left(\left|X_T - \tilde{X}_T^h\right|\right) \le C_T\, h^\gamma.$$

A numerical scheme is weakly convergent of order γ, if for each $h < h_0$

$$\left|\mathbb{E}f(X_T) - \mathbb{E}f(\tilde{X}_T^h)\right| \le C_T^f\, h^\gamma,$$

for every f of class $C^{2(1+\gamma)}$, where f and its derivatives up to order $2(1+\gamma)$ have polynomial growth. The constants C_T and C_T^f depend on the SDE and the parameters indicated as indices (T, or T and f).

Remark 4.20. The relevant order of convergence is $1/2, 1, 3/2, 2, 5/2, \ldots$, i.e., an integer multiplicity of $1/2$. Then $2(1+\gamma)$ is an integer, and $C^{2(1+\gamma)}$ is a usual space of functions continuous together with their derivatives.

4.3 Proofs of Convergence

We will analyze the convergence rates of the Euler–Maruyama and Milstein schemes in a one-dimensional case. The proofs of convergence in many dimensions are described in the monograph by Kloeden and Platen [51]. We begin with the strong convergence of the Euler–Maruyama scheme. A more complete discussion of several formulations of this convergence can be found in the book by Pagès [70].

Theorem 4.21. *Consider the stochastic differential equation* (4.2) *with the coefficients satisfying the following conditions:*

(A1) $|b(t,x) - b(t,y)| + |\sigma(t,x) - \sigma(t,y)| \leq K|x-y|;$
(A2) $|b(t,x)| + |\sigma(t,x)| \leq K(1+|x|);$
(A3) $|b(t,x) - b(s,x)| + |\sigma(t,x) - \sigma(s,x)| \leq K(1+|x|)\sqrt{t-s};$

for $x, y \in \mathbb{R}$ and $t, s \in [0,T]$, $t > s$.

The Euler-Maruyama scheme for equation (4.2) *reads*

$$X_{n+1}^h = X_n^h + b(t_n, X_n^h)h + \sigma(t_n, X_n^h)\delta W_n,$$

where

$$h = \frac{T}{N}, \quad t_n = nh, \quad n = 0, \ldots, N;$$
$$\delta W_n = W_{t_{n+1}} - W_{t_n}, \quad n = 0, \ldots, N-1,$$

and superscript h in X_n^h indicates the dependence on time step h.

The obtained sequence of random variables is extended by linear approximation to a continuous process on $[0,T]$ called the continuous Euler–Maruyama scheme *which for $t \in [t_n, t_{n+1})$ is given by the* *expression*

$$\tilde{X}_t^h = X_n^h + \int_{t_n}^t b(t_n, X_n^h)ds + \int_{t_n}^t \sigma(t_n, X_n^h)dW_s,$$
$$n = 0, \ldots, N-1, \quad \tilde{X}_T^h = X_N^h.$$

Then

$$\mathbb{E}\left(\sup_{t\in[0,T]} \left|X_t - \tilde{X}_t^h\right|\right) = O(h^{1/2}).$$

It is convenient to simplify notation by defining for $t \in [0,T]$ the function

$$\Psi_t = \max\{t_n, n = 0, \ldots, N\colon\ t_n \le t\}.$$

With this function, the continuous Euler–Maruyama scheme can be written as

$$\tilde{X}_t^h = x + \int_0^t b(\Psi_s, \tilde{X}_{\Psi_s}^h)ds + \int_0^t \sigma(\Psi_s, \tilde{X}_{\Psi_s}^h)dW_s, \tag{4.11}$$

where $\tilde{X}_{\Psi_t}^h$ defines the stepwise constant process $\tilde{X}_{\Psi_t}^h = X_n^h$ for $t \in [t_n, t_{n+1})$.

Example 4.22. For some equations, the discretization error of the Euler-Maruyama scheme can be eliminated. Consider a process X_t that satisfies the stochastic differential equation

$$dS_t = rdt + \sigma(t)dW_t$$

for constant r and deterministic function $\sigma(t)$.

On $[0,T]$, we select a sequence of points $0 = t_0 < t_1 < \cdots < t_N = T$ and compute the solutions of the stochastic equation at these points

$$\begin{aligned} S_{t_{n+1}} - S_{t_n} &= r\big(t_{n+1} - t_n\big) + \int_{t_n}^{t_{n+1}} \sigma(t)dW_t \\ &= r\big(t_{n+1} - t_n\big) + Z_{n+1}\sqrt{\int_{t_n}^{t_{n+1}} \sigma^2(t)dt}, \end{aligned}$$

where Z_{n+1} are standard normal random variables. On the other hand, we obtain with the same sequence of time points the following Euler–Maruyama algorithm

$$S_0^h = S_0, \quad S_{t_{n+1}}^h = S_{t_n}^h + r\big(t_{n+1} - t_n\big) + Z_{n+1}\sqrt{\int_{t_n}^{t_{n+1}} \sigma^2(t)dt},$$

where $(Z_1, \ldots, Z_N)$ are i.i.d. standard normal variables. It is easy to see that $S_{t_n}^h$ has the same distribution as S_{t_n} for every n, and, thus, there is no discretization error.

The proof of Theorem 4.21 requires a uniform bound on the solution $\tilde{X}_t^h$ obtained with the help of the Burkholder–Davis–Gundy inequality [48].

Lemma 4.23 (Burkholder–Davis–Gundy inequality). *Let $\big(M_t\big)_{t\in[u,v]}$ be a continuous, square integrable martingale. For each $m > 0$ there exist constants $0 < k_m < K_m < \infty$ such that*

$$k_m \mathbb{E}\left(\left(\langle M\rangle_v\right)^m\right) \le \mathbb{E}\left(\sup_{t\in[u,v]} |M_t|^{2m}\right) \le K_m \mathbb{E}\left(\left(\langle M\rangle_v\right)^m\right),$$

where $\langle M\rangle_v$ denotes the quadratic variation of M.

Then we can prove the following estimate.

Lemma 4.24. *Let $\tilde{X}_t^h$ be the Euler–Maruyama approximation defined in Theorem 4.21. Under assumptions (A1) and (A2) of this theorem, we get for each $p \ge 1$ the estimate*

$$\sup_{h<1} \mathbb{E}\left(\sup_{t\in[0,T]} |\tilde{X}_t^h|^p\right)^{1/p} < +\infty.$$

Proof. Since $h = \frac{T}{N}$ is now fixed, we omit the superscript h in the proof. Then the equation for $\tilde{X}_t := \tilde{X}_t^h$ reads

$$\tilde{X}_t = x + \int_0^t b(\Psi_s, \tilde{X}_{\Psi_s})ds + \int_0^t \sigma(\Psi_s, \tilde{X}_{\Psi_s})dW_s.$$

From the above equation, we have the estimate

$$\begin{aligned} \sup_{s\le t} |\tilde{X}_s|^p \le 3^{p-1}\Bigg(|x|^p &+ \sup_{s\le t}\left| \int_0^s b(\Psi_v, \tilde{X}_{\Psi_v})dv\right|^p \\ &+ \sup_{s\le t}\left| \int_0^s \sigma(\Psi_v, \tilde{X}_{\Psi_v})dW_v\right|^p\Bigg), \end{aligned} \tag{4.12}$$

which follows from Jensen's inequality for the convex function $|x|^p$

$$|a_1 + \cdots + a_n|^p \leq n^{p-1}\big(|a_1|^p + \cdots + |a_n|^p\big).$$

We separately estimate each term in (4.12). By Jensen's inequality, we get

$$\begin{aligned}
&\left|\int_0^s b(\Psi_v, \tilde{X}_{\Psi_v})dv\right|^p \\
&\quad = s^p\left|\frac{1}{s}\int_0^s b(\Psi_v, \tilde{X}_{\Psi_v})dv\right|^p \leq s^{p-1}\int_0^s \big|b(\Psi_v, \tilde{X}_{\Psi_v})\big|^p dv \\
&\quad \leq s^{p-1}K^p \int_0^s (1 + |\tilde{X}_{\Psi_v}|)^p dv \leq C\left(1 + \int_0^s |\tilde{X}_{\Psi_v}|^p dv\right).
\end{aligned}$$

For fixed h and $n = 0, \ldots, N$, we have $|\tilde{X}_{t_n}| < +\infty$. Hence, by assumption (A2) of Theorem 4.21 the stochastic integral

$$\left(\int_0^t \sigma(\Psi_v, \tilde{X}_{\Psi_v})dW_v\right)_{t\leq T}$$

is a square-integrable martingale. By the Burkholder–Davis–Gundy inequality, assumption (A2) of Theorem 4.21, and Hölder's inequality, we get

$$\begin{aligned}
&\mathbb{E}\left(\sup_{s\leq t}\left|\int_0^s \sigma(\Psi_v, \tilde{X}_{\Psi_v})dW_v\right|^p\right) \leq K\,\mathbb{E}\left(\left(\int_0^t \big|\sigma(\Psi_v, \tilde{X}_{\Psi_v})\big|^2 dv\right)^{p/2}\right) \\
&\quad \leq K\,\mathbb{E}\left(t^{p/2-1}\int_0^t \left(\big|\sigma(\Psi_v, \tilde{X}_{\Psi_v})\big|^2\right)^{p/2} dv\right) \\
&\quad \leq C\left(1 + \int_0^t \mathbb{E}|\tilde{X}_{\Psi_v}|^p dv\right).
\end{aligned}$$

Collecting the estimates, we obtain

$$\begin{aligned}
\mathbb{E}\left(\sup_{s\leq t}|\tilde{X}_s|^p\right) &\leq C\left(1 + \int_0^t \mathbb{E}|\tilde{X}_{\Psi_v}|^p dv\right) \\
&\leq C\left(1 + \int_0^t \mathbb{E}\left(\sup_{r\leq v}|\tilde{X}_r|^p\right) dv\right).
\end{aligned}$$

Using Gronwall's inequality, we obtain the desired estimate

$$\mathbb{E}\left(\sup_{s\leq t}|\tilde{X}_s|^p\right) < +\infty.$$

□

The following technical lemma will be useful in the proof of Theorem 4.21.

Lemma 4.25. *Let $\tilde{X}_t^h$ be the continuous Euler–Maruyama approximation defined in Theorem* 4.21. *Under assumptions (A1) and (A2) of this theorem, we have for each $p \geq 1$ the estimate*

$$\sup_{h<1} \mathbb{E}\left(\sup_{t\in[0,T]} |\tilde{X}_t^h - \tilde{X}_{\Psi_t}^h|^p \right) \leq Ch^{p/2}.$$

Proof. As in the previous proof, we omit the index h. It is sufficient to prove the estimate in a single interval $[t_n, t_{n+1})$. Let $t \in [t_n, t_{n+1})$, then

$$\tilde{X}_t = \tilde{X}_{\Psi_t} + \int_{t_n}^t b(t_n, X_n)dv + \int_{t_n}^t \sigma(t_n, X_n)dW_v.$$

By Jensen's inequality

$$|\tilde{X}_t - \tilde{X}_{\Psi_t}|^p \leq C\left(\left|\int_{t_n}^t b(t_n, X_n)dv\right|^p + \left|\int_{t_n}^t \sigma(t_n, X_n)dW_v\right|^p \right).$$

By assumption (A2) and Lemma 4.24, we have

$$\mathbb{E}\left(\left|\int_{t_n}^t b(t_n, X_n)dv\right|^p \right) \leq Ch^p\, \mathbb{E}\left(1 + |X_n|^p\right) \leq Ch^p.$$

Since the stochastic integral

$$\int_{t_n}^t \sigma(t_n, X_n)dW_v$$

is a square-integrable martingale, then, similarly to Lemma 4.24, we obtain

$$\begin{aligned}\mathbb{E}\left(\left|\int_{t_n}^t \sigma(t_n, X_n)dW_v\right|^p \right) &\leq C\mathbb{E}\left(\left(\int_{t_n}^{t_{n+1}} |\sigma(t_n, X_n)|^2 dv \right)^{p/2} \right)\\ &\leq Ch^{p/2}\mathbb{E}(1 + |X_n|^p) \leq Ch^{p/2}.\end{aligned}$$

Collecting the above estimates, we get

$$\mathbb{E}\left(\sup_{t\in[t_n,t_{n+1})} |\tilde{X}_t - \tilde{X}_{\Psi_t}|^p \right) \leq Ch^p + Ch^{p/2} \leq Ch^{p/2},$$

from where the result follows. □

Proof of Theorem 4.21. With the help of function Ψ_t, we can write

$$\tilde{X}_t = x + \int_0^t b(\Psi_s, \tilde{X}_{\Psi_s})ds + \int_0^t \sigma(\Psi_s, \tilde{X}_{\Psi_s})dW_s,$$

where, as previously, we omit the superscript h in $\tilde{X}_t^h$. Then for $t \in [t_n, t_{n+1})$, we get

$$X_t - \tilde{X}_t = R_1(t) + R_2(t),$$

where

$$R_1(t) = \int_0^t b(s, X_s)ds - \int_0^t b(\Psi_s, \tilde{X}_{\Psi_s})ds,$$

$$R_2(t) = \int_0^t \sigma(s, X_s)dW_s - \int_0^t \sigma(\Psi_s, \tilde{X}_{\Psi_s})dW_s.$$

Let

$$z(t) = \mathbb{E}\big(X_t - \tilde{X}_t\big)^2, \quad r_1(t) = \mathbb{E}\big(R_1(t)\big)^2, \quad r_2(t) = \mathbb{E}\big(R_2(t)\big)^2.$$

Then

$$z(t) = \mathbb{E}\big(R_1(t) + R_2(t)\big)^2 \leq 2r_1(t) + 2r_2(t).$$

We now separately estimate $r_1(t)$ and $r_2(t)$.

$$R_1(t) = \int_0^t \Big(b(s, X_s)ds - b(s, \tilde{X}_{\Psi_s})\Big)\, ds$$
$$+ \int_0^t \Big(b(s, \tilde{X}_{\Psi_s}) - b(\Psi_s, \tilde{X}_{\Psi_s})\Big)\, ds.$$

For the first integral, we obtain the estimate

$$\mathbb{E}\left(\left(\int_0^t \Big(b(s, X_s) - b(s, \tilde{X}_{\Psi_s})\Big)ds\right)^2\right)$$
$$\leq \mathbb{E}\left(\left(\int_0^t K|X_s - \tilde{X}_{\Psi_s}|ds\right)^2\right)$$
$$\leq 2K^2T\,\mathbb{E}\left(\int_0^t \Big((X_s - \tilde{X}_s)^2 + (\tilde{X}_s - \tilde{X}_{\Psi_s})^2\Big)\, ds\right)$$

$$\leq 2K^2T\int_0^t z(s)ds + 2K^2T\,\mathbb{E}\left(\int_0^t (\tilde{X}_s - \tilde{X}_{\Psi_s})^2 ds\right)$$
$$\leq C\int_0^t z(s)ds + Ch,$$

which follows from the definition $z(s) = \mathbb{E}\big(X_s - \tilde{X}_s\big)^2$ and the estimate of $\big(\tilde{X}_s - \tilde{X}_{\Psi_s}\big)^2$ obtained in Lemma 4.25.

For the second integral, we obtain

$$\mathbb{E}\left(\left(\int_0^t \Big(b(s,\tilde{X}_{\Psi_s}) - b(\Psi_s,\tilde{X}_{\Psi_s})\Big)ds\right)^2\right)$$
$$\leq T\,\mathbb{E}\left(\int_0^t \Big(b(s,\tilde{X}_{\Psi_s}) - b(\Psi_s,\tilde{X}_{\Psi_s})\Big)^2 ds\right)$$
$$\leq 2T\,\mathbb{E}\left(\int_0^t K^2(1+|\tilde{X}_{\Psi_s}|^2)(s-\Psi_s)ds\right)$$
$$\leq 2TK^2(1+M)\sum_{k\leq n}\left(\int_{t_k}^{t_{k+1}}(s-t_k)ds\right)$$
$$\leq 2TK^2(1+M)\cdot\frac{1}{2}h^2n \leq T^2K^2(1+M)h,$$

where $M = \mathbb{E}\big(\sup_{s\leq T}|\tilde{X}_s|^2\big) < +\infty$ by Lemma 4.24.

Collecting these estimates and assuming $h \leq 1$, we obtain

$$r_1(t) = \mathbb{E}\big(R_1(s)\big)^2 \leq C_1h + C_2\int_0^t z(s)ds.$$

For $r_2(t)$, we perform similar computations.

$$R_2(t) = \int_0^t \Big(\sigma(s,X_s) - \sigma(s,\tilde{X}_{\Psi_s})\Big)dW_s$$
$$+ \int_0^t \Big(\sigma(s,\tilde{X}_{\Psi_s}) - \sigma(\Psi_s,\tilde{X}_{\Psi_s})\Big)dW_s.$$

For the first integral, we obtain the estimate

$$\mathbb{E}\left(\left(\int_0^t \Big(\sigma(s,X_s) - \sigma(s,\tilde{X}_{\Psi_s})\Big)dW_s\right)^2\right)$$
$$= \mathbb{E}\left(\int_0^t \Big(\sigma(s,X_s) - \sigma(s,\tilde{X}_{\Psi_s})\Big)^2 ds\right)$$

$$\leq 2K^2\,\mathbb{E}\left(\int_0^t (X_s - \tilde{X}_s)^2 ds\right) + 2K^2\,\mathbb{E}\left(\int_0^t (\tilde{X}_s - \tilde{X}_{\Psi_s})^2 ds\right)$$
$$\leq C\int_0^t z(s)ds + Ch.$$

The second integral is estimated as follows

$$\mathbb{E}\left(\left(\int_0^t \left(\sigma(s, \tilde{X}_{\Psi_s}) - \sigma(\Psi_s, \tilde{X}_{\Psi_s})\right) dW_s\right)^2\right)$$
$$= \mathbb{E}\left(\int_0^t \left(\sigma(s, \tilde{X}_{\Psi_s}) - \sigma(\Psi_s, \tilde{X}_{\Psi_s})\right)^2 ds\right)$$
$$\leq 2\mathbb{E}\left(\int_0^t K^2(1 + |\tilde{X}_{\Psi_s}|^2)(s - \Psi_s)ds\right)$$
$$\leq 2K^2(1+M)\cdot\frac{1}{2}h^2 n = (nh)K^2(1+M)h \leq TK^2(1+M)h.$$

Collecting the estimates, we write

$$r_2(t) = \mathbb{E}\big(R_2(t)\big)^2 \leq C_1 h + C_2\int_0^t z(s)ds.$$

The estimates of r_1 and r_2 give together

$$z(t) \leq C_1 h + C_2\int_0^t z(s)ds.$$

By Gronwall's inequality, we get

$$z(t) \leq C_1 h \exp(C_2 t).$$

Hence, using the Doob maximal inequality, we complete the proof

$$\mathbb{E}\left(\sup_{t\in[0,T]} |X_t - \tilde{X}_t|\right) \leq \left(\mathbb{E}\left(\sup_{t\in[0,T]} |X_t - \tilde{X}_t|\right)^2\right)^{1/2}$$
$$\leq 2\left(\mathbb{E}\left(|X_T - \tilde{X}_T|^2\right)\right)^{1/2} \leq C\big(z(T)\big)^{1/2} \leq C\,h^{1/2}.$$

□

The Milstein scheme gives the $O(h)$ order of convergence. To make the proof of convergence simpler, we impose assumptions that are stronger than required. For more general assumptions, the reader can consult the monograph by Kloeden and Platen [51].

Theorem 4.26. *Let the coefficients of equation* (4.2) *be of class* $C^{1,2}([0,T]\times\mathbb{R})$. *In addition, these coefficients fulfill the conditions:*

(B1) $|b(t,x)| \le K(1+|x|)$ *and* $|b(t,x)-b(s,x)| \le K(1+|x|)\sqrt{t-s}$;
(B2) $|\sigma(t,x)| \le K$ *and* $|\sigma(t,x)-\sigma(s,x)| \le K\sqrt{t-s}$;
(B3) $|\partial b/\partial x\,(t,x)|+|\partial\sigma/\partial x\,(t,x)|+|\partial^2 b/\partial x^2\,(t,x)|+|\partial^2\sigma/\partial x^2\,(t,x)| \le K$;
(B4) $|\partial b/\partial t\,(t,x)|+|\partial\sigma/\partial t\,(t,x)| \le K(1+|x|)$.

In the notation of Theorem 4.21, *the Milstein scheme for equation* (4.2) *reads*

$$X_{n+1}^h = X_n^h + b(t_n,X_n^h)h + \sigma(t_n,X_n^h)\delta W_n + \frac{1}{2}\frac{\partial\sigma}{\partial x}(t_n,X_n^h)\sigma(t_n,X_n^h)\big((\delta W_n)^2-h\big).$$

The above sequence of random variables is extended to a process on $[0,T]$ *by the linear approximation that for* $t\in[t_n,t_{n+1})$ *is given by the expression*

$$\tilde{X}_t^h = X_n^h + \int_{t_n}^t b(t_n,X_n^h)ds + \int_{t_n}^t \sigma(t_n,X_n^h)dW_s + \int_{t_n}^t\int_{t_n}^s \frac{\partial\sigma}{\partial x}(t_n,X_n^h)\sigma(t_n,X_n^h)dW_v dW_s,$$

for $n=0,\ldots,N-1$ *with* $\tilde{X}_T^h = X_N^h$.

Under the above assumptions, we have the estimate

$$\mathbb{E}\left(\sup_{t\in[0,T]}\left|X_t-\tilde{X}_t^h\right|\right) = O(h).$$

Proof. To simplify the proof, we investigate the time-independent coefficients. Then the derivatives $\partial f/\partial x$ and $\partial^2 f/\partial x^2$ are denoted by f' and f'', respectively.

We rewrite equation (4.7) in a more convenient form for the proof. For $t\in[t_n,t_{n+1})$ we apply the Itô–Taylor expansion (4.8) with $t_0 = t_n$. Iterating this expansion over all subintervals $[t_k, t_{k+1})$ for $k < n$ we obtain

$$X_t = x + \int_0^t b(X_{\Psi_s})ds + \int_0^t \sigma(X_{\Psi_s})dW_s + \int_0^t \int_{\Psi_s}^s \sigma'(X_{\Psi_s})\sigma(X_{\Psi_s})dW_v dW_s + R(t),$$

where the function $\Psi_t = \max\{t_n\colon t_n \leq t\}$ is used to simplify notation. The remainder $R(t)$ is

$$\begin{aligned} R(t) = & \int_0^t \int_{\Psi_s}^s \big(b'(X_v)b(X_v) + \frac{1}{2}b''(X_v)\sigma^2(X_v)\big)dvds \\ & + \int_0^t \int_{\Psi_s}^s b'(X_v)\sigma(X_v)dW_v ds \\ & + \int_0^t \int_{\Psi_s}^s \big(b(X_v)\sigma'(X_v) + \frac{1}{2}\sigma''(X_v)\sigma^2(X_v)\big)dvdW_s \\ & + \int_0^t \int_{\Psi_s}^s \big(\sigma(X_v)\sigma'(X_v) - \sigma(X_{\Psi_s})\sigma'(X_{\Psi_s})\big)dW_v dW_s. \end{aligned}$$

For the Milstein approximation, we have

$$\tilde{X}_t = x + \int_0^t b(\tilde{X}_{\Psi_s})ds + \int_0^t \sigma(\tilde{X}_{\Psi_s})dW_s + \int_0^t \int_{\Psi_s}^s \sigma'(\tilde{X}_{\Psi_s})\sigma(\tilde{X}_{\Psi_s})dW_v dW_s.$$

Then for $t \in [t_n, t_{n+1})$, we get

$$X_t - \tilde{X}_t = A_1(t) + A_2(t) + A_3(t) + R(t),$$

where

$$A_1(t) = \int_0^t \big(b(X_{\Psi_s}) - b(\tilde{X}_{\Psi_s})\big)ds,$$

$$A_2(t) = \int_0^t \big(\sigma(X_{\Psi_s}) - \sigma(\tilde{X}_{\Psi_s})\big)dW_s,$$

$$A_3(t) = \int_0^t \int_{\Psi_s}^s \big(\sigma'(X_{\Psi_s})\sigma(X_{\Psi_s}) - \sigma'(\tilde{X}_{\Psi_s})\sigma(\tilde{X}_{\Psi_s})\big)dW_v dW_s.$$

Let

$$z(t) = \sup_{s\le t} \mathbb{E}(X_s - \tilde{X}_s)^2, \quad a_i(t) = \sup_{s\le t} \mathbb{E}(A_i(s))^2, \quad i = 1, 2, 3,$$

$$r(t) = \sup_{s\le t} \mathbb{E}(R(s))^2.$$

Then

$$\begin{aligned} z(t) &= \sup_{s\le t} \mathbb{E}\big(A_1(s) + A_2(s) + A_3(s) + R(s)\big)^2 \\ &\le 4\big(a_1(t) + a_2(t) + a_3(t) + r(t)\big). \end{aligned}$$

We now separately estimate each term.

Since $b(x)$ and $\sigma(x)$ have bounded first derivatives, both functions are globally Lipschitz continuous. By this Lipschitz continuity and the Cauchy–Schwarz inequality, we get for A_1

$$\begin{aligned} \mathbb{E}\big(A_1^2(t)\big) &= \mathbb{E}\left(\left(\int_0^t (b(X_{\Psi_s}) - b(\tilde{X}_{\Psi_s}))ds\right)^2\right) \\ &\le K^2 T \int_0^t \mathbb{E}\Big(\big(X_{\Psi_s} - \tilde{X}_{\Psi_s}\big)^2\Big) ds \le C \int_0^t z(s) ds. \end{aligned}$$

For A_2, we use the Itô isometry of stochastic integrals

$$\begin{aligned} \mathbb{E}\big(A_2^2(t)\big) &= \mathbb{E}\left(\left(\int_0^t (\sigma(X_{\Psi_s}) - \sigma(\tilde{X}_{\Psi_s}))dW_s\right)^2\right) \\ &= \int_0^t \mathbb{E}\Big(\big(\sigma(X_{\Psi_s}) - \sigma(\tilde{X}_{\Psi_s})\big)^2\Big) ds \\ &\le K^2 \int_0^t \mathbb{E}\Big(\big(X_{\Psi_s} - \tilde{X}_{\Psi_s}\big)^2\Big) ds \le C \int_0^t z(s) ds. \end{aligned}$$

To estimate A_3, we use the boundedness of $\sigma(x)$ and the Lipschitz continuity of $\sigma'(x)$ which follows from the boundedness of $\sigma''(x)$. Applying the Itô isometry twice, we obtain

$$\begin{aligned} &\mathbb{E}\big(A_3^2(t)\big) \\ &= \mathbb{E}\left(\left(\int_0^t \int_{\Psi_s}^s (\sigma'(X_{\Psi_s})\sigma(X_{\Psi_s}) - \sigma'(\tilde{X}_{\Psi_s})\sigma(\tilde{X}_{\Psi_s}))dW_v dW_s\right)^2\right) \end{aligned}$$

$$= \int_0^t \mathbb{E}\Big(\Big(\int_{\Psi_s}^s (\sigma'(X_{\Psi_s})\sigma(X_{\Psi_s}) - \sigma'(\tilde{X}_{\Psi_s})\sigma(\tilde{X}_{\Psi_s}))dW_v\Big)^2\Big)ds$$

$$= \int_0^t \int_{\Psi_s}^s \mathbb{E}\Big((\sigma'(X_{\Psi_s})\sigma(X_{\Psi_s}) - \sigma'(\tilde{X}_{\Psi_s})\sigma(\tilde{X}_{\Psi_s}))^2\Big)dvds$$

$$\leq Ch \int_0^t \mathbb{E}\Big((X_{\Psi_s} - \tilde{X}_{\Psi_s})^2\Big)ds \leq C\int_0^t z(s)ds.$$

We split the remainder $R(t)$ into its four components R_1 to R_4, and estimate each component separately.

By assumptions (B2), (B3), and Theorem 4.13, we get

$$\begin{aligned}
\mathbb{E}\big(R_1^2(t)\big) &= \mathbb{E}\Big(\Big(\int_0^t \int_{\Psi_s}^s (b'(X_v)b(X_v) + \frac{1}{2}b''(X_v)\sigma^2(X_v))dvds\Big)^2\Big) \\
&\leq T\,\mathbb{E}\Big(\int_0^t \Big(\int_{\Psi_s}^s (b'(X_v)b(X_v) + \frac{1}{2}b''(X_v)\sigma^2(X_v))dv\Big)^2 ds\Big) \\
&\leq Ch \int_0^t \int_{\Psi_s}^s \mathbb{E}\big(1 + |X_v|^2\big)dvds \leq Ch^2\big(1 + |x|^2\big).
\end{aligned}$$

In the estimate of R_3, we apply additionally the Itô isometry

$$\begin{aligned}
\mathbb{E}\big(R_3^2(t)\big) &= \mathbb{E}\Big(\Big(\int_0^t \int_{\Psi_s}^s (b(X_v)\sigma'(X_v) + \frac{1}{2}\sigma''(X_v)\sigma^2(X_v))dvdW_s\Big)^2\Big) \\
&= \int_0^t \mathbb{E}\Big(\Big(\int_{\Psi_s}^s (b'(X_v)b(X_v) + \frac{1}{2}b''(X_v)\sigma^2(X_v))dv\Big)^2\Big)ds \\
&\leq Ch \int_0^t \int_{\Psi_s}^s \mathbb{E}\big(1 + |X_v|^2\big)dvds \leq Ch^2\big(1 + |x|^2\big).
\end{aligned}$$

The estimation of R_2 is more complicated. First, we split the domain of integration $[0, t]$ into the subintervals defined by the grid point of the Milstein approximation

$$\mathbb{E}\big(R_2^2(t)\big) = \mathbb{E}\left(\left(\int_0^t \int_{\Psi_s}^s b'(X_v)\sigma(X_v)dW_v ds\right)^2\right)$$
$$\leq 2\,\mathbb{E}\left(\left(\sum_{k=0}^{n_t-1} \int_{t_k}^{t_{k+1}} \int_{t_k}^s b'(X_v)\sigma(X_v)dW_v ds\right)^2\right)$$
$$+ 2\,\mathbb{E}\left(\left(\int_{t_{n_t}}^t \int_{t_{n_t}}^s b'(X_v)\sigma(X_v)dW_v ds\right)^2\right),$$

where $n_t = \max\{n\colon t_n \leq t\}$.

By Fubini's theorem, we get

$$\mathbb{E}\big(R_2^2(t)\big) \leq 2\,\mathbb{E}\left(\left(\sum_{k=0}^{n_t-1} \int_{t_k}^{t_{k+1}} \int_v^{t_{k+1}} b'(X_v)\sigma(X_v)ds dW_v\right)^2\right)$$
$$+ 2\,\mathbb{E}\left(\left(\int_{t_{n_t}}^t \int_v^t b'(X_v)\sigma(X_v)ds dW_v\right)^2\right).$$

To estimate the first term, let us observe that, since the intervals $[t_k, t_{k+1})$ and $[t_j, t_{j+1})$ are disjoint for $k \neq j$, then

$$\mathbb{E}\left(\int_{t_k}^{t_{k+1}} (\dots)dW_v \int_{t_j}^{t_{j+1}} (\dots)dW_v\right) = 0.$$

Using this identity in computing the square of the sum on the right-hand side and applying the Itô isometry, we obtain the estimate

$$\mathbb{E}\big(R_2^2(t)\big) \leq 2\sum_{k=0}^{n_t-1} \int_{t_k}^{t_{k+1}} \mathbb{E}\left(\left(\int_v^{t_{k+1}} b'(X_v)\sigma(X_v)ds\right)^2\right)dv$$
$$+ 2\int_{t_{n_t}}^t \mathbb{E}\left(\left(\int_v^t b'(X_v)\sigma(X_v)ds\right)^2\right)dv$$

$$\le C\int_0^t \mathbb{E}\left(\left(\int_v^{\Psi_v+h} b'(X_v)\sigma(X_v)ds\right)^2\right)dv$$

$$\le Ch\int_0^t\int_v^{\Psi_v+h} dsdv \le Ch^2.$$

To estimate R_4 we use the Itô isometry twice, assumptions (B2) and (B3), and the estimates of Theorem 4.13 to obtain

$$\begin{aligned}
&\mathbb{E}\big(R_4^2(t)\big)\\
&= \mathbb{E}\left(\left(\int_0^t\int_{\Psi_s}^s (\sigma(X_v)\sigma'(X_v) - \sigma(X_{\Psi_s})\sigma'(X_{\Psi_s}))dW_v dW_s\right)^2\right)\\
&= \int_0^t \mathbb{E}\left(\left(\int_{\Psi_s}^s (\sigma(X_v)\sigma'(X_v) - \sigma(X_{\Psi_s})\sigma'(X_{\Psi_s}))dW_v\right)^2\right)ds\\
&= \int_0^t\int_{\Psi_s}^s \mathbb{E}\left(\left(\sigma(X_v)\sigma'(X_v) - \sigma(X_{\Psi_s})\sigma'(X_{\Psi_s})\right)^2\right)dvds\\
&\le C\int_0^t\int_{\Psi_s}^s \mathbb{E}\big((X_v - X_{\Psi_s})^2\big)dvds\\
&\le C\big(1+|x|^2\big)\int_0^t\int_{\Psi_s}^s |v-\Psi_s|dvds \le Ch^2\big(1+|x|^2\big).
\end{aligned}$$

Collecting the estimates, we obtain

$$z(t) \le C_1h^2 + C_2\int_0^t z(s)ds.$$

Using Gronwall's inequality, we have

$$z(t) \le C_1h^2\exp(C_2t).$$

Similarly as in the proof of Theorem 4.21, we apply the Doob maximal inequality to conclude the proof

$$\mathbb{E}\left(\sup_{t\in[0,T]}|X_t-\tilde{X}_t|\right) \le \left(\mathbb{E}\left(\sup_{t\in[0,T]}|X_t-\tilde{X}_t|\right)^2\right)^{1/2}$$

$$\le 2\left(\mathbb{E}\left(|X_T-\tilde{X}_T|^2\right)\right)^{1/2} \le C\big(z(T)\big)^{1/2} \le C\,h. \qquad \square$$

Remark 4.27. The limitation of the proofs to one-dimensional equations is not accidental. For the Euler–Maruyama scheme, the proof of convergence in many dimensions remains similar to the proof of Theorem 4.21. The case of the Milstein scheme is different. As we have mentioned, deriving this scheme in many dimensions, we must evaluate the iterated stochastic integrals

$$\int_{t_k}^{t_{k+1}} \int_{t_k}^{s} dW_v^j dW_s^i, \quad i, j = 1, \ldots, m.$$

The simulations of these integrals have a very large computational complexity making the gain of the better convergence rate problematic.

Example 4.28 (Lamperti transform). Consider the stochastic Itô equation

$$dX_t = b(t, X_t)dt + \sigma(t)dW_t,$$

with $\sigma(t)$ independent of x. The Euler–Maruyama scheme for this equation

$$X_{n+1}^h = X_n^h + b(t_n, X_n^h)h + \sigma(t_n)\delta W_n,$$

is the same as the Milstein scheme. Hence, the convergence order of the Euler–Maruyama scheme is 1 (similar to the order of convergence of the Milstein scheme). This shows that for a general Itô equation, the order of convergence of the Euler–Maruyama scheme can be improved by transforming process X_t into a process with constant volatility.

Consider a general form of the Itô equation

$$dX_t = b(t, X_t)dt + \sigma(t, X_t)dW_t,$$

with a continuously differentiable and strictly positive volatility $\sigma(t, X_t) \geq \delta > 0$. Define a function ψ and a process Y as follows

$$\psi(t, x) = \int \frac{1}{\sigma(t, x)} dx, \quad Y_t = \psi(t, X_t) = \int_{\xi}^{x} \frac{1}{\sigma(t, u)} du \Big|_{x = X_t},$$

where ξ is an arbitrary point inside the state space of X_t.

The process Y_t is said to be the *Lamperti transform* of X_t. Y_t is a one-to-one mapping from the state-space of X_t to $\mathbb{R}$ for $t \in [0, \infty)$. By the definition of ψ, we have

$$\frac{\partial \psi(t,x)}{\partial x}\bigg|_{x=X_t} = \frac{1}{\sigma(t,X_t)}, \quad \frac{\partial^2 \psi(t,x)}{\partial x^2}\bigg|_{x=X_t} = -\frac{\frac{\partial \sigma(t,x)}{\partial x}}{\sigma^2(t,x)}\bigg|_{x=X_t}.$$

Combining Itô's formula with these results and applying identity $X_t = \psi^{-1}(t, Y_t)$, we get

$$dY_t = \left(\frac{\partial \psi(t,\psi^{-1}(t,Y_t))}{\partial t} + \frac{b(t,\psi^{-1}(t,Y_t))}{\sigma(t,\psi^{-1}(t,Y_t))} - \frac{1}{2}\frac{\partial \sigma(t,\psi^{-1}(t,Y_t))}{\partial x}\right)dt$$
$$+ dW_t.$$

Thus, Y_t is a process with constant volatility equal to 1, and the Euler–Maruyama scheme applied to this last equation strongly converges with order 1.

We now investigate the order of weak convergence of the Euler–Maruyama scheme. To simplify the presentation, we consider only the equation with time-independent coefficients

$$dX_s = b(X_s)ds + \sigma(X_s)dW_s, \quad s > t, \quad X_t = x. \tag{4.13}$$

We write $X_s^{t,x}$ to indicate the dependence of the solution on initial conditions. By Theorem 5.4, we know that if $b, \sigma \in C^4(\mathbb{R}^d)$ with bounded derivatives and $g \in C^4(\mathbb{R}^d)$ with polynomial growth together with its derivatives, then

$$u(t,x) = \mathbb{E}\Big(g(X_T^{t,x})\Big)$$

is a solution of the Cauchy problem

$$\frac{\partial u}{\partial t} + \sum_{i=1}^{d} b_i(x)\frac{\partial u}{\partial x_i} + \sum_{i,j=1}^{d} a_{ij}(x)\frac{\partial^2 u}{\partial x_i \partial x_j} = 0, \quad t \in [0,T), x \in \mathbb{R}^d,$$
$$u(T,x) = g(x), \tag{4.14}$$

where $a_{ij} = 1/2\sum_{k=1}^{m} \sigma_i^k \sigma_j^k$, and u is a C^1 function with respect to t and C^4 function with respect to x which together with its x-derivatives grows polynomially in x uniformly in t.

Corollary 4.29. *When X_t is a strong solution of* (4.13) *and u is a solution of class $C^{1,2}([0,T] \times \mathbb{R}^d)$ of* (4.14), *then $Y_t = u(t, X_t)$ is a local martingale.*

Proof. By Itô's formula, we have

$$
\begin{aligned}
dY_t &= \frac{\partial u}{\partial t}dt + \sum_{i=1}^{d} \frac{\partial u}{\partial x_i}\left(b_i dt + \sum_{k=1}^{m} \sigma_i^k dW_t^k\right) + \sum_{i,j=1}^{d} a_{ij}\frac{\partial^2 u}{\partial x_i \partial x_j}dt \\
&= \left(\frac{\partial u}{\partial t} + \sum_{i=1}^{d} b_i \frac{\partial u}{\partial x_i} + \sum_{i,j=1}^{d} a_{ij}\frac{\partial^2 u}{\partial x_i \partial x_j}\right)dt + \sum_{i=1}^{d}\sum_{k=1}^{m}\frac{\partial u}{\partial x_i}\sigma_i^k dW_t^k \\
&= \sum_{i=1}^{d}\sum_{k=1}^{m}\frac{\partial u}{\partial x_i}\sigma_i^k dW_t^k,
\end{aligned}
$$

which shows that Y_t is the Itô integral. □

For the Euler–Maruyama scheme, we have the following result, which was originally proved in two papers: by Talay and Tubaro [86] and by Bally and Talay [5].

Theorem 4.30. *Let assumptions (A1), (A2) of Theorem 4.21 be fulfilled and $b, \sigma \in C^4(\mathbb{R}^d)$ that grow polynomially together with their derivatives up to order 4. If X_t is a solution of (4.13) with $X_0 = x$, then for each $g \in C^4(\mathbb{R}^d)$, which has polynomial growth together with its derivatives, and $T > 0$, there exists a constant C_g such that*

$$
\left|\mathbb{E}\left(g(X_T)\right) - \mathbb{E}\left(g(\tilde{X}_T^h)\right)\right| \le C_g\, h.
$$

Proof. We present partial proof, omitting some tedious computations. We assume $d = 1$ to simplify the presentation and omit the superscript h in $\tilde{X}^h$.

By Corollary 4.29, we have

$$
\mathbb{E}\left(g(X_T)\right) = \mathbb{E}\left(u(T, X_T)\right) = u(0, x).
$$

Then

$$
\begin{aligned}
\mathbb{E}\left(g(\tilde{X}_T) - g(X_T)\right) &= \mathbb{E}\left(u(T, \tilde{X}_T)\right) - u(0, x) \\
&= \sum_{n=1}^{N} \mathbb{E}\left(u(t_n, \tilde{X}_{t_n}) - u(t_{n-1}, \tilde{X}_{t_{n-1}})\right).
\end{aligned}
$$

To prove the theorem, it is enough to estimate the local error

$$\left|\mathbb{E}\Big(u(t_n, \tilde{X}_{t_n}) - u(t_{n-1}, \tilde{X}_{t_{n-1}})\Big)\right| \le Ch^2$$

since then

$$\begin{aligned}\left|\mathbb{E}\Big(g(\tilde{X}_T) - g(X_T)\Big)\right| &\le \sum_{n=1}^{N} \left|\mathbb{E}\Big(u(t_n, \tilde{X}_{t_n}) - u(t_{n-1}, \tilde{X}_{t_{n-1}})\Big)\right| \\ &\le \sum_{n=1}^{N} Ch^2 = CTh.\end{aligned}$$

By Corollary 4.29, we obtain

$$\mathbb{E}\Big(u(t_n, X_{t_n}^{t_{n-1}, \tilde{X}_{t_{n-1}}})|\mathcal{F}_{t_{n-1}}\Big) = u(t_{n-1}, \tilde{X}_{t_{n-1}}).$$

Inserting this equality into the expression for the local error, we get

$$\begin{aligned}&\mathbb{E}\Big(u(t_n, \tilde{X}_{t_n}) - u(t_{n-1}, \tilde{X}_{t_{n-1}})\Big) \\ &\quad = \mathbb{E}\Big(\mathbb{E}\Big(u(t_n, \tilde{X}_{t_n}) - u(t_{n-1}, \tilde{X}_{t_{n-1}})|\mathcal{F}_{t_{n-1}}\Big)\Big) \\ &\quad = \mathbb{E}\Big(\mathbb{E}\Big(u(t_n, \tilde{X}_{t_n}) - u(t_{n-1}, \tilde{X}_{t_{n-1}}) - u\left(t_n, X_{t_n}^{t_{n-1}, \tilde{X}_{t_{n-1}}}\right) \\ &\qquad + u(t_{n-1}, \tilde{X}_{t_{n-1}})\Big|\mathcal{F}_{t_{n-1}}\Big)\Big) \\ &\quad = \mathbb{E}\left(\mathbb{E}\left(u(t_n, \tilde{X}_{t_n}) - u\left(t_n, X_{t_n}^{t_{n-1}, \tilde{X}_{t_{n-1}}}\right) \Big|\mathcal{F}_{t_{n-1}}\right)\right).\end{aligned}$$

We rewrite the conditional expectation in the above expression as the difference of two terms

$$\begin{aligned}&\mathbb{E}\left(u(t_n, \tilde{X}_{t_n}) - u\left(t_n, X_{t_n}^{t_{n-1}, \tilde{X}_{t_{n-1}}}\right) |\mathcal{F}_{t_{n-1}}\right) \\ &\quad = \mathbb{E}\Big(u(t_n, \tilde{X}_{t_n}) - u(t_n, \tilde{X}_{t_{n-1}})|\mathcal{F}_{t_{n-1}}\Big) \\ &\qquad - \mathbb{E}\left(u\left(t_n, X_{t_n}^{t_{n-1}, \tilde{X}_{t_{n-1}}}\right) - u(t_n, \tilde{X}_{t_{n-1}})|\mathcal{F}_{t_{n-1}}\right)\end{aligned}$$

and estimate each of these terms expanding $u(t, x+\delta x) - u(t,x)$ in Taylor's series with respect to δx. Then we obtain

$$\Big|\mathbb{E}\Big(\mathbb{E}\Big(u(t_n, \tilde{X}_{t_n}) - u(t_n, X_{t_n}^{t_{n-1},\tilde{X}_{t_{n-1}}})|\mathcal{F}_{t_{n-1}}\Big)\Big)\Big|$$

$$\leq \mathbb{E}\Big(\sum_{k=1}^{3} \frac{1}{k!}\Big|\frac{\partial^k u(t_n, \tilde{X}_{t_{n-1}})}{\partial x^k}\Big|$$

$$\times \Big|\mathbb{E}\Big((\tilde{X}_{t_n} - \tilde{X}_{t_{n-1}})^k - (X_{t_n}^{t_{n-1},\tilde{X}_{t_{n-1}}} - \tilde{X}_{t_{n-1}})^k|\mathcal{F}_{t_{n-1}}\Big)\Big|$$

$$+ \mathbb{E}(|R(\tilde{X}_{t_n})|\,|F_{t_{n-1}}) + \mathbb{E}(|R(X_{t_n}^{t_{n-1},\tilde{X}_{t_{n-1}}})|\,|F_{t_{n-1}})\Big),$$

where

$$R(Z) = \frac{1}{4!}\frac{\partial^4 u(t_n, \tilde{X}_{t_{n-1}} + \theta(Z)(Z - \tilde{X}_{t_{n-1}}))}{\partial x^4}(Z - \tilde{X}_{t_{n-1}})^4.$$

Since $u(t,x)$ is a C^4 function with respect to x growing polynomially together with all its derivatives, then we can find constants $2q$ and $C > 0$ such that for $k = 1, 2, 3$

$$\left|\frac{\partial^k u(t_n, \tilde{X}_{t_{n-1}})}{\partial x^k}\right| \leq C(1 + |\tilde{X}_{t_{n-1}}|^{2q}).$$

After some modifications this estimate remains valid in point $\tilde{X}_{t_{n-1}} + \theta(Z)(Z - \tilde{X}_{t_{n-1}})$ for the fourth derivative $\frac{\partial^4 u}{\partial x^4}$ appearing in the remainder $R(Z)$.

The expression

$$\mathbb{E}\Big((\tilde{X}_{t_n} - \tilde{X}_{t_{n-1}})^k - (X_{t_n}^{t_{n-1},\tilde{X}_{t_{n-1}}} - \tilde{X}_{t_{n-1}})^k|\mathcal{F}_{t_{n-1}}\Big) \tag{4.15}$$

is estimated separately for each $k = 1, 2, 3$.

For $k = 1$, we have

$$\Big|\mathbb{E}\Big((\tilde{X}_{t_n} - \tilde{X}_{t_{n-1}}) - (X_{t_n}^{t_{n-1},\tilde{X}_{t_{n-1}}} - \tilde{X}_{t_{n-1}})|\mathcal{F}_{t_{n-1}}\Big)\Big|$$

$$= \Big|\mathbb{E}\Big(X_{t_n}^{t_{n-1},\tilde{X}_{t_{n-1}}} - \tilde{X}_{t_n}|\mathcal{F}_{t_{n-1}}\Big)\Big| \leq \mathbb{E}\Big(|r(t_n)||\mathcal{F}_{t_{n-1}}\Big)$$

$$\leq \mathbb{E}\left(\left|\int_{t_{n-1}}^{t_n}\int_{t_{n-1}}^{s} L^0 b(X_v)dvds\right|\,\middle|\mathcal{F}_{t_{n-1}}\right),$$

where $r(t)$, given by (4.9), is the remainder in the Itô–Taylor expansion of the Euler–Maruyama approximation and operator L^0 is defined in Section 4.2.

Since $L^0 b$ has a polynomial growth, there are constants $2q$ and $C > 0$ such that

$$\mathbb{E}\left(\left|\int_{t_{n-1}}^{t_n}\int_{t_{n-1}}^{s} L^0 b(X_v)dvds\right|\Big|\mathcal{F}_{t_{n-1}}\right) \le C\big(1 + |\tilde{X}_{t_{n-1}}|^{2q}\big)h^2.$$

To estimate (4.15) for $k = 3$, we first note the estimate

$$\mathbb{E}\Big(|r(t_n)|^2|\mathcal{F}_{t_{n-1}}\Big) \le C\big(1 + |\tilde{X}_{t_{n-1}}|^{2q}\big)h^2,$$

which can be proved using the above considerations.

Then applying the Hölder inequality to $x^3 - y^3 = (x - y)(x^2 + xy + y^2)$, using the estimate of $|r(t_n)|^2$, and the observation that in $\big(\tilde{X}_{t_n} - \tilde{X}_{t_{n-1}}\big)$ and $\big(X_{t_n}^{t_{n-1},\tilde{X}_{t_{n-1}}} - \tilde{X}_{t_{n-1}}\big)$ all terms have the order of smallness at least $1/2$ with respect to h, we obtain for $k = 3$

$$\begin{aligned}&\left|\mathbb{E}\Big(\big(\tilde{X}_{t_n} - \tilde{X}_{t_{n-1}}\big)^3 - \big(X_{t_n}^{t_{n-1},\tilde{X}_{t_{n-1}}} - \tilde{X}_{t_{n-1}}\big)^3|\mathcal{F}_{t_{n-1}}\Big)\right|\\ &\quad \le C\big(1 + |\tilde{X}_{t_{n-1}}|^{2q}\big)h^2.\end{aligned}$$

To estimate (4.15) for $k = 2$, we write

$$\begin{aligned}&\mathbb{E}\Big(\big(\tilde{X}_{t_n} - \tilde{X}_{t_{n-1}}\big)^2 - \big(X_{t_n}^{t_{n-1},\tilde{X}_{t_{n-1}}} - \tilde{X}_{t_{n-1}}\big)^2|\mathcal{F}_{t_{n-1}}\Big)\\ &\quad = \mathbb{E}\Big(r(t_n)\big(\tilde{X}_{t_n} - \tilde{X}_{t_{n-1}} + X_{t_n}^{t_{n-1},\tilde{X}_{t_{n-1}}} - \tilde{X}_{t_{n-1}}\big)|\mathcal{F}_{t_{n-1}}\Big).\end{aligned}$$

Since

$$\begin{aligned}&\big(\tilde{X}_{t_n} - \tilde{X}_{t_{n-1}} + X_{t_n}^{t_{n-1},\tilde{X}_{t_{n-1}}} - \tilde{X}_{t_{n-1}}\big)\\ &\quad = \int_{t_{n-1}}^{t_n}\big(b(\tilde{X}_{t_{n-1}}) + b(X_s^{t_{n-1},\tilde{X}_{t_{n-1}}})\big)ds\\ &\qquad + \int_{t_{n-1}}^{t_n}\big(\sigma(\tilde{X}_{t_{n-1}}) + \sigma(X_s^{t_{n-1},\tilde{X}_{t_{n-1}}})\big)dW_s,\end{aligned}$$

we separately estimate

$$\mathbb{E}\left(r(t_n)\int_{t_{n-1}}^{t_n}(b(\tilde{X}_{t_{n-1}})+b(X_s^{t_{n-1},\tilde{X}_{t_{n-1}}}))ds\big|\mathcal{F}_{t_{n-1}}\right) \tag{4.16}$$

and

$$\mathbb{E}\left(r(t_n)\int_{t_{n-1}}^{t_n}(\sigma(\tilde{X}_{t_{n-1}})+\sigma(X_s^{t_{n-1},\tilde{X}_{t_{n-1}}}))dW_s\big|\mathcal{F}_{t_{n-1}}\right). \tag{4.17}$$

Taking into account that all terms in $r(t_n)$ are at least of the first order in h, we obtain for (4.16)

$$\mathbb{E}\left(r(t_n)\int_{t_{n-1}}^{t_n}(b(\tilde{X}_{t_{n-1}})+b(X_s^{t_{n-1},\tilde{X}_{t_{n-1}}}))ds\big|\mathcal{F}_{t_{n-1}}\right)$$
$$\leq C(1+|\tilde{X}_{t_{n-1}}|^{2q})h^2.$$

To estimate (4.17) let us recall the remainder $r(t_n)$

$$r(t_n)=\int_{t_{n-1}}^{t_n}\int_{t_{n-1}}^{s}L^0b(X_v)dvds+\int_{t_{n-1}}^{t_n}\int_{t_{n-1}}^{s}L^1b(X_v)dW_vds$$
$$+\int_{t_{n-1}}^{t_n}\int_{t_{n-1}}^{s}L^0\sigma(X_v)dvdW_s+\int_{t_{n-1}}^{t_n}\int_{t_{n-1}}^{s}L^1\sigma(X_v)dW_vdW_s.$$

Inserting this expansion into (4.17) and considering the order of smallness with respect to h, we can estimate all terms by h^2 except the last term. To estimate the last term

$$\mathbb{E}\Bigg(\left(\int_{t_{n-1}}^{t_n}\int_{t_{n-1}}^{s}L^1\sigma(X_v)dW_vdW_s\right.$$
$$\left.\cdot\int_{t_{n-1}}^{t_n}(\sigma(\tilde{X}_{t_{n-1}})+\sigma(X_z^{t_{n-1},\tilde{X}_{t_{n-1}}}))dW_z\big|\mathcal{F}_{t_{n-1}}\right),$$

we rewrite the second integral as the sum

$$\int_{t_{n-1}}^{t_n}(\sigma(X_z^{t_{n-1},\tilde{X}_{t_{n-1}}})-\sigma(\tilde{X}_{t_{n-1}}))dW_z+\int_{t_{n-1}}^{t_n}2\sigma(\tilde{X}_{t_{n-1}})dW_z.$$

Then the integral

$$\mathbb{E}\Bigg(\int_{t_{n-1}}^{t_n}\int_{t_{n-1}}^{s} L^1\sigma(X_v)dW_v dW_s$$

$$\cdot\int_{t_{n-1}}^{t_n}\left(\sigma(X_z^{t_{n-1},\tilde{X}_{t_{n-1}}})-\sigma(\tilde{X}_{t_{n-1}})\right)dW_z\big|\mathcal{F}_{t_{n-1}}\Bigg)$$

is of order h^2 due to the Hölder inequality, the Lipschitz property of σ, and the estimate of Theorem 4.13

$$\mathbb{E}\left(\left|X_z^{t_{n-1},\tilde{X}_{t_{n-1}}} - X_{t_{n-1}}^{t_{n-1},\tilde{X}_{t_{n-1}}}\right|^2\right) \le C|z-t_{n-1}|.$$

The estimate is completed, observing that

$$\mathbb{E}\left(\int_{t_{n-1}}^{t_n}\int_{t_{n-1}}^{s} L^1\sigma(X_v)dW_v dW_s\cdot\int_{t_{n-1}}^{t_n} 2\sigma(\tilde{X}_{t_{n-1}})dW_s\big|\mathcal{F}_{t_{n-1}}\right)$$

$$=\mathbb{E}\left(\int_{t_{n-1}}^{t_n} 2\sigma(\tilde{X}_{t_{n-1}})\int_{t_{n-1}}^{s} L^1\sigma(X_v)dW_v ds\big|\mathcal{F}_{t_{n-1}}\right)$$

$$=\mathbb{E}\left(\int_{t_{n-1}}^{t_n}\int_{v}^{t_n} 2\sigma(\tilde{X}_{t_{n-1}})L^1\sigma(X_v)ds dW_v\big|\mathcal{F}_{t_{n-1}}\right)=0.$$

Hence, we have proved that for $k=1,2,3$

$$\left|\mathbb{E}\Big((\tilde{X}_{t_n}-\tilde{X}_{t_{n-1}})^k-(X_{t_n}^{t_{n-1},\tilde{X}_{t_{n-1}}}-\tilde{X}_{t_{n-1}})^k\big|\mathcal{F}_{t_{n-1}}\Big)\right|$$

$$\le C\big(1+|\tilde{X}_{t_{n-1}}|^{2q}\big)h^2.$$

Since the terms $\big(\tilde{X}_{t_n}-\tilde{X}_{t_{n-1}}\big)$ and $\big(X_{t_n}^{t_{n-1},\tilde{X}_{t_{n-1}}}-\tilde{X}_{t_{n-1}}\big)$ are of order $1/2$ with respect to h, as mentioned above, then we obtain for the remainders

$$\mathbb{E}\big(|R(\tilde{X}_{t_n})|\,|F_{t_{n-1}}\big)=C\big(1+|\tilde{X}_{t_{n-1}}|^{2q}\big)h^2,$$

$$\mathbb{E}\big(|R(X_{t_n}^{t_{n-1},\tilde{X}_{t_{n-1}}})|\,|F_{t_{n-1}}\big)=C\big(1+|\tilde{X}_{t_{n-1}}|^{2q}\big)h^2.$$

Collecting all the above estimates, we obtain the desired estimate of the local error

$$\left|\mathbb{E}\Big(\mathbb{E}\Big(u(t_n,\tilde{X}_{t_n}) - u(t_n, X_{t_n}^{t_{n-1},\tilde{X}_{t_{n-1}}})|\mathcal{F}_{t_{n-1}}\Big)\Big)\right|$$
$$\leq C\mathbb{E}\Big(\big(1+|\tilde{X}_{t_{n-1}}|^{2q}\big)\big(1+|\tilde{X}_{t_{n-1}}|^{2q}\big)\Big)h^2 \leq C\big(1+|x|^{4q}\big)h^2,$$

where x is the deterministic initial condition, and the last estimate follows from Theorem 4.13. □

Example 4.31 (The Euler–Maruyama scheme as a control variate). Consider the Monte Carlo estimation of $\mathbb{E}\big(g(X_T)\big)$, where X_t is a solution of the stochastic equation

$$dX_s = b(X_s)ds + \sigma(X_s)dW_s, \quad X_t = x.$$

An MC estimator of $\mathbb{E}\big(g(X_T)\big)$ can be computed as the sample mean of n replicates of $g(X_T)$ obtained by applying the Euler–Maruyama scheme to the above equation.

Let $u(t,x) = \mathbb{E}\big(g(X_T^{t,x})\big)$. If $u(t,x)$ is sufficiently smooth, it fulfills equation (4.14), and $Y_t = u(t,X_t)$ is a local martingale due to Corollary 4.29. Integrating

$$dY_t = \frac{\partial u}{\partial x}(X_t)\sigma(X_t)dW_t,$$

we obtain

$$g(X_T) - \mathbb{E}\big(g(X_T)\big) = \int_0^T \frac{\partial u}{\partial x}(X_t)\sigma(X_t)dW_t.$$

The above identity suggests the following control variate for the estimation of $\mathbb{E}\big(g(X_T)\big)$. Let $v(t,x)$ be a bounded $C^{1,2}$ function. Then

$$\int_0^T \frac{\partial v}{\partial x}(X_t)\sigma(X_t)dW_t$$

has the mean zero. To estimate $\mathbb{E}\big(g(X_T)\big)$ we simulate n replicates of the random variable

$$M_T = g(X_T) - \int_0^T \frac{\partial v}{\partial x}(X_t)\sigma(X_t)dW_t.$$

We compute the estimator of $\mathbb{E}\big(g(X_T)\big)$ as the average over n replicates of the following approximations of M_T

$$M_T^h = g(X_T^h) - \sum_{i=0}^{N-1} \frac{\partial v}{\partial x}(X_{t_i}^h)\sigma(X_{t_i}^h)\sqrt{t_{i+1} - t_i}Z_{i+1}$$

obtained by the Euler–Maruyama algorithm with a discretization $0 = t_0 < \cdots < t_N = T$ of interval $[0, T]$, where $(Z_1, \ldots, Z_N)$ are i.i.d. samples from standard normal distribution.

Observe that if $v(t, x)$ is equal $u(t, x)$, then we obtain a zero variance estimator of $\mathbb{E}\big(g(X_T)\big)$. Hence, finding v such that $\partial v/\partial x \approx \partial u/\partial x$, we can get a substantial reduction of variance.

For the Milstein scheme, we omit the proof of weak convergence because the order of weak convergence of this scheme is equal to 1, i.e., is the same as the order of strong convergence. The fact that the order of weak convergence of the Euler–Maruyama scheme is the same as that of the Milstein scheme shows that, in a sense, the Euler–Maruyama is "better" than its order of strong convergence suggests. This is also demonstrated in Example 4.28.

4.4 Exercises

Exercise 4.1. Let X_t be the Ornstein–Uhlenbeck process

$$dX_t = -X_t dt + dW_t, \quad X_0 = x.$$

Write the Itô–Taylor expansion for a scalar function $f(X_t)$ at point $t_0 = 0$ up to terms of second order. For simplicity, omit the remainder term.

Exercise 4.2. Write the Milstein scheme for the scalar equation

$$dX_t = -\frac{1}{2}X_t dt + X_t dW_t^1 + X_t dW_t^2,$$

where W_t^1 and W_t^2 are independent scalar Wiener processes.

Exercise 4.3. Consider the Black–Scholes stochastic equation

$$dS_t = rS_t dt + \sigma S_t dW_t, \quad S_0 = x,$$

where r and σ are positive constants and x is deterministic. Let S_{2h} be its exact solution at point $t = 2h$ and $\hat{S}_2$ an approximate solution at point $t = 2h$ obtained by the Euler–Maruyama scheme with time step h.

Calculate the bias $\mathbb{E}(\hat{S}_2) - \mathbb{E}(S_{2h})$ and $\mathrm{Var}(\hat{S}_2) - \mathrm{Var}(S_{2h})$ with accuracy $O\big(h^3\big)$.

Exercise 4.4. Consider the Itô process X_t satisfying a linear stochastic equation with constant coefficients

$$dX_t = \mu X_t dt + \sigma X_t dW_t, \quad t \in (0, T], \quad X_0 = x_0,$$

with $x_0 = 1.0$, $\mu = 1.5$, $\sigma = 1.0$, and $T = 1$. Simulate $L = 50$ trajectories of the Wiener process W_t on $[0, T]$ with equidistant time steps of size h. Compute X_T^k, $k = 1, \ldots, L$, on these paths using an analytical solution of the equation. Compute the approximate solution Y_T^k implementing the Euler–Maruyama scheme corresponding to the same sample paths of the Wiener process. Evaluate the absolute error

$$\varepsilon = \frac{1}{L} \sum_{k=1}^{L} |X_T^k - Y_T^k|.$$

(a) Perform the computations for step sizes $h = 2^{-4}$, 2^{-5}, 2^{-6}, and 2^{-7}. Compare the results.
(b) Repeat the computations for 20 different batches of 50 trajectories and $h = 2^{-4}$. Evaluate the 95% confidence interval for the obtained absolute error.

Exercise 4.5. Investigate experimentally the rate of convergence of the Euler–Maruyama scheme for the one-dimensional stochastic equation

$$dX_t = -aX_t dt + \sigma dW_t, \quad X_0 = x,$$

with $a = 1$, $\sigma = 0.3$, and $x = 1$.

Perform $L = 50$ simulations of this equation on a grid $0 = t_0 < t_1 < \cdots < t_N = T$, for $T = 1$, with a constant time step h. Let Y_T^k, $k = 1, \ldots, L$, denote the results of these simulations and X_T^k the corresponding exact solutions with the same paths of the Wiener process W_t. Compute the error

$$\varepsilon_h = \frac{1}{L} \sum_{k=1}^{L} |Y_T^k - X_T^k|,$$

that is an absolute error of the strong approximation.

Repeat the computations for $h_0 = T/100$, $h_{j+1} = h_j/2$, $j = 0, 1, \ldots, J$ taking J not greater than 5. From the relation $\log \varepsilon_{h_j} \sim \log h_j$ find an approximate order of convergence of the Euler–Maruyama scheme.

Exercise 4.6. Let X_t be a solution of equation (4.2) with coefficients satisfying the conditions of Theorem 4.21. Denote by $\tilde{X}_t^h$ the Euler–Maruyama approximation of X_t. Consider a payoff of a European option $g\colon\ [0,\infty] \to [0,\infty]$ that is a Hölder continuous function with exponent $\gamma \in (0,1]$ and Hölder norm $\|g\|_{C^{0,\gamma}} = \sup_{x \neq y} \frac{|g(x)-g(y)|}{|x-y|^\gamma}$. Prove that

$$\left|\mathbb{E}(g(X_T)) - \mathbb{E}(g(\tilde{X}_T^h))\right| \leq \|g\|_{C^{0,\gamma}} \mathbb{E}\left|X_T - \tilde{X}_T^h\right|^\gamma.$$

Exercise 4.7. A variance swap is a contract that pays at maturity date T the average of (daily) realized variance of the stock during the life of the contract (usually from 0 to T) minus the strike

$$\frac{1}{N}\sum_{n=1}^{N}\left(\ln\frac{S_n}{S_{n-1}}\right)^2 - K\frac{1}{D},$$

where S_n is the stock price in day t_n (t_0 is the initial date and $t_N = T$), K is the strike expressed as yearly variance and D is a factor used to recalculate yearly variance in terms of daily variance, i.e., D is the number of days in a year.

Consider the Black–Scholes model given by the stochastic equation

$$dS_t = rS_t dt + \sigma S_t dW_t,$$

where r and σ are positive constants.

Compute in this model the price of a corridor variance swap defined as

$$\frac{1}{N}\sum_{n=1}^{N} f(S_n)\left(\ln\frac{S_n}{S_{n-1}}\right)^2 - K\frac{1}{D},$$

with

$$f(S) = \begin{cases} 1, & \text{if } \frac{S}{S_0} \in [A,B], \\ 0, & \text{otherwise.} \end{cases}$$

In the computations use the Euler–Maruyama scheme taking $S_0 = 50$, $r = 5\%$, $\sigma = 30\%$, $T = 0.25$, $K = 0.077$, $A = 0.6$, $B = 1.4$, and assume 30/360 day-count-convention. Select the step size h and the number of simulated paths L to get an error of the swap price smaller than 10^{-3}.

Exercise 4.8. The stock price follows the SABR stochastic volatility model

$$dS_t = rS_t dt + S_t^{\beta}\sqrt{v_t}dW_t^S,$$
$$dv_t = \kappa(\theta - v_t)dt + \nu\sqrt{v_t}dW_t^v,$$

where r is interest rate, ν is volatility of volatility, κ, θ are positive constants, and $\beta \in (0, 1)$.

Processes W_t^S and W_t^v are standard one-dimensional *correlated* Wiener processes with a constant in time correlation

$$d\langle W^S, W^v\rangle_t = \rho dt,$$

where $\rho \in [-1, 1]$.

Price in this model a European supershare option, i.e., a contract with the payoff

$$g(S_T, K_1, K_2) = \frac{S_T}{K_1}\mathbb{1}_{\{K_1 \le S_T \le K_2\}}.$$

Compute trajectories of S_t using the Euler–Maruyama scheme and trajectories of v_t via the Milstein scheme taking $S_0 = 50$, $v_0 = 0.06$, $r = 0.05$, $\nu = 0.4$, $T = 2$, $\kappa = 2$, $\theta = 0.04$, $\rho = 0.1$, $\beta = 0.7$, $K_1 = 40$, and $K_2 = 70$. Select the step size h and the number of simulated paths L to get an error of the option price smaller than 10^{-3}.

Exercise 4.9 (Stochastic stability [51]). Consider a scalar Itô equation

$$dX_s = b(s, X_s)ds + \sigma(s, X_s)dW_s, \tag{4.18}$$

with a unique solution denoted $X_s^{t,x}$, for each $s \ge t$ and each deterministic initial value $X_t = x$. Let $b(s, 0) = 0$ and $\sigma(s, 0) = 0$ for all

$s \geq t$. Then $X_s \equiv 0$ is a stationary solution of the considered equation. This steady solution is called *stochastically stable* if for any $\varepsilon > 0$ and $t \geq 0$

$$\lim_{x \to 0} \mathbb{P}\left(\sup_{s \geq t} |X_s^{t,x}| > \varepsilon\right) = 0.$$

This solution is called *stochastically asymptotically stable* if, in addition,

$$\lim_{x \to 0} \mathbb{P}\left(\lim_{s \to \infty} |X_s^{t,x}| = 0\right) = 1.$$

Similarly to ordinary differential equations, stochastic stability can be investigated by Lyapunov functions. Consider a function $V(s,x)$ that is sufficiently smooth so that Itô's formula can be applied. Let $\alpha(z)$ and $\beta(z)$ for $z \geq 0$ be increasing monotonically, continuous functions with $\alpha(0) = \beta(0) = 0$ such that

$$\alpha(|x|) \leq V(s,x) \leq \beta(|x|). \tag{4.19}$$

The Itô formula gives

$$dV(s,X_s) = \left(\frac{\partial V}{\partial s} + b(s,X_s)\frac{\partial V}{\partial x} + \frac{1}{2}\sigma^2(s,X_s)\frac{\partial^2 V}{\partial x^2}\right) ds$$
$$+ \sigma(s,X_s)\frac{\partial V}{\partial x} dW_s.$$

Assume that $V(s,X_s)$ is such that

$$\frac{\partial V}{\partial s} + b(s,X_s)\frac{\partial V}{\partial x} + \frac{1}{2}\sigma^2(s,X_s)\frac{\partial^2 V}{\partial x^2} \leq 0.$$

Then the integration of the differential $dV(s,X_s)$ gives

$$V(s,X_s) - V(t,x) \leq \int_t^s \sigma(\tau,X_\tau)\frac{\partial V}{\partial x} dW_\tau.$$

After taking the expectation, one gets

$$\mathbb{E}\big(V(s,X_s)|\mathcal{F}_t\big) \leq V(t,x),$$

where $\mathcal{F}_s$ is a σ-field generated by processes X_τ, $\tau \in [t,s]$. This implies that $V(s,X_s)$ is a Lyapunov function, and along the solution X_s, $V(s,X_s)$ is a supermartingale.

Applying the above estimate and Doob's maximal inequality

$$\mathbb{P}\left(\sup_{t\leq s\leq\tau}|Y_s|\geq\varepsilon\right)\leq\frac{1}{\varepsilon}\mathbb{E}(|Y_\tau|),$$

yields the estimate

$$\mathbb{P}\left(\sup_{t\leq s\leq\tau}V(s,X_s)\geq\varepsilon\right)\leq\frac{C}{\varepsilon}V(t,x)$$

for $C,\varepsilon>0$ and $\tau>t$. The last inequality implies

$$\mathbb{P}\left(\sup_{s\geq t}V(s,X_s)\geq\varepsilon\right)\leq\frac{C}{\varepsilon}V(t,x)$$

that together with equation (4.19) proves the stochastic stability of the zero solution of equation (4.18).

(a) Consider a linear stochastic equation with constant coefficients

$$dX_t=bX_tdt+\sigma X_tdW_t, \tag{4.20}$$

and the Lyapunov function $V(x)=x^2$.
Prove that

$$\frac{\partial V}{\partial t}+b\frac{\partial V}{\partial x}+\frac{1}{2}\sigma^2\frac{\partial^2 V}{\partial x^2}\leq 0,$$

provided $(b+\sigma^2/2)<0$. Conclude that for b and σ fulfilling this condition, the zero solution is stochastically asymptotically stable for all deterministic initial conditions.

(b) Equation (4.20), as a linear equation with constant coefficients, has an explicit solution. Find this solution for any deterministic initial condition. Note that this solution converge to 0 with probability 1 for $(b-\sigma^2/2)<0$.

Exercise 4.10 (Strongly consistent schemes [51]). Consider a scalar Itô equation on an interval $[0,T]$

$$dX_t=b(t,X_t)dt+\sigma(t,X_t)dW_t$$

that possesses a unique solution X_t. Approximate this solution on a grid $0 = t_0 < t_1 < \cdots < t_N = T$ with time steps $\delta t_n = t_{n+1} - t_n$, $n = 0, \ldots, N-1$. Let $h = \max_n \delta t_n$ and Y_n^h be the discrete approximation of X_t on the defined grid. This approximation is called *strongly consistent* if there exists a nonnegative function $c(h)$ with $\lim_{h \to 0} c(h) = 0$ such that

$$\mathbb{E}\left(\left|\mathbb{E}\left(\frac{Y_{n+1}^h - Y_n^h}{\delta t_n}\middle|\mathcal{F}_{t_n}\right) - b(t_n, Y_n^h)\right|^2\right) \le c(h),$$

$$\mathbb{E}\left(\frac{1}{\delta t_n}\left|Y_{n+1}^h - Y_n^h - \mathbb{E}(Y_{n+1}^h - Y_n^h|\mathcal{F}_{t_n}) - \sigma(t_n, Y_n^h)\delta W_n\right|^2\right) \le c(h),$$

where $\delta W_n = W_{t_{n+1}} - W_{t_n}$.

Consider a stochastic equation with time-independent coefficients

$$dX_t = b(X_t)dt + \sigma(X_t)dW_t.$$

Prove that for one-dimensional equations with time-independent, Lipschitz continuous coefficients with linear growth, a strongly consistent approximation Y_n^h on an equidistant grid is strongly convergent to X_t.

Exercise 4.11. The Heun scheme, known for ordinary differential equations, can be extended to stochastic differential equations with time-independent coefficients

$$dX_t = b(X_t)dt + \sigma(X_t)dW_t.$$

Let Y_n be a discrete approximation to X_t with $\delta t_n = t_{n+1} - t_n$, $\delta W_n = W_{t_{n+1}} - W_{t_n}$. Then the stochastic Heun scheme reads

$$\begin{aligned} Y_{n+1} = Y_n &+ \frac{1}{2}\Big(b(Y_n) + b\big(Y_n + b(Y_n)\delta t_n + \sigma(Y_n)\delta W_n\big)\Big)\delta t_n \\ &+ \frac{1}{2}\Big(\sigma(Y_n) + \sigma\big(Y_n + b(Y_n)\delta t_n + \sigma(Y_n)\delta W_n\big)\Big)\delta W_n. \end{aligned}$$

(a) Show that this scheme is not strongly consistent.
(b) Find the conditions on the coefficients of the equation which make the Heun scheme consistent.

Exercise 4.12. Prove that the Milstein scheme is strongly consistent provided $\sigma\frac{\partial \sigma}{\partial x}$ is bounded.

Exercise 4.13 (Weakly consistent schemes [51]). Consider a multidimensional Itô equation on interval $[0, T]$

$$dX_t = b(t, X_t)dt + \sigma(t, X_t)dW_t$$

that possesses a unique solution X_t. Approximate this solution on a grid $0 = t_0 < t_1 < \cdots < t_N = T$ with time steps $\delta t_n = t_{n+1} - t_n$, $n = 0, \ldots, N-1$. Let $h = \max_n \delta t_n$ and Y_n^h be the discrete approximation of X_t on the defined grid. This approximation is called *weakly consistent* if there exists a nonnegative function $c(h)$ with $\lim_{h \to 0} c(h) = 0$ such that

$$\mathbb{E}\left(\left|\mathbb{E}\left(\frac{Y_{n+1}^h - Y_n^h}{\delta t_n}\middle|\mathcal{F}_{t_n}\right) - b(t_n, Y_n^h)\right|^2\right) \le c(h),$$

$$\mathbb{E}\left(\left|\mathbb{E}\left(\frac{\left(Y_{n+1}^h - Y_n^h\right)^2}{\delta t_n}\middle|\mathcal{F}_{t_n}\right) - \sigma^2(t_n, Y_n^h)\right|^2\right) \le c(h).$$

(a) Prove that the Euler–Maruyama scheme is weakly consistent.
(b) Consider the following scheme for a one-dimensional Itô equation

$$Y_{n+1} = Y_n + b(t_n, Y_n)\delta t_n + \sigma(t_n, Y_n)\xi_n\sqrt{\delta t_n},$$

where $\delta t_n = t_{n+1} - t_n$ and ξ_n are independent random variables with two-point distribution $\mathbb{P}(\xi_n = \pm 1) = 1/2$. Prove that this scheme is weakly consistent.

Exercise 4.14. Consider an m-dimensional Bessel process, $m \ge 2$, defined by the Itô equation

$$dY_t = \frac{m-1}{2Y_t}dt + dW_t, \quad 0 < t < \infty, \quad Y_0 = y \ge 0.$$

(a) Prove that the Bessel process never attains the origin, i.e.,

$$\mathbb{P}(Y_t > 0\colon\ 0 < t < \infty) = 1.$$

(b) Consider the approximation of the Bessel process by the finite difference scheme with constant time step δt

$$Y_{n+1} = Y_n + \frac{m-1}{2Y_{n,\theta}}\delta t + \delta W_n,$$

where $Y_{n,\theta} = \theta Y_{n+1} + (1-\theta)Y_n$.

Simulate the approximate solution for different choices of θ and time steps δt for a finite time interval $[0, T]$. Investigate whether the approximate solutions hit the origin.

Exercise 4.15. Consider the CEV model of stock prices

$$dS_t = rS_t dt + \sigma_0 S_t^{\beta} dW_t,$$

where interest rate r and volatility σ_0 are constants, and $0 < \beta \leq 1$.

(a) Show that for the Euler–Maruyama scheme

$$S_{n+1} = S_n + rS_n \delta t + \sigma_0 S_n^{\beta} \delta W_n$$

S_n can be negative for some n. Explain that for $\beta = 1$ the problem can be resolved by log transformation $X_t = \ln S_t$.

(b) Show that an analogous transformation for $\beta < 1$

$$X_t = \frac{1}{1-\beta} S_t^{1-\beta}$$

does not solve the problem. Find the stochastic equation for X_t and show by simulations that the Euler–Maruyama scheme can produce negative values in the approximation of X_t. Note that for negative X_t, there is no inverse transformation giving real values of S_t.

Exercise 4.16. Consider the Black–Scholes model

$$dS_t = rS_t dt + \sigma S_t dW_t, \quad S_0 = x$$

with constant r and σ, and deterministic $x > 0$. Approximate S_t on a grid with constant time step h using the Milstein scheme

$$S_{n+1} = S_n + \left(r - \sigma^2/2\right) h S_n + \sigma \sqrt{h} S_n Z_n + 1/2\, \sigma^2 h S_n (Z_n)^2,$$

where Z_n, $n = 0, 1, \ldots, N-1$, are i.i.d. random variables with standard normal distribution.

Prove that the scheme is positive, i.e., $S_n > 0 \Rightarrow S_{n+1} > 0$, if and only if $\sigma^2 \leq 2r$.

Exercise 4.17. In the Cox–Ingersoll–Ross (CIR) model of short interest rates, the short rate X_t follows the stochastic equation

$$dX_t = \kappa(\theta - X_t)dt + \nu\sqrt{X_t}dW_t,$$

where κ, θ, $\nu > 0$, and $X_0 = x > 0$. If the Feller condition $2\kappa\theta \geq \nu^2$ is satisfied, then X_t is always positive. Nevertheless, the Euler–Maruyama scheme applied to this equation gives negative values of the solution with a positive probability.

This problem can be overcome, also for a more general class of stochastic differential equations with time-independent coefficients

$$dY_t = a(Y_t)dt + b(Y_t)dW_t,$$

by the application of the "semi-implicit" Euler scheme

$$Y_{n+1} = Y_n + a(Y_{n+1})\delta t + b(Y_n)\delta W_n.$$

Prove that this scheme applied appropriately to the equation obtained from the CIR equation by the substitution $Z_t = \sqrt{X_t}$ gives a unique positive solution for the CIR model.

Exercise 4.18. Consider the CIR model of short interest rate

$$dX_t = \kappa(\theta - X_t)dt + \nu\sqrt{X_t}dW_t, \quad X_0 = x > 0,$$

with positive coefficients κ, θ, and ν, and with $\nu^2 \leq 2\kappa\theta$.

Let $Y_t = e^{\kappa t}X_t$. Derive the stochastic equation for Y_t, and prove that the Milstein scheme for Y_t is *almost surely* positive.

Exercise 4.19. Consider the CIR model of short interest rate

$$dX_t = \kappa(\theta - X_t)dt + \nu\sqrt{X_t}dW_t, \quad X_0 = x > 0,$$

with positive coefficients κ, θ, and ν, and with $\nu^2 \leq 2\kappa\theta$.

(a) Find the Lamperti transform for this model.
(b) Compute in this model the price of a zero-coupon bond with maturity T, assuming $X_0 = 0.12$, $\kappa = 1$, $\theta = 0.10$, $\nu = 0.2$, and $T = 1$. Perform the computations using the Euler–Maruyama scheme for the original equation and the equation obtained after the Lamperti transformation. In simulations use $N = 25, 50, 100$ time steps and $M = 10000$ sample paths. Compare the accuracy of different simulations.

Hint: The price of a zero-coupon bond is given by the formula

$$B(t,T) = \mathbb{E}\left(\exp\left(-\int_t^T X_r dr\right)\right).$$

Exercise 4.20. Let W_t be a standard Wiener process. The *standard Brownian bridge* on $[0,T]$ is given by the conditional distribution $B_t = (W_t | W_T = 0)$ and can be defined by the formula

$$B_t = W_t - \frac{t}{T} W_T, \quad t \in [0,T].$$

(a) Prove that B_t is normally distributed $B_t \sim \mathcal{N}(0,\sigma^2)$. Find σ^2.
(b) Consider a multidimensional random vector X and split its components into two groups $(X_{(1)}, X_{(2)})$. Assume that $(X_{(1)}, X_{(2)})$ possesses a multivariate normal distribution

$$\begin{bmatrix} X_{(1)} \\ X_{(2)} \end{bmatrix} \sim \mathcal{N}\left(\begin{bmatrix} \mu_{(1)} \\ \mu_{(2)} \end{bmatrix}, \begin{bmatrix} \Sigma_{(11)} & \Sigma_{(12)} \\ \Sigma_{(21)} & \Sigma_{(22)} \end{bmatrix}\right).$$

Prove that if $\Sigma_{(22)}$ has full rank, then

$$\begin{aligned}(X_{(1)} | X_{(2)} = x) \sim \mathcal{N}\big(&\mu_{(1)} + \Sigma_{(12)}\Sigma_{(22)}^{-1}(x - \mu_{(2)}), \\ &\Sigma_{(11)} - \Sigma_{(12)}\Sigma_{(22)}^{-1}\Sigma_{(21)}\big).\end{aligned}$$

(c) Design an algorithm for generating sample paths of W_t, $t \in [T_0, T_1]$, under the condition $W_{T_0} = x$ and $W_{T_1} = y$.
Hint: Use the result of the previous subpoint.

Exercise 4.21 (Pricing the down-and-out call option). Barrier options are difficult to simulate since they are strongly path-dependent and discontinuous with respect to the path of the monitored process. The difficulty in simulating such payoffs is that one must compare the asset value and the barrier value at any time before expiration, whereas the paths are simulated only at a fixed number of grid points. If it is not detected that a trigger has occurred between two successive grid points, the option price can be overestimated. To take into account that the option may be knocked out between grid points, the barrier crossing can be conditionally simulated on the known values of asset prices using the Brownian bridge technique.

(a) Consider the standard Black–Scholes model with constant coefficients

$$dS_t = rS_t dt + \sigma S_t dW_t.$$

To price the down-and-out call option with strike K and barrier H, simulate final stock price S_T using the explicit solution

$$S_T = S_0 \exp\Big((r - \sigma^2/2)T + \sigma\sqrt{T}Z\Big),$$

where $Z \sim \mathcal{N}(0,1)$.

Let $P(x, y, T, H, \sigma)$ denote the probability that process S_t, starting at $S_0 = x$ and ending at $S_T = y$, crosses barrier H in the interval $(0, T)$

$$P(x, y, T, H, \sigma) = \mathbb{P}\big(\exists t < T\colon\ S_t \le H | S_0 = x, S_T = y\big).$$

The down-and-out call price is then given by the formula

$$V_{DO} = e^{-rT}\mathbb{E}\big((1 - P(S_0, S_T, T, H, \sigma))(S_T - K)^+\big).$$

Let B_t be a standard Brownian bridge on interval $[0, T]$. Prove that

$$\mathbb{P}\bigg(\sup_{t\in[0,T]}\Big(x + (y - x)\frac{t}{T} + \sigma B_t\Big) \le z\bigg)$$
$$= \begin{cases} 1 - \exp\Big(-\frac{2(z-x)(z-y)}{\sigma^2 T}\Big) & \text{if } z \ge \max(x, y), \\ 0 & \text{if } z < \max(x, y). \end{cases}$$

Using the exact solution of the Black–Scholes model and the above formula, show that

$$P(x, y, T, H, \sigma) = \begin{cases} 1 & \text{if } \min(x, y) < H, \\ \exp\Big(-\frac{2\ln(x/H)\ln(y/H)}{\sigma^2 T}\Big) & \text{otherwise.} \end{cases}$$

Hint: Let $M_T = \sup_{t\in[0,T]} W_t$. Using the reflection principle, show that $\mathbb{P}(W_T < y, M_T > z) = \mathbb{P}(W_T > 2z - y)$. Using the density of the standard normal distribution, obtain

$$\mathbb{P}\big(M_T > z | W_T = y\big) = \exp\Big(-\frac{2z(z-y)}{T}\Big).$$

Derive from this expression that if $B_t^y = \frac{t}{T}y + W_t - \frac{t}{T}W_T$, then

$$\mathbb{P}\left(\sup_{t\in[0,T]} B_t^y\right) = \begin{cases} 1 - \exp\Big(-\frac{2z(z-y)}{T}\Big) & \text{if } z \geq \max(0,y), \\ 0 & \text{if } z < \max(0,y). \end{cases}$$

(b) Simulate the price of the down-and-out call option in the Black–Scholes model using the Brownian bridge technique described above. Use the following model parameters: $S_0 = 50$, $r = 5\%$, $\sigma = 30\%$, $K = 50$, $T = 0.5$, and $H = 40$. Compare the results with the crude Monte Carlo simulations (paths that cross the barrier have payoff zero) and the exact price formula

$$V_{DO} = S_0\Phi(x) - Ke^{-rT}\Phi(x - \sigma\sqrt{T}) - S_0\left(\frac{H}{S_0}\right)^{2\lambda}\Phi(y) + Ke^{-rT}\left(\frac{H}{S_0}\right)^{2\lambda-2}\Phi(y - \sigma\sqrt{T}),$$

where

$$x = \frac{\ln(S_0/K) + (r + \sigma^2/2)T}{\sigma\sqrt{T}}, \quad y = \frac{\ln(H^2/(S_0K)) + \lambda\sigma^2 T}{\sigma\sqrt{T}},$$

and

$$\lambda = \frac{r + \sigma^2/2}{\sigma^2}.$$

(c) The Brownian bridge technique can also be applied to pricing barrier options in a general market model defined by the equation

$$dX_t = \mu(t, X_t)dt + \sigma(t, X_t)dW_t.$$

Introducing a regular grid $0 = t_0 < t_1 < \cdots < t_N = T$ with time step $h = T/N$, generate sample paths by the Euler–Maruyama scheme

$$X_{t_{n+1}}^h = X_{t_n}^h + \mu(t_n, X_{t_n}^h)h + \sigma(t_n, X_{t_n}^h)(W_{t_{n+1}} - W_{t_n}).$$

In each time interval $[t_n, t_{n+1}]$ the process

$$X_t^h = X_{t_n}^h + \mu(t_n, X_{t_n}^h)(t - t_n) + \sigma(t_n, X_{t_n}^h)(W_t - W_{t_n})$$

is the Wiener process and, conditionally on $X_{t_n}^h = x$ and $X_{t_{n+1}}^h = y$, has the same law as $\hat{X}_t = x + \sigma(t_n, x)(W_t - W_{t_n})$ for $t \in [t_n, t_{n+1}]$.

Thus, the probability of crossing the barrier in the interval $[t_n, t_{n+1}]$ is given by

$$\begin{aligned}\mathbb{P}\big(\exists t \in [t_n, t_{n+1}]\colon \hat{X}_t < H | X_{t_n}^h, X_{t_{n+1}}^h\big) \\ = P\big(X_{t_n}^h, X_{t_{n+1}}^h, h, H, \sigma(t_n, X_{t_n}^h)\big),\end{aligned}$$

where according to subpoint (a).

$$P(x, y, h, H, \sigma) = \begin{cases} 1 & \text{if } \min(x, y) < H, \\ \exp\Big(-\frac{2(x-H)(y-H)}{\sigma^2 h}\Big) & \text{otherwise.} \end{cases}$$

Using the above formula, compute the down-and-out call option in the CEV model

$$dS_t = rS_t dt + \sigma S_t^{\beta} dW_t,$$

with $S_0 = 50$, $r = 5\%$, $\sigma = 30\%$, $\beta = 0.7$, $K = 50$, and $H = 40$. Compare the result with the crude Monte Carlo simulations.

Chapter 5

Introduction to Elliptic and Parabolic Equations

5.1 From Stochastic to Partial Differential Equations

There is an inspiring interplay between stochastic processes and partial differential equations. In particular, solutions to many elliptic or parabolic differential equations can be represented as expectations of the functionals of stochastic processes. In this section, we briefly present the relationship between Itô's stochastic processes and second-order elliptic and parabolic equations.

Consider a stochastic process given by the Itô equation

$$dX_s = b(s, X_s)ds + \sigma(s, X_s)dW_s, \quad X_t = x. \tag{5.1}$$

Let us assume that the coefficients in this equation fulfill the conditions of Theorem 4.13. Hence, the equation possesses a unique strong solution, which we denote $X_s^{t,x}$ to indicate the dependence on the initial data.

Definition 5.1. Let $X_s^{t,x}$ be a solution of (5.1) with the coefficients b and σ independent of s. The *(infinitesimal) generator* $\mathcal{A}$ of X_s is defined by

$$\mathcal{A}u(x) = \lim_{s \to t} \frac{\mathbb{E}\big(u(X_s^{t,x})\big) - u(x)}{s - t}, \quad x \in \mathbb{R}^d.$$

The set of functions $u\colon \mathbb{R}^d \to \mathbb{R}$ for which the limit exists for all $x \in \mathbb{R}^d$ is denoted by $\mathcal{D}_{\mathcal{A}}$ and is called the domain of $\mathcal{A}$.

For a function $u \in \mathcal{D}_{\mathcal{A}}$

$$\mathcal{A}u(x) = \sum_{i,j=1}^{d} a_{ij}(x)\frac{\partial^2 u}{\partial x_i \partial x_j} + \sum_{i=1}^{d} b_i(x)\frac{\partial u}{\partial x_i}, \quad \text{where } a_{ij} = \frac{1}{2}\sum_{k=1}^{m} \sigma_i^k \sigma_j^k.$$

When the coefficients in (5.1) are time dependent $b = b(t, x)$ and $\sigma = \sigma(t, x)$, we have the family of operators $\mathcal{A}^t$

$$\mathcal{A}^t u(t,x) = \sum_{i,j=1}^{d} a_{ij}(t,x)\frac{\partial^2 u}{\partial x_i \partial x_j} + \sum_{i=1}^{d} b_i(t,x)\frac{\partial u}{\partial x_i}.$$

A fundamental relation between expectations of Itô's functionals and partial differential equations was established by Feynman and Kac. The proof of their theorem can be found in many textbooks, in particular in the book by Karatzas and Shreve [48].

Theorem 5.2 (Feynman–Kac theorem). *Consider the Cauchy problem*

$$\begin{aligned} &\frac{\partial u}{\partial t} + \mathcal{A}^t u - cu = f, \quad t \in [0,T), x \in \mathbb{R}^d, \\ &u(T,x) = g(x), \quad x \in \mathbb{R}^d, \end{aligned} \tag{5.2}$$

where $\mathcal{A}^t$*, introduced in Definition* 5.1*, is a family of operators generated by the stochastic process of equation* (5.1)*. Let* $\mathcal{A}^t$ *be uniformly elliptic, i.e.,*

$$\exists \delta > 0, \quad \sum_{i,j=1}^{d} a_{ij}(t,x)\xi_i\xi_j \geq \delta|\xi|^2, \quad \forall t \in [0,T], \; x \in \mathbb{R}^d, \; \xi \in \mathbb{R}^d \backslash \{0\}.$$

Assume that the functions c: $[0,T] \times \mathbb{R}^d \to [0,\infty)$, f: $[0,T] \times \mathbb{R}^d \to \mathbb{R}$ *and* g: $\mathbb{R}^d \to \mathbb{R}$ *are continuous and satisfy (with some constants* C *and* $q \geq 2$*)*

$$\begin{aligned} &|g(x)| \leq C(1 + |x|^q), \quad \forall x \in \mathbb{R}^d, \\ &|f(t,x)| \leq C(1 + |x|^q), \quad t \in [0,T], \forall x \in \mathbb{R}^d. \end{aligned}$$

Let $u(t,x)$ *be a solution of* (5.2) *which is continuous in* $[0,T] \times \mathbb{R}^d$ *and of class* $C^{1,2}([0,T) \times \mathbb{R}^d)$ *with the polynomial growth condition*

(for some constants $C > 0$ and $p \geq 2$)

$$\sup_{t\in[0,T]} |u(t,x)| \leq C(1+|x|^p), \quad x \in \mathbb{R}^d.$$

Then $u(t,x)$ is a unique solution of (5.2) *and admits the stochastic representation called* the Feynman–Kac formula

$$\begin{aligned} u(t,x) = \mathbb{E}\bigg(& g(X_T^{t,x}) \exp\Big(-\int_t^T c(r, X_r^{t,x})dr\Big) \\ & + \int_t^T f(s, X_s^{t,x}) \exp\Big(-\int_t^s c(r, X_r^{t,x})dr\Big)\, ds\bigg). \end{aligned} \tag{5.3}$$

By the Feynman–Kac theorem, the computation of expectations $\mathbb{E}(g(X_T))$, very often encountered in computational finance, can be reduced to the construction of a smooth solution of a certain partial differential equation. Numerical approximations of solutions of such equations will be discussed in subsequent chapters.

The following theorem shows that, under suitable assumptions, the Feynman–Kac formula gives a solution to equation (5.2). This can be regarded as a converse to the Feynman–Kac theorem.

Theorem 5.3. *Let $X_s^{t,x}$ be a strong solution of* (5.1). *We assume that the coefficients $b(s,y)$ and $\sigma(s,y)$ of this equation satisfy the assumptions of Theorem* 4.13. *In addition, they are twice continuously differentiable with respect to y for any $s \in [0,T]$, and all their partial derivatives with respect to y up to the second order are bounded.*

Let c: $[0,T]\times\mathbb{R}^d \to [0,\infty)$, f: $[0,T]\times\mathbb{R}^d \to \mathbb{R}$, and g: $\mathbb{R}^d \to \mathbb{R}$ be Borel functions that are twice continuously differentiable with respect to x for any $t \in [0,T]$. Assume that the absolute values of these functions and all their partial derivatives with respect to x up to the second order are bounded by $C(1+|x|^q)$ (with some constants $C > 0$ and $q \geq 2$). Then $u(t,x)$ given by the Feynman–Kac formula (5.3) *is a well-defined function in $[0,T]\times\mathbb{R}^d$ which is twice differentiable with respect to x continuously in (t,x) and continuously differentiable with respect to t in $[0,T]\times\mathbb{R}^d$ with the growth estimate (for some* *constants* $C > 0$ *and* $p \geq 2$*)*

$$\sup_{0 \leq t \leq T} |u(t,x)| \leq C(1 + |x|^p), \quad x \in \mathbb{R}^d.$$

The function $u(t,x)$ *is a solution of equation* (5.2) *which fulfills the terminal condition* $\lim_{t \to T} u(t,x) = g(x)$.

The proof of Theorem 5.3 under the assumed regularity of the coefficients requires the construction of probabilistic solutions to partial differential equations (see the book by Krylov[53]). Results of this type are necessary in proofs of convergence for weak solutions of stochastic differential equations (cf. Chapter 4). Unfortunately, the regularity required in the proof of Theorem 4.30 is stronger than the regularity of function $u(t,x)$ from Theorem 5.3. The following theorem gives the smoothness required in the proof of Theorem 4.30. It is quoted in many publications discussing the weak convergence of the Euler–Maruyama scheme. Its complete proof can be found in [71].

Theorem 5.4. *Let* $X_s^{t,x}$ *be a strong solution of* (5.1). *Assume that coefficients* $b(s,y)$ *and* $\sigma(s,y)$ *of this equation are* (s,y)*-continuous for* $(s,y) \in [0,T] \times \mathbb{R}^d$ *and growth linearly with* y. *Assume that for* $n \geq 2$, *these coefficients are* n *times continuously differentiable with respect to* y *for any* $s \in [0,T]$ *and all partial derivatives of these functions with respect to* y *up to order* n *are uniformly bounded.*

We also assume that operator $\mathcal{A}^t$ *in equation* (5.2) *is uniformly elliptic. Functions* c, f, *and* g *in this equation are* n *times continuously differentiable with respect to* x *for any* $t \in [0,T]$, *and the absolute values of these functions and all their partial derivatives with respect to* x *up to order* n *are bounded by* $C(1 + |x|^q)$. *Then* $u(t,x)$ *defined by the Feynman–Kac formula* (5.3) *is* n *times differentiable with respect to* x *continuously in* (t,x) *and continuously differentiable with respect to* t *in* $[0,T] \times \mathbb{R}^d$ *with the absolute values of all its partial derivatives with respect to* x *up to order* n *bounded by* $C(1 + |x|^p)$ *for some constants* $C > 0$ *and* $p \geq q$.

The following examples demonstrate that the Feynman–Kac Theorem is essential for deriving partial differential equations that model financial markets.

Example 5.5. In the Black–Scholes model, the price of the underlying in a risk-neutral measure fulfills the equation

$$dS_t = rS_t dt + \sigma S_t dW_t.$$

Then the price of the contingent claim with payoff $g(S_T)$ is

$$V_g(t) = \mathbb{E}\Big(e^{-r(T-t)} g(S_T) \big| S_t = x\Big).$$

By the Feynman–Kac theorem $G(t,x) = \mathbb{E}\big(g(S_T)|S_t = x\big)$ fulfills the equation

$$\frac{\partial G}{\partial t} + rx\frac{\partial G}{\partial x} + \frac{1}{2}\sigma^2 x^2 \frac{\partial^2 G}{\partial x^2} = 0.$$

Since $F(t,x) := V_g(t) = e^{-r(T-t)}G(t,x)$, we have

$$\frac{\partial F}{\partial t} + rx\frac{\partial F}{\partial x} + \frac{1}{2}\sigma^2 x^2 \frac{\partial^2 F}{\partial x^2} - rF = 0, \quad F(T,x) = g(x),$$

which is the Black–Scholes partial differential equation.

Example 5.6. The Heston stochastic volatility model is given by the system of stochastic differential equations

$$\begin{aligned} dS_t &= r(t)S_t dt + \sqrt{v_t} S_t dW_t^S, \\ dv_t &= \kappa(\theta - v_t)dt + \nu\sqrt{v_t} dW_t^v, \end{aligned}$$

with correlation ρ between Wiener processes W_t^S and W_t^v.

The straightforward application of the Feynman–Kac theorem gives the following differential equation for the Heston model

$$\begin{aligned} \frac{\partial V}{\partial t} + \frac{1}{2}vS^2\frac{\partial^2 V}{\partial S^2} + \rho\nu v S\frac{\partial^2 V}{\partial S \partial v} + \frac{1}{2}\nu^2 v\frac{\partial^2 V}{\partial v^2} + rS\frac{\partial V}{\partial S} \\ + \kappa(\theta - v)\frac{\partial V}{\partial v} - rV = 0. \end{aligned}$$

This market model is incomplete as v_t is not a tradable asset. Thus, many equivalent martingale measures can be used in pricing derivatives on this market, and it is not clear in which of these measures the above equation holds. One can rather expect different equations for different martingale measures. We derive these equations for European options, assuming that the price of that option depends on t, the stock price S_t, and on v_t. Denote this price by $V(t, S_t, v_t)$.

To derive the pricing equation for a European option, we construct a self-financing portfolio hedging the option with price $V^1(t, S_t, v_t)$ and expiration date T_1. The portfolio contains ϕ_t^0 units of currency in banking account $B_t = e^{rt}$, where r is a risk-free interest rate, ϕ_t^1 shares of stock, and ϕ_t^2 options with price $V^2(t, S_t, v_t)$ and expiration date $T_2 > T_1$, where option V^2 is added to hedge the risk of stochastic volatility. Then the hedging strategy is $V^1(t, S_t, v_t) = \phi_t^0 B_t + \phi_t^1 S_t + \phi_t^2 V^2(t, S_t, v_t)$. The self-financing of the portfolio means that

$$dV^1(t, S_t, v_t) = \phi_t^0 r B_t dt + \phi_t^1 dS_t + \phi_t^2 dV^2(t, S_t, v_t).$$

Using the no-arbitrage principle and Itô's formula, we obtain the equality

$$\begin{aligned}
&\left(\frac{\partial V^1}{\partial t} + \frac{1}{2} v S^2 \frac{\partial^2 V^1}{\partial S^2} + \rho \nu v S \frac{\partial^2 V^1}{\partial S \partial v} + \frac{1}{2} \nu^2 v \frac{\partial^2 V^1}{\partial v^2}\right) dt \\
&\quad + \frac{\partial V^1}{\partial S} dS_t + \frac{\partial V^1}{\partial v} dv_t \\
&\quad = \phi_t^2 \left(\frac{\partial V^2}{\partial t} + \frac{1}{2} v S^2 \frac{\partial^2 V^2}{\partial S^2} + \rho \nu v S \frac{\partial^2 V^2}{\partial S \partial v} + \frac{1}{2} \nu^2 v \frac{\partial^2 V^2}{\partial v^2}\right) dt \\
&\quad + \phi_t^0 r B_t dt + \left(\phi_t^1 + \phi_t^2 \frac{\partial V^2}{\partial S}\right) dS_t + \phi_t^2 \frac{\partial V^2}{\partial v} dv_t.
\end{aligned}$$

Equating the terms with dW_t^v, we obtain

$$\phi_t^2 = \frac{\partial V^1 / \partial v}{\partial V^2 / \partial v}.$$

Similarly, equating the terms with dW_t^S, we find

$$\phi_t^1 = \frac{\partial V^1}{\partial S} - \phi_t^2 \frac{\partial V^2}{\partial S}.$$

Substituting these values and $\phi_t^0 = (V^1 - \phi_t^1 S_t - \phi_t^2 V^2)/B_t$ to the self-financing equality and comparing the obtained dt

terms, yields

$$\frac{1}{\frac{\partial V^1}{\partial v}}\left(\frac{\partial V^1}{\partial t}+\frac{1}{2}vS^2\frac{\partial^2 V^1}{\partial S^2}+\rho\nu vS\frac{\partial^2 V^1}{\partial S\partial v}\right.$$
$$\left.+\frac{1}{2}\nu^2 v\frac{\partial^2 V^1}{\partial v^2}+rS\frac{\partial V^1}{\partial S}-rV^1\right)$$
$$=\frac{1}{\frac{\partial V^2}{\partial v}}\left(\frac{\partial V^2}{\partial t}+\frac{1}{2}vS^2\frac{\partial^2 V^2}{\partial S^2}+\rho\nu vS\frac{\partial^2 V^2}{\partial S\partial v}\right.$$
$$\left.+\frac{1}{2}\nu^2 v\frac{\partial^2 V^2}{\partial v^2}+rS\frac{\partial V^2}{\partial S}-rV^2\right).$$

In the above equation, the left-hand side depends only on V^1, and the right-hand side depends only on V^2. Thus, there exists a function $F(t,S,v)$ equal to each side of this equation. Then $V(t,S,v)$ fulfills the equation

$$\frac{\partial V}{\partial t}+\frac{1}{2}vS^2\frac{\partial^2 V}{\partial S^2}+\rho\nu vS\frac{\partial^2 V}{\partial S\partial v}+\frac{1}{2}\nu^2 v\frac{\partial^2 V}{\partial v^2}+rS\frac{\partial V}{\partial S}-rV=F\frac{\partial V}{\partial v}.$$

To recover the complete generator of the two-dimensional process (S_t, v_t), from which we started this example, we assume $F(t,S,v) = -\kappa(\theta-v)+\lambda(t,S,v)$ and obtain the pricing equation

$$\frac{\partial V}{\partial t}+\frac{1}{2}vS^2\frac{\partial^2 V}{\partial S^2}+\rho\nu vS\frac{\partial^2 V}{\partial S\partial v}+\frac{1}{2}\nu^2 v\frac{\partial^2 V}{\partial v^2}$$
$$+rS\frac{\partial V}{\partial S}+\kappa(\theta-v)\frac{\partial V}{\partial v}-rV$$
$$=\lambda(t,S,v)\frac{\partial V}{\partial v}.$$

The unspecified term $\lambda(t,S,v)$ defines the entire family of pricing equations for the Heston model. It represents the *price of volatility risk*, the market value assigned to the unhedged risk of the volatility process.

5.2 Sobolev Spaces

Partial differential equations require a certain smoothness of their solutions to make the equations meaningful. For many practically important equations, it is difficult to achieve that goal if the derivatives are understood in the classical sense. A space suitable for the analysis of equations with nonsmooth solutions is a space of functions with derivatives defined in a weak sense, namely, Sobolev's space. (There are many books on the theory of partial differential equations in Sobolev's spaces. Our presentation follows the book by Evans [29] where the reader can find more complete theory, in particular the proofs omitted in this short outline.) To define Sobolev's spaces, we begin by weakening the notion of derivatives. In the following, we consider functions defined on U, an open, bounded subset of $\mathbb{R}^d$.

Definition 5.7. Let $u, v \in L^1_{loc}(U)$ and $\alpha = (\alpha_1, \ldots, \alpha_d)$ be a multi-index. We call v the weak derivative of order α of u and write

$$D^\alpha u = v$$

if

$$\int_U u(x) D^\alpha \varphi(x) dx = (-1)^{|\alpha|} \int_U v(x)\varphi(x) dx$$

for each $\varphi \in C_0^\infty(U)$, where $C_0^\infty(U)$ is the space of infinitely differentiable functions in U with compact support, and $D^\alpha \varphi(x) = \frac{\partial^{|\alpha|}\varphi(x)}{\partial x_1^{\alpha_1} \ldots \partial x_d^{\alpha_d}}$ with $|\alpha| = \alpha_1 + \cdots + \alpha_d$.

By Du we denote the weak gradient of u, i.e., the vector $(\frac{\partial u}{\partial x_1}, \ldots, \frac{\partial u}{\partial x_d})$ with the partial derivatives understood in the weak sense.

Example 5.8. Consider a one-dimensional example with $U = (0, 2)$. Define in U

$$u(x) = \begin{cases} x, & \text{if } 0 < x \le 1, \\ 1, & \text{if } 1 \le x < 2. \end{cases}$$

We show that the weak derivative of u is

$$v(x) = \begin{cases} 1, & \text{if } 0 < x \le 1, \\ 0, & \text{if } 1 < x < 2. \end{cases}$$

To see this, we must show that for $\varphi \in C_0^\infty(U)$

$$\int_0^2 u(x)\varphi'(x)dx = -\int_0^2 v(x)\varphi(x)dx.$$

By the definitions of u and v, we obtain

$$\begin{aligned}\int_0^2 u(x)\varphi'(x)dx &= \int_0^1 u(x)\varphi'(x)dx + \int_1^2 u(x)\varphi'(x)dx \\ &= \int_0^1 x\varphi'(x)dx + \int_1^2 \varphi'(x)dx \\ &= \varphi(1) - \int_0^1 \varphi(x)dx - \varphi(1) = -\int_0^2 v(x)\varphi(x)dx.\end{aligned}$$

Example 5.9. Let $U = (-1,1)$ and $u(x) = |x|$. We show that the weak derivative of u is $v(x) = \operatorname{sgn} x$. Taking $\varphi \in C_0^\infty(U)$ and integrating by parts, we get

$$\begin{aligned}\int_{-1}^1 u(x)\varphi'(x)dx &= \int_{-1}^0 -x\varphi'(x)dx + \int_0^1 x\varphi'(x)dx \\ &= \int_{-1}^0 \varphi(x)dx - \int_0^1 \varphi(x)dx = -\int_{-1}^1 \operatorname{sgn} x\varphi(x)dx.\end{aligned}$$

Example 5.10. Let in $U = (0,2)$

$$u(x) = \begin{cases} x, & \text{if } 0 < x \le 1, \\ 2, & \text{if } 1 \le x < 2. \end{cases}$$

Then u does not have a weak derivative, i.e., does not exist a function $v \in L^1_{loc}(U)$ such that

$$\int_0^2 u(x)\varphi'(x)dx = -\int_0^2 v(x)\varphi(x)dx$$

for any $\varphi \in C_0^\infty(U)$.

Let v be assumed to exist. Then ($\varphi(0) = \varphi(2) = 0$)

$$-\int_0^2 v(x)\varphi(x)dx = \int_0^2 u(x)\varphi'(x)dx = \int_0^1 x\varphi'(x)dx + 2\int_1^2 \varphi'(x)dx$$
$$= -\varphi(1) - \int_0^1 \varphi(x)dx.$$

We replace φ in the above identity by a sequence φ_n such that $0 \leq \varphi_n \leq 1$, $\varphi_n(1) = 1$ and $\varphi_n(x) \to 0$ for all $x \neq 1$. Passing to the limit $n \to \infty$, we obtain

$$1 = \lim_{n\to\infty} \varphi_n(1) = \lim_{n\to\infty}\left(\int_0^2 v(x)\varphi_n(x)dx - \int_0^1 \varphi(x)dx\right) = 0,$$

which gives a contradiction.

We now define Sobolev's spaces as spaces of functions that are differentiable in the weak sense (their weak derivatives are well defined).

Definition 5.11. The Sobolev space $W^{k,p}(U)$ is a space of functions $u\colon U \to \mathbb{R}$ such that u and all weak derivatives $D^\alpha u$, for $|\alpha| \leq k$, belong to $L^p(U)$.

If $p = 2$, we write $H^k(U)$ instead of $W^{k,2}(U)$.

Theorem 5.12. *For each integer $k \geq 1$ and $1 \leq p \leq \infty$ the Sobolev space $W^{k,p}(U)$ is a Banach space with the norm*

$$\|u\|_{W^{k,p}(U)} = \left(\sum_{|\alpha|\leq k} \int_U |D^\alpha u|^p dx\right)^{1/p}, \quad 1 \leq p < \infty,$$
$$\|u\|_{W^{k,\infty}(U)} = \sum_{|\alpha|\leq k} \operatorname{ess\,sup}_U |D^\alpha u|, \quad p = \infty.$$

The Sobolev space $W^{k,2}(U) \equiv H^k(U)$ is a Hilbert space.

The scalar product in Hilbert spaces $H^k(U)$ will be denoted $(\cdot,\cdot)_{H^k(U)}$. The only exception from this notation will be the scalar product in $L^2(U)$ denoted $(\cdot,\cdot)$.

Definition 5.13. $W_0^{k,p}(U)$ is the closure of $C_0^\infty(U)$ in $W^{k,p}(U)$.

Example 5.14. Let $U = \{x \in \mathbb{R}^d\colon |x| < 1\}$. For $\gamma > 0$ consider the function

$$u(x) = |x|^{-\gamma}, \quad x \in U, x \neq 0.$$

We demonstrate that $u \in W^{k,p}(U)$ if and only if $\gamma < d/p - k$.

For $k = 0$, we have

$$\int_U |u(x)|^p dx = \int_U |x|^{-\gamma p} dx = C(d) \int_0^1 r^{d-\gamma p-1} dr$$
$$= \begin{cases} \frac{C(d)}{d-\gamma p}, & \text{if } d - \gamma p > 0, \\ \infty, & \text{otherwise.} \end{cases}$$

Hence, $u \in L^p(U)$ when $\gamma < d/p$.

For $k = 1$, we have

$$\frac{\partial u}{\partial x_i} = -\gamma x_i |x|^{-\gamma-2}, \quad i = 1, \ldots, d.$$

For $Du = (u_{x_1}, \ldots, u_{x_d})$, we obtain $|Du| = \gamma |x|^{-\gamma-1}$. Then $Du \in L^p(U)$ when $\gamma < d/p - 1$. We must check whether the computed Du is a weak derivative of u. On the open set $U \backslash \{0\}$ the weak derivatives Du coincide with the classical derivatives. We show that u_{x_i} defines the weak derivative on the entire domain U.

Let $\varphi \in C_0^\infty(U)$ and $B_\varepsilon = \{x \in \mathbb{R}^d\colon |x| < \varepsilon\}$. Integration-by-parts gives

$$\int_{U \backslash B_\varepsilon} u \varphi_{x_i} dx = -\int_{U \backslash B_\varepsilon} u_{x_i} \varphi dx + \int_{\partial B_\varepsilon} u \varphi \nu_i dS,$$

where ν_i is the ith coordinate of the inward normal to ∂B_ε and dS is the surface measure on ∂B_ε. Since $d - \gamma - 1 > 0$, then

$$\left| \int_{\partial B_\varepsilon} u \varphi \nu_i dS \right| \leq \|\varphi\|_\infty \int_{\partial B_\varepsilon} \varepsilon^{-\gamma} dS \leq C \varepsilon^{d-\gamma-1} \to 0 \text{ as } \varepsilon \to 0,$$

$$\lim_{\varepsilon \to 0} \int_{U \backslash B_\varepsilon} u \varphi_{x_i} dx = \int_U u \varphi_{x_i} dx,$$

$$\lim_{\varepsilon \to 0} \int_{U \backslash B_\varepsilon} u_{x_i} \varphi dx = \int_U u_{x_i} \varphi dx.$$

The above equalities prove that u_{x_i} is a weak derivative of u over the whole U

$$\int_U u\varphi_{x_i}dx = -\int_U u_{x_i}\varphi dx.$$

Similarly, we obtain $D^\alpha u \in L^p(U)$ for $|\alpha| = k$ when $\gamma < d/p - k$.

Theorem 5.15 (Properties of Sobolev's spaces). *Let $u, v \in W^{k,p}(U)$ and $|\alpha| \le k$. Then:*

(1) *$D^\alpha u \in W^{k-|\alpha|,p}(U)$ and $D^\beta(D^\alpha u) = D^\alpha(D^\beta u) = D^{\alpha+\beta}u$ for all multi-indices α, β such that $|\alpha| + |\beta| \le k$.*
(2) *For all $a_1, a_2 \in \mathbb{R}$ the linear combination $a_1 u + a_2 v \in W^{k,p}(U)$ and $D^\alpha(a_1 u + a_2 v) = a_1 D^\alpha u + a_2 D^\alpha v$.*
(3) *If V is an open subset of U, then $u\big|_V \in W^{k,p}(V)$.*
(4) *If $\varphi \in C_0^\infty(U)$, then $\varphi u \in W^{k,p}(U)$, and*

$$D^\alpha(\varphi u) = \sum_{\beta\le\alpha} \binom{\alpha}{\beta} D^\beta \varphi D^{\alpha-\beta}u.$$

It appears that although functions in Sobolev's spaces are not smooth, they can be approximated by smooth functions. The following theorem describes the procedure of this approximation.

Theorem 5.16. *Let U be an open, bounded set in $\mathbb{R}^d$ with ∂U of class C^1. If $u \in W^{k,p}(U)$ for $1 \le p < \infty$, then there exists a sequence $u_m \in C^\infty(\bar{U})$ converging to u in the norm of $W^{k,p}(U)$.*

The space H^{-1}. The space $H^{-1}(U)$ is the dual space to $H_0^1(U)$, i.e., a space of continuous linear functionals on $H_0^1(U)$. The duality product $\langle f, u\rangle$ between $H^{-1}(U)$ and $H_0^1(U)$ denotes the action of functional $f \in H^{-1}(U)$ on element $u \in H_0^1(U)$. The norm in $H^{-1}(U)$ is given by the formula

$$\|f\|_{H^{-1}(U)} = \sup\Big\{\langle f, u\rangle\colon\ u \in H_0^1(U), \|u\|_{H_0^1(U)} \le 1\Big\}.$$

Traces of functions. Since functions in $L^p(U)$ have no values at "point x", there is no natural meaning of "restricting u to ∂U" and formulation of boundary value problems. Analyzing such problems, we must attach "boundary values" to functions in $L^p(U)$. The following theorem explains how to define "boundary values".

Theorem 5.17 (Trace Theorem). *Let U be an open, bounded set in $\mathbb{R}^d$ with ∂U of class C^1. There exists a linear, bounded operator*

$$T\colon W^{1,p}(U) \to L^p(\partial U), \quad 1 \le p < \infty$$

such that

(1) $Tu = u\big|_{\partial U}$ *for* $u \in W^{1,p}(U) \cap C(\bar{U})$.
(2) $\|Tu\|_{L^p(\partial U)} \le C\|u\|_{W^{1,p}(U)}$, *where the constant C depends on p and U.*

5.2.1 *Embedding theorems*

We present several inequalities between the norms of various Sobolev spaces. These inequalities prove the boundedness of the embeddings between different Sobolev spaces, which can serve to characterize the regularity of solutions of differential equations.

Theorem 5.18 (Poincaré's inequality). *Let U be an open, bounded set in $\mathbb{R}^d$. For $u \in W_0^{1,p}(U)$, $1 \le p < d$, we have the estimate*

$$\|u\|_{L^q(U)} \le C\|Du\|_{L^p(U)}$$

for $q \in [1, p^*]$, where p^* is defined as $1/p^* = 1/p - 1/d$ and is called the Sobolev conjugate *of p, and the constant C depends on p, q, d, and U but is independent of u.*

The next theorem proves the embedding of Sobolev's spaces into Hölder's spaces defined below.

Definition 5.19. Let U be an open set in $\mathbb{R}^d$. A function $u\colon U \to \mathbb{R}$ is called *Hölder continuous* with exponent γ if its *Hölder norm* is finite

$$\|u\|_{C^{0,\gamma}(U)} = \sup_{\substack{x,y\in U\\ x\neq y}} \left(\frac{|u(x) - u(y)|}{|x-y|^\gamma} \right) < +\infty.$$

The Hölder space $C^{k,\gamma}(U)$ is a space of functions of class $C^k(U)$ whose derivatives of order k are Hölder continuous with exponent γ. The norm in $C^{k,\gamma}(U)$ is defined by the expression

$$\|u\|_{C^{k,\gamma}(U)} = \sum_{|\alpha|\le k} \sup_{x\in U} |D^\alpha u| + \sum_{|\alpha|=k} \|D^\alpha u\|_{C^{0,\gamma}(U)}.$$

Theorem 5.20 (Sobolev inequalities). *Let U be an open, bounded set in $\mathbb{R}^d$ with a C^1 boundary or the whole $\mathbb{R}^d$. For $u \in W^{k,p}(U)$, $1 \le p < \infty$, we have:*

(1) *If $k < d/p$ and $l \le k$, then $u \in W^{k-l,q}(U)$, where $1/q = 1/p - l/d$. In particular, for $l = k$ we have $u \in L^q(U)$. In addition, for a constant C depending only on k, l, p, d, and U, we have the estimate*

$$\|u\|_{W^{k-l,q}(U)} \le C\|u\|_{W^{k,p}(U)}.$$

(2) *If $k = d/p$ and $l \le k$, then $u \in W^{k-l,q}(U)$, for $p \le q \le \infty$, and there is a constant C depending only on k, l, p, d, and U such that*

$$\|u\|_{W^{k-l,q}(U)} \le C\|u\|_{W^{k,p}(U)}.$$

(3) *If $k > d/p$, then $u \in C^{k-[d/p]-1,\gamma}(\bar{U})$ and for a constant C depending only on k, p, d, γ, and U, we have the estimate*

$$\|u\|_{C^{k-[d/p]-1,\gamma}(\bar{U})} \le C\|u\|_{W^{k,p}(U)}.$$

The constant γ is given by

$$\gamma = \begin{cases} \left[\frac{d}{p}\right] + 1 - \frac{d}{p}, & \text{if } d/p \text{ is not an integer,} \\ \text{any positive number} < 1, & \text{if } d/p \text{ is an integer,} \end{cases}$$

where $[a]$ denotes the integer part of a.

For functions that also depend on the time variable, embedding theorems can be more complicated because the function can belong to one functional space, and its time derivative can belong to another space. We present a theorem that will be used for parabolic equation analysis.

Theorem 5.21. *Let $u \in L^2(0,T; H_0^1(U))$, $du/dt \in L^2(0,T; H^{-1}(U))$. Then $u \in C([0,T]; L^2(U))$ and we have the estimate*

$$\max_{0\le t\le T} \|u(t)\|_{L^2(U)} \le C\left(\|u\|_{L^2(0,T;H_0^1(U))} + \|du/dt\|_{L^2(0,T;H^{-1}(U))}\right),$$

where the constant C depends only on T.

5.3 Elliptic Equations of Second-Order

We will now study the existence of solutions to elliptic differential equations in an open, bounded set $U \subset \mathbb{R}^d$. The condition that the trace of a solution on the boundary ∂U is equal to a given function is called the *Dirichlet boundary condition* and the differential problem with the Dirichlet boundary condition is called the *Dirichlet problem*. We limit the investigation to the Dirichlet problem with zero boundary conditions

$$\begin{aligned} \mathcal{A}u &= f, \quad \text{in } U, \\ u|_{\partial U} &= 0. \end{aligned} \tag{5.4}$$

$\mathcal{A}$ is a second-order differential operator. Depending on the situation, this operator is considered in the *divergence* form

$$\mathcal{A}u(x) = \sum_{i=1}^{d}\sum_{j=1}^{d} -\frac{\partial}{\partial x_i}\left(a_{ij}(x)\frac{\partial u(x)}{\partial x_j}\right) + \sum_{i=1}^{d} b_i(x)\frac{\partial u(x)}{\partial x_i} + c(x)u(x) \tag{5.5}$$

or the *nondivergence* form

$$\mathcal{A}u(x) = \sum_{i=1}^{d}\sum_{j=1}^{d} -a_{ij}(x)\frac{\partial^2 u(x)}{\partial x_i \partial x_j} + \sum_{i=1}^{d} b_i(x)\frac{\partial u(x)}{\partial x_i} + c(x)u(x). \tag{5.6}$$

Remark 5.22. If the coefficients a_{ij} are of class C^1, an operator written in divergence form can be rewritten in nondivergence form with b_i replaced by

$$\bar{b}_i = b_i - \sum_{j=1}^{d} \frac{\partial a_{ij}}{\partial x_j}.$$

We assume that $\mathcal{A}$ is a uniformly elliptic operator.

Definition 5.23. The differential operator $\mathcal{A}$ defined by (5.5) or (5.6) is called *uniformly elliptic* if $a_{ij} = a_{ji}$, $i, j = 1, \ldots, d$, and

$$\exists \delta > 0 \ \forall x \in U \ \forall \xi \in \mathbb{R}^d \setminus \{0\} \quad \sum_{i=1}^{d}\sum_{j=1}^{d} a_{ij}(x)\xi_i\xi_j \geq \delta |\xi|^2.$$

Our goal is to prove the existence (and uniqueness) of solutions of the Dirichlet problem with a uniformly elliptic operator $\mathcal{A}$. For the Dirichlet problem (5.4), we define a weak solution.

Definition 5.24. Let a_{ij}, b_i, $c \in L^\infty(U)$, $i, j = 1, \dots, d$, and $f \in L^2(U)$. We call $u \in H_0^1(U)$ a *weak solution* of the Dirichlet problem (5.4) with $\mathcal{A}$ given in divergence form if

$$\begin{aligned}
&\int_U \left(\sum_{i,j=1}^d a_{ij}(x) \frac{\partial u(x)}{\partial x_i} \frac{\partial v(x)}{\partial x_j} \right. \\
&\qquad \left. + \sum_{i=1}^d b_i(x) \frac{\partial u(x)}{\partial x_i} v(x) + c(x)u(x)v(x) \right) dx \\
&\quad = \int_U f(x)v(x)dx,
\end{aligned}$$

for each $v \in H_0^1(U)$.

Fundamental to investigating second-order elliptic equations and also to solving some problems of second-order parabolic equations is the following theorem.

Theorem 5.25 (Energy estimates). *Let $u, v \in H_0^1(U)$ and*

$$B[u, v] = \int_U \left(\sum_{i,j=1}^d a_{ij} \frac{\partial u}{\partial x_i} \frac{\partial v}{\partial x_j} + \sum_{i=1}^d b_i \frac{\partial u}{\partial x_i} v + cuv \right) dx,$$

with a_{ij}, b_i, $c \in L^\infty(U)$, $i, j = 1, \dots, d$.

There exist constants $\alpha, \beta > 0$, and $\gamma \ge 0$ such that

$$\begin{aligned}
|B[u, v]| &\le \alpha \|u\|_{H_0^1(U)} \|v\|_{H_0^1(U)}, \\
\beta \|u\|_{H_0^1(U)}^2 &\le B[u, u] + \gamma \|u\|_{L^2(U)}^2.
\end{aligned}$$

Proof. Since a_{ij}, b_i, $c \in L^\infty(U)$, we have the estimate

$$|B[u,v]| \le \sum_{i,j=1}^{d} \|a_{ij}\|_{L^\infty(U)} \int_U |Du||Dv|dx$$
$$+ \sum_{i=1}^{d} \|b_i\|_{L^\infty(U)} \int_U |Du||v|dx$$
$$+ \|c\|_{L^\infty(U)} \int_U |u||v|dx \le C\|u\|_{H_0^1(U)}\|v\|_{H_0^1(U)}.$$

By the uniform ellipticity,

$$\delta \int_U |Du|^2 dx$$
$$\le \int_U \sum_{i,j=1}^{d} a_{ij} \frac{\partial u}{\partial x_i}\frac{\partial u}{\partial x_j} dx = B[u,u] - \int_U \left(\sum_{i=1}^{d} b_i \frac{\partial u}{\partial x_i} u + cu^2 \right) dx$$
$$\le B[u,u] + \sum_{i=1}^{d} \|b_i\|_{L^\infty(U)} \int_U |Du||u|dx + \|c\|_{L^\infty(U)} \int_U |u|^2 dx.$$

In Cauchy's inequality

$$\int_U |Du||u|dx \le \varepsilon \int_U |Du|^2 dx + \frac{1}{4\varepsilon} \int_U |u|^2 dx$$

we select ε such that $\varepsilon \sum_{i=1}^{d} \|b_i\|_{L^\infty(U)} < \delta/2$. Then

$$\frac{\delta}{2} \int_U |Du|^2 dx \le B[u,u] + C \int_U |u|^2 dx.$$

By Poincaré's inequality $\|u\|_{L^2(U)} \le C\|Du\|_{L^2(U)}$, we get the estimate

$$\|u\|_{H_0^1(U)} \le C\|Du\|_{L^2(U)}.$$

It easily follows that

$$\beta\|u\|_{H_0^1(U)}^2 \le B[u,u] + \gamma\|u\|_{L^2(U)}^2.$$

□

The existence of weak solutions of problem (5.4) follows from the above energy estimates and the Lax–Milgram theorem.

Theorem 5.26 (Lax–Milgram Theorem). *Let $B\colon H \times H \to \mathbb{R}$ be a bilinear functional in a Hilbert space H such that*

$$\forall u, v \in H \quad |B[u,v]| \leq \alpha \|u\| \|v\|, \ \alpha > 0,$$

$$\forall u \in H \quad |B[u,u]| \geq \beta \|u\|^2, \ \beta > 0.$$

If $f\colon H \to \mathbb{R}$ is a bounded linear functional in H, then there exists a unique element $u \in H$ such that

$$B[u,v] = (f,v), \quad \forall v \in H,$$

where $\|\cdot\|$ and $(\cdot,\cdot)$ denote the norm and scalar product in H, respectively.

Theorem 5.27 (Existence of weak solutions). *There is a constant $\gamma \geq 0$ such that for each $\mu \geq \gamma$ and $f \in L^2(U)$ there exists a unique weak solution $u \in H_0^1(U)$ of the Dirichlet problem with $\mathcal{A}$ in divergence form*

$$\begin{aligned} \mathcal{A}u + \mu u &= f, \quad \text{in } U, \\ u|_{\partial U} &= 0. \end{aligned} \tag{5.7}$$

Proof. Let γ be the constant from Theorem 5.25. Taking $\mu \geq \gamma$, we define

$$B_\mu[u,v] = B[u,v] + \mu(u,v), \quad u,v \in H_0^1(U).$$

$B_\mu[u,v]$ fulfills the assumptions of the Lax–Milgram theorem. For $f \in L^2(U)$ we define linear functional $\langle f, v\rangle = (f,v)$. Applying the Lax–Milgram theorem to the equation

$$B_\mu[u,v] = (f,v),$$

we find a unique $u \in H_0^1(U)$ satisfying the conclusion of the theorem. Therefore, u is a unique weak solution of the Dirichlet problem (5.7). □

We close our analysis of Dirichlet's problem, pointing to the improvement of solution regularity for more regular data.

Remark 5.28. If the coefficients of operator $\mathcal{A}$ are of class $C^{m+1}(\bar{U})$, and $f \in H^m(U)$, then $u \in H_0^1(U)$, the weak solution of the Dirichlet problem (5.7) with ∂U of class C^{m+2}, belongs to $H^{m+2}(U)$ and

$$\|u\|_{H^{m+2}(U)} \leq C \|f\|_{H^m(U)}.$$

5.4 Parabolic Equations of Second-Order

Let $U \subset \mathbb{R}^d$ be an open, bounded domain and $U_T = (0,T] \times U$, $T > 0$. We will study the initial-boundary value problem with the Dirichlet boundary conditions

$$\begin{aligned} &\frac{\partial u}{\partial t} + \mathcal{A}^t u = f, \quad \text{in } U_T, \\ &u = 0, \quad \text{on } [0,T] \times \partial U, \\ &u = g, \quad \text{on } \{t = 0\} \times U. \end{aligned} \tag{5.8}$$

Similarly to the elliptic case, we consider the operator $\mathcal{A}^t$ in the divergence form

$$\begin{aligned} \mathcal{A}^t u(t,x) = &\sum_{i=1}^{d}\sum_{j=1}^{d} -\frac{\partial}{\partial x_i}\left(a_{ij}(t,x)\frac{\partial u(t,x)}{\partial x_j}\right) \\ &+ \sum_{i=1}^{d} b_i(t,x)\frac{\partial u(t,x)}{\partial x_i} + c(t,x)u(t,x) \end{aligned}$$

and the nondivergence form

$$\begin{aligned} \mathcal{A}^t u(t,x) = &\sum_{i=1}^{d}\sum_{j=1}^{d} -a_{ij}(t,x)\frac{\partial^2 u(t,x)}{\partial x_i \partial x_j} \\ &+ \sum_{i=1}^{d} b_i(t,x)\frac{\partial u(t,x)}{\partial x_i} + c(t,x)u(t,x). \end{aligned}$$

Definition 5.29. The second-order operator $\partial/\partial t + \mathcal{A}^t$ is called *uniformly parabolic* if $a_{ij} = a_{ji}$, $i,j = 1,\dots,d$, and

$$\exists \delta > 0 \ \forall (t,x) \in U_T \ \forall \xi \in \mathbb{R}^d \backslash \{0\} \quad \sum_{i=1}^{d}\sum_{j=1}^{d} a_{ij}(t,x)\xi_i\xi_j \geq \delta|\xi|^2.$$

The function $u(t,x)$ that solves problem (5.8) will be treated as a mapping $u\colon [0,T] \to H_0^1(U)$. Then $u(t)$ denotes the value of this function in $H_0^1(U)$.

Definition 5.30. Let a_{ij}, b_i, $c \in L^\infty(U_T)$, $i,j = 1,\dots,d$, $f \in L^2(U_T)$, and $g \in L^2(U)$. A function $u \in L^2(0,T; H_0^1(U))$ is called a *weak solution* of the initial-boundary value problem (5.8) with $\mathcal{A}^t$ in divergence form if $du/dt \in L^2(0,T; H^{-1}(U))$ and

(1) For any $v \in H_0^1(U)$

$$\left\langle \frac{du}{dt}(t), v \right\rangle + B^t[u(t), v] = (f(t), v),$$

where the equality holds almost everywhere in t and

$$B^t[u,v] = \int_U \left(\sum_{i,j=1}^{d} a_{ij}(t,x) \frac{\partial u}{\partial x_i} \frac{\partial v}{\partial x_j} + \sum_{i=1}^{d} b_i(t,x) \frac{\partial u}{\partial x_i} v + c(t,x)uv \right) dx.$$

(2) $u(0) = g$.

If $u \in L^2(0,T; H_0^1(U))$ and $du/dt \in L^2(0,T; H^{-1}(U))$, then $u \in C([0,T]; L^2(U))$, which means that the equality of point (2) makes sense (cf. Theorem 5.21).

Example 5.31. Some parabolic equations possess solutions in the classical sense, i.e., solutions are functions with continuous derivatives that inserted into the equation fulfill that equation pointwise. The best-known example is the *heat equation*

$$\frac{\partial u}{\partial t} = \Delta u \equiv \sum_{i=1}^{d} \frac{\partial^2 u}{\partial x_i^2}.$$

To find a solution to this equation, observe that: if $u(t,x)$ is a solution, then $u(a^2t, ax)$ also solves the equation for any $a \in \mathbb{R}$. This scaling indicates that the solution can be searched in the form

$$u(t,x) = \frac{1}{\sqrt{t^d}} w(y), \quad y = \frac{|x|}{\sqrt{t}}.$$

Elementary computations give

$$\frac{\partial u}{\partial t} = -\frac{1}{2t^{(d+2)/2}} \left(dw(y) + yw'(y) \right),$$

$$\Delta u = \frac{1}{2t^{(d+2)/2}} \left(w''(y) + \frac{d-1}{y} w'(y) \right).$$

Inserting these expressions into the heat equation yields the ordinary differential equation

$$yw''(y) + (d-1)w'(y) + \frac{y^2}{2}w'(y) + \frac{d}{2}yw(y) = 0.$$

Multiplying by y^{d-2}, we can write this equation in the form

$$\big(y^{d-1}w'(y)\big)' + \frac{1}{2}\big(y^d w(y)\big)' = 0.$$

Integrating the last equation, we obtain

$$y^{d-1}w'(y) + \frac{1}{2}y^d w(y) = C,$$

where C is a real constant. Assuming that w and w' are finite at $y = 0$, we deduce $C = 0$ and therefore

$$w'(y) + \frac{1}{2}yw(y) = 0.$$

This gives the family of solutions

$$w(y) = c_0 \exp\left(-\frac{y^2}{4}\right).$$

Normalizing the solution of the heat equation

$$\int_{\mathbb{R}^d} u(t,x)dx = 1,$$

we find

$$\begin{aligned} 1 &= \frac{1}{\sqrt{t^d}}\int_{\mathbb{R}^d} w\left(\frac{|x|}{\sqrt{t}}\right)dx = \frac{c_0}{\sqrt{t^d}}\int_{\mathbb{R}^d}\exp\left(-\frac{|x|^2}{4t}\right)dx \\ &= c_0\int_{\mathbb{R}^d} e^{-|z|^2}dz = c_0(4\pi)^{d/2}. \end{aligned}$$

Then we conclude that

$$u(t,x) = \frac{1}{(4\pi t)^{d/2}}\exp\left(-\frac{|x|^2}{4t}\right)$$

is a solution of the heat equation. This solution is called the *fundamental solution* of the heat equation.

Example 5.32. The fundamental solution of the heat equation is a solution in the whole $\mathbb{R}^d$. An approach that fits well to bounded domains is the *separation of variables* method. This method is particularly efficient for the heat equation in a rectangular domain (the method is also suitable for many other partial differential equations in bounded domains). To demonstrate how the method works, we consider the one-dimensional heat equation in $U = (0,1)$ with zero boundary conditions

$$\begin{aligned} &\frac{\partial u}{\partial t}(t,x) - \frac{\partial^2 u}{\partial x^2}(t,x) = 0, \quad x \in U, t \geq 0, \\ &u(t,0) = 0, \quad u(t,1) = 0, \quad t > 0, \\ &u(0,x) = g(x), \quad x \in U. \end{aligned} \tag{5.9}$$

We look for solutions of the form $u(t,x) = w(t)v(x)$. Substituting this form of $u(t,x)$ into the differential equation, we obtain

$$\frac{w'(t)}{w(t)} = \frac{v''(x)}{v(x)}.$$

In this last equation, the left-hand side is independent of x, and the right-hand side is independent of t. Thus, both sides must be constant. Writing this constant as $-\lambda^2$, we obtain

$$w'(t) = -\lambda^2 w(t),$$

that gives the solution with an arbitrary constant C

$$w(t) = C \exp\big(-\lambda^2 t\big). \tag{5.10}$$

For $v(x)$, we have the following boundary value problem

$$\begin{aligned} &v''(x) + \lambda^2 v(x) = 0, \quad x \in U, \\ &v(0) = v(1) = 0. \end{aligned}$$

The general solution of this problem has the form

$$v(x) = A \sin \lambda x + B \cos \lambda x.$$

The boundary conditions can only be fulfilled for $B = 0$. Then $\lambda = n\pi$, $n = 1, 2, \ldots$.

Thus, we have

$$v(x) = \sum_{n=1}^{\infty} A_n \sin n\pi x. \tag{5.11}$$

Collecting results (5.10) and (5.11), we obtain

$$u(t,x) = \sum_{n=1}^{\infty} c_n \exp(-n^2\pi^2 t) \sin n\pi x$$

with arbitrary constants c_n. We find these constants by the Fourier expansion of the initial condition $g(x)$

$$g(x) = \sum_{n=1}^{\infty} c_n \sin n\pi x, \text{ where } c_n = 2\int_0^1 g(x) \sin n\pi x \, dx.$$

For the nonhomogeneous Dirichlet boundary problem

$$\begin{aligned}
&\frac{\partial u}{\partial t}(t,x) - \frac{\partial^2 u}{\partial x^2}(t,x) = 0, \quad x \in U, t \geq 0, \\
&u(t,0) = q_0, \quad u(t,1) = q_1, \quad t > 0, \\
&u(0,x) = g(x), \quad x \in U,
\end{aligned}$$

with constant q_0 and q_1, we can apply the change of variables

$$z(t,x) = \frac{u(t,x) - q_0}{q_1 - q_0}$$

to reduce the problem to the boundary conditions

$$z(t,0) = 0, \quad z(t,1) = 1.$$

Subtracting from $z(t,x)$ the steady-state solution $z_{st}(x) = x$, which is the solution of the stationary problem $\partial^2 z/\partial x^2 = 0$, we obtain function $\bar{u}(t,x) = z(t,x) - z_{st}(x)$ which solves the homogeneous problem (5.9).

To solve the heat equation with the Dirichlet–Neumann boundary conditions

$$\frac{\partial u}{\partial t}(t,x) - \frac{\partial^2 u}{\partial x^2}(t,x) = 0, \quad x \in U, t \geq 0,$$

$$u(t,0)=0, \quad \frac{\partial u}{\partial x}(t,1)=0, \quad t>0,$$
$$u(0,x)=g(x), \quad x\in U,$$

we must reconsider the eigenvalue problem

$$\begin{aligned} &v''(x)+\lambda^2 v(x)=0, \quad x\in U,\\ &v(0)=0, \quad \frac{\partial v}{\partial x}(1)=0 \end{aligned} \tag{5.12}$$

and its general solution

$$v(x)=A\sin\lambda x + B\cos\lambda x, \quad x\in U.$$

Problem (5.12) has a nonzero solutions for $B=0$ and $\lambda=(2n-1)\pi/2$, $n=1,2,\ldots$.

Then the solution of the mixed problem for the heat equation is

$$u(t,x)=\sum_{n=1}^{\infty} c_n \exp\bigl(-(2n-1)^2\pi^2 t/4\bigr)\sin\bigl((2n-1)\pi x/2\bigr)$$

with constants c_n obtained by the Fourier expansion of the initial condition $g(x)$

$$g(x)=\sum_{n=1}^{\infty} c_n \sin\bigl((2n-1)\pi x/2\bigr),$$

$$\text{where } c_n = 2\int_0^1 g(x)\sin\bigl((2n-1)\pi x/2\bigr)\,dx.$$

5.4.1 *Galerkin approximation*

Since $H_0^1(U)\subset L^2(U)$ and both spaces are Hilbert spaces, we can select the basis $\{\phi_k\}_{k=1}^{\infty}$ which is an orthonormal basis of $L^2(U)$ and an orthogonal basis of $H_0^1(U)$. We can choose as ϕ_k the basis of eigenvectors in $H_0^1(U)$ of a uniformly elliptic operator $\mathcal{A}_0 = \sum_{i,j=1}^{d} -\frac{\partial}{\partial x_i}\Bigl(a_{ij}(x)\frac{\partial u(x)}{\partial x_j}\Bigr)$ (for details see Evans [29] [Section 6.5]). For fixed m, we define the function

$$u_m(t)=\sum_{k=1}^{m} d_m^k(t)\phi_k.$$

We search for coefficients d_m^k which make u_m an approximation of the solution to (5.8). Thus, we seek u_m as a solution of the discrete approximation of (5.8):

$$\left(\frac{du_m}{dt}(t), \phi_k\right) + B^t[u_m(t), \phi_k] = (f(t), \phi_k),$$
$$0 < t \leq T, k = 1, \ldots, m, \tag{5.13}$$
$$d_m^k(0) = (g, \phi_k), \quad k = 1, \ldots, m.$$

Theorem 5.33. *For every $m \geq 1$, there exists a unique function u_m which solves* (5.13).

Proof. By the definition of u_m, we have $(du_m/dt, \phi_k) = dd_m^k/dt$. We also have the following equality

$$B^t[u_m(t), \phi_k] = \sum_{i=1}^{m} e^{ki}(t) d_m^i(t),$$

where $e^{ki}(t) = B^t[\phi_i, \phi_k]$.

Denoting $f_k(t) = (f, \phi_k)$ and using the above equalities, we transform (5.13) into a linear system of ordinary differential equations

$$\frac{dd_m^k}{dt} + \sum_{i=1}^{m} e^{ki} d_m^i = f_k, \quad k = 1, \ldots, m,$$

with initial conditions $d_m^k(0) = (g, \phi_k)$.

This linear system possesses a unique solution. Thus, we obtain a unique solution of (5.13). □

Theorem 5.34 (Energy estimates). *If u_m is a solution of* (5.13), *then*

$$\max_{0 \leq t \leq T} \|u_m(t)\|_{L^2(U)} + \|u_m\|_{L^2(0,T;H_0^1(U))} + \|du_m/dt\|_{L^2(0,T;H^{-1}(U))}$$
$$\leq C\Big(\|f\|_{L^2(0,T;L^2(U))} + \|g\|_{L^2(U)}\Big), \quad m = 1, 2, \ldots, \tag{5.14}$$

where the constant C depends on U, T, and the coefficients of $\mathcal{A}^t$.

Proof. We separately estimate each term on the left-hand side of (5.14).

Multiplying (5.13) by d_m^k and summing over k from 1 to m, we get

$$\left(\frac{du_m}{dt}(t), u_m(t)\right) + B^t[u_m(t), u_m(t)] = (f(t), u_m(t)). \qquad (5.15)$$

By Theorem 5.25 and the uniform boundedness in t of the coefficients of $B^t[u,v]$, we obtain the estimate

$$\beta\|u_m(t)\|^2_{H_0^1(U)} \le B^t[u_m(t), u_m(t)] + \gamma\|u_m(t)\|^2_{L^2(U)},$$

where $\beta > 0$, $\gamma \ge 0$.

Since $(du_m/dt(t), u_m(t)) = 1/2\, d/dt\big(\|u_m(t)\|^2_{L^2(U)}\big)$ and

$$|(f(t), u_m(t))| \le \frac{1}{2}\|f(t)\|^2_{L^2(U)} + \frac{1}{2}\|u_m(t)\|^2_{L^2(U)},$$

we can use the estimate of Theorem 5.25 to replace (5.15) by the inequality

$$\frac{d}{dt}\|u_m(t)\|^2_{L^2(U)} + 2\beta\|u_m(t)\|^2_{H_0^1(U)} \le C_1\|u_m(t)\|^2_{L^2(U)} + C_2\|f(t)\|^2_{L^2(U)}, \qquad (5.16)$$

which holds a.e. in t.

Inequality (5.16) remains valid if we neglect $2\beta\|u_m(t)\|^2_{H_0^1(U)}$ on the left-hand side. Then we obtain $\eta' \le C_1\eta + C_2\xi$, where $\eta = \|u_m(t)\|^2_{L^2(U)}$ and $\xi = \|f(t)\|^2_{L^2(U)}$. By Gronwall's lemma, we get

$$\eta(t) \le e^{C_1 t}\left(\eta(0) + C_2\int_0^t \xi(s)ds\right).$$

Since $\eta(0) = \|u_m(0)\|^2_{L^2(U)} \le \|g\|^2_{L^2(U)}$, then

$$\max_{0\le t\le T}\|u_m(t)\|^2_{L^2(U)} \le C\left(\|g\|^2_{L^2(U)} + \|f\|^2_{L^2(0,T;L^2(U))}\right). \qquad (5.17)$$

To estimate the second term in (5.14), we integrate (5.16) over $[0,T]$ and apply (5.17)

$$\begin{aligned}\|u_m\|^2_{L^2(0,T;H_0^1(U))} &= \int_0^T \|u_m(t)\|^2_{H_0^1(U)}dt \\ &\le C\left(\|f\|^2_{L^2(0,T;L^2(U))} + \|g\|^2_{L^2(U)}\right).\end{aligned}$$

To estimate the last term of (5.14), we select $v \in H_0^1(U)$, $\|v\|_{H_0^1(U)} \le 1$, and split this v into orthogonal components $v = v_1 + v_2$, where $v_1 \in \mathrm{Lin}(\phi_1, \ldots, \phi_m)$ and $(v_2, \phi_k) = 0$, $k = 1, \ldots, m$. Then $\|v_1\|_{H_0^1(U)} \le \|v\|_{H_0^1(U)} \le 1$.

From (5.13), we obtain

$$\left(\frac{du_m}{dt}(t), v_1\right) + B^t[u_m(t), v_1] = (f(t), v_1).$$

Since

$$\begin{aligned}\left\langle\frac{du_m}{dt}(t), v\right\rangle = \left(\frac{du_m}{dt}(t), v\right) &= \left(\frac{du_m}{dt}(t), v_1\right)\\ &= (f(t), v_1) - B^t[u_m(t), v_1],\end{aligned}$$

then by the elementary inequality $|a - b| \le |a| + |b|$ and the estimate $\|v_1\|_{H_0^1(U)} \le 1$, we get

$$\left|\left\langle\frac{du_m}{dt}(t), v\right\rangle\right| \le C\left(\|f(t)\|_{L^2(U)} + \|u_m(t)\|_{H_0^1(U)}\right).$$

Thus,

$$\|du_m/dt(t)\|_{H^{-1}(U)} \le C\left(\|f(t)\|_{L^2(U)} + \|u_m(t)\|_{H_0^1(U)}\right).$$

Squaring the above inequality and integrating, we obtain the desired estimate

$$\begin{aligned}\int_0^T \|du_m/dt(t)\|^2_{H^{-1}(U)} dt &\le C\int_0^T \left(\|f(t)\|^2_{L^2(U)} + \|u_m(t)\|^2_{H_0^1(U)}\right) dt\\ &\le C\left(\|f\|^2_{L^2(0,T;L^2(U))} + \|g\|^2_{L^2(U)}\right).\end{aligned}$$

□

Theorem 5.35. *Let a_{ij}, b_i, $c \in L^\infty(U_T)$, $i, j = 1, \ldots, d$, $f \in L^2(U_T)$ and $g \in L^2(U)$. Then there exists a unique weak solution $u(t)$ of (5.8) with $\mathcal{A}^t$ in divergence form. For this solution, we have $u \in L^2(0, T; H_0^1(U))$ and $du/dt \in L^2(0, T; H^{-1}(U))$.*

Proof. We begin with the proof of existence. The sequences of Galerkin's approximations $u_m \in L^2(0, T; H_0^1(U))$ and $du_m/dt \in L^2(0, T; H^{-1}(U))$ are bounded because of the estimates of the previous theorem. Thus, there exists a function $u \in L^2(0, T; H_0^1(U))$

with $du/dt \in L^2(0,T;H^{-1}(U))$ and a weakly convergent subsequence (which we also index with m)

$$u_m \rightharpoonup u, \quad \text{in } L^2(0,T;H_0^1(U)),$$
$$\frac{du_m}{dt} \rightharpoonup \frac{du}{dt}, \quad \text{in } L^2(0,T;H^{-1}(U)).$$

Let us define

$$v = \sum_{k=1}^{N} w^k(t)\phi_k, \tag{5.18}$$

with smooth $w^k(t)$ such that $v \in C^1(0,T;H_0^1(U))$. We multiply (5.13) for $m \geq N$ by $w^k(t)$, sum with respect to k from 1 to N, and integrate the sum with respect to t in $[0,T]$

$$\int_0^T \left(\left\langle \frac{du_m}{dt}(t), v(t)\right\rangle + B^t[u_m(t), v(t)]\right) dt = \int_0^T (f(t), v(t))dt.$$

Passing to the limit with m (weak convergence), we obtain

$$\int_0^T \left(\left\langle \frac{du}{dt}(t), v(t)\right\rangle + B^t[u(t), v(t)]\right) dt = \int_0^T (f(t), v(t))dt, \tag{5.19}$$

where the equality holds for any $v \in L^2(0,T;H_0^1(U))$ because functions of the form (5.18) are dense in $L^2(0,T;H_0^1(U))$. Since $v \in L^2(0,T;H_0^1(U))$ is arbitrary, we obtain for each $z \in H_0^1(U)$ and a.e. $t \in [0,T]$ the equality

$$\left\langle \frac{du}{dt}(t), z\right\rangle + B^t[u(t), z] = (f(t), z). \tag{5.20}$$

Furthermore, $u \in C([0,T];L^2(U))$ by Theorem 5.21.

To prove $u(0) = g$, we use the smoothness of $w^k(t)$. Integrating by parts, we can write (5.19) as

$$\int_0^T \left(-\left\langle \frac{dv}{dt}(t), u(t)\right\rangle + B^t[u(t), v(t)]\right) dt$$
$$= \int_0^T (f(t), v(t))dt + (u(0), v(0))$$

for $v \in C^1(0,T;H_0^1(U))$ such that $v(T) = 0$.

Similarly,

$$\int_0^T \left(-\left\langle \frac{dv}{dt}(t), u_m(t) \right\rangle + B^t[u_m(t), v(t)] \right) dt$$
$$= \int_0^T (f(t), v(t))dt + (u_m(0), v(0)).$$

Passing in the last equality to the limit with m, we obtain

$$\int_0^T \left(-\left\langle \frac{dv}{dt}(t), u(t) \right\rangle + B^t[u(t), v(t)] \right) dt$$
$$= \int_0^T (f(t), v(t))dt + (g, v(0))$$

since $u_m(0) \to g$ in $L^2(U)$, which follows from the initial condition $d_m^k(0) = (g, \phi_k)$ in Theorem 5.33. The arbitrariness of $v(0)$ gives $u(0) = g$.

Let us now prove uniqueness. Choosing $f = 0$ and $g = 0$, we prove $u = 0$.

Inserting $z = u(t)$ in (5.20), we get

$$\frac{d}{dt} \left(\frac{1}{2} \|u(t)\|^2_{L^2(U)} \right) + B^t[u(t), u(t)] = 0$$

for a.e. t.

Since, by Theorem 5.25, we have the inequality

$$B^t[u(t), u(t)] \geq \beta \|u(t)\|^2_{H_0^1(U)} - \gamma \|u(t)\|^2_{L^2(U)} \geq -\gamma \|u(t)\|^2_{L^2(U)},$$

then

$$\frac{d}{dt} \left(\frac{1}{2} \|u(t)\|^2_{L^2(U)} \right) - \gamma \|u(t)\|^2_{L^2(U)} \leq 0.$$

By Gronwall's lemma, we get $u = 0$ for $u(0) = g = 0$. □

Theorem 5.36 (Regularity of solutions). *Let the coefficients of equation (5.8) be C^1 in x and independent of t. Assume $g \in H_0^1(U)$ and $f \in L^2(0, T; L^2(U))$ with ∂U smooth enough. Then u, which is* *a weak solution of* (5.8) *such that* $u \in L^2(0,T;H_0^1(U))$, $du/dt \in L^2(0,T;H^{-1}(U))$, *is in fact more regular*

$$u \in L^2(0,T;H^2(U)) \cap L^\infty(0,T;H_0^1(U)), \quad du/dt \in L^2(0,T;L^2(U)).$$

If, in addition, $g \in H^2(U)$, $df/dt \in L^2(0,T;L^2(U))$, *then*

$$u \in L^\infty(0,T;H^2(U)), \quad du/dt \in L^\infty(0,T;L^2(U)) \cap L^2(0,T;H_0^1(U)),$$
$$d^2u/dt^2 \in L^2(0,T;H^{-1}(U)).$$

Remark 5.37. For $g \in H^{2m+1}(U) \cap H_0^1(U)$ and $d^k f/dt^k \in L^2(0,T;H^{2m-2k}(U))$, $k = 0,1,\dots,m$, we can show that $d^k u/dt^k \in L^2(0,T;H^{2m+2-2k}(U))$, $k = 0,1,\dots,m+1$, if ∂U is sufficiently smooth.

We now present the *maximum principle* for second-order parabolic equations. Contrary to integral energy estimates, the maximum principle can be considered as a pointwise estimate. The maximum principle is based on the observation that if a function u is a solution of a second-order parabolic equation in domain U, then it attains its maximum or minimum at the boundary ∂U. In fact, we consider u, which does not fulfill a parabolic equation but a parabolic inequality. This approach allows us to obtain separate results for the maximum and minimum of u.

Theorem 5.38 (Maximum principle). *Let* $\mathcal{A}^t$ *be given in the nondivergence form with* $c = 0$ *and* $u \in C^{1,2}(U_T) \cap C(\bar{U}_T)$.

If

$$\frac{\partial u}{\partial t} + \mathcal{A}^t u \le 0 \quad \text{in } U_T,$$

then

$$\max_{\bar{U}_T} u = \max_{\Gamma_T} u, \quad \text{where } \Gamma_T = \bar{U}_T \backslash U_T.$$

If

$$\frac{\partial u}{\partial t} + \mathcal{A}^t u \ge 0 \quad \text{in } U_T,$$

then

$$\min_{\bar{U}_T} u = \min_{\Gamma_T} u.$$

Theorem 5.39. *Let $\mathcal{A}^t$ be given in the nondivergence form with $c \geq 0$ in U_T and $u \in C^{1,2}(U_T) \cap C(\bar{U}_T)$.*

If

$$\frac{\partial u}{\partial t} + \mathcal{A}^t u \leq 0 \quad \text{in } U_T,$$

then

$$\max_{\bar{U}_T} u \leq \max_{\Gamma_T} u^+,$$

where $u^+ = \max(u, 0)$.

If

$$\frac{\partial u}{\partial t} + \mathcal{A}^t u \geq 0 \quad \text{in } U_T,$$

then

$$\min_{\bar{U}_T} u \geq -\max_{\Gamma_T} u^-,$$

where $u^- = \max(-u, 0)$.

5.5 The Black–Scholes Equation

The Black–Scholes equation is a standard example of a second-order parabolic equation. Let us recall that this equation describes the time dynamics of option prices as functions of the underlying price S and time t

$$\frac{\partial V(t,S)}{\partial t} + \frac{1}{2}\sigma^2(t,S)S^2\frac{\partial^2 V(t,S)}{\partial S^2} + rS\frac{\partial V(t,S)}{\partial S} - rV(t,S) = 0, \tag{5.21}$$

with the terminal condition of option payoff

$$V(T,S) = g(S),$$

and the problem is defined on $[0,T] \times [0,\infty)$.

The theory of parabolic equations developed in the previous section cannot be directly applied to the Black–Scholes equation:

(1) The domain is unbounded as $S \in [0,\infty)$.
(2) The coefficients in the equation are unbounded.

These problems can be resolved by

(1) Building a separate theory suitable for the Black–Scholes equation. Such a theory requires special functional spaces that mimic the Sobolev space approach. We briefly describe this method at the end of this section.
(2) Making a suitable change of variables to reduce the Black–Scholes equation to a problem analyzed in this chapter. We describe that approach below, omitting technical details.

We can eliminate the unbounded coefficients substituting $x = \ln S$. We also substitute $\tau = T - t$, replacing terminal conditions with initial conditions. Due to these substitutions, we obtain the initial value problem

$$\begin{aligned} &\frac{\partial u}{\partial \tau} - \frac{1}{2}\tilde{\sigma}^2(\tau, x)\frac{\partial^2 u}{\partial x^2} + b(\tau, x)\frac{\partial u}{\partial x} + c(\tau, x)u = 0, \\ &u(0, x) = \tilde{g}(x), \end{aligned} \tag{5.22}$$

where $u(\tau, x) = V(T - \tau, e^x)$. The coefficients $\tilde{\sigma}$, b, and c are bounded (the boundedness follows by their financial meaning), but the domain is unbounded: $x \in \mathbb{R}$ ($\tilde{\sigma}$, $\tilde{g}$ denote functions σ and g after the above change of variables).

Assuming additionally that $\tilde{\sigma}(\tau, \cdot)$ is of class C^1 in x and the following estimates are uniform in τ

$$0 < \sigma_L \leq \tilde{\sigma}(\tau, x) \leq \sigma_U, \quad \left|\frac{\partial \tilde{\sigma}(\tau, x)}{\partial x}\right| \leq C, \tag{5.23}$$

we can transform (5.22) to the divergence form

$$\begin{aligned} &\frac{\partial u}{\partial \tau} - \frac{1}{2}\frac{\partial}{\partial x}\left(\tilde{\sigma}^2(\tau, x)\frac{\partial u}{\partial x}\right) + \bar{b}(\tau, x)\frac{\partial u}{\partial x} + c(\tau, x)u = 0, \\ &u(0, x) = \tilde{g}(x). \end{aligned} \tag{5.24}$$

Equation (5.24) is an example of a second-order parabolic equation in an unbounded domain $U_T = (0, T] \times \mathbb{R}^d$. Such equations are investigated in weighted Sobolev spaces (for details of the analysis of second-order parabolic equations in weighted Sobolev spaces, see the lecture notes by Bonnans [10]). Let us consider the problem in full generality

$$\begin{aligned} &\frac{\partial u}{\partial t} + \mathcal{A}^t u = f, \quad \text{in } U_T, \\ &u = g, \quad \text{on } \{t=0\} \times \mathbb{R}^d, \end{aligned} \tag{5.25}$$

where $\partial/\partial t + \mathcal{A}^t$ is uniformly parabolic and

$$\begin{aligned} \mathcal{A}^t u(t,x) = &\sum_{i,j=1}^{d} -\frac{\partial}{\partial x_i}\left(a_{ij}(t,x)\frac{\partial u(t,x)}{\partial x_j}\right) \\ &+ \sum_{i=1}^{d} b_i(t,x)\frac{\partial u(t,x)}{\partial x_i} + c(t,x)u(t,x). \end{aligned}$$

Let $L^2_\rho(\mathbb{R}^d)$ denote the space with weight ρ

$$L^2_\rho(\mathbb{R}^d) = \left\{u\colon \int_{\mathbb{R}^d} |u(x)|^2 \rho(x)dx < +\infty\right\}.$$

The norm in this space is defined by the formula

$$\|u\|_{L^2_\rho} = \left(\int_{\mathbb{R}^d} |u(x)|^2 \rho(x)dx\right)^{1/2}.$$

We also define spaces $H^k_\rho(\mathbb{R}^d)$ with the norm

$$\|u\|_{H^k_\rho} = \|u\|_{L^2_\rho} + \sum_{|\alpha|\le k} \|D^\alpha u\|_{L^2_\rho}.$$

Definition 5.40. The weight functions $\rho(x)$ are functions of class $C^1(\mathbb{R}^d)$ such that $\rho(x)^{-1}D\rho(x)$ are bounded uniformly in $x \in \mathbb{R}^d$.

The proof of existence and uniqueness of problem (5.25) is analogous to the proof for a bounded domain U.

First, integrating by parts the second-order terms in $\mathcal{A}^t$, we define for every $u, v \in H^1_\rho(\mathbb{R}^d)$ the bilinear form

$$B^t_\rho[u,v] = \int_{\mathbb{R}^d} \left(\sum_{i,j=1}^{d} a_{ij}(t,x) \frac{\partial u}{\partial x_i} \frac{\partial v}{\partial x_j} + \sum_{i=1}^{d} \hat{b}_i(t,x) \frac{\partial u}{\partial x_i} v + c(t,x)uv \right) \rho(x)dx, \qquad (5.26)$$

where

$$\hat{b}_i(t,x) = b_i(t,x) + \sum_{j=1}^{d} a_{ij}(t,x) \frac{1}{\rho(x)} \frac{\partial \rho(x)}{\partial x_j}.$$

Assuming a_{ij}, b_i, $c \in L^\infty(U_T)$, $i,j = 1, \ldots, d$, and the symmetry $a_{ij} = a_{ji}$, we obtain the energy estimates for $B^t_\rho[u,v]$ with $u, v \in H^1_\rho(\mathbb{R}^d)$

$$|B^t_\rho[u,v]| \le \alpha \|u\|_{H^1_\rho} \|v\|_{H^1_\rho},$$

$$\beta \|u\|^2_{H^1_\rho} \le B^t_\rho[u,u] + \gamma \|u\|^2_{L^2_\rho}.$$

The proof of the above estimates is similar to the proof for a bounded U. The only difference is the passage from the estimate

$$\beta \|Du\|^2_{L^2_\rho} \le B^t_\rho[u,u] + \gamma \|u\|^2_{L^2_\rho}$$

to the estimate

$$\beta \|u\|^2_{H^1_\rho} \le B^t_\rho[u,u] + \gamma \|u\|^2_{L^2_\rho}.$$

For a bounded U, we have used Poincaré's inequality. In $\mathbb{R}^d$, we replace $\|Du\|^2_{L^2_\rho}$ with $\|u\|^2_{H^1_\rho}$ by adding $\beta\|u\|^2_{L^2_\rho}$ to both sides which only increases the constant γ.

Similarly to the case of a bounded U, we consider a solution of (5.25) as a mapping $u\colon\ [0,T] \to H^1_\rho(\mathbb{R}^d)$. Multiplying (5.25) by

$\rho(x)v(x)$, with $v \in H^1_\rho(\mathbb{R}^d)$, and integrating on $[0,T]$, we obtain the weak form of the equation

$$\begin{aligned}&\left\langle \frac{du}{dt}(t), v\right\rangle + B^t_\rho[u(t), v] = \langle f(t), v\rangle,\\ &u(0) = g,\end{aligned} \tag{5.27}$$

where $\langle v^*, v\rangle$ denotes the value of functionals v^* from H^{-1}_ρ, the space dual to H^1_ρ, on elements $v \in H^1_\rho$. Similarly to a bounded U, H^1_ρ is densely embedded in L^2_ρ, which from its part is densely embedded in H^{-1}_ρ.

Remark 5.41. To prove the existence of solutions for (5.25) by the Lax-Milgram theorem we need *coerciveness* of the bilinear form $B^t_\rho[u, u]$

$$\beta\|u\|^2_{H^1_\rho} \leq B^t_\rho[u, u].$$

This cannot be obtained by adding to $c(x)$ a large constant as in Theorem 5.27 since now $c(x)$ has a clear financial meaning. We can achieve the same effect by the change of variables $u_\gamma(t) = e^{-\gamma t}u(t)$. Then $u_\gamma(t)$ solves (5.25) in which the bilinear form $B^t_\rho[u, v]$ is replaced by

$$B^t_{\rho,\gamma}[u, v] = B^t_\rho[u, v] + \gamma(u, v)_{L^2_\rho},$$

where $(u, v)_{L^2_\rho}$ denotes the scalar product in $L^2_\rho(\mathbb{R}^d)$. It is obvious that $B^t_{\rho,\gamma}[u, u]$ is already coercive.

Making the change of variables described above, integrating equation (5.27) on $[0, \tau]$ and applying the coerciveness of $B^t_{\rho,\gamma}[u, u]$, we obtain the estimate for $\tau \in [0, T]$

$$\begin{aligned}&e^{-2\gamma\tau}\|u(\tau)\|^2_{L^2_\rho} + (2\beta - \varepsilon)\int_0^\tau e^{-2\gamma s}\|u(s)\|^2_{H^1_\rho}ds\\ &\leq \|g\|^2_{L^2_\rho} + \varepsilon^{-1}\int_0^\tau \|f(s)\|^2_{H^{-1}_\rho}ds,\end{aligned} \tag{5.28}$$

where β is the constant from the coerciveness estimate for $B^t_{\rho,\gamma}[u, u]$ and $\varepsilon > 0$ is a small constant.

Estimate (5.28) is the energy estimate for (5.25). Given this estimate, the Galerkin approximation of (5.25) has a convergent subsequence. Then we have the following theorem.

Theorem 5.42. *Assume* a_{ij}, b_i, $c \in L^\infty(U_T)$, $i, j = 1, \ldots, d$, $g \in L^2_\rho$, *and* $f \in L^2(0,T;H^{-1}_\rho)$. *There exists a unique weak solution* $u(t)$ *of the initial value problem* (5.25) *such that* $u \in L^2(0,T;H^1_\rho)$ *with* $du/dt \in L^2(0,T;H^{-1}_\rho)$. *For this* u *estimate* (5.28) *holds for* $\tau \in [0,T]$.

The above theorem enables us to select the appropriate weight function $\rho(x)$. For the theorem to work, we need $g \in L^2_\rho$. Since g is the option payoff, we must choose ρ that makes this payoff an element of L^2_ρ.

Consider an example of a vanilla call option with payoff $(S-K)^+$. Passing to $x = \ln S$, we get $g(x) = (e^x - K)^+$. Then a proper weight function is $\rho(x) = e^{-\lambda\varphi(x)}$, where $\varphi(x) = (1 + |x|^2)^{1/2}$ and $\lambda > 0$ is sufficiently large.

The Black–Scholes equation in the original variables

It is possible to perform an analysis for equation (5.21) similar to the analysis of problem (5.8) without changing variables and introducing weighted Sobolev spaces. In particular, we can prove the existence of weak solutions to (5.21). This approach is described in detail in the book by Achdou and Pironneau [1]. For the mathematical analysis of the Black–Scholes equation in its original variables, we must replace the space $H^1_0(U)$ with the space

$$\mathcal{W} = \left\{ u \in L^2(\mathbb{R}_+) \colon x\frac{du}{dx} \in L^2(\mathbb{R}_+) \right\}$$

with the norm

$$\|u\|_{\mathcal{W}} = \left\| x\frac{du}{dx} \right\|_{L^2(\mathbb{R}_+)},$$

where the derivative $\frac{du}{dx}$ is understood in the weak sense.

Definition 5.43. $V(t,\cdot)$ is called a *weak solution* of the Black–Scholes equation (5.21) if $V \in C([0,T];L^2(\mathbb{R}_+)) \cap L^2(0,T;\mathcal{W})$,

$dV/dt \in L^2(0,T;\mathcal{W}')$, where $\mathcal{W}'$ is the dual space to $\mathcal{W}$, and V solves the following problem for each $u \in \mathcal{W}$

$$\begin{aligned} &\left\langle \frac{dV}{dt}(t), u \right\rangle + B^t[V(t), u] = 0, \quad t \in [0,T), \\ &V(T) = g, \quad \text{on} \quad \mathbb{R}_+, \end{aligned} \tag{5.29}$$

where

$$\begin{aligned} B^t[v,u] = &\int_{\mathbb{R}_+} \frac{1}{2} S^2 \sigma^2(t,S) \frac{\partial v}{\partial S}\frac{\partial u}{\partial S} dS \\ &+ \int_{\mathbb{R}_+} \left(-r(t) + \sigma^2(t,S) + S\sigma(t,S)\frac{\partial \sigma}{\partial S} \right) S\frac{\partial v}{\partial S} u dS \\ &+ r(t) \int_{\mathbb{R}_+} vu dS. \end{aligned}$$

An energy estimate is crucial for the existence of weak solutions. In the case of the Black–Scholes equation (5.21), we have the following energy estimate.

Theorem 5.44 (Energy estimate for Eq. (5.21)). *Assume*

(1) $0 < \sigma_L \le \sigma(t,S) \le \sigma_U$, *where* σ_L *and* σ_U *are constants.*
(2) $|S\partial\sigma/\partial S| \le C_\sigma$ *for* $t \in [0,T]$, $S \in \mathbb{R}_+$ *and* $C_\sigma > 0$.

Then there exist constants $\alpha > 0$ *and* $\gamma > 0$ *such that*

$$\begin{aligned} &|B^t[v,u]| \le \alpha \|v\|_{\mathcal{W}} \|u\|_{\mathcal{W}}, \\ &\frac{\sigma_L^2}{4} \|v\|_{\mathcal{W}}^2 \le B^t[v,v] + \gamma \|v\|_{L^2(\mathbb{R}_+)}^2. \end{aligned}$$

The proof of this energy estimate is similar to that of Theorem 5.25 if we use the $\mathbb{R}^d$ version of Poincaré's inequality

$$\forall v \in \mathcal{W}, \quad \|v\|_{L^2(\mathbb{R}_+)} \le 2 \left\| x\frac{dv}{dx} \right\|_{L^2(\mathbb{R}_+)},$$

which can be obtained from the integral identity

$$2\int_{\mathbb{R}_+} xv(x)\frac{dv}{dx}dx = -\int_{\mathbb{R}_+} v^2(x)dx.$$

Using the above energy estimate, we obtain the following existence theorem.

Theorem 5.45. *If $g \in L^2(\mathbb{R}_+)$ and the assumptions of Theorem 5.44 are fulfilled, then there exists a unique weak solution $V(t)$ of problem (5.29) and for each t, $0 \le t < T$, we have the estimate*

$$e^{-2\gamma(T-t)}\|V(t)\|^2_{L^2(\mathbb{R}_+)} + \frac{1}{2}\sigma_L^2 \int_t^T e^{-2\gamma(T-s)}\|V(s)\|^2_{\mathcal{W}} ds \le \|g\|^2_{L^2(\mathbb{R}_+)},$$

where γ is the constant from Theorem 5.44.

Computations of numerical solutions of the Black–Scholes equation are usually simpler when we transform the equation into the one-dimensional heat equation. In the following example, we show the relevant change of variables.

Example 5.46. Assume that σ and r in the Black–Scholes equation (5.21) are constant. Then there is a change of variables that transforms the Black–Scholes equation to the heat equation.

Introducing the new variables $\tau = T - t$, $x = \ln S$, and $u(\tau, x) = V(T - \tau, e^x)$, we obtain the equation

$$\frac{\partial u(\tau,x)}{\partial \tau} - \frac{1}{2}\sigma^2 \frac{\partial^2 u(\tau,x)}{\partial x^2} - (r - \sigma^2/2)\frac{\partial u(\tau,x)}{\partial x} + ru(\tau,x) = 0.$$

Defining the new dependent variable $v(\tau,x) = u(\tau,x)e^{-a\tau - bx}$, where $b = 1/2 - r/\sigma^2$ and $a = -r - b^2\sigma^2/2$, we get the equation

$$\frac{\partial v(\tau,x)}{\partial \tau} - \frac{1}{2}\sigma^2 \frac{\partial^2 v(\tau,x)}{\partial x^2} = 0.$$

With $s = \sigma^2\tau/2$ the above equation becomes the heat equation

$$\frac{\partial v(s,x)}{\partial s} - \frac{\partial^2 v(s,x)}{\partial x^2} = 0.$$

The terminal condition $V(T, S) = g(S)$ becomes

$$v(0,x) = e^{(q-1)x/2} g(e^x), \quad x \in \mathbb{R}, \quad q = \frac{2r}{\sigma^2}.$$

For several exchange-traded exotic options, we derive pricing equations that are analogous to the Black–Scholes equation. These pricing equations can be numerically solved using methods described later in this book.

Example 5.47 (Asian options). In this example, we provide a fairly general analysis of European path-dependent options with payoffs that depend on S, the price of the underlying asset, and the continuously sampled average

$$A_t = \int_0^t f(s, S_s)ds,$$

where f is a deterministic function of its variables and S_s the stochastic process of the Black–Scholes model

$$dS_t = rS_t dt + \sigma S_t dW_t$$

with constant interest rate r and constant volatility σ.

Since S_t is a Markov process, then S_t and A_t are independent processes. Because we assumed that the payoff depends on S and A, the option price should depend on both of these variables. Then $V(t, S, A)$ is a function of three variables. To derive the differential equation for the option price, we apply Itô's formula to obtain the differential of V

$$dV = \frac{\partial V}{\partial t}dt + \frac{\sigma^2}{2}S^2\frac{\partial^2 V}{\partial S^2}dt + \frac{\partial V}{\partial S}dS + \frac{\partial V}{\partial A}dA.$$

The differential dS is known from the market model. A simple consideration shows that

$$dA_t = f(t, S_t)dt.$$

Then

$$dV = \left(\frac{\partial V}{\partial t} + \frac{\sigma^2}{2}S^2\frac{\partial^2 V}{\partial S^2} + rS\frac{\partial V}{\partial S} + f(t, S)\frac{\partial V}{\partial A}\right)dt + \sigma S\frac{\partial V}{\partial S}dW_t.$$

By standard hedging considerations, we obtain the differential equation for these options

$$\frac{\partial V}{\partial t} + \frac{1}{2}\sigma^2 S^2\frac{\partial^2 V}{\partial S^2} + rS\frac{\partial V}{\partial S} + f(t, S)\frac{\partial V}{\partial A} - rV = 0. \tag{5.30}$$

As a more specific example, we take the average strike Asian option with arithmetic averaging. For this option, $f(t, S) = S$,

$$A_t = \int_0^t S_s ds,$$

and the payoff is

$$\max\left(S_T - \frac{1}{T}\int_0^T S_t dt, 0\right)$$

for the call option and

$$\max\left(\frac{1}{T}\int_0^T S_t dt - S_T, 0\right)$$

for the put option.

The payoff can be expressed as $S_T F(T, A_T/S_T)$. This suggests the so-called *similarity reduction*. Introducing the new variable $R = A/S$, the option price V can be factorized $V(t, S, A) = SH(t, R)$. Inserting this factorization into equation (5.30), we obtain the equation

$$\frac{\partial H}{\partial t} + (1 - rR)\frac{\partial H}{\partial R} + \frac{1}{2}\sigma^2 R^2 \frac{\partial^2 H}{\partial R^2} = 0, \quad \text{for} \quad t \in [0, T), \; R > 0. \tag{5.31}$$

We now consider an Asian call option. For this option, the terminal condition is

$$H(T, R) = \left(1 - \frac{1}{T}R\right)^+, \quad \text{for} \quad R > 0.$$

To obtain the boundary condition for $R \to \infty$, we note that R tends to infinity only when $S \to 0$. In this case, the option will not be exercised, and $\lim_{R\to\infty} H(t, R) = 0$. To obtain the boundary condition at $R = 0$, we observe that H must be finite at $R = 0$. Returning to the differential equation (5.31), we find that for very small R, the term $R\partial H/\partial R$ is negligible compared to $\partial H/\partial R$. We also claim that the term $R^2\partial^2 H/\partial R^2$ is negligible. If not, then

$$\frac{\partial^2 H}{\partial R^2} \sim O\left(\frac{1}{R^2}\right),$$

which contradicts the finiteness of H near zero. Hence, at $R = 0$ the terms remaining in equation (5.31) give the boundary condition

$$\frac{\partial H}{\partial t} + \frac{\partial H}{\partial R} = 0, \quad \text{for} \quad R = 0, \; t \in [0, T).$$

Example 5.48 (Lookback options). In the basic *lookback* contract, the payoff comes in two varieties: the fixed strike and the floating strike. These options have payoffs that are the same as those of vanilla options, except that in the fixed strike option, it is the asset value that is replaced by the maximum or minimum of the asset price during the option life, in the floating strike option, the strike is replaced by the above maximum or minimum.

Depending on how the maximum or minimum is monitored, we distinguish: continuous monitoring, in which asset prices are monitored continuously between the issue and expiry of the option, and discrete monitoring, in which asset prices are monitored only in selected moments of time (e.g., weekly or monthly).

Consider a floating strike lookback option with continuous monitoring. The option is called floating put when the payoff is

$$V_T = M_T - S_T, \quad \text{where } M_T = \max_{0\le t\le T} S_t,$$

and the floating call when the payoff is

$$V_T = S_T - m_T, \quad \text{where } m_T = \min_{0\le t\le T} S_t.$$

Concentrate on a floating put. Let the price at time t of the option be denoted by $V(t, S_t, M_t)$. The value of this option in the Black–Scholes model can be computed similarly to the previous example. Define

$$M_n(t) = \left(\int_0^t (S_\tau)^n\right)^{1/n}.$$

Then function $V(t, S, M_n)$ can be thought of as the price of an instrument depending on variable M_n. With computations similar to those in the previous example, we obtain the following equation

$$\frac{\partial V(t,S,M_n)}{\partial t} + rS\frac{\partial V(t,S,M_n)}{\partial S} + \frac{1}{n}\frac{S^n}{M_n^{n-1}}\frac{\partial V(t,S,M_n)}{\partial M_n} + \frac{1}{2}\sigma^2 S^2\frac{\partial^2 V(t,S,M_n)}{\partial S^2} - rV(t,S,M_n) = 0.$$

Since $S_t \le \max_{0\le\tau\le t} S_\tau = M_t$, then

$$\lim_{n\to\infty}\frac{1}{n}\frac{S^n}{(M_n)^{n-1}} = 0.$$

Observing that $\lim_{n\to\infty} M_n(t) = M_t$, we obtain the equation for $V(t,S,M)$

$$\frac{\partial V(t,S,M)}{\partial t} + rS\frac{\partial V(t,S,M)}{\partial S} + \frac{1}{2}\sigma^2 S^2 \frac{\partial^2 V(t,S,M)}{\partial S^2} - rV(t,S,M) = 0.$$

The above equation is the standard one-dimensional Black–Scholes equation in which variable M plays the role of a parameter. This parameter enters, however, boundary and terminal conditions.

The terminal condition for this option is (observe that always $M_t \geq S_t$)

$$V(T,S,M) = M - S.$$

To impose boundary conditions, we observe that the problem is posed only in the region $0 \leq S \leq M$. For $S = 0$, the payoff is M, therefore, the boundary condition at $S = 0$ is the discounted payoff. At $S = M$, the changes to the option price are negligible to small changes in the maximum (if the maximum is changing, it is due to changes in S, hence, both changes compensate). These considerations lead to the boundary conditions

$$V(t,0,M) = Me^{-r(T-t)},$$
$$\frac{\partial V(t,S,M)}{\partial M} = 0 \quad \text{at } S = M.$$

To the above boundary value problem, we apply similarity reduction. Thus, we introduce the new variable $x = S/M$ and the factorization $V(t,S,M) = MW(t,x)$. For the floating put, payoff $h(S_T, M_T) = M_T - S_T$ can be expressed as $h(M,S) = M - S = M(1-x)$ and fits the above factorization of the option price. Inserting this factorization into the Black–Scholes equation, we obtain the equation for $W(t,x)$

$$\frac{\partial W(t,x)}{\partial t} + rx\frac{\partial W(t,x)}{\partial x} + \frac{1}{2}\sigma^2 x^2 \frac{\partial^2 W(t,x)}{\partial x^2} - rW(t,x) = 0, \;\; x \in (0,1), t \in [0,T),$$

with the terminal condition

$$W(T, x) = 1 - x, \quad x \in [0, 1],$$

and the boundary conditions

$$W(t, 0) = e^{-r(T-t)}, \quad t \in [0, T],$$
$$\frac{\partial W}{\partial x}(t, 1) = W(t, 1), \quad t \in [0, T].$$

The existence of solutions for vanilla and exotic options in $\mathbb{R}^d$ is not important in practice since obtaining numerical solutions on $\mathbb{R}^d$ is impossible. For numerical algorithms, we must limit considerations to a bounded domain $U \subset \mathbb{R}^d$ and introduce *artificial* boundaries and *artificial* boundary conditions. For initial-boundary value problems localized on bounded sets, the theory developed in Sobolev spaces without weights is applicable. The choice of a bounded domain U must be a compromise between the numerical error, which usually decreases with the size of U, and the computational complexity, which increases with the size of U.

A crucial problem in controlling numerical errors is the selection of artificial boundary conditions. In quantitative finance, hints can be found by analyzing the economic aspects of a problem. The nature of such hints is clearly visible in an example of vanilla options (we consider these options in variables (t, S), leaving to the reader the task of translating the obtained artificial boundary conditions into the variables used in transformed equations). For a call option, we have $\lim_{S\to 0} V(t, S) = 0$, which has an obvious economic interpretation. For large S, we can approximate the option price by $V(t, S) \approx S(t) - Ke^{-r(T-t)}$. This approximation is obtained by computing the present value at t of the payoff $(S(T) - K)$ (valid for large S). For the put option we have the obvious condition $\lim_{S\to\infty} V(t, S) = 0$ and the condition $\lim_{S\to 0} V(t, S) = Ke^{-r(T-t)}$, which is the discounted to t payoff K at T.

5.6 Exercises

Exercise 5.1. A function u: $U \to \mathbb{R}$ is called absolutely continuous on interval $U \subset \mathbb{R}$ if and only if for every $\varepsilon > 0$ there exists $\delta > 0$

such that for every finite sequence of pairwise disjoint subintervals $\{(x_k, y_k)\}_{k=1}^{L}$ of U

$$\sum_{k=1}^{L}(y_k - x_k) < \delta \Rightarrow \sum_{k=1}^{L} |u(y_k) - u(x_k)| < \varepsilon.$$

Let u be absolutely continuous on interval $U = (a, b)$. Show that u admits a weak derivative $v \in L^1(U)$ and that the weak derivative coincides with the classical derivative almost everywhere.

Exercise 5.2. Let $f \in L^p(\mathbb{R}^n)$, $1 \le p < \infty$. Let $f_h(x) = f(x - h)$, $h \in \mathbb{R}^n$. Prove that

$$\|f_h - f\|_{L^p} \to 0, \quad \text{as } |h| \to 0.$$

Hint: C^∞ functions with compact support in $\mathbb{R}^n$ are dense in L^p, $p \in [0, \infty)$.

Exercise 5.3. Let $U \subset \mathbb{R}^d$ be an open and bounded set. Prove that for $u \in W_0^{1,p}(U)$, $1 \le p < d$, the norm $\|u\|_{W^{1,p}(U)}$ is equivalent to $\|Du\|_{L^p(U)}$.

Exercise 5.4. Let $U = \{x \in \mathbb{R}^d : |x| < 1\}$, and

$$u(x) = \ln\left(\ln\left(1 + \frac{1}{|x|}\right)\right) \quad \text{on } U\backslash\{0\}.$$

Show that $u \in L^d(U)$.

Exercise 5.5. A function u: $\mathbb{R}^d \to \mathbb{R}$ is called harmonic if $\Delta u = 0$.

Prove that $\Delta(uv) = 2\nabla u \cdot \nabla v$ for harmonic functions $u, v : \mathbb{R}^d \to \mathbb{R}$.

Exercise 5.6. Compute a weak derivative of the function

$$f(x) = \begin{cases} x \ln|x|, & \text{for } x \in (-1, 0) \cup (0, 1), \\ 0, & \text{for } x = 0. \end{cases}$$

Find p, $1 \le p \le \infty$, such that $f \in W^{1,p}(-1, 1)$.

Exercise 5.7. Let

$$u(x) = \frac{|x|}{1+|x|^2}, \quad \text{for } x \in \mathbb{R}.$$

Prove that $u \in H^1(\mathbb{R})$.

Exercise 5.8. Let $U = \{x \in \mathbb{R}^d : |x| < 1\}$. Define

$$f(x) = (1-|x|)^s, s \in \mathbb{R}, \ x \in U.$$

Find p, $1 \le p \le \infty$, such that $f \in W^{1,p}(U)$.

Exercise 5.9. Solve the initial-boundary value problem for the heat equation

$$\begin{aligned}
&\frac{\partial u(t,x)}{\partial t} = \frac{\partial^2 u(t,x)}{\partial x^2}, \quad (t,x) \in (0,\infty) \times (0,\pi),\\
&u(t,0) = u(t,\pi) = 0, \quad 0 \le t < \infty,\\
&u(0,x) = \sin 2x, \quad x \in [0,\pi].
\end{aligned}$$

Exercise 5.10. Let U be an open domain in $\mathbb{R}^3$ with smooth boundary ∂U. Consider the Dirichlet problem

$$\begin{aligned}
&-\frac{\partial^2 u}{\partial x^2} - \frac{\partial^2 u}{\partial y^2} - 4\frac{\partial^2 u}{\partial z^2} + \frac{\partial u}{\partial x} + 2\frac{\partial u}{\partial y} + \frac{\partial u}{\partial z} + u = f,\\
&u(x,y,z) = 0, \quad \text{for } (x,y,z) \in \partial U,
\end{aligned}$$

where $f \in L^2(U)$.

Prove the existence of a weak solution to this Dirichlet problem. To which space does this solution belong?

Exercise 5.11. Let $u(t,x)$ be a smooth solution of the problem

$$\begin{aligned}
&\frac{\partial u}{\partial t} + u\frac{\partial u}{\partial x} = a^2\frac{\partial^2 u}{\partial x^2}, \quad 0 < x < 1, \quad t > 0,\\
&u(t,0) = u(t,1) = 0, \quad t > 0,\\
&u(0,x) = g(x), \quad 0 \le x \le 1,
\end{aligned}$$

where a is a real constant.

Prove that the L^2-norm of this solution

$$\|u(t)\|^2 = \int_0^1 |u(t,x)|^2 dx$$

is a decreasing function of time.

Exercise 5.12. Let u be a smooth solution of the Dirichlet problem

$$\begin{aligned}
&\frac{\partial u}{\partial t} - \Delta u + c(x)u = 0, \quad (t,x) \in (0,\infty) \times U,\\
&u = 0, \quad (t,x) \in [0,\infty) \times \partial U,\\
&u = g, \quad (t,x) \in \{t = 0\} \times U,
\end{aligned}$$

where U is a bounded domain in $\mathbb{R}^n$ with a smooth boundary ∂U.

Prove that if $g(x) \geq 0$ and $c(x) \geq \gamma$ for $x \in U$, where γ is a real constant, then $u(t,x) \geq 0$ for $(t,x) \in [0,T] \times U$.

Exercise 5.13. Define a weak solution to the Neumann problem for Poisson's equation

$$\begin{aligned}
-\Delta u &= f, \quad x \in U,\\
\frac{\partial u}{\partial \nu} &= 0, \quad x \in \partial U,
\end{aligned}$$

where $U \subset \mathbb{R}^d$ is a bounded domain with a smooth boundary, $f \in L^2(U)$, and ν is a unit normal vector outward to ∂U. Prove that the problem has a weak solution if and only if

$$\int_U f(x)dx = 0.$$

Exercise 5.14. Consider the initial-boundary value problem for the heat equation

$$\begin{aligned}
&\frac{\partial u}{\partial t} = \frac{\partial^2 u}{\partial x^2}, \quad x \in (0,1), t > 0,\\
&\frac{\partial u}{\partial x}(t,0) = \frac{\partial u}{\partial x}(t,1) = 0, \quad t > 0,\\
&u(0,x) = g(x), \quad x \in (0,1),
\end{aligned}$$

where $g(x)$ is a bounded, continuous function.

Show that the solution $u(t,x)$ satisfies

$$\lim_{t\to\infty} u(t,x) = C, \quad \text{for all } x \in (0,1),$$

for constant C. Compute this constant.

Exercise 5.15. Consider the Black–Scholes model with a risky asset price S_t. The geometric average-rate call option for that asset has the payoff

$$\max\left(\exp\left(\frac{1}{T}\int_0^T \ln(S_t)dt\right) - K, 0\right),$$

with an obvious change in the formula for the put option.

Show that the price $V(t,S,A)$ of a geometric average-rate option satisfies the equation

$$\frac{\partial V}{\partial t} + \frac{1}{2}\sigma^2 S^2 \frac{\partial^2 V}{\partial S^2} + rS\frac{\partial V}{\partial S} + \ln S\frac{\partial V}{\partial A} = rV,$$

where $A(t) = \int_0^t \ln S(u)du$.

Exercise 5.16. Consider the Black–Scholes model with two assets of prices $S_1(t)$ and $S_2(t)$. The dynamics of these prices are given by the equations

$$dS_i(t) = rS_i(t)dt + \sigma_i S_i(t)dW_i(t), \quad i = 1,2,$$

where the Wiener processes W_1 and W_2 are correlated with correlation ρ.

Show that the differential equation for the option price $V(t,S_1,S_2)$ is

$$\frac{\partial V}{\partial t} + \frac{1}{2}\sum_{i=1}^{2}\sigma_i^2 S_i^2 \frac{\partial^2 V}{\partial S_i^2} + \sum_{i=1}^{2} rS_i\frac{\partial V}{\partial S_i} + \rho\sigma_1\sigma_2 S_1 S_2 \frac{\partial^2 V}{\partial S_1 \partial S_2} = rV.$$

Exercise 5.17. A strangle is an option combination in which an investor takes a long position in a call and in a put on the same share with price S_t and with the same expiry date T but with different strike prices (K_1 for the call, and K_2 for the put, with $K_1 > K_2$). Write the Black–Scholes equation for the strangle pricing. Determine suitable boundary conditions, i.e., values at $S = 0$ and for S "large", and a terminal condition (value at $t = T$).

Exercise 5.18. The cash-or-nothing binary call/put option has the payoff

$$V(T, S_T) = B\mathbb{1}_{\{S_T > K\}}, \quad \text{for call,}$$
$$V(T, S_T) = B\mathbb{1}_{\{S_T < K\}}, \quad \text{for put,}$$

where B is a constant (the payoff if the option is in-the-money).

For the asset-or-nothing options, the payoffs are

$$V(T, S_T) = S_T\mathbb{1}_{\{S_T > K\}}, \quad \text{for call,}$$
$$V(T, S_T) = S_T\mathbb{1}_{\{S_T < K\}}, \quad \text{for put.}$$

Show that in the Black–Scholes model, the closed-form solutions of the cash-or-nothing puts are

$$V(t, S_t) = Be^{-r(T-t)}\Phi(-d_2),$$

and for the asset-or-nothing puts

$$V(t, S_t) = S_t\Phi(-d_1),$$

where

$$d_1 = \frac{\ln(S_t/K) + (r + \sigma^2/2)(T-t)}{\sigma\sqrt{T-t}},$$

$$d_2 = \frac{\ln(S_t/K) + (r - \sigma^2/2)(T-t)}{\sigma\sqrt{T-t}}.$$

Exercise 5.19. Let $V(t, S)$ be a solution of the problem

$$\frac{\partial V(t,S)}{\partial t} + \frac{1}{2}\sigma^2 S^2 \frac{\partial^2 V(t,S)}{\partial S^2} + \mu S \frac{\partial V(t,S)}{\partial S} - rV(t,S) = 0, \; S \geq 0,$$
$$V(T, S) = g(S), \quad 0 \leq S < \infty$$

with $r = r(t)$, $\mu = \mu(t)$, and $\sigma = \sigma(t)$ nonconstant, known functions of t.

Introduce new independent variables $x = \ln(S)$, $\tau = T - t$ and define

$$a(\tau) = \frac{1}{2}\int_0^\tau \sigma^2(T-s)ds,$$

$$b(\tau) = \int_0^\tau \mu(T-s)ds,$$

$$c(\tau) = \int_0^\tau r(T-s)ds.$$

Define $y = x + b(\tau) - a(\tau)$ and a new time variable $\eta = a(\tau)$.

Show that $u(\eta, y) = e^{c(\tau)}V(T-\tau, e^{y+a(\tau)-b(\tau)})$, where $\tau = a^{-1}(\eta)$, fulfills the heat equation

$$\frac{\partial u}{\partial \eta} = \frac{\partial^2 u}{\partial y^2},$$
$$u(0, y) = g(e^y).$$

Exercise 5.20. Derive the pricing equation for a European option, assuming the stock price is governed by the arithmetic Brownian motion

$$dS_t = \mu dt + \sigma dW_t.$$

Exercise 5.21. Assume that European call prices are available for all strikes K. Consider call prices $V(t, K)$ for a fixed S as a function of strike K. Prove that price $V(t, K)$ satisfies the equation called the *Dupire equation*

$$\frac{\partial V(t,K)}{\partial t} + \frac{1}{2}\sigma^2 K^2 \frac{\partial^2 V(t,K)}{\partial K^2} - rK\frac{\partial V(t,K)}{\partial K} = 0.$$

Exercise 5.22. Prove that the formula

$$e^{-rT}\int_K^\infty (y-K)\frac{1}{\sigma y\sqrt{2\pi T}}\exp\left(-\frac{\ln(y/S_0)-(r-\sigma^2/2)T}{2\sigma^2 T}\right)dy$$

is equivalent to the Black–Scholes formula for European calls.

Chapter 6

Finite Difference Methods for Parabolic Equations

The finite difference approximation is the oldest method of solving numerically differential equations. The first applications were developed already by Euler. Finite difference methods are based on estimating derivatives by differential quotients.

In this chapter, we shall be concerned with the numerical solution of parabolic equations by finite differences. We first discuss, in Section 6.1, elementary finite difference algorithms applied to the heat equation and one-dimensional linear parabolic equations and examine their basic properties. Following this, the important concepts of convergence, consistency, and stability will be presented and shown to be related by the Lax equivalence theorem. Special attention will be given to the concept of the stability of difference schemes. The discussion of the schemes' stability in Section 6.4 will begin with the stability in the maximum norm and then extended to a thorough analysis of the von Neumann stability in the L^2 norm. The chapter concludes by discussing difference schemes in two and three dimensions.

The reader interested in a deeper understanding of difference schemes is referred to advanced textbooks on finite difference methods, e.g., Larsson and Thomée [59], Morton and Mayers [65], Strikwerda [85], or Thomas [87]. Financial applications of finite differences are treated in many computational finance textbooks, particularly in the books by Achdou and Pironneau [1], Duffy [23], Hirsa [39], and Seydel [79].

6.1 Introduction to Finite Differences

We begin by presenting finite difference methods for the model problem of one-dimensional heat conduction

$$\frac{\partial u(t,x)}{\partial t} - \frac{\partial^2 u(t,x)}{\partial x^2} = 0.$$

We consider the problem in a bounded interval $(x_{\min}, x_{\max})$ for $t \in [0,T]$. The interval $(x_{\min}, x_{\max})$ is divided into M subintervals and the time interval $[0,T]$ into N subintervals. We set

$$\delta x = \frac{x_{\max} - x_{\min}}{M}, \qquad \delta t = \frac{T}{N}.$$

The points

$$x_k := x_{\min} + k \cdot \delta x, \quad k = 0, 1, \ldots, M, \quad t_n := n \cdot \delta t, \quad n = 0, 1, \ldots, N,$$

are called the *grid points* (or the *mesh points*).

The heat equation derivatives are approximated by finite differences

$$\begin{aligned} \frac{\partial u}{\partial t}(t_n, x_k) &\approx \frac{u(t_{n+1}, x_k) - u(t_n, x_k)}{\delta t} \\ \frac{\partial^2 u}{\partial x^2}(t_n, x_k) &\approx \frac{u(t_n, x_{k+1}) - 2u(t_n, x_k) + u(t_n, x_{k-1})}{(\delta x)^2}. \end{aligned}$$

The approximation of $u(t_n, x_k)$ is denoted by u_k^n.

We now define several simple difference schemes that approximate a solution of the heat equation.

Euler explicit scheme. In the Euler explicit scheme, we approximate the time derivative by a forward difference

$$\frac{u_k^{n+1} - u_k^n}{\delta t} - \frac{u_{k+1}^n - 2u_k^n + u_{k-1}^n}{(\delta x)^2} = 0.$$

Thus, the heat equation approximation satisfies

$$u_k^{n+1} = \lambda u_{k+1}^n + (1 - 2\lambda) u_k^n + \lambda u_{k-1}^n,$$

where $\lambda = \delta t / (\delta x)^2$.

Introducing the vector

$$U^n = (u_1^n, u_2^n, \dots, u_{M-1}^n)$$

(u_0^n and u_M^n are omitted as known from the boundary conditions), we can write the scheme in matrix form

$$BU^{n+1} = AU^n + d^n,$$

where B is identity matrix of dimension $(M-1) \times (M-1)$ and

$$A = \begin{pmatrix} 1-2\lambda & \lambda & & 0 \\ \lambda & \ddots & \lambda & \\ & \ddots & \ddots & \ddots \\ 0 & & \ddots & \ddots \end{pmatrix}, \quad d^n = \begin{pmatrix} \lambda u_0^n \\ 0 \\ \vdots \\ 0 \\ \lambda u_M^n \end{pmatrix},$$

with A of dimension $(M-1) \times (M-1)$ and d^n of dimension $M-1$.

Euler implicit scheme. In that scheme, we approximate the time derivative by a backward difference to obtain

$$\frac{u_k^{n+1} - u_k^n}{\delta t} - \frac{u_{k+1}^{n+1} - 2u_k^{n+1} + u_{k-1}^{n+1}}{(\delta x)^2} = 0.$$

Then we get the equation

$$-\lambda u_{k+1}^{n+1} + (1+2\lambda)u_k^{n+1} - \lambda u_{k-1}^{n+1} = u_k^n,$$

which can be written in matrix form

$$BU^{n+1} = AU^n + d^n$$

with identity matrix A of dimension $(M-1) \times (M-1)$ and

$$B = \begin{pmatrix} 1+2\lambda & -\lambda & & 0 \\ -\lambda & \ddots & -\lambda & \\ & \ddots & \ddots & \ddots \\ 0 & & \ddots & \ddots \end{pmatrix}, \quad d^n = \begin{pmatrix} \lambda u_0^{n+1} \\ 0 \\ \vdots \\ 0 \\ \lambda u_M^{n+1} \end{pmatrix},$$

where B is $(M-1) \times (M-1)$-dimensional and d^n, $(M-1)$-dimensional.

Crank–Nicolson scheme. This scheme can be considered a "linear combination" of the explicit and implicit Euler schemes

$$-\frac{\lambda}{2}u_{k-1}^{n+1} + (1+\lambda)u_k^{n+1} - \frac{\lambda}{2}u_{k+1}^{n+1} = \frac{\lambda}{2}u_{k-1}^{n} + (1-\lambda)u_k^{n} + \frac{\lambda}{2}u_{k+1}^{n}.$$

The matrix form of this scheme is similar to the previous two schemes

$$BU^{n+1} = AU^n + d^n$$

but with different matrices

$$B = \begin{pmatrix} 1+\lambda & -\frac{\lambda}{2} & & 0 \\ -\frac{\lambda}{2} & \ddots & -\frac{\lambda}{2} & \\ & \ddots & \ddots & \ddots \\ 0 & & \ddots & \ddots \end{pmatrix}, \quad d^n = \frac{\lambda}{2}\begin{pmatrix} u_0^n + u_0^{n+1} \\ 0 \\ \vdots \\ 0 \\ u_M^n + u_M^{n+1} \end{pmatrix},$$

$$A = \begin{pmatrix} 1-\lambda & \frac{\lambda}{2} & & 0 \\ \frac{\lambda}{2} & \ddots & \frac{\lambda}{2} & \\ & \ddots & \ddots & \ddots \\ 0 & & \ddots & \ddots \end{pmatrix}.$$

Consider now a general, one-dimensional, linear, parabolic equation

$$\frac{\partial u}{\partial t} - a^2(t,x)\frac{\partial^2 u}{\partial x^2} + b(t,x)\frac{\partial u}{\partial x} + c(t,x)u = 0. \tag{6.1}$$

To obtain a finite difference approximation of this equation, we approximate the first-order x derivative by the expression

$$\frac{\partial u}{\partial x}(t_n, x_k) \approx \frac{u(t_n, x_{k+1}) - u(t_n, x_{k-1})}{2\delta x}.$$

Denoting, as previously, by u_k^n the approximation of $u(t_n, x_k)$ we obtain for the schemes defined above the matrix equation

$$B^{n+1}U^{n+1} = A^n U^n + d^n.$$

Since the coefficients in (6.1) are time-dependent, we obtain different matrices A^n and B^n on different time levels. The forms of A^n, B^{n+1}, and d^n depend on the scheme employed.

For the Euler explicit scheme B^{n+1} is an identity matrix and A^n is tridiagonal with the elements:

$$\begin{aligned} A^n_{k,k} &= 1 - 2\lambda\left(a^n_k\right)^2 - \delta t\, c^n_k, \\ A^n_{k,k+1} &= -\frac{\gamma}{2} b^n_{k+1} + \lambda\left(a^n_{k+1}\right)^2, \\ A^n_{k,k-1} &= \frac{\gamma}{2} b^n_{k-1} + \lambda\left(a^n_{k-1}\right)^2, \end{aligned}$$

where

$$\lambda = \frac{\delta t}{(\delta x)^2}, \quad \gamma = \frac{\delta t}{\delta x}.$$

The vector d^n has all zero elements except the first and last elements given by the expressions

$$d^n_1 = \lambda\left(a^n_0\right)^2 u^n_0 + \frac{\gamma}{2} b^n_0 u^n_0, \quad d^n_{M-1} = \lambda\left(a^n_M\right)^2 u^n_M - \frac{\gamma}{2} b^n_M u^n_M.$$

For the Euler implicit scheme A^n is an identity matrix and B^{n+1} is tridiagonal with the elements:

$$\begin{aligned} B^{n+1}_{k,k} &= 1 + 2\lambda\left(a^{n+1}_k\right)^2 + \delta t\, c^{n+1}_k, \\ B^{n+1}_{k,k+1} &= \frac{\gamma}{2} b^{n+1}_{k+1} - \lambda\left(a^{n+1}_{k+1}\right)^2, \\ B^{n+1}_{k,k-1} &= -\frac{\gamma}{2} b^{n+1}_{k-1} - \lambda\left(a^{n+1}_{k-1}\right)^2. \end{aligned}$$

For the first and last elements of d^n, we have

$$\begin{aligned} d^n_1 &= \lambda\left(a^{n+1}_0\right)^2 u^{n+1}_0 + \frac{\gamma}{2} b^{n+1}_0 u^{n+1}_0, \\ d^n_{M-1} &= \lambda\left(a^{n+1}_M\right)^2 u^{n+1}_M - \frac{\gamma}{2} b^{n+1}_M u^{n+1}_M. \end{aligned}$$

For the Crank–Nicolson scheme the corresponding matrices are tridiagonal with the elements:

$$\begin{aligned} B^{n+1}_{k,k} &= 1 + \lambda\left(a^{n+1}_k\right)^2 + \frac{\delta t}{2} c^{n+1}_k, \\ B^{n+1}_{k,k+1} &= \frac{\gamma}{4} b^{n+1}_{k+1} - \frac{\lambda}{2}\left(a^{n+1}_{k+1}\right)^2, \\ B^{n+1}_{k,k-1} &= -\frac{\gamma}{4} b^{n+1}_{k-1} - \frac{\lambda}{2}\left(a^{n+1}_{k-1}\right)^2, \end{aligned}$$

and

$$A^n_{k,k} = 1 - \lambda\big(a^n_k\big)^2 - \frac{\delta t}{2}c^n_k,$$

$$A^n_{k,k+1} = -\frac{\gamma}{4}b^n_{k+1} + \frac{\lambda}{2}\big(a^n_{k+1}\big)^2,$$

$$A^n_{k,k-1} = \frac{\gamma}{4}b^n_{k-1} + \frac{\lambda}{2}\big(a^n_{k-1}\big)^2.$$

For d^n, we have

$$d^n_1 = \frac{\lambda}{2}\Big(\big(a^n_0\big)^2 u^n_0 + \big(a^{n+1}_0\big)^2 u^{n+1}_0\Big) + \frac{\gamma}{4}\Big(b^n_0 u^n_0 + b^{n+1}_0 u^{n+1}_0\Big),$$

$$d^n_{M-1} = \frac{\lambda}{2}\Big(\big(a^n_M\big)^2 u^n_M + \big(a^{n+1}_M\big)^2 u^{n+1}_M\Big) - \frac{\gamma}{4}\Big(b^n_M u^n_M + b^{n+1}_M u^{n+1}_M\Big).$$

6.2 Convergence Analysis of Two-Level Schemes

We restrict the analysis of convergence to two-time-level schemes for the linear, parabolic initial-boundary value problem

$$\begin{aligned} &\frac{\partial u}{\partial t} + \mathcal{A}^t u = f, \quad \text{in} \ \ (0,T] \times U, \\ &u = 0, \quad \text{on} \ \ [0,T] \times \partial U, \\ &u = g, \quad \text{on} \ \ \{t = 0\} \times U, \end{aligned} \tag{6.2}$$

where $\mathcal{A}^t$ is the uniformly parabolic operator of Definition 5.29.

We introduce a grid in U, i.e., a discrete set J_U of grid points $x_{\boldsymbol{k}}$ indexed by vectors $\boldsymbol{k}$ with integer components k_i, $i = 1, \ldots, d$. For $U \subset \mathbb{R}^d$, the discretization spacing δx_i can depend on the direction x_i; however, all δx_i are of the same order h, and we assume that all $\delta x_i \to 0$ with $h \to 0$. The interval $[0, T]$ is discretized with points t_n, $n = 0, 1, \ldots, N$, and the time step δt (this time step can be a function of h as well) such that $N\delta t = T$.

Let us define the localization operator

$$I_{\delta t,h}\colon\ C([0,T] \times U) \to \mathbb{R}^{(N+1)\times \# J_U}$$

which maps continuous functions to their values at grid nodes $u^n_{\boldsymbol{k}} = u(t_n, x_{\boldsymbol{k}})$, $x_{\boldsymbol{k}} \in J_U$, $n = 0, 1, \ldots, N$. For each t_n, we introduce a grid function $U^n = \{u^n_{\boldsymbol{k}}\}$ which is defined in the grid points of J_U.

We approximate the derivatives in the differential operator $\mathcal{A}^t$ by finite differences in the x variable and the time derivative by forward or backward finite differences. Then we obtain the following finite difference approximation for the differential problem (6.2)

$$L^{n+1}U^{n+1} = R^n U^n + F^n,$$

where the terms for time level $n+1$ are on the left-hand side of the equation, and the terms for time level n are on the right-hand side, and F^n is the localization of the nonhomogeneous term f. For the one-dimensional schemes of the previous section matrices L^n and R^n straightforwardly correspond to matrices B^n and A^n

$$B^n = \delta t L^n, \quad A^n = \delta t R^n.$$

Definition 6.1. The system of equations

$$L^{n+1}U^{n+1} = R^n U^n + F^n, \quad n = 0, 1, \ldots, N-1, \tag{6.3}$$

is called the *two-time-level difference scheme* for problem (6.2).

The difference scheme (6.3) is said to be *solvable* if

$$\|(L^n)^{-1}\| \leq C\delta t,$$

where the constant C is independent of n.

The solvability condition means that starting from U^0, we can compute grid function U^n in all subsequent time levels.

If u is a smooth function and U^n is a grid function obtained by localization of u, then we can expect the convergence

$$L^{n+1}U^{n+1} - R^n U^n - F^n \to \frac{\partial u}{\partial t} + \mathcal{A}^t u - f, \quad \text{as } \delta t, h \to 0.$$

This leads to the notion of *consistency* of a difference scheme.

Definition 6.2. For sufficiently smooth functions φ we define the *truncation error*

$$\Psi^n(\varphi) = L^{n+1} I^{n+1}_{\delta t,h} \varphi - R^n I^n_{\delta t,h}\varphi - F^n - I^n_{\delta t,h}\left(\frac{\partial \varphi}{\partial t} + \mathcal{A}^t \varphi - f\right),$$

where $I^n_{\delta t,h}\varphi$ denotes the localization of φ in the nth time level.

It is said that the difference scheme (6.3) is *consistent* with the differential problem (6.2) in norm $\|\cdot\|$ if

$$\lim_{h,\delta t\to 0} \|\Psi^n(\varphi)\| = 0 \quad \text{for } n = 0, \dots, N-1.$$

When there exist constants $C(\varphi)$, k_1, and k_2 such that

$$\|\Psi^n(\varphi)\| \le C(\varphi)\big(h^{k_1} + (\delta t)^{k_2}\big),$$

scheme is said to have the *order of approximation* k_1 in x and k_2 in t.

If the initial-boundary value problem (6.2) possesses a smooth solution, then, to simplify the definition, it is often assumed that φ is just this solution. Then the truncation error is

$$\Psi^n(\varphi) = L^{n+1} I^{n+1}_{\delta t,h}\varphi - R^n I^n_{\delta t,h}\varphi - F^n.$$

To compute the truncation errors of difference schemes, we use Taylor's expansions summarized in the following lemma.

Lemma 6.3. *Let $z \in C^4(J)$, where J is an open, bounded interval in $\mathbb{R}$. Then:*

$$\frac{z(x+h) - 2z(x) + z(x-h)}{h^2} = z''(x) + \frac{h^2}{12} z^{(4)}(x) + O(h^3),$$

$$\frac{z(x+h) - z(x-h)}{2h} = z'(x) + \frac{h^2}{6} z^{(3)}(x) + O(h^4),$$

$$\frac{z(x+h) - z(x)}{h} = z'(x) + \frac{h}{2} z''(x) + O(h^2).$$

Applying the above lemma, we compute the truncation errors for some well-known schemes.

Example 6.4. Let us compute the truncation error of the one-dimensional heat equation

$$\frac{\partial u}{\partial t} - \frac{\partial^2 u}{\partial x^2} = 0$$

approximated by the Euler explicit scheme

$$\frac{u_k^{n+1} - u_k^n}{\delta t} - \frac{u_{k+1}^n - 2u_k^n + u_{k-1}^n}{(\delta x)^2} = 0.$$

Assuming that u is a smooth solution of the heat equation and applying Taylor's expansions of Lemma 6.3, we obtain the truncation error

$$\Psi(u) = \left(\frac{1}{2}u_{tt}\delta t - \frac{1}{12}u_{xxxx}(\delta x)^2\right) + O\big((\delta t)^2\big) + O\big((\delta x)^3\big).$$

Thus, the accuracy of the Euler explicit scheme is $O(\delta t) + O\big((\delta x)^2\big)$.

Example 6.5. To the one-dimensional heat equation

$$\frac{\partial u}{\partial t} - \frac{\partial^2 u}{\partial x^2} = 0,$$

we apply the Du Fort–Frankel scheme

$$\frac{u_k^{n+1} - u_k^{n-1}}{2\delta t} - \frac{u_{k+1}^n - u_k^{n+1} - u_k^{n-1} + u_{k-1}^n}{(\delta x)^2} = 0.$$

The truncation error of this scheme computed up to order $O\big((\delta t)^2 + (\delta x)^2\big)$ is

$$\Psi(u) = \frac{1}{6}u_{ttt}(\delta t)^2 - \frac{1}{12}u_{xxxx}(\delta x)^2 + u_{tt}(\delta t)^2(\delta x)^{-2}.$$

Consistency with the heat equation, therefore, requires that not only $\delta t \to 0$ and $\delta x \to 0$ but also $\delta t/\delta x \to 0$. When $\delta t/\delta x = \gamma$, with constant γ, the scheme approximates

$$\gamma^2\frac{\partial^2 u}{\partial t^2} + \frac{\partial u}{\partial t} - \frac{\partial^2 u}{\partial x^2} = 0.$$

Definition 6.6. The difference scheme (6.3) is said to be *stable* with respect to initial conditions in norm $\|\cdot\|$ if for any two solutions U^n, V^n, with initial conditions U^0, V^0, respectively, and the same right-hand side F^n, there exists a constant C such that

$$\|U^n - V^n\| \le C\|U^0 - V^0\|, \quad n\delta t \le T.$$

If R^n and L^n are time-independent (they are constant in n), then the stability condition of the two-time-level scheme (6.3) can be written as

$$\|(L^{-1}R)^n\| \le C, \quad n\delta t \le T.$$

It is also possible to investigate stability with respect to the non-homogeneous term F^n, but that analysis will be not carried on.

Example 6.7. We show on a simple example of the advection equation

$$\frac{\partial u}{\partial t} + b\frac{\partial u}{\partial x} = 0,$$

how to analyze stability in the l^2-norm.

The equation is approximated by the forward-time, forward-space scheme

$$\frac{u_k^{n+1} - u_k^n}{\delta t} + b\frac{u_{k+1}^n - u_k^n}{\delta x} = 0.$$

To find a sufficient stability condition, we rewrite the scheme in the form

$$u_k^{n+1} = \alpha u_k^n + \beta u_{k+1}^n,$$

where $\alpha = 1 + b\gamma$ and $\beta = -b\gamma$, with $\gamma = \delta t/\delta x$.

To avoid the discussion of boundary conditions, we consider the problem for $x \in \mathbb{R}$. Then

$$\begin{aligned}
&\sum_{k=-\infty}^{\infty} |u_k^{n+1}|^2 \\
&\quad = \sum_{k=-\infty}^{\infty} \left|\alpha u_k^n + \beta u_{k+1}^n\right|^2 \\
&\quad \leq \sum_{k=-\infty}^{\infty} \left(|\alpha|^2|u_k^n|^2 + 2|\alpha||\beta||u_k^n||u_{k+1}^n| + |\beta|^2|u_{k+1}^n|^2\right) \\
&\quad \leq \sum_{k=-\infty}^{\infty} \left(|\alpha|^2|u_k^n|^2 + |\alpha||\beta|(|u_k^n|^2 + |u_{k+1}^n|^2) + |\beta|^2|u_{k+1}^n|^2\right) \\
&\quad = \sum_{k=-\infty}^{\infty} \left(|\alpha|^2|u_k^n|^2 + |\alpha||\beta||u_k^n|^2\right) \\
&\qquad + \sum_{k=-\infty}^{\infty} \left(|\beta|^2|u_{k+1}^n|^2 + |\alpha||\beta||u_{k+1}^n|^2\right)
\end{aligned}$$

$$= \sum_{k=-\infty}^{\infty} \left(|\alpha|^2 + 2|\alpha||\beta| + |\beta|^2\right)|u_k^n|^2 = \left(|\alpha| + |\beta|\right)^2 \sum_{k=-\infty}^{\infty} |u_k^n|^2.$$

This gives the relation

$$\sum_{k=-\infty}^{\infty} \left|u_k^n\right|^2 \leq \left(|\alpha| + |\beta|\right)^{2n} \sum_{k=-\infty}^{\infty} |u_k^0|^2.$$

If $\left(|\alpha| + |\beta|\right) \leq 1$, then the scheme is stable. This corresponds to the stability condition $-1 \leq b\gamma \leq 0$.

The above-defined stability of a difference scheme is closely related to the well-posedness of the corresponding differential problem.

Definition 6.8. The problem (6.2) is called *well-posed* in norm $\|\cdot\|$ if:

(1) There exists a unique solution of problem (6.2) for each initial data g such that $\|g\| < \infty$.
(2) There is a constant C such that for any two solutions u_1, u_2 of problem (6.2) with data g_1, g_2, f_1, f_2, respectively, we have the estimate

$$\|u_1(t) - u_2(t)\| \leq C\left(\|g_1 - g_2\| + \sup_{\tau\in[0,t]} \|f_1(\tau) - f_2(\tau)\|\right) \text{ for } t \leq T.$$

The following theorem explains the connection between consistency, stability, and convergence of difference schemes for well-posed differential problems.

Theorem 6.9 (Lax Equivalence Theorem). *If the problem* (6.2) *is linear, well-posed, and its discrete approximation is solvable and consistent, then the solution of the difference scheme* (6.3) *converges to the solution of* (6.2) *if and only if the difference scheme* (6.3) *is stable.*

Thus, if U^n is a solution of (6.3) *for a given discretization with grid J_U and time step δt and u is a solution of* (6.2), *then*

$$\|U^n - I_{\delta t,h}^n u\| \to 0 \quad \textit{for} \quad h, \delta t \to 0, \quad n\delta t \to t, \quad t \leq T.$$

When the scheme has the order of approximation k_1 in x and k_2 in t, then there is a constant C such that

$$\|U^n - I_{\delta t,h}^n u\| \leq C\left(h^{k_1} + (\delta t)^{k_2}\right).$$

Proof. We prove only that consistency and stability imply convergence. We assume that the operators L^n and R^n are time-independent. Hence, these operators are constant in n, and this superscript will be omitted. To simplify notation, we write u^n instead of $I^n_{\delta t,h}u$.

Assume that u is a smooth solution of (6.2) and consider the difference $U^n - u^n$. Then we have

$$L(U^{n+1} - u^{n+1}) = R(U^n - u^n) - \Psi^n,$$

where Ψ^n is the truncation error. Thus, we obtain

$$U^{n+1} - u^{n+1} = L^{-1}R(U^n - u^n) - L^{-1}\Psi^n,$$

and iterating

$$U^{n+1} - u^{n+1} = -\left(L^{-1}\Psi^n + L^{-1}RL^{-1}\Psi^{n-1} + \cdots + \left(L^{-1}R\right)^n L^{-1}\Psi^0\right).$$

By the stability and solvability conditions, we have the inequality

$$\|\left(L^{-1}R\right)^k L^{-1}\| \leq C\delta t,$$

which gives the estimate

$$\|U^n - u^n\| \leq C\delta t \sum_{i=0}^{n-1} \|\Psi^i\|.$$

If the scheme is consistent, then

$$\delta t \sum_{i=0}^{n-1} \|\Psi^i\| \leq N\delta t \max_{0\leq i\leq N-1} \|\Psi^i\| \to 0 \quad \text{as } h, \delta t \to 0,$$

which completes the proof.

Now assume u is not smooth. For smooth initial data $\tilde{g}$ and nonhomogeneous terms $\tilde{f}$, we obtain smooth solutions of (6.2) by Theorem 5.36 and Remark 5.37. Let $\tilde{g} \in C^\infty(U)$ and $\tilde{f} \in C^\infty(U_T)$ be such that ($\tilde{g}$ and $\tilde{f}$ exist due to Theorem 5.16)

$$\|g - \tilde{g}\| + \sup_{t\in[0,T]} \|f(t) - \tilde{f}(t)\| \leq \varepsilon.$$

Let now $\tilde{u}$ be a smooth solution of (6.2) with the above $\tilde{g}$ and $\tilde{f}$. By the well-posedness of (6.2), we get

$$\|u(t) - \tilde{u}(t)\| \le C(t) \left(\|g - \tilde{g}\| + \sup_{\tau \in [0,t]} \|f(\tau) - \tilde{f}(\tau)\| \right) \le \varepsilon C.$$

Taking $\widetilde{U}^n$ a solution of the difference scheme (6.3) corresponding to $\tilde{u}$, we obtain the convergence

$$\begin{aligned} \|U^n - u^n\| &= \|U^n - \widetilde{U}^n + \widetilde{U}^n - \tilde{u}^n + \tilde{u}^n - u^n\| \\ &\le \|U^n - \widetilde{U}^n\| + \|\widetilde{U}^n - \tilde{u}^n\| + \|\tilde{u}^n - u^n\| \to 0, \\ &\text{for} \quad h, \delta t \to 0, \end{aligned}$$

where the convergence $\|U^n - \widetilde{U}^n\| \to 0$ follows from the stability of (6.3), the convergence $\|\widetilde{U}^n - \tilde{u}^n\| \to 0$, from the consistency, and $\|\tilde{u}^n - u^n\| \to 0$ from the well-posedness of (6.2). □

Example 6.10. We show, without applying the Lax theorem, that the approximation for the heat equation with zero boundary conditions

$$\frac{\partial u}{\partial t} - \frac{\partial^2 u}{\partial x^2} = 0, \quad u(t,0) = u(t,1) = 0, \quad u(0,x) = g(x),$$

obtained by the Euler explicit scheme, converges in the maximum norm.

Let $\phi_k^n = u_k^n - u(t_n, x_k)$ be the approximation error at grid point (t_n, x_k), where $u(t_n, x_k)$ denotes the localization of solution u at (t_n, x_k). Comparing the Euler scheme with the exact equation, we obtain the error equation

$$\phi_k^{n+1} = \lambda \phi_{k-1}^n + (1 - 2\lambda)\phi_k^n + \lambda \phi_{k+1}^n + \delta t \Psi_k^n,$$

where Ψ_k^n is the truncation error at point (t_n, x_k), and $\lambda = \delta t/(\delta x)^2$. This equation gives the estimate

$$|\phi_k^{n+1}| \le \lambda |\phi_{k-1}^n| + |1 - 2\lambda||\phi_k^n| + \lambda |\phi_{k+1}^n| + \delta t |\Psi_k^n|.$$

Taking the maximum norm of the right-hand side, we obtain the estimate

$$|\phi_k^{n+1}| \le \big(\lambda + |1 - 2\lambda| + \lambda\big) \|\phi^n\|_\infty + \delta t \|\Psi^n\|_\infty,$$

where $\|w\|_\infty = \max_{0 \le k \le M} |w_k|$.

Assuming that $\lambda \leq 1/2$, we obtain

$$\|\phi^{n+1}\|_\infty \leq \|\phi^n\|_\infty + \delta t \|\Psi^n\|_\infty.$$

Iterating this estimate, we have

$$\|\phi^{n+1}\|_\infty \leq \|\phi^{n-1}\|_\infty + \delta t\big(\|\Psi^n\|_\infty + \|\Psi^{n-1}\|_\infty\big).$$

Thus,

$$\|\phi^n\|_\infty \leq \|\phi^0\|_\infty + n\delta t Y,$$

where $Y = \max_{1\leq n\leq N} \|\Psi^n\|_\infty$. Assuming that the initial data for the Euler scheme are obtained by the localization of function $g(x)$, the initial data for the heat equation, we have the same initial data for both problems and $\|\phi^0\|_\infty = 0$. Then

$$\|\phi^n\|_\infty \leq TY.$$

Let us recall that the truncation error for the Euler explicit scheme up to terms $O\big(\delta t + (\delta x)^2\big)$ is (cf. Example 6.4)

$$\Psi(u) = \frac{1}{2} u_{tt}\delta t - \frac{1}{12} u_{xxxx}(\delta x)^2.$$

Assuming that the solution of the heat equation is sufficiently smooth, we have bounded derivatives u_{tt} and u_{xxxx} for $t \in [0, T]$ and $x \in (0, 1)$. Then $Y \to 0$ for $\delta t \to 0$ and $\delta x \to 0$, and the approximation error $\|\phi^n\|_\infty \to 0$. Hence, the Euler explicit scheme converges to the solution of the heat equation in the maximum norm when $\lambda \leq 1/2$.

Example 6.11. We now demonstrate how the convergence result of the previous example can be obtained using the Lax theorem. We know from Example 6.4 that the Euler scheme is consistent. To obtain convergence by the Lax theorem, we must prove stability.

Writing the Euler explicit scheme in the form

$$u_k^{n+1} = \lambda\left(u_{k-1}^n + u_{k+1}^n\right) + (1 - 2\lambda)u_k^n$$

and assuming that $\lambda \leq 1/2$, we notice that all coefficients on the right-hand side of the above equation are nonnegative. Hence,

$$\|U^{n+1}\|_\infty \leq 2\lambda\|U^n\|_\infty + (1-2\lambda)\|U^n\|_\infty.$$

The rearrangement of terms in the inequality yields

$$\|U^{n+1}\|_\infty \leq \|U^n\|_\infty,$$

which proves stability

$$\|U^n\|_\infty \leq \|U^0\|_\infty.$$

This, due to the Lax theorem, proves convergence in the maximum norm.

6.3 θ-schemes

Consider a one-dimensional version of problem (6.2). Then U is an open interval, and we can assume $U = (0,1)$ without loss of generality. Problem (6.2) can now be replaced by

$$\begin{aligned}
&\frac{\partial u}{\partial t} + \mathcal{A}^t u = f, \quad (t,x) \in (0,T] \times (0,1),\\
&u(t,0) = u(t,1) = 0, \quad t \in [0,T],\\
&u(0,x) = g(x), \quad x \in (0,1).
\end{aligned} \tag{6.4}$$

Assume that the coefficients of $\mathcal{A}^t$ and the nonhomogeneous term f in (6.4) are t independent. Then we can drop the superscript t from $\mathcal{A}^t$ and write

$$\mathcal{A}u = -a^2(x)\frac{\partial^2 u}{\partial x^2} + b(x)\frac{\partial u}{\partial x} + c(x)u.$$

Thus, the Euler explicit and implicit schemes, and the Crank–Nicolson scheme can be written by a single formula, the so-called *θ-scheme*,

$$(I + \theta A)U^{n+1} = \big(I - (1-\theta)A\big)U^n + \phi, \tag{6.5}$$

where

$$A_{k,k} = 2\lambda a_k^2 + \delta t\, c_k, \quad A_{k,k+1} = \frac{\gamma}{2} b_{k+1} - \lambda a_{k+1}^2,$$
$$A_{k,k-1} = -\frac{\gamma}{2} b_{k-1} - \lambda a_{k-1}^2,$$

when, as previously,

$$\lambda = \frac{\delta t}{(\delta x)^2}, \quad \gamma = \frac{\delta t}{\delta x},$$

and ϕ is a localization of f.

In the following theorem, we estimate the order of approximation for the θ-scheme (6.5).

Theorem 6.12. *The θ-scheme for the one-dimensional, linear, parabolic problem* (6.4) *has the order of approximation*

$$O\big((\theta - 1/2)\delta t\big) + O\big((\delta x)^2 + (\delta t)^2\big).$$

Proof. Consider the solution u of (6.4) of class $C^{2,4}\big((0,T)\times(0,1)\big)$. Since we consider the action of a finite difference operator on functions of continuous variables, we introduce the following notation:

$$u = u(\tau, \xi), \quad \text{the localization of } u \text{ at fixed point } (\tau, \xi),$$
$$u_t = \frac{\partial u}{\partial t}(\tau, \xi), \quad u_x = \frac{\partial u}{\partial x}(\tau, \xi),$$
$$\hat{u} = u(\tau + \delta t, \xi), \quad \bar{u} = u(\tau + \delta t/2, \xi), \quad u_\Delta = \frac{\hat{u} - u}{\delta t}.$$

For simplicity, assume that the coefficients of operator $\mathcal{A}$ are constant. Under this assumption, we define the grid difference operator

$$\Lambda u = -a^2 \frac{S^+u - 2u + S^-u}{(\delta x)^2} + b\frac{S^+u - S^-u}{2\delta x} + cu,$$

where S^+ and S^- denote shift operators $S^\pm u = S^\pm u(\tau, \xi) = u(\tau, \xi \pm \delta x)$. Then the θ-scheme for (6.4) has the form

$$u_\Delta + \Lambda\big(\theta\hat{u} + (1-\theta)u\big) = \phi,$$

where ϕ is a localization of f.

Since u is a solution of (6.4), then by Definition 6.2 the truncation error ψ is given by the expression

$$\psi = u_\Delta + \Lambda\big(\theta\hat{u} + (1-\theta)u\big) - \phi,$$

and is only a function of u. By Lemma 6.3, we get

$$\begin{aligned}\Lambda u &= -a^2 u_{xx} - a^2\frac{(\delta x)^2}{12}u_{xxxx} + O\big((\delta x)^3\big) + bu_x \\ &\quad + b\frac{(\delta x)^2}{6}u_{xxx} + O\big((\delta x)^4\big) \\ &\quad + cu = \mathcal{A}u + \frac{(\delta x)^2}{12}\mathcal{A}u_{xx} + O\big((\delta x)^2\big).\end{aligned}$$

To estimate the truncation error, we apply the identities that follow from the definition of u_Δ

$$\begin{aligned}\hat{u} &= \frac{1}{2}(\hat{u}+u) + \frac{1}{2}(\hat{u}-u) = \frac{1}{2}(\hat{u}+u) + \frac{1}{2}\delta t\, u_\Delta, \\ u &= \frac{1}{2}(\hat{u}+u) - \frac{1}{2}(\hat{u}-u) = \frac{1}{2}(\hat{u}+u) - \frac{1}{2}\delta t\, u_\Delta, \\ \theta\hat{u} + (1-\theta)u &= \frac{1}{2}(\hat{u}+u) + (\theta - 1/2)\delta t\, u_\Delta.\end{aligned}$$

Thus,

$$\psi = u_\Delta + \frac{1}{2}\Lambda(\hat{u}+u) + (\theta - 1/2)\delta t \Lambda u_\Delta - \phi. \tag{6.6}$$

By Taylor's expansion, we get

$$\begin{aligned}\hat{u} &= \bar{u} + \frac{1}{2}\delta t\,\bar{u}_t + \frac{(\delta t)^2}{8}\bar{u}_{tt} + O\big((\delta t)^3\big), \\ u &= \bar{u} - \frac{1}{2}\delta t\,\bar{u}_t + \frac{(\delta t)^2}{8}\bar{u}_{tt} + O\big((\delta t)^3\big), \\ \frac{1}{2}(\hat{u}+u) &= \bar{u} + \frac{(\delta t)^2}{8}\bar{u}_{tt} + O\big((\delta t)^3\big).\end{aligned}$$

Then the comparison of

$$u = \frac{1}{2}(\hat{u}+u) - \frac{1}{2}\delta t\, u_\Delta = \bar{u} + \frac{(\delta t)^2}{8}\bar{u}_{tt} - \frac{1}{2}\delta t\, u_\Delta + O\big((\delta t)^3\big)$$

with

$$u = \bar{u} - \frac{1}{2}\delta t\, \bar{u}_t + \frac{(\delta t)^2}{8}\bar{u}_{tt} + O\big((\delta t)^3\big)$$

gives

$$u_\Delta = \bar{u}_t + O\big((\delta t)^2\big).$$

Inserting into (6.6) the above expression for u_Δ and the expression for $(\hat{u}+u)/2$, we obtain

$$\psi = \bar{u}_t + \mathcal{A}\bar{u} + \frac{(\delta x)^2}{12}\mathcal{A}\bar{u}_{xx} + (\theta - 1/2)\delta t \mathcal{A}\bar{u}_t + \frac{(\delta x)^2}{12}(\theta - 1/2)\delta t \mathcal{A}\bar{u}_{txx} + O\big((\delta x)^2 + (\delta t)^2\big) - \phi.$$

We have $\bar{u}_t + \mathcal{A}\bar{u} = \bar{f}$ due to (6.4). Assuming the equality $\bar{f} = \phi$ (f is independent of t and the localization of f is properly chosen), we have

$$\psi = (\theta - 1/2)\delta t \mathcal{A}\bar{u}_t + O\big((\delta x)^2 + (\delta t)^2\big).$$

□

6.4 Stability of Difference Schemes

We now analyze the stability of the two-time-level difference schemes for the linear, parabolic problem (6.2). To simplify the presentation, we assume that the coefficients of (6.2) are time-independent and limit our analysis to stability with respect to the initial data. Let U^n and V^n be two solutions of scheme (6.3) with initial conditions U^0 and V^0, respectively. Put $W^n = U^n - V^n$. To prove that a scheme is stable in norm $\|\cdot\|$, we have to prove the following implication

$$LW^{n+1} = RW^n \quad \Longrightarrow \quad \|W^n\| \le C\|W^0\|, \quad n\delta t \le T,$$

where W^n fulfills zero boundary conditions.

The constant C is independent of n but generally depends on T, and, with increasing T, can lead to exponential growth of the numerical solution. Only when $C \le 1$ the solution is bounded by a universal constant for any T.

For parabolic problems, due to the maximum principle, it is very natural to prove stability in the l^∞ norm. As an example, we show the stability of θ-schemes.

Example 6.13. Consider the θ-schemes for the heat equation

$$\frac{u_k^{n+1}-u_k^n}{\delta t}=\theta\frac{u_{k+1}^{n+1}-2u_k^{n+1}+u_{k-1}^{n+1}}{(\delta x)^2}+(1-\theta)\frac{u_{k+1}^n-2u_k^n+u_{k-1}^n}{(\delta x)^2}.$$

We rewrite this equation in the form

$$\begin{aligned}(1+2\theta\lambda)u_k^{n+1}=&\,\theta\lambda(u_{k-1}^{n+1}+u_{k+1}^{n+1})+(1-\theta)\lambda(u_{k-1}^n+u_{k+1}^n)\\&+\big(1-2(1-\theta)\lambda\big)u_k^n.\end{aligned}$$

Assume that $\theta\geq 1-1/(2\lambda)$. Then all the coefficients on the right-hand side are nonnegative, which gives the estimate

$$\begin{aligned}(1+2\theta\lambda)\|U^{n+1}\|_\infty&\leq 2\theta\lambda\|U^{n+1}\|_\infty+2(1-\theta)\lambda\|U^n\|_\infty\\&+\big(1-2(1-\theta)\lambda\big)\|U^n\|_\infty,\end{aligned}$$

where $\|U^n\|_\infty=\max_{0\leq k\leq M}|u_k^n|$ is the l^∞ norm in $\mathbb{R}^{M+1}$. The rearrangement of terms in the inequality yields

$$\|U^{n+1}\|_\infty\leq\|U^n\|_\infty.$$

This gives

$$\|U^n\|_\infty\leq\|U^0\|_\infty$$

which proves for $\theta\geq 1-\frac{1}{2\lambda}$ the stability of θ-schemes with $C=1$.

The maximum principle for parabolic equations can help establish stability in the supremum norm. However, there are numerical schemes that do not satisfy the discrete maximum principle. It appears that a more convenient is the stability analysis in the l^2 norm. In addition, in the l^2 setting, we can use Fourier's analysis, which is particularly suitable for constant-coefficient problems. Before proceeding to the stability analysis of the two-time-level schemes, we recall some facts from linear algebra.

Lemma 6.14. *Let A be a symmetric matrix in $\mathbb{R}^M$. Then*

$$\rho(A) = \|A\|,$$

where $\|A\|$ denotes the operator norm of A implied by the Euclidean norm in $\mathbb{R}^M$, and $\rho(A)$ denotes the spectral radius of A

$$\rho(A) = \max_{\mu \in \sigma(A)} |\mu|,$$

where $\sigma(A)$ is the spectrum of A, the set of all eigenvalues of A.

For nonsymmetric matrices in $\mathbb{R}^M$, we have only the inequality

$$\rho(A) \leq \|A\|.$$

Lemma 6.15. *Let A be the matrix defined for the θ-scheme (6.5) implied by the operator $\mathcal{A}$ with constant coefficients. Then A is tridiagonal with elements*

$$A_{k,k} = 2\lambda a^2 + \delta t\, c, \quad A_{k,k+1} = \frac{\gamma}{2}b - \lambda a^2, \quad A_{k,k-1} = -\frac{\gamma}{2}b - \lambda a^2.$$

For $\gamma b \neq 2\lambda a^2$, the eigenproblem

$$Ar^{(j)} = \mu_j r^{(j)}$$

has the eigenvalues

$$\mu_j = \delta t\, c + 2\lambda a^2 - \sqrt{4\lambda^2 a^4 - \gamma^2 b^2} \cos \frac{j\pi}{M}, \quad j = 1, \ldots, M-1,$$

and the eigenvectors

$$r^{(j)} = \left(\left(\frac{2\lambda a^2 + \gamma b}{2\lambda a^2 - \gamma b} \right)^{1/2} \sin \frac{j\pi}{M}, \ldots, \left(\frac{2\lambda a^2 + \gamma b}{2\lambda a^2 - \gamma b} \right)^{1/2} \sin \frac{(M-1)j\pi}{M} \right).$$

We now consider problem (6.2) for constant coefficients. Then, in the l^2 setting, we have the following stability result for the θ-schemes.

Theorem 6.16. *Let A be the matrix defined in Lemma 6.15. Assume that the eigenvalues of the symmetric part of this matrix, obtained by setting $b = 0$, are positive. This assumption corresponds to the inequality*

$$c > -\frac{4a^2}{(\delta x)^2} \sin^2 \frac{\pi}{2M} \approx -a^2\pi^2, \tag{6.7}$$

where we have substituted $\delta x\, M = 1$, the size of the spatial domain $U = (0,1)$.

If A is symmetric ($b = 0$), then the θ-scheme

$$(I + \theta A)U^{n+1} = (I - (1-\theta)A)U^n$$

is stable in the l^2-norm for

$$\theta \geq \frac{1}{2} - \frac{1}{4\lambda a^2 + \delta t\, c}.$$

For the nonsymmetric matrix A (with $b \neq 0$), the θ-scheme is stable if (6.7) holds and $\theta \geq 1/2$.

Proof. Taking into account equation (6.5) defining θ-schemes, a sufficient condition for stability is

$$\left\| (I + \theta A)^{-1}\big(I - (1-\theta)A\big) \right\| \leq 1.$$

Since

$$\big(I - (1-\theta)A\big) = I + \theta A - \frac{1}{\theta}(I + \theta A) + \frac{1}{\theta}I = \left(1 - \frac{1}{\theta}\right)(I + \theta A) + \frac{1}{\theta}I,$$

we have

$$(I + \theta A)^{-1}\big(I - (1-\theta)A\big) = \left(1 - \frac{1}{\theta}\right)I + \frac{1}{\theta}(I + \theta A)^{-1}.$$

Let A be symmetric ($b = 0$). Then also $(I + \theta A)^{-1}$ is symmetric and the norm of

$$\left(1 - \frac{1}{\theta}\right)I + \frac{1}{\theta}(I + \theta A)^{-1}$$

is equal to its spectral radius. Then the estimate we are looking for can be reduced to

$$\max_{\mu_j} \left| \left(1 - \frac{1}{\theta}\right) + \frac{1}{\theta(1 + \theta \mu_j)} \right| \leq 1,$$

where μ_j are the eigenvalues of A.

By Lemma 6.15, we have

$$\mu_j = \delta t\, c + 2\lambda a^2 - 2\lambda a^2 \cos\frac{j\pi}{M} = \delta t\, c + 4\lambda a^2 \sin^2\frac{j\pi}{2M},$$
$$j = 1, \ldots, M-1.$$

The condition

$$\left(1 - \frac{1}{\theta}\right) + \frac{1}{\theta(1+\theta\mu_j)} \leq 1$$

gives

$$\theta - 1 + \frac{1}{1+\theta\mu_j} \leq \theta \Rightarrow \theta\mu_j \geq 0 \Rightarrow \mu_j \geq 0,$$

which is (6.7).

The condition

$$\left(1 - \frac{1}{\theta}\right) + \frac{1}{\theta(1+\theta\mu_j)} \geq -1$$

gives

$$\theta - 1 + \frac{1}{1+\theta\mu_j} \geq -\theta \Rightarrow -1 + \frac{1}{1+\theta\mu_j} \geq -2\theta$$
$$\Rightarrow \frac{\mu_j}{1+\theta\mu_j} \leq 2 \Rightarrow \theta \geq \frac{1}{2} - \frac{1}{\mu_j}.$$

Taking into account the values of μ_j given by Lemma 6.15, we obtain

$$\max_j\left(-\frac{1}{\mu_j}\right) = -\frac{1}{\max_j \mu_j} \leq -\frac{1}{\delta t\, c + 4\lambda a^2}.$$

Hence, if

$$\theta \geq \frac{1}{2} - \frac{1}{\delta t\, c + 4\lambda a^2}$$

and (6.7) holds, then the spectral radius is not greater than 1.

The stability of the nonsymmetric matrix A (with $b \neq 0$) follows from the estimate

$$\|(I+\theta A)^{-1}(I-(1-\theta)A)\| = \left\| \left(1-\frac{1}{\theta}\right) I + \frac{1}{\theta}(I+\theta A)^{-1} \right\| \leq 1.$$

Taking $U \in \mathbb{R}^{M-1}$, we get ($\|\cdot\|_2$ and $(\cdot,\cdot)$ denote the l^2-norm and the corresponding scalar product in $\mathbb{R}^{M-1}$)

$$\begin{aligned}
&\left\| \left(\left(1-\frac{1}{\theta}\right) I + \frac{1}{\theta}(I+\theta A)^{-1} \right) U \right\|_2^2 \\
&= \left(1-\frac{1}{\theta}\right)^2 \|U\|_2^2 + \frac{1}{\theta}\left(1-\frac{1}{\theta}\right)(U,(I+\theta A)^{-1}U) \\
&\quad + \frac{1}{\theta}\left(1-\frac{1}{\theta}\right)((I+\theta A)^{-1}U,U) + \frac{1}{\theta^2}\|(I+\theta A)^{-1}U\|_2^2 \\
&= \left(\frac{1}{\theta}-1\right)^2 \|U\|_2^2 \\
&\quad - \frac{1}{\theta}\left(\frac{1}{\theta}-1\right)((I+\theta A)(I+\theta A)^{-1}U,(I+\theta A)^{-1}U) \\
&\quad - \frac{1}{\theta}\left(\frac{1}{\theta}-1\right)((I+\theta A)^{-1}U,(I+\theta A)(I+\theta A)^{-1}U) \\
&\quad + \frac{1}{\theta^2}\|(I+\theta A)^{-1}U\|_2^2 \\
&= \left(\frac{1}{\theta}-1\right)^2 \|U\|_2^2 \\
&\quad - \frac{1}{\theta}\left(\frac{1}{\theta}-1\right)((I+\theta A)^{-1}U,(I+\theta A)^{\top}(I+\theta A)^{-1}U) \\
&\quad - \frac{1}{\theta}\left(\frac{1}{\theta}-1\right)((I+\theta A)^{-1}U,(I+\theta A)(I+\theta A)^{-1}U) \\
&\quad + \frac{1}{\theta^2}\|(I+\theta A)^{-1}U\|_2^2 \\
&= \left(\frac{1}{\theta}-1\right)^2 \|U\|_2^2 + \left(\frac{2}{\theta}-\frac{1}{\theta^2}\right)\|(I+\theta A)^{-1}U\|_2^2 \\
&\quad - \left(\frac{1}{\theta}-1\right)((I+\theta A)^{-1}U,(A+A^{\top})(I+\theta A)^{-1}U).
\end{aligned}$$

To complete the proof, we show that the last expression is bounded by $\|U\|_2^2$.

This proof proceeds in several steps. First, we prove that if all eigenvalues of the symmetric part of A are positive, then $(U, AU) \geq C\|U\|_2^2$ with $C > 0$. Let A_0 denote matrix A for $a^2 = 1$, $b = 0$, and $c = 0$. By simple computations, we obtain

$$(U, A_0 U) = \lambda \sum_{i=0}^{M-1} (u_i - u_{i+1})^2,$$

where the zero boundary conditions $u_0 = u_M = 0$ are used.

On the other hand, expanding U in a series of eigenvectors of A_0 and using the positivity of the eigenvalues of A_0, we get

$$(U, A_0 U) \geq \min_j \mu_j \|U\|_2^2 = 4\lambda \sin^2 \frac{\pi}{2M} \|U\|_2^2.$$

For matrix A, we obtain similarly

$$\begin{aligned}(U, AU) &= \lambda a^2 \sum_{i=0}^{M-1} (u_i - u_{i+1})^2 + c\delta t \|U\|_2^2 \\ &\geq \left(c\delta t + 4\lambda a^2 \sin^2 \frac{\pi}{2M}\right) \|U\|_2^2 \geq C\|U\|_2^2.\end{aligned}$$

This proves that $(U, (I + \theta A)U) \geq C\|U\|_2^2$, with $C \geq 1$, which implies that $(I + \theta A)$ is invertible and gives

$$\left\|(I + \theta A)^{-1} U\right\|_2^2 \leq \|U\|_2^2.$$

The estimate for (U, AU) also shows that $(A + A^\top)$ is positive definite and

$$\left(\frac{1}{\theta} - 1\right) \left((I + \theta A)^{-1} U, (A + A^\top)(I + \theta A)^{-1} U\right) \geq 0.$$

Then we get

$$\begin{aligned}&\left\| \left(\left(1 - \frac{1}{\theta}\right) I + \frac{1}{\theta}(I + \theta A)^{-1} \right) U \right\|_2^2 \\ &\quad \leq \left(\frac{1}{\theta} - 1\right)^2 \|U\|_2^2 + \left(\frac{2}{\theta} - \frac{1}{\theta^2}\right) \|U\|_2^2 = \|U\|_2^2\end{aligned}$$

since for $\theta \geq 1/2$ both coefficients on the right-hand side are non-negative and sum to 1. □

Remark 6.17. Let us observe that the above theorem gives for the heat equation the stability condition

$$\theta \geq \frac{1}{2} - \frac{1}{4\lambda}$$

which holds for much smaller θ than the l^∞ stability condition of Example 6.13

$$\theta \geq 1 - \frac{1}{2\lambda}.$$

We now carry out the stability analysis of problem (6.2) with constant coefficients by applying the discrete Fourier transform to the solutions of (6.3). To simplify the presentation, we limit the consideration of stability with respect to the initial data. Then we consider only initial-value problems in the whole $\mathbb{R}^d$.

Let $\delta x_1 = \delta x_2 = \cdots = \delta x_d = 1/M$. The grid points of $\mathbb{R}^d$ are indexed by vectors $\boldsymbol{k} \in \mathbb{Z}^d$ with components k_i, $i = 1, \ldots, d$. For a function $\{U_{\boldsymbol{k}}\}_{\boldsymbol{k} \in \mathbb{Z}^d}$ defined on the grid in $\mathbb{R}^d$, we introduce the discrete Fourier transform

$$\hat{U}(\xi) = \frac{1}{(2\pi)^{d/2}} \sum_{\boldsymbol{k} \in \mathbb{Z}^d} U_{\boldsymbol{k}} e^{-i(\boldsymbol{k} \cdot \Delta x, \xi)} |\Delta x|,$$

where Δx is a vector with components $(\delta x_1, \delta x_2, \ldots, \delta x_d)$, $\boldsymbol{k} \cdot \Delta x$ denotes a vector with components $k_i \delta x_i$, and $|\Delta x| = \prod_{i=1}^d \delta x_i$.

The functions $\hat{U}$ are defined on the whole $\mathbb{R}^d$ and are periodic with period $2\pi M$ in the direction of each coordinate. Hence, we can restrict these functions to cube $[-\pi M, \pi M]^d$ and get the inverse Fourier transform

$$U_{\boldsymbol{k}} = \frac{1}{(2\pi)^{d/2}} \int_{[-\pi M, \pi M]^d} e^{i(\boldsymbol{k} \cdot \Delta x, \xi)} \hat{U}(\xi) d\xi.$$

We consider grid functions U as elements of the space l^2 with the norm

$$\|U\|_2^2 = \sum_{\boldsymbol{k} \in \mathbb{Z}^d} \left|U_{\boldsymbol{k}}\right|^2 |\Delta x|,$$

Their Fourier transforms $\hat{U}$ belong to the space $L^2([-\pi M, \pi M]^d)$ with the norm

$$\|\hat{U}\|_{L^2}^2 = \frac{1}{(2\pi)^d} \int_{[-\pi M, \pi M]^d} \left|\hat{U}(\xi)\right|^2 d\xi.$$

Functions $\hat{U}(\xi)$ for a fixed ξ are from the Euclidean space $\mathbb{R}^d$ with the Euclidean norm denoted $|\cdot|$.

For the discrete Fourier transform, similarly to the continuous Fourier transform, holds the Parseval identity

$$\|\hat{U}\|_{L^2}^2 = \|U\|_2^2.$$

Taking the discrete Fourier transform of the difference scheme

$$LU^{n+1} = RU^n \tag{6.8}$$

corresponding to the initial-value problem with constant coefficients and zero free-term

$$\frac{\partial u}{\partial t} + \mathcal{A}u = 0, \quad \text{in} \quad (0,T] \times \mathbb{R}^d,$$

$$u = g, \quad \text{on} \quad \{t = 0\} \times \mathbb{R}^d,$$

we obtain

$$\sum_{\boldsymbol{k}} \left(LU^{n+1}\right)_{\boldsymbol{k}} e^{-i(\boldsymbol{k}\cdot\Delta x,\xi)} = \sum_{\boldsymbol{k}} \left(RU^n\right)_{\boldsymbol{k}} e^{-i(\boldsymbol{k}\cdot\Delta x,\xi)}.$$

Since

$$\left(LU^{n+1}\right)_{\boldsymbol{k}} = \sum_{\boldsymbol{j}} l_{\boldsymbol{j}} U_{\boldsymbol{k}-\boldsymbol{j}}^{n+1}, \quad \left(RU^n\right)_{\boldsymbol{k}} = \sum_{\boldsymbol{j}} r_{\boldsymbol{j}} U_{\boldsymbol{k}-\boldsymbol{j}}^{n},$$

equation (6.8) leads to the equation for the Fourier transforms

$$\hat{L}(\xi)\hat{U}^{n+1}(\xi) = \hat{R}(\xi)\hat{U}^n(\xi),$$

where

$$\hat{L}(\xi) = \sum_{\boldsymbol{j}} l_{\boldsymbol{j}} e^{-i(\boldsymbol{j}\cdot\Delta x,\xi)}, \quad \hat{R}(\xi) = \sum_{\boldsymbol{j}} r_{\boldsymbol{j}} e^{-i(\boldsymbol{j}\cdot\Delta x,\xi)}.$$

The matrix

$$G(\xi) = \hat{L}^{-1}(\xi)\hat{R}(\xi)$$

is called the *amplification matrix* and is a continuous function of ξ. Then the equation for the Fourier transforms is

$$\hat{U}^n(\xi) = \left(G(\xi)\right)^n \hat{U}^0(\xi).$$

Theorem 6.18 (von Neumann stability condition). *A necessary condition for the stability in the norm l^2 with respect to initial* *data for the problem (6.2) with constant coefficients is the existence of a constant K such that the spectral radius of $G(\xi)$ has the estimate*

$$\rho\big(G(\xi)\big) \leq 1 + K\delta t, \quad \forall \xi.$$

Since the spectral radius of A is the greatest absolute value of the eigenvalues of A, we can reformulate the above estimate in terms of the eigenvalues of $G(\xi)$

$$\forall \xi \quad |\mu_j(\xi)| \leq 1 + K\delta t,$$

for each eigenvalue $\mu_j(\xi)$ of the amplification matrix $G(\xi)$.

Proof. Assume that the necessary condition is not satisfied. Then for each K, there exist a vector ξ_K and an eigenvalue $\mu(\xi_K)$ of $G(\xi_K)$ such that $|\mu(\xi_K)| > 1 + K\delta t$. Thus, for $T = n\delta t$ we have

$$|\mu(\xi_K)|^n > 1 + Kn\delta t = 1 + KT \quad \Rightarrow \quad \rho\big(G^n(\xi_K)\big) > 1 + KT.$$

Due to Lemma 6.14, we obtain

$$\|G^n(\xi_K)\| > 1 + KT,$$

where $\|G^n(\xi_K)\|$ is the operator norm of matrix $G^n(\xi_K)$.

Since $G^n(\xi)$ is a continuous function, there exists an open neighborhood I_K of ξ_K, with a positive volume, where we have the estimate $\|G^n(\xi)\| > 1 + KT$ for $\xi \in I_K$. We can now select an initial condition U^0_K such that $\hat{U}^0_K$ is zero in the exterior of I_K and $|G^n(\xi)\hat{U}^0_K(\xi)| > (1+KT)|\hat{U}^0_K(\xi)|$ for $\xi \in I_K$. Since the volume of I_K is positive, we get the estimate for l^2 norms with smaller, but still unbounded from the above constant K_1

$$\|G^n\hat{U}^0_K\|_{L^2} > (1 + K_1T)\|\hat{U}^0_K\|_{L^2}.$$

By the Parseval identity and the above inequality, we have

$$\sup_{U^0} \frac{\|U^n\|_2}{\|U^0\|_2} = \sup_{\hat{U}^0} \frac{\|\hat{U}^n\|_{L^2}}{\|\hat{U}^0\|_{L^2}} \geq \frac{\|G^n\hat{U}^0_K\|_{L^2}}{\|\hat{U}^0_K\|_{L^2}} > (1 + K_1T),$$

which contradicts the stability because K_1 is arbitrarily large. □

Corollary 6.19. *The proof of the above theorem shows that the sufficient condition for stability is*

$$\sup_{\xi} \|G^n(\xi)\| \le C$$

for each n such that $n\delta t \le T$ *and* $C > 0$ *independent of* n.

Example 6.20. To the advection equation

$$\frac{\partial u}{\partial t} + b\frac{\partial u}{\partial x} = 0$$

approximated by the forward-time, central-space scheme

$$\frac{u_k^{n+1} - u_k^n}{\delta t} + b\frac{u_{k+1}^n - u_{k-1}^n}{2\delta x} = 0,$$

we apply the von Neumann stability analysis.

Applying the discrete Fourier transform, we obtain the amplification function

$$G(\xi) = 1 + \frac{\nu}{2}\left(e^{-i\delta x\,\xi} - e^{i\delta x\,\xi}\right) = 1 - i\nu\sin(\delta x\,\xi),$$

where $\nu = b\,\delta t/\delta x$. Hence,

$$|G(\xi)|^2 = 1 + \nu^2\sin^2(\delta x\,\xi).$$

Since $|G(\xi)|$ is greater than 1 for $\delta x\,\xi$ not equal to 0 or π, then by Theorem 6.18 this scheme is unstable.

Example 6.21. We apply to the advection equation of the previous example the Lax–Friedrichs scheme

$$\frac{u_k^{n+1} - (u_{k+1}^n + u_{k-1}^n)/2}{\delta t} + b\frac{u_{k+1}^n - u_{k-1}^n}{2\delta x} = 0.$$

Applying the discrete Fourier transform, we obtain the amplification function

$$\begin{aligned} G(\xi) &= \frac{1}{2}\left(e^{-i\delta x\,\xi} + e^{i\delta x\,\xi}\right) + \frac{\nu}{2}\left(e^{-i\delta x\,\xi} - e^{i\delta x\,\xi}\right) \\ &= \cos(\delta x\,\xi) - i\nu\sin(\delta x\,\xi). \end{aligned}$$

Then

$$|G(\xi)|^2 = \cos^2(\delta x\,\xi) + \nu^2\sin^2(\delta x\,\xi).$$

For $\nu \le 1$, we get $|G(\xi)| \le 1$. Then the condition of Theorem 6.18 is fulfilled, and the scheme is stable.

Example 6.22. Consider the multidimensional heat equation

$$u_t = Au_{xx}, \quad x \in \mathbb{R}, \quad t > 0,$$

where $u = (u^1, \ldots, u^d)$ is a d-dimensional vector and A a constant, symmetric, positive definite matrix. This equation is approximated by the Euler explicit scheme

$$\frac{u_k^{n+1} - u_k^n}{\delta t} = A\frac{u_{k+1}^n - 2u_k^n + u_{k-1}^n}{(\delta x)^2}.$$

To investigate the stability of this difference scheme, we apply the discrete Fourier transform to obtain the equation

$$\hat{U}^{n+1} = \big(I - 4\lambda \sin^2(\delta x\,\xi/2)A\big)\hat{U}^n, \quad \lambda = \frac{\delta t}{(\delta x)^2}.$$

The above equation implies the amplification matrix

$$G(\xi) = I - 4\lambda \sin^2(\delta x\,\xi/2)A.$$

Then the eigenvalues of G are

$$\mu_j(\xi) = 1 - 4\lambda \sin^2(\delta x\,\xi/2)\alpha_j, \quad j = 1, \ldots, d,$$

where α_j are the eigenvalues of matrix A.

Since A is a symmetric, positive definite matrix, then all $\alpha_j > 0$. Hence,

$$|\mu_j| \leq 1 \quad \text{for all } j$$

provided $\lambda\alpha_j \leq 1/2$ for all j. This is a natural extension of the stability condition for the explicit Euler scheme applied to the one-dimensional heat equation.

The von Neumann stability condition for an initial value problem is also a necessary condition for the stability of an initial-boundary value problem. The extension of the von Neumann stability analysis to a sufficient condition for initial-boundary value problems is complicated and beyond the scope of this book.

However, initial-boundary value problems in a rectangular domain, say $U = (-1, 1)^d$ with periodic boundary data, can be easily reduced to the already discussed initial value problems. Let as previously $\delta x_1 = \delta x_2 = \cdots = \delta x_d = 1/M$. The grid points of J_U are indexed by the vectors

$$\boldsymbol{k} \in Z_M = \{\boldsymbol{k} = (k_1, \ldots, k_d)\colon\ k_i = 0, \pm 1, \pm 2, \ldots, \pm M\}.$$

A grid function $\{U_{\boldsymbol{k}}\}_{\boldsymbol{k}\in Z_M}$ defined on a discrete grid J_U can be expanded into a series of trigonometric polynomials

$$U_{\boldsymbol{k}} = U(\boldsymbol{k}\cdot\Delta x) = \frac{1}{(2\pi)^{d/2}} \sum_{\boldsymbol{l}\in Z_M}{}' \hat{U}(\xi_{\boldsymbol{l}}) e^{-i(\boldsymbol{k}\cdot\Delta x, \xi_{\boldsymbol{l}})} \quad \text{for } \xi_{\boldsymbol{l}} = \boldsymbol{l}\pi,$$

where the prime in the summation sign indicates that the summation must be modified for $l_i = \pm M$ to account for the periodicity of the boundary conditions.

The coefficients $\hat{U}(\xi_{\boldsymbol{l}})$ are defined by the *finite Fourier transform*

$$\hat{U}(\xi_{\boldsymbol{l}}) = \frac{1}{(2\pi)^{d/2}} \sum_{\boldsymbol{k}\in Z_M}{}' U_{\boldsymbol{k}} e^{-i(\boldsymbol{k}\cdot\Delta x, \xi_{\boldsymbol{l}})} |\Delta x|, \quad \text{for } \xi_{\boldsymbol{l}} = \boldsymbol{l}\pi.$$

Functions $\hat{U}$ belong to the space l^2 with the norm

$$\|\hat{U}\|_2^2 = \sum_{\boldsymbol{l}\in Z_M}{}' |\hat{U}(\xi_{\boldsymbol{l}})|^2,$$

whereas functions U belong to the space l^2 with the norm

$$\|U\|_2^2 = \sum_{\boldsymbol{k}\in Z_M}{}' |U_{\boldsymbol{k}}|^2 |\Delta x|.$$

With the above norms, we have the Parseval identity $\|U\|_2 = \|\hat{U}\|_2$. Similarly to the initial value problems, we define the amplification matrix $G = G(\xi_{\boldsymbol{l}})$, which is now defined for a discrete set of points $\xi_{\boldsymbol{l}}$. For this amplification matrix, the von Neumann stability condition (Theorem 6.18 and Corollary 6.19) remains valid; however, the proof of Theorem 6.18 requires some modifications.

Proof of Theorem 6.18 for the finite Fourier transform. Since G^n is an operator of multiplication by a matrix, we can compute its norm by applying a well-known property of multiplication operators.

If B is an operator of multiplication by function $b(x)$ in spaces L^2 (or l^2), then the operator norm of B is given by the formula

$$\|B\| = \sup_{u \in L^2} \frac{\left(\int |b(x)u(x)|^2 dx\right)^{1/2}}{\left(\int |u(x)|^2 dx\right)^{1/2}} = \sup_x |b(x)|.$$

By the Parseval identity and the above property of multiplication operators, we have

$$\sup_{U^0} \frac{\|U^n\|_2}{\|U^0\|_2} = \sup_{\hat{U}^0} \frac{\|\hat{U}^n\|_2}{\|\hat{U}^0\|_2} = \sup_{\hat{U}^0} \frac{\|G^n \hat{U}^0\|_2}{\|\hat{U}^0\|_2} = \sup_{l} \|\big(G(\xi_l)\big)^n\|.$$

Since

$$\|\big(G(\xi_l)\big)^n\| \geq \rho\big(G^n(\xi_l)\big) = \big(\rho\big(G(\xi_l)\big)\big)^n,$$

the existence of a constant $K > 1$ such that

$$\big(\rho\big(G(\xi_l)\big)\big)^n > K \quad \text{for some } \boldsymbol{l} \in Z_M$$

contradicts stability.

Then the necessary condition for stability is the existence of a constant $K > 1$ such that

$$\big(\rho\big(G(\xi_l)\big)\big)^n < K \quad \forall \boldsymbol{l} \in Z_M.$$

Taking into account that $n\delta t \leq T$, we obtain

$$\rho\big(G(\xi_l)\big) \leq K^{\delta t/T} \leq 1 + K_1 \delta t \quad \forall \boldsymbol{l} \in Z_M,$$

which completes the proof. □

It can be shown that if G is a normal matrix, its operator norm is equal to its spectral radius. Then the von Neumann condition is also sufficient, in particular, is sufficient for one-dimensional problems. It appears, however, that even when the condition is sufficient, the constant in the condition can lead to the rapid growth of the grid solution. The following example illustrates the problem.

Example 6.23. Consider the advection-diffusion equation

$$\frac{\partial u}{\partial t} + b\frac{\partial u}{\partial x} = a^2\frac{\partial^2 u}{\partial x^2}.$$

Applying the discrete Fourier transform to the Euler explicit scheme

$$\frac{u_k^{n+1} - u_k^n}{\delta t} + b\frac{u_{k+1}^n - u_{k-1}^n}{2\delta x} = a^2\frac{u_{k+1}^n - 2u_k^n + u_{k-1}^n}{(\delta x)^2},$$

we obtain the amplification function ($d = 1$, hence, G is one-dimensional)

$$\begin{aligned} G(\xi) &= 1 - 2\kappa + (\kappa + \nu/2)e^{-i\delta x\,\xi} + (\kappa - \nu/2)e^{i\delta x\,\xi} \\ &= 1 - 2\kappa + 2\kappa\cos(\delta x\,\xi) - i\nu\sin(\delta x\,\xi), \end{aligned}$$

where $\kappa = a^2\delta t/(\delta x)^2$, $\nu = b\delta t/\delta x$. Denoting $s = \sin(\delta x\,\xi/2)$, we get

$$|G(\xi)|^2 = (1 - 4\kappa s^2)^2 + 4\nu^2 s^2(1 - s^2).$$

Taking $s^2 = 1$, we obtain $|G| \leq 1$ for $\kappa \leq 1/2$, which is the necessary condition for stability. Since $\nu^2 = (b^2/a^2)\kappa\delta t$ and $\max_{s^2\in[0,1]} s^2(1 - s^2) = 1/4$, we get for $\kappa \leq 1/2$ the estimate

$$\begin{aligned} |G(\xi)|^2 &= (1 - 4\kappa s^2)^2 + 4\nu^2 s^2(1 - s^2) \leq 1 + 4\nu^2 s^2(1 - s^2) \\ &\leq 1 + \nu^2 \leq 1 + \frac{b^2}{2a^2}\delta t, \end{aligned}$$

so the von Neumann condition is satisfied and — since the problem is one-dimensional — the condition is sufficient for stability. On the other hand, taking $\nu = 1$, $\kappa = 1/4$, and $s^2 = 1/2$, we obtain $|G|^2 = 5/4$ which gives a rapid growth of Fourier's modes.

The above example suggests the introduction of a stronger notion of stability.

Definition 6.24. A two-time-level difference scheme is said to be *strongly stable* in the norm l^2 with respect to initial conditions if the following estimate holds for the amplification matrix

$$\forall\xi \quad \|G(\xi)\| \leq 1.$$

Example 6.25. For the advection-diffusion equation of Example 6.23 the condition $|G(\xi)| \leq 1$ gives

$$\nu^2 \leq 2\kappa \leq 1. \tag{6.9}$$

Indeed, from the expression

$$|G(\xi)|^2 = (1 - 4\kappa s^2)^2 + 4\nu^2 s^2(1 - s^2),$$

we obtain for $s^2 = 1$ the estimate $2\kappa \leq 1$. Rewriting $|G(\xi)|^2$ as

$$|G(\xi)|^2 = 1 - 4s^2(2\kappa - \nu^2) + 4s^4(4\kappa^2 - \nu^2),$$

we obtain $|G(\xi)| \leq 1$ provided that

$$4s^4(4\kappa^2 - \nu^2) \leq 4s^2(2\kappa - \nu^2).$$

Thus, for $s^2 > 0$, we get

$$s^2(4\kappa^2 - \nu^2) \leq (2\kappa - \nu^2).$$

Excluding the case $2\kappa = \nu^2 = 1$ and taking the limit $s^2 \to 0$, we obtain from the above inequality $2\kappa - \nu^2 \geq 0$. Since the excluded case falls into the general inequality, it proves (6.9).

Number ν/κ is called the *Peclet mesh number* and relates the convection term $b\partial u/\partial x$ to the diffusion term $a^2\partial^2 u/\partial x^2$. The condition $\nu^2/\kappa \leq 2$ means that the convection term cannot be too large with respect to the diffusion term. The maximal admissible $\kappa = 1/2$ restricts the Peclet mesh number to $\nu/\kappa \leq 2$, which implies $\delta x \leq 2a^2/b$. The violation of this restriction can generate spurious oscillations of the scheme.

Example 6.26. We can improve the stability by taking an *upwind scheme*, which applies a different approximation of the first-order x derivative. Let us consider the equation of Example 6.23

$$\frac{\partial u}{\partial t} + b\frac{\partial u}{\partial x} = a^2\frac{\partial^2 u}{\partial x^2}.$$

If $b > 0$, the left-hand side of the equation is a first-order operator with the traveling wave solution $u(t, x) = F(x - bt)$, where $F(\cdot) = g(\cdot)$ is given by the initial condition. We can say that the profile $F(\cdot)$ drifts in the positive x direction ("wind blows to the right"). Looking from the node (k, n), the node $(k-1, n)$ is "upwind". Applying this approximation of the first-order derivative, we obtain for the Euler explicit scheme

$$\frac{u_k^{n+1} - u_k^n}{\delta t} + b\frac{u_k^n - u_{k-1}^n}{\delta x} = a^2 \frac{u_{k+1}^n - 2u_k^n + u_{k-1}^n}{(\delta x)^2},$$

the amplification function

$$\begin{aligned} G(\xi) &= 1 - 2\kappa - \nu + (\kappa + \nu)e^{-i\delta x\,\xi} + \kappa e^{i\delta x\,\xi} \\ &= 1 - 2\kappa - \nu + 2\kappa\cos(\delta x\,\xi) + \nu\cos(\delta x\,\xi) - i\nu\sin(\delta x\,\xi). \end{aligned}$$

Denoting $s = \sin(\delta x\,\xi/2)$, we get

$$|G(\xi)|^2 = (1 - 2(2\kappa + \nu)s^2)^2 + 4\nu^2 s^2(1 - s^2).$$

The condition of strong stability $|G(\xi)| \leq 1$ implies the inequality

$$2\kappa + \nu \leq 1. \tag{6.10}$$

To prove this inequality observe that condition $|G(\xi)|^2 \leq 1$ gives $2\kappa + \nu \leq 1$ for $s^2 = 1$. Since $0 < \nu^2 \leq \nu \leq 2\kappa + \nu$ for $b > 0$, then for $2\kappa + \nu \leq 1$ and arbitrary $s^2 \in [0, 1]$, we have

$$\begin{aligned} |G(\xi)|^2 &= (1 - 2(2\kappa + \nu)s^2)^2 + 4\nu^2 s^2(1 - s^2) \\ &\leq (1 - 2(2\kappa + \nu)s^2)^2 + 4(2\kappa + \nu)s^2(1 - s^2) \\ &= 1 + 4s^4(2\kappa + \nu)(2\kappa + \nu - 1) \leq 1, \end{aligned}$$

thus, the condition of strong stability holds.

Inequality (6.10) is called the **CFL** condition (Courant, Friedrichs and Lewy [17]) and for small κ is less restrictive than (6.9). For example, taking $\kappa = 1/50$, we obtain from inequality (6.10) $\nu \leq 0.96$ and $\nu^2/\kappa \approx 46$, a value much larger than $\nu^2/\kappa \leq 2$ permitted by inequality (6.9).

Remark 6.27. The von Neumann stability condition applies only to constant-coefficient equations where the Fourier transform is well defined. Nevertheless, the von Neumann analysis is also used for variable-coefficient equations by "freezing" coefficients in their constant values. Because stability is a local property, "freezing" works well for many variable-coefficient equations.

Example 6.28 (Black–Scholes equation in the original variables). We consider the initial value problem for the Black–Scholes equation with variable coefficients (t in the equation is the time to maturity)

$$\frac{\partial V(t,S)}{\partial t} - \frac{1}{2}\sigma^2(t,S)S^2\frac{\partial^2 V(t,S)}{\partial S^2} - r(t)S\frac{\partial V(t,S)}{\partial S} + r(t)V(t,S) = 0$$

with the initial condition

$$V(0,S) = g(S).$$

To write a finite difference scheme for that equation, we divide the time interval $[0,T]$ into N subintervals of length δt, truncate the domain of the S variable to a finite interval $(0, S_{\max})$, and divide it into M subintervals of length δx. In rectangle $[0,T] \times [0, S_{\max}]$, we define a uniform grid (t_n, S_k), where $t_n = n\delta t$ and $S_k = k\delta x$. Let u_k^n be the grid approximation of $V(t_n, S_k)$ and $U^n = (u_1^n, \ldots, u_{M-1}^n)$ be a vector of approximation at time level t_n (u_0^n and u_M^n are omitted as known from boundary conditions). The Euler implicit scheme can then be written as

$$(I + \delta t\, A^{n+1})U^{n+1} = U^n, \tag{6.11}$$

where A^n is a tridiagonal matrix of dimension $(M-1) \times (M-1)$ with entries

$$A_{k,k}^n = (k\sigma_k^n)^2 + r^n, \quad k = 1, \ldots M-1,$$

$$A_{k,k+1}^n = -\frac{1}{2}\big((k\sigma_k^n)^2 + kr^n\big), \quad k = 1, \ldots, M-2,$$

$$A_{k,k-1} = -\frac{1}{2}\big((k\sigma_k^n)^2 - kr^n\big), \quad k = 2, \ldots, M-1.$$

Numerical experiments show that the scheme converges independently from the fact that the coefficients are unbounded.

This convergence can be rigorously proved, and we present this proof, following the approach from [1], under the simplified assumptions that σ and r are positive constants.

First, we prove that the scheme is solvable, which means that $(I + \delta t A)$ is invertible (we drop index n since for constant σ and r matrices A^n are the same on each time level).

Let $\|\cdot\|_2$ denote the Euclidean norm and $\|\cdot\|_M$ the norm in $\mathbb{R}^{M-1}$ defined by the formula (by assumption $u_0 = u_M = 0$)

$$\|U\|_M^2 = \sum_{k=1}^{M} k^2 (u_k - u_{k-1})^2.$$

We split matrix A as follows $A = \sigma^2 A_0 + A_1 + rI$, where A_0 is a matrix with entries

$$a_{k,k}^0 = k^2, \quad a_{k,k-1}^0 = a_{k,k+1}^0 = -\frac{k^2}{2},$$

and A_1 has entries

$$a_{k,k}^1 = 0, \quad a_{k,k-1}^1 = \frac{kr}{2}, \quad a_{k,k+1}^1 = -\frac{kr}{2}.$$

Assuming $u_0 = u_M = 0$ and applying Cauchy's inequality, we obtain for matrix A_0

$$\begin{aligned}
&(U, A_0 U) \\
&= \frac{1}{2}\sum_{k=1}^{M-1} k^2 u_k \big(2u_k - u_{k-1} - u_{k+1}\big) \\
&= \frac{1}{2}\sum_{k=1}^{M} k^2 \big(u_k - u_{k-1}\big)^2 + \frac{1}{2}\sum_{k=1}^{M} \big((k-1)^2 - k^2\big) u_{k-1} \big(u_{k-1} - u_k\big) \\
&= \frac{1}{2}\sum_{k=1}^{M} k^2 \big(u_k - u_{k-1}\big)^2 - \frac{1}{2}\sum_{k=1}^{M} (2k-1) u_{k-1} \big(u_{k-1} - u_k\big) \\
&\geq \frac{1}{2}\sum_{k=1}^{M} k^2 \big(u_k - u_{k-1}\big)^2 - \frac{\eta}{4}\sum_{k=1}^{M} u_{k-1}^2 \\
&\quad - \frac{1}{4\eta}\sum_{k=1}^{M} (2k-1)^2 \big(u_{k-1} - u_k\big)^2 \geq \left(\frac{1}{2} - \frac{1}{\eta}\right) \|U\|_M^2 - \frac{\eta}{4}\|U\|_2^2.
\end{aligned}$$

For A_1, we get

$$(U, A_1 U) = -\frac{r}{2}\sum_{k=1}^{M-1} k u_k \big(u_{k+1} - u_{k-1}\big).$$

Then

$$
\begin{aligned}
|(U, A_1 U)| &= \left| -\frac{r}{2} \sum_{k=1}^{M-1} k u_k (u_{k+1} - u_{k-1}) \right| \\
&= \frac{r}{2} \left| \sum_{k=1}^{M} k u_k (u_k - u_{k-1}) + \sum_{k=1}^{M} (k-1) u_{k-1} (u_k - u_{k-1}) \right| \\
&\le r \|U\|_2 \|U\|_M \le \frac{r}{2\eta} \|U\|_M^2 + \frac{r\eta}{2} \|U\|_2^2.
\end{aligned}
$$

Collecting the above estimates, we obtain

$$
(U, AU) \ge \left(\frac{\sigma^2}{2} - \frac{\sigma^2}{\eta} - \frac{r}{2\eta} \right) \|U\|_M^2 + \left(r - \frac{\sigma^2 \eta}{4} - \frac{r\eta}{2} \right) \|U\|_2^2.
$$

Taking η sufficiently large, we have the estimate

$$
(U, AU) \ge C_1 \|U\|_M^2 - C_2 \|U\|_2^2 \tag{6.12}
$$

with positive constants C_1 and C_2. From estimate (6.12), we obtain

$$
\big(U, (I + \delta t A) U\big) \ge (1 - C_2 \delta t) \|U\|_2^2
$$

which proves that for $\delta t < 1/C_2$ matrix $(I + \delta t A)$ is invertible. Therefore, the implicit Euler scheme is solvable.

To show the stability of the scheme, observe that, due to the scheme's linearity, it is sufficient to prove the estimate

$$
\|U^n\|_2 \le C \|U^0\|_2
$$

for the constant C independent of n.

From formula (6.11) defining the scheme, we obtain

$$
\delta t (U^n, AU^n) = \big(U^n, (U^{n-1} - U^n)\big).
$$

The above identity can be rewritten as

$$
\|U^n\|_2^2 + \|U^n - U^{n-1}\|_2^2 + 2\delta t (U^n, AU^n) = \|U^{n-1}\|_2^2.
$$

Applying estimate (6.12) to this identity, we obtain

$$
(1 - 2C_2 \delta t) \|U^n\|_2^2 + \|U^n - U^{n-1}\|_2^2 + 2C_1 \delta t \|U^n\|_M^2 \le \|U^{n-1}\|_2^2.
$$

Assuming that $(1 - 2C_2\delta t) > 0$, which corresponds to $\delta t < 1/(2C_2)$, we can divide the above inequality by $(1 - 2C_2\delta t)$ and iterate from $n = 0$ to N. Then we obtain

$$\|U^N\|_2^2 + \sum_{n=1}^{N}(1 - 2C_2\delta t)^{n-N-1}\|U^n - U^{n-1}\|_2^2$$
$$+ 2C_1\delta t\sum_{n=1}^{N}(1 - 2C_2\delta t)^{n-N-1}\|U^n\|_M^2 \le (1 - 2C_2\delta t)^{-N}\|U^0\|_2^2.$$

Since $\ln(1 - x) > -x$, we have the estimate

$$(1 - 2C_2\delta t)^{-N} \le e^{2C_2N\delta t} = e^{2C_2T}.$$

This gives the desired estimate and proves the scheme stability with $C = e^{2C_2T}$

$$\|U^N\|_2^2 \le C\|U^0\|_2^2.$$

Since the consistency of this scheme can be easily proved similarly to the θ-schemes, then by the Lax theorem, we obtain the scheme convergence.

It can be proved that the θ-schemes for the Black–Scholes equation in its original variables are convergent for $\theta \ge 1/2$. However, for $\theta < 1$, the proof is more involved.

6.5 Finite Differences in Many Dimensions

6.5.1 *Generalizations of one-dimensional methods*

The one-dimensional finite difference schemes of Section 6.1 can be straightforwardly extended to many dimensions. Before we proceed, we would like to emphasize that the concepts introduced for one-dimensional schemes of consistency, stability, and convergence remain valid for multidimensional finite differences. Our basic tools are the Lax equivalence theorem (Theorem 6.9) and the von Neumann analysis of stability.

We begin by solving the Dirichlet problem for the two-dimensional heat equation in the rectangular domain $U = (0,1)^2$

$$\begin{aligned}
&\frac{\partial u}{\partial t} - a^2\left(\frac{\partial^2 u}{\partial x^2} + \frac{\partial^2 u}{\partial y^2}\right) = 0, \quad (t,x,y) \in (0,T] \times U, \\
&u(t,x,y) = q(t,x,y), \quad (x,y) \in \partial U, \quad t \in [0,T], \\
&u(0,x,y) = g(x,y), \quad (x,y) \in U.
\end{aligned} \tag{6.13}$$

In analogy to the one-dimensional approach, we introduce in U a rectangular grid with spacing $\delta x \times \delta y$ where

$$\delta x = \frac{1}{M_x}, \quad \delta y = \frac{1}{M_y},$$

and divide the time interval into N subintervals of length $\delta t = T/N$. The grid points of this mesh are denoted

$$(x_j, y_k) = (j \cdot \delta x, k \cdot \delta y), \quad j = 0, \dots, M_x, \quad k = 0, \dots, M_y,$$
$$t_n = n \cdot \delta t, \quad n = 0, \dots, N.$$

The time derivative in the heat equation is approximated by the forward difference

$$\frac{\partial u(t_n, x_j, y_k)}{\partial t} \approx \frac{u(t_{n+1}, x_j, y_k) - u(t_n, x_j, y_k)}{\delta t},$$

or the backward differences defined analogously, and the second-order space derivatives are approximated by the central differences

$$\frac{\partial^2 u(t_n, x_j, y_k)}{\partial x^2} \approx \frac{u(t_n, x_{j+1}, y_k) - 2u(t_n, x_j, y_k) + u(t_n, x_{j-1}, y_k)}{(\delta x)^2},$$
$$\frac{\partial^2 u(t_n, x_j, y_k)}{\partial y^2} \approx \frac{u(t_n, x_j, y_{k+1}) - 2u(t_n, x_j, y_k) + u(t_n, x_j, y_{k-1})}{(\delta y)^2}.$$

We denote by $u^n_{j,k}$ the approximation of $u(t_n, x_j, y_k)$. To simplify notation, we define several difference operators. We begin with the first-order difference operator

$$\delta_x u_{j,k}^n = \frac{u_{j+1/2,k}^n - u_{j-1/2,k}^n}{\delta x}.$$

Since points $x_j \pm \delta x/2$ are not grid points, we use the central differences

$$\delta_x u_{j,k}^n = \frac{u_{j+1,k}^n - u_{j-1,k}^n}{2\delta x}.$$

This leads to the following second-order difference operator

$$\delta_{xx} u_{j,k}^n = \frac{u_{j+1,k}^n - 2u_{j,k}^n + u_{j-1,k}^n}{(\delta x)^2}.$$

Analogously, we define the operators δ_y and δ_{yy}.

We begin with the two-dimensional explicit Euler scheme

$$\frac{u_{j,k}^{n+1} - u_{j,k}^n}{\delta t} - a^2(\delta_{xx} + \delta_{yy})u_{j,k}^n = 0.$$

Solving for $u_{j,k}^{n+1}$, we obtain

$$\begin{aligned} u_{j,k}^{n+1} &= a^2\lambda_x\big(u_{j-1,k}^n + u_{j+1,k}^n\big) + a^2\lambda_y\big(u_{j,k-1}^n + u_{j,k+1}^n\big) \\ &\quad + (1 - 2a^2\lambda_x - 2a^2\lambda_y)u_{j,k}^n, \end{aligned}$$

where

$$\lambda_x = \frac{\delta t}{(\delta x)^2}, \quad \lambda_y = \frac{\delta t}{(\delta y)^2}.$$

By the above equation, we can compute $u_{j,k}^{n+1}$ at all internal points (x_j, y_k), $j = 1, \ldots, M_x - 1$, $k = 1, \ldots, M_y - 1$.

The boundary conditions

$$u_{j,k}^{n+1} = q(t_{n+1}, x_j, y_k),$$

$$\text{for } (j,k) \in \{0, M_x\} \times \{0, \ldots, M_y\} \cup \{0, \ldots, M_x\} \times \{0, M_y\}$$

supplement the solution on ∂U.

To compute the truncation error of the scheme, we assume that u is a smooth solution of the equation. Applying Taylor's expansions of Lemma 6.3, we obtain the truncation error

$$\Psi(u) = \frac{1}{2}u_{tt}\delta t - \frac{1}{12}\big(u_{xxxx}(\delta x)^2 + u_{yyyy}(\delta y)^2\big) + O\big((\delta t)^2\big) + O\big((\delta x)^3 + (\delta y)^3\big).$$

This gives the truncation error of the scheme of order $O(\delta t) + O\big((\delta x)^2 + (\delta y)^2\big)$.

Applying the discrete Fourier transform into the scheme, we obtain the following amplification function

$$\begin{aligned} G(\xi_x, \xi_y) &= 1 + a^2\lambda_x\left(e^{-i\delta x\,\xi_x} - 2 + e^{i\delta x\,\xi_x}\right) \\ &\quad + a^2\lambda_y\left(e^{-i\delta y\,\xi_y} - 2 + e^{i\delta y\,\xi_y}\right) \\ &= 1 - 4a^2\lambda_x\sin^2\frac{\delta x\,\xi_x}{2} - 4a^2\lambda_y\sin^2\frac{\delta y\,\xi_y}{2}. \end{aligned}$$

The maximum of G occurs at $(0,0)$ and is equal 1, and the minimum, at (π,π), is equal $1 - 4a^2(\lambda_x + \lambda_y)$. Thus, $|G(\xi_x, \xi_y)| \le 1$ if

$$1 - 4a^2(\lambda_x + \lambda_y) \ge -1 \implies \lambda_x + \lambda_y \le \frac{1}{2a^2}.$$

Hence, we have obtained a numerical method easy to implement and with a small computational complexity but with a restrictive stability condition. This is not a surprise as we have used an explicit scheme.

To improve stability, we apply the Crank–Nicolson scheme

$$\frac{u_{j,k}^{n+1} - u_{j,k}^{n}}{\delta t} - \frac{a^2}{2}(\delta_{xx} + \delta_{yy})\big(u_{j,k}^{n+1} + u_{j,k}^{n}\big) = 0.$$

Solving for $u_{j,k}^{n+1}$, we obtain

$$\left(1 - \frac{\delta t}{2}a^2(\delta_{xx} + \delta_{yy})\right)u_{j,k}^{n+1} = \left(1 + \frac{\delta t}{2}a^2(\delta_{xx} + \delta_{yy})\right)u_{j,k}^{n}.$$

Introducing the matrix

$$U^n = \big(u_{j,k}^n\big), \quad j = 1, \ldots, M_x - 1, \quad k = 1, \ldots, M_y - 1,$$

we can write the above equation as

$$\left(I - \frac{1}{2}C\right)U^{n+1} = \left(I + \frac{1}{2}C\right)U^n,$$

where C is a $(M_y - 1) \times (M_y - 1)$ tridiagonal block matrix

$$C = \begin{pmatrix} D_x & D_y & & \\ D_y & D_x & D_y & \\ & \ddots & \ddots & \\ & & D_y & D_x \end{pmatrix}$$

with the matrix entries of dimension $(M_x - 1) \times (M_x - 1)$

$$D_x = \begin{pmatrix} \alpha & \beta & & \\ \beta & \alpha & \beta & \\ & \ddots & \ddots & \\ & & \beta & \alpha \end{pmatrix}, \qquad D_y = \lambda_y a^2 I,$$

where

$$\alpha = -2a^2(\lambda_x + \lambda_y), \quad \beta = \lambda_x a^2.$$

The truncation error of the scheme is of order $O\big((\delta t)^2 + (\delta x)^2 + (\delta y)^2\big)$ which can be computed as in Theorem 6.12. The von Neumann stability analysis gives

$$\left(1 + 2a^2\lambda_x \sin^2\frac{\delta x\,\xi_x}{2} + 2a^2\lambda_y \sin^2\frac{\delta y\,\xi_y}{2}\right)G(\xi_x, \xi_y)$$
$$= \left(1 - 2a^2\lambda_x \sin^2\frac{\delta x\,\xi_x}{2} - 2a^2\lambda_y \sin^2\frac{\delta y\,\xi_y}{2}\right).$$

Since $|(1-z)/(1+z)| \le 1$ for all $z \ge 0$, then $|G(\xi_x, \xi_y)| \le 1$ and the scheme is unconditionally stable.

Thus, we obtain a scheme with good approximation and stability properties but very costly in implementation. In each time step, we solve a linear system of $(M_x - 1) \times (M_y - 1)$ equations. Since the system is not tridiagonal, its solution is very expensive. The fact that the system is block tridiagonal can reduce the cost; however, this reduction is minor.

6.5.2 *Alternating direction method*

A significant reduction of computational complexity can be achieved by splitting a two-dimensional problem into a sequence of one-dimensional problems. Before proceeding to rigorous mathematical considerations, we informally describe the concept behind the time-splitting method.

Consider the semi-discrete equation

$$\frac{dU}{dt} = \Lambda U,$$

where Λ is a discrete matrix representation of a differential operator.

The solution of this equation can be written formally as

$$U(t) = \exp(\Lambda t)U(0).$$

Assume that Λ can be split into

$$\Lambda = \Lambda_1 + \Lambda_2.$$

We can think about splitting with Λ_1 corresponding to x derivatives and Λ_2, to y derivatives; however, the splitting can be quite general.

We want to apply the above splitting to replace $e^{(\Lambda_1+\Lambda_2)t}$ with $e^{\Lambda_1 t}e^{\Lambda_2 t}$. These two operators are equal only if Λ_1 and Λ_2 commute ($\Lambda_1\Lambda_2 = \Lambda_2\Lambda_1$). However, when the time increment is small, the error generated by substituting $e^{(\Lambda_1+\Lambda_2)t}$ with $e^{\Lambda_1 t}e^{\Lambda_2 t}$ is small.

Applying the above splitting to a multidimensional finite difference scheme with the introduced earlier time discretization, we obtain by Taylor's expansion

$$\begin{aligned} U^{n+1} &= e^{\delta t(\Lambda_1+\Lambda_2)}U^n \\ &= \left(e^{\delta t\Lambda_1}e^{\delta t\Lambda_2} + \frac{(\delta t)^2}{2}(\Lambda_2\Lambda_1 - \Lambda_1\Lambda_2) + O\big((\delta t)^3\big)\right)U^n. \end{aligned} \tag{6.14}$$

Hence, up to the local error term $O\big((\delta t)^2\big)$, we can replace $e^{\delta t(\Lambda_1+\Lambda_2)}$ with $e^{\delta t\Lambda_1}e^{\delta t\Lambda_2}$.

The idea of operator splitting is the basis of a powerful method that is especially useful for solving parabolic equations. This method is called the *alternating direction implicit* (ADI) method. We present various ADI algorithms for the previously introduced Dirichlet problem for the two-dimensional heat equation.

Peaceman–Rachford scheme: This scheme is obtained by splitting the Crank–Nicolson scheme

$$\left(1-\frac{\delta t}{2}a^2(\delta_{xx}+\delta_{yy})\right)u_{j,k}^{n+1}=\left(1+\frac{\delta t}{2}a^2(\delta_{xx}+\delta_{yy})\right)u_{j,k}^{n}. \quad (6.15)$$

Since

$$\begin{aligned}1 &\pm \frac{\delta t}{2}a^2\delta_{xx}\pm\frac{\delta t}{2}a^2\delta_{yy}\\ &=\left(1\pm\frac{\delta t}{2}a^2\delta_{xx}\right)\left(1\pm\frac{\delta t}{2}a^2\delta_{yy}\right)-\frac{(\delta t)^2}{4}a^4\delta_{xx}\delta_{yy},\end{aligned}$$

we can write (6.15) as

$$\begin{aligned}&\left(1-\frac{\delta t}{2}a^2\delta_{xx}\right)\left(1-\frac{\delta t}{2}a^2\delta_{yy}\right)u_{j,k}^{n+1}\\ &\quad=\left(1+\frac{\delta t}{2}a^2\delta_{xx}\right)\left(1+\frac{\delta t}{2}a^2\delta_{yy}\right)u_{j,k}^{n}\\ &\quad\quad+\frac{(\delta t)^2}{4}a^4\delta_{xx}\delta_{yy}\big(u_{j,k}^{n+1}-u_{j,k}^{n}\big).\end{aligned}$$

By the Taylor expansion, we have $u_{j,k}^{n+1}=u_{j,k}^{n}+O(\delta t)$. Thus, the term

$$\frac{(\delta t)^2}{4}a^4\delta_{xx}\delta_{yy}\big(u_{j,k}^{n+1}-u_{j,k}^{n}\big)$$

is of order $O\big((\delta t)^3\big)$ that is the order of the discretization error.

Neglecting this term as we neglect the discretization error, we arrive at the scheme

$$\begin{aligned}&\left(1-\frac{\delta t}{2}a^2\delta_{xx}\right)\left(1-\frac{\delta t}{2}a^2\delta_{yy}\right)u_{j,k}^{n+1}\\ &\quad=\left(1+\frac{\delta t}{2}a^2\delta_{xx}\right)\left(1+\frac{\delta t}{2}a^2\delta_{yy}\right)u_{j,k}^{n}. \quad (6.16)\end{aligned}$$

This scheme is up to $O\big((\delta t)^3\big)$ equivalent to the Crank–Nicolson scheme. In this scheme, however, the finite differences in the directions x and y are separated. Introducing the intermediate level

$U^{n+1/2}$, we get

$$\left(1 - \frac{\delta t}{2} a^2 \delta_{xx}\right) u_{j,k}^{n+1/2} = \left(1 + \frac{\delta t}{2} a^2 \delta_{yy}\right) u_{j,k}^{n}, \tag{6.17}$$

$$\left(1 - \frac{\delta t}{2} a^2 \delta_{yy}\right) u_{j,k}^{n+1} = \left(1 + \frac{\delta t}{2} a^2 \delta_{xx}\right) u_{j,k}^{n+1/2}. \tag{6.18}$$

To find $U^{n+1/2}$, we must solve $(M_y - 1)$ systems of $(M_x - 1)$ equations and then $(M_x - 1)$ systems of $(M_y - 1)$ equations to compute U^{n+1}. Each of these systems is tridiagonal, which makes their solution very fast.

We must supplement the solutions of equations (6.17–6.18) with boundary conditions. The boundary conditions for (6.18) follow from the Dirichlet boundary condition for the differential problem (6.13). Deriving the boundary conditions for equation (6.17), we should keep in mind the accuracy of the scheme because it can be easily destroyed by a wrong choice of boundary data.

Adding the left-hand side of (6.18) to the right-hand side of (6.17), solving for $u_{j,k}^{n+1/2}$, and neglecting terms of order $(\delta t)^2$, we get

$$u_{j,k}^{n+1/2} = \frac{1}{2}\left(1 - \frac{\delta t}{2} a^2 \delta_{yy}\right) u_{j,k}^{n+1} + \frac{1}{2}\left(1 + \frac{\delta t}{2} a^2 \delta_{yy}\right) u_{j,k}^{n}.$$

Thus, for the Peaceman–Rachford scheme with Dirichlet boundary conditions, we should use the following boundary conditions for $u_{j,k}^{n+1/2}$

$$\begin{aligned} u_{0,k}^{n+1/2} &= \frac{1}{2}\left(1 - \frac{\delta t}{2} a^2 \delta_{yy}\right) q(t_{n+1}, 0, y_k) \\ &\quad + \frac{1}{2}\left(1 + \frac{\delta t}{2} a^2 \delta_{yy}\right) q(t_n, 0, y_k), \\ u_{M_x,k}^{n+1/2} &= \frac{1}{2}\left(1 - \frac{\delta t}{2} a^2 \delta_{yy}\right) q(t_{n+1}, 1, y_k) \\ &\quad + \frac{1}{2}\left(1 + \frac{\delta t}{2} a^2 \delta_{yy}\right) q(t_n, 1, y_k). \end{aligned}$$

The boundary conditions for $u_{j,k}^{n+1/2}$ on the boundaries $y = 0$ and $y = 1$ are not required because these values can be computed from (6.17).

The truncation error of the Peaceman–Rachford scheme is readily calculated from the unsplit form (6.16). Expanding the terms in equation (6.16), we obtain the Peaceman–Rachford scheme in the form

$$\frac{u_{j,k}^{n+1}-u_{j,k}^{n}}{\delta t} = \frac{1}{2}a^2\delta_{xx}\big(u_{j,k}^{n+1}+u_{j,k}^{n}\big)+\frac{1}{2}a^2\delta_{yy}\big(u_{j,k}^{n+1}+u_{j,k}^{n}\big) - \frac{\delta t}{4}a^4\delta_{xx}\delta_{yy}\big(u_{j,k}^{n+1}-u_{j,k}^{n}\big).$$

Multiplying this equation by δt and expanding all terms in Taylor's series, we compute the leading terms of the truncation error

$$\begin{aligned}\Psi^n(u) &\approx \frac{1}{24}(\delta t)^2\frac{\partial^3 u}{\partial t^3}-\frac{1}{12}(\delta x)^2\frac{\partial^4 u}{\partial x^4}-\frac{1}{12}(\delta y)^2\frac{\partial^4 u}{\partial y^4}\\ &\quad -\frac{1}{8}(\delta t)^2\frac{\partial^4 u}{\partial t^2\partial x^2}-\frac{1}{8}(\delta t)^2\frac{\partial^4 u}{\partial t^2\partial y^2}+\frac{1}{4}(\delta t)^2\frac{\partial^5 u}{\partial t\partial x^2\partial y^2}\\ &= O\big((\delta t)^2+(\delta x)^2+(\delta y)^2\big).\end{aligned}$$

Hence, the Peaceman–Rachford scheme is second-order accurate in δt, δx, and δy, similarly to the two-dimensional Crank–Nicolson scheme.

To analyze the scheme's stability, it is more convenient to use the two-step version of the scheme. Applying the discrete Fourier transform to equations (6.17–6.18), we obtain

$$\left(1+2a^2\lambda_x\sin^2\frac{\delta x\,\xi_x}{2}\right)\hat{U}^{n+1/2} = \left(1-2a^2\lambda_y\sin^2\frac{\delta y\,\xi_y}{2}\right)\hat{U}^{n},$$

$$\left(1+2a^2\lambda_y\sin^2\frac{\delta y\,\xi_y}{2}\right)\hat{U}^{n+1} = \left(1-2a^2\lambda_x\sin^2\frac{\delta x\,\xi_x}{2}\right)\hat{U}^{n+1/2}.$$

From these two equations, we obtain the amplification function

$$G(\xi_x,\xi_y)=\frac{\left(1-2a^2\lambda_x\sin^2\frac{\delta x\,\xi_x}{2}\right)\left(1-2a^2\lambda_y\sin^2\frac{\delta y\,\xi_y}{2}\right)}{\left(1+2a^2\lambda_x\sin^2\frac{\delta x\,\xi_x}{2}\right)\left(1+2a^2\lambda_y\sin^2\frac{\delta y\,\xi_y}{2}\right)}.$$

From that expression, we see that $|G(\xi_x,\xi_y)|\le 1$. Therefore, the Peaceman–Rachford scheme is unconditionally stable. Since we have a consistent and stable scheme, the scheme is convergent according to the Lax equivalence theorem.

Douglas–Rachford scheme: The Douglas–Rachford scheme is obtained by splitting the two-dimensional Euler implicit scheme

$$\big(1 - \delta t\, a^2(\delta_{xx} + \delta_{yy})\big)u_{j,k}^{n+1} = u_{j,k}^n. \tag{6.19}$$

To factor the left-hand side of this equation into

$$(1 - \delta t\, a^2\delta_{xx})(1 - \delta t\, a^2\delta_{yy})u_{j,k}^{n+1},$$

we must add to the left-hand side of (6.19) the term

$$(\delta t)^2 a^4 \delta_{xx}\delta_{yy}u_{j,k}^{n+1}.$$

To compensate for this term, we add to the right-hand side

$$(\delta t)^2 a^4 \delta_{xx}\delta_{yy}u_{j,k}^{n}.$$

We already know from the analysis of the Peaceman–Rachford scheme that the difference

$$(\delta t)^2 a^4 \delta_{xx}\delta_{yy}\big(u_{j,k}^{n+1} - u_{j,k}^n\big) \tag{6.20}$$

is a higher-order term.

Then we obtain the one-step version of the Douglas–Rachford scheme

$$(1 - \delta t\, a^2\delta_{xx})(1 - \delta t\, a^2\delta_{yy})u_{j,k}^{n+1} = \big(1 + (\delta t)^2 a^4\delta_{xx}\delta_{yy}\big)u_{j,k}^n.$$

Since this scheme differs from the Euler implicit scheme by the higher-order term (6.20), the accuracy of the Douglas–Rachford scheme is the same as the Euler implicit scheme, i.e., first-order in δt and second-order in δx and δy.

The splitting form of the Douglas–Rachford scheme is

$$\begin{aligned} (1 - \delta t\, a^2\delta_{xx})u_{j,k}^* &= (1 + \delta t\, a^2\delta_{yy})u_{j,k}^n, \\ (1 - \delta t\, a^2\delta_{yy})u_{j,k}^{n+1} &= u_{j,k}^* - \delta t\, a^2\delta_{yy}u_{j,k}^n. \end{aligned} \tag{6.21}$$

As in the Peaceman–Rachford scheme, we carefully select the boundary conditions for U^*. From (6.21), we find

$$u_{j,k}^* = (1 - \delta t\, a^2\delta_{yy})u_{j,k}^{n+1} + \delta t\, a^2\delta_{yy}u_{j,k}^n.$$

Thus, the boundary conditions for U^* at $j = 0$ and $j = M_x$ can be derived from the Dirichlet boundary conditions

$$\begin{aligned} u_{0,k}^* &= (1 - \delta t\, a^2\delta_{yy})q(t_{n+1}, 0, y_k) + \delta t\, a^2\delta_{yy}q(t_n, 0, y_k), \\ u_{M_x,k}^* &= (1 - \delta t\, a^2\delta_{yy})q(t_{n+1}, 1, y_k) + \delta t\, a^2\delta_{yy}q(t_n, 1, y_k). \end{aligned}$$

We now proceed to the stability analysis of the Douglas–Rachford scheme using the unsplit version of the scheme. Applying the discrete Fourier transform, we get

$$\left(1 + 4a^2\lambda_x \sin^2 \frac{\delta x\, \xi_x}{2}\right)\left(1 + 4a^2\lambda_y \sin^2 \frac{\delta y\, \xi_y}{2}\right)\hat{U}^{n+1}$$
$$= \left(1 + 16a^4\lambda_x\lambda_y \sin^2 \frac{\delta x\, \xi_x}{2} \sin^2 \frac{\delta y\, \xi_y}{2}\right)\hat{U}^{n}.$$

From the above equation, we obtain the amplification function

$$G(\xi_x, \xi_y) = \frac{\left(1 + 16a^4\lambda_x\lambda_y \sin^2 \frac{\delta x\, \xi_x}{2} \sin^2 \frac{\delta y\, \xi_y}{2}\right)}{\left(1 + 4a^2\lambda_x \sin^2 \frac{\delta x\, \xi_x}{2}\right)\left(1 + 4a^2\lambda_y \sin^2 \frac{\delta y\, \xi_y}{2}\right)}.$$

It is easy to see that $0 \leq G(\xi_x, \xi_y) \leq 1$. Therefore, the scheme is unconditionally stable. As a consistent scheme, it also converges.

6.5.3 *Additional topics*

Arbitrary domain

We investigated two-dimensional finite difference schemes in a unit square to simplify the presentation. Real problems require a domain U that is complicated in shape. When setting up difference schemes, we can use a regular grid and adopt finite differences to the irregular boundary of U. An alternative approach is based on irregular grids better adapted to the boundary. Both approaches have some advantages but also specific difficulties. Below, we present the use of regular grids. The analysis of irregular meshes is beyond the scope of this book.

Consider an open, bounded domain $U \subset \mathbb{R}^2$, which is embedded in a larger rectangular set D_U. A regular mesh J_U covers the entire D_U. The regularity of J_U means that the spacing between grid points on any line parallel to the $0x$ axis is constant and equals δx; the same applies to spacing δy along the $0y$ axis. However, the regularity does not exclude that $\delta x \neq \delta y$.

The points of J_U inside U are called the *interior points*. Points at the intersections of the mesh lines with the boundary of U are called the *boundary points*. A boundary point can be a point belonging to

J_U, but in most cases, it is situated between two points of J_U. We call a point $(x_j, y_k) \in J_U$ *regular* if it is an interior point and its distance from any boundary point is not less than the grid spacing. The interior points that are closer to some boundary point are called *irregular*. For regular points operators δ_{xx} and δ_{yy} act in the way defined earlier for $U = (0,1)^2$. To define these operators for irregular points, we take an irregular point (x_j, y_k) and assume that the irregularity only holds in the x direction. Then only δ_{xx} is changed. We have the following three cases:

(1) If (x^*_{j-1}, y_k) is a boundary point (the star superscript indicates that the distance between x^*_{j-1} and x_j can be smaller than δx) and (x_{j+1}, y_k) is a regular point, then

$$\delta_{xx} u^n_{j,k} = \frac{1}{\delta x}\left(\frac{u(t_n, x_{j+1}, y_k) - u(t_n, x_j, y_k)}{\delta x} - \frac{u(t_n, x_j, y_k) - u(t_n, x^*_{j-1}, y_k)}{\delta x^-}\right),$$

where $\delta x^- = |x_j - x^*_{j-1}|$ and obviously $\delta x^- \le \delta x$.

(2) If (x^*_{j+1}, y_k) is a boundary point and (x_{j-1}, y_k) is a regular point, then

$$\delta_{xx} u^n_{j,k} = \frac{1}{\delta x}\left(\frac{u(t_n, x^*_{j+1}, y_k) - u(t_n, x_j, y_k)}{\delta x^+} - \frac{u(t_n, x_j, y_k) - u(t_n, x_{j-1}, y_k)}{\delta x}\right),$$

where $\delta x^+ = |x^*_{j+1} - x_j|$.

(3) Both points (x^*_{j+1}, y_k) and (x^*_{j-1}, y_k) are boundary points, then

$$\delta_{xx} u^n_{j,k} = \frac{1}{\delta x}\left(\frac{u(t_n, x^*_{j+1}, y_k) - u(t_n, x_j, y_k)}{\delta x^+} - \frac{u(t_n, x_j, y_k) - u(t_n, x^*_{j-1}, y_k)}{\delta x^-}\right).$$

Similar modifications of δ_{yy} are required when (x_j, y_k) is irregular in the y direction.

These modifications make the implementation of the ADI algorithms more complicated. However, the essential advantage of solving linear systems with tridiagonal matrices remains valid.

Mixed derivatives

We now extend the considerations to anisotropic diffusion equations with mixed second-order derivatives

$$\frac{\partial u}{\partial t} - a_{11}\frac{\partial^2 u}{\partial x^2} - 2a_{12}\frac{\partial^2 u}{\partial x \partial y} - a_{22}\frac{\partial^2 u}{\partial y^2} = 0 \tag{6.22}$$

defined on $U = (0,1)^2$ with Dirichlet boundary conditions.

The difference schemes we have used for the heat equation now involve nine points at each time level to approximate the spatial derivatives. These cause much greater difficulty in computations than the five-point schemes used for the heat equation. In addition, the use of the ellipticity condition $a_{11}a_{22} > a_{12}^2$ to control the growth of terms arising from the approximation of mixed derivatives can be insufficient, particularly when the coefficients a_{11} and a_{22} are of different magnitude. Hence, numerical schemes for such equations require careful design to obtain accurate and convergent algorithms.

Fortunately, in ADI schemes, we can put the approximation of mixed derivatives into the explicit part of the algorithm. We confine the discussion to the Peaceman–Rachford scheme. For equation (6.22), we have the following extension of the Peaceman–Rachford scheme

$$\left(1 - \frac{\delta t}{2}a_{11}\delta_{xx}\right)u_{j,k}^{n+1/2} = \left(1 + \frac{\delta t}{2}a_{22}\delta_{yy} + \delta t\, a_{12}\delta_x\delta_y\right)u_{j,k}^{n},$$

$$\left(1 - \frac{\delta t}{2}a_{22}\delta_{yy}\right)u_{j,k}^{n+1} = \left(1 + \frac{\delta t}{2}a_{11}\delta_{xx} + \delta t\, a_{12}\delta_x\delta_y\right)u_{j,k}^{n+1/2}.$$

Unfortunately, this scheme is only first-order accurate in time. The scheme can be upgraded to a second-order accurate scheme in time by introducing additional intermediate values

$$\widetilde{U}^n = \frac{3}{2}U^n - \frac{1}{2}U^{n-1}.$$

The improved scheme is as follows

$$\left(1 - \frac{\delta t}{2}a_{11}\delta_{xx}\right)u_{j,k}^{n+1/2} = \left(1 + \frac{\delta t}{2}a_{22}\delta_{yy}\right)u_{j,k}^{n} + \delta t\, a_{12}\delta_x\delta_y\widetilde{u}_{j,k}^{n},$$

$$\left(1 - \frac{\delta t}{2}a_{22}\delta_{yy}\right)u_{j,k}^{n+1} = \left(1 + \frac{\delta t}{2}a_{11}\delta_{xx}\right)u_{j,k}^{n+1/2} + \delta t\, a_{12}\delta_x\delta_y\widetilde{u}_{j,k}^{n}.$$

The boundary conditions for this scheme can be obtained similarly to those of the original Peaceman–Rachford scheme

$$u_{0,k}^{n+1/2} = \frac{1}{2}\left(1 - \frac{\delta t}{2}a_{22}\delta_{yy}\right) q(t_{n+1}, 0, y_k) + \frac{1}{2}\left(1 + \frac{\delta t}{2}a_{22}\delta_{yy}\right) q(t_n, 0, y_k),$$

$$u_{M_x,k}^{n+1/2} = \frac{1}{2}\left(1 - \frac{\delta t}{2}a_{22}\delta_{yy}\right) q(t_{n+1}, 1, y_k) + \frac{1}{2}\left(1 + \frac{\delta t}{2}a_{22}\delta_{yy}\right) q(t_n, 1, y_k).$$

Lower order terms

There is no doubt where first-order derivatives should be placed in ADI schemes. The first-order derivative with respect to x should go with the second-order x derivative. The same applies to derivatives with respect to y. As we know from Section 6.4, the way we approximate the first-order derivatives greatly influences the scheme stability. These results extend straightforwardly to ADI schemes. The formulas used for approximating first-order derivatives and decisions of placing corresponding terms in the implicit or explicit part of the scheme determine the accuracy of the scheme. These effects can be investigated easily by adapting the considerations of Section 6.4.

For nonhomogeneous equations with a nonhomogeneous term $f(t, x, y)$, it is not always clear where such a term should go in an ADI scheme. Using an incorrect approximation, we can destroy the scheme's accuracy. The suggested solution is to use an integral form of the differential equation (in an analogy with equations of mathematical physics, this integral form is called the conservation law formulation) and approximate the integral of $f(t, x, y)$ in a way that preserves the desired order of accuracy. We do not discuss these considerations in detail. To illustrate that the good placement of the nonhomogeneous term is not obvious, we describe, following the presentation in the book by Thomas [87], the derivation of the Peaceman–Rachford scheme for the equation

$$\frac{\partial u}{\partial t} - a^2\left(\frac{\partial^2 u}{\partial x^2} + \frac{\partial^2 u}{\partial y^2}\right) = f(t, x, y).$$

Integrating the equation in a bounded domain $U \subset \mathbb{R}^2$ and applying Green's theorem, we obtain

$$\int_U \frac{\partial u}{\partial t} dxdy = \int_U f(t,x,y)dxdy + \int_{\partial U} a^2 \nu \cdot \nabla u dS,$$

where ν is the outward normal to ∂U.

Applying this equation to the domain

$$U = \big((j-1/2)\delta x, (j+1/2)\delta x\big) \times \big((k-1/2)\delta y, (k+1/2)\delta y\big),$$

which is the cell centered at the (j,k) grid point, we obtain the following version of the integral form of the conservation law

$$\begin{aligned}
&\int_{y_{k-1/2}}^{y_{k+1/2}} \int_{x_{j-1/2}}^{x_{j+1/2}} u_t dxdy \\
&\quad = \int_{y_{k-1/2}}^{y_{k+1/2}} \int_{x_{j-1/2}}^{x_{j+1/2}} f(t,x,y)dxdy \\
&\qquad + a^2 \int_{y_{k-1/2}}^{y_{k+1/2}} u_x(t, x_{j+1/2}, y)dy - a^2 \int_{y_{k-1/2}}^{y_{k+1/2}} u_x(t, x_{j-1/2}, y)dy \\
&\qquad + a^2 \int_{x_{j-1/2}}^{x_{j+1/2}} u_y(t, x, y_{k+1/2})dx - a^2 \int_{x_{j-1/2}}^{x_{j+1/2}} u_y(t, x, y_{k-1/2})dx.
\end{aligned}$$

Integrating this equation from t_n to t_{n+1}, we get

$$\begin{aligned}
&\int_{y_{k-1/2}}^{y_{k+1/2}} \int_{x_{j-1/2}}^{x_{j+1/2}} (u^{n+1} - u^n) dxdy \\
&\quad = \int_{t_n}^{t_{n+1}} \int_{y_{k-1/2}}^{y_{k+1/2}} \int_{x_{j-1/2}}^{x_{j+1/2}} f(t,x,y)dxdydt \\
&\qquad + a^2 \int_{t_n}^{t_{n+1}} \int_{y_{k-1/2}}^{y_{k+1/2}} u_x(t, x_{j+1/2}, y)dydt \\
&\qquad - a^2 \int_{t_n}^{t_{n+1}} \int_{y_{k-1/2}}^{y_{k+1/2}} u_x(t, x_{j-1/2}, y)dydt
\end{aligned}$$

$$+ a^2 \int_{t_n}^{t_{n+1}} \int_{x_{j-1/2}}^{x_{j+1/2}} u_y(t, x, y_{k+1/2}) dx dt$$
$$- a^2 \int_{t_n}^{t_{n+1}} \int_{x_{j-1/2}}^{x_{j+1/2}} u_y(t, x, y_{k-1/2}) dx dt.$$

Approximating the first integral and the integral of the x-derivative by the midpoint rule and the integral of the y-derivative by the trapezoidal rule, we obtain

$$\begin{aligned}
&\delta x\, \delta y(u_{j,k}^{n+1} - u_{j,k}^n) + O\big(\delta t(\delta x)^3 \delta y\big) + O\big(\delta t\, \delta x(\delta y)^3\big) \\
&\quad = \int_{t_n}^{t_{n+1}} \int_{y_{k-1/2}}^{y_{k+1/2}} \int_{x_{j-1/2}}^{x_{j+1/2}} f(t, x, y) dx dy dt \\
&\quad + a^2(\delta t\, \delta x\, \delta y)\delta_{xx} u_{j,k}^{n+1/2} + O\big(\delta t\, \delta x(\delta y)^3\big) + O\big((\delta t)^3 \delta x\, \delta y\big) \\
&\quad + a^2(\delta t\, \delta x\, \delta y)\delta_{yy}\big(u_{j,k}^{n+1} + u_{j,k}^n\big) + O\big(\delta t(\delta x)^3 \delta y\big) + O\big((\delta t)^3 \delta x\, \delta y\big).
\end{aligned}$$

To preserve the order of approximation of the differential part of the equation, we must approximate the nonhomogeneous integral at least to the order

$$O\big((\delta t)^3 \delta x\, \delta y\big) + O\big(\delta t(\delta x)^3 \delta y\big) + O\big(\delta t\, \delta x(\delta y)^3\big).$$

Hence, if we approximate the nonhomogeneous integral by the midpoint rule with respect to x and y, and either the midpoint rule or the trapezoidal rule with respect to t, we obtain the proper order of approximation. With the trapezoidal approximation of the integral with respect to t, we get the scheme

$$\begin{aligned}
\delta x\, \delta y(u_{j,k}^{n+1} - u_{j,k}^n) &= \frac{\delta t\, \delta x\, \delta y}{2}\big(f_{j,k}^n + f_{j,k}^{n+1}\big) + a^2(\delta t\, \delta x\, \delta y)\delta_{xx} u_{j,k}^{n+1/2} \\
&\quad + a^2 \frac{\delta t\, \delta x\, \delta y}{2} \delta_{yy}\big(u_{j,k}^{n+1} + u_{j,k}^n\big).
\end{aligned}$$

This gives the following splitting form of the Peaceman–Rachford scheme which preserves the second-order accuracy

$$\left(1 - \frac{\delta t}{2} a^2 \delta_{xx}\right) u_{j,k}^{n+1/2} = \left(1 + \frac{\delta t}{2} a^2 \delta_{yy}\right) u_{j,k}^n + \frac{\delta t}{2} f_{j,k}^n,$$
$$\left(1 - \frac{\delta t}{2} a^2 \delta_{yy}\right) u_{j,k}^{n+1} = \left(1 + \frac{\delta t}{2} a^2 \delta_{xx}\right) u_{j,k}^{n+1/2} + \frac{\delta t}{2} f_{j,k}^{n+1}.$$

Approximating the nonhomogeneous integral by the midpoint rule with respect to t, we obtain also the second-order accurate scheme

$$\left(1-\frac{\delta t}{2}a^2\delta_{xx}\right)u_{j,k}^{n+1/2}=\left(1+\frac{\delta t}{2}a^2\delta_{yy}\right)u_{j,k}^{n}+\frac{\delta t}{2}f_{j,k}^{n+1/2},$$
$$\left(1-\frac{\delta t}{2}a^2\delta_{yy}\right)u_{j,k}^{n+1}=\left(1+\frac{\delta t}{2}a^2\delta_{xx}\right)u_{j,k}^{n+1/2}+\frac{\delta t}{2}f_{j,k}^{n+1/2}.$$

Three-dimensional schemes

Below, we give a brief presentation of three-dimensional ADI schemes. As before, we consider the heat equation

$$\frac{\partial u}{\partial t}-a^2\left(\frac{\partial^2 u}{\partial x^2}+\frac{\partial^2 u}{\partial y^2}+\frac{\partial^2 u}{\partial z^2}\right)=0.$$

The extension of two-dimensional ADI schemes to three dimensions is not straightforward, as the example of the Peaceman–Rachford scheme shows. The three-dimensional Peaceman–Rachford scheme is not unconditionally stable and is only first-order accurate in time. In contrast, the three-dimensional Douglas–Rachford scheme

$$(1-\delta t\, a^2\delta_{xx})u_{j,k,l}^{*}=\big(1+\delta t\, a^2(\delta_{yy}+\delta_{zz})\big)u_{j,k,l}^{n},$$
$$(1-\delta t\, a^2\delta_{yy})u_{j,k,l}^{**}=u_{j,k,l}^{*}-\delta t\, a^2\delta_{yy}u_{j,k,l}^{n},$$
$$(1-\delta t\, a^2\delta_{zz})u_{j,k,l}^{n+1}=u_{j,k,l}^{**}-\delta t\, a^2\delta_{zz}u_{j,k,l}^{n}$$

is unconditionally stable and $O\big((\delta t)+(\delta x)^2+(\delta y)^2+(\delta z)^2\big)$ accurate, exactly as in two dimensions.

To obtain unconditionally stable ADI schemes, we have to proceed as in two dimensions, i.e., take a stable scheme such as the Crank–Nicolson or the implicit Euler scheme and perform an appropriate splitting. We now illustrate such splitting for the three-dimensional Crank–Nicolson scheme

$$\left(1-\frac{\delta t}{2}a^2(\delta_{xx}+\delta_{yy}+\delta_{zz})\right)u_{j,k,l}^{n+1}$$
$$=\left(1+\frac{\delta t}{2}a^2(\delta_{xx}+\delta_{yy}+\delta_{zz})\right)u_{j,k,l}^{n} \qquad (6.23)$$

which is unconditionally stable and $O\big((\delta t)^2 + (\delta x)^2 + (\delta y)^2 + (\delta z)^2\big)$ accurate. Adding to the left-hand side the expression

$$\frac{(\delta t)^2}{4} a^4(\delta_{xx}\delta_{yy} + \delta_{xx}\delta_{zz} + \delta_{yy}\delta_{zz})u^{n+1}_{j,k,l} - \frac{(\delta t)^3}{8} a^6 \delta_{xx}\delta_{yy}\delta_{zz} u^{n+1}_{j,k,l}$$

and a similar expression for $u^n_{j,k,l}$ to the right-hand side, we obtain the scheme

$$\begin{aligned}&\left(1 - \frac{\delta t}{2} a^2 \delta_{xx}\right)\left(1 - \frac{\delta t}{2} a^2 \delta_{yy}\right)\left(1 - \frac{\delta t}{2} a^2 \delta_{zz}\right) u^{n+1}_{j,k,l} \\ &\quad = \left(1 + \frac{\delta t}{2} a^2 \delta_{xx}\right)\left(1 + \frac{\delta t}{2} a^2 \delta_{yy}\right)\left(1 + \frac{\delta t}{2} a^2 \delta_{zz}\right) u^{n}_{j,k,l}. \qquad (6.24)\end{aligned}$$

Collecting the added terms

$$\begin{aligned}&\frac{(\delta t)^2}{4} a^4(\delta_{xx}\delta_{yy} + \delta_{xx}\delta_{zz} + \delta_{yy}\delta_{zz})\big(u^{n+1}_{j,k,l} - u^n_{j,k,l}\big) \\ &\quad - \frac{(\delta t)^3}{8} a^6 \delta_{xx}\delta_{yy}\delta_{zz}\big(u^{n+1}_{j,k,l} + u^n_{j,k,l}\big),\end{aligned}$$

we obtain an expression of order $O\big((\delta t)^3\big)$. Hence, up to $O\big((\delta t)^2\big)$ the schemes (6.23) and (6.24) are equivalent.

We now write (6.24) in the form

$$\begin{aligned}&\left(1 - \frac{\delta t}{2} a^2 \delta_{xx}\right)\left(1 - \frac{\delta t}{2} a^2 \delta_{yy}\right)\left(1 - \frac{\delta t}{2} a^2 \delta_{zz}\right) \big(u^{n+1}_{j,k,l} - u^n_{j,k,l}\big) \\ &\quad = \delta t\, a^2(\delta_{xx} + \delta_{yy} + \delta_{zz})u^n_{j,k,l} + \frac{(\delta t)^3}{4} a^6 \delta_{xx}\delta_{yy}\delta_{zz} u^n_{j,k,l}. \qquad (6.25)\end{aligned}$$

Since the last term in equation (6.25) is of order $O\big((\delta t)^3\big)$, it can be dropped without destroying the scheme's accuracy. We split the modified scheme using the so-called Δ-formulation. Then we arrive at the Douglas–Gunn scheme

$$\begin{aligned}\left(1 - \frac{\delta t}{2} a^2 \delta_{xx}\right) \Delta u^{*}_{j,k,l} &= \delta t\, a^2(\delta_{xx} + \delta_{yy} + \delta_{zz})u^n_{j,k,l}, \\ \left(1 - \frac{\delta t}{2} a^2 \delta_{yy}\right) \Delta u^{**}_{j,k,l} &= \Delta u^{*}_{j,k,l},\end{aligned}$$

$$\left(1-\frac{\delta t}{2}a^2\delta_{zz}\right)\Delta u_{j,k,l}=\Delta u^{**}_{j,k,l},$$

$$\Delta u_{j,k,l}=u^{n+1}_{j,k,l}-u^{n}_{j,k,l}.$$

The scheme is $O\big((\delta t)^2+(\delta x)^2+(\delta y)^2+(\delta z)^2\big)$ accurate as the Crank–Nicolson scheme. Applying the discrete Fourier transform to this scheme, we find

$$\begin{aligned}
&\left(1+2a^2\lambda_x\sin^2\frac{\delta x\,\xi_x}{2}\right)\left(1+2a^2\lambda_y\sin^2\frac{\delta y\,\xi_y}{2}\right)\\
&\quad\times\left(1+2a^2\lambda_z\sin^2\frac{\delta z\,\xi_z}{2}\right)\hat{U}^{n+1}\\
&=\left(1-2a^2\lambda_x\sin^2\frac{\delta x\,\xi_x}{2}-2a^2\lambda_y\sin^2\frac{\delta y\,\xi_y}{2}-2a^2\lambda_z\sin^2\frac{\delta z\,\xi_z}{2}\right.\\
&\quad+4a^4\lambda_x\lambda_y\sin^2\frac{\delta x\,\xi_x}{2}\sin^2\frac{\delta y\,\xi_y}{2}+4a^4\lambda_x\lambda_z\sin^2\frac{\delta x\,\xi_x}{2}\sin^2\frac{\delta z\,\xi_z}{2}\\
&\quad+4a^4\lambda_y\lambda_z\sin^2\frac{\delta y\,\xi_y}{2}\sin^2\frac{\delta z\,\xi_z}{2}\\
&\quad\left.+8a^6\lambda_x\lambda_y\lambda_z\sin^2\frac{\delta x\,\xi_x}{2}\sin^2\frac{\delta y\,\xi_y}{2}\sin^2\frac{\delta z\,\xi_z}{2}\right)\hat{U}^{n}.
\end{aligned}$$

It is easy to check that the amplification function $G(\xi_x,\xi_y,\xi_z)$ which follows from this expression fulfills the condition

$$-1\le G(\xi_x,\xi_y,\xi_z)\le 1.$$

Therefore, the scheme is unconditionally stable. Being stable and consistent, the scheme is convergent.

6.6 Exercises

Exercise 6.1. To solve the initial value problem for the advection equation

$$\frac{\partial u}{\partial t}+b\frac{\partial u}{\partial x}=0,\quad u(0,x)=g(x),$$

apply the two-step scheme

$$u_k^{n+1/2} = u_k^n - \frac{b\gamma}{2}(u_{k+1}^n - u_{k-1}^n),$$

$$u_k^{n+1} = u_k^n - \frac{b\gamma}{2}(u_{k+1}^{n+1/2} - u_{k-1}^{n+1/2}),$$

where $\gamma = \delta t/\delta x$.

Write this scheme as a one-step scheme. Find the order of approximation of this scheme and analyze its stability.

Exercise 6.2. Approximate the advection equation

$$\frac{\partial u}{\partial t} + b\frac{\partial u}{\partial x} = f(t,x)$$

by the box scheme

$$\frac{u_k^{n+1} + u_{k+1}^{n+1} - u_k^n - u_{k+1}^n}{2\delta t} + \frac{b}{2}\left(\frac{u_{k+1}^{n+1} - u_k^{n+1}}{\delta x} + \frac{u_{k+1}^n - u_k^n}{\delta x}\right) = f_k^n.$$

Prove that the scheme is stable for all values of $\gamma = \delta t/\delta x$.

Exercise 6.3. Approximate the advection-diffusion equation

$$\frac{\partial u}{\partial t} + b\frac{\partial u}{\partial x} = a^2\frac{\partial^2 u}{\partial x^2}$$

by the MacCormack scheme

$$\tilde{u}_k^n = u_k^n - b\delta t\frac{u_k^n - u_{k-1}^n}{\delta x},$$

$$u_k^{n+1} = u_k^n - \frac{b}{2}\delta t\left(\frac{u_k^n - u_{k-1}^n}{\delta x} + \frac{\tilde{u}_{k+1}^n - \tilde{u}_k^n}{\delta x}\right)$$

$$+ \frac{a^2}{2}\delta t\left(\frac{u_{k+1}^n - 2u_k^n + u_{k-1}^n}{(\delta x)^2} + \frac{\tilde{u}_{k+1}^n - 2\tilde{u}_k^n + \tilde{u}_{k-1}^n}{(\delta x)^2}\right).$$

Find the conditions for the von Neumann stability.

Exercise 6.4. Approximate the equation

$$\frac{\partial u}{\partial t} + b\frac{\partial^3 u}{\partial x^3} = f(t,x)$$

by the scheme

$$\frac{u_k^{n+1} - (u_{k+1}^n + u_{k-1}^n)/2}{\delta t} + \frac{b}{2}\frac{u_{k+2}^n - 2u_{k+1}^n + 2u_{k-1}^n - u_{k-2}^n}{(\delta x)^3} = f_k^n.$$

(a) Prove that the scheme is consistent with the equation if $(\delta x)^2/\delta t$ tends to zero as δx and δt tend to zero.

(b) Prove that the scheme is stable if $4|b|\delta t/(\delta x)^3$ is bounded.
Note that the consistency and stability conditions cannot be satisfied simultaneously. Thus, this scheme cannot converge because it cannot be consistent and stable.

(c) Show that the scheme

$$\frac{u_k^{n+1} - u_k^n}{\delta t} + b\frac{u_{k+2}^n - 3u_{k+1}^n + 3u_k^n - u_{k-1}^n}{(\delta x)^3} = f_k^n$$

is consistent with the equation.
Prove that the scheme is stable if $\delta t/(\delta x)^3$ is constant and $0 \leq b\delta t/(\delta x)^3 \leq 1/4$.

Exercise 6.5. Consider the equation

$$\frac{\partial u}{\partial t} + \frac{1}{2}\sigma^2 x^2 \frac{\partial u^2}{\partial x^2} = 0, \quad 0 \leq x \leq x_{\max}, \quad t \in [0, T),$$

with the terminal condition

$$u(T, x) = g(x), \quad x \in [0, x_{\max}],$$

and the boundary conditions

$$u(t, 0) = q_1(t), \quad u(t, x_{\max}) = q_2(t).$$

The above terminal-boundary value problem is approximated by the explicit Euler scheme on an equidistant grid in (t, x). Investigate the stability of this scheme.

Exercise 6.6. Consider the equation

$$\frac{\partial u}{\partial t} + \frac{1}{2}\sigma^2 x^2 \frac{\partial^2 u}{\partial x^2} = 0, \quad t \in [0, T), \quad x \in (0, x_{\max})$$

with the terminal condition

$$u(T, x) = (K - x)^+, \quad x \in [0, x_{\max}], \quad K > 0,$$

and the boundary conditions

$$\frac{\partial u}{\partial x} = 0, \quad x = 0, \quad t \in [0, T),$$

$$u = 0, \quad x = x_{\max}, \quad t \in [0, T).$$

The problem is approximated by the Crank–Nicolson scheme on an equidistant grid. Write the discretization of the boundary conditions that give the same order of approximation as the order of the Crank–Nicolson scheme.

Exercise 6.7. For the heat equation

$$\frac{\partial u}{\partial t} = \frac{\partial^2 u}{\partial x^2}$$

apply the scheme called *the leapfrog scheme*

$$\frac{u_k^{n+1} - u_k^{n-1}}{2\delta t} = \frac{u_{k+1}^n - 2u_k^n + u_{k-1}^n}{\delta x^2}.$$

Compute its order of approximation and analyze the scheme stability.

Exercise 6.8. Consider the parabolic equation with variable coefficients

$$a(x)\frac{\partial u}{\partial t} = \frac{\partial}{\partial x}\left(\sigma(x)\frac{\partial u}{\partial x}\right),$$

with $0 < a_{\min} \leq a(x) \leq a_{\max} < +\infty$ and $0 < \sigma_{\min} \leq \sigma(x) \leq \sigma_{\max} < +\infty$.

To solve this equation on a bounded interval $U = (0, x_{\max})$ with zero boundary conditions, apply a finite difference scheme in which the term

$$\frac{\partial}{\partial x}\left(\sigma\frac{\partial u}{\partial x}\right)(x_k)$$

is approximated by

$$\frac{1}{\delta x}\left[\left(\sigma\frac{\partial u}{\partial x}\right)(x_{k+1/2}) - \left(\sigma\frac{\partial u}{\partial x}\right)(x_{k-1/2})\right],$$

$$\text{where} \quad x_{k\pm1/2} = x_k \pm \frac{\delta x}{2}.$$

To obtain a numerical scheme, approximate $\partial u/\partial t\,(x_{k\pm1/2})$ by central differences and $\partial u/\partial t\,(t_n)$ by forward differences.

Write the final version of the scheme and compute its order of approximation assuming that $\sigma(x)$ is sufficiently smooth.

Exercise 6.9. For the heat equation

$$\frac{\partial u}{\partial t} = a^2 \frac{\partial^2 u}{\partial x^2}$$

apply the following two-step scheme

$$\tilde{u}_k^{n+1/2} = u_k^n + \frac{1}{2} a^2 \delta t \frac{u_{k+1}^n - 2u_k^n + u_{k-1}^n}{(\delta x)^2},$$

$$u_k^{n+1} = u_k^n + a^2 \delta t \frac{\tilde{u}_{k+1}^{n+1/2} - 2\tilde{u}_k^{n+1/2} + \tilde{u}_{k-1}^{n+1/2}}{(\delta x)^2}.$$

(a) Prove that this scheme has the order of approximation $O\big((\delta t)^2 + (\delta x)^2\big)$.
(b) Prove that the scheme is stable for $a^2 \delta t/(\delta x)^2 \le 1/2$.

Exercise 6.10. Consider a one-dimensional parabolic equation with the Dirichlet–Neumann boundary conditions

$$\frac{\partial u}{\partial t} - a^2(t,x) \frac{\partial^2 u}{\partial x^2} + b(t,x) \frac{\partial u}{\partial x} + c(t,x) u = f(t,x),$$
$$x \in (0,1), \quad t \in (0,T],$$
$$u(t,0) = 0, \quad \frac{\partial u}{\partial x}(t,1) = 0, \quad t \in [0,T],$$
$$u(0,x) = g(x), \quad x \in (0,1).$$

Write the Euler explicit scheme for this problem on an equidistant grid. Investigate its consistency and stability.

Exercise 6.11. The backward and forward finite differences are one-sided and give first-order approximations. In contrast, the central difference that uses function values on both sides of the point of approximation is second-order accurate. One-sided second-order approximations of first-order derivatives can be obtained by selecting the appropriate parameters α_1, α_2, and α_3 in the expression

$$\frac{\alpha_1 u(x) + \alpha_2 u(x-h) + \alpha_3 u(x-2h)}{h} - u'(x) = O(h^2).$$

(a) Prove that the following estimate holds for a one-sided approximation of a C^3 function $u(x)$

$$\frac{3u(x) - 4u(x-h) + u(x-2h)}{2h} - u'(x) = \frac{h^2}{3} u'''(\eta),$$

where $\eta \in (x - 2h, x)$.

(b) The above concept of second-order accuracy applied to a one-dimensional parabolic equation

$$\frac{\partial u}{\partial t} - a^2(t,x)\frac{\partial^2 u}{\partial x^2} + b(t,x)\frac{\partial u}{\partial x} + c(t,x)u = f(t,x)$$

gives the Gear scheme

$$\begin{aligned}\left(3u_k^n - 4u_k^{n-1} + u_k^{n-2}\right) - \lambda(a_k^n)^2\left(u_{k+1}^n - 2u_k^n + u_{k-1}^n\right)\\ + \gamma b_k^n\left(u_{k+1}^n - u_{k-1}^n\right) + 2\delta t\, c_k^n u_k^n = 2\delta t\, f_k^n,\end{aligned}$$

where

$$\lambda = \frac{\delta t}{(\delta x)^2}, \quad \gamma = \frac{\delta t}{\delta x}.$$

Prove that this scheme is second-order accurate with respect to δt and δx. Analyze the stability of this scheme.

Exercise 6.12. Prove that the truncation error of the Crank–Nicolson scheme for the heat equation

$$\frac{\partial u}{\partial t} = \frac{\partial^2 u}{\partial x^2}$$

at point $(t_{n+1/2}, x_k)$ takes the following form

$$(\delta t)^2\left(\frac{1}{24}\frac{\partial^3 u}{\partial t^3}(\eta^{(1)}, x_k) - \frac{1}{8}\frac{\partial^4 u}{\partial t^2 \partial x^2}(\eta^{(2)}, x_k)\right) - \frac{(\delta x)^2}{12}\frac{\partial^4 u}{\partial x^4}(\eta^{(3)}, \xi),$$

where $\xi \in (x_{k-1}, x_{k+1})$, $\eta^{(i)} \in (t_n, t_{n+1})$, $i = 1, 2, 3$.
Hint: Approximate the derivative $\partial u/\partial t\,(t_{n+1/2}, x_k)$ by the central difference between points (t_{n+1}, x_k) and (t_n, x_k). The second-order derivative $\partial^2 u/\partial x^2(t_{n+1/2}, x_k)$ approximate by the average of values in points (t_{n+1}, x_k) and (t_n, x_k).

Exercise 6.13. Consider the three-point explicit finite difference scheme

$$u_k^{n+1} = a_k u_{k-1}^n + b_k u_k^n + c_k u_{k+1}^n, \quad k = 0, 1, \ldots, M,$$

where $a_k \geq 0$, $b_k = 1 - a_k - c_k \geq 0$, $c_k \geq 0$, and $a_0 = c_M = 0$. Prove the scheme stability under the maximum norm

$$\max_{0 \leq k \leq M} |u_k^{n+1}| \leq \max_{0 \leq k \leq M} |u_k^n|.$$

Exercise 6.14. To the nonhomogeneous heat equation

$$\frac{\partial u}{\partial t} = a^2 \frac{\partial^2 u}{\partial x^2} + f(t, x),$$

apply the Du Fort–Frankel scheme

$$\frac{u_k^{n+1} - u_k^{n-1}}{2\delta t} = a^2 \frac{u_{k+1}^n - (u_k^{n+1} + u_k^{n-1}) + u_{k-1}^n}{(\delta x)^2} + f_k^n.$$

Prove that the scheme is unconditionally stable.

Exercise 6.15. Approximate the advection equation

$$\frac{\partial u}{\partial t} + b\frac{\partial u}{\partial x} = 0$$

by the scheme

$$\frac{u_k^{n+1} - u_k^n}{\delta t} + \frac{b}{2}\left(\frac{u_{k+1}^{n+1} - u_k^{n+1}}{\delta x} + \frac{u_k^n - u_{k-1}^n}{\delta x}\right) = 0.$$

Multiplying the scheme by $u_k^{n+1} + u_k^n$ and summing over k, obtain the relation

$$\sum_{k=-\infty}^{\infty} \left(\left(1 - \frac{b\gamma}{2}\right) |u_k^{n+1}|^2 + \frac{b\gamma}{2} u_k^{n+1} u_{k+1}^{n+1}\right)$$
$$= \sum_{k=-\infty}^{\infty} \left(\left(1 - \frac{b\gamma}{2}\right) |u_k^n|^2 + \frac{b\gamma}{2} u_k^n u_{k+1}^n\right),$$

where $\gamma = \delta t / \delta x$.

Prove that the scheme is stable for $b\gamma < 1$.

Exercise 6.16. Apply to the Black–Scholes equation with variable volatility

$$\frac{\partial V}{\partial t}+\frac{1}{2}\sigma^2(S)S^2\frac{\partial^2 V}{\partial S^2}+rS\frac{\partial V}{\partial S}-rV=0,\quad S\geq 0, t\in[0,T]$$

the change of variables

$$\begin{aligned}\xi&=\frac{S}{S+K},\\ \tau&=T-t,\\ V(t,S)&=(S+K)\bar{V}(\tau,\xi).\end{aligned}$$

Show that the obtained equation is parabolic in a bounded domain (τ,ξ) with $\tau\in[0,T]$ and $\xi\in[0,1)$

$$\frac{\partial\bar{V}}{\partial\tau}=\frac{1}{2}\bar{\sigma}^2(\xi)\xi^2(1-\xi)^2\frac{\partial^2\bar{V}}{\partial\xi^2}+r\xi(1-\xi)\frac{\partial\bar{V}}{\partial\xi}-r(1-\xi)\bar{V},$$

where $\bar{\sigma}(\xi)=\sigma\big(K\xi/(1-\xi)\big)$.

Consider the following explicit scheme for this equation

$$\begin{aligned}\frac{v_k^{n+1}-v_k^n}{\delta\tau}&=(\xi_k(1-\xi_k)\bar{\sigma}_k)^2\frac{v_{k-1}^n-2v_k^n+v_{k+1}^n}{2(\delta\xi)^2}\\ &\quad+r\xi_k(1-\xi_k)\frac{v_{k+1}^n-v_{k-1}^n}{2\delta\xi}-r(1-\xi_k)v_k^n,\end{aligned}$$

where $v_k^n=\bar{V}(n\delta\tau,\xi_k)$, $\bar{\sigma}_k=\bar{\sigma}(\xi_k)$, and $\xi_k=k\delta\xi$.

Prove that if

$$\max_{0\leq k\leq M}\frac{\big(\xi_k(1-\xi_k)\bar{\sigma}_k\big)^2}{2}\frac{\delta\tau}{(\delta\xi)^2}\leq\frac{1}{2},$$

then the von Neumann stability condition holds.

Exercise 6.17 (Separation of singularities). The truncation error can be better controlled when the solution of the problem is sufficiently smooth. In pricing financial derivatives, we encounter the problem of smoothness caused by terminal conditions (even a simple vanilla option has a terminal condition that is only continuous). To overcome the lack of smoothness, we introduce a function obtained by subtracting from the original solution a function that bears non-smooth singularities. If the function with singularities is easily computable and fulfills an equation similar to the equation of the original problem, the truncation error of the equation for the difference can be controlled better.

(a) Consider pricing a vanilla call option in the Black–Scholes model with variable volatility

$$\frac{\partial V}{\partial t} + \frac{1}{2}\sigma^2(S)S^2\frac{\partial^2 V}{\partial S^2} + rS\frac{\partial V}{\partial S} - rV = 0, \quad 0 \le S, t \in [0,T],$$
$$V(T,S) = \max(S-K,0), \quad 0 \le S.$$

Since the final condition is not smooth, subtract from $V(t,S)$ the solution $V_K(t,S)$ of the Black–Scholes equation with constant volatility $\sigma(K)$. Let $\bar{V}(t,S) = V(t,S) - V_K(t,S)$. This function fulfills the equation

$$\frac{\partial \bar{V}}{\partial t} + \frac{1}{2}\sigma^2(S)S^2\frac{\partial^2 \bar{V}}{\partial S^2} + rS\frac{\partial \bar{V}}{\partial S} - r\bar{V} = f(t,S), \quad 0 \le S, t \in [0,T],$$
$$\bar{V}(T,S) = 0, \quad 0 \le S,$$

where

$$f(t,S) = \frac{1}{2}\left(\sigma^2(K) - \sigma^2(S)\right)S^2\frac{\partial^2 V_K}{\partial S^2}.$$

The exact form of function $f(t,S)$ is known because the price V_K is given by the Black–Scholes formula.

Apply the change of variables described in problem (6.16) and reformulate the problem for $V(t,S)$ and $V_K(t,S)$ on a bounded domain $\xi \in [0,1]$, $\tau \in [0,T]$.

(b) Investigate the effectiveness of the singularity separation method on the CEV model of local volatility

$$dS_t = rS_t dt + \sigma_0 S_t^{\beta} dW_t,$$

where interest rate r and volatility σ_0 are constants, and $0 < \beta \le 1$.

Following the Feynman–Kac theorem (Theorem 5.2), prove that the option price in the CEV model fulfills the equation

$$\frac{\partial V}{\partial t} + \frac{1}{2}\sigma_0^2 S^{2\beta}\frac{\partial^2 V}{\partial S^2} + rS\frac{\partial V}{\partial S} - rV = 0, \quad 0 \le S, t \in [0, T],$$

with an appropriate terminal condition.

Approximate the price of a call option in (τ, ξ) variables by the Crank–Nicolson scheme on an equidistant grid. Compute the option prices with and without separation of singularities taking $S_0 = 45$, $K = 50$, $\sigma_0 = 25\%$, $r = 5\%$, $T = 1$, and $\beta = 0.7$. Use grids with $M = N = 50, 100, 200, 400$. Compare the accuracy of both methods.

(c) The call option price in the CEV model for $\beta < 1$ can be evaluated analytically by the formula due to Schroder [78]

$$V(0, S_0) = S_0\left(1 - W\left(2y; 2 + \frac{2}{2-2\beta}, 2x\right)\right) - Ke^{-rT}W\left(2x; \frac{2}{2-2\beta}, 2y\right),$$

where $W(x; \nu, \lambda)$ is the cumulative distribution function for the noncentral chi-squared random variable with ν degrees of freedom and noncentrality parameter λ. The parameters x and y are defined as follows

$$k = \frac{2r}{\sigma_0^2(2-2\beta)\left(e^{r(2-2\beta)T} - 1\right)}, \quad x = kS_0^{2-2\beta}e^{r(2-\beta)T},$$
$$y = kK^{2-2\beta}.$$

Using the noncentral chi-squared distribution, compute the exact option price (the distribution function for the noncentral chi-squared random variable is available in many computer packages such as MATLAB, R, and S-PLUS). Compare the result with the solution obtained by the Crank–Nicolson scheme. Compute the truncation error of the numerical approximation.

Exercise 6.18. Derive a differential equation satisfied by the option Delta in the classical Black–Scholes model. Find the appropriate boundary conditions for this equation.

Exercise 6.19. Consider an arithmetic average Asian option. The price of this Asian call option fulfills the equation (cf. Example 5.47 in Chapter 5)

$$\frac{\partial H}{\partial t} + (1 - rR)\frac{\partial H}{\partial R} + \frac{1}{2}\sigma^2 R^2 \frac{\partial^2 H}{\partial R^2} = 0, \quad \text{for} \quad t \in [0, T), \quad R > 0,$$

with the terminal condition

$$H(T, R) = \left(1 - \frac{1}{T}R\right)^+ \quad \text{for} \quad R > 0$$

and the boundary conditions

$$H = 0 \quad \text{for} \quad R \to \infty, \quad t \in [0, T),$$

$$\frac{\partial H}{\partial t} + \frac{\partial H}{\partial R} = 0 \quad \text{for} \quad R = 0, \quad t \in [0, T).$$

Approximate the equation for $H(t, R)$ by the Crank–Nicolson scheme on an equidistant grid in a bounded domain $[0, T] \times [0, R_{\max}]$. Write the discretization of the boundary conditions that give the same order of approximation as the order of the Crank–Nicolson scheme. Compute the price of the average strike Asian call option with arithmetic averaging assuming $S_0 = 50$, $\sigma = 30\%$, $r = 5\%$, and $T = 0.5$.

Exercise 6.20. Consider a floating strike lookback put option with continuous monitoring. By similarity reduction, the option price is given by the equation (cf. Example 5.48 in Chapter 5)

$$\frac{\partial W(t, x)}{\partial t} + rx\frac{\partial W(t, x)}{\partial x} + \frac{1}{2}\sigma^2 x^2 \frac{\partial^2 W(t, x)}{\partial x^2} - rW(t, x) = 0,$$

for $t \in [0, T)$ and $x \in (0, 1)$ with the terminal condition

$$W(x, T) = 1 - x \quad \text{for } x \in [0, 1],$$

and the boundary conditions

$$W(0, t) = e^{-r(T-t)} \quad \text{for } t \in [0, T],$$

$$\frac{\partial W}{\partial x}(1, t) = W(1, t) \quad \text{for } t \in [0, T].$$

Approximate this problem by the implicit Euler scheme on an equidistant grid with the order of approximation $O\big(\delta t + (\delta x)^2\big)$. Write the discretization of the boundary conditions that give the same order of approximation as the order of the implicit Euler scheme.

Exercise 6.21. Apply to the first order equation in two space dimensions

$$\frac{\partial u}{\partial t} + b_1 \frac{\partial u}{\partial x} + b_2 \frac{\partial u}{\partial y} = 0$$

the Lax–Friedrichs scheme

$$\frac{u_{j,k}^{n+1} - (u_{j+1,k}^n + u_{j-1,k}^n + u_{j,k+1}^n + u_{j,k-1}^n)/4}{\delta t} + b_1 \frac{u_{j+1,k}^n - u_{j-1,k}^n}{2\delta x} + b_2 \frac{u_{j,k+1}^n - u_{j,k-1}^n}{2\delta y} = 0.$$

Prove that the scheme is stable if and only if

$$|b_1|^2 \frac{\delta t}{(\delta x)^2} + |b_2|^2 \frac{\delta t}{(\delta y)^2} \leq \frac{1}{2}.$$

Exercise 6.22. To the two-dimensional heat equation

$$\frac{\partial u}{\partial t} = a^2 \left(\frac{\partial^2 u}{\partial x^2} + \frac{\partial^2 u}{\partial y^2} \right),$$

apply the two-dimensional Du Fort–Frankel scheme with $\delta x = \delta y = h$

$$\frac{u_{j,k}^{n+1} - u_{j,k}^{n-1}}{2\delta t} = a^2 \frac{u_{j+1,k}^n + u_{j-1,k}^n + u_{j,k+1}^n + u_{j,k-1}^n - 2(u_{j,k}^{n+1} + u_{j,k}^{n-1})}{h^2}.$$

Prove that the scheme is unconditionally stable.

Exercise 6.23. The following two-dimensional parabolic equation

$$\frac{\partial u}{\partial t} + b_1 \frac{\partial u}{\partial x} + b_2 \frac{\partial u}{\partial y} = a_{11}^2 \frac{\partial^2 u}{\partial x^2} + a_{22}^2 \frac{\partial^2 u}{\partial y^2},$$

is approximated by the explicit Euler scheme

$$\frac{u_{j,k}^{n+1}-u_{j,k}^{n}}{\delta t}+b_1\frac{u_{j+1,k}^{n}-u_{j-1,k}^{n}}{2\delta x}+b_2\frac{u_{j,k+1}^{n}-u_{j,k-1}^{n}}{2\delta y}$$
$$=a_{11}^2\frac{u_{j+1,k}^{n}-2u_{j,k}^{n}+u_{j-1,k}^{n}}{(\delta x)^2}+a_{22}^2\frac{u_{j,k+1}^{n}-2u_{j,k}^{n}+u_{j,k-1}^{n}}{(\delta y)^2}.$$

Prove that the scheme is stable if

$$a_{11}^2\frac{\delta t}{(\delta x)^2}+a_{22}^2\frac{\delta t}{(\delta y)^2}\le\frac{1}{2}.$$

Exercise 6.24. To the equation

$$\frac{\partial u}{\partial t}-a_{11}\frac{\partial^2 u}{\partial x^2}-2a_{12}\frac{\partial^2 u}{\partial x\partial y}-a_{22}\frac{\partial^2 u}{\partial y^2}=0,$$

apply the scheme

$$\left(1-\frac{\delta t}{2}a_{11}\delta_{xx}\right)u_{j,k}^{n+1/2}=\left(1+\frac{\delta t}{2}a_{22}\delta_{yy}\right)u_{j,k}^{n}+\delta t\,a_{12}\delta_x\delta_y\widetilde{u}_{j,k}^{n},$$
$$\left(1-\frac{\delta t}{2}a_{22}\delta_{yy}\right)u_{j,k}^{n+1}=\left(1+\frac{\delta t}{2}a_{11}\delta_{xx}\right)u_{j,k}^{n+1/2}+\delta t\,a_{12}\delta_x\delta_y\widetilde{u}_{j,k}^{n},$$

where $\widetilde{u}^n=3u^n/2-u^{n-1}/2$.

Prove that this scheme is second-order accurate in time.

Chapter 7

Finite Element Methods

Finite difference methods with uniform grids are easy to implement in computer codes; however, they are not sufficiently flexible for complex domains and data with low regularity. An alternative approach is based on the Galerkin approximation described in Chapter 5 and is called the *finite element method.*

The finite element method has become the most important numerical method for solving partial differential equations, particularly elliptic and parabolic equations. The method is based on a variational formulation of boundary value problems and approximates the exact solution using piecewise polynomial functions. In this approach, one can easily handle complicated domains and solutions of minimal regularity. It allows accurate error analysis, thereby estimating the computational cost of the applied algorithms. The method results in a finite algebraic system of equations for approximate solutions. In addition, unlike the finite difference method, the approximate solution is known as a piecewise polynomial function in the entire domain and not just as a collection of values at grid points.

In this chapter, we consider only finite element approximations for space variables. Therefore, we present the whole mathematical apparatus at the level of finite elements for elliptic equations. The extension to parabolic equations is obtained by applying finite elements to spatial variables and approximating the time derivatives using finite differences. Hence, for parabolic problems, we explore the properties of the method established in the analysis of elliptic problems. Readers interested in extending their knowledge beyond the material presented in this chapter should consult Larson and

Bengzon [58], Quarteroni [74], Quarteroni and Valli [75], or Thomée [88]. Applications of finite elements in computational finance can also be found in Achdou and Pironneau [1], Hilber *et al.* [38], or Seydel [79].

7.1 Finite Elements for Elliptic Equations

The Galerkin method, which is applied in Section 5.4 to second-order parabolic equations, can also be applied to the elliptic equation

$$\begin{aligned} \mathcal{A}u &= f \quad \text{in } U, \\ u|_{\partial U} &= 0, \end{aligned} \tag{7.1}$$

where $\mathcal{A}$ is the second-order uniformly elliptic operator in divergence form given by (5.5) with coefficients a_{ij}, b_i, and c sufficiently smooth.

Before implementing the Galerkin approximation, we slightly modify the elliptic problem (7.1). Let us recall that, in the proof of the existence of weak solutions in Section 5.3, we have modified the elliptic problem (7.1) to the following

$$\begin{aligned} \mathcal{A}u + \mu u &= f, \quad \text{in } U, \\ u|_{\partial U} &= 0, \end{aligned}$$

and proved that for a sufficiently large μ, this problem possesses a unique solution. This corresponds to adding to the function $c(x)$ in the definition of $\mathcal{A}$ a large constant μ. To simplify the presentation, we assume that this large constant has already been added to $c(x)$, and the bilinear form $B[u,v]$ (see Theorem 5.25) is given by the expression

$$B[u,v] = \int_U \left(\sum_{i,j=1}^{d} a_{ij}(x) \frac{\partial u}{\partial x_i} \frac{\partial v}{\partial x_j} + \sum_{i=1}^{d} b_i(x) \frac{\partial u}{\partial x_i} v + \bar{c}(x) uv \right) dx, \tag{7.2}$$

where $\bar{c}(x) = c(x) + \mu$. In what follows, we will skip the bar over $c(x)$, assuming that the function $c(x)$ in the definition of $\mathcal{A}$ is such that estimate (7.5) (see below) holds.

Hence, we consider the weak formulation of the Dirichlet problem (7.1):

$$\text{find } u \in H_0^1(U) \text{ such that } B[u,v] = (f,v) \quad \forall v \in H_0^1(U). \tag{7.3}$$

The following estimates can be derived from Theorem 5.25

$$|B[u, v]| \leq \alpha \|u\|_{H_0^1(U)} \|v\|_{H_0^1(U)}, \tag{7.4}$$

$$\beta \|u\|^2_{H_0^1(U)} \leq B[u, u]. \tag{7.5}$$

The bilinear form $B[u, v]$ is said to be *coercive* when it fulfills inequality (7.5).

To implement the Galerkin approximation, we must select a basis $\{\phi_i\}_{i=1}^{\infty}$ and define functions

$$u_m = \sum_{i=1}^{m} d_m^i \phi_i,$$

to approximate the Dirichlet problem (7.3)

$$B[u_m, \phi_i] = (f, \phi_i), \quad i = 1, \ldots, m. \tag{7.6}$$

Using the definition of u_m, we can reduce (7.6) to the linear system

$$\sum_{j=1}^{m} e^{ij} d_m^j = f_i, \quad i = 1, \ldots, m, \tag{7.7}$$

where $e^{ij} = B[\phi_i, \phi_j]$ and $f_i = (f, \phi_i)$. This system of linear equations possesses a unique solution since $\{e^{ij}\}_{i,j=1}^{m}$ is a nonsingular matrix due to the coerciveness of B.

In Section 5.4, we have chosen as $\{\phi_i\}_{i=1}^{\infty}$ the eigenfunctions of operator $\mathcal{A}_0 = \sum_{i,j=1}^{d} -\frac{\partial}{\partial x_i}\left(a_{ij}(x)\frac{\partial u}{\partial x_j}\right)$ which form an orthonormal basis in $L^2(U)$ and an orthogonal basis in $H_0^1(U)$. However, using the eigenfunctions of $\mathcal{A}_0$ as the basis is not an efficient numerical implementation. The construction of a basis suitable for numerical computations is the most challenging problem in the implementation of the Galerkin approximation. One possibility is to use the so-called *finite elements*. First, we present their construction in one dimension.

The finite element method in the one-dimensional case. Let U be a finite interval. Without loss of generality, we take $U = (0, 1)$ and

$$\mathcal{A}u(x) := -\frac{d}{dx}\left(a^2(x)\frac{du(x)}{dx}\right) + b(x)\frac{du(x)}{dx} + c(x)u(x) = f(x) \quad \text{in } U,$$

with $u(0) = u(1) = 0$.

We define a partition $\mathcal{T}_h$ dividing interval $(0,1)$ into M subintervals $K_j = (x_{j-1}, x_j)$, called *elements*, of width $h_j = x_j - x_{j-1}$ such that

$$0 = x_0 < x_1 < \cdots < x_{M-1} < x_M = 1.$$

We set $h = \max_j h_j$ and construct the family of spaces indexed with h

$$X_h^r = \{v_h \in C(\bar{U}) \colon v_h\big|_{K_j} \in \Pi^r(K_j), \quad \forall K_j \in \mathcal{T}_h\}, \quad r = 1, 2, \ldots, \tag{7.8}$$

where $\Pi^r(K_j)$ denotes the space of polynomials of degree not greater than r defined in K_j.

We replace $H_0^1(U)$, the functional space of the Galerkin approximation, with the finite-dimensional space $V_h = X_h^r \cap H_0^1(U)$ with a fixed r. We begin with the definition of a basis $\{\phi_i\}$ in X_h^1. X_h^1 is a space of piecewise linear functions. Each such function is uniquely determined by its values in the vertices x_j. Since we have $M+1$ vertices, then defining $M+1$ basis functions ϕ_i, $i = 0, \ldots, M$, we define the space X_h^1. The basis mostly used is the so-called *nodal basis* consisting of functions ϕ_i such that

$$\phi_i(x_j) = \delta_{ij}, \quad i, j = 0, 1, \ldots, M, \tag{7.9}$$

where δ_{ij} is the Kronecker delta.

These functions, called the *"hat" functions* due to their shape, are given by the expression

$$\phi_i(x) = \begin{cases} \frac{x - x_{i-1}}{x_i - x_{i-1}}, & \text{for } x_{i-1} \le x \le x_i, \quad i = 1, \ldots, M, \\ \frac{x_{i+1} - x}{x_{i+1} - x_i}, & \text{for } x_i \le x \le x_{i+1}, \quad i = 0, 1, \ldots, M-1, \\ 0, & \text{otherwise.} \end{cases} \tag{7.10}$$

Next, we define X_h^2 a space of piecewise quadratic functions. Since a quadratic function is uniquely defined by its values in three distinct points, to define the basis of quadratic functions in each subinterval, we must supplement vertices x_j by the midpoints of each subinterval (x_{j-1}, x_j) obtaining points

$$0 = x_0 < x_1 < \cdots < x_{2M} = 1.$$

Then the $2M + 1$ basis functions ϕ_i of X_h^2 can be such that

$$\phi_i(x_j) = \delta_{ij}, \quad i, j = 0, 1, \ldots, 2M.$$

This construction can be extended to an arbitrary integer $r > 0$.

We now return to the one-dimensional elliptic problem

$$-\frac{d}{dx}\Big(a^2(x)\frac{du(x)}{dx}\Big) + b(x)\frac{du(x)}{dx} + c(x)u(x) = f(x), \quad 0 < x < 1,$$
$$u(0) = u(1) = 0. \tag{7.11}$$

Our goal is to approximate a solution of this problem in spaces V_h

$$V_h = \{v_h \in X_h^1\colon v_h(0) = 0 = v_h(1)\}.$$

These spaces are finite-dimensional subspaces of $H_0^1(0,1)$ since functions from X_h^1 are differentiable on $(0,1)$ except a finite number of vertices x_j.

We construct the Galerkin approximation by finding $u_h \in V_h$ which for each $v_h \in V_h$ solves the equation

$$B_F[u_h, v_h] := \int_0^1 \Big(a^2(x)\frac{du_h}{dx}\frac{dv_h}{dx} + b(x)\frac{du_h}{dx}v_h + c(x)u_h v_h\Big)dx$$
$$= \int_0^1 f(x)v_h dx. \tag{7.12}$$

Using the basis of the hat functions in X_h^1, we can expand $u_h(x) = \sum_{i=1}^{M-1} w_i\phi_i(x)$. Then by taking the basis functions $\phi_j(x)$ as functions v_h, we can rewrite (7.12) as the linear system

$$A_h W = F, \tag{7.13}$$

where A_h is the so-called *stiffness matrix* with elements $a_{ij} = B_F[\phi_i, \phi_j]$, $W = (w_1, \ldots w_{M-1})$ is the vector of components of u_h in the basis ϕ_i, and F is the *load vector* with components $f_i = (f, \phi_i)$ (lack of indices $i = 0$ and $i = M$ is due to the boundary conditions $u_h(0) = u_h(1) = 0$).

According to our assumptions, $B_F[u,v]$ is coercive, therefore, A_h is nonsingular, and there is a unique solution of system (7.13). Then

$u_h(x) = \sum_{i=1}^{M-1} w_i\phi_i(x)$ is an approximate weak solution of the Dirichlet problem (7.11).

Example 7.1. We illustrate the finite element method by solving the two-point boundary value problem with constant coefficients

$$-a^2u''(x) + cu(x) = f(x), \quad 0 < x < 1,$$
$$u(0) = u(1) = 0,$$

where $c \geq 0$.

We approximate this problem introducing in interval $(0,1)$ a grid of M subintervals $K_j = (x_{j-1}, x_j)$ of length $h_j = x_j - x_{j-1}$, with $x_0 = 0$ and $x_M = 1$. We take as a finite element space the space of hat functions X_h^1. The approximate problem is

$$\int_0^1 \Big(a^2u_h'\phi_i' + cu_h\phi_i\Big)dx = \int_0^1 f(x)\phi_i dx, \ i = 1, \ldots, M-1,$$

with $u_h = \sum_{i=1}^{M-1} w_i\phi_i(x)$ expanded in the basis of hat functions ϕ_i.

The approximate problem is a system of linear equations

$$A_hW = F,$$

where matrix A_h has elements

$$a_{i,j} = \int_0^1 \Big(a^2\phi_i'(x)\phi_j'(x) + c\phi_i(x)\phi_j(x)\Big)dx,$$

and F is a vector with entries

$$f_i = \int_0^1 f(x)\phi_i(x)dx.$$

By simple computations, we get

$$\begin{aligned}
a_{i,i} &= \int_0^1 \Big(a^2\phi_i'^2 + c\phi_i{}^2\Big)dx \\
&= \int_{x_{i-1}}^{x_i} \Big(a^2\phi_i'^2 + c\phi_i{}^2\Big)dx + \int_{x_i}^{x_{i+1}} \Big(a^2\phi_i'^2 + c\phi_i{}^2\Big)dx \\
&= a^2\left(\frac{1}{h_i^2}h_i + \frac{(-1)^2}{h_{i+1}^2}h_{i+1}\right) + \frac{c}{3}(h_i + h_{i+1}) \\
&= a^2\left(\frac{1}{h_i} + \frac{1}{h_{i+1}}\right) + \frac{c}{3}(h_i + h_{i+1}),
\end{aligned}$$

and

$$\begin{aligned}
a_{i,i+1} &= \int_0^1 \left(a^2\phi_i'\phi_{i+1}' + c\phi_i\phi_{i+1}\right)dx \\
&= \int_{x_i}^{x_{i+1}} \left(a^2\phi_i'\phi_{i+1}' + c\phi_i\phi_{i+1}\right)dx \\
&= a^2\frac{(-1)}{h_{i+1}}\frac{1}{h_{i+1}}h_{i+1} + \frac{c}{6}h_{i+1} = -a^2\frac{1}{h_{i+1}} + \frac{c}{6}h_{i+1}.
\end{aligned}$$

We obviously have the equality $a_{i+1,i} = a_{i,i+1}$. Thus, the stiffness matrix A_h is the sum of two matrices A and C, where

$$A = a^2\begin{pmatrix}
\left(\frac{1}{h_1}+\frac{1}{h_2}\right) & -\frac{1}{h_2} & & \\
-\frac{1}{h_2} & \left(\frac{1}{h_2}+\frac{1}{h_3}\right) & -\frac{1}{h_3} & \\
& \ddots & \ddots & \ddots \\
& & -\frac{1}{h_{M-1}} & \left(\frac{1}{h_{M-1}}+\frac{1}{h_M}\right)
\end{pmatrix},$$

$$C = \frac{c}{6}\begin{pmatrix}
(2h_1+2h_2) & h_2 & & \\
h_2 & (2h_2+2h_3) & h_3 & \\
& \ddots & \ddots & \ddots \\
& & h_{M-1} & (2h_{M-1}+2h_M)
\end{pmatrix}.$$

Because of the constant values of a^2 and c, the stiffness matrix A_h is evaluated exactly. The load vector F cannot be evaluated exactly for arbitrary functions $f(x)$. Using the trapezoidal rule to approximate f_i, we obtain the load vector

$$F = \frac{1}{2}\begin{pmatrix}
f(x_1)(h_1+h_2) \\
f(x_2)(h_2+h_3) \\
\vdots \\
f(x_{M-1})(h_{M-1}+h_M)
\end{pmatrix}.$$

Let us observe that matrix A can be split into the sum of M simpler matrices

$$
\begin{aligned}
A =& \frac{a^2}{h_1}\begin{pmatrix} 1 & & & & \\ & & & & \\ & & & & \\ & & & & \\ & & & & \end{pmatrix} + \frac{a^2}{h_2}\begin{pmatrix} 1 & -1 & & & \\ -1 & 1 & & & \\ & & & & \\ & & & & \\ & & & & \end{pmatrix} + \dots \\
&+ \frac{a^2}{h_{M-1}}\begin{pmatrix} & & & & \\ & & & & \\ & & & & \\ & & & 1 & -1 \\ & & & -1 & 1 \end{pmatrix} + \frac{a^2}{h_M}\begin{pmatrix} & & & & \\ & & & & \\ & & & & \\ & & & & \\ & & & & 1 \end{pmatrix} \\
=& A^{K_1} + A^{K_2} + \cdots + A^{K_M}.
\end{aligned}
$$

An analogous split holds for C

$$
\begin{aligned}
C =& \frac{ch_1}{6}\begin{pmatrix} 2 & & & & \\ & & & & \\ & & & & \\ & & & & \\ & & & & \end{pmatrix} + \frac{ch_2}{6}\begin{pmatrix} 2 & 1 & & & \\ 1 & 2 & & & \\ & & & & \\ & & & & \\ & & & & \end{pmatrix} + \dots \\
&+ \frac{ch_{M-1}}{6}\begin{pmatrix} & & & & \\ & & & & \\ & & & & \\ & & & 2 & 1 \\ & & & 1 & 2 \end{pmatrix} + \frac{ch_M}{6}\begin{pmatrix} & & & & \\ & & & & \\ & & & & \\ & & & & \\ & & & & 2 \end{pmatrix} \\
=& C^{K_1} + C^{K_2} + \cdots + C^{K_M}.
\end{aligned}
$$

Matrices $A^{K_j} + C^{K_j}$, $j = 1, 2, \dots, M$, are obtained by restricting the integration of elements $a_{i,j}$ to one subinterval or element K_i.

The summation of these (element) matrices into the global matrix is called *assembling.* The assembly process is essential for finite element algorithms because it allows the formation of stiffness matrices by computing element matrices over a single element.

The procedure for load vector F is analogous except that, instead of adding element matrices to form the global matrix A_h, we add local vectors to form the global vector F.

The goal of the subsequent analysis is to estimate the error of approximation (7.13). We begin by defining an interpolation operator in X_h^1 and discussing its properties. For $v \in C([0,1])$, we define the *interpolant* $I_h^1 v$ determined by the partition $\mathcal{T}_h$. For each node x_i, $i = 0, \ldots, M$, we set

$$I_h^1 v(x_i) = v(x_i).$$

Using the basis $\{\phi_i\}_{i=0}^M$ of X_h^1, we define the interpolant as follows

$$I_h^1 v(x) = \sum_{i=0}^{M} v(x_i)\phi_i(x).$$

The operator $I_h^1\colon C([0,1]) \to X_h^1$ is called the *interpolation operator.* Let us observe that functions from $H^1(0,1)$ are continuous. Hence, the interpolation operator is also well defined in $H^1(0,1)$.

Analogously, we can define the interpolation operator $I_h^r : C([0,1]) \to X_h^r$ for $r > 1$. First, we interpolate v on each $K_j \in \mathcal{T}_h$ projecting v on $\Pi^r(K_j)$. This projection is defined, similarly to the case of X_h^1, on the basis functions $\phi_{i,j} \in \Pi^r(K_j)$ such that

$$\phi_{i,j}(x_{j,l}) = \delta_{il},$$

where $x_{j,l}$, $l = 0, \ldots, r$, are $r+1$ nodes of K_j. Denoting this interpolation as $I_{K_j}^r v$, we can write

$$I_h^r v\Big|_{K_j} = I_{K_j}^r\left(v\big|_{K_j}\right) \quad \forall K_j \in \mathcal{T}_h. \tag{7.14}$$

Then we have the following theorem.

Theorem 7.2. *Let $v \in H^{r+1}(0,1)$ for $r \geq 1$, and $I_h^r v$ be its interpolant in X_h^r defined by (7.14). Then the following estimate holds*

$$|v - I_h^r v|_{H^m(0,1)} \leq C_{m,r} h^{r+1-m} |v|_{H^{r+1}(0,1)}, \quad m = 0, 1,$$

where the constant $C_{m,r}$ is independent of v and h.

Here, $|\cdot|_{H^k(U)}$ denotes the seminorm in $H^k(U)$ defined by the derivatives of order k, i.e.,

$$|u|_{H^k(U)} = \left(\sum_{|\alpha|=k} \int_U |D^\alpha u|^2 dx \right)^{1/2}.$$

Proof. We prove the theorem only for $r = 1$. Due to the Sobolev inequality if $v \in H^2(0,1)$, then $v \in C^1(0,1)$, and $I_h^1 v$ is differentiable except a finite number of nodes x_j. Let $z = v - I_h^1 v$. Since $z(x_j) = 0$, $j = 0, \ldots, M$, then by Rolle's theorem, in each $K_j = (x_{j-1}, x_j)$ there exists $\xi_j \in K_j$ such that $z'(\xi_j) = 0$.

Since $I_h^1 v$ is a linear function in each K_j, we have

$$z'(x) = \int_{\xi_j}^{x} z''(s)ds = \int_{\xi_j}^{x} v''(s)ds, \quad \text{for } x \in K_j,$$

where the last integral is well defined since $v \in H^2(0,1)$.

By the Hölder inequality, we obtain

$$|z'(x)| \leq \int_{x_{j-1}}^{x_j} |v''(s)|ds \leq \left(|x_j - x_{j-1}|\right)^{1/2} \left(\int_{x_{j-1}}^{x_j} |v''(s)|^2 ds \right)^{1/2}$$

$$\leq h^{1/2} \left(\int_{x_{j-1}}^{x_j} |v''(s)|^2 ds \right)^{1/2}. \tag{7.15}$$

Hence,

$$\int_{x_{j-1}}^{x_j} |z'(s)|^2 ds \leq h^2 \int_{x_{j-1}}^{x_j} |v''(s)|^2 ds.$$

Since for $x \in K_j$

$$z(x) = \int_{x_{j-1}}^{x} z'(s)ds,$$

then using estimate (7.15), we obtain

$$|z(x)| \leq \int_{x_{j-1}}^{x_j} |z'(s)|ds \leq h^{3/2} \left(\int_{x_{j-1}}^{x_j} |v''(s)|^2 ds \right)^{1/2}.$$

This gives

$$\int_{x_{j-1}}^{x_j} |z(s)|^2 ds \le h^4 \int_{x_{j-1}}^{x_j} |v''(s)|^2 ds.$$

Summing over all K_j, $j = 1, \dots, M$, we obtain

$$\int_0^1 |z'(s)|^2 ds \le h^2 \int_0^1 |v''(s)|^2 ds,$$
$$\int_0^1 |z(s)|^2 ds \le h^4 \int_0^1 |v''(s)|^2 ds.$$

These estimates prove the theorem for $r = 1$ with $C_{m,1} = 1$, $m = 0, 1$. □

To obtain an error estimate for Galerkin's approximation, we need the following lemma, also valid for multidimensional finite element approximations discussed in the next section.

Theorem 7.3 (Céa's Lemma). *Let $u \in H_0^1(U)$ be a weak solution of the Dirichlet problem* (7.3) *with U an open, bounded domain in $\mathbb{R}^d$. Let its Galerkin approximation $u_h \in V_h$ solve* (7.26)*, a multi-dimensional version of problem* (7.12)*. Then*

$$\|u - u_h\|_{H_0^1(U)} \le \frac{\alpha}{\beta} \inf_{v_h \in V_h} \|u - v_h\|_{H_0^1(U)}.$$

Proof. The proof follows from properties of the bilinear form $B[u, v]$. Let $u \in H_0^1(U)$ solve

$$B[u, v] = (f, v), \quad \forall v \in H_0^1(U),$$

and $u_h \in V_h$ solve

$$B[u_h, v] = (f, v), \quad \forall v \in V_h.$$

Since $V_h \subset H_0^1(U)$, then taking both equalities with $v \in V_h$, we obtain the orthogonality relation

$$B[u - u_h, v] = 0, \quad \forall v \in V_h. \tag{7.16}$$

Let $v_h \in V_h$. Taking $v = u_h - v_h$ in (7.16), we have

$$B[u - u_h, u - u_h] = B[u - u_h, u - v_h] \le \alpha \|u - u_h\|_{H_0^1(U)} \|u - v_h\|_{H_0^1(U)}.$$

On the other hand, the coerciveness of B gives

$$\beta\|u - u_h\|^2_{H^1_0(U)} \leq B[u - u_h, u - u_h].$$

By the above estimates, we have

$$\|u - u_h\|_{H^1_0(U)} \leq \frac{\alpha}{\beta}\|u - v_h\|_{H^1_0(U)}.$$

Since v_h is an arbitrary vector in V_h, this proves the assertion of the theorem. □

A simple corollary from the Céa lemma is the following H^1 error estimate of the Galerkin approximation.

Theorem 7.4. *Let $u \in H^1_0(0,1)$ be a solution of problem* (7.11) *and u_h a solution of its finite element approximation* (7.12) *in $V_h = H^1_0(0,1) \cap X^r_h$. In addition, let $u \in H^{m+1}(0,1)$ for $m \geq r$. Then the following* a priori *estimate holds*

$$\|u - u_h\|_{H^1_0(0,1)} \leq \frac{\alpha}{\beta} C h^r |u|_{H^{r+1}(0,1)},$$

where the constant C is independent of u and h.

Proof. Inserting in Céa's lemma $v_h = I^r_h u$, we get

$$\|u - u_h\|_{H^1_0(0,1)} \leq \frac{\alpha}{\beta}\|u - I^r_h u\|_{H^1_0(0,1)}.$$

By the estimate of Theorem 7.2, we obtain the claim of the theorem. □

In $L^2(0,1)$, we can obtain a better error estimate.

Theorem 7.5. *Let $u \in H^1_0(0,1)$ be a solution of problem* (7.11) *and u_h a solution of its finite element approximation* (7.12) *in $V_h = H^1_0(0,1) \cap X^r_h$. In addition, let $u \in H^{m+1}(0,1)$ for $m \geq r$. Then the following* a priori *estimate holds*

$$\|u - u_h\|_{L^2(0,1)} \leq C\, h^{r+1} |u|_{H^{r+1}(0,1)},$$

where the constant C is independent of u and h.

Proof. For an arbitrary $g \in L^2(0,1)$, we consider the following dual problem with $B_F[v,z]$ defined by (7.12):

$$\text{find } z \in H_0^1(0,1) \text{ such that } B_F[v,z] = (v,g), \quad \forall v \in H_0^1(0,1).$$

It can be shown (similarly to problem (7.11)) that the dual problem has a unique solution $z = z(g)$, and the following regularity result holds

$$\|z\|_{H^2(0,1)} \le C\|g\|_{L^2(0,1)}, \quad \forall g \in L^2(0,1), \tag{7.17}$$

(see the regularity result of Remark 5.28).

Let $e_h = u - u_h$. Choosing $g = e_h$ and $v = e_h$, we obtain

$$B_F[e_h, z(e_h)] = \|e_h\|^2_{L^2(0,1)}.$$

Given the Galerkin orthogonality property (7.16), we have

$$B_F[e_h, z] = B_F[u - u_h, z] = B_F[u - u_h, z - I_h^1 z] = B_F[e_h, z - I_h^1 z].$$

Then using the estimate of Theorem 7.2 and estimate (7.17), we have

$$\begin{aligned}\|e_h\|^2_{L^2(0,1)} &= |B_F[e_h, z]| = |B_F[e_h, z - I_h^1 z]| \\ &\le C\|e_h\|_{H^1(0,1)}\|z - I_h^1 z\|_{H^1(0,1)} \le C\,h\|e_h\|_{H^1(0,1)}\|z\|_{H^2(0,1)} \\ &\le C\,h\|e_h\|_{H^1(0,1)}\|e_h\|_{L^2(0,1)}.\end{aligned}$$

Thus, we obtain

$$\|e_h\|_{L^2(0,1)} \le C\,h\|e_h\|_{H^1(0,1)}$$

which together with Theorem 7.4 gives the desired estimate. □

The multidimensional case: To extend the finite element method to multidimensional domains, we must define finite elements for multidimensional boundary-value problems. Let $U \subset \mathbb{R}^d$ be an open, bounded, convex domain with a Lipschitz boundary. The first step is to define a triangulation of U. Contrary to the one-dimensional case, there are now many possibilities for triangulations. The most popular method is to split U into simplices. If $\{x_0, \ldots, x_d\}$ are $d+1$ points in $\mathbb{R}^d$, then the convex hull of $\{x_0, \ldots, x_d\}$ is called a *simplex* when vectors $\{x_1 - x_0, \ldots, x_d - x_0\}$ are linearly independent (in other words $\{x_0, \ldots, x_d\}$ do not belong to a single hyperplane in $\mathbb{R}^d$). Points $\{x_0, \ldots, x_d\}$ are then called the *vertices of the simplex.* The standard simplex in $\mathbb{R}^d$ is the set

$$\hat{K}_d = \left\{ x \in \mathbb{R}^d \colon \ x_i \geq 0, \sum_{i=1}^{d} x_i \leq 1 \right\}. \tag{7.18}$$

This is a unit interval in $\mathbb{R}^1$, a unit triangle in $\mathbb{R}^2$, and a unit tetrahedron in $\mathbb{R}^3$.

The triangulation $\mathcal{T}_h$ of $U \subset \mathbb{R}^d$ is a division of U into nonoverlapping simplices such that the intersection of any two simplices of $\mathcal{T}_h$ is either empty or a common face, where a face of dimension $m < d$ of a simplex is the convex hull of a subset of $m+1$ its vertices. For a simplex $K \in \mathcal{T}_h$, we define its diameter $h_K = diam(K)$. Then the diameter of triangulation $\mathcal{T}_h$ is $h = \max_{K \in \mathcal{T}_h} h_K$.

In general, for a convex domain U with a Lipschitz boundary, the sum of all simplices of a triangulation

$$U_h = \operatorname{int} \left(\bigcup_{K \in \mathcal{T}_h} K \right)$$

is a proper subset of U. This leads to additional difficulties with an error estimate on $U \backslash U_h$. In the following, we omit this problem by assuming that the shape of U is such that $U = U_h$.

Definition 7.6. For each simplex $K \in \mathcal{T}_h$, we define a finite element as a triple $(K, \Pi^r(K), \Sigma)$ where

(i) K is a closed simplex with a Lipschitz boundary;
(ii) $\Pi^r(K)$ is a space of polynomials of degree not greater than r, of dimension $M_r = \binom{r+d}{r}$, and with a basis $\{\phi_i\}_{i=1}^{M_r}$;
(iii) Σ is a space of linear functionals σ: $\Pi^r(K) \to \mathbb{R}$, i.e., Σ is the adjoint space of $\Pi^r(K)$ with a basis $\{\sigma_i\}_{i=1}^{M_r}$ and elements σ_i called the *degrees of freedom.*

The basis of $\Pi^r(K)$ is selected to be dual to Σ, i.e., $\sigma_i(\phi_j) = \delta_{ij}$.

The space $\Pi^r(K)$ is called *unisolvent* with respect to the functionals $\{\sigma_i\}_{i=1}^{M_r}$ if for each $a = (\alpha_1, \ldots, \alpha_{M_r}) \in \mathbb{R}^{M_r}$ there is exactly one polynomial $p \in \Pi^r(K)$ such that $\sigma_i(p) = \alpha_i$, $i = 1, \ldots, M_r$. When the space $\Pi^r(K)$ is unisolvent, we also say that the functionals $\{\sigma_i\}_{i=1}^{M_r}$ are unisolvent.

Definition 7.7. Let $\Pi^r(K)$ be unisolvent. There exists in K a set of points $\{a_i\}_{i=1}^{M_r}$ such that for $\forall p \in \Pi^r(K)$ $\sigma_i(p) = p(a_i)$, $i = 1, \ldots, M_r$. These points are called *nodes.*

The finite elements whose linear functionals are defined by evaluations on the nodes in K are called the *Lagrangian finite elements.* For the Lagrangian finite elements, we have for every $p \in \Pi^r(K)$ the expansion $p(x) = \sum_{i=1}^{M_r} \sigma_i(p)\phi_i(x)$. The functionals σ_i for the Lagrangian elements are often identified with nodes a_i, and then a_i are called the degrees of freedom.

The Lagrange finite elements represent a function u as a piecewise polynomial function with discontinuous derivatives at the cell boundaries. Sometimes, it is desirable to have continuous derivatives. A typical example is the solution of a differential equation with derivatives of order higher than two where one needs basis functions with continuous first-order derivatives. This can be achieved by introducing the Hermite finite elements with cubic polynomials as basis functions. To define the Hermite finite elements in many dimensions, it is convenient to use barycentric coordinates.

Barycentric coordinates: *Barycentric coordinates* form a coordinate system in $\mathbb{R}^d$ alternative to the Cartesian one. Let K be a simplex in $\mathbb{R}^d$ defined by $d+1$ points $\{a_0, \ldots, a_d\}$. Assume that a_i, $i = 0, 1, \ldots, d$, have Cartesian coordinates $a_i = (a_{i,1}, a_{i,2}, \ldots, a_{i,d})$.

The *barycentric coordinates* $\lambda_i = \lambda_i(x)$, $0 \le i \le d$, of any point $x \in \mathbb{R}^d$, with respect to the $(d+1)$ points a_i, are the (unique) solutions of the linear system

$$\sum_{i=0}^{d} a_{i,j}\lambda_i = x_j, \quad 1 \le j \le d, \quad \sum_{i=0}^{d} \lambda_i = 1.$$

This system can be written as

$$\begin{pmatrix} x \\ 1 \end{pmatrix} = A\lambda,$$

where

$$A = \begin{pmatrix} a_{0,1} & a_{1,1} & \dots & a_{d,1} \\ a_{0,2} & a_{1,2} & \dots & a_{d,2} \\ \vdots & \vdots & & \vdots \\ a_{0,d} & a_{1,d} & \dots & a_{d,d} \\ 1 & 1 & \dots & 1 \end{pmatrix}.$$

Inverting the above linear system, one sees that the barycentric coordinates are affine functions of the Cartesian coordinates of x

$$\lambda = A^{-1}\begin{pmatrix} x \\ 1 \end{pmatrix}.$$

Barycentric coordinates allow to define compactly finite elements of a given order. For example, linear finite elements are defined by the degrees of freedom $\sigma_i(p) = p(a_i)$ and the basis functions in barycentric coordinates $\phi_i(\lambda) = \lambda_i$. Then for a polynomial $p \in \Pi^1(K)$, we have

$$p(x) = \sum_{i=0}^{d} p(a_i)\lambda_i(x).$$

For quadratic finite elements, the degrees of freedom are

$$\sigma_i(p) = p(a_i), \quad \sigma_{ij}(p) = p(a_{ij}), \quad i, j = 0, \dots, d, \ i < j,$$

where $a_{ij} = (a_i + a_j)/2$, and the basis functions in barycentric coordinates have the form

$$\phi_i(\lambda) = \lambda_i(2\lambda_i - 1), \quad \phi_{ij}(\lambda) = 4\lambda_i\lambda_j.$$

For $p \in \Pi^2(K)$, we get

$$p(\lambda) = \sum_{i=0}^{d} \sigma_i(p)\phi_i(\lambda) + \sum_{i<j}^{d} \sigma_{ij}(p)\phi_{ij}(\lambda).$$

Similar expressions are also available for higher-order finite elements.

Example 7.8 (Hermite finite elements). In one dimension, the Hermite element is a simplex $K = [0, 1]$ and the space of third-degree polynomials $\Pi^3(K)$. The degrees of freedom are defined as the values of the function and its first-order derivative at the endpoints of the interval. These four degrees of freedom correspond to the four basis functions written in general form as follows

$$\phi_i(x) = \sum_{n=0}^{3} c_{i,n} x^n,$$

with coefficients $c_{i,n}$ to be determined. The constraints that the basis function number i must be 1 for the degree of freedom number i and zero for the other three degrees of freedom yield four equations to determine $c_{i,n}$. Solving these equations, we obtain

$$\begin{aligned}
\phi_0(x) &= 1 - 3x^2 + 2x^3, \\
\phi_1(x) &= x - 2x^2 + x^3, \\
\phi_2(x) &= 1 - 3x^2 + 2x^3, \\
\phi_3(x) &= -x^2 + x^3.
\end{aligned}$$

The Hermite finite element in $\mathbb{R}^d$ forms: a simplex K spanned by points a_i, $i = 0, \ldots, d$, the finite element space $\Pi^3(K)$ of dimension $(d+1)(d+2)(d+3)/6$, and the functionals which are the values of the function in the vertices of the simplex ($(d+1)$ values), the directional derivatives at the vertices in the direction of other vertices ($d(d+1)$ values), and the value of the barycenter at the two-faces of K ($(d+1)(d-1)d/6$ values):

$$\begin{aligned}
\sigma_i(p) &= p(a_i), \quad i = 0, \ldots, d, \\
\sigma_{ij}(p) &= Dp(a_i)(a_j - a_i), \quad i, j = 0, \ldots, d, \quad i \neq j, \\
\sigma_{ijk}(p) &= p(a_{ijk}), \quad i, j, k = 0, \ldots, d, \quad i < j < k,
\end{aligned}$$

where $a_{ijk} = (a_i + a_j + a_k)/3$ and Dp denotes the gradient of p.

The corresponding basis functions expressed in barycentric coordinates are as follows:

$$\begin{aligned}
\phi_i(\lambda) &= -2\lambda_i^3 + 3\lambda_i^2 - 7\lambda_i \sum_{j<k; j\neq i\neq k} \lambda_j \lambda_k, \\
\phi_{ij}(\lambda) &= \lambda_i \lambda_j (2\lambda_i - \lambda_j - 1), \\
\phi_{ijk}(\lambda) &= 27\lambda_i \lambda_j \lambda_k.
\end{aligned}$$

Then, through laborious computations, we can show that each $p \in \Pi^3(K)$ is uniquely defined by its valuation on functionals σ and

$$p(\lambda) = \sum_i \sigma_i(p)\phi_i(\lambda) + \sum_{i \neq j} \sigma_{ij}(p)\phi_{ij}(\lambda) + \sum_{i<j<k} \sigma_{ijk}(p)\phi_{ijk}(\lambda).$$

Definition 7.9. A family of triangulations $\mathcal{T}_h$ parametrized by a mesh parameter h belonging to $H_F \subset (0, \infty)$ forms regular triangulations if:

(i) 0 is the limit point of H_F;
(ii) there is a constant $C \geq 1$ such that

$$h_K \leq C\,\rho(K), \quad \forall K \in \mathcal{T}_h,$$

where $\rho(K)$ is the radius of the greatest sphere inscribed in K.

Definition 7.10. Consider a finite element $(\hat{K}, \hat{\Pi}^r(\hat{K}), \hat{\Sigma})$, where $\hat{K}$ is a standard simplex in $\mathbb{R}^d$ defined by (7.18), $\hat{\Pi}^r(\hat{K})$ is the space of polynomials on $\hat{K}$ of degree not greater than r, and $\hat{\Sigma}$ is a set of unisolvent functionals on $\hat{\Pi}^r(\hat{K})$.

Mappings G_K: $\hat{K} \to K$ defined for each $K \in \mathcal{T}_h$ by the expression $G_K(\hat{x}) = J_K\hat{x} + b_K$, $\hat{x} \in \hat{K}$, where J_K is a nonsingular matrix and b_K is a vector, are called *affine mappings*. The collection of finite elements $(K, \Pi^r(K), \Sigma)$, for $K \in \mathcal{T}_h$, is an *affine family of finite elements* if:

(i) $K = G_K(\hat{K})$;
(ii) $\Pi^r(K) = \{p\colon p = \hat{p} \circ G_K^{-1}, \hat{p} \in \hat{\Pi}^r(\hat{K})\}$;
(iii) $\Sigma = \{\sigma_i\colon \sigma_i(p(x)) = \hat{\sigma}_i\big(p(G_K(\hat{x}))\big), \hat{\sigma}_i \in \hat{\Sigma}, x = G_K(\hat{x})\}$.

Lemma 7.11. *Let $\mathcal{T}_h$ be a family of regular triangulations of affine finite elements. For any integer $m \geq 0$ and each function $v \in H^m(K)$, we define function $\hat{v} = v \circ G_K$: $\hat{K} \to \mathbb{R}$. Then $\hat{v} \in H^m(\hat{K})$ and the following estimates hold*

$$|\hat{v}|_{H^m(\hat{K})} \leq C\|J_K\|^m |\det J_K|^{-1/2} |v|_{H^m(K)}, \tag{7.19}$$

$$|v|_{H^m(K)} \leq C\|J_K^{-1}\|^m |\det J_K|^{1/2} |\hat{v}|_{H^m(\hat{K})}, \tag{7.20}$$

with the constant C depending only on m.

The operator norm $\|\cdot\|$ *is implied by the Euclidean norm in* $\mathbb{R}^d$, *and we have the following estimates*

$$\|J_K\| \le \frac{h_K}{\rho(\hat{K})}, \quad \|J_K^{-1}\| \le \frac{h_{\hat{K}}}{\rho(K)}. \tag{7.21}$$

Proof. Let us recall that

$$|\hat{v}|_{H^m(\hat{K})} = \left(\sum_{|\alpha|=m} \int_{\hat{K}} |D^\alpha \hat{v}|^2 d\hat{x} \right)^{1/2}.$$

By the definition of $\hat{v}$ and the chain rule, we have for $|\alpha| = m$

$$\begin{aligned}\|D^\alpha \hat{v}\|_{L^2(\hat{K})} &\le C\|J_K\|^m \sum_{|\beta|=m} \|(D^\beta v)\circ G_K\|_{L^2\hat{K})} \\ &\le C\|J_K\|^m |\det J_K|^{-1/2} \sum_{|\beta|=m} \|D^\beta v\|_{L^2(K)}.\end{aligned}$$

Summing the last inequality over all multi-indices α with $|\alpha| = m$, we get (7.19). The proof of (7.20) is analogous.

To prove estimates (7.21), let us recall the definition of the operator norm

$$\|J_K\| = \frac{1}{\rho(\hat{K})} \sup_{|\xi|=\rho(\hat{K})} |J_K \xi|.$$

For each ξ such that $|\xi| = \rho(\hat{K})$, we can find two points $\hat{x}, \hat{y} \in \hat{K}$ with $\hat{x} - \hat{y} = \xi$. Since $J_K\xi = G_K(\hat{x}) - G_K(\hat{y})$, we have the estimate $|J_K\xi| \le h_K$ which gives the first of estimates (7.21). The proof of the second is similar. □

Similarly to the one-dimensional case, we define the spaces

$$X_h^r = \{v_h \in C(\bar{U})\colon\ v_h\big|_K \in \Pi^r(K), \quad \forall K \in \mathcal{T}_h\},$$

and the finite element space $V_h = X_h^r \cap H_0^1(U)$. For X_h^r, we define the interpolation operator

$$I_h^r\colon C(\bar{U}) \to X_h^r$$

which, for a given triangulation $\mathcal{T}_h$ of U, is defined on each finite element $K \in \mathcal{T}_h$ as the local interpolation operator associating to a continuous function v the polynomial $I_h^r v \in \Pi^r(K)$ such that

$$I_h^r v(x) = \sum_{i=1}^{M_r} v(a_i)\phi_i(x),$$

where $\{\phi_i\}$ is a basis of $\Pi^r(K)$ and $\{a_i\}$ are nodes in K.

To estimate the interpolation error, we need the following improved version of the Bramble–Hilbert lemma [20].

Lemma 7.12. *Let U be a bounded, convex domain in $\mathbb{R}^d$. If $v \in H^m(U)$, $m \geq 1$, then for $0 \leq j < m$*

$$\inf_{Q \in \Pi^{m-1}(U)} |v - Q|_{H^j(U)} \leq C|v|_{H^m(U)},$$

where the constant $C = C(d, m, j, U)$.

We begin with a local estimate of the interpolation error.

Theorem 7.13. *Let $\mathcal{T}_h$ be a family of regular triangulations of affine finite elements in $\mathbb{R}^d$. Let $2(r+1) > d$ and $0 \leq m \leq r+1$. Then there exists a constant $C = C(r, m, \hat{K})$ such that*

$$|v - I_h^r v|_{H^m(K)} \leq C \frac{h_K^{r+1}}{\rho^m(K)} |v|_{H^{r+1}(K)}, \quad \forall v \in H^{r+1}(K).$$

Proof. Since K is bounded and convex, we have for $2(r+1-s) > d$ the Sobolev embedding (Theorem 5.20) of $H^{r+1}(K) = H^{(r+1-s)+s}(K)$ into $C^s(K)$. The interpolation operator I_h^r is then well defined in $H^{r+1}(K)$.

Let the interpolation operator $\hat{I}_h^r\colon C^s(\hat{K}) \to H^{r+1}(\hat{K})$ be defined by the expression $I_h^r v \circ G_K = \hat{I}_h^r \hat{v}$. An immediate consequence of this definition is the following equality

$$|(v - I_h^r v) \circ G_K|_{H^m(\hat{K})} = |\hat{v} - \hat{I}_h^r \hat{v}|_{H^m(\hat{K})}. \tag{7.22}$$

Since $\hat{I}_h^r \hat{v}(\hat{x}) = \sum_{i=1}^{M_r} \hat{v}(\hat{a}_i)\hat{\phi}_i(\hat{x})$, the boundedness of this operator follows from the estimate

$$\|\hat{I}_h^r \hat{v}\|_{H^{r+1}(\hat{K})} \leq \sum_{i=1}^{M_r} |\hat{v}(\hat{a}_i)| \|\hat{\phi}_i\|_{H^{r+1}(\hat{K})} \leq C \sup_{\hat{x}} |\hat{v}(\hat{x})| = C\|\hat{v}\|_{C(\hat{K})}.$$

We now demonstrate that, for all $0 \le j \le r+1$, the following estimate holds

$$|\hat{v} - \hat{I}_h^r \hat{v}|_{H^j(\hat{K})} \le C|\hat{v}|_{H^{r+1}(\hat{K})}. \tag{7.23}$$

Taking a polynomial $\hat{Q} \in \Pi^r(\hat{K})$, we obtain by the boundedness of $\hat{I}_h^r$ and the Sobolev embedding

$$\begin{aligned}
\|\hat{v} - \hat{I}_h^r \hat{v}\|_{H^{r+1}(\hat{K})} &= \|\hat{v} - \hat{Q} - \hat{I}_h^r(\hat{v} - \hat{Q})\|_{H^{r+1}(\hat{K})} \\
&\le \|\hat{v} - \hat{Q}\|_{H^{r+1}(\hat{K})} + \|\hat{I}_h^r(\hat{v} - \hat{Q})\|_{H^{r+1}(\hat{K})} \\
&\le \|\hat{v} - \hat{Q}\|_{H^{r+1}(\hat{K})} + C\|\hat{v} - \hat{Q}\|_{C(\hat{K})} \\
&\le C\|\hat{v} - \hat{Q}\|_{H^{r+1}(\hat{K})}.
\end{aligned}$$

By Lemma 7.12, we have for $j \le r$

$$|\hat{v} - \hat{Q}|_{H^j(\hat{K})} \le C|\hat{v}|_{H^{r+1}(\hat{K})}.$$

For $j = r+1$, we get

$$|\hat{v} - \hat{Q}|_{H^{r+1}(\hat{K})} = |\hat{v}|_{H^{r+1}(\hat{K})}$$

since $\hat{Q}$ is a polynomial of degree r.

Because $\hat{Q}$ is arbitrary, we obtain

$$\|\hat{v} - \hat{I}_h^r \hat{v}\|_{H^{r+1}(\hat{K})} \le C|\hat{v}|_{H^{r+1}(\hat{K})}.$$

Estimate (7.23) follows immediately from the above inequality.

By Lemma 7.11, equality (7.22), and estimate (7.23), we have

$$\begin{aligned}
|v - I_h^r v|_{H^m(K)} &\le C\|J_K^{-1}\|^m |\det J_K|^{1/2} |\hat{v} - \hat{I}_h^r \hat{v}|_{H^m(\hat{K})} \\
&\le C\frac{h_{\hat{K}}^m}{\rho^m(K)} |\det J_K|^{1/2} |\hat{v} - \hat{I}_h^r \hat{v}|_{H^m(\hat{K})} \\
&\le C\frac{h_{\hat{K}}^m}{\rho^m(K)} |\det J_K|^{1/2} |\hat{v}|_{H^{r+1}(\hat{K})} \\
&\le C\frac{1}{\rho^m(K)} |\det J_K|^{1/2} |\hat{v}|_{H^{r+1}(\hat{K})},
\end{aligned}$$

where the constant C is a function of $(r, m, \hat{K})$.

Applying (7.19) and (7.21) to the above inequality, we obtain

$$|v - I_h^r v|_{H^m(K)} \le C \frac{1}{\rho^m(K)} |\det J_K|^{1/2} |\hat{v}|_{H^{r+1}(\hat{K})}$$
$$\le C \frac{1}{\rho^m(K)} \|J_K\|^{r+1} |v|_{H^{r+1}(K)} \le C \frac{h_K^{r+1}}{\rho^m(K)} |v|_{H^{r+1}(K)},$$

which completes the proof. □

Finally, we have the following global estimate.

Theorem 7.14. *Let $\{\mathcal{T}_h\}_{h>0}$ be a family of regular triangulations of affine finite elements in a convex domain $U \subset \mathbb{R}^d$ and $v \in H^{r+1}(U)$, $2(r+1) > d$. Then for $m = 0, 1$, the following estimates hold*

$$|v - I_h^r v|_{H^m(U)} \le C \left(\sum_{K \in \mathcal{T}_h} h_K^{2(r+1-m)} |v|^2_{H^{r+1}(K)} \right)^{1/2}, \tag{7.24}$$

$$|v - I_h^r v|_{H^m(U)} \le C\, h^{r+1-m} |v|_{H^{r+1}(U)}, \tag{7.25}$$

where $C = C(r, m, d)$. The restriction $m = 0, 1$ is the result of the requirement $I_h^r v \in H^m(\Omega)$, which holds only for $m \le 1$.

Proof. By Theorem 7.13, we have

$$|v - I_h^r v|^2_{H^m(U)} = \sum_{K \in \mathcal{T}_h} |v - I_h^r v|^2_{H^m(K)} \le C \sum_{K \in \mathcal{T}_h} \frac{h_K^{2(r+1)}}{\rho^{2m}(K)} |v|^2_{H^{r+1}(K)}$$
$$= C \sum_{K \in \mathcal{T}_h} \frac{h_K^{2m}}{\rho^{2m}(K)} h_K^{2(r+1-m)} |v|^2_{H^{r+1}(K)}$$
$$\le C \sum_{K \in \mathcal{T}_h} h_K^{2(r+1-m)} |v|^2_{H^{r+1}(K)},$$

which proves (7.24) with $C = C(r, m, d)$. Estimate (7.25) follows from the fact that simplices K are not overlapping, then for $k \ge 0$

$$|v|_{H^k(U)} = \left(\sum_{K \in \mathcal{T}_h} |v|^2_{H^k(K)} \right)^{1/2}.$$

□

Let $V_h = X_h^r \cap H_0^1(U)$. We consider the following finite element problem for the second-order elliptic equation (7.1) with the Dirichlet boundary conditions:

$$\text{find } u_h \in V_h \text{ such that } B[u_h, v_h] = (f, v_h), \quad \forall v_h \in V_h. \tag{7.26}$$

The existence of a unique u_h which solves (7.26) follows from the equivalence of (7.26) with (7.6) and the unique solvability of the linear system (7.7). Once the interpolation error is estimated, we can estimate the approximation errors similarly to the one-dimensional case. Then we have the following theorems.

Theorem 7.15. *Let $u \in H_0^1(U)$ be a solution of (7.3), $U \subset \mathbb{R}^d$, and $u_h \in V_h$ be its approximate finite element solution, i.e., a solution of (7.26) obtained with affine finite elements of degree r for a family of regular triangulations $\mathcal{T}_h$. If $u \in H^{r+1}(U)$, $2(r+1) > d$, then the following* a priori *error estimates hold*

$$\begin{aligned} \|u - u_h\|_{H_0^1(U)} &\le \frac{\alpha}{\beta} C \left(\sum_{K \in \mathcal{T}_h} h_K^{2r} |u|_{H^{r+1}(K)}^2 \right)^{1/2}, \\ \|u - u_h\|_{H_0^1(U)} &\le \frac{\alpha}{\beta} C\, h^r |u|_{H^{r+1}(U)}, \end{aligned} \tag{7.27}$$

where the constant C is independent of h and u.

Theorem 7.16. *Let $u \in H_0^1(U)$ be a solution of (7.3), $U \subset \mathbb{R}^d$, and $u_h \in V_h$ be its approximate solution, i.e., a solution of (7.26) obtained with affine finite elements of degree r for a family of regular triangulations $\mathcal{T}_h$. If $u \in H^{m+1}(U) \cap C(\bar{U})$ for $m > 0$, then the following* a priori *error estimate holds*

$$\|u - u_h\|_{L^2(U)} \le C\, h^{s+1} |u|_{H^{s+1}(U)}, \quad s = \min(m, r), \tag{7.28}$$

where the constant C is independent of h and u.

We conclude this section with a few remarks about error control. Due to the estimates of Theorem 7.15, we can reduce the approximation error by decreasing the size of the finite element mesh or increasing r. The increase of r is not very common because higher-order polynomials lead to unstable numerical schemes. Hence, to reduce the approximation error, the grid should be refined. However, decreasing h over the entire domain is not the most efficient strategy. It is more convenient to rely on the first estimate (7.27) and refine the grid only for elements K that make large contributions to the global error. This strategy is called *grid adaptivity*, and its implementation requires the grid refinement for elements K on which the seminorm $|u|_{H^{r+1}(K)}$ is large. This is called *a priori adaptivity* because we use *a priori* estimates. The strategy seems to be of little use since the exact solution u is not known. However, we can replace u in the *a priori* estimate by a well-chosen approximation. That strategy is not that simple as, even for a two-dimensional problem, we need the seminorm in H^2. Assume that we use linear elements. Then u_h is continuous and even piecewise differentiable. However, the computation of the approximate second-order derivatives of u_h is not a straightforward operation because a special reconstruction technique is required for the first-order derivatives. For some problems, we can omit the difficulty using more smooth finite elements as the Hermite finite elements. We are not going into details of these procedures. Nevertheless, it is clear that using grid adaptivity, we need sophisticated software for automatic grid generation (cf. [74]).

In use is also *a posteriori adaptivity* since it is possible to obtain an error estimate in terms of the approximate solution u_h, so-called *a posteriori estimates* (cf. [58]). This approach is not much easier for a computer implementation because we enter the domain of numerically demanding *a posteriori* estimates.

7.2 Finite Elements for Parabolic Equations

We now consider the linear, parabolic initial-boundary value problem

$$\begin{aligned} &\frac{\partial u}{\partial t} + \mathcal{A}^t u = f, \quad \text{in } (0,T] \times U, \\ &u = 0, \quad \text{on } [0,T] \times \partial U, \\ &u = g, \quad \text{on } \{t = 0\} \times U, \end{aligned} \tag{7.29}$$

where $U \subset \mathbb{R}^d$ and $\mathcal{A}^t$ is the uniformly parabolic operator in divergence form defined in Section 5.4. To simplify the presentation, we assume that the coefficients of $\mathcal{A}^t$ are time-independent. Similarly to the elliptic case, we assume that the bilinear form generated by operator $\mathcal{A}^t$ is coercive and given by equation (7.2). Then we drop the superscript t from $\mathcal{A}^t$ and $B^t[u,v]$ since these operators are independent of time. By a weak solution of problem (7.29), we mean a function $u(t) = u(t,\cdot)$, $u(t) \in H_0^1(U)$ for $t \in [0,T]$, which fulfills the following initial value problem

$$\begin{aligned} &\left\langle \frac{du}{dt}(t), v \right\rangle + B[u(t),v] = (f(t),v), \quad \forall v \in H_0^1(U), \\ &u(0) = g. \end{aligned} \tag{7.30}$$

To find a numerical solution, we approximate (7.30) by finite elements in space variables. Let V_h be an M_r-dimensional space of finite elements and $\{\phi_i\}_{i=1}^{M_r}$ a basis in V_h. First, we consider the so-called *spatially semi-discrete problem*: find a function $u_h(t) = u_h(t,\cdot)$ such that $u_h(t) \in V_h$ for all $t \in [0,T]$, and $u_h(t)$ is a solution of the following initial value problem

$$\begin{aligned} &\left\langle \frac{du_h}{dt}(t), v \right\rangle + B[u_h(t),v] = (f(t),v), \quad \forall v \in V_h, \\ &u_h(0) = g_h, \end{aligned} \tag{7.31}$$

where $g_h \in V_h$ is an approximation of g.

Expanding u_h in the basis of V_h

$$u_h(t,x) = \sum_{i=1}^{M_r} w_i(t)\phi_i(x)$$

and inserting this series into (7.31), we obtain

$$\sum_{i=1}^{M_r} \frac{\partial w_i(t)}{\partial t}(\phi_i,\phi_j) + \sum_{i=1}^{M_r} w_i(t)B[\phi_i,\phi_j] = (f(t),\phi_j), \quad j = 1,\dots,M_r.$$

Denoting by $W(t) = \big(w_1(t),\dots,w_{M_r}(t)\big)$ the vector of unknowns, by E_h the mass matrix with elements

$$\left(E_h\right)_{ij} = (\phi_i,\phi_j), \quad i,j = 1,\dots,M_r,$$

by A_h the stiffness matrix with elements

$$\left(A_h\right)_{ij} = B[\phi_i,\phi_j], \quad i,j = 1,\dots,M_r,$$

and by $F_h(t) = \big(f_1(t), \ldots, f_{M_r}(t)\big)$ the load vector with components

$$f_i(t) = (f(t), \phi_i), \quad i = 1, \ldots, M_r,$$

we reduce the Galerkin approximation to the following system of ordinary differential equations

$$E_h \frac{dW(t)}{dt} + A_h W(t) = F_h(t). \tag{7.32}$$

E_h is a positive definite matrix since $\{\phi_i\}$ is a basis of V_h. A_h is also a positive definite matrix by the coerciveness of $B[u, v]$. Hence, the system (7.32) possesses a unique solution, and also u_h which solves (7.31) is uniquely defined.

Example 7.17. We analyze the one-dimensional heat equation

$$\frac{\partial u}{\partial t} - a^2 \frac{\partial^2 u}{\partial x^2} = f(t, x), \quad 0 < x < 1, \quad t > 0,$$
$$u(t, 0) = u(t, 1) = 0, \quad t > 0,$$
$$u(0, x) = g(x),$$

using the computations for the stationary two-point boundary value problem of Example 7.1.

We approximate the heat equation introducing in interval $(0, 1)$ a grid with M subintervals $K_j = (x_{j-1}, x_j)$ of length $h_j = x_j - x_{j-1}$. We take as a finite element space the space of hat functions X_h^1. The approximate problem is

$$\int_0^1 \frac{\partial u_h}{\partial t} \phi_i(x) dx + \int_0^1 a^2 \frac{\partial u_h}{\partial x} \phi_i'(x) dx$$
$$= \int_0^1 f(t, x) \phi_i dx, \; i = 1, \ldots, M - 1,$$

with $u_h(t, x) = \sum_{i=1}^{M-1} w_i(t) \phi_i(x)$.

The approximate problem is a system of linear differential equations

$$E_h \frac{dW}{dt} + A_h W(t) = F(t),$$

where mass matrix E_h has elements

$$e_{i,j} = \int_0^1 \phi_i(x)\phi_j(x)dx,$$

stiffness matrix A_h has elements

$$a_{i,j} = \int_0^1 a^2\phi_i'(x)\phi_j'(x)dx,$$

and $F(t)$ is a vector with entries

$$f_i(t) = \int_0^1 f(t,x)\phi_i(x)dx.$$

From Example 7.1, we know that

$$a_{i,i} = a^2\left(\frac{1}{h_i} + \frac{1}{h_{i+1}}\right), \quad a_{i,i+1} = -a^2\frac{1}{h_{i+1}}.$$

The elements of the mass matrix can also be recovered from Example 7.1

$$e_{i,i} = \frac{1}{3}(h_i + h_{i+1}), \quad e_{i,i+1} = \frac{1}{6}h_{i+1}.$$

Hence,

$$E_h = \frac{1}{6}\begin{pmatrix} (2h_1+2h_2) & h_2 & & \\ h_2 & (2h_2+2h_3) & h_3 & \\ & \ddots & \ddots & \ddots \\ & & h_{M-1} & (2h_{M-1}+2h_M) \end{pmatrix}$$

and

$$A_h = a^2\begin{pmatrix} \left(\frac{1}{h_1}+\frac{1}{h_2}\right) & -\frac{1}{h_2} & & \\ -\frac{1}{h_2} & \left(\frac{1}{h_2}+\frac{1}{h_3}\right) & -\frac{1}{h_3} & \\ & \ddots & \ddots & \ddots \\ & & -\frac{1}{h_{M-1}} & \left(\frac{1}{h_{M-1}}+\frac{1}{h_M}\right) \end{pmatrix}.$$

For the load vector $F(t)$, we apply the trapezoidal rule to obtain

$$F(t) = \frac{1}{2}\begin{pmatrix} f(t,x_1)(h_1+h_2) \\ f(t,x_2)(h_2+h_3) \\ \vdots \\ f(t,x_{M-1})(h_{M-1}+h_M) \end{pmatrix}.$$

The obtained system of ordinary differential equations

$$E_h\frac{dW}{dt} + A_hW(t) = F(t),$$

possesses a unique solution as a linear system in which matrix E_h is invertible (by its definition).

The proof of convergence of the finite element approximation will go in two steps. First, we prove an error estimate for the semi-discrete problem (7.31). The convergence will be carried on under the simplified assumption that the bilinear form $B[u,v]$ is symmetric. This corresponds to the assumption that the operator $\mathcal{A}$ in problem (7.29) is self-adjoint.

Definition 7.18. Let the bilinear form $B[u,v]$ implied by the operator $\mathcal{A}$ of problem (7.29) be symmetric and fulfill estimates (7.4) and (7.5). The *Ritz projection* R_h: $H_0^1(U) \to V_h$ is defined by the equality

$$B[R_hu, v_h] = B[u, v_h], \quad \forall u \in H_0^1(U), \quad \forall v_h \in V_h.$$

The properties of the Ritz projection most relevant for the proofs of subsequent theorems are summarized in the following lemma.

Lemma 7.19.

(1) *For each* $u \in H_0^1(U)$ *and* $v_h \in V_h$ *the following orthogonality relation holds*

$$B[R_hu - u, v_h] = 0.$$

(2) *For all* $u \in H_0^1(U)$, *we have*

$$\|R_hu - u\|_{\mathcal{H}} = \min_{v_h\in V_h} \|v_h - u\|_{\mathcal{H}},$$

where $\|v\|_{\mathcal{H}} = \big(B[v,v]\big)^{1/2}$ *is the norm in* $H_0^1(U)$ *equivalent to the standard norm of this space due to the symmetry of the bilinear form* $B[u,v]$, *and estimates* (7.4) *and* (7.5).

(3) *If u is a weak solution of (7.3), then the Ritz projection $R_h u = u_h$, where u_h is a finite element solution of (7.26).*

Proof. Statement (1) follows from the definition of the Ritz projection. To prove Statement (2), let us recall that, due to (7.4) and (7.5), the norm $\big(B[\cdot,\cdot]\big)^{1/2}$ is equivalent to the norm $\|\cdot\|_{H_0^1(U)}$. Statement (1) implies that R_h is the orthogonal projection of $H_0^1(U)$ on V_h in the norm $\|\cdot\|_{\mathcal{H}}$. Then Statement (2) is a property of orthogonal projections in a Hilbert space.

To prove Statement (3), we observe that the orthogonality relation for the Ritz projection is the orthogonality relation (7.16), which is valid for the finite element solution u_h. Since $R_h u$ is uniquely defined as an orthogonal projection in $H_0^1(U)$, then $R_h u = u_h$. □

The following lemma extends the error estimates of the interpolation operator in V_h to the Ritz projection.

Lemma 7.20. *Let U be an open, convex, bounded domain in $\mathbb{R}^d$. Then for $m = 1, 2$, we have the estimate*

$$\|R_h u - u\|_{L^2(U)} + h|R_h u - u|_{H_0^1(U)} \le C\, h^m \|u\|_{H^m(U)},$$
$$\forall u \in H^m(U) \cap H_0^1(U).$$

Proof. Given the assumptions on $B[u,v]$ and the Poincaré inequality for a bounded U, we have the inequalities

$$\begin{aligned} C_1\|v\|_{H_0^1(U)} &\le \|v\|_{\mathcal{H}} \le C_2\|v\|_{H_0^1(U)}, \\ C_1|v|_{H_0^1(U)} &\le \|v\|_{H_0^1(U)} \le C_2|v|_{H_0^1(U)}. \end{aligned} \tag{7.33}$$

The H_0^1 estimate of the lemma follows from the fact that R_h is an orthogonal projection in $\mathcal{H}$. Then $\|R_h u\|_{\mathcal{H}} \le \|u\|_{\mathcal{H}}$ and, by inequalities (7.33), $|R_h u|_{H_0^1(U)} \le C|u|_{H_0^1(U)}$. Hence,

$$|R_h u - u|_{H_0^1(U)} \le C|u|_{H_0^1(U)} \le C\|u\|_{H_0^1(U)}. \tag{7.34}$$

Since the Ritz projection is an orthogonal projection $\mathcal{H} \to V_h$, we have

$$\|R_h u - u\|_{\mathcal{H}} = \min_{v \in V_h} \|v - u\|_{\mathcal{H}}$$

which gives

$$\|R_h u - u\|_{\mathcal{H}} \le \|I_h^1 u - u\|_{\mathcal{H}}.$$

Then by (7.33)

$$|R_h u - u|_{H_0^1(U)} \le C\|R_h u - u\|_{\mathcal{H}} \le C\|I_h^1 u - u\|_{H_0^1(U)}.$$

Hence, by (7.33) and the estimates of Theorem 7.14, we obtain

$$|R_h u - u|_{H_0^1(U)} \le C\,|I_h^1 u - u|_{H_0^1(U)} \le C\,h|u|_{H^2(U)} \le C\,h\|u\|_{H^2(U)}. \tag{7.35}$$

To obtain the L^2 estimate of $(R_h u - u)$, we consider the following weak dual problem with the right-hand side $e = R_h u - u$:

$$\text{find } g \in H_0^1(U) \text{ such that } B[v, g] = (v, e), \quad \forall v \in H_0^1(U).$$

Given the assumptions on B, this problem possesses a unique weak solution, and the following regularity estimate holds (cf. Remark 5.28)

$$\|g\|_{H^2(U)} \le C\|e\|_{L^2(U)}.$$

Taking $v = e$, using the orthogonality of the Ritz projection (Statement (1) of Lemma 7.19), estimates (7.4) and (7.33), the estimates of Theorem 7.14, and the above regularity estimate, we get

$$\begin{aligned}\|e\|_{L^2(U)}^2 = |B[e, g]| = |B[e, g - I_h^1 g]| &\le C\,\|e\|_{H_0^1(U)}\|g - I_h^1 g\|_{H_0^1(U)} \\ &\le C\,h\|e\|_{H_0^1(U)}\|g\|_{H^2(U)} \le C\,h\|e\|_{H_0^1(U)}\|e\|_{L^2(U)}.\end{aligned}$$

Hence, $\|e\|_{L^2(U)} \le C\,h\|e\|_{H_0^1(U)}$. Since by (7.33) and (7.35), we have

$$\|R_h u - u\|_{H_0^1(U)} \le C\,|R_h u - u|_{H_0^1(U)} \le C\,h\|u\|_{H^2(U)},$$

that completes the proof for $m = 2$.

Since for $m = 2$, we have proven the estimate

$$\|e\|_{L^2(U)} \le C\,h\|e\|_{H_0^1(U)} \le C\,h|e|_{H_0^1(U)},$$

then by (7.34), we get

$$\|R_h u - u\|_{L^2(U)} \le C\,h|R_h u - u|_{H_0^1(U)} \le C\,h|u|_{H_0^1(U)} \le C\,h\|u\|_{H_0^1(U)}.$$

□

Remark 7.21. The above estimates can be extended immediately to finite elements of order $r > 2$. It is sufficient to apply the estimates of Theorem 7.14 with an appropriate r. Then we obtain for $2 \le s \le r$

$$\|R_h u - u\|_{L^2(U)} + h|R_h u - u|_{H_0^1(U)} \le C\, h^s \|u\|_{H^s(U)},$$
$$\forall u \in H^s(U) \cap H_0^1(U).$$

These estimates apply to solutions of elliptic or parabolic equations in domains with smooth boundaries because only for such domains we can expect that $u \in H^r(U)$ for $r > 2$ (cf. Remarks 5.28 and 5.37). In polyhedral domains, we cannot expect a higher regularity of solutions because singularities can develop at the corners of the domain. Hence, there is no justification for using finite elements of order higher than 2 in polyhedral domains. For convex domains with smooth boundaries, the regularity of solutions is not a problem; however, to obtain a high-order approximation error, a special consideration of the boundary layer $U \backslash U_h$ is required.

Theorem 7.22. *Let $u \in L^2(0,T; H^4(U))$ be a solution of* (7.30) *with $g \in H^3(U)$ and a sufficiently smooth f, and $u_h(t)$ be a solution of* (7.31) *with g_h obtained by an orthogonal projection of g onto space V_h. Then for $t \ge 0$*

$$\|u_h(t) - u(t)\|_{L^2(U)}$$
$$\le \|g_h - g\|_{L^2(U)} + C\, h^2 \left(\|g\|_{H^2(U)} + \int_0^t \left\| \frac{du}{dt}(s) \right\|_{H^2(U)} ds \right).$$

Proof. Using the Ritz projection, we can write

$$u_h - u = (u_h - R_h u) + (R_h u - u).$$

The second term can be estimated using Lemma 7.20

$$\|R_h u(t) - u(t)\|_{L^2(U)}$$
$$\le C\, h^2 \|u(t)\|_{H^2(U)} = C\, h^2 \left\| g + \int_0^t \frac{du}{dt}(s) ds \right\|_{H^2(U)}$$
$$\le C\, h^2 \left(\|g\|_{H^2(U)} + \int_0^t \left\| \frac{du}{dt}(s) \right\|_{H^2(U)} ds \right).$$

Let $D(t) = u_h(t) - R_h u(t)$. Then using the definition of the Ritz projection and the commutation of R_h with time differentiation, we obtain

$$\begin{aligned}
&\left(\frac{dD}{dt}(t), v_h\right) + B[D(t), v_h] \\
&= \left(\frac{du_h}{dt}(t), v_h\right) + B[u_h(t), v_h] - \left(R_h\frac{du}{dt}(t), v_h\right) - B[R_h u(t), v_h] \\
&= (f(t), v_h) - \left(R_h\frac{du}{dt}(t), v_h\right) - B[R_h u(t), v_h] \\
&= (f(t), v_h) - \left(R_h\frac{du}{dt}(t), v_h\right) - B[u(t), v_h] \\
&= \left(\frac{du}{dt}(t) - R_h\frac{du}{dt}(t), v_h\right).
\end{aligned}$$

Taking $v_h = D(t)$ and using the coerciveness of B, we obtain

$$\begin{aligned}
\frac{1}{2}\frac{d}{dt}\|D(t)\|^2_{L^2(U)} &\le \left(\frac{du}{dt}(t) - R_h\frac{du}{dt}(t), D(t)\right) \\
&\le \|D(t)\|_{L^2(U)}\left\|\frac{du}{dt}(t) - R_h\frac{du}{dt}(t)\right\|_{L^2(U)},
\end{aligned}$$

which gives the estimate

$$\frac{d}{dt}\|D(t)\|_{L^2(U)} \le \left\|\frac{du}{dt}(t) - R_h\frac{du}{dt}(t)\right\|_{L^2(U)}.$$

Integrating the above inequality, we have

$$\|D(t)\|_{L^2(U)} \le \|D(0)\|_{L^2(U)} + \int_0^t \left\|\frac{du}{dt}(s) - R_h\frac{du}{dt}(s)\right\|_{L^2(U)} ds.$$

Using the estimate from Lemma 7.20, we obtain

$$\left\|\frac{du}{dt}(t) - R_h\frac{du}{dt}(t)\right\|_{L^2(U)} \le C\,h^2\left\|\frac{du}{dt}(t)\right\|_{H^2(U)}$$

and

$$\begin{aligned}
\|D(0)\|_{L^2(U)} = \|g_h - R_h g\|_{L^2(U)} &\le \|g_h - g\|_{L^2(U)} + \|R_h g - g\|_{L^2(U)} \\
&\le \|g_h - g\|_{L^2(U)} + c\,h^2\|g\|_{H^2(U)}. \quad \square
\end{aligned}$$

The above result can be extended to finite elements of order $r > 1$. When a weak solution v of (7.3) is a function in $H_0^1(U) \cap H^r(U)$, then, due to Remark 7.21, we have the estimate

$$\|v - R_h v\|_{L^2(U)} \leq C\, h^r \|v\|_{H^r(U)}. \tag{7.36}$$

In the finite element space V_h in which estimate (7.36) holds, we have a result stronger than given by Theorem 7.22. However, this stronger result has limited applicability in polyhedral domains (see Remark 7.21).

Theorem 7.23. *Let $u(t)$ be a solution of (7.30) and $u_h(t)$ a solution of (7.31). Then*

$$\|u_h(t) - u(t)\|_{L^2(U)} \leq C\, h^r \left(\|g_h - g\|_{H^r(U)} + \int_0^t \left\| \frac{du}{dt}(s) \right\|_{H^r(U)} ds \right),$$

where $g_h \in X_h^r \cap H_0^1(U) \cap H^{r+1}(U)$, $g \in H_0^1(U) \cap H^{r+1}(U)$ and $u(t) \in H_0^1(U) \cap H^{r+1}(U)$, $du/dt(t) \in H_0^1(U) \cap H^r(U)$.

To obtain a fully discretized problem, we can apply various discretizations. The most popular approach is to approximate the time derivative by finite differences and apply two-time-level schemes. However, finite element discretization in the time variable is also used (cf. [75]). To apply finite differences, we divide the time interval $[0, T]$ into N subintervals, set $\delta t = T/N$ and obtain the time grid $t_n = n \cdot \delta t$, $n = 0, 1, \ldots, N$. Denoting $W^n = W(t_n)$ and $F^n = F_h(t_n)$, we approximate system (7.32) by the θ-scheme

$$E_h \frac{W^{n+1} - W^n}{\delta t} + A_h\big(\theta W^{n+1} + (1-\theta) W^n\big) = \big(\theta F^{n+1} + (1-\theta) F^n\big). \tag{7.37}$$

Then we define the fully discrete Galerkin approximation

$$u_h^n(x) = \sum_{i=1}^{M_r} w_i^n \phi_i(x), \tag{7.38}$$

where $w_i^n = w_i(t_n)$ according to the notation introduced earlier.

Our goal is to prove that u_h^n converge to $u(t, x)$, a solution of the continuous problem (7.29). We begin by proving the stability of the

θ-schemes. An important step in the proof is based on the following *inverse estimate.*

Lemma 7.24. *Let $\mathcal{T}_h$ be a family of regular triangulations of $U \subset \mathbb{R}^d$. There exists a constant C_{inv} such that for all $v_h \in V_h$*

$$\|Dv_h\|_{L^2(U)} \leq C_{inv}\, h^{-1} \|v_h\|_{L^2(U)},$$

where Dv denotes the gradient of v.

Proof. It is sufficient to prove the above estimate in a single finite element $K \in \mathcal{T}_h$

$$\int_K |Dv_h|^2 dx \leq C\, h^{-2} \int_K |v_h|^2 dx.$$

Let $\hat{K}$ be a standard simplex given by formula (7.18) and G: $\hat{K} \to K$ an affine map. We define $\hat{v}_h(\hat{x}) = v_h(G(\hat{x}))$ for $\hat{x} \in \hat{K}$. Denoting $J = \left(\dfrac{\partial x}{\partial \hat{x}}\right)$, the Jacobian matrix of G, we get $D\hat{v}_h = JDv_h$. By the triangulation regularity, we have $\|J\| \sim h$. From that relation follows that $\|J^{-1}\| \sim h^{-1}$, and the following estimates hold

$$|D\hat{v}_h| \leq Ch|Dv_h|, \quad |Dv_h| \leq Ch^{-1}|D\hat{v}_h|.$$

By the change of variables $dx = |\det J| d\hat{x} \simeq h^d d\hat{x}$, we obtain

$$\int_K |Dv_h|^2 dx \leq C\, h^{d-2} \int_{\hat{K}} |D\hat{v}_h|^2 d\hat{x}.$$

Let us observe that since V_h is a finite-dimensional space, all norms in V_h are equivalent. In particular, the H^k-norm is equivalent to the L^2-norm. Then

$$\int_U \sum_{|\alpha| \leq k} |D^\alpha v_h|^2 dx \leq C \int_U |v_h|^2 dx, \quad \forall v_h \in V_h.$$

Applying this inequality to the H^1 norm, we obtain

$$\begin{aligned}\int_K |Dv_h|^2 dx &\leq C\, h^{d-2} \int_{\hat{K}} |D\hat{v}_h|^2 d\hat{x} \\ &\leq C\, h^{d-2} \int_{\hat{K}} \sum_{|\alpha| \leq 1} |D^\alpha \hat{v}_h|^2 d\hat{x} \leq C\, h^{d-2} \int_{\hat{K}} |\hat{v}_h|^2 d\hat{x} \\ &\leq C\, h^{-2} \int_K |v_h|^2 dx.\end{aligned}$$

□

Theorem 7.25. *Assume that the bilinear form $B[u, v]$ fulfills conditions (7.4) and (7.5), and $\|f(t)\|_{L^2(U)}$ is bounded on $[0, T]$. For $\theta < 1/2$, we assume additionally that the following time step restriction holds*

$$\delta t(1 + C_{inv}h^{-1})^2 < \frac{2\beta}{(1-2\theta)\alpha^2}, \tag{7.39}$$

where C_{inv} is the constant from the estimate in Lemma 7.24, and α, β are the constants from (7.4) and (7.5).

Then u_h^n, which solves the weak formulation of the fully discrete approximation

$$\begin{aligned}
\frac{1}{\delta t}\left(u_h^{n+1} - u_h^n, v_h\right) &= -B\left[\theta u_h^{n+1} + (1-\theta)u_h^n, v_h\right] \\
&\quad + \left(\theta f(t_{n+1}) + (1-\theta)f(t_n), v_h\right), \quad \forall v_h \in V_h, \\
u_h^0 &= I_h^1 g,
\end{aligned} \tag{7.40}$$

have the estimate

$$\|u_h^n\|_{L^2(U)} \le C\left(\|u_h^0\|_{L^2(U)} + \delta t\sum_{i=0}^{n}\|f(t_i)\|_{L^2(U)}\right),$$

where the constant C depends on θ but is independent of h, δt and N, and is a nondecreasing function of α, β^{-1}, and T.

Proof. Taking $v_h = \theta u_h^{n+1} + (1-\theta)u_h^n$ in (7.40) and applying the elementary identity

$$\begin{aligned}
&(u_h^{n+1} - u_h^n, u_h^n) + \frac{1}{2}(u_h^{n+1} - u_h^n, u_h^{n+1} - u_h^n) \\
&= \frac{1}{2}\|u_h^{n+1}\|_{L^2(U)} - \frac{1}{2}\|u_h^n\|_{L^2(U)},
\end{aligned}$$

we obtain

$$\begin{aligned}
&\frac{1}{2}\|u_h^{n+1}\|_{L^2(U)}^2 - \frac{1}{2}\|u_h^n\|_{L^2(U)}^2 + (\theta - 1/2)\|u_h^{n+1} - u_h^n\|_{L^2(U)}^2 \\
&\quad + \delta t B\left[\theta u_h^{n+1} + (1-\theta)u_h^n, \theta u_h^{n+1} + (1-\theta)u_h^n\right] \\
&\le \delta t\left(\theta f(t_{n+1}) + (1-\theta)f(t_n), \theta u_h^{n+1} + (1-\theta)u_h^n\right).
\end{aligned}$$

By the coerciveness of $B[u,v]$ and the Cauchy inequality, we get for $0 < \varepsilon \le 1$

$$\begin{aligned}\|u_h^{n+1}\|^2_{L^2(U)} - \|u_h^n\|^2_{L^2(U)} + (2\theta - 1)\|u_h^{n+1} - u_h^n\|^2_{L^2(U)} \\ + 2(1-\varepsilon)\beta\delta t\|\theta u_h^{n+1} + (1-\theta)u_h^n\|^2_{H_0^1(U)} \\ \le \frac{\delta t}{2\varepsilon\beta}\|\theta f(t_{n+1}) + (1-\theta)f(t_n)\|^2_{H^{-1}(U)}.\end{aligned} \tag{7.41}$$

For $\theta \ge 1/2$, inequality (7.41) gives the estimate of $\|u_h^{n+1}\|^2_{L^2(U)} - \|u_h^n\|^2_{L^2(U)}$ which is sufficient to complete the proof. For $\theta < 1/2$, we need a better estimate. To this end, we insert $v_h = u_h^{n+1} - u_h^n$ into (7.40) to obtain

$$\begin{aligned}&\|u_h^{n+1} - u_h^n\|^2_{L^2(U)} \\ &= -\delta t B\big[\theta u_h^{n+1} + (1-\theta)u_h^n, u_h^{n+1} - u_h^n\big] \\ &\quad + \delta t\big(\theta f(t_{n+1}) + (1-\theta)f(t_n), u_h^{n+1} - u_h^n\big) \\ &\le \alpha\delta t\|\theta u_h^{n+1} + (1-\theta)u_h^n\|_{H_0^1(U)}\|u_h^{n+1} - u_h^n\|_{H_0^1(U)} \\ &\quad + \delta t\|\theta f(t_{n+1}) + (1-\theta)f(t_n)\|_{H^{-1}(U)}\|u_h^{n+1} - u_h^n\|_{H_0^1(U)}.\end{aligned}$$

By Lemma 7.24, we have

$$\begin{aligned}\|u_h^{n+1} - u_h^n\|_{L^2(U)} \le \delta t(1 + C_{inv}h^{-1})\Big(\alpha\|\theta u_h^{n+1} + (1-\theta)u_h^n\|_{H_0^1(U)} \\ + \|\theta f(t_{n+1}) + (1-\theta)f(t_n)\|_{H^{-1}(U)}\Big).\end{aligned} \tag{7.42}$$

Inserting this estimate into (7.41) and defining for $\eta > 0$ the constant

$$\kappa = 2(1-\varepsilon)\beta - (1-2\theta)\alpha^2(1+\eta)\delta t(1 + C_{inv}h^{-1})^2,$$

we obtain

$$\begin{aligned}\|u_h^{n+1}\|^2_{L^2(U)} - \|u_h^n\|^2_{L^2(U)} + \delta t\kappa\|\theta u_h^{n+1} + (1-\theta)u_h^n\|^2_{H_0^1(U)} \\ \le C\,\delta t(1 + \delta t\, h^{-2})\|\theta f(t_{n+1}) + (1-\theta)f(t_n)\|^2_{H^{-1}(U)}.\end{aligned} \tag{7.43}$$

For sufficiently small ε, η, and $\theta < 1/2$, we have $0 < \kappa < +\infty$ due to (7.39). This gives the estimate of $\|u_h^{n+1}\|^2_{L^2(U)} - \|u_h^n\|^2_{L^2(U)}$.

Let m be fixed, $1 \leq m \leq N$. By summing the estimates for $\theta < 1/2$ from $n = 0$ to $n = m - 1$ and similarly the estimates for $\theta \geq 1/2$, we obtain

$$\|u_h^m\|_{L^2(U)}^2 \leq \|u_h^0\|_{L^2(U)}^2 + C\,\delta t \sum_{n=0}^{m-1} \|\theta f(t_{n+1}) + (1-\theta) f(t_n)\|_{H^{-1}(U)}^2.$$

Since $\|\cdot\|_{H^{-1}} \leq \|\cdot\|_{L^2}$, the assertion of the theorem follows. □

To prove the convergence of the fully discrete Galerkin method, we consider separately the θ-schemes with different θ.

Theorem 7.26. *Let u_h^n be computed by the implicit Euler scheme (scheme (7.40) with $\theta = 1$) with $g_h = I_h^1 g$. Let $u \in L^2(0,T;H^4(U))$ be a solution of (7.30) with $g \in H^3(U)$ and a sufficiently smooth f (cf. Remark 5.37). Then*

$$\|u_h^n - u(t_n)\|_{L^2(U)} \leq C\,h^2 \left(\|g\|_{H^2(U)} + \int_0^{t_n} \left\| \frac{du}{dt}(s) \right\|_{H^2(U)} ds \right) + C\,\delta t \int_0^{t_n} \left\| \frac{d^2u}{dt^2}(s) \right\|_{L^2(U)} ds. \tag{7.44}$$

The interpolant $I_h^1 g$ is well defined only when $U \subset \mathbb{R}^d$ for $d \leq 5$ (g is continuous due to Theorem 5.20). For $d > 5$, we must additionally assume that $g \in H^m(U)$, $2m > d$, and reformulate the theorem.

Proof. For the implicit Euler scheme, u_h^n solves the equation

$$\frac{1}{\delta t}\left(u_h^{n+1} - u_h^n, v_h\right) + B[u_h^{n+1}, v_h] = (f(t_{n+1}), v_h), \quad \forall v_h \in V_h. \tag{7.45}$$

Using the Ritz projection, we can write

$$\|u_h^n - u(t_n)\|_{L^2(U)} \leq \|u_h^n - R_h u(t_n)\|_{L^2(U)} + \|R_h u(t_n) - u(t_n)\|_{L^2(U)}.$$

From Lemma 7.20, we estimate the second term

$$\|R_h u(t_n) - u(t_n)\|_{L^2(U)} \leq C\,h^2 \left(\|g\|_{H^2(U)} + \int_0^{t_n} \left\| \frac{du}{dt}(s) \right\|_{H^2(U)} ds \right).$$

To estimate the first term, we define $D_h^n = u_h^n - R_h u(t_n)$. Inserting D_h^n into equation (7.45), we obtain

$$\frac{1}{\delta t}\left(D_h^{n+1} - D_h^n, v_h\right) + B[D_h^{n+1}, v_h] = (e^{n+1}, v_h), \quad \forall v_h \in V_h, \tag{7.46}$$

where

$$(e^{n+1}, v_h) = (f(t_{n+1}), v_h) - \frac{1}{\delta t}(R_h(u(t_{n+1}) - u(t_n)), v_h) - B[u(t_{n+1}), v_h].$$

Equation (7.46) for D_h^n is analogous to equation (7.40) for u_h^n with $\theta = 1$. Thus, the stability result of Theorem 7.25 gives

$$\|D_h^n\|_{L^2(U)} \leq C\left(\|D_h^0\|_{L^2(U)} + \delta t \sum_{i=1}^{n} \|e^i\|_{L^2(U)}\right).$$

For D_h^0, we have the estimate

$$\begin{aligned}\|D_h^0\|_{L^2(U)} = \|g_h - R_h g\|_{L^2(U)} &\leq \|g_h - g\|_{L^2(U)} + \|g - R_h g\|_{L^2(U)} \\ &\leq C h^2 \|g\|_{H^2(U)}\end{aligned}$$

by Lemma 7.20 and Theorem 7.14.

To estimate $\|e^i\|_{L^2(U)}$, let us observe that

$$(f(t_i), v_h) - B[u(t_i), v_h] = \left(\frac{du}{dt}(t_i), v_h\right).$$

Then

$$\begin{aligned}(e^i, v_h) &= \left(\frac{du}{dt}(t_i), v_h\right) - \frac{1}{\delta t}(R_h(u(t_i) - u(t_{i-1})), v_h) \\ &= \left(\frac{du}{dt}(t_i) - \frac{u(t_i) - u(t_{i-1})}{\delta t}, v_h\right) \\ &\quad + \left((I - R_h)\frac{u(t_i) - u(t_{i-1})}{\delta t}, v_h\right).\end{aligned}$$

Using the Taylor formula, we have

$$\frac{du}{dt}(t_i) - \frac{u(t_i) - u(t_{i-1})}{\delta t} = \frac{1}{\delta t}\int_{t_{i-1}}^{t_i} (s - t_{i-1})\frac{d^2u}{dt^2}(s)ds.$$

Since R_h commutes with time differentiation, then

$$(I - R_h)(u(t_i) - u(t_{i-1})) = \int_{t_{i-1}}^{t_i} (I - R_h)\frac{du}{dt}(s)ds.$$

Applying Lemma 7.20, we obtain

$$\|(I - R_h)(u(t_i) - u(t_{i-1}))\|_{L^2(U)} \leq C\,h^2 \int_{t_{i-1}}^{t_i} \left\|\frac{du}{dt}(s)\right\|_{H^2(U)} ds.$$

Then

$$\begin{aligned}
\|e^i\|_{L^2(U)} &\leq \frac{1}{\delta t}\left\|\int_{t_{i-1}}^{t_i} (s - t_{i-1})\frac{d^2u}{dt^2}(s)ds\right\|_{L^2(U)} \\
&\quad + \frac{C\,h^2}{\delta t}\int_{t_{i-1}}^{t_i} \left\|\frac{du}{dt}(s)\right\|_{H^2(U)} ds \\
&\leq \int_{t_{i-1}}^{t_i} \left\|\frac{d^2u}{dt^2}(s)\right\|_{L^2(U)} ds + \frac{C\,h^2}{\delta t}\int_{t_{i-1}}^{t_i} \left\|\frac{du}{dt}(s)\right\|_{H^2(U)} ds.
\end{aligned}$$

Together, these estimates yield

$$\begin{aligned}
\|D_h^n\|_{L^2(U)} &\leq C\,h^2\|g\|_{H^2(U)} + C\,\delta t\sum_{i=1}^{n} \frac{C\,h^2}{\delta t}\int_{t_{i-1}}^{t_i} \left\|\frac{du}{dt}(s)\right\|_{H^2(U)} ds \\
&\quad + C\,\delta t\sum_{i=1}^{n}\int_{t_{i-1}}^{t_i} \left\|\frac{d^2u}{dt^2}(s)\right\|_{L^2(U)} ds \\
&\leq C\left(h^2\|g\|_{H^2(U)} + h^2\int_0^{t_n} \left\|\frac{du}{dt}(s)\right\|_{H^2(U)} ds \right. \\
&\qquad \left. + \,\delta t\int_0^{t_n} \left\|\frac{d^2u}{dt^2}(s)\right\|_{L^2(U)} ds\right).
\end{aligned}$$

□

Remark 7.27. The theorem holds under the weaker assumption $g \in H^2(U)$. However, with this weaker assumption, the formulation of the theorem requires a change of norms on the right-hand side of estimate (7.44) adequate to the regularity of the time derivatives $du/dt(t) \in H_0^1(U)$ and $d^2u/dt^2(t) \in H^{-1}(U)$ (cf. Theorem 5.36). In addition, the dimension of $U \subset \mathbb{R}^d$ must be restricted to $d \leq 3$.

The above theorem remains valid for the θ-schemes with $\theta > 1/2$, and the proof is essentially the same. For $\theta < 1/2$, we can obtain an analogous theorem by imposing an additional assumption similar to (7.39) that controls the time step. The obtained result is only first-order accurate in time. To obtain second-order accuracy in time, we apply the Crank–Nicolson scheme ($\theta = 1/2$). Then we obtain the following theorem.

Theorem 7.28. *Let u_h^n be computed by the Crank–Nicolson scheme (scheme (7.40) with $\theta = 1/2$) with $g_h = I_h^1 g$. Let $u \in L^2(0,T;H^6(U))$ be a solution of (7.30) with $g \in H^5(U)$ and a sufficiently smooth f. Then*

$$\|u_h^n - u(t_n)\|_{L^2(U)} \le C\,h^2\left(\|g\|_{H^2(U)} + \int_0^{t_n}\left\|\frac{du}{dt}(s)\right\|_{H^2(U)} ds\right) + C\,(\delta t)^2\int_0^{t_n}\left\|\frac{d^3u}{dt^3}(s)\right\|_{L^2(U)} ds.$$

The mentioned in Theorem 7.26 restrictions on the dimensionality of U and the smoothness of g also apply in this case.

Proof. The proof goes along the same lines as the proof of Theorem 7.26. The Crank–Nicolson scheme for u_h^n is

$$\begin{aligned}\frac{1}{\delta t}\left(u_h^{n+1} - u_h^n, v_h\right) + B\left[\frac{1}{2}(u_h^{n+1} + u_h^n), v_h\right]\\ = \left(\frac{1}{2}(f(t_{n+1}) + f(t_n)), v_h\right), \quad \forall v_h \in V_h.\end{aligned} \tag{7.47}$$

Then we split

$$\|u_h^n - u(t_n)\|_{L^2(U)} \le \|u_h^n - R_h u(t_n)\|_{L^2(U)} + \|R_h u(t_n) - u(t_n)\|_{L^2(U)},$$

and estimate the second term by Lemma 7.20

$$\|R_h u(t_n) - u(t_n)\|_{L^2(U)} \le C\,h^2\left(\|g\|_{H^2(U)} + \int_0^{t_n}\left\|\frac{du}{dt}(s)\right\|_{H^2(U)} ds\right).$$

To estimate the first term, we define $D_h^n = u_h^n - R_h u(t_n)$. Inserting D_h^n into equation (7.47), we obtain

$$\begin{aligned}\frac{1}{\delta t}\left(D_h^{n+1} - D_h^n, v_h\right) + B\left[\frac{1}{2}(D_h^{n+1} + D_h^n), v_h\right]\\ = \left(\frac{1}{2}(e^{n+1} + e^n), v_h\right), \quad \forall v_h \in V_h,\end{aligned}$$

where

$$
\begin{aligned}
&\left(\frac{1}{2}(e^{n+1}+e^{n}), v_h\right)\\
&\quad = \left(\frac{1}{2}(f(t_{n+1})+f(t_n)), v_h\right) - \frac{1}{\delta t}(R_h(u(t_{n+1})-u(t_n)), v_h)\\
&\qquad - B\left[\frac{1}{2}(u(t_{n+1})+u(t_n)), v_h\right].
\end{aligned}
$$

Similarly to the proof of Theorem 7.26, we get the estimates of D_h^n

$$
\|D_h^n\|_{L^2(U)} \le C\left(\|D_h^0\|_{L^2(U)} + \delta t\sum_{i=1}^{n}\left\|\frac{1}{2}(e^i+e^{i-1})\right\|_{L^2(U)}\right)
$$

and D_h^0

$$
\begin{aligned}
\|D_h^0\|_{L^2(U)} = \|g_h - R_h g\|_{L^2(U)} &\le \|g_h - g\|_{L^2(U)} + \|g - R_h g\|_{L^2(U)}\\
&\le C\,h^2\|g\|_{H^2(U)}.
\end{aligned}
$$

To estimate $\left\|(e^i+e^{i-1})/2\right\|_{L^2(U)}$, we use the identity

$$
(f(t_i), v_h) - B[u(t_i), v_h] = \left(\frac{du}{dt}(t_i), v_h\right).
$$

Then

$$
\begin{aligned}
&\left(\frac{1}{2}(e^{i}+e^{i-1}), v_h\right)\\
&\quad = \left(\frac{1}{2}\left(\frac{du}{dt}(t_i)+\frac{du}{dt}(t_{i-1})\right), v_h\right) - \frac{1}{\delta t}(R_h(u(t_i)-u(t_{i-1})), v_h)\\
&\quad = \left((I-R_h)\frac{u(t_i)-u(t_{i-1})}{\delta t}, v_h\right)\\
&\qquad + \left(\frac{du}{dt}(t_{i-1/2}) - \frac{u(t_i)-u(t_{i-1})}{\delta t}, v_h\right)\\
&\qquad + \left(\frac{1}{2}\left(\frac{du}{dt}(t_i)+\frac{du}{dt}(t_{i-1})\right) - \frac{du}{dt}(t_{i-1/2}), v_h\right),
\end{aligned}
$$

where $t_{i-1/2} = (t_i + t_{i-1})/2$.

For the first term on the right-hand side, we obtain, as in Theorem 7.26,

$$\|(I - R_h)(u(t_i) - u(t_{i-1}))\|_{L^2(U)} \leq C\, h^2 \int_{t_{i-1}}^{t_i} \left\|\frac{du}{dt}(s)\right\|_{H^2(U)} ds.$$

Integrating twice by parts, we obtain for the second term

$$\begin{aligned}
&\frac{1}{2}\int_{t_{i-1}}^{t_{i-1/2}} (s - t_{i-1})^2 \frac{d^3u}{dt^3}(s)ds + \frac{1}{2}\int_{t_{i-1/2}}^{t_i} (s - t_i)^2 \frac{d^3u}{dt^3}(s)ds \\
&\quad = (t_i - t_{i-1}) \left(\frac{u(t_i) - u(t_{i-1})}{\delta t} - \frac{du}{dt}(t_{i-1/2})\right).
\end{aligned}$$

By the above formula, we obtain

$$\delta t \left\|\frac{du}{dt}(t_{i-1/2}) - \frac{u(t_i) - u(t_{i-1})}{\delta t}\right\|_{L^2(U)} \leq C(\delta t)^2 \int_{t_{i-1}}^{t_i} \left\|\frac{d^3u}{dt^3}(s)\right\|_{L^2(U)} ds.$$

By the Taylor formula, we obtain for the last term

$$\begin{aligned}
&\frac{1}{2}\left(\frac{du}{dt}(t_i) + \frac{du}{dt}(t_{i-1})\right) - \frac{du}{dt}(t_{i-1/2}) \\
&\quad = \frac{1}{2}\int_{t_{i-1}}^{t_{i-1/2}} (s - t_{i-1}) \frac{d^3u}{dt^3}(s)ds + \frac{1}{2}\int_{t_{i-1/2}}^{t_i} (t_i - s) \frac{d^3u}{dt^3}(s)ds,
\end{aligned}$$

which gives the estimate

$$\begin{aligned}
&\left\|\frac{1}{2}\left(\frac{du}{dt}(t_i) + \frac{du}{dt}(t_{i-1})\right) - \frac{du}{dt}(t_{i-1/2})\right\|_{L^2(U)} \\
&\quad \leq C\delta t \int_{t_{i-1}}^{t_i} \left\|\frac{d^3u}{dt^3}(s)\right\|_{L^2(U)} ds.
\end{aligned}$$

Together, these estimates yield

$$\begin{aligned}
\|D_h^n\|_{L^2(U)} &\leq C\, h^2 \|g\|_{H^2(U)} + C\, h^2 \int_0^{t_n} \left\|\frac{du}{dt}(s)\right\|_{H^2(U)} ds \\
&\quad + C\,(\delta t)^2 \sum_{i=1}^{n} \int_{t_{i-1}}^{t_i} \left\|\frac{d^3u}{dt^3}(s)\right\|_{L^2(U)} ds
\end{aligned}$$

$$\leq C\left(h^2\|g\|_{H^2(U)} + h^2\int_0^{t_n}\left\|\frac{du}{dt}(s)\right\|_{H^2(U)} ds\right.$$
$$\left. + (\delta t)^2\int_0^{t_n}\left\|\frac{d^3u}{dt^3}(s)\right\|_{L^2(U)} ds\right).$$

□

The error estimates of Theorems 7.26 and 7.28 are given in terms of the solution $u(t)$. Using the regularity estimates of Theorem 5.34, we can estimate the error in terms of the initial data g and the nonhomogeneous term f (cf. [75]).

Example 7.29. Let us analyze a fully discretized initial problem (after the change of variables $t \to T - t$) for the Black–Scholes equation with time-dependent volatility and interest rate

$$\frac{\partial V(t,S)}{\partial t} - \frac{1}{2}\sigma^2(t)S^2\frac{\partial^2 V(t,S)}{\partial S^2} - r(t)S\frac{\partial V(t,S)}{\partial S} + r(t)V(t,S) = 0,$$

with the initial condition, which is the option payoff

$$V(0,S) = g(S).$$

We restrict the problem to a finite interval $(0, S_{\max})$ and introduce a grid with M subintervals of length $h_j = S_j - S_{j-1}$. The finite element space is the space of hat functions X_h^1. We apply time discretization using the implicit Euler scheme with N equidistant time intervals and $\delta t = T/N$. Let V^n be a finite element approximation of $V(t,S)$ on time level t_n. Then the Galerkin approximation has the form

$$\left(\frac{V^n - V^{n-1}}{\delta t}, v_h\right) + B[V^n, v_h] = 0,$$

where

$$B[u,v] = \frac{\sigma^2}{2}\int_0^{S_{\max}} S^2\frac{\partial u}{\partial S}\frac{\partial v}{\partial S}dS$$
$$+ \left(\sigma^2 - r\right)\int_0^{S_{\max}} S\frac{\partial u}{\partial S}v dS + r\int_0^{S_{\max}} uv dS.$$

Approximating V^n by the hat functions $V^n = \sum_{i=1}^{M-1} w_i^n\phi_i$ and denoting $W^n = (w_1^n, \ldots, w_{M-1}^n)$ the vector of the coefficients in the expansion of V^n in the basis of hat functions (w_0^n and w_M^n have to be recovered from the boundary conditions), we obtain the option price in the Black–Scholes model as a solution of the following system of linear equations

$$E_h(W^n - W^{n-1}) + \delta t A_h^n W^n = 0,$$

with starting value W^0 obtained by expanding the payoff function $g(S)$ in the basis of hat functions.

To obtain entries of the stiffness matrix A_h^n, we first compute the elementary integrals:

$$\int_0^{S_{\max}} \phi_i \phi_i dS = \frac{1}{3}(h_i + h_{i+1}),$$

$$\int_0^{S_{\max}} \phi_i \phi_{i+1} dS = \frac{1}{6} h_{i+1}, \quad \int_0^{S_{\max}} \phi_i \phi_{i-1} dS = \frac{1}{6} h_i,$$

$$\int_0^{S_{\max}} S\phi_i \frac{\partial \phi_i}{\partial S} dS = -\frac{1}{6}(h_i + h_{i+1}),$$

$$\int_0^{S_{\max}} S\phi_i \frac{\partial \phi_{i+1}}{\partial S} dS = \frac{S_{i+1}}{2} - \frac{h_{i+1}}{3},$$

$$\int_0^{S_{\max}} S\phi_i \frac{\partial \phi_{i-1}}{\partial S} dS = -\frac{S_{i-1}}{2} - \frac{h_i}{3}.$$

The following integrals are computed using the trapezoidal rule for quadratures:

$$\int_0^{S_{\max}} S^2 \frac{\partial \phi_i}{\partial S} \frac{\partial \phi_i}{\partial S} dS = S_i^2 \left(\frac{1}{h_i} + \frac{1}{h_{i+1}} \right) + \frac{1}{2}(h_i + h_{i+1}),$$

$$\int_0^{S_{\max}} S^2 \frac{\partial \phi_i}{\partial S} \frac{\partial \phi_{i+1}}{\partial S} dS = -\left(\frac{S_i^2}{h_{i+1}} + S_i + \frac{h_{i+1}}{2} \right),$$

$$\int_0^{S_{\max}} S^2 \frac{\partial \phi_i}{\partial S} \frac{\partial \phi_{i-1}}{\partial S} dS = -\left(\frac{S_i^2}{h_i} - S_i + \frac{h_i}{2} \right).$$

Then we obtain the following entries of the stiffness matrix

$$\begin{aligned} a^n_{i,i} &= \frac{S_i^2\sigma^2(t_n)}{2}\left(\frac{1}{h_i}+\frac{1}{h_{i+1}}\right)+\frac{\sigma^2(t_n)}{12}(h_i+h_{i+1}) \\ &\quad +\frac{r(t_n)}{2}(h_i+h_{i+1}), \\ a^n_{i,i+1} &= -\frac{S_i^2\sigma^2(t_n)}{2h_{i+1}}-\frac{\sigma^2(t_n)}{12}h_{i+1}-\frac{r(t_n)}{2}S_i, \\ a^n_{i,i-1} &= -\frac{S_i^2\sigma^2(t_n)}{2h_i}-\frac{\sigma^2(t_n)}{12}h_i+\frac{r(t_n)}{2}S_i. \end{aligned}$$

The mass matrix E_h has entries that can be recovered from Example 7.1

$$e_{i,i}=\frac{1}{3}(h_i+h_{i+1}),\quad e_{i,i+1}=e_{i+1,i}=\frac{1}{6}h_{i+1}.$$

7.3 Exercises

Exercise 7.1. Let K be a simplex in $\mathbb{R}^d$ with vertices a_i, $0\le i\le d$. Show that a polynomial in K of degree not greater than k, $k\ge 1$, is uniquely defined by its values in the set $L_k(K)$, called *the principal lattice* of order k of simplex K, given by

$$L_k(K)=\left\{x=\sum_{i=0}^d \lambda_i a_i\colon \sum_{i=0}^d \lambda_i=1, \lambda_i\in\left\{0,\frac{1}{k},\ldots,\frac{k-1}{k}\right\}, 0\le i\le d\right\}.$$

Exercise 7.2. Given a triangle $K\subset\mathbb{R}^2$ with vertices a_i, $1\le i\le 3$, and mid-points $a_{ij}=(a_i+a_j)/2$, $1\le i<j\le 3$, show that polynomial $p\in\Pi^4(K)$ is completely determined by the following values:

$$p(a_i),\frac{\partial^2 p}{\partial x_1^2}(a_i),\frac{\partial^2 p}{\partial x_1\partial x_2}(a_i),\frac{\partial^2 p}{\partial x_2^2}(a_i),\quad 1\le i\le 3,$$

$$p(a_{ij}),\quad 1\le i<j\le 3,$$

where x_1, x_2 are the coordinates in $\mathbb{R}^2$.

Exercise 7.3. The following finite element is defined: the set $K \subset \mathbb{R}^2$ is a triangle with vertices a_i, $1 \le i \le 3$, the space of polynomials is the space $\Pi_*^3(K)$ defined as

$$\Pi_*^3 = \left\{ p\colon\ p(x_1, x_2) = \sum_{i+j \le 3} \gamma_{ij} x_1^i x_2^j, \quad \gamma_{ij} = \gamma_{ji} \right\},$$

and

$$\Sigma = \left\{ p(a_i), \frac{\partial p}{\partial x_1}(a_i), \frac{\partial p}{\partial x_2}(a_i), 1 \le i \le 3 \right\}$$

so that this finite element is of class C^0.

Investigate if Σ is $\Pi_*^3(K)$-unisolvent.

Exercise 7.4. The following important result is called the Bramble–Hilbert lemma. Let F be a nonnegative functional on $W^{k,p} = W^{k,p}(U)$, where U is a bounded, convex domain in $\mathbb{R}^d$, and assume that

$$F(v + w) \le F(v) + F(w), \quad \forall v, w \in W^{k,p},$$

$$F(v) \le C\|v\|_{W^{k,p}}, \quad \forall v \in W^{k,p},$$

$$F(v) = 0, \quad \forall v \in \Pi^{k-1}.$$

Then F is bounded with respect to the seminorm in $W^{k,p}$

$$|v|_{W^{k,p}} = \left(\sum_{|\alpha|=k} \int_U |D^\alpha v|^p dx \right)^{1/p},$$

i.e., there exists a constant $C = C(U, k, p)$ such that

$$F(v) \le C|v|_{W^{k,p}}, \quad \forall v \in W^{k,p}.$$

Prove the Bramble–Hilbert lemma for $d = 1$, $U = (0, 1)$, and $k = p = 2$.

Hint: Consider a function $v(x)$ in element $K_j = (x_{j-1}, x_j)$. Expand $v(x_{j-1} + h)$ at x_{j-1} by Taylor's formula. Let $Q_1 v$ be the polynomial of degree 1 obtained by the truncation of this expansion in each element K_j of a triangulation of U. Show that $\|v - Q_1 v\|_{L^2(U)} \le C|v|_{H^2(U)}$. Then $F(v) \le F(v - Q_1 v) + F(Q_1 v) = F(v - Q_1 v) \le C\|v - Q_1 v\|_{L^2(U)} \le C|v|_{H^2(U)}$.

Exercise 7.5. Consider the one-dimensional problem

$$\frac{d}{dx}\left(a^2(x)\frac{du}{dx}\right) = f(x).$$

This problem is approximated by linear Lagrangian elements on a uniform grid with step h.

Prove that the Galerkin approximation has the form

$$a^2_{i+1/2}\frac{u_{i+1}-u_i}{h^2} - a^2_{i-1/2}\frac{u_i-u_{i-1}}{h^2} = \frac{f_{i-1}+4f_i+f_{i+1}}{6},$$

where

$$a^2_{i+1/2} = \frac{1}{h}\int_{x_i}^{x_{i+1}} a^2(x)dx, \quad a^2_{i-1/2} = \frac{1}{h}\int_{x_{i-1}}^{x_i} a^2(x)dx.$$

Exercise 7.6. Consider the one-dimensional problem

$$\frac{d}{dx}\left(a^2\frac{du}{dx}\right) = f(x)$$

with constant a. Approximate the problem by second-order Lagrangian elements on a uniform grid with step h. Consider the two elements formed by the points (x_{i-2}, x_{i-1}, x_i) and (x_i, x_{i+1}, x_{i+2}). Show that for an interior point, such as x_{i-1}, we obtain

$$a^2\frac{u_{i-2}-2u_{i-1}+u_i}{h^2} = \frac{f_{i-2}+8f_{i-1}+f_i}{10}$$

and for a boundary point, such as x_i,

$$a^2\frac{-u_{i-2}+8u_{i-1}-14u_i+8u_{i+1}-u_{i+2}}{4h^2}$$
$$= \frac{f_{i-2}-2f_{i-1}-8f_i-2f_{i+1}+f_{i+2}}{10}.$$

Exercise 7.7. Consider the following one-dimensional boundary-value problem

$$-\frac{d}{dx}\left(\alpha\frac{du}{dx}\right) + \gamma u = f, \quad x \in (0,1),$$
$$u(0) = 0,$$
$$\alpha\frac{du}{dx}(1) + \delta u(1) = 0,$$

where $\alpha = \alpha(x)$, $\gamma = \gamma(x)$, $f = f(x)$ are known functions with $0 \leq \gamma(x) \leq \gamma_1$, $0 < \alpha_0 \leq \alpha(x) \leq \alpha_1$ for all $x \in [0,1]$, and $\delta \geq 0$. Assuming $f \in L_2(0,1)$, find the weak formulation of the problem. Design the Galerkin approximation of this problem using linear finite elements on a uniform grid with step h.

Exercise 7.8. Consider the two-point boundary value problem

$$-\frac{d^2u}{dx^2} + u = 2x, \quad x \in (0,1),$$
$$u(0) = u(1) = 0.$$

Apply the finite element method based on linear Lagrangian elements on a uniform grid with $h = 1/10, 1/20$. Find the exact solution and compute the maximum of the error at grid points.

Exercise 7.9. Consider the two-point boundary value problem

$$-\frac{d^2u}{dx^2} = f(x), \quad x \in (0,1),$$
$$u(0) = u(1) = 0.$$

Approximate this problem by the Galerkin method dividing interval $(0,1)$ into a finite sum of disjoint subintervals K_j of length h_j. Prove the following *a posteriori* error estimate for the finite element solution u_h

$$\|(u - u_h)'\|^2_{L^2(0,1)} \leq C \sum_{j=1}^{M} \rho_j^2(u_h),$$

where ρ_j are defined as follows

$$\rho_j(u_h) = h_j \|f + u_h''\|_{L_2(K_j)}.$$

Exercise 7.10. Consider the Dirichlet problem in a two-dimensional domain U

$$\Delta u = f, \quad \text{in } U,$$
$$u|_{\partial U} = u_0.$$

Approximate the problem with linear Lagrangian elements on a uniform Cartesian mesh ($\delta x = \delta y = h$).

Prove that the approximation for interior grid points has the form

$$\frac{-4u_{j,k}+u_{j+1,k}+u_{j-1,k}+u_{j,k+1}+u_{j,k-1}}{h^2}$$
$$=\frac{6f_{j,k}+f_{j+1,k}+f_{j-1,k}+f_{j+1,k+1}+f_{j,k+1}+f_{j-1,k-1}+f_{j,k-1}}{12}.$$

Exercise 7.11. Consider the one-dimensional heat equation

$$\begin{aligned}\frac{\partial u}{\partial t}-\frac{\partial^2 u}{\partial x^2}=f, \quad x\in(0,\pi), t>0,\\ u(t,0)=u(t,\pi)=0, \quad t>0,\\ u(0,x)=g(x), \quad x\in(0,\pi).\end{aligned}$$

(a) Prove that if $g(x)=\pi-x$, then

$$\left\|\frac{\partial u(t,\cdot)}{\partial t}\right\|_{L^2(0,\pi)}\le Ct^{-3/4}, \quad \text{for } t\to 0.$$

(b) Discretize the problem in space using piecewise linear functions on a uniform grid with step h and determine the corresponding ordinary differential equation (an analog of equation (7.32)).

Exercise 7.12. Consider the problem:

$$\begin{aligned}\frac{\partial u}{\partial t}-\frac{\partial}{\partial x}\left(\alpha\frac{\partial u}{\partial x}\right)-\beta u=0, \quad (t,x)\in(0,\infty)\times(0,1),\\ u(t,0)=\eta, \quad t>0,\\ \alpha\frac{\partial u}{\partial x}(t,1)+\gamma u(t,1)=0, \quad t>0,\\ u(0,x)=g(x), \quad x\in(0,1),\end{aligned}$$

where $\alpha=\alpha(x)$ and $g(x)$ are given functions, $\gamma,\eta\in\mathbb{R}$, and $\beta>0$.

(a) Prove the existence and uniqueness of a weak solution for varying γ, provide suitable limitations on the coefficients and suitable regularity hypotheses for the functions α and g.
(b) Introduce the spatial semi-discretization of the problem using the Galerkin finite element method and conduct its stability and convergence analysis.

Exercise 7.13. Consider the homogeneous heat equation

$$\frac{\partial u}{\partial t} - \Delta u = 0, \quad (t,x) \in (0,T] \times U,$$
$$u = 0, \quad (t,x) \in [0,T] \times \partial U,$$
$$u = g, \quad t = 0, x \in U.$$

Let us recall that there exists an orthonormal basis $(\phi_i)_{i=1}^{\infty}$ of smooth eigenfunctions and the corresponding eigenvalues $(\lambda_i)_{i=1}^{\infty}$ such that

$$-\Delta\phi_i = \lambda_i \phi_i, \quad \text{in } U.$$

In the weak formulation, the eigenvalue problem is given by

$$(-\Delta\phi_i, v) = (\nabla\phi_i, \nabla v) = \lambda_i(\phi_i, v), \quad v \in H_0^1(U).$$

(a) Let $u(t,x)$ be a solution of the homogeneous heat equation. Prove that there exists a constant C such that

$$\|\nabla u(x,t)\|_{L^2(U)}^2 \leq Ct^{-1}\|g\|_{L^2(U)}^2.$$

Hint: Use the eigenfunction expansion of u and the inequality $x^k e^{-x} \leq C$ which holds for $x > 0$ and some positive constant C.

(b) Let Δ_h denote the discrete Laplacian defined by

$$\Delta_h u_h = \sum_{i=1}^{M_r} \lambda_i (u_h, \varphi_i)\varphi_i,$$

where λ_i and φ_i, $i = 1, \ldots, M_r$, form a complete set of eigenvalues and eigenvectors of the following eigenvalue problem

$$(\nabla\varphi, \nabla v_h) = \lambda(\varphi, v_h), \quad \forall v_h \in V_h.$$

Assume that u_h is the solution of

$$\left\langle \frac{\partial u_h}{\partial t}(t), v \right\rangle - (\Delta_h u_h(t), v) = 0, \quad \forall v \in V_h,$$
$$u_h(0) = g_h.$$

Prove that

$$|u_h(t)|_{H^1(U)} \leq Ct^{-1/2}\|g_h\|_{L^2(U)}, \text{ for } t > 0.$$

Exercise 7.14. Consider the initial-boundary value problem

$$\begin{aligned} \frac{\partial u}{\partial t} - \Delta u = 0, &\quad (t,x) \in \mathbb{R}_+ \times U, \\ u = 0, &\quad (t,x) \in \mathbb{R}_+ \times \partial U, \\ u(0) = g, &\quad x \in U, \end{aligned}$$

in a bounded, convex domain $U \subset \mathbb{R}^2$ with smooth boundary ∂U.

Let u_h be a solution of the finite element approximation of this problem

$$\begin{aligned} \left\langle \frac{\partial u_h}{\partial t}(t), v \right\rangle + \int_U \nabla u_h(t) \nabla v dx = 0, &\quad \forall v \in V_h, \\ u_h(0) = g_h, & \end{aligned}$$

with $g_h = I_h^1 g$ and $g \in H^2 \cap H_0^1$.

Show that

$$\|u_h(t) - u(t)\|_{L^2(U)} \leq Ch^2 \|g\|_{H^2(U)}, \quad \text{for } t \geq 0.$$

Exercise 7.15. Under the assumptions of Theorem 7.22, prove that for $t \geq 0$

$$\begin{aligned} |u_h(t) - u(t)|_{H^1(U)} &\leq |g_h - g|_{H^1(U)} \\ &+ Ch \left(\|g\|_{H^2(U)} + \|u(t)\|_{H^2(U)} + \left(\int_0^t \left\| \frac{du}{dt}(s) \right\|_{H^1(U)}^2 ds \right)^{1/2} \right). \end{aligned}$$

Exercise 7.16. Introducing variables $\tau = T - t$ and $x = \ln S$, we obtain the following form of the Black–Scholes equation

$$\frac{\partial u}{\partial \tau} - \frac{\sigma^2}{2} \frac{\partial^2 u}{\partial x^2} - \left(r - \frac{\sigma^2}{2} \right) \frac{\partial u}{\partial x} + ru = 0.$$

This equation is used to compute the price of a vanilla call option by the finite element method for $\tau \in [0, T]$ and $x \in [x_{\min}, x_{\max}]$ with the boundary conditions

$$u(\tau, x_{\min}) = 0, \quad u(\tau, x_{\max}) = x_{\max}, \quad \tau \in (0, T],$$

and the initial condition $u(0, x) = g(x)$.

(a) Write the variational formulation of the above initial-boundary problem.
(b) Divide the time interval $[0, T]$ into N equal subintervals and apply the implicit Euler scheme in time. In the approximation in the x-direction, use finite elements with piecewise linear functions on an equidistant grid with step size $h = (x_{\max} - x_{\min})/M$. Write the obtained system of discrete equations.
(c) Compute in the above model the price of a European call option with parameters: initial stock prices $S_0 = e^{x_j}$ for all grid points $x_j \in [x_{\min}, x_{\max}]$, risk-free interest rate $r = 5\%$, volatility $\sigma = 30\%$, strike $K = 45$, and time to maturity $T = 0.5$ year. In the computations, take $x_{\min} = -6$, $x_{\max} = 2.5$, $N = 50$, and $M = 170$ (this choice assures that the strike K will be one of the nodes of the partition — the property important for minimizing the approximation error). Estimate the approximation error by comparing the results of the numerical computations with the option prices computed from the Black–Scholes formula.

Exercise 7.17 (Option price in a local volatility model). The option price equation in the Black–Scholes local volatility model has the form

$$\frac{\partial V}{\partial t} + \frac{1}{2}\sigma^2(S)S^2\frac{\partial^2 V}{\partial S^2} + rS\frac{\partial V}{\partial S} - rV = 0,$$
$$V(T, S) = g(S).$$

Approximate this price using a finite element algorithm.

(a) Switch to time-to-maturity $t \to T - t$ and log-price $x = \ln(S)$, and localize the equation to a bounded domain $U = (-R, R)$, $R > 0$. Derive the equation for $u(t, x) = V(T - t, e^x)$.
(b) Assume that the volatility function in the new variable $\tilde{\sigma}(x) = \sigma(e^x)$ is of class C^1 and

$$0 < \sigma_* \leq \tilde{\sigma}(x) \leq \sigma^*, \quad \left|\frac{d\tilde{\sigma}}{dx}\right| \leq C.$$

Under these assumptions, find a bilinear form $B[u(t), v]$ of the weak formulation of the Black–Scholes equation

$$\left\langle \frac{du}{dt}(t), v \right\rangle + B[u(t), v] = 0, \quad v \in H^1(U).$$

Prove that $B[u(t), v]$ fulfills the energy estimates analogous to those of Theorem 5.25.

(c) Introduce a partition of $[-R, R]$ into subintervals $K_j = (x_{j-1}, x_j)$, $1 \leq j \leq M$, such that $-R = x_0 < x_1 < \cdots < x_M = R$. The size of the interval K_j is h_j, and we set $h = \max_j h_j$. Define the discrete space V_h of linear hat functions

$$V_h = \{v_h \in X_h^1 \colon v_h(-R) = g(e^{-R}), v_h(R) = g(e^R)\}.$$

Compute the mass matrix E_h and the stiffness matrix A_h. To simplify the computations, assume that $g(S) = (K - S)^+$, i.e., consider a put option with strike K.

(d) Approximate the weak formulation of the Black–Scholes equation by the implicit Euler scheme with finite elements from V_h. Take a uniform grid $h_j = h$, for each j, and compare the obtained scheme with a scheme for finite difference approximation. Observe that for finite differences, the matrix corresponding to the mass matrix is an identity matrix, and for finite elements, it is a tridiagonal matrix. However, there is a procedure called the *mass lumping* that can map the mass matrix into a diagonal matrix (for details, see Quateroni [74]). Therefore, when the mesh is uniform, the finite element method with mass lumping is equivalent to the finite difference scheme (the statement remains valid for any θ-scheme).

Exercise 7.18. A popular example of a local volatility model is the *constant elasticity of variance* (CEV) model. In this model, the price $V(t, S)$ of a European vanilla option fulfills the equation (cf. Problem 6.17 of Chapter 6)

$$\frac{\partial V}{\partial t} + \frac{1}{2}\sigma_0^2 S^{2\beta} \frac{\partial^2 V}{\partial S^2} + rS\frac{\partial V}{\partial S} - rV = 0, \quad 0 \leq S, t \in [0, T].$$

(a) Using the results of the previous problem, compute the price of the call option in the CEV model, assuming: initial stock price $S_0 = 40$, strike $K = 35$, risk-free interest rate $r = 5\%$, maturity $T = 0.5$ year, volatility $\sigma_0 = 30\%$, and $\beta = 0.5$. In the computations, use linear elements with no more than 100 nodes in x-direction and the implicit Euler scheme in t-direction with no more than 50 time steps.

(b) Compare the obtained result with the exact formula for call options in the CEV model given in Problem 6.17 of Chapter 6. Compute the approximation error.

Exercise 7.19. Consider in the Black–Scholes model an option based on two assets with prices S_1 and S_2. The price $V(t, S_1, S_2)$ of this option fulfills the equation

$$\begin{aligned}\frac{\partial V}{\partial t} &+ \frac{1}{2}\sigma_1^2 S_1^2 \frac{\partial^2 V}{\partial S_1^2} + \frac{1}{2}\sigma_2^2 S_2^2 \frac{\partial^2 V}{\partial S_2^2} + \rho\sigma_1\sigma_2 S_1 S_2 \frac{\partial^2 V}{\partial S_1 \partial S_2} \\ &+ rS_1 \frac{\partial V}{\partial S_1} + rS_2 \frac{\partial V}{\partial S_2} - rV = 0, \\ V(T, S_1, S_2) &= g(S_1, S_2).\end{aligned}$$

Switch to time-to-maturity $t \to T - t$, introduce new dependent variable $u(t, x, y) = V(T - t, S_1, S_2)$, localize the equation to a bounded domain $U = (0, x_{\max}) \times (0, y_{\max})$, and find the bilinear form $B[u(t), v]$ of the weak formulation of the Black–Scholes equation

$$\left\langle \frac{du}{dt}(t), v \right\rangle + B[u(t), v] = 0, \quad v \in H^1(U)..$$

(a) Consider the call option with the payoff $g\big(S_1(T), S_2(T)\big) = \max\big(S_1(T) + S_2(T) - K, 0\big)$, where $S_1(T)$, $S_2(T)$ are the prices of these two assets at time T. Find the boundary conditions for the Black–Scholes equation for this option.
Hint: Analyze separately each side of U. If $x_{\max}$ and $y_{\max}$ are sufficiently large compared to K then on the side $(x, y_{\max})$ assume $u(t, x, y_{\max}) = x + y_{\max}$, and similarly on the side $(x_{\max}, y)$. On sides $(x, 0)$ and $(0, y)$, the option is, in fact, a vanilla call option on a single asset with the price given by the Black–Scholes formula.
(b) Implementing two-dimensional finite elements is a demanding exercise. To simplify the problem, introduce a fixed structured grid obtained by triangulation of U by three families of parallel lines: with two families of lines U is divided into rectangles with sides parallel to the Cartesian axes, and then every mesh rectangle is divided into two triangles using always the same diagonal (cf. Fig. 7.1). As basis functions take affine functions in

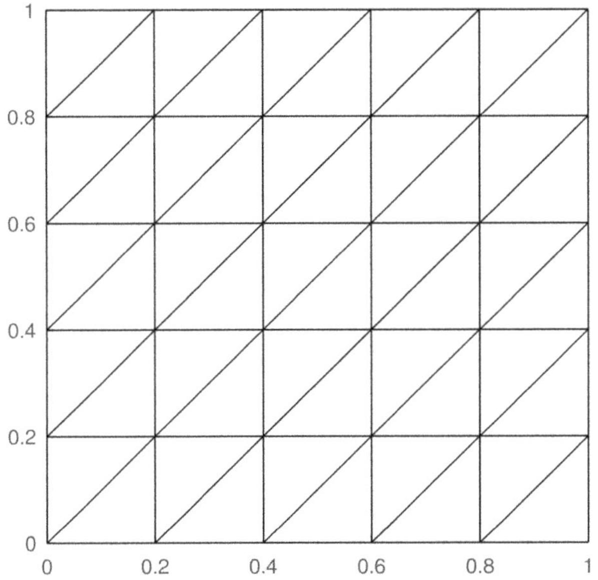

Fig. 7.1. Triangulation by a fixed grid.

two dimensions $\phi(x, y) = a + bx + cy$ with $a, b, c \in \mathbb{R}$. For each triangle K_j of the above partition $\mathcal{T}_h$ with vertices a_i, $i = 1, 2, 3$, the space $\Pi^1(K_j)$ is spanned by three basis affine functions ϕ_j defined uniquely by its values on vertices a_i

$$\phi_j(a_i) = \delta_{ij}, \quad i, j = 1, 2, 3.$$

Define the discrete space V_h as the space of these affine functions

$$V_h = \{v_h \in X_h^1\colon v_h \text{ fulfills the boundary conditions}\}.$$

Compute the mass matrix E_h and the stiffness matrix A_h.

(c) Approximate the weak formulation of the Black–Scholes equation by the implicit Euler scheme with finite elements from V_h. Compute the option price with parameters: initial stock prices $S_1(0) = S_2(0) = 25$, strike $K = 50$, risk-free interest rate $r = 5\%$, maturity $T = 0.5$ year, annual volatilities $\sigma_1 = \sigma_2 = 25\%$, correlation $\rho = -0.3$. Take $x_{\max} = y_{\max} = 200$, the number of time steps $N = 50$, and the number of grid points in each direction $M = 40$.

Exercise 7.20. The pricing equation in the Heston stochastic volatility model reads (cf. Example 5.6 in Chapter 5)

$$\frac{\partial V}{\partial t} + \frac{1}{2} v S^2 \frac{\partial^2 V}{\partial S^2} + \rho \nu v S \frac{\partial^2 V}{\partial S \partial v} + \frac{1}{2} \nu^2 v \frac{\partial^2 V}{\partial v^2} + rS \frac{\partial V}{\partial S}$$
$$+ \big(\kappa(\theta - v) - \lambda\big) \frac{\partial V}{\partial v} - rV = 0.$$

Let the martingale measure be chosen such that the market price of volatility risk $\lambda = 0$.

(a) Consider a European call option. Show that the proper boundary and terminal values for this option are as follows:

$$V(T, S, v) = (S - K)^+,$$
$$V(t, 0, v) = 0,$$
$$\lim_{S \to \infty} \frac{\partial V}{\partial S}(t, S, v) = 1,$$
$$\lim_{v \to \infty} V(t, S, v) = S,$$
$$rS \frac{\partial V}{\partial S}(t, S, 0) + \kappa\theta \frac{\partial V}{\partial v}(t, S, 0) + \frac{\partial V}{\partial t}(t, S, 0) - rV(t, S, 0) = 0.$$

(b) Change variables to $t \to T - t$, $x = \ln(S)$, and $z = 2\sqrt{v}$. Derive the equation for $u(t, x, z) = V(T - t, e^x, z^2/4) \exp(-1/2\alpha z^2)$ with a positive constant α and find the bilinear form of the weak formulation.

(c) Solve the obtained weak form of the Heston PDE by finite elements. Take as the domain of integration the rectangle $U = [-R, R] \times [-V, V]$. Analogously to Problem 7.19, introduce a fixed structured grid obtained by triangulation of U by three families of parallel lines (cf. Fig. 7.1). Take affine functions in two dimensions as the basis functions. Use the implicit Euler scheme for time discretization. Compute the price of a European call option with parameters: initial stock price $S_0 = 50$, risk-free interest rate $r = 5\%$, volatility of volatility $\nu = 50\%$, mean variance $\theta = 4\%$, $\kappa = 2$, correlation $\rho = 0.5$, strike $K = 45$, time to maturity $T = 2$ years. In the computations take $\alpha < 5$ and the integration domain $U = [-6, 6] \times [-2, 2]$.

Chapter 8

American Options

An American option is a contract that grants the holder the right to buy or sell a security at an agreed-upon price during a period of time up to and including its maturity date. The option is Bermudan if it can only be exercised at a discrete, finite set of points in time prior to and including the maturity date. Such contracts are traded in all major financial markets, so identifying efficient techniques for pricing them is an important problem.

The computation of American option prices is a challenging problem, especially when several underlying assets are involved. In mathematical formulation, this is an optimal stopping problem. In diffusion models, this problem is reduced to a variational inequality, which is solved by PDE methods. Independently, numerical methods based on the Monte Carlo technique were introduced in the late 1990s. The starting point of all these numerical methods is the replacement of the interval of exercise dates by a finite set of dates. This approach reduces the pricing of American options to the pricing of Bermudan options.

In this chapter, we analyze both the abovementioned numerical methods. We will present the Monte Carlo procedure of Longstaff and Schwartz implementing effectively the dynamic programming principle supplemented with least squares regression on a finite set of functions that approximates conditional expectations. We will also analyze algorithms that approximate variational inequalities, limiting the presentation to the two most popular algorithms: projected successive over-relaxation (PSOR) and penalization.

8.1 Pricing American Options

We begin by collecting results from the theory of optimal stopping in continuous time. In this presentation, we follow the paper by El Karoui [27], where the reader can find more complete results and relevant proofs. We consider stopping problems in a probability space $(\Omega, \mathcal{F}, \mathbb{P})$ with filtration $\mathbb{F} = (\mathcal{F}_t)_{0 \le t \le T}$ satisfying usual conditions of completeness and right-continuity. In addition, we assume that the σ-field $\mathcal{F}_0$ is trivial. $\mathcal{T}_{t,T}$ denotes the set of all stopping times $\tau \in [t, T]$ with respect to filtration $\mathbb{F}$

$$\mathcal{T}_{t,T} = \{\tau\colon \mathbb{P}(\tau \in [t, T]) = 1\}, \quad 0 \le t < T < +\infty.$$

Definition 8.1. An adapted, right-continuous process $(X_t)_{0 \le t \le T}$ is called *regular* if X_τ is integrable for every $\tau \in \mathcal{T}_{0,T}$, and for every nondecreasing sequence τ_n of stopping times with $\lim_{n\to\infty} \tau_n = \tau$, we have $\lim_{n\to\infty} \mathbb{E}(X_{\tau_n}) = \mathbb{E}(X_\tau)$.

Theorem 8.2. *Let $Z = (Z_t)_{0 \le t \le T}$ be an adapted, right-continuous process satisfying $Z_t \ge 0$ for all $t \in [0, T]$, and $\mathbb{E}(\sup_{0 \le t \le T} Z_t) < +\infty$.*

For $t \in [0, T]$, we define

$$U_t = \operatorname*{ess\,sup}_{\tau \in \mathcal{T}_{t,T}} \mathbb{E}(Z_\tau | \mathcal{F}_t).$$

Then:

(1) *$(U_t)_{0 \le t \le T}$ is a supermartingale;*
(2) *$\mathbb{E}(U_t) = \sup_{\tau \in \mathcal{T}_{t,T}} \mathbb{E}(Z_\tau)$;*
(3) *U admits a right-continuous modification.*

Definition 8.3. A right-continuous modification of the process U from the above theorem is called the *Snell envelope* of Z.

Definition 8.4. For the process Z a stopping time $\hat{\tau} \in \mathcal{T}_{0,T}$ is called *optimal* if $\mathbb{E}(Z_{\hat{\tau}}) = \sup_{\tau \in \mathcal{T}_{0,T}} \mathbb{E}(Z_\tau)$.

Theorem 8.5. *The stopping time $\hat{\tau} \in \mathcal{T}_{0,T}$ is optimal if and only if the following conditions are satisfied:*

(1) *$U_{\hat{\tau}} = Z_{\hat{\tau}}$ a.s.;*
(2) *$U_t^{\hat{\tau}} = U_{\hat{\tau} \wedge t}$, $0 \le t \le T$, is a martingale.*

Theorem 8.6. *If process Z is regular, then its Snell envelope U is also regular, and*

$$\tau_0 = \inf\{s \in [t,T]\colon\, U_s = Z_s\}$$

is the smallest optimal stopping time in $\mathcal{T}_{t,T}$.

Then $v(t) := \mathbb{E}(U_t)$ is called the value function of the optimal stopping problem *for the process Z with stopping in $\mathcal{T}_{t,T}$ and is given by the expression*

$$v(t) = \mathbb{E}(U_t) = \sup_{\tau\in\mathcal{T}_{t,T}} \mathbb{E}(Z_\tau) = \mathbb{E}(Z_{\tau_0}).$$

After this brief review of the results concerning optimal stopping, we return to American options. The problem of pricing American options will be considered in a financial market of d risky assets whose prices are given by stochastic processes $S_s = (S_s^1, \ldots, S_s^d)$ in $(\Omega, \mathcal{F}, \mathbb{P})$. We assume that these processes are adapted to filtration $\mathbb{F}$, right-continuous with left limits, strictly positive semimartingales. There is a riskless asset S_s^0 in that market that defines discount factor $\beta_s = (S_s^0)^{-1}$.

Since the prices S_s^i are nonnegative, we introduce, as in Chapter 5, a new variable $X_s = \ln S_s$. The dynamics of X_s is described by the following stochastic differential equation

$$dX_s = b(s, X_s)ds + \sigma(s, X_s)dW_s. \tag{8.1}$$

We denote by $X_s^{t,x}$ a solution of (8.1) with initial condition $X_t = x$.

Definition 8.7. An American option for underlying X_s is a nonnegative, adapted stochastic process $(Z_s)_{0\le s\le T}$, where $Z_s = g(s, X_s)$ is the payoff of the option exercised at time s. We assume that $g(s, x)$, called the *option reward*, is a continuous function of (s, x) with exponential growth in x

$$|g(s,x)| \le Ce^{C|x|}, \quad C > 0.$$

Under the condition that the coefficients of equation (8.1) fulfill the assumptions of Theorem 4.13, Z_s is a continuous and regular process and satisfies

$$\mathbb{E}\left(\sup_{s\in[0,T]} Z_s\right) < +\infty.$$

Theorem 8.8. *Let $X_s = \ln S_s$ be a solution of equation (8.1) with the coefficients fulfilling the assumptions of Theorem 4.13 in a probability space $(\Omega, \mathcal{F}, \mathbb{P})$, and $\beta_s = \exp\big(-\int_0^s r(\eta)d\eta\big)$ be the deterministic discount factor, where $r(\eta)$ is a nonnegative, continuous function in $[0, T]$. Assume that $\mathbb{P}^*$ is a risk-neutral probability measure, i.e., a measure equivalent to $\mathbb{P}$ such that processes $\beta_s S_s^i$, $i = 1, \ldots, d$, are martingales with respect to $\mathbb{P}^*$. Consider an American option written on asset X_s with payoff process $Z_s = g(s, X_s)$, where the reward function $g(s, x)$ fulfills the conditions of Definition 8.7. There exists an admissible trading strategy φ for the considered American option, which is optimal for both the seller and buyer of the option. The value process of strategy φ is given by the expression*

$$\mathcal{V}_\varphi(0) = \sup_{\tau \in \mathcal{T}_{0,T}} \mathbb{E}^*\big(\beta_\tau Z_\tau\big).$$

Furthermore, there is a stopping time $\hat{\tau}$ attaining this supremum.

The above-defined value $\mathcal{V}_\varphi(0)$ is called the "fair price" *or the* arbitrage-free price *of the American option with payoff process Z_s.*

The following theorem is due to Jaillet *et al.* [43]. This theorem solves the pricing problem for an American option in terms of the value function of an optimal stopping problem.

Theorem 8.9. *Let the assumptions of the previous theorem be satisfied and $X_s^{t,x}$ be a solution of (8.1) with a deterministic initial condition $X_t = x$. Let $g(s, x)$ be the reward function of Definition 8.7. Define the function*

$$V(t, x) = \frac{1}{\beta_t} \sup_{\tau \in \mathcal{T}_{t,T}} \mathbb{E}^*\left(\beta_\tau g\big(\tau, X_\tau^{t,x}\big)\right) \quad (t, x) \in [0, T] \times \mathbb{R}^d. \tag{8.2}$$

This function is continuous, and at time t defines the value function of the optimal stopping problem for the American option with reward $g(s, x)$. For any solution X_s of equation (8.1) this function defines the nonnegative supermartingale

$$V(t, X_t) = \frac{1}{\beta_t} \operatorname*{ess\,sup}_{\tau \in \mathcal{T}_{t,T}} \mathbb{E}^*\left(\beta_\tau g\big(\tau, X_\tau\big)\Big|\mathcal{F}_t\right).$$

The process $\big(\beta_s V(s, X_s)\big)_{t \le s \le T}$ is the Snell envelope of $\tilde{Z}_s = \beta_s g(s, X_s)$, $s \in [t, T]$.

For simplicity, we assume in the rest of this chapter that $\mathbb{P}$ is a risk-neutral measure and processes $\beta_s S_s^i$, $i = 1, \ldots, d$, are martingales with respect to this measure. Then the value function $V(t, x)$ computed with respect to $\mathbb{P}$ is the arbitrage-free price of the American option with reward $g(s, x)$.

8.2 Monte Carlo Pricing

The most popular Monte Carlo implementation of the valuation formula from Theorem 8.9 is the Longstaff–Schwartz algorithm [60]. To describe this algorithm, we replace the continuous optimal stopping problem of Definition 8.4 with the following discrete optimal stopping problem.

We consider in space $(\Omega, \mathcal{F}, \mathbb{P})$ a Markov chain $(X_n)_{n=0}^N$ with values in $\mathbb{R}^d$, and a discrete filtration $(\mathcal{F}_n)_{n=0}^N$, generated by this Markov chain, corresponding to time discretization $0 = t_0 < t_1 < \cdots < t_N = T$.

Let $g(t, x)$ be a reward function of an American option. Given a nonnegative, adapted, discrete, square-integrable stochastic process $(Z_n)_{n=0}^N$ with $Z_n = g(t_n, X_n)$, we want to compute $\sup_{\tau \in \mathcal{T}_{0,N}} Z_\tau$, where $\mathcal{T}_{n,N}$ denotes the set of all stopping times with values in $\{t_n, \ldots, t_N\}$. To simplify the computations, we assume that discount factor $\beta_t = 1$ for all $t \in [0, T]$.

Let $U = (U_n)_{n=0}^N$ be the Snell envelope of Z

$$U_n = \operatorname*{ess\,sup}_{\tau \in \mathcal{T}_{n,N}} \mathbb{E}\big(Z_\tau \big| \mathcal{F}_n\big), \quad n = 0, \ldots, N.$$

The discrete optimal stopping problem for Z_n and its Snell envelope U_n is solved by dynamic programming:

$$\begin{aligned} U_N &= Z_N, \\ U_n &= \max\big(Z_n, \mathbb{E}(U_{n+1} | \mathcal{F}_n)\big), \quad n = 0, \ldots, N-1. \end{aligned}$$

Let

$$\tau_n = \min\{j \geq n \colon U_j = Z_j\}.$$

Then

$$U_n = \mathbb{E}(Z_{\tau_n} \big| \mathcal{F}_n) = \max\big(Z_n, \mathbb{E}(Z_{\tau_{n+1}} | \mathcal{F}_n)\big). \tag{8.3}$$

The above relation enables us to write the dynamic programming principle in terms of the stopping times τ_k:

$$\tau_N = t_N = T,$$
$$\tau_n = t_n \mathbb{1}_{\{Z_n \geq \mathbb{E}(Z_{\tau_{n+1}}|\mathcal{F}_n)\}} + \tau_{n+1} \mathbb{1}_{\{Z_n < \mathbb{E}(Z_{\tau_{n+1}}|\mathcal{F}_n)\}},$$
$$n = 0, \dots, N-1,$$

and obtain the value function for the discrete stopping problem

$$U_0 = \max\bigl(Z_0, \mathbb{E}(Z_{\tau_1})\bigr).$$

Because $Z_0 = g(0, x)$ is known, this gives an approximation of the American option price $V(0, x)$.

The algorithm

Step 1. Since $(X_n)_{n=0}^N$ is a Markov chain, then $\mathbb{E}(Z_{\tau_{n+1}}|\mathcal{F}_n) = \mathbb{E}(Z_{\tau_{n+1}}|X_n)$. The state space of $\mathbb{E}(Z_{\tau_{n+1}}|X_n)$ is $L^2(\mathbb{R}^d, \mu_n)$, where μ_n is the measure generated by the random variable X_n. Let $\bigl(e_m^n(X_n)\bigr)_{m\geq 1}$ be a basis in $L^2(\mathbb{R}^d, \mu_n)$. Then

$$\mathbb{E}(Z_{\tau_{n+1}}|X_n) = \sum_{m=1}^{\infty} \lambda_m^n e_m^n(X_n). \tag{8.4}$$

We approximate $\mathbb{E}(Z_{\tau_{n+1}}|X_n)$ in an M-dimensional space $\mathcal{H}_n \subset L^2(\mathbb{R}^d, \mu_n)$ defining an orthogonal projection (for simplicity we assume all spaces $\mathcal{H}_n$ of the same dimension M)

$$\pi_n^M : L^2(\Omega, \mathbb{P}) \to \mathcal{H}_n.$$

The construction of the sequence of approximate stopping times is recursive. We begin with $\tau_N^M = t_N = T$. Assuming that τ_{n+1}^M is known, we define

$$\pi_n^M\bigl(Z_{\tau_{n+1}^M}\bigr) = F_n^M,$$

where F_n^M are approximated in the basis $e^n(X_n) = \{e_1^n(X_n), \dots, e_M^n(X_n)\}$ of $\mathcal{H}_n$

$$F_n^M = \sum_{m=1}^{M} \lambda_m^{M,n} e_m^n(X_n).$$

The coefficients $\lambda_m^{M,n}$ of this expansion are determined as solutions of the minimization problem

$$\lambda^{M,n} = \arg\min_{a\in\mathbb{R}^M} \mathbb{E}\left(Z_{\tau_{n+1}^M} - \sum_{m=1}^M a_m e_m^n(X_n)\right)^2 .$$

Using the above F_n^M, we define the stopping times

$$\tau_n^M = t_n \mathbb{1}_{\{Z_n \geq F_n^M\}} + \tau_{n+1}^M \mathbb{1}_{\{Z_n < F_n^M\}},$$

and the processes $Z_{\tau_n^M}$:

$$\begin{aligned} Z_{\tau_N^M} &= Z_N, \\ Z_{\tau_n^M} &= Z_n \mathbb{1}_{\{Z_n \geq F_n^M\}} + Z_{\tau_{n+1}^M} \mathbb{1}_{\{Z_n < F_n^M\}}. \end{aligned}$$

This approximation gives the approximate value function

$$U_0^M = \max\big(Z_0, \mathbb{E}(Z_{\tau_1^M})\big).$$

Step 2. To obtain a working algorithm, we must know the projections π_n^M. This is achieved by a Monte Carlo simulation. To this end, we simulate L independent paths $(X_n^k)_{k=1}^L$ and compute $Z_n^k = g(t_n, X_n^k)$. The values of Z_n^k are used to compute recursively coefficients $\hat{\lambda}_m^{M,n}$ approximating $\lambda_m^{M,n}$, and stopping times $\hat{\tau}_n^M$ approximating τ_n^M.

We define the stopping time $\hat{\tau}_n^M$ on each path separately beginning the recursion with $\hat{\tau}_{N,k}^M = t_N = T$ and $Z^k_{\hat{\tau}_{N,k}^M} = Z_N^k$, $k = 1, \ldots, L$. Knowing $\hat{\tau}_{n+1,k}^M$ and $Z^k_{\hat{\tau}_{n+1,k}^M}$, we compute $\hat{\lambda}^{M,n}$

$$\hat{\lambda}^{M,n} = \arg\min_{a\in\mathbb{R}^M} \sum_{k=1}^L \left(Z^k_{\hat{\tau}_{n+1,k}^M} - \sum_{m=1}^M a_m e_m^n(X_n^k)\right)^2 .$$

This procedure returns values $\hat{\lambda}_m^{M,n}$. Then for $k = 1, \ldots, L$, we define

$$\hat{F}_{n,k}^M = \sum_{m=1}^M \hat{\lambda}_m^{M,n} e_m^n(X_n^k),$$

the stopping times

$$\hat{\tau}^M_{n,k} = t_n \mathbb{1}_{\{Z^k_n \geq \hat{F}^M_{n,k}\}} + \hat{\tau}^M_{n+1,k} \mathbb{1}_{\{Z^k_n < \hat{F}^M_{n,k})\}},$$

and the processes

$$Z^k_{\hat{\tau}^M_{n,k}} = Z^k_n \mathbb{1}_{\{Z^n_k \geq \hat{F}^M_{n,k}\}} + Z^k_{\hat{\tau}^M_{n+1,k}} \mathbb{1}_{\{Z^k_n < \hat{F}^M_{n,k})\}}.$$

Recursively, beginning from $\hat{\tau}^M_{N,k}$, we compute all $\hat{\tau}^M_{n,k}$ for $n = N - 1, \ldots, 0$ and $k = 1, \ldots, L$. Finally, we obtain the approximation of the Snell envelope at $t_0 = 0$

$$U_0^{M,L} = \max\left(Z_0, \frac{1}{L}\sum_{k=1}^{L} Z^k_{\hat{\tau}^M_{1,k}}\right),$$

which gives a numerical approximation of the value function $V(0, x)$.

Remark 8.10. The above presentation of the algorithm is useful for convergence analysis. In practical computations, Step 1 is limited to fixing the dimensions of $\mathcal{H}_n$ and the choice of basis functions in these spaces. Only Step 2 is implemented in computer code. The choice of basis functions means the choice of a class of functions universal for all spaces $\mathcal{H}_n$ (Longstaff–Schwartz used the Laguerre polynomials). In Step 2 of the algorithm, we evaluate these basis functions at points X^k_n.

Let us observe that since $e^n(X_n) = (e^n_1(X_n), \ldots, e^n_M(X_n))$ is a basis in $\mathcal{H}_n$, the coefficients $\lambda^{M,n}_m$ are uniquely defined by

$$\left(\lambda^{M,n}_m\right)^M_{m=1} = (A^n)^{-1}\mathbb{E}\Big(Z_{\tau^M_{n+1}} e^n(X_n)\Big),$$

where

$$(A^n)_{ij} = \mathbb{E}\big(e^n_i(X_n), e^n_j(X_n)\big)$$

and A^n is invertible by the linear independence of e^n_m, $m = 1, \ldots, M$.

Similarly,

$$\left(\hat{\lambda}^{M,n}_m\right)^M_{m=1} = (\hat{A}^n)^{-1}\frac{1}{L}\sum_{k=1}^{L} Z^k_{\hat{\tau}^M_{n+1,k}} e^n(X^k_n),$$

where

$$(\hat{A}^n)_{ij} = \frac{1}{L}\sum_{k=1}^{L} e_i^n(X_n^k), e_j^n(X_n^k).$$

Example 8.11 (Computing Delta by the Longstaff-Schwartz algorithm). In this example, we show how to compute the price and Delta of the American put option with payoff $g(x) = (K - x)^+$. We assume that the stock price follows the Black–Scholes model; however, the option price can also be computed in more complicated models of local volatility (for the computation of Delta, the Black–Scholes model is necessary).

In the forward pass, we generate L independent sample paths of stock prices at N time steps t_n, $n = 0, \dots, N$, denoting by X_n^k the price at time t_n on path k, $k = 1, \dots, L$. Then following the theoretical description of the algorithm, we select the space $\mathcal{H}_n$, or strictly speaking, a basis in $\mathcal{H}_n$. Following Longstaff and Schwartz, we take as basis functions the weighted Laguerre polynomials $e(x) = (e_1, \dots, e_M)$ and assume that all spaces $\mathcal{H}_n$ are of the same dimension M. (M sufficient for pricing vanilla American options is rather low $M = 5, 6$.)

In the backward pass, we compute on each path the values $\hat{Z}_n^k$ beginning from $\hat{Z}_N^k = g(X_N^k)$ where, to simplify notation, we write $\hat{Z}_n^k$ for the value $Z^k_{\hat{\tau}^M_{n,k}}$. Assume that $\hat{Z}_{n+1}^k$ are already computed. To compute $\hat{Z}_n^k$, we must compare $g(X_n^k)$ with $\mathbb{E}(\hat{Z}_{n+1}^k|X_n^k)$. This requires the projection of the conditional expectation into the basis of $\mathcal{H}$. The coefficients of this projection form a vector $\hat{\lambda}^{M,n}$ given by the formula known from the description of the algorithm

$$\hat{\lambda}^{M,n} = (\hat{A}^n)^{-1}\frac{1}{L}\sum_{k=1}^{L} \hat{Z}_{n+1}^k e(X_n^k),$$

where

$$(\hat{A}^n)_{ij} = \frac{1}{L}\sum_{k=1}^{L} e_i(X_n^k)e_j(X_n^k).$$

If $g(X_n^k) < \sum_{m=1}^{M} \hat{\lambda}_m^{M,n} e_m(X_n^k)$, then $\hat{Z}_n^k = \exp(-r\delta t)\hat{Z}_{n+1}^k$; else $\hat{Z}_n^k = g(X_n^k)$. Going backward from $t_N = T$ to $t_0 = 0$, we find all $\hat{Z}_n^k$ and obtain an approximation of the price of the American put option

$$V = \max\left(Z_0, \frac{1}{L}\sum_{k=1}^{L} \hat{Z}_1^k\right).$$

To compute the sensitivities of this option, we use the method of path differentiation known from Chapter 3. The pathwise estimate of the sensitivity $dV/d\theta$ for the American put option can be approximated as

$$\frac{dV}{d\theta} = \lim_{\varepsilon \to 0} \frac{V(\theta+\varepsilon) - V(\theta)}{\varepsilon} \tag{8.5}$$

provided that the limit exists with probability 1.

We can compute this limit separately for individual paths. Thus, the computation of the option sensitivities reduces to the interchangeability of differentiation and the expectation operator. Due to Lemma 3.23 for many sensitivity parameters and vanilla options in the Black–Scholes model, the interchangeability holds, and we can use pathwise differentiation to compute the option sensitivities.

Applying this approach to the Longstaff–Schwartz algorithm, we use computed exercise times $t^{(k)}$ and discounted payoff functions $V^{(k)} = e^{-rt^{(k)}} g(X^k_{t^{(k)}})$ on each sample path. Assume that the conditions of Lemma 3.23 hold and the equality (8.5) can be transferred to the level of each $V^{(k)}$. Taking into account time discretization, we can expect that, for a sufficiently small ε, the exercise time on the sample path with parameter $(\theta+\varepsilon)$ is the same as that on the sample path with parameter θ. Then

$$\frac{\partial V^{(k)}}{\partial \theta} = e^{-rt^{(k)}} \frac{\partial g}{\partial X}\frac{\partial X}{\partial \theta}\bigg|_{X=X^k_{t^{(k)}}}.$$

Assuming this relation, consider the computation of the option Delta where θ equals X_0. In the Black–Scholes model, the stock price is

$$X_t = X_0 \exp\big((r - \sigma^2/2)t + \sigma W_t\big).$$

Thus, we have

$$\frac{\partial g}{\partial X} = \frac{\partial (K-X)^+}{\partial X} = \mathbb{1}_{\{X<K\}}, \quad \frac{\partial X}{\partial X_0} = \frac{X}{X_0}.$$

Introducing the function

$$f(X) = \frac{\partial g}{\partial X}\frac{\partial X}{\partial X_0} = \frac{X}{X_0}\mathbb{1}_{\{X<K\}},$$

we define a stochastic process $Y = f(X)$ with the realization $\hat{Y}_n^k$ on the kth path for $n = 0, \dots, N$. For $t_N = T$, we set $\hat{Y}_N^k = f(X_N^k)$. Assume that $\hat{Y}_{n+1}^k$ are already computed. We compute $\hat{Y}_n^k$ using vectors $\hat{\lambda}^{M,n}$. If $g(X_n^k) < \sum_{m=1}^{M} \hat{\lambda}_m^{M,n} e_m(X_n^k)$, then $\hat{Y}_n^k = \hat{Y}_{n+1}^k$; else $\hat{Y}_n^k = f(X_n^k)$. Going backward from $t_N = T$ to $t_0 = 0$, we find all $\hat{Y}_n^k$. Let us note the lack of discounting between levels $(n+1)$ and n. Since all intermediate values must be discounted to time zero, this can be performed in one step at time $t = 0$. Then

$$\Delta = e^{-rT}\frac{1}{L}\sum_{k=1}^{L}\hat{Y}_0^k.$$

A similar procedure can be applied (with some modifications) to compute other Greek parameters. For Rho, the sensitivity of the option price to changes in the risk-free interest rate r, we have in the Black–Scholes model

$$\frac{\partial V^{(k)}}{\partial r} = \left(-t^{(k)}\exp(-rt^{(k)})g(X) + \exp(-rt^{(k)})\frac{\partial g}{\partial X}\frac{\partial X}{\partial r}\right)\bigg|_{X=X^k_{t^{(k)}}},$$

where

$$\frac{\partial X}{\partial r} = tX_0\exp\Big((r-\sigma^2/2)t + \sigma W_t\Big) = tX.$$

Hence, we can compute Rho similarly to Delta defining the function

$$f(t, X_t) = -te^{-rt}g(X_t) + te^{-rt}X_t\mathbb{1}_{\{X_t<K\}}$$

and performing similar computations as in the case of Delta.

8.2.1 *Convergence*

Our goal here is to prove that for M, L going to infinity $U_0^{M,L}$ converge to U_0 the value function of the discrete optimal stopping problem. Our proof follows the approach of Clément *et al.* [16].

First, for vectors $a^l \in \mathbb{R}^M$ and $x_l \in \mathbb{R}^d$, we define functions $F_n^M(a^l, x_l) = \sum_{m=1}^M a_m^l e_m^n(x_l)$. Then for parameters $a = (a^1, \ldots, a^{N-1})$, $x = (x_1, \ldots, x_N)$ and $z = (z_1, \ldots, z_N)$, with $a^n \in \mathbb{R}^M$, $x_n \in \mathbb{R}^d$, and $z_n \in \mathbb{R}$, we define the scalar functions:

$$W_N(a, x, z) = z_N,$$
$$W_n(a, x, z) = z_n \mathbb{1}_{\{z_n \geq F_n^M(a^n, x_n)\}} + W_{n+1}(a, x, z) \mathbb{1}_{\{z_n < F_n^M(a^n, x_n)\}}.$$

Clearly,

$$W_n(\lambda^M, X, Z) = Z_{\tau_n^M}, \quad \text{where } \lambda^M = (\lambda^{M,1}, \ldots, \lambda^{M,N-1}),$$

and

$$W_n(\hat{\lambda}^M, X^k, Z^k) = Z^k_{\hat{\tau}^M_{n,k}}, \quad \text{where } \hat{\lambda}^M = (\hat{\lambda}^{M,1}, \ldots, \hat{\lambda}^{M,N-1}).$$

Lemma 8.12. *For $n \in \{1, \ldots, N-1\}$*

$$|W_n(a, x, z) - W_n(b, x, z)|$$
$$\leq \left(\sum_{i=n}^{N} |z_i| \right) \sum_{i=n}^{N-1} \mathbb{1}_{\{|z_i - F_i^M(b^i, x_i)| \leq |F_i^M(b^i, x_i) - F_i^M(a^i, x_i)|\}}.$$

Proof. Let $B_n(a) = \{z_n \geq F_n^M(a^n, x_n)\}$, $B_n(b) = \{z_n \geq F_n^M(b^n, x_n)\}$. Denote $\mathbb{1}_{A^c} = \mathbb{1} - \mathbb{1}_A$ and $\mathbb{1}_{AB} = \mathbb{1}_A + \mathbb{1}_B - \mathbb{1}_A \mathbb{1}_B$. From the formula

$$W_n(a, x, z) = z_n \mathbb{1}_{B_n(a)} + \sum_{i=n+1}^{N-1} z_i \mathbb{1}_{B_n^c(a) \ldots B_{i-1}^c(a) B_i(a)}$$
$$+ z_N \mathbb{1}_{B_n^c(a) \ldots B_{N-1}^c(a)},$$

we have

$$W_n(a, x, z) - W_n(b, x, z)$$
$$= z_n (\mathbb{1}_{B_n(a)} - \mathbb{1}_{B_n(b)})$$
$$+ \sum_{i=n+1}^{N-1} z_i (\mathbb{1}_{B_n^c(a) \ldots B_{i-1}^c(a) B_i(a)} - \mathbb{1}_{B_n^c(b) \ldots B_{i-1}^c(b) B_i(b)})$$
$$+ z_N (\mathbb{1}_{B_n^c(a) \ldots B_{N-1}^c(a)} - \mathbb{1}_{B_n^c(b) \ldots B_{N-1}^c(b)}).$$

Since

$$\left|\mathbb{1}_{B_n^c(a)\dots B_{i-1}^c(a)B_i(a)} - \mathbb{1}_{B_n^c(b)\dots B_{i-1}^c(b)B_i(b)}\right|$$
$$\le \sum_{j=n}^{i-1}\left|\mathbb{1}_{B_j^c(a)} - \mathbb{1}_{B_j^c(b)}\right| + \left|\mathbb{1}_{B_i(a)} - \mathbb{1}_{B_i(b)}\right| = \sum_{j=n}^{i}\left|\mathbb{1}_{B_j(a)} - \mathbb{1}_{B_j(b)}\right|$$

and

$$\left|\mathbb{1}_{B_n^c(a)\dots B_{N-1}^c(a)} - \mathbb{1}_{B_n^c(b)\dots B_{N-1}^c(b)}\right| \le \sum_{j=n}^{N-1}\left|\mathbb{1}_{B_j(a)} - \mathbb{1}_{B_j(b)}\right|,$$

we obtain

$$|W_n(a,x,z) - W_n(b,x,z)| \le \left(\sum_{i=n}^{N}|z_i|\right)\sum_{i=n}^{N-1}\left|\mathbb{1}_{B_i(a)} - \mathbb{1}_{B_i(b)}\right|.$$

Because $|\mathbb{1}_A - \mathbb{1}_B| = \mathbb{1}_{(A\setminus B)\cup(B\setminus A)}$, we get

$$\begin{aligned}
&\left|\mathbb{1}_{B_n(a)} - \mathbb{1}_{B_n(b)}\right| \\
&\quad = \mathbb{1}_{\{F_n^M(a^n,x_n)\le z_n < F_n^M(b^n,x_n)\}} + \mathbb{1}_{\{F_n^M(b^n,x_n)\le z_n < F_n^M(a^n,x_n)\}} \\
&\quad = \mathbb{1}_{\{F_n^M(a^n,x_n)-F_n^M(b^n,x_n)\le z_n - F_n^M(b^n,x_n)<0\}} \\
&\qquad + \mathbb{1}_{\{0\le z_n - F_n^M(b^n,x_n)<F_n^M(a^n,x_n)-F_n^M(b^n,x_n)\}} \\
&\quad = \mathbb{1}_{\{0< F_n^M(b^n,x_n)-z_n\le F_n^M(b^n,x_n)-F_n^M(a^n,x_n)\}} \\
&\qquad + \mathbb{1}_{\{0\le z_n - F_n^M(b^n,x_n)<F_n^M(a^n,x_n)-F_n^M(b^n,x_n)\}} \\
&\quad \le \mathbb{1}_{\{|z_n - F_n^M(b^n,x_n)|\le|F_n^M(b^n,x_n)-F_n^M(a^n,x_n)|\}}.
\end{aligned}$$

The application of the above estimate concludes the proof. □

Proving the convergence of $U_0^{M,L}$ to U_0 is not an easy task. First, we keep M constant and consider the limit $L \to \infty$ proving that $U_0^{M,L}$ converge to U_0^M.

Lemma 8.13. *Let the simulated paths $X^k = (X_0^k, \dots, X_N^k)$, $k = 1, \dots, L$, be independent. We assume that in the finite-dimensional space $\mathcal{H}_n$*

(LS) $\mathbb{P}(Z_n = F_n^M) = 0, \quad n = 1, \dots, N-1.$

Under the above assumptions $(\hat{\lambda}_m^{M,n})_{m=1}^M$ *converge almost surely to* $(\lambda_m^{M,n})_{m=1}^M$, $n = 1, \dots, N-1$.

Proof. The proof goes by induction in n. For $n = N-1$, the result follows from the strong law of large numbers. Assume that the result is true for $i = n, \dots, N-1$. Then

$$(\hat{\lambda}_m^{M,n-1})_{m=1}^M = (\hat{A}^{n-1})^{-1}\frac{1}{L}\sum_{k=1}^L Z^k_{\hat{\tau}^M_{n,k}} e^{n-1}(X^k_{n-1}).$$

$1/L\sum_{k=1}^L W_n(\hat{\lambda}^M, X^k, Z^k)e^{n-1}(X^k_{n-1})$ converge by the law of large numbers to $\mathbb{E}\Big(W_n(\hat{\lambda}^M, X, Z)e^{n-1}(X_{n-1})\Big)$ and by the same reason $\hat{A}^{n-1}$ converge to A^{n-1}. Since

$$Z^k_{\hat{\tau}^M_{n,k}} = W_n(\hat{\lambda}^M, X^k, Z^k),$$

it suffices to prove

$$\lim_{L\to\infty}\frac{1}{L}\sum_{k=1}^L\Big(W_n(\hat{\lambda}^M, X^k, Z^k) - W_n(\lambda^M, X^k, Z^k)\Big)e^{n-1}(X^k_{n-1}) = 0.$$

By Lemma 8.12, we get

$$\begin{aligned}&\frac{1}{L}\Big|\sum_{k=1}^L\Big(W_n(\hat{\lambda}^M, X^k, Z^k) - (W_n(\lambda^M, X^k, Z^k)\Big)e^{n-1}(X^k_{n-1})\Big|\\ &\quad\le \sum_{k=1}^L \|e^{n-1}(X^k_{n-1})\|\sum_{i=n}^N |Z_i^k|\\ &\qquad\times\sum_{i=n}^{N-1}\mathbb{1}_{\{|Z_i^k - F_i^M(\lambda^{M,i}, X_i^k)|\le|F_i^M(\hat{\lambda}^{M,i}, X_i^k) - F_i^M(\lambda^{M,i}, X_i^k)|\}}.\end{aligned}$$

Since $\hat{\lambda}^{M,i}$ converge to $\lambda^{M,i}$ for $i \ge n$, then

$$\limsup_{L\to\infty}\frac{1}{L}\Big|\sum_{k=1}^L\Big(W_n(\hat{\lambda}^M, X^k, Z^k) - (W_n(\lambda^M, X^k, Z^k)\Big)e^{n-1}(X^k_{n-1})\Big|$$

$$\leq \limsup_{L\to\infty} \frac{1}{L}\sum_{k=1}^{L} \|e^{n-1}(X_{n-1}^k)\| \sum_{i=n}^{N} |Z_i^k|$$
$$\times \sum_{i=n}^{N-1} \mathbb{1}_{\{|Z_i^k - F_i^M(\lambda^{M,i}, X_i^k)| \leq \varepsilon \|e^i(X_i^k)\|\}}$$
$$= \mathbb{E}\left(\|e^{n-1}(X_{n-1})\| \sum_{i=n}^{N} |Z_i| \sum_{i=n}^{N-1} \mathbb{1}_{\{|Z_i - F_i^M(\lambda^{M,i}, X_i)| \leq \varepsilon \|e^i(X_i)\|\}} \right),$$

where, in the last equality, we have applied the strong law of large numbers. Since $\mathbb{P}(Z_i = F_i^M) = 0$ for each i by assumption (LS), letting ε to zero yields the desired convergence. □

Let us remark that assumption (LS) is essential for a correct convergence of optimal stopping times $\hat{\tau}_k^*$ of Z^k computed on paths X^k, $k = 1, \ldots, L$, to the optimal stopping time τ^* of Z. It can happen that the values of $\hat{F}_{n,k}^M$, which converge to F_n^M, are always on one side of F_n^M, say $\hat{F}_{n,k}^M > F_n^M$. Then it can be suboptimal to exercise for any k. However, it is optimal to exercise in the limit. Thus, the optimal stopping time τ^* will not be approximated correctly. Condition (LS) ensures that such an event has probability zero.

Theorem 8.14. *If under the assumptions of Lemma* 8.13 $(\hat{\lambda}_m^{M,n})_{m=1}^M$ *converge almost surely to* $(\lambda_m^{M,n})_{m=1}^M$ *as* L *tends to infinity, then* $U_0^{M,L}$ *converge to* U_0^M *in probability.*

Proof. Since Z_0 is deterministic, it is sufficient to prove that $1/L\sum_{k=1}^{L} Z_{\hat{\tau}_{1,k}^M}^k$ converge to $\mathbb{E}(Z_{\tau_1^M})$.

Because paths X^k are independent, then $1/L\sum_{k=1}^{L}\sum_{m=1}^{M} \hat{\lambda}_m^{M,n}$ $e_m^n(X_n^k)$ converge to $\mathbb{E}(Z_{\tau_{n+1}^M}|X_n)$. Thus, we must prove

$$\lim_{L\to\infty} \frac{1}{L}\sum_{k=1}^{L}\Big(Z_{\hat{\tau}_{n,k}^M}^k - W_n(\lambda^M, X, Z)\Big) = 0,$$

where $\lambda^M = (\lambda^{M,1}, \ldots, \lambda^{M,N-1})$.

Since $Z^k_{\hat{\tau}^M_{n,k}} = W_n(\hat{\lambda}^M, X^k, Z^k)$, we have

$$\frac{1}{L}\Big|\sum_{k=1}^{L} W_n(\hat{\lambda}^M, X^k, Z^k) - W_n(\lambda^M, X, Z)\Big|$$
$$\leq \frac{1}{L}\sum_{k=1}^{L}\Big(|W_n(\hat{\lambda}^M, X^k, Z^k) - W_n(\lambda^M, X^k, Z^k)|$$
$$+ |W_n(\lambda^M, X^k, Z^k) - W_n(\lambda^M, X, Z)|\Big).$$

By Lemma 8.12, we have

$$\frac{1}{L}\sum_{k=1}^{L} |W_n(\hat{\lambda}^M, X^k, Z^k) - W_n(\lambda^M, X^k, Z^k)|$$
$$\leq \frac{1}{L}\sum_{k=1}^{L}\sum_{i=n}^{N} |Z_i^k|$$
$$\times \sum_{i=n}^{N-1} \mathbb{1}_{\{|Z_i^k - F_i^M(\lambda^{M,i}, X_i^k)| \leq |F_i^M(\hat{\lambda}^{M,i}, X_i^k) - F_i^M(\lambda^{M,i}, X_i^k)|\}}.$$

$\hat{\lambda}^M$ converge to λ^M almost surely, then for some $\varepsilon > 0$, we have

$$\limsup_{L\to\infty} \frac{1}{L}\sum_{k=1}^{L} |W_n(\hat{\lambda}^M, X^k, Z^k) - W_n(\lambda^M, X^k, Z^k)|$$
$$\leq \limsup_{L\to\infty} \frac{1}{L}\sum_{k=1}^{L}\sum_{i=n}^{N} |Z_i^k| \sum_{i=n}^{N-1} \mathbb{1}_{\{|Z_i^k - F_i^M(\lambda^{M,i}, X_i^k)| \leq \varepsilon\}}$$
$$= \mathbb{E}\left(\sum_{i=n}^{N} |Z_i| \sum_{i=n}^{N-1} \mathbb{1}_{\{|Z_i - F_i^M(\lambda^{M,i}, X_i)| \leq \varepsilon\}}\right),$$

where the last equality follows from the strong law of large numbers. Letting ε to zero and using the assumption (LS), we get for $L \to \infty$

$$\frac{1}{L}\sum_{k=1}^{L}(W_n(\hat{\lambda}^M, X^k, Z^k) - W_n(\lambda^M, X^k, Z^k)) \to 0.$$

The convergence

$$\frac{1}{L}\sum_{k=1}^{L}\left(W_n(\lambda^M, X^k, Z^k) - W_n(\lambda^M, X, Z)\right) \to 0$$

follows straightforwardly from the law of large numbers. □

The convergence of U_0^M to U_0 is a consequence of the following theorem and the properties of orthogonal projections in Hilbert space.

Theorem 8.15. *The following convergence holds in* $L^2(\mathbb{R}^d, \mu_n)$

$$\lim_{M\to\infty} \mathbb{E}(Z_{\tau_n^M}|X_n) = \mathbb{E}(Z_{\tau_n}|X_n)$$

for $n = 1, \ldots, N$.

Proof. The proof goes by induction in n. For $n = N$, the result is true since $Z_{\tau_N^M} = Z_{\tau_N} = Z_T$. Now, assume that the result is true for $n+1$. We show that it is also true for n.

From the definition

$$Z_{\tau_n^M} = Z_n \mathbb{1}_{\{Z_n \geq F_n^M\}} + Z_{\tau_{n+1}^M} \mathbb{1}_{\{Z_n < F_n^M\}},$$

we obtain using (8.3)

$$\begin{aligned}
&\mathbb{E}(Z_{\tau_n^M} - Z_{\tau_n}|X_n)\\
&\quad = \left(Z_n - \mathbb{E}(Z_{\tau_{n+1}}|X_n)\right)\left(\mathbb{1}_{\{Z_n \geq F_n^M\}} - \mathbb{1}_{\{Z_n \geq \mathbb{E}(Z_{\tau_{n+1}}|X_n)\}}\right)\\
&\qquad + \mathbb{E}(Z_{\tau_{n+1}^M} - Z_{\tau_{n+1}}|X_n)\mathbb{1}_{\{Z_n < F_n^M\}}.
\end{aligned}$$

The second term on the right-hand side converges to zero by the inductive assumption. For the first term, using the identity $|\mathbb{1}_A - \mathbb{1}_B| = \mathbb{1}_{(A\setminus B)\cup(B\setminus A)}$, we get, as in the proof of Lemma 8.12,

$$\begin{aligned}
&\left|\left(Z_n - \mathbb{E}(Z_{\tau_{n+1}}|X_n)\right)\left(\mathbb{1}_{\{Z_n \geq F_n^M\}} - \mathbb{1}_{\{Z_n \geq \mathbb{E}(Z_{\tau_{n+1}}|X_n)\}}\right)\right|\\
&\quad = \left|Z_n - \mathbb{E}(Z_{\tau_{n+1}}|X_n)\right|\\
&\qquad \times \left|\mathbb{1}_{\{\mathbb{E}(Z_{\tau_{n+1}}|X_n) > Z_n \geq F_n^M\}} - \mathbb{1}_{\{F_n^M > Z_n \geq \mathbb{E}(Z_{\tau_{n+1}}|X_n)\}}\right|
\end{aligned}$$

$$\le \left|Z_n - \mathbb{E}(Z_{\tau_{n+1}}|X_n)\right| \mathbb{1}_{\{|Z_n - \mathbb{E}(Z_{\tau_{n+1}}|X_n)| \le |F_n^M - \mathbb{E}(Z_{\tau_{n+1}}|X_n)|\}}$$
$$\le |F_n^M - \mathbb{E}(Z_{\tau_{n+1}}|X_n)|$$
$$\le \left|F_n^M - \pi_n^M\big(\mathbb{E}(Z_{\tau_{n+1}}|X_n)\big)\right|$$
$$+ \left|\pi_n^M\big(\mathbb{E}(Z_{\tau_{n+1}}|X_n)\big) - \mathbb{E}(Z_{\tau_{n+1}}|X_n)\right|.$$

Since by definition

$$F_n^M = \pi_n^M\big(Z_{\tau_{n+1}^M}\big) = \pi_n^M\big(\mathbb{E}(Z_{\tau_{n+1}^M}|X_n)\big),$$

then

$$\left|\big(Z_n - \mathbb{E}(Z_{\tau_{n+1}}|X_n)\big)\big(\mathbb{1}_{\{Z_n \ge F_n^M\}} - \mathbb{1}_{\{Z_n \ge \mathbb{E}(Z_{\tau_{n+1}}|X_n)\}}\big)\right|$$
$$\le \left|\mathbb{E}(Z_{\tau_{n+1}^M}|X_n) - \mathbb{E}(Z_{\tau_{n+1}}|X_n)\right|$$
$$+ \left|\pi_n^M\big(\mathbb{E}(Z_{\tau_{n+1}}|X_n)\big) - \mathbb{E}(Z_{\tau_{n+1}}|X_n)\right|.$$

The first term on the right-hand side converges to zero by the inductive assumption and the second, by the properties of the orthogonal projections. □

Hence, we have two independent convergences: $U_0^{M,L} \to U_0^M$, as L goes to infinity, and $U_0^M \to U_0$, for $M \to \infty$. This is, however, not sufficient to obtain convergence $U_0^{M,L} \to U_0$. The problem of this last convergence has been discussed in many recent papers. Several results were obtained with the help of mathematical techniques that are too advanced for the presentation in this book (cf. [25, 84, 92, 93]). Some of these papers, in addition to the proofs of convergence, also provide (complicated) formulas for error estimates.

8.3 Variational Inequalities

As we have mentioned in the introduction to this chapter, optimal stopping problems can be reduced to variational inequalities. Variational inequalities are a classical mathematical technique used in many problems in mathematical physics; thus, numerical algorithms for solving them have long been known. Below, we briefly present that approach to the optimal stopping problem for American options and find its value function. We begin by presenting theorems that guarantee the existence and uniqueness of solutions. Then we describe numerical schemes that give finite difference approximations. These approximations are formulated as *linear complementarity problems* (LCP). The solution of LCP creates a numerical challenge of its own. There is a large number of numerical algorithms for treating LCP. We present a rather old and not very fast approach of *projected successive over-relaxation* (PSOR), which is popular due to the simplicity of its computer implementation. We prove that the approximation generated by PSOR converges to the exact solution of LCP. We discuss as well another popular and more efficient algorithm of *penalization.*

We begin by presenting the most significant theoretical results for variational inequalities applied to optimal stopping problems. In this presentation, we follow the paper by Jaillet *et al.* [43]. The reader is also advised to consult the book by Bensoussan and Lions [8], where more complete proofs can be found. In our approach, the solutions of variational inequalities are understood in the weak (variational) sense, which corresponds to the weak solutions of the elliptic and parabolic equations analyzed in Chapter 5. This problem is also studied in the framework of the theory of viscosity solutions (cf. [28, 68]) and strong solutions (cf. [73]).

Let us recall the stochastic differential equation

$$dX_s = b(s, X_s)ds + \sigma(s, X_s)dW_s, \quad X_t = x, \tag{8.6}$$

describing the dynamics of risky assets. Process X_s defines the family of differential operators (minus sign has been added to conform to the notation of Chapter 5)

$$\mathcal{A}^t u = \sum_{i,j=1}^{d} -\frac{\partial}{\partial x_i}\left(a_{ij}(t,x)\frac{\partial u}{\partial x_j}\right) + \sum_{i=1}^{d} \bar{b}_i(t,x)\frac{\partial u}{\partial x_i} + c(t,x)u. \tag{8.7}$$

Discussing the Black–Scholes model in Chapter 5, we defined operator $\mathcal{A}^t$ in the nondivergent form. The above divergent form is more convenient for the analysis of variational inequalities. The coefficients of operator $\mathcal{A}^t$ are defined by the coefficients of the stochastic equation (8.6)

$$a_{ij} = \frac{1}{2}\sum_{k=1}^{d} \sigma_i^k \sigma_j^k, \quad \bar{b}_i = -b_i + \sum_{j=1}^{d} \frac{\partial a_{ij}}{\partial x_j}, \tag{8.8}$$

and function $c(t,x)$ equals the risk-free interest rate $r(t)$, which we assume as a deterministic function of time.

Since the stochastic process X_s describes the logarithmic price, it takes values in $\mathbb{R}^d$. Then operator $\mathcal{A}^t$ should also be considered in $\mathbb{R}^d$. Hence, similarly to Section 5.5, we investigate this operator in weighted Sobolev spaces. We consider Sobolev's spaces with weight functions that satisfy the conditions of Definition 5.40. Similarly as in Section 5.5, we limit our analysis to spaces $L^2_\rho(\mathbb{R}^d)$ and $H^1_\rho(\mathbb{R}^d)$.

Together with the differential operator $\mathcal{A}^t$ we consider in $H^1_\rho(\mathbb{R}^d)$ the associated bilinear form $B^t_\rho[u,v]$

$$B^t_\rho[u,v] = \int_{\mathbb{R}^d} \left(\sum_{i,j=1}^{d} a_{ij}(t,x) \frac{\partial u}{\partial x_i} \frac{\partial v}{\partial x_j} + \sum_{i=1}^{d} \hat{b}_i(t,x) \frac{\partial u}{\partial x_i} v + c(t,x)uv \right) \rho(x)dx,$$

where

$$\hat{b}_i(t,x) = \bar{b}_i(t,x) + \sum_{j=1}^{d} a_{ij}(t,x) \frac{1}{\rho(x)} \frac{\partial \rho(x)}{\partial x_j}.$$

It is easy to notice, following the proof of Theorem 5.25, that if ρ fulfills the conditions of Definition 5.40, and a_{ij}, b_i, c, $i,j = 1,\ldots,d$, are in $L^\infty([0,T] \times \mathbb{R}^d)$ with symmetric a_{ij}, then the energy estimates of Theorem 5.25 hold

$$\begin{aligned} &\left|B^t_\rho[u(t),v(t)]\right| \le \alpha \|u(t)\|_{H^1_\rho} \|v(t)\|_{H^1_\rho}, \\ &u(t), v(t) \in H^1_\rho(\mathbb{R}^d) \ a.e.\ t \in [0,T], \\ &\beta \|u(t)\|^2_{H^1_\rho} \le B^t_\rho[u(t),u(t)] + \gamma \|u(t)\|^2_{L^2_\rho}, \\ &u(t) \in H^1_\rho(\mathbb{R}^d) \ a.e.\ t \in [0,T]. \end{aligned} \tag{8.9}$$

We already know from Section 5.5, that it is more convenient when the bilinear form is coercive. The coerciveness of $B^t_\rho[u,v]$ can be achieved by the change of variables $u_\gamma(t) = e^{-\gamma t}u(t)$ (see Remark 5.41 in Section 5.5). We perform this change of variables and obtain the coercive bilinear form $B^t_{\rho,\gamma}$. To simplify notation, we drop the index γ. Hence, our assumptions on operator $\mathcal{A}^t$ and bilinear form B^t_ρ are formulated as follows.

Assumption 8.16. Let $\mathcal{A}^t$ be defined by (8.7) and $B^t_\rho[u,v]$ be the corresponding bilinear form. We assume that operator $\partial/\partial t + \mathcal{A}^t$ is uniformly parabolic in the sense of Definition 5.29. About the coefficients of operator $\mathcal{A}^t$ and form B^t_ρ we assume:

(A1) The coefficients $a_{i,j} \in C^{1,2}([0,T] \times \mathbb{R}^d)$, $i,j = 1,\ldots,d$, are bounded with uniformly bounded first derivatives with respect to t and x.
(A2) The coefficients $\hat{b}_i \in C^{1,1}([0,T] \times \mathbb{R}^d)$, $i = 1,\ldots,d$, are bounded with bounded first derivatives with respect to t.
(A3) The free term c is a function of t only and $c(t) \in C^1(0,T)$ is bounded together with its first derivative.

These assumptions correspond to the following conditions for the coefficients of equation (8.6):

(1) The entries $\sigma_{i,j}$ of the volatility matrix are of class $C^{1,2}([0,T] \times \mathbb{R}^d)$ and are bounded with uniformly bounded first derivatives with respect to t and x, and second derivatives with respect to x.
(2) The entries b_i of the drift vector are of class $C^{1,1}([0,T] \times \mathbb{R}^d)$ and are bounded with uniformly bounded first derivatives with respect to t and x.
(3) $c(t)$ represents the risk-free interest rate and is a bounded, nonnegative function of class $C^1(0,T)$ with a bounded first derivative.
(4) Additionally, we impose on the weight function $\rho(x)$ requirements stronger than in Definition 5.40 assuming that this function is of class $C^2(\mathbb{R}^d)$ and $\rho(x)^{-1}D^\alpha\rho(x)$ is uniformly bounded in $x \in \mathbb{R}^d$ for $|\alpha| \le 2$.

Under the above assumptions $B^t_\rho[u,v]$ is t-uniformly continuous, coercive in $H^1_\rho(\mathbb{R}^d)$, and fulfills the energy estimates (8.9).

The proof of the following theorem is presented in Section 2 of Chapter 3 in the book by Bensoussan and Lions [8] (see also the paper by Jaillet *et al.* [43]). The proof by Bensoussan and Lions is under much weaker assumptions of the boundedness of the coefficients of operator $\mathcal{A}^t$, but we retain the stronger assumptions because they are required in the proof of the subsequent theorem.

Theorem 8.17. *Assume that* B_ρ^t *fulfills the conditions of Assumption* 8.16 *and* $g \in H_\rho^1(\mathbb{R}^d)$. *Then for each* $v \in H_\rho^1(\mathbb{R}^d)$ *such that* $v \geq g$, *there exists a unique solution* u *defined on* $[0, T] \times \mathbb{R}^d$ *of the following variational inequality*

$$\begin{aligned}
&-\left(\frac{du}{dt}(t), v - u(t)\right)_{L_\rho^2} + B_\rho^t[u(t), v - u(t)] \geq 0, \quad a.e.\ t \in [0, T), \\
&u(t) \geq g, \quad a.e.\ t \in [0, T], \\
&u(T) = g,
\end{aligned} \tag{8.10}$$

with $u \in L^2(0, T; H_\rho^1(\mathbb{R}^d))$ *and* $du/dt \in L^2(0, T; H_\rho^{-1}(\mathbb{R}^d))$.

Remark 8.18. From Theorem 5.36, we know that in fact $du/dt \in L^2(0, T; L_\rho^2(\mathbb{R}^d))$ and, due to Theorem 5.21, $u \in C(0, T; L_\rho^2(\mathbb{R}^d))$. Hence, it is legitimate to use the scalar product $\left(du/dt(t), v - u(t)\right)_{L_\rho^2}$. For the same reason, $u(T) = g$ has the standard meaning of equality between two L_ρ^2-functions.

We are now in a position to justify that the price of an American option defined in terms of the value function of an optimal stopping problem can also be obtained as a solution of the variational inequality (8.10).

Theorem 8.19. *Let the option reward function* $g \in H_\rho^1(\mathbb{R}^d) \cap C^0(\mathbb{R}^d)$. *If the hypotheses of Assumption* 8.16 *are satisfied and* $V(t, x)$ *is the value function defined in Theorem* 8.9, *then* $V(t, x)$ *is a solution of the variational inequality* (8.10) *with the coefficients of* $B_\rho^t[u, v]$ *given by* (8.8). *(In fact,* (8.10) *is solved by* $e^{-\gamma t} V(t, x)$ *due to the mentioned earlier change of variables.)*

The proof of the above theorem can be derived from the results in Section 4 of Chapter 3 in the book by Bensoussan and Lions [8]. Bensoussan and Lions prove that if g is continuous, then $V(t,x)$ is a solution of the weak variational inequality (cf. Definition 8.21). Since Theorem 8.22 implies that the solution of the weak inequality is also a solution of the strong inequality, the combination of Theorem 8.22 with the result of Bensoussan and Lions justifies the above theorem. The direct proof that $V(t,x)$ is a solution of the strong variational inequality (8.10) requires an analysis in weighted Sobolev's spaces $W^{k,p}(\mathbb{R}^d)$ for $p > d$ (cf. Theorem 3.4.1 in Bensoussan and Lions and Theorem 3.2 in Jaillet *et al.*). This approach is not compatible with our L^2 setting.

Theorem 8.20. *Under the assumptions of Theorem* 8.17 *variational inequality* (8.10) *is equivalent to the following integral version which holds for each* $v \in L^2(0,T;H^1_\rho(\mathbb{R}^d))$ *such that* $dv/dt \in L^2(0,T;H^{-1}_\rho(\mathbb{R}^d))$ *and* $v(t) \geq g$*, for almost each* $t \in [0,T]$,

$$\begin{aligned}
&\int_0^T -\Big(\frac{du}{dt}(t), v(t)-u(t)\Big)_{L^2_\rho} dt + \int_0^T B^t_\rho[u(t), v(t)-u(t)]dt \geq 0,\\
&u(t) \geq g, \quad a.e.\ t \in [0,T],\\
&u(T) = g.
\end{aligned} \tag{8.11}$$

In addition, for such v*, we have*

$$\begin{aligned}
&\int_0^T -\Big\langle\frac{dv}{dt}(t), v(t)-u(t)\Big\rangle dt + \int_0^T B^t_\rho[u(t), v(t)-u(t)]dt\\
&\quad\geq \frac{1}{2}\|v(0)-u(0)\|^2_{L^2_\rho} - \frac{1}{2}\|v(T)-u(T)\|^2_{L^2_\rho},\\
&u(t) \geq g, \quad a.e.\ t \in [0,T],\\
&u(T) = g.
\end{aligned} \tag{8.12}$$

Proof. The fact that (8.10) implies (8.11) follows by integration and properties of functions $u(t)$ and $v(t)$. The converse holds because $v(t)$ is an arbitrary L^2 function of $t \in [0,T]$.

To obtain (8.12), we have to add to (8.11) the obvious identity

$$\int_0^T \left\langle \frac{du}{dt}(t) - \frac{dv}{dt}(t), v(t) - u(t) \right\rangle dt$$
$$= \frac{1}{2}\|v(0) - u(0)\|^2_{L^2_\rho} - \frac{1}{2}\|v(T) - u(T)\|^2_{L^2_\rho}.$$

□

Definition 8.21. The following problem is called the *weak formulation of variational inequality*:
find $u \in L^2(0,T; H^1_\rho(\mathbb{R}^d))$ such that $du/dt \in L^2(0,T; H^{-1}_\rho(\mathbb{R}^d))$ and $u(t) \geq g$, for a.e. $t \in [0,T]$, which fulfills the following inequality

$$\int_0^T -\left\langle \frac{dv}{dt}(t), v(t) - u(t) \right\rangle dt + \int_0^T B^t_\rho[u(t), v(t) - u(t)]dt$$
$$\geq -\frac{1}{2}\|v(T) - u(T)\|^2_{L^2_\rho}, \tag{8.13}$$

for each $v \in L^2(0,T; H^1_\rho(\mathbb{R}^d))$ such that $dv/dt \in L^2(0,T; H^{-1}_\rho(\mathbb{R}^d))$ and $v(t) \geq g$, for a.e. $t \in [0,T]$.

Theorem 8.20 shows that a solution of (8.10) is also a solution of the weak formulation (8.13). The following theorem, due to Brésis [13], gives the conditions for the converse of Theorem 8.20 to be valid.

Theorem 8.22. *If the bilinear form $B^t_\rho[u,v]$ is t-uniformly continuous and coercive in $H^1_\rho(\mathbb{R}^d)$, the weak formulation* (8.13) *possesses a unique solution u which is also a solution of variational inequality* (8.10).

Remark 8.23. In general, the weak formulation of variational inequality possesses many solutions (the advantage of the weak formulation is that a solution always exists). Due to the special properties of B^t_ρ, there is only one solution of the weak formulation, which is then a solution of (8.10).

For numerical applications, it is convenient to formulate variational inequalities as linear complementarity problems.

Lemma 8.24. *Under the assumptions of Theorem* 8.17*, a solution of* (8.10) *is equivalent to a solution of the following linear complementarity problem*

(i) $-\left(\frac{du}{dt}(t), w\right)_{L^2_\rho} + B^t_\rho[u(t), w] \geq 0, a.e.\ t \in [0, T),$

$w \in H^1_\rho(\mathbb{R}^d), w \geq 0,$

(ii) $u(t) \geq g,\ \ a.e.\ t \in [0, T],$

(iii) $-\left(\frac{du}{dt}(t), g - u(t)\right)_{L^2_\rho} + B^t_\rho[u(t), g - u(t)] = 0,\ \ a.e.\ t \in [0, T),$

(iv) $u(T) = g.$

Proof. Let u be a solution of (8.10). For $w \in H^1_\rho(\mathbb{R}^d)$, $w \geq 0$, we put $v = u + w$. Then $v(t) \geq g$, $v(t) \in H^1_\rho(\mathbb{R}^d)$, and due to (8.10)

$$\begin{aligned} &-\left(\frac{du}{dt}(t), w\right)_{L^2_\rho} + B^t_\rho[u(t), w] \\ &= -\left(\frac{du}{dt}(t), v(t) - u(t)\right)_{L^2_\rho} + B^t_\rho[u(t), v(t) - u(t)] \geq 0, \end{aligned}$$

which proves (i).

Taking $v(t) = g$ in the above inequality, we obtain

$$-\left(\frac{du}{dt}(t), g - u(t)\right)_{L^2_\rho} + B^t_\rho[u(t), g - u(t)] \geq 0.$$

On the other hand, taking $w = u(t) - g \geq 0$ in (i), we obtain the opposite inequality. This gives

$$-\left(\frac{du}{dt}(t), g - u(t)\right)_{L^2_\rho} + B^t_\rho[u(t), g - u(t)] = 0,$$

which proves (iii).

Conversely, let u solve the LCP of the lemma. Then any $v \in H^1_\rho(\mathbb{R}^d)$, $v \geq g$, can be written as $v = g + w$ with $w \geq 0$ and $w \in$

$H^1_\rho(\mathbb{R}^d)$. By inequality (i), we get

$$-\left(\frac{du}{dt}(t), v-g\right)_{L^2_\rho} + B^t_\rho[u(t), v-g] \geq 0.$$

Adding this inequality to (iii), we obtain inequality (8.10).

Since points (ii) and (iv) are the same as in Theorem 8.17, that completes the proof. □

Under the assumptions of Theorem 8.17, it can be proved that variational inequality (8.10) can be reduced to the following strong linear complementarity problem also called *the obstacle problem* (cf. the book by Pascucci [73])

$$\begin{aligned}
&\frac{\partial u}{\partial t} - \mathcal{A}^t u \leq 0, \quad t \in [0,T), \quad x \in \mathbb{R}^d, \\
&u \geq g, \quad t \in [0,T), \quad x \in \mathbb{R}^d, \\
&(u-g)\left(\frac{\partial u}{\partial t} - \mathcal{A}^t u\right) = 0, \quad t \in [0,T), \quad x \in \mathbb{R}^d, \\
&u(T,x) = g(x), \quad x \in \mathbb{R}^d,
\end{aligned} \tag{8.14}$$

where $u \in W^{1,p}_{loc}(0,T; W^{2,p}_{loc}(\mathbb{R}^d))$, $p \geq 1$, and equalities are understood in the sense of L^p.

This formulation can be interpreted as a *free boundary problem*:

(1) In the region of $\mathbb{R}^d$ called *the continuation region* $u > g$ and the equation $\partial u/\partial t - \mathcal{A}^t u = 0$ holds.
(2) In the region called *the exercise region* or *the stopping region* the equality $u = g$ holds and $\partial u/\partial t - \mathcal{A}^t u < 0$.

The boundary of the exercise region is called *the free boundary.*

Example 8.25 (American put option). We analyze the free boundary problem for an American option in the Black–Scholes model. We restrict our considerations to an American put (an American call option has a price equal to a European call). Let $P(t,S)$ be the price of the American put written for simplicity in the original variables (t is the time from the issuing date, and S is the stock price).

Operator $\mathcal{A}^t$ is given by the formula (we drop superscript t since this operator is time independent)

$$\mathcal{A}P = -\frac{1}{2}\sigma^2 S^2 \frac{\partial^2 P}{\partial S^2} - rS\frac{\partial P}{\partial S} + rP$$

and the payoff is $g(S) = (K - S)^+$.

Then the linear complementarity problem for the American put is as follows. For each time t, the half line $S \in [0, \infty)$ is divided by a point $S_f < K$ into two regions. For $S \in [0, S_f)$ early exercise of the option is optimal and

$$P(t, S) = (K - S), \quad t \in [0, T],$$
$$\frac{\partial P}{\partial t} + \frac{1}{2}\sigma^2 S^2 \frac{\partial^2 P}{\partial S^2} + rS\frac{\partial P}{\partial S} - rP < 0.$$

In the region $S \in [S_f, \infty)$, it is optimal to keep the option and

$$\frac{\partial P}{\partial t} + \frac{1}{2}\sigma^2 S^2 \frac{\partial^2 P}{\partial S^2} + rS\frac{\partial P}{\partial S} - rP = 0,$$
$$P(t, S) > (K - S)^+, \quad t \in [0, T),$$
$$P(T, S) = (K - S)^+.$$

The function $S_f = S_f(t)$ defines the free boundary. When computing the price of the American put, we must determine this boundary and impose boundary conditions for the option price.

The following properties of the American put can be derived from the pricing formula of Theorem 8.9:

(1) $P(t, S)$ is continuous on $[0, T] \times [0, \infty)$;
(2) $P(t, S)$ as a function of S is nonincreasing and convex for every $t \in [0, T]$;
(3) $P(t, S)$ as a nonincreasing function of $t \in [0, T]$ for every $S \in [0, \infty)$.

The following behavior of the option price near the free boundary can be considered as a condition that determines the location of the free boundary and the conditions on this boundary:

(1) $\lim_{S \to S_f(t)} P(t, S) = K - S_f(t)$, for $t \in [0, T]$;
(2) $\lim_{S \to S_f(t)} \partial P(t, S)/\partial S = -1$, for $t \in [0, T]$.

The first assertion easily follows from the continuity of the option price. To justify the second, we follow the arguments from the book by Elliot and Kopp [26]. We begin by observing that

$$\frac{\partial P}{\partial S} \geq -1.$$

Let $S < S'$ be two initial values of process S_s in the Black–Scholes model

$$dS_s = rS_s ds + \sigma S_s dW_s, \quad S_t = S \text{ or } S'.$$

Let τ be the optimal stopping time for $P(t, S)$. Then

$$\begin{aligned}
P(t, S') - P(t, S) &= P(t, S') - \mathbb{E}\Big(e^{-r(\tau-t)}(K - S_\tau^{t,S})^+\Big) \\
&\geq \mathbb{E}\Big(e^{-r(\tau-t)}((K - S_\tau^{t,S'})^+ - (K - S_\tau^{t,S})^+)\Big) \\
&= \mathbb{E}\Big(e^{-r(\tau-t)}((K - S_\tau^{t,S'}) - (K - S_\tau^{t,S}))\Big) \\
&\quad + \mathbb{E}\Big(e^{-r(\tau-t)}((K - S_\tau^{t,S'})^- - (K - S_\tau^{t,S})^-)\Big).
\end{aligned}$$

The last expectation in the above sequence of inequalities is non-negative for $S < S'$. This follows from considerations similar to the proof that $P(t, S)$ is a nonincreasing function of S.

Using the formula

$$S_s^{t,S} = S \exp\Big((r - \sigma^2/2)(s - t) + \sigma W_{s-t}\Big),$$

we obtain

$$\begin{aligned}
&P(t, S') - P(t, S) \\
&\quad \geq \mathbb{E}\Big(e^{-r(\tau-t)}(S_\tau^{t,S} - S_\tau^{t,S'})\Big) \\
&\quad = (S - S')\mathbb{E}\Big(\exp(-\sigma^2/2(\tau - t) + \sigma W_{\tau-t})\Big) = (S - S'),
\end{aligned}$$

which proves that $\partial P/\partial S \geq -1$.

To prove that $\lim_{S\to S_f} \partial P(t,S)/\partial S = -1$, we return to variable $x = \ln S$. Let $u(t,x) = P(t,e^x)$ and $x^* = \ln S_f$. Then from the linear complementarity problem for function $u(t,x)$, we have

$$\frac{\sigma^2}{2}u_{xx} \leq \left(\frac{\sigma^2}{2} - r\right)u_x - u_t + ru.$$

Integrating the above inequality in $Q = (t_1,t_2)\times\big(x^*(t)-\varepsilon, x^*(t)+\varepsilon\big)$, we obtain

$$\begin{aligned}
&\frac{\sigma^2}{2}\int_{t_1}^{t_2}\big(u_x(t,x^*(t)+\varepsilon) - u_x(t,x^*(t)-\varepsilon)\big)dt\\
&\quad\leq \left(\frac{\sigma^2}{2} - r\right)\int_{t_1}^{t_2}\big(u(t,x^*(t)+\varepsilon) - u(t,x^*(t)-\varepsilon)\big)dt\\
&\qquad + \int_Q \big(ru - u_t\big)dxdt.
\end{aligned}$$

Due to the continuity of u, the first integral on the right-hand side tends to zero as $\varepsilon \to 0$ by the dominated convergence theorem. We rewrite the second integral on the right-hand side as follows

$$\int_Q \big(ru - u_t\big)dxdt = \int_Q rudxdt - \int_{Q_x}\big(u(t^+,x) - u(t^-,x)\big)dx,$$

where Q_x is a line in Q for fixed x, which begins at time $t^-(x)$ and end at time $t^+(x)$. By the continuity of u and the dominated convergence theorem, the last two integrals also tend to zero as $\varepsilon \to 0$. Hence,

$$\int_{t_1}^{t_2}\big(u_x(t,x^*(t)+\varepsilon) - u_x(t,x^*(t)-\varepsilon)\big)dt \leq 0.$$

Since the point $(x^*(t)-\varepsilon)$ is in the stopping region where $u(t,x) = K - e^x$, then $u_x = -e^x$. Passing to the limit $\varepsilon \to 0$, we have

$$\int_{t_1}^{t_2}\left(\lim_{x\to x^*} u_x(t,x) + e^{x^*}\right)dt \leq 0. \tag{8.15}$$

The elementary formula

$$\frac{\partial P}{\partial S} = \frac{\partial u}{\partial x}\frac{dx}{dS},$$

and the condition $\partial P/\partial S \geq -1$ give $\partial u/\partial x \geq -e^x$, i.e., $u_x + e^x \geq 0$.

By the above inequality and formula (8.15), we obtain the *smooth fit* across the boundary

$$\lim_{x \to x^*} u_x(t,x) = -e^{x^*},$$

which, in terms of function $P(t, S)$, says that

$$\lim_{S \to S_f} \frac{\partial P(t,S)}{\partial S} = -1.$$

To compute a numerical approximation of variational inequality (8.10), we restrict our considerations to a bounded subset of $\mathbb{R}^d$. First, we demonstrate how a solution of the variational inequality in a bounded domain converges to a solution of the original problem in $\mathbb{R}^d$.

To simplify the considerations, we limit the analysis to a stochastic differential equation with time-independent coefficients

$$dX_s = b(X_s)ds + \sigma(X_s)dW_s, \quad X_t = x.$$

We replace the value function of the optimal stopping problem

$$V(t,x) = \frac{1}{\beta_t} \sup_{\tau \in \mathcal{T}_{t,T}} \mathbb{E}\Big(\beta_\tau g\big(X_\tau^{t,x}\big)\Big)$$

by the approximate value function

$$V_K(t,x) = \frac{1}{\beta_t} \sup_{\tau \in \mathcal{T}_{t,T}} \mathbb{E}\Big(\beta_{\tau \wedge T_K^{t,x}}\, g\big(X^{t,x}_{\tau \wedge T_K^{t,x}}\big)\Big),$$

where $T_K^{t,x} = \inf\{s > t \colon |X_s^{t,x}| > K\}$.

Then we have uniform convergence of V_K to V on compact sets (cf. [43, 94]).

Theorem 8.26. *Let functions b, σ, and r fulfill Assumption* 8.16, *and the reward function g be such that $\rho(x)g(x)$ is a bounded, continuous function on $\mathbb{R}^d$ with $\|\rho g\|_{L^\infty(\mathbb{R}^d)} \le C$ and $\|D(\rho g)\|_{L^\infty(\mathbb{R}^d)} \le C$ for $C > 0$, where ρ is the weight function of Definition* 5.40. *Then for all $U_R = \{x \in \mathbb{R}^d \colon |x| < R\}$, $R > 0$,*

$$\lim_{K \to \infty} \max_{t \in [0,T]} \|V(t,\cdot) - V_K(t,\cdot)\|_{L^\infty(\bar{U}_R)} = 0.$$

Theorem 8.27. *Consider the bilinear form $B_R[u,v]$ defined for $u, v \in H^1(U_R)$ by the formula*

$$B_R[u,v] = \int_{U_R} \left(\sum_{i,j=1}^{d} a_{ij}(x) \frac{\partial u}{\partial x_i} \frac{\partial v}{\partial x_j} + \sum_{i=1}^{d} \bar{b}_i(x) \frac{\partial u}{\partial x_i} v + c(x)uv \right) dx,$$

where the coefficients of B_R are defined by (8.8). *If the assumptions of Theorem* 8.26 *are fulfilled, the value function $V_K(t,x)$ for $K = R$ is a unique solution of the following variational inequality*

$$\begin{aligned} &- \int_0^T \left(\frac{du}{dt}(t), v(t) - u(t) \right)_{L^2(U_R)} dt + \int_0^T B_R[u(t), v(t) - u(t)]dt \geq 0, \\ &u(t) \geq g, \quad a.e.\ t \in [0,T], \\ &u(T) = g, \\ &u(t) = g, \quad on \quad \partial U_R, t \in [0,T], \end{aligned} \tag{8.16}$$

which holds for $v \in L^2(0,T; H^1(U_R))$, $dv/dt \in L^2(0,T; H^{-1}(U_R))$ and $v(t) \geq g$ for almost all $t \in [0,T]$, with $u \in L^2(0,T; H^1(U_R))$ and $du/dt \in L^2(0,T; L^2(U_R))$.

Remark 8.28. Restricting considerations to a bounded set U_R, we must complement the problem with boundary conditions on ∂U_R. In general, we can impose $u(t) = g_0$ on ∂U_R, where g_0 is an arbitrary function such that $g_0 \geq g$. The result of Theorem 8.26 justifies any boundary condition. By this theorem, the behavior of the solution near the distant boundary ∂U_R does not affect the solution on any fixed bounded region in the limit $R \to \infty$. Therefore, any well-posed problem on U_R can be an approximation of the original problem on $\mathbb{R}^d$ provided R is sufficiently large. The choice $g_0 \equiv g$ is the simplest possible choice.

8.3.1 *Discrete variational inequalities*

We now construct a numerical algorithm approximating variational inequality (8.16). A large part of this section follows the ideas of the book by Glowinski *et al.* [35]. However, the proofs are slightly different because we use finite differences instead of finite elements used in Ref. [35]. For simplicity, we consider only a one-dimensional problem with constant coefficients. Without loss of generality, we assume $U_R = (-1, 1)$ with boundary conditions $u(t, -1) = g(-1)$, $u(t, 1) = g(1)$. We consider the bilinear form

$$B_R[u, v] = \int_{U_R} \left(a^2 \frac{\partial u}{\partial x} \frac{\partial v}{\partial x} + b \frac{\partial u}{\partial x} v + cuv \right) dx, \tag{8.17}$$

generated by the operator

$$\mathcal{A}u = -a^2 \frac{\partial^2 u}{\partial x^2} + b \frac{\partial u}{\partial x} + cu. \tag{8.18}$$

Under the conditions discussed at the beginning of this section, we have

$$B_R[u, u] \geq \beta \|u\|^2_{H^1(U_R)},$$
$$|B_R[u, v]| \leq \alpha \|u\|_{H^1(U_R)} \|v\|_{H^1(U_R)}.$$

We approximate operator $-\partial/\partial t + \mathcal{A}$ by finite differences in time and space. We divide $[-1, 1]$ into M subintervals of length $\delta x = 2/M$ and the time interval $[0, T]$ into N subintervals of length $\delta t = T/N$. With grid points $x_k = -1 + k\delta x$, $k = 0, \ldots, M$, we define a grid function $v_M = (v_{(0)}, \ldots, v_{(M)})$ which is an $(M + 1)$-dimensional vector. Similarly, taking $t_n = n\delta t$, $n = 0, \ldots, N$, we define a grid function $v_{N,M} = (v_M^{(0)}, \ldots, v_M^{(N)})$ in both time and spatial variables. We write v_M for a vector and $v_{(k)}$ for its components if we consider a grid function only in the spatial variable. The notation $v_{N,M}$ and $v_{(k)}^{(n)}$ is used for a vector and its entries in the case of a grid function in the time and spatial variables.

To define a finite difference approximation of $-\partial/\partial t + \mathcal{A}$, we approximate the derivatives by finite differences. The finite difference operators in the x directions are extensions of the operators defined in Section 6.5. The first-order operator δ_x is acting on a grid function v_M by central differences

$$(\delta_x v_M)_k = \frac{v_{(k+1)} - v_{(k-1)}}{2\delta x}$$

and similarly, the second-order operator

$$(\delta_{xx} v_M)_k = \frac{v_{(k+1)} - 2v_{(k)} + v_{(k-1)}}{(\delta x)^2}.$$

The derivative with respect to time is approximated by forward differences

$$(\delta_t v_{N,M})^{(n)} = \frac{v_M^{(n+1)} - v_M^{(n)}}{\delta t}.$$

Definition 8.29. With the above definitions of finite difference operators, we define the following spaces for grid functions in spatial variables:

$$L_M^2 = \left\{ v_M = (v_{(k)})_{k=0}^M \colon \sum_{k=1}^{M-1} |v_{(k)}|^2 < +\infty \right\}$$

with the norm

$$\|v_M\|_{L_M^2}^2 = \sum_{k=0}^{M} \delta x |v_{(k)}|^2,$$

and

$$H_M^1 = \left\{ v_M = (v_{(k)})_{k=0}^M \colon \sum_{k=0}^{M} \left| \frac{v_{(k+1)} - v_{(k-1)}}{2\delta x} \right|^2 < +\infty \right\}$$

with the norm (assuming $v_{-1} = v_{M+1} = 0$)

$$\|v_M\|_{H_M^1}^2 = \sum_{k=0}^{M} \delta x |v_{(k)}|^2 + \sum_{k=0}^{M} \delta x \left| \frac{v_{(k+1)} - v_{(k-1)}}{2\delta x} \right|^2.$$

Similarly, we define the L^2-type spaces for grid functions in time and space

$$L_N^2(0,T; L_M^2) = \left\{ v_{N,M} = (v_M^{(n)})_{n=0}^N \colon \sum_{n=0}^{N} \sum_{k=0}^{M} |v_{(k)}^{(n)}|^2 < +\infty \right\}$$

with the norm

$$\|v_{N,M}\|_{L_N^2(L_M^2)}^2 = \sum_{n=0}^{N} \sum_{k=0}^{M} \delta t \delta x |v_{(k)}^{(n)}|^2,$$

and

$$L_N^2(0,T;H_M^1)$$
$$= \left\{ v_{N,M} = (v_M^{(n)})_{n=0}^N \colon \sum_{n=0}^{N}\sum_{k=1}^{M-1} \left| \frac{v_{(k+1)}^{(n)} - v_{(k-1)}^{(n)}}{2\delta x} \right|^2 < +\infty \right\}$$

with the norm (similarly as previously assuming $v_{-1} = v_{M+1} = 0$)

$$\|v_{N,M}\|^2_{L_N^2(H_M^1)} = \sum_{n=0}^{N}\sum_{k=0}^{M} \delta t \delta x |v_{(k)}^{(n)}|^2 + \sum_{n=0}^{N}\sum_{k=0}^{M} \delta t \delta x \left| \frac{v_{(k+1)}^{(n)} - v_{(k-1)}^{(n)}}{2\delta x} \right|^2.$$

We now define matrix Λ, which is a discrete approximation of operator $\mathcal{A}$.

Definition 8.30. Let Λ be an $(M+1)\times(M+1)$-dimensional matrix acting on grid functions v_M by the formula

$$(\Lambda v_M)_{(k)} = -a^2(\delta_{xx} v_M)_{(k)} + b(\delta_x v_M)_{(k)} + c(v_M)_{(k)},$$
$$k = 1, \ldots, M-1,$$
$$(\Lambda v_M)_{(0)} = v_{(0)}, \quad (\Lambda v_M)_{(M)} = v_{(M)}.$$

Then for $v_M, w_M \in H_M^1$, we define

$$(\Lambda v_M, w_M)_{L_M^2} = \sum_{k=0}^{M} \delta x (\Lambda v_M)_{(k)} w_{(k)}$$

as an approximation of the bilinear form $B_R[v,w]$.

By elementary computations, we obtain the analogous estimates as for $B_R[v,w]$

$$|(\Lambda v_M, w_M)_{L_M^2}| \le \alpha \|v_M\|_{H_M^1} \|w_M\|_{H_M^1},$$
$$(\Lambda v_M, v_M)_{L_M^2} \ge \beta \|v_M\|^2_{H_M^1}.$$

Our goal is to prove that the grid functions obtained by solving an appropriate discrete variational inequality converge to a solution of the continuous variational inequality (8.16). This requires an extension of grid functions to functions defined on $[0, T] \times U_R$. For this purpose, we use a piecewise constant extension.

Let $\chi(x_k)$ denote the characteristic function of interval $(x_k - \delta x/2, x_k + \delta x/2)$ and $\chi(t_n)$, the characteristic function of interval $(t_n - \delta t/2, t_n + \delta t/2)$, with obvious modifications for $\chi(x_0)$, $\chi(x_M)$, $\chi(t_0)$, and $\chi(t_N)$. Then we define the step functions

$$\hat{v}_{N,M} = \sum_{n=0}^{N} \sum_{k=0}^{M} v_{(k)}^{(n)} \chi(x_k) \chi(t_n) \tag{8.19}$$

and

$$\hat{v}_M^{(n)} = \sum_{k=0}^{M} v_{(k)}^{(n)} \chi(x_k).$$

The following technical lemma summarizes the essential properties of these step functions.

Lemma 8.31. *Let $v \in L^2(0, T; H^1(U_R))$ and $dv/dt \in L^2(0, T; H^{-1}(U_R))$. For a family of grids defined by uniform partitions of U_R with steps $\delta x \to 0$ and $[0, T]$ with steps $\delta t \to 0$ there exists a sequence of grid functions $v_{N,M}$ such that for the corresponding piecewise constant extensions $\hat{v}_{N,M}$, we have the following convergences for $\delta x, \delta t \to 0$:*

$$\begin{aligned} &\hat{v}_{N,M} \to v \quad \text{in } L^2(0, T; L^2(U_R)), \\ &(\delta_x v_{N,M})^{\curlyvee} \to Dv \quad \text{in } L^2(0, T; L^2(U_R)), \\ &(\delta_t v_{N,M})^{\curlyvee} \to \frac{dv}{dt} \quad \text{in } L^2(0, T; H^{-1}(U_R)). \end{aligned}$$

Here, we write Dv (despite the one-dimensionality of v) to stress that the derivative is in the weak sense.

Proof. Assuming $v \in H^1(U_R)$, we prove that there exists a sequence of grid functions v_M such that $\hat{v}_M \to v$ in $L^2(U_R)$ and $(\delta_x v_M)^{\curlyvee} \to Dv$ in $L^2(U_R)$.

Since a function in $H^1(U_R)$ can be approximated by a sequence of C^∞ functions (cf. Theorem 5.16), the proof can be reduced to

$v \in C^\infty(\bar{U}_R)$. For a C^∞ function v, a weak derivative is a classical derivative denoted by v'.

Let x_k, $k = 0, \ldots, M$, be grid points in U_R. We define the grid function $v_M = (v_{(0)}, \ldots, v_{(M)})$ by the localization of v

$$v_{(k)} = v(x_k).$$

Then there exists a sequence of grid functions v_M such that the step functions $\hat{v}_M$ converge uniformly to v on U_R. Since v is a continuous function on a compact set, this function is uniformly continuous. Hence, for a given $\varepsilon > 0$, there exists a grid step $\delta x = h_1$ such that

$$|v(x) - v(x_k)| < \varepsilon \quad \text{for} \quad |x - x_k| < h_1.$$

Then

$$\sup_{U_R} |\hat{v}_M - v| < \varepsilon$$

for grid step h_1. This proves the uniform convergence of $\hat{v}_M$ to v on U_R.

Next, we prove that there exists a grid step h_2 such that $(\delta_x v_M)\hat{}$ converge uniformly to v' on U_R.

By the Taylor expansion, we have

$$\left| \frac{v(x_k + h_2) - v(x_k)}{h_2} - v'(x_k) \right| \leq \frac{1}{2} h_2 |v''(x_k + \theta h_2)| \leq C h_2^2,$$

where $C = 1/2 \sup_{U_R} |v''|$.

Let v'_M denote the localization of v'. Then the above Taylor estimate yields

$$\sup_{U_R} \left| (\delta_x v_M)\hat{} - \hat{v}'_M \right| \leq C h_2 < \varepsilon/2$$

for $h_2 < \varepsilon/(2C)$.

Because v' is uniformly continuous on U_R, for sufficiently small h_2, we have

$$\sup_{U_R} |\hat{v}'_M - v'| < \varepsilon/2.$$

Together, these estimates prove the uniform convergence of $(\delta_x v_M)\hat{}$ to v' on U_R.

The proof of convergence $(\delta_t v_{N,M})\hat{} \to dv/dt$ is analogous and is omitted. $\square$

Remark 8.32. We cannot obtain $\hat{v}_{N,M} \to v$ in $L^2(0,T;H^1(U_R))$ since $\hat{v}_{N,M}$ is not in $H^1(U_R)$. This is the reason why we separately consider the convergence of $\hat{v}_{N,M}$ to v and $(\delta_x v_{N,M})\hat{}$ to Dv.

The consistency of finite difference approximations requires a slightly different definition than in Chapter 6.

Definition 8.33. We say that the finite-dimensional bilinear form $(Av_M, w_M)_{L^2_M}$ defined by matrix A is consistent with the bilinear form $B[v,w]$ associated with a second-order uniformly elliptic operator $\mathcal{A}$ in divergence form if for each $v_M, w_M \in H^1_M$ and their piecewise constant extensions $\hat{v}_M, \hat{w}_M$ the convergences

$$\hat{v}_M \rightharpoonup v, \quad (\delta_x v_M)\hat{} \rightharpoonup Dv \text{ weakly in } L^2(U_R),$$
$$\hat{w}_M \to w, \quad (\delta_x w_M)\hat{} \to Dw \text{ strongly in } L^2(U_R)$$

for $\delta x \to 0$ imply the following convergence

$$(A\hat{v}_M, \hat{w}_M)_{L^2(U_R)} \to B[v,w],$$
$$(A\hat{w}_M, \hat{v}_M)_{L^2(U_R)} \to B[w,v].$$

With some abuse of notation, we write $A\hat{v}_M$ understanding this expression as the abbreviation of $(Av_M)\hat{}$.

Lemma 8.34. *The bilinear form $(\Lambda v_M, w_M)_{L^2_M}$ defined by matrix Λ of Definition 8.30 is consistent in the sense of the above definition with the bilinear form $B_R[v,w]$ given by (8.17).*

In addition, for $v_{N,M} \in L^2_N(0,T;H^1_M)$ such that for $\delta t, \delta x \to 0$

$$\hat{v}_{N,M} \rightharpoonup v, \quad (\delta_x v_{N,M})\hat{} \rightharpoonup Dv \textit{ weakly in } L^2(0,T;L^2(U_R)),$$

we have

$$\liminf_{\delta t,\delta x \to 0} \int_0^T (\Lambda\hat{v}_{N,M}, \hat{v}_{N,M})_{L^2(U_R)} dt \geq \int_0^T B_R[v,v]dt. \tag{8.20}$$

Proof. By elementary computations, we get (with natural modifications for $k = 0$ and $k = M$)

$$-(\delta_{xx}v_M)w_M = -\sum_{k=0}^{M} \frac{1}{\delta x}\Big(\frac{v_{(k+1)} - v_{(k)}}{\delta x} - \frac{v_{(k)} - v_{(k-1)}}{\delta x}\Big)w_{(k)}$$

$$= \sum_{k=0}^{M} \frac{v_{(k)} - v_{(k-1)}}{\delta x}\frac{w_{(k)} - w_{(k-1)}}{\delta x}.$$

The above identity gives

$$\int_{U_R} -(\delta_{xx}\hat{v}_M)\hat{w}_M dx = \int_{U_R} (\delta_x\hat{v}_M)(\delta_x\hat{w}_M)dx,$$

which enables the rewriting of $(\Lambda\hat{v}_M, \hat{w}_M)_{L^2(U_R)}$ as the bilinear form

$$(\Lambda\hat{v}_M, \hat{w}_M)_{L^2(U_R)}$$
$$= \int_{U_R} \big(a^2(\delta_x\hat{v}_M)(\delta_x\hat{w}_M) + b(\delta_x\hat{v}_M)\hat{w}_M + c\hat{v}_M\hat{w}_M\big)\, dx.$$

Let now $\hat{v}_M$ and $\hat{w}_M$ be sequences that fulfill the conditions of Definition 8.33. Then $(\Lambda\hat{v}_M, \hat{w}_M)_{L^2(U_R)}$ and $(\Lambda\hat{w}_M, \hat{v}_M)_{L^2(U_R)}$ can be expressed in terms of the above bilinear form as linear combinations of scalar products (u_n^1, u_m^2) in $L^2(U_R)$, where u_n^1 is a sequence weakly convergent to u^1 and u_m^2, a sequence strongly convergent to u^2. From the definitions of weak and strong convergence, we have

$$(u_n^1, u_m^2)_{L^2(U_R)} \to (u^1, u_m^2)_{L^2(U_R)} \to (u^1, u^2)_{L^2(U_R)}.$$

This proves the consistency of $(\Lambda v_m, w_M)_{L^2_M}$ with $B_R[v, w]$.

The proof of (8.20) follows from the definition of weak convergence and the Fatou lemma

$$\liminf_{\delta t, \delta x \to 0} \int_0^T \Big((\Lambda\hat{v}_{N,M}, \hat{v}_{N,M})_{L^2(U_R)} - (\Lambda\hat{v}_{N,M}, v)_{L^2(U_R)}\Big)dt$$

$$\geq \liminf_{\delta t, \delta x \to 0} \int_0^T \Big((\Lambda v, \hat{v}_{N,M})_{L^2(U_R)} - B_R[v, v]\Big)dt.$$

Then

$$\liminf_{\delta t,\delta x\to 0}\int_0^T (\Lambda\hat{v}_{N,M},\hat{v}_{N,M})_{L^2(U_R)}dt$$

$$\geq \liminf_{\delta t,\delta x\to 0}\int_0^T \Big((\Lambda\hat{v}_{N,M},v)_{L^2(U_R)} + (\Lambda v,\hat{v}_{N,M})_{L^2(U_R)} - B_R[v,v]\Big)dt$$

$$\geq \int_0^T B_R[v,v]dt,$$

which ends the proof. □

We approximate the variational inequality (8.16) by finite differences applying the θ-scheme in time. Finite differences in spatial variables create additional difficulties in the proof of convergence as $\hat{v}_M$ is not in $H^1(U_R)$. In one dimension, we can omit this difficulty by using finite elements, which are in $H^1(U_R)$. We decided to carry on the proof for finite differences in a way that can be easily extended to the finite element approximation in a multidimensional case when $\hat{v}_M$ is not in $H^1(U_R)$. In this way, we obtain simultaneously the proof for finite differences and finite elements.

Definition 8.35. Let $g_h = (g_{(0)},\ldots,g_{(M)})$, $g_{(k)} = g(x_k)$, be an approximation of reward function g. The *finite difference approximation* $w_{N,M}$ of the variational inequality (8.16) is defined recursively by the following θ-scheme:

(i) $w_M^{(N)} = g_h$;

(ii) knowing $w_M^{(n+1)} \in H_M^1$, $w_M^{(n+1)} \geq g_h$, find $w_M^{(n)} \in H_M^1$, $w_M^{(n)} \geq g_h$, $n = N-1,\ldots,0$, such that for all $v_M \in H_M^1$, $v_M \geq g_h$,

$$\Big(w_M^{(n+1)} - w_M^{(n)} - \delta t\Lambda\big((1-\theta)w_M^{(n+1)} + \theta w_M^{(n)}\big), v_M - w_M^{(n)}\Big)_{L_M^2} \leq 0. \tag{8.21}$$

Since the iterations go downwards, then $\theta = 1$ corresponds to the fully implicit scheme.

Let us assume, for a moment, that the recursion of the above definition possesses a unique solution. The existence of this solution can be proved by constructing a relevant numerical algorithm (cf. Theorems 8.40 and 8.42). Our goal is to prove that $w_{N,M}$ given by

(8.21) converges to a solution of (8.16). We begin by proving the stability of the finite difference approximation.

Theorem 8.36. *Let operator* Λ *fulfill the conditions of Definition* 8.30. *Then* $w_{N,M}$, *a solution of the discrete variational inequality* (8.21), *has the following estimate, for* $(1-\theta)\delta t(\delta x)^{-2}$ *small enough,*

$$\begin{aligned}\max_{0\le n\le N}\left\|w_M^{(n)}-g_h\right\|_{L_M^2}^2&+C\sum_{n=0}^{N-1}\left\|w_M^{(n+1)}-w_M^{(n)}\right\|_{L_M^2}^2\\&+C\sum_{n=0}^{N}\delta t\left\|w_M^{(n)}\right\|_{H_M^1}^2\\&\le CT\|g_h\|_{H_M^1}^2.\end{aligned}$$

Proof. Inserting $v_M=g_h$ into (8.21), we have

$$\begin{aligned}&\left(w_M^{(n+1)}-w_M^{(n)},g_h-w_M^{(n)}\right)_{L_M^2}\\&\quad-\delta t\left(\Lambda\left((1-\theta)w_M^{(n+1)}+\theta w_M^{(n)}\right),g_h-w_M^{(n)}\right)_{L_M^2}\le 0.\end{aligned}\tag{8.22}$$

By the identities

$$\begin{aligned}&\left(w_M^{(n+1)}-w_M^{(n)},g_h-w_M^{(n)}\right)_{L_M^2}\\&\quad=\frac{1}{2}\left(\left\|w_M^{(n)}-g_h\right\|_{L_M^2}^2+\left\|w_M^{(n+1)}-w_M^{(n)}\right\|_{L_M^2}^2-\left\|w_M^{(n+1)}-g_h\right\|_{L_M^2}^2\right),\end{aligned}$$

$$\begin{aligned}&\left(\Lambda\left((1-\theta)w_M^{(n+1)}+\theta w_M^{(n)}\right),w_M^{(n)}\right)_{L_M^2}=\theta\left(\Lambda w_M^{(n)},w_M^{(n)}\right)_{L_M^2}\\&\quad+(1-\theta)\left(\Lambda w_M^{(n+1)},w_M^{(n+1)}\right)_{L_M^2}\\&\quad-(1-\theta)\left(\Lambda w_M^{(n+1)},w_M^{(n+1)}-w_M^{(n)}\right)_{L_M^2},\end{aligned}$$

and the estimates of Definition 8.30, we obtain from (8.22)

$$\left\|w_M^{(n)} - g_h\right\|_{L_M^2}^2 + \left\|w_M^{(n+1)} - w_M^{(n)}\right\|_{L_M^2}^2 + 2\delta t\theta\beta\left\|w_M^{(n)}\right\|_{H_M^1}^2$$
$$+ 2\delta t(1-\theta)\beta\left\|w_M^{(n+1)}\right\|_{H_M^1}^2$$
$$\leq \left\|w_M^{(n+1)} - g_h\right\|_{L_M^2}^2 + 2\delta t(1-\theta)\alpha\left\|w_M^{(n+1)}\right\|_{H_M^1}\left\|w_M^{(n+1)} - w_M^{(n)}\right\|_{H_M^1}$$
$$+ 2\delta t\alpha\Big((1-\theta)\left\|w_M^{(n+1)}\right\|_{H_M^1} + \theta\left\|w_M^{(n)}\right\|_{H_M^1}\Big)\|g_h\|_{H_M^1}.$$

Since

$$\|v\|_{H_M^1} \leq C_0(\delta x)^{-1}\|v\|_{L_M^2}, \tag{8.23}$$

then using the Cauchy inequality, we obtain

$$\left\|w_M^{(n)} - g_h\right\|_{L_M^2}^2 + \left(1 - \frac{C_0^2}{\varepsilon}(1-\theta)\alpha\delta t(\delta x)^{-2}\right)\left\|w_M^{(n+1)} - w_M^{(n)}\right\|_{L_M^2}^2$$
$$+ 2\delta t\theta(\beta - \alpha\varepsilon)\left\|w_M^{(n)}\right\|_{H_M^1}^2 + 2\delta t(1-\theta)(\beta - 2\alpha\varepsilon)\left\|w_M^{(n+1)}\right\|_{H_M^1}^2$$
$$\leq \delta t\frac{\alpha}{\varepsilon}\|g_h\|_{H_M^1}^2 + \|w_M^{(n+1)} - g_h\|_{L_M^2}^2.$$

Taking $\delta t(\delta x)^{-2}$ such small that $\left(1 - C_0^2(1-\theta)\alpha\varepsilon^{-1}\delta t(\delta x)^{-2}\right) \geq \gamma > 0$, and ε such that $2\alpha\varepsilon < \beta$, we obtain

$$\left\|w_M^{(n)} - g_h\right\|_{L_M^2}^2 + \gamma\left\|w_M^{(n+1)} - w_M^{(n)}\right\|_{L_M^2}^2$$
$$+ C\delta t\left\|w_M^{(n)}\right\|_{H_M^1}^2 + C\delta t\left\|w_M^{(n+1)}\right\|_{H_M^1}^2$$
$$\leq C\delta t\|g_h\|_{H_M^1}^2 + \left\|w_M^{(n+1)} - g_h\right\|_{L_M^2}^2.$$

Summing the above inequality from N down to $m \geq 0$, we obtain

$$\left\|w_M^{(m)} - g_h\right\|_{L_M^2}^2 + \gamma\sum_{n=m}^{N-1}\left\|w_M^{(n+1)} - w_M^{(n)}\right\|_{L_M^2}^2$$
$$+ C\sum_{n=m}^{N-1}\delta t\|w_M^{(n+1)}\|_{H_M^1}^2 + C\sum_{n=m}^{N}\delta t\|w_M^{(n)}\|_{H_M^1}^2$$
$$\leq CT\|g_h\|_{H_M^1}^2.$$

□

In the proof of convergence, we use the weak formulation of variational inequalities. The theorem below shows that the weak discrete formulation follows from the strong formulation, the result analogous to Theorem 8.20.

Theorem 8.37. *Let $w_{N,M}$ be a solution of the strong formulation of the discrete variational inequality*

$$\begin{aligned}
&\sum_{n=0}^{N-1} -\delta t\Big(\frac{w_M^{(n+1)} - w_M^{(n)}}{\delta t}, v_M^{(n)} - w_M^{(n)}\Big)_{L_M^2} \\
&\qquad + \sum_{n=0}^{N-1} \delta t\Big(\Lambda\big((1-\theta)w_M^{(n+1)} + \theta w_M^{(n)}\big), v_M^{(n)} - w_M^{(n)}\Big)_{L_M^2} \geq 0, \\
&w_M^{(n)} \geq g_h, \quad n = 0, \dots, N, \\
&w_M^{(N)} = g_h,
\end{aligned}$$

for each $v_{N,M}$ such that $v_M^{(n)} \in H_M^1$ and $v_M^{(n)} \geq g_h$, $n = 0, \dots, N$.
Then $w_{N,M}$ solves the following weak formulation

$$\begin{aligned}
&\sum_{n=0}^{N-1} -\delta t\Big(\frac{v_M^{(n+1)} - v_M^{(n)}}{\delta t}, v_M^{(n)} - w_M^{(n)}\Big)_{L_M^2} \\
&\qquad + \sum_{n=0}^{N-1} \delta t\Big(\Lambda\big((1-\theta)w_M^{(n+1)} + \theta w_M^{(n)}\big), v_M^{(n)} - w_M^{(n)}\Big)_{L_M^2} \\
&\qquad \geq -\frac{1}{2}\|v_M^{(N)} - w_M^{(N)}\|_{L_M^2}, \\
&w_M^{(n)} \geq g_h, \quad n = 0, \dots, N, \\
&w_M^{(N)} = g_h,
\end{aligned}$$

for each $v_{N,M}$ as above.

Theorem 8.38. *Let $w_{N,M}$ be a sequence of solutions of the discrete variational inequality (8.21) for δt and δx tending to zero ($N, M \to \infty$). Let u be a unique solution of the continuous variational inequality (8.16) with the bilinear form $B_R[u, v]$ defined by (8.17). Let $\hat{w}_{N,M}$ denote a piecewise constant extension of $w_{N,M}$.*

Then for $(1-\theta)\delta t(\delta x)^{-2} \to 0$ *as* δt, δx *go to zero, we obtain the convergence*

$$\begin{aligned} &\hat{w}_{N,M} \to u \quad \text{in } L^2(0,T;L^2(U_R)),\\ &(\delta_x w_{N,M})\check{} \to Du \quad \text{in } L^2(0,T;L^2(U_R)). \end{aligned}$$

Proof. From the stability results of Theorem 8.36 follow the boundedness of sequence $\hat{w}_{N,M}$. This sequence contains a weakly convergent subsequence, which we also denote $\hat{w}_{N,M}$. Let

$$\begin{aligned} &\hat{w}_{N,M} \rightharpoonup w \text{ in } L^2(0,T;L^2(U_R)),\\ &(\delta_x w_{N,M})\check{} \rightharpoonup Dw \text{ in } L^2(0,T;L^2(U_R)). \end{aligned}$$

Our goal is to prove that w solves the variational inequality (8.16) with $B_R[u,v]$ defined by (8.17). We take $v \in L^2(0,T;H^1(U_R))$ such that $dv/dt \in L^2(0,T;H^{-1}(U_R))$, $v(T) = g$, and $v(t) \geq g$ for $t \in [0,T)$. Let $\hat{v}_{N,M}$ be a sequence of piecewise constant approximations of v that exists due to Lemma 8.31. Inserting $v_{N,M}$ into the weak inequality of Theorem 8.37, we obtain

$$\begin{aligned} &\sum_{n=0}^{N-1} -\delta t\Big(\frac{v_M^{(n+1)} - v_M^{(n)}}{\delta t}, v_M^{(n)} - w_M^{(n)}\Big)_{L_M^2}\\ &\quad + \sum_{n=0}^{N-1} \delta t\Big(\Lambda((1-\theta)w_M^{(n+1)} + \theta w_M^{(n)}), v_M^{(n)} - w_M^{(n)}\Big)_{L_M^2} \geq 0. \end{aligned}$$

After a rearrangement, we have

$$\begin{aligned} &\sum_{n=0}^{N-1} -\delta t\left(\frac{v_M^{(n+1)} - v_M^{(n)}}{\delta t}, v_M^{(n)} - w_M^{(n)}\right)_{L_M^2}\\ &\quad + \sum_{n=0}^{N-1} \delta t\Big(\Lambda w_M^{(n)}, v_M^{(n)} - w_M^{(n)}\Big)_{L_M^2}\\ &\quad \geq (1-\theta)\sum_{n=0}^{N-1} \delta t\Big(\Lambda(w_M^{(n)} - w_M^{(n+1)}), v_M^{(n)} - w_M^{(n)}\Big)_{L_M^2}. \end{aligned} \tag{8.24}$$

Since $\hat{w}_{N,M}$ converges to w weakly, then due to Lemma 8.34, we have

$$\liminf_{\delta t,\delta x\to 0}\int_0^T \left(\Lambda\hat{w}_{N,M},\hat{w}_{N,M}\right)_{L^2(U_R)}dt \geq \int_0^T B_R[w,w]dt.$$

Because $\hat{v}_{N,M}\to v$ and $(\delta_t v_{N,M})\check{}\to dv/dt$ strongly, then passing to the limit $\delta t,\delta x\to 0$ on the left-hand side of (8.24) (with the change from $v_{N,M}$ and $w_{N,M}$ to $\hat{v}_{N,M}$ and $\hat{w}_{N,M}$) and using the consistency results of Definition 8.33, one gets

$$\begin{aligned}\int_0^T -\left\langle \frac{dv}{dt}(t),v(t)-w(t)\right\rangle dt + \int_0^T B_R\big[w(t),v(t)-w(t)\big]dt\\ \geq \limsup_{\delta t,\delta x\to 0}(1-\theta)\sum_{n=0}^{N-1}\delta t\Big(\Lambda\big(w_M^{(n)}-w_M^{(n+1)}\big),v_M^{(n)}-w_M^{(n)}\Big)_{L_M^2}.\end{aligned}$$

It remains to prove that

$$X_{N,M}=(1-\theta)\sum_{n=0}^{N-1}\delta t\Big(\Lambda\big(w_M^{(n)}-w_M^{(n+1)}\big),v_M^{(n)}-w_M^{(n)}\Big)_{L_M^2}$$

tends to zero.

Due to the estimates of Definition 8.30 and (8.23), we obtain

$$\begin{aligned}|X_{N,M}| &\leq (1-\theta)\alpha\sum_{n=0}^{N-1}\delta t\|(w_M^{(n)}-w_M^{(n+1)}\|_{H_M^1}\|v_M^{(n)}-w_M^{(n)}\|_{H_M^1}\\ &\leq C_0(1-\theta)\alpha(\delta x)^{-1}\\ &\quad\times\sum_{n=0}^{N-1}\delta t\|(w_M^{(n)}-w_M^{(n+1)}\|_{L_M^2}\|v_M^{(n)}-w_M^{(n)}\|_{H_M^1}\\ &\leq C_0(1-\theta)\alpha(\delta x)^{-1}(\delta t)^{1/2}\left(\sum_{n=0}^{N-1}\|(w_M^{(n)}-w_M^{(n+1)}\|_{L_M^2}^2\right)^{1/2}\\ &\quad\times\left(\sum_{n=0}^{N-1}\delta t\|v_M^{(n)}-w_M^{(n)}\|_{H_M^1}^2\right)^{1/2}.\end{aligned}$$

The term

$$\sum_{n=0}^{N-1} \|(w_M^{(n)} - w_M^{(n+1)}\|_{L_M^2}^2$$

is bounded due to Theorem 8.36. Since $v_{N,M}, w_{N,M} \in L_N^2(0,T;H_M^1)$, the term

$$\sum_{n=0}^{N-1} \delta t \|v_M^{(n)} - w_M^{(n)}\|_{H_M^1}^2$$

is also bounded.

Since $(1-\theta)(\delta x)^{-2}\delta t \to 0$ for $\delta t, \delta x \to 0$, then $X_{N,M} \to 0$ and we have

$$\int_0^T -\left\langle \frac{dv}{dt}(t), v(t) - w(t) \right\rangle dt + \int_0^T B_R\big[w(t), v(t) - w(t)\big] dt \geq 0.$$

This proves that w is a solution of the weak formulation of variational inequality (8.13). Due to Theorem 8.22, a solution of the weak variational inequality (8.13) is also a solution of the strong variational inequality (8.16). Since (8.16) possesses a unique solution, then $w \equiv u$.

We must prove that the convergence of $\hat{w}_{N,M}$ to u and $(\delta_x w_{N,M})\hat{}$ to Du is strong in $L^2(0,T;L^2(U_R))$. Let $\hat{u}_{N,M}$ be a piecewise constant approximation of u which exists due to Lemma 8.31. We show that

$$Y_{N,M} = \sum_{n=0}^{N} \delta t \big(\Lambda w_M^{(n)} - \Lambda u_M^{(n)}, w_M^{(n)} - u_M^{(n)}\big)_{L_M^2}$$

converges to zero for $\delta x, \delta t \to 0$.

Taking $v_{N,M} = u_{N,M}$ in the weak variational inequality of Theorem 8.37, we obtain (observe that $u(T) = g$)

$$\begin{aligned} &\sum_{n=0}^{N-1} \delta t \Big(\Lambda\big((1-\theta)w_M^{(n+1)} + \theta w_M^{(n)}\big), w_M^{(n)}\Big)_{L_M^2} \\ &\quad\leq \sum_{n=0}^{N-1} -\delta t \left(\frac{u_M^{(n+1)} - u_M^{(n)}}{\delta t}, u_M^{(n)} - w_M^{(n)}\right)_{L_M^2} \qquad (8.25) \\ &\qquad + \sum_{n=0}^{N-1} \delta t \Big(\Lambda\big((1-\theta)w_M^{(n+1)} + \theta w_M^{(n)}\big), u_M^{(n)}\Big)_{L_M^2}. \end{aligned}$$

Since

$$\begin{aligned} Y_{N,M} = &\sum_{n=0}^{N} \delta t\big(\Lambda w_M^{(n)}, w_M^{(n)}\big)_{L_M^2} - \sum_{n=0}^{N} \delta t\big(\Lambda w_M^{(n)}, u_M^{(n)}\big)_{L_M^2} \\ &+ \sum_{n=0}^{N} \delta t\big(\Lambda u_M^{(n)}, u_M^{(n)} - w_M^{(n)}\big)_{L_M^2} \end{aligned} \tag{8.26}$$

and

$$\begin{aligned} &\sum_{n=0}^{N-1} \delta t\Big(\Lambda\big((1-\theta)w_M^{(n+1)} + \theta w_M^{(n)}\big), w_M^{(n)}\Big)_{L_M^2} \\ &\qquad + (1-\theta)\sum_{n=0}^{N-1} \delta t\Big(\Lambda w_M^{(n)} - \Lambda w_M^{(n+1)}, w_M^{(n)}\Big)_{L_M^2} \\ &= \sum_{n=0}^{N-1} \delta t\Big(\Lambda w_M^{(n)}, w_M^{(n)}\Big)_{L_M^2}, \end{aligned} \tag{8.27}$$

we can insert (8.25) and (8.27) into (8.26) to obtain

$$\begin{aligned} Y_{N,M} \le &\sum_{n=0}^{N-1} -\delta t \left(\frac{u_M^{(n+1)} - u_M^{(n)}}{\delta t}, u_M^{(n)} - w_M^{(n)}\right)_{L_M^2} \\ &+ \sum_{n=0}^{N-1} \delta t\Big(\Lambda\big((1-\theta)w_M^{(n+1)} + \theta w_M^{(n)}\big), u_M^{(n)}\Big)_{L_M^2} \\ &+ (1-\theta)\sum_{n=0}^{N-1} \delta t\Big(\Lambda w_M^{(n)} - \Lambda w_M^{(n+1)}, w_M^{(n)}\Big)_{L_M^2} \\ &- \sum_{n=0}^{N} \delta t\big(\Lambda w_M^{(n)}, u_M^{(n)}\big)_{L_M^2} + \sum_{n=0}^{N} \delta t\big(\Lambda u_M^{(n)}, u_M^{(n)} - w_M^{(n)}\big)_{L_M^2}. \end{aligned}$$

Using the equality

$$(1-\theta)w_M^{(n+1)} + \theta w_M^{(n)} = w_M^{(n)} - (1-\theta)\big(w_M^{(n)} - w_M^{(n+1)}\big),$$

we obtain the estimate

$$Y_{N,M} \le \sum_{n=0}^{N-1} \delta t \left(-\frac{u_M^{(n+1)} - u_M^{(n)}}{\delta t} + \Lambda u_M^{(n)}, u_M^{(n)} - w_M^{(n)} \right)_{L_M^2}$$

$$- (1-\theta) \sum_{n=0}^{N-1} \delta t \left(\Lambda w_M^{(n)} - \Lambda w_M^{(n+1)}, u_M^{(n)} - w_M^{(n)} \right)_{L_M^2}.$$

We now prove that

$$Z := (1-\theta) \sum_{n=0}^{N-1} \delta t \left(\Lambda w_M^{(n)} - \Lambda w_M^{(n+1)}, u_M^{(n)} - w_M^{(n)} \right)_{L_M^2} \to 0.$$

From the estimates of Definition 8.30 and (8.23), we have

$$|Z| \le (1-\theta)\alpha \sum_{n=0}^{N-1} \delta t \left\| w_M^{(n)} - w_M^{(n+1)} \right\|_{H_M^1} \left\| u_M^{(n)} - w_M^{(n)} \right\|_{H_M^1}$$

$$\le C_0(1-\theta)\alpha(\delta x)^{-1} \sum_{n=0}^{N-1} \delta t \left\| w_M^{(n)} - w_M^{(n+1)} \right\|_{L_M^2} \left\| u_M^{(n)} - w_M^{(n)} \right\|_{H_M^1}$$

$$\le C(1-\theta)(\delta x)^{-1}(\delta t)^{1/2} \left(\sum_{n=0}^{N-1} \left\| w_M^{(n)} - w_M^{(n+1)} \right\|_{L_M^2}^2 \right)^{1/2}$$

$$\times \left(\sum_{n=0}^{N-1} \delta t \left\| u_M^{(n)} - w_M^{(n)} \right\|_{H_M^1}^2 \right)^{1/2}.$$

Similarly,

$$\sum_{n=0}^{N-1} \left\| w_M^{(n)} - w_M^{(n+1)} \right\|_{L_M^2}^2 < +\infty,$$

due to Theorem 8.36, and since $v_{N,M}, w_{N,M} \in L_N^2(0,T;H_M^1)$, then also

$$\sum_{n=0}^{N-1} \delta t \left\| u_M^{(n)} - w_M^{(n)} \right\|_{H_M^1}^2 < +\infty.$$

Since $(1-\theta)\delta t(\delta x)^{-2} \to 0$ for $\delta t, \delta x \to 0$, then $Z \to 0$.

The remaining expression

$$\sum_{n=0}^{N-1} \delta t \left(-\frac{u_M^{(n+1)} - u_M^{(n)}}{\delta t} + \Lambda u_M^{(n)}, u_M^{(n)} - w_M^{(n)} \right)_{L^2_M}$$

also converges to zero. Because $\hat{u}_{N,M} \to u$ strongly, hence, also weakly, and $\hat{w}_{N,M} \rightharpoonup u$ weakly, then $\hat{u}_{N,M} - \hat{w}_{N,M}$ converges to zero weakly. Since $(\delta_t u_{N,M})\check{} \to du/dt$ strongly, then

$$\sum_{n=0}^{N-1} \delta t \left(-\frac{u_M^{(n+1)} - u_M^{(n)}}{\delta t}, u_M^{(n)} - w_M^{(n)} \right)_{L^2_M} \to 0.$$

By the strong convergence $\hat{u}_{N,M} \to u$, the weak convergence $\hat{u}_{N,M} - \hat{w}_{N,M} \rightharpoonup 0$, and the consistency result of Lemma 8.34, we have

$$\begin{aligned} &\sum_{n=0}^{N} \delta t (\Lambda u_M^{(n)}, u_M^{(n)} - w_M^{(n)})_{L^2_M} \\ &\qquad = \int_0^T (\Lambda \hat{u}_{N,M}, \hat{u}_{N,M} - \hat{w}_{N,M})_{L^2(U_R)} dt \to 0. \end{aligned}$$

That proves $Y_{N,M} \to 0$ for $\delta t, \delta x \to 0$.

By the estimates of Definition 8.30 and the convergence $Y_{N,M} \to 0$

$$\sum_{n=0}^{N} \delta t (\Lambda w_M^{(n)} - \Lambda u_M^{(n)}, w_M^{(n)} - u_M^{(n)})_{L^2_M} dt \geq \beta \sum_{n=0}^{N} \delta t \| w_M^{(n)} - u_M^{(n)} \|^2_{H^1_M}.$$

Hence,

$$\int_0^T \| \hat{w}_{N,M} - \hat{u}_{N,M} \|^2_{L^2(U_R)} dt \to 0,$$

and

$$\int_0^T \| (\delta_x w_{N,M})\check{} - (\delta_x u_{N,M})\check{} \|^2_{L^2(U_R)} dt \to 0,$$

which gives the desired convergence

$$\begin{aligned} &\hat{w}_{N,M} \to u \text{ strongly in } \; L^2(0,T; L^2(U_R)), \\ &(\delta_x w_{N,M})\check{} \to Du \text{ strongly in } \; L^2(0,T; L^2(U_R)). \end{aligned}$$

□

8.3.2 *Projected SOR algorithm*

We begin by reformulating the discrete variational inequality (8.21) as a linear complementarity problem. The following lemma is a discrete version of Lemma 8.24.

Lemma 8.39. *Let $w_{N,M}$ be a solution of the discrete variational inequality of Definition 8.35. Then $w_{N,M}$ is a solution of the following discrete linear complementarity problem:*
knowing $w_M^{(n+1)} \in H_M^1$ such that $w_M^{(n+1)} \geq g_h$, find $w_M^{(n)} \in H_M^1$, $n = N-1, \ldots, 0$, such that for all $v_M \in H_M^1$, $v_M \geq 0$,

(i) $w_M^{(N)} = g_h$,

(ii) $\left(w_M^{(n+1)} - w_M^{(n)} - \delta t \Lambda\big((1-\theta) w_M^{(n+1)} + \theta w_M^{(n)}\big), v_M\right)_{L_M^2} \leq 0$,

(iii) $w_M^{(n)} \geq g_h$,

(iv) $\left(w_M^{(n+1)} - w_M^{(n)} - \delta t \Lambda\big((1-\theta) w_M^{(n+1)} + \theta w_M^{(n)}\big), g_h - w_M^{(n)}\right)_{L_M^2} = 0$.

By the above lemma, the solution of the discrete variational inequality is reduced to the solution of the linear problem at each time step $n = N-1, \ldots, 0$:

$$
\begin{aligned}
&QX \geq G, \\
&X \geq \Phi, \\
&(QX - G, X - \Phi) = 0,
\end{aligned}
\tag{8.28}
$$

where $(\cdot, \cdot)$ denotes the scalar product in $\mathbb{R}^{M+1} \equiv L_M^2$ and

$$
\begin{aligned}
Q &= I + \theta \delta t \Lambda, \\
X &= w_M^{(n)}, \\
G &= (I - (1-\theta)\delta t \Lambda) w_M^{(n+1)}, \\
\Phi &= g_h.
\end{aligned}
$$

Introducing new variables $Z = X - \Phi$ and $V = G - Q\Phi$, we rewrite the linear complementarity problem in the following form:
find $W = (W_k)_{k=0}^M$ and $Z = (Z_k)_{k=0}^M$ such that

$$\begin{aligned} &QZ - W = V, \\ &W \geq 0, \quad Z \geq 0, \\ &(W, Z) = 0. \end{aligned} \tag{8.29}$$

Theorem 8.40. *Let* Λ *fulfill the estimates of Definition* 8.30. *Then a solution of* (8.29) *is unique.*

Proof. Given the estimates of Definition 8.30, we have (δt is fixed)

$$C_1 \|v\|_{H_M^1}^2 \geq (Qv, v)_{L_M^2} \geq C_2 \|v\|_{H_M^1}^2.$$

Since now δx is fixed, the norms $\|\cdot\|_{L_M^2}$ and $\|\cdot\|_{H_M^1}$ are equivalent. Hence, Q is a bounded, positive definite matrix.

For proof simplicity, assume that Q is symmetric (this assumption will be used further in the PSOR algorithm).

Let us consider the following optimization problem

$$\max_{Z \geq 0} V^\top Z - \frac{1}{2} Z^\top Q Z.$$

The Lagrange function for this problem is

$$L(Z, W) = \frac{1}{2} Z^\top Q Z - V^\top Z - W^\top Z,$$

where W is the vector of Lagrange multipliers. Let us observe that the Lagrange function is convex. Hence, there is a unique solution of this optimization problem, and this solution fulfills the Kuhn–Tucker conditions. Computing the Kuhn–Tucker conditions, we obtain

$$\begin{aligned} &QZ - V - W = 0, \\ &W \geq 0, \quad Z \geq 0, \\ &W_k Z_k = 0, \quad k = 0, \ldots, M, \text{ hence,} \quad (W, Z) = 0. \end{aligned}$$

This is exactly (8.29). □

In the above proof, we assume that Q is a symmetric, positive definite matrix. The positive definiteness of matrix Q is essential for the algorithm (see Theorem 8.42). The assumption of symmetry can be partially relaxed to diagonally dominant matrices or a particular type of tridiagonal matrices. We omit such extensions to simplify the proof of convergence.

The PSOR algorithm
Step 1. Select relaxation parameter $\omega \in (1,2)$, the accuracy $\varepsilon > 0$, and starting point $Z^0 \geq 0$. Put $p = 0$.
Step 2. Compute successively,

$$\begin{aligned}
Y_i^{p+1} &= V_i - \sum_{j=1}^{i-1} Q_{ij} Z_j^{p+1} - \sum_{j=i}^{M} Q_{ij} Z_j^p, \\
Z_i^{p+1} &= \max\left(0, Z_i^p + \omega \frac{Y_i^{p+1}}{Q_{ii}}\right), \\
W_i^{p+1} &= -Y_i^{p+1} + Q_{ii}\big(Z_i^{p+1} - Z_i^p\big).
\end{aligned}$$

Step 3. If $|Z^{p+1} - Z^p| > \varepsilon$, increase p by 1 and return to Step 2; otherwise **stop**. Z^{p+1} is the solution.

Example 8.41. Before proving the convergence of the PSOR algorithm, we illustrate its action on a simple example of the American put option in the Black–Scholes model.

The linear complementarity problem for the American put is given by the following system of inequalities (cf. equation (8.14))

$$\begin{aligned}
&\frac{\partial u}{\partial t} + \frac{1}{2}\sigma^2 \frac{\partial^2 u}{\partial x^2} + \big(r - \sigma^2/2\big)\frac{\partial u}{\partial x} - ru \leq 0, \quad t \in [0,T], \quad x \in \mathbb{R}, \\
&u(t,x) \geq g(x) \equiv \big(K - e^x\big)^+, \quad t \in [0,T], \quad x \in \mathbb{R}, \\
&\left(\frac{\partial u}{\partial t} + \frac{1}{2}\sigma^2 \frac{\partial^2 u}{\partial x^2} + \big(r - \sigma^2/2\big)\frac{\partial u}{\partial x} - ru\right)\big(u(t,x) - g(x)\big) = 0, \\
&u(T,x) = g(x), \quad x \in \mathbb{R}.
\end{aligned}$$

Restricting the spatial domain to a finite interval $(-R, R)$, dividing this domain into M subintervals of equal size δx, and dividing the time interval $[0,T]$ into N equal subintervals of size δt, we approximate the differential formula by the fully implicit Euler scheme. Let u_k^n denote the approximation of $u(t_n, x_k)$, where $t_n = n\delta t$,

$n = 1, \ldots, N$, and $x_k = -R + k\delta x$, $k = 0, \ldots, M$. Then we obtain the following system of algebraic inequalities

$$\begin{aligned} u_k^{n+1} &\le (1 + \sigma^2\lambda + r\delta t)u_k^n - \big(\lambda\sigma^2/2 + (r - \sigma^2/2)\gamma/2\big)u_{k+1}^n \\ &\quad - \big(\lambda\sigma^2/2 - (r - \sigma^2/2)\gamma/2\big)u_{k-1}^n, \\ u_k^n &\ge g_k, \\ &\Big(u_k^{n+1} - (1 + \sigma^2\lambda + r\delta t)u_k^n + \big(\lambda\sigma^2/2 + (r - \sigma^2/2)\gamma/2\big)u_{k+1}^n \\ &\quad + \big(\lambda\sigma^2/2 - (r - \sigma^2/2)\gamma/2\big)u_{k-1}^n\Big)\big(u_k^n - g_k\big) = 0, \\ u_k^N &= g_k, \end{aligned}$$

where, as previously, $\lambda = \delta t/(\delta x)^2$ and $\gamma = \delta t/\delta x$.

Defining the vectors

$$U^n = (u_1^n, \ldots, u_{M-1}^n), \quad G = (g_1, \ldots, g_{M-1}),$$

we rewrite the above inequalities in the matrix form

$$\begin{aligned} &AU^n \ge U^{n+1} + d^n, \\ &U^n \ge G, \\ &\big(AU^n - U^{n+1} - d^n\big)\big(U^n - G\big) = 0, \\ &U^N = G, \end{aligned} \tag{8.30}$$

where d^n is the vector of boundary values obtained from the option boundary conditions $\lim_{x\to-\infty} u(t,x) = K$ and $\lim_{x\to\infty} u(t,x) = 0$, and A is a tridiagonal matrix with entries

$$\begin{aligned} a_{k,k} &= 1 + \sigma^2\lambda + r\delta t, \\ a_{k,k+1} &= -\lambda\sigma^2/2 - (r - \sigma^2/2)\gamma/2, \\ a_{k-1,k} &= -\lambda\sigma^2/2 + (r - \sigma^2/2)\gamma/2. \end{aligned}$$

To solve the above problem, we must know how to solve efficiently a system of linear equations

$$Aw = b$$

for a given matrix A and vector b.

A system of linear equations can be efficiently solved by the LU method, which is a direct method of computing the solution in one pass. The fact that the solution is found in one pass limits the possibility of using the method for solving linear inequalities. More suitable for that purpose are iterative methods. We begin by demonstrating how different iterative methods solve a system of linear equations. Then it will be easier to understand the modifications required to solve inequalities.

The main idea behind iterative methods can be described as follows. The system of equations $Aw = b$ can be rewritten in the form

$$Bw = (B - A)w + b,$$

where B is a suitable matrix. For nonsingular B, we obtain

$$w = (I - B^{-1}A)w + B^{-1}b,$$

which leads to the iterations

$$w^{[k+1]} = (I - B^{-1}A)w^{[k]} + B^{-1}b.$$

To find a good candidate for matrix B, we split A in the form $A = D - L - U$, where D is a diagonal matrix, L is a strict lower triangular matrix, and U is a strict upper-triangular matrix.

The simplest possibility is explored by the Jacobi method, where B is equal to D, the diagonal of A, which implies $B - A = L + U$ and the iterations are

$$Dw^{[k+1]} = (L + U)w^{[k]} + b.$$

Starting from an initial guess $w^{[0]}$, the whole process is iterated until a chosen measure of error becomes sufficiently small.

A development of the Jacobi method is the Gauss–Seidel method in which $B = D - L$. This implies $B - A = U$ and the iterations are

$$(D - L)w^{[k+1]} = Uw^{[k]} + b.$$

Solving this system componentwise, we get

$$w_i^{[k+1]} = \frac{1}{a_{ii}}\left(b_i - \sum_{j=1}^{i-1} a_{ij}w_j^{[k+1]} - \sum_{j=i+1}^{M-1} a_{ij}w_j^{[k]}\right).$$

Hence, the inversion of matrix B can be reduced to division by the diagonal elements of matrix A. Since in the Gauss–Seidel method we update $w_i^{[k+1]}$ using already computed updates $w_j^{[k+1]}$ for $j < i$, the method converges more rapidly than the Jacobi method.

The *Successive Over-Relaxation* (SOR) method refines the Gauss–Seidel algorithm. In the SOR method, we set $B = D/\omega - L$, where ω is the *relaxation parameter*, and $B - A = (\omega^{-1} - 1)D + U$. With the choice $\omega = 1$, we get the Gauss–Seidel method, and by choosing $1 \leq \omega < 2$, we get over-relaxation. Solving the linear system componentwise as before, we obtain the SOR algorithm

$$w_i^{[k+1]} = w_i^{[k]} + \frac{\omega}{a_{ii}} \left(b_i - \sum_{j=1}^{i-1} a_{ij} w_j^{[k+1]} - \sum_{j=i}^{M-1} a_{ij} w_j^{[k]} \right).$$

The relaxation parameter ω is a factor that improves the convergence of the iterations. It can be shown that there is an optimal value of ω, which gives the best rate of convergence. There are ways for theoretical computation of this optimal value; however, practically more effective is to find a near-optimal value by changing ω during iterations to obtain a value that minimizes the number of iterations in the loop.

The *projected SOR* algorithm (PSOR) is a minor modification of SOR. The construction of the algorithm and its proof of convergence follow the paper by Cryer [19]. To describe how PSOR works for an American put, let us write equation (8.30) in the form

$$\begin{aligned} &Aw \geq b, \\ &w \geq g, \\ &(Aw - b)(w - g) = 0, \end{aligned}$$

where $w = U^n$, $b = U^{n+1} + d^n$, and $g = G$.

Let us write the SOR as a two-step algorithm introducing an auxiliary vector y, which is also computed iteratively

$$\begin{aligned} y_i^{[k+1]} &= b_i - \sum_{j=1}^{i-1} a_{ij} w_j^{[k+1]} - \sum_{j=i}^{M-1} a_{ij} w_j^{[k]}, \\ w_i^{[k+1]} &= w_i^{[k]} + \frac{\omega}{a_{ii}} y_i^{[k+1]}. \end{aligned}$$

To satisfy the constraint $w \geq g$, we modify the second equation in the above two-step algorithm (that fits the description of the PSOR algorithm for a general linear complementarity problem)

$$y_i^{[k+1]} = b_i - \sum_{j=1}^{i-1} a_{ij} w_j^{[k+1]} - \sum_{j=i}^{M-1} a_{ij} w_j^{[k]},$$

$$w_i^{[k+1]} = \max\left(g_i, w_i^{[k]} + \frac{\omega}{a_{ii}} y_i^{[k+1]} \right).$$

To show that this modification is already the solution of the linear complementarity problem for an American put, consider the ith component of the solution vector w. We have two possibilities: (i) $w_i > g_i$, or (ii) $w_i = g_i$. Condition $w_i > g_i$ means that holding the option is optimal and that inequality means also $\left(Aw\right)_i = b_i$. Hence, $(Aw - b)_i (w - g)_i = 0$. When $w_i = g_i$, it is optimal to exercise the option. Then the PSOR gives $\left(Aw\right)_i > b_i$ and again the condition $(Aw - b)_i (w - g)_i = 0$ is fulfilled. This proves that the PSOR algorithm computes the price of the American put option.

Theorem 8.42. *Let Z^p, W^p be generated by the PSOR algorithm. Then $Z^p \to Z$, $W^p \to W$, where (Z, W) is a solution of* (8.29).

Proof. Let $F(u) = u^\top Q u - 2u^\top V$. Then by the symmetry of Q,

$$F(u) - F(v) = (u - v)^\top Q(u - v) + 2(u - v)^\top (Qv - V).$$

Define the vectors $z^{(p,l)}$, $l = -1, 0, \ldots, M$,

$$z_i^{(p+1,l)} = \begin{cases} Z_i^{p+1}, & \text{for } 0 \le i \le l, \\ Z_i^p, & \text{for } l < i \le M. \end{cases}$$

Then $z^{(p+1,-1)} = Z^p$ and $z^{(p+1,M)} = Z^{p+1}$. With vectors $z^{(p+1,l)}$, we can write

$$Y_i^{p+1} = (V - Qz^{(p+1,i-1)})_i.$$

Let

$$\omega_{(p+1,i)} = \begin{cases} \left(Z_i^{p+1} - Z_i^p\right) \frac{Q_{ii}}{Y_i^{p+1}}, & \text{if } Y_i^{p+1} \neq 0\,, \\ \omega, & \text{if } Y_i^{p+1} = 0. \end{cases}$$

We have $0 \le \omega_{(p+1,i)} \le \omega$. Indeed, there are two possibilities: (i) if $Y_i^{p+1} \neq 0$ and $Z_i^p + \omega Y_i^{p+1}/Q_{ii} \ge 0$, then $\omega_{(p+1,i)} = \omega$; (ii) if

$Z_i^p + \omega Y_i^{p+1}/Q_{ii} < 0$, then $Y_i^{p+1} < 0$ and $0 \le \omega_{(p+1,i)} < \omega$. Thus, we can write

$$Z_i^{p+1} = Z_i^p + \omega_{(p+1,i)} \frac{Y_i^{p+1}}{Q_{ii}}.$$

We have

$$\begin{aligned} &F(z^{(p+1,i)}) - F(z^{(p+1,i-1)}) \\ &\quad = \left(z^{(p+1,i)} - z^{(p+1,i-1)}\right)^\top Q\left(z^{(p+1,i)} - z^{(p+1,i-1)}\right) \\ &\qquad + 2\left(z^{(p+1,i)} - z^{(p+1,i-1)}\right)^\top \left(Qz^{(p+1,i-1)} - V\right) \end{aligned}$$

and after simplification

$$\begin{aligned} &F(z^{(p+1,i)}) - F(z^{(p+1,i-1)}) \\ &\quad = Q_{ii}\left(Z_i^{p+1} - Z_i^p\right)^2 - 2\left(Z_i^{p+1} - Z_i^p\right)Y_i^{p+1} \\ &\quad = -\omega_{(p+1,i)}(2 - \omega_{(p+1,i)}) \frac{\left(Y_i^{p+1}\right)^2}{Q_{ii}}. \end{aligned}$$

Since $0 \le \omega_{(p+1,i)} \le \omega < 2$, then $F(z^{(p+1,i)}) \le F(z^{(p+1,i-1)})$ and the sequence $F(z^{(p,i)})$ is decreasing. By the definition of $z^{(p,i)}$, we have $F(Z^{p+1}) \le F(Z^p)$. $F(u)$ is bounded from below as a quadratic function with positive-definite matrix Q. Then

$$F(Z^p) \searrow F_\infty, \quad p \to \infty.$$

Let $a = \min_{0 \le i \le M} Q_{ii}$ then, by the definition of $\omega_{(p+1,i)}$, we obtain

$$\begin{aligned} &F(z^{(p+1,i-1)}) - F(z^{(p+1,i)}) = Q_{ii}\left(Z_i^{p+1} - Z_i^p\right)^2\left(-1 + \frac{2}{\omega_{(p+1,i)}}\right) \\ &\ge a\left(-1 + \frac{2}{\omega}\right)\left(Z_i^{p+1} - Z_i^p\right)^2. \end{aligned}$$

This gives

$$\left|Z_i^{p+1} - Z_i^p\right| \le \left(a\left(-1 + \frac{2}{\omega}\right)\right)^{-1/2}\left(F(z^{(p+1,i-1)}) - F(z^{(p+1,i)})\right)^{1/2}.$$

The convergence of $F(z^{(p,i)})$ implies

$$\left|Z_i^{p+1} - Z_i^p\right| \to 0, \quad p \to \infty.$$

Let Z be a condensation point of Z^p. There exists a sequence $p_k \to \infty$, for $k \to \infty$, such that

$$Z^{p_k} \to Z, \quad \text{for } k \to \infty.$$

Then we have

$$\begin{aligned} Y^{p_k} &\to Y = V - QZ, \\ W^{p_k} &\to W = -Y. \end{aligned}$$

We must prove $Z \geq 0$ and $Y \leq 0$. Condition $Z \geq 0$ follows from the inequality $Z^p \geq 0$ for all p. Let us now assume that $Y > 0$. Then there exist $\varepsilon > 0$, p_0, and i_0 such that $Y_{i_0}^{p_k} \geq \varepsilon$ for $p_k \geq p_0$. On the other hand, from Step 2 of the PSOR algorithm, we obtain

$$Z_{i_0}^{p_k} - Z_{i_0}^{p_k - 1} \geq \frac{\varepsilon\omega}{Q_{i_0 i_0}} \quad \text{for} \quad p_k \geq p_0$$

which contradicts the convergence $Z_i^{p_k} - Z_i^{p_k - 1} \to 0$.

We now prove that $Y^\top Z = 0$. Assume that it is not true. Then there exist $\varepsilon > 0$, i_0, and p_0 such that

$$Z_{i_0}^{p_k} \geq \varepsilon, \quad Y_{i_0}^{p_k} \leq -\varepsilon \quad \text{for} \quad p_k \geq p_0.$$

Then from Step 2 of the PSOR algorithm

$$Z_{i_0}^{p_k - 1} \geq Z_{i_0}^{p_k} \quad \text{and} \quad \left|Z_{i_0}^{p_k} - Z_{i_0}^{p_k - 1}\right| \geq \frac{\varepsilon\omega}{Q_{i_0 i_0}} \quad \text{for} \quad p_k \geq p_0,$$

which again contradicts the convergence $Z_i^{p_k} - Z_i^{p_k - 1} \to 0$.

For the proof completeness, we must demonstrate that the sequence Z^p possesses a condensation point. To this end, let us observe that $Z^p \in R = \{z\colon\ F(z) \leq F(Z^0)\}$ for all p. Since $F(u)$ is bounded from below, R is compact as the inverse image of a compact set under continuous mapping. Then Z^p has a condensation point as an infinite sequence in a compact set. □

8.3.3 Penalty method

The basic concept of the penalty method is to replace the variational inequality (8.16) with the nonlinear differential equation

$$
\begin{aligned}
&-\frac{\partial u_\varepsilon}{\partial t} + \mathcal{A}^t u_\varepsilon + \frac{1}{\varepsilon} j(u_\varepsilon(t)) = 0, \quad \text{on} \quad [0,T) \times U_R, \\
&u_\varepsilon(t) = g, \quad \text{on} \quad \partial U_R, \ a.e.\ t \in [0,T), \\
&u_\varepsilon(T) = g, \quad \text{on} \quad U_R,
\end{aligned} \tag{8.31}
$$

where $j(u) = [u-g]^-$ and $[x]^- = \min(x,0)$.

We begin the investigation of (8.31) with the following useful lemma.

Lemma 8.43. *Operator $j(u)$ is monotone in $L^2(U_R)$, i.e.,*

$$(j(u_1) - j(u_2), u_1 - u_2) \geq 0, \quad \forall u_1, u_2 \in L^2(U_R).$$

This operator is also continuous in $L^2(U_R)$.

Proof. By the elementary estimate

$$(x^- - y^-)(x-y) \geq (x^- - y^-)^2, \quad x, y \in \mathbb{R},$$

we obtain taking $u_1, u_2 \in L^2(U_R)$

$$
\begin{aligned}
\big(j(u_1) - j(u_2), u_1 - u_2\big) &= \big([u_1 - g]^- - [u_2 - g]^-, u_1 - u_2\big) \\
&= \big([u_1 - g]^- - [u_2 - g]^-, (u_1 - g) - (u_2 - g)\big) \\
&\geq \|[u_1 - g]^- - [u_2 - g]^-\|^2 = \|j(u_1) - j(u_2)\|^2 \geq 0.
\end{aligned}
$$

The same estimate proves that $j(u)$ is continuous. □

From Chapter 3 of the book by Bensoussan and Lions [8], we have the following two theorems.

Theorem 8.44. *Let Assumption* 8.16 *hold in U_R. There exists a unique weak solution $u_\varepsilon(t)$ of* (8.31) *with $u_\varepsilon \in L^2(0,T;H^1(U_R))$ and $du_\varepsilon/dt \in L^2(0,T;L^2(U_R))$.*

Theorem 8.45. *Let $u(t)$ be a solution of* (8.16) *with $u \in L^2(0,T;H^1(U_R))$ and $du/dt \in L^2(0,T;L^2(U_R))$. Let $u_\varepsilon(t)$ solve*

(8.31) *with* $u_\varepsilon \in L^2(0,T;H^1(U_R))$ *and* $du_\varepsilon/dt \in L^2(0,T;L^2(U_R))$. *Then*

$$\max_{t\in[0,T]} \|u(t) - u_\varepsilon(t)\|_{L^2(U_R)} \le C\sqrt{\varepsilon}$$

for $C > 0$.

We now construct a numerical solution of (8.31). Similarly to the investigation of variational inequalities, we restrict the considerations to a one-dimensional case. We assume that operator $\mathcal{A}^t$ is time-independent and given by formula (8.18). We consider the weak formulation of the differential equation (8.31)

$$\left(-\frac{du_\varepsilon}{dt}(t), v\right)_{L^2(U_R)} + B_R\big[u_\varepsilon(t), v\big] + \frac{1}{\varepsilon}\big(j(u_\varepsilon(t)), v\big)_{L^2(U_R)} = 0, \tag{8.32}$$

which holds, $t \in [0,T)$ a.e. for each $v \in H^1(U_R)$.

We approximate the differential problem by finite differences. As described previously, we define space and time grids, the corresponding functional spaces L^2_M, H^1_M and $L^2_N(0,T;L^2_M)$, $L^2_N(0,T;H^1_M)$, and grid functions v_M, $v_{N,M}$. Matrix Λ is given by Definition 8.30, and due to Lemma 8.34, $(\Lambda v_M, w_M)_{L^2_M}$ is consistent with $B_R[v,w]$.

Problem (8.31) is approximated by the following θ-scheme for grid function $w_{N,M}$

$$w_M^{(n)} - w_M^{(n+1)} + \delta t \Lambda\left((1-\theta)w_M^{(n+1)} + \theta w_M^{(n)}\right) + \frac{\delta t}{\varepsilon} j_h\left(w_M^{(n)}\right) = 0, \tag{8.33}$$

where $j_h(w_M^{(n)}) = [w_M^{(n)} - g_h]^-$.

We postpone, for a moment, the existence of the solution of equation (8.33) (cf. Theorem 8.52) and concentrate on the convergence of $\hat{w}_{N,M}$ to u_ε, a weak solution of the continuous penalty problem (8.31). The first step in this proof is the following result.

Theorem 8.46. *Let matrix* Λ *fulfill the conditions of Definition* 8.30. *Then* $w_{N,M}$, *a solution of the discrete penalty problem* (8.33), *has,* *for $(1-\theta)\delta t(\delta x)^{-2}$ small enough, the following estimate*

$$\max_{0\le n\le N}\left\|w_M^{(n)}-g_h\right\|_{L_M^2}^2+C\sum_{n=0}^{N-1}\left\|w_M^{(n+1)}-w_M^{(n)}\right\|_{L_M^2}^2$$
$$+C\sum_{n=0}^{N}\delta t\left\|w_M^{(n)}\right\|_{H_M^1}^2\le CT\|g_h\|_{H_M^1}^2.$$

Proof. Multiplying equation (8.33) scalarly by $(w_M^{(n)}-g_h)$, we obtain

$$\begin{aligned}&\left(w_M^{(n)}-w_M^{(n+1)},w_M^{(n)}-g_h\right)_{L_M^2}\\&+\delta t\Big(\Lambda\big((1-\theta)w_M^{(n+1)}+\theta w_M^{(n)}\big),w_M^{(n)}-g_h\Big)_{L_M^2}\\&+\frac{\delta t}{\varepsilon}\Big(j_h(w_M^{(n)}),w_M^{(n)}-g_h\Big)_{L_M^2}=0.\end{aligned}\tag{8.34}$$

We have

$$\Big(j_h(w_M^{(n)}),w_M^{(n)}-g_h\Big)_{L_M^2}=\Big(j_h(w_M^{(n)})-j_h(g_h),w_M^{(n)}-g_h\Big)_{L_M^2}\ge 0$$

by the monotonicity of j_h which follows from Lemma 8.43 and the observation that $j_h(g_h)=0$.

Then (8.34) can be reduced to

$$\begin{aligned}&\left(w_M^{(n)}-w_M^{(n+1)},w_M^{(n)}-g_h\right)_{L_M^2}\\&+\delta t\Big(\Lambda\big((1-\theta)w_M^{(n+1)}+\theta w_M^{(n)}\big),w_M^{(n)}-g_h\Big)_{L_M^2}\le 0\end{aligned}$$

and this is exactly inequality (8.22) from the proof of Theorem 8.36. Thus, the rest of the proof follows exactly the proof of Theorem 8.36. □

With the above estimate, we can prove that solutions of problem (8.33) converge to a weak solution of problem (8.31) for $\delta t,\delta x\to 0$.

Theorem 8.47. *Let $w_{N,M}$ be a sequence of solutions of the discrete penalty problem* (8.33) *for δt and δx tending to zero ($N, M \to \infty$). Let u_ε be a unique weak solution of the continuous penalty problem* (8.31). *Let $\hat{w}_{N,M}$ denote a piecewise constant extension of $w_{N,M}$. Then for $(1-\theta)\delta t(\delta x)^{-2}$ sufficiently small to satisfy the conditions of Theorem* 8.46, *we obtain the convergence*

$$\hat{w}_{N,M} \rightharpoonup u_\varepsilon \text{ in } L^2(0,T;L^2(U_R)),$$

$$(\delta_x w_{N,M})\hat{} \rightharpoonup Du_\varepsilon \text{ in } L^2(0,T;L^2(U_R)).$$

Proof. From the stability results of Theorem 8.46, it follows that the sequence $\hat{w}_{N,M}$ is bounded. Thus, this sequence contains a weakly convergent subsequence, which we also denote $\hat{w}_{N,M}$. Let

$$\hat{w}_{N,M} \rightharpoonup w \text{ in } L^2(0,T;L^2(U_R)),$$

$$(\delta_x w_{N,M})\hat{} \rightharpoonup Dw \text{ in } L^2(0,T;L^2(U_R)).$$

Our goal is to prove that w is a weak solution of the penalty problem (8.31). This proof is analogous to the proof of Theorem 5.35. We take $v \in L^2(0,T;H^1(U_R))$ such that $v(t) \geq g$ for $t \in [0,T]$. Let $\hat{v}_{N,M}$ be a sequence of piecewise constant approximations of v. We rewrite (8.33) for $\hat{w}_M^{(n)}$, multiply scalarly the obtained equality by $\hat{v}_M^{(n)}$, and sum over n

$$\sum_{n=0}^{N-1}\Bigg(\bigg(-\frac{\hat{w}_M^{(n+1)}-\hat{w}_M^{(n)}}{\delta t}, \hat{v}_M^{(n)}\bigg)_{L^2(U_R)} + \Big(\Lambda\big((1-\theta)\hat{w}_M^{(n+1)} + \theta\hat{w}_M^{(n)}\big), \hat{v}_M^{(n)}\Big)_{L^2(U_R)} + \frac{1}{\varepsilon}\big(j_h(\hat{w}_M^{(n)}), \hat{v}_M^{(n)}\big)_{L^2(U_R)}\Bigg) = 0.$$

Passing to the limit $\delta t, \delta x \to 0$, using the consistency of $(\Lambda w_M, v_M)$ with $B_R[w,v]$, and the continuity (hence, also the weak continuity) of $j(x)$, we obtain

$$\int_0^T\bigg(\Big(-\frac{dw}{dt}(t), v(t)\Big)_{L^2(U_R)} + B_R[w(t),v(t)] + \frac{1}{\varepsilon}\big(j(w(t)), v(t)\big)_{L^2(U_R)}\bigg)dt = 0.$$

Since $v \in L^2(0,T;H^1(U_R))$ is arbitrary, we have

$$\left(-\frac{dw}{dt}(t), z\right)_{L^2(U_R)} + B_R[w(t), z] + \frac{1}{\varepsilon}(j(w(t)), z)_{L^2(U_R)} = 0$$

for each $z \in H^1(U_R)$. Hence, $w(t)$ is a weak solution of (8.31). We also have $w \geq g$ because all $\hat{w}_{N,M} \geq g_h$, and $w(T) = g$ since $w_M^{(N)} = g_h$. □

Remark 8.48. Delicate analytical considerations exploring the regularity of solutions of penalty problem (8.31) and the estimates of Theorem 8.46 reveal that the weakly convergent sequence $\hat{w}_{N,M}$ of Theorem 8.47 is, in fact, converging strongly to $w = u_\varepsilon$ in $L^2(0,T;L^2(U_R))$.

Definition 8.49. A square matrix A is called the *M-matrix* if nondiagonal entries of A are nonpositive ($a_{ij} \leq 0$, $i \neq j$) and all principal minors of A are positive definite. This property can be expressed in terms of the entries of A stating that $\forall i$ $a_{ii} \geq 0$, $a_{ij} \leq 0$, $i \neq j$, and $\forall i$ $\sum_j a_{ij} \geq 0$ with at least one i_0 such that $\sum_j a_{i_0 j} > 0$.

The property of an M-matrix A that is particularly important for our future considerations is the positivity of A^{-1}.

Example 8.50. Consider the Black–Scholes model with operator $\mathcal{A}$ given for $x = \ln S$ by the formula

$$\mathcal{A}u = -\frac{1}{2}\sigma^2\frac{\partial^2 u}{\partial x^2} - \left(r - \frac{1}{2}\sigma^2\right)\frac{\partial u}{\partial x} + ru.$$

Due to Definition 8.30, matrix Λ corresponding to operator $\mathcal{A}$ is tridiagonal with the entries

$$\Lambda_{k,k} = \sigma^2\frac{1}{(\delta x)^2} + r,$$

$$\Lambda_{k,k+1} = -\frac{1}{2}\sigma^2\frac{1}{(\delta x)^2} + \left(\frac{1}{2}\sigma^2 - r\right)\frac{1}{\delta x},$$

$$\Lambda_{k,k-1} = -\frac{1}{2}\sigma^2\frac{1}{(\delta x)^2} - \left(\frac{1}{2}\sigma^2 - r\right)\frac{1}{\delta x}.$$

It is easy to observe that Λ is an M-matrix for $\delta x < \min(1, \sigma^2/(2r))$. Obviously also $Q = (I + \delta t\theta\Lambda)$ is an M-matrix. Q is an M-matrix even for negative interest rates provided δt is sufficiently small.

Denoting

$$Q = I + \theta\delta t\Lambda,$$
$$X = w_M^{(n)},$$
$$Q_p = (I - (1-\theta)\delta t\Lambda),$$
$$X_p = w_M^{(n+1)},$$
$$\Phi = g_h,$$

we can write the penalty problem (8.33) in the compact form

$$QX + \frac{\delta t}{\varepsilon}[X - \Phi]^- = Q_p X_p. \tag{8.35}$$

We solve (8.35) assuming that Q is an M-matrix. To solve equation (8.35), we apply an iterative method. We first prove the following estimate.

Lemma 8.51. *Let* $w_{N,M}$ *be a solution of* (8.33). *Then for* $0 \le n \le N$

$$\left\| [w_M^{(n)} - \Phi]^- \right\|_{L_M^2} \le C\frac{\varepsilon}{\delta t}.$$

Proof. We denote $Y_\varepsilon = w_M^{(n)} - \Phi$. Then (8.35) can be written as

$$QY_\varepsilon + \frac{\delta t}{\varepsilon}[Y_\varepsilon]^- = Q_p X_p - Q\Phi. \tag{8.36}$$

Without loss of generality, we can assume that $Y_\varepsilon = (y_1, y_2)$, where $y_1 = [Y_\varepsilon]^-$, and $y_2 = [Y_\varepsilon]^+$. Then matrix Q is decomposed accordingly

$$Q = \begin{pmatrix} Q_{11} & Q_{12} \\ Q_{21} & Q_{22} \end{pmatrix}.$$

Let $Q_p X_p - Q\Phi = b$. Due to Theorem 8.46, $\|b\|_{L_M^2}$ is bounded for all $w_{N,M}$.

We multiply scalarly (8.36) by $[Y_\varepsilon]^-$ to obtain

$$(Q_{11}y_1, y_1)_{L_M^2} + (Q_{12}y_2, y_1)_{L_M^2} + \frac{\delta t}{\varepsilon}\|[Y_\varepsilon]^-\|_{L_M^2}^2 = (b, [Y_\varepsilon]^-)_{L_M^2}. \tag{8.37}$$

$(Q_{11}y_1, y_1)_{L_M^2} \ge 0$ since Q is an M-matrix. We have $y_1 \le 0$ and $Q_{12}y_2 \le 0$ since $y_2 \ge 0$ and $Q_{12} \le 0$. Then $(Q_{12}y_2, y_1)_{L_M^2} \ge 0$.

Dropping these nonnegative terms from the left-hand side of (8.37), we obtain

$$\|[Y_\varepsilon]^-\|^2_{L^2_M} \le \frac{\varepsilon}{\delta t}\big|(b,[Y_\varepsilon]^-)_{L^2_M}\big| \le \frac{\varepsilon}{\delta t}\|[Y_\varepsilon]^-\|_{L^2_M}\|b\|_{L^2_M}.$$

□

A solution of (8.35) is obtained by nonlinear iterations (we follow here the approach by Forsyth and Vetzal [31]). To define these iterations, we introduce the diagonal matrix

$$P(X)_{ij} = \begin{cases} 1 & \text{if } X < \Phi \text{ and } i = j, \\ 0 & \text{otherwise.} \end{cases} \tag{8.38}$$

Then we can write equation (8.35) as

$$\left(Q + \frac{\delta t}{\varepsilon}P(X)\right)X = Q_p X_p + \frac{\delta t}{\varepsilon}P(X)\Phi.$$

The above equation can be solved by the following Newton iterations:

$$\begin{aligned} &X^0 = X_p, \\ &\left(Q + \frac{\delta t}{\varepsilon}P(X^k)\right)X^{k+1} = Q_p X_p + \frac{\delta t}{\varepsilon}P(X^k)\Phi. \end{aligned} \tag{8.39}$$

The iteration process terminates when for a given tolerance η

$$\frac{\|X^{k+1} - X^k\|_{L^\infty(U_R)}}{\max\big(1, \|X^{k+1}\|_{L^\infty(U_R)}\big)} < \eta, \quad \text{or} \quad P(X^{k+1}) = P(X^k).$$

Theorem 8.52. *Let Λ be an M-matrix. Then:*

(a) *the iterates* (8.39) *converge to a unique solution of* (8.35) *for any initial value X_p;*
(b) *the iterates converge monotonically: if $X^1 \ge X^0$, then $X^{k+1} \ge X^k$ for $k \ge 1$.*

Proof. *Monotone convergence*: Subtracting from equation (8.39) for X^{k+1} the same equation for X^k, we obtain

$$\left(Q + \frac{\delta t}{\varepsilon}P(X^k)\right)(X^{k+1} - X^k) = \frac{\delta t}{\varepsilon}\big(P(X^k) - P(X^{k-1})\big)(\Phi - X^k).$$

Let us examine the term $\big(P(X^k) - P(X^{k-1})\big)(\Phi - X^k)$:

(1) if $X_i^k < \Phi_i$, then $P(X^k)_{ii} = 1$ and $\big(P(X^k) - P(X^{k-1})\big)_{ii}(\Phi - X^k)_i \geq 0$;
(2) if $X_i^k \geq \Phi_i$, then $P(X^k)_{ii} = 0$ and $\big(P(X^k) - P(X^{k-1})\big)_{ii}(\Phi - X^k)_i = -P(X^{k-1})_{ii}(\Phi - X^k)_i \geq 0$.

Thus, we always have

$$\big(P(X^k) - P(X^{k-1})\big)(\Phi - X^k) \geq 0, \quad k \geq 1.$$

Since Λ is an M-matrix, then also $(I + \theta\delta t\Lambda + \delta t\, \varepsilon^{-1} P(X^k))$ is an M-matrix. Thus, for $k \geq 1$, we have

$$\begin{aligned}(X^{k+1} - X^k)\\ &= \left(I + \theta\delta t\Lambda + \frac{\delta t}{\varepsilon} P(X^k)\right)^{-1} \big(P(X^k) - P(X^{k-1})\big)(\Phi - X^k) \geq 0.\end{aligned}$$

Bounded iterates: From (8.39), we have for $k \geq 1$

$$\begin{aligned}&\|X^{k+1}\|_{L^\infty(U_R)}\\ &\leq \left\| \left(Q + \frac{\delta t}{\varepsilon} P(X^k)\right)^{-1} \right\|_{\mathcal{L}(L^\infty, L^\infty)} \left\| Q_p X_p + \frac{\delta t}{\varepsilon} P(X^k)\Phi \right\|_{L^\infty(U_R)}\\ &\leq C,\end{aligned}$$

since matrix $\left(Q + \delta t\, \varepsilon^{-1} P(X^k)\right)^{-1}$ is bounded as the inverse of an M-matrix and also matrices Q_p and $P(X^k)$ are bounded (in the norm of any finite-dimensional space). Then X^k as a sequence of bounded, monotone iterates converges to a solution of (8.35).

Uniqueness: Assume that there are two solutions of (8.35): V^1 and V^2. Subtracting equation (8.35) for V^2 from the same equation for V^1, we obtain

$$\left(Q + \frac{\delta t}{\varepsilon} P(V^2)\right)(V^1 - V^2) = \frac{\delta t}{\varepsilon}\big(P(V^1) - P(V^2)\big)(\Phi - V^1).$$

Using similar computations as in the proof of monotonicity, we have

$$\big(P(V^1) - P(V^2)\big)(\Phi - V^1) \geq 0.$$

Since $\big(Q + \delta t\, \varepsilon^{-1} P(V^2)\big)$ is an M-matrix, then $(V^1 - V^2) \geq 0$. Performing the same computations with the roles of V^1 and V^2 interchanged, we get $(V^2 - V^1) \geq 0$. Therefore, $V^1 = V^2$. □

8.4 Exercises

Exercise 8.1. Consider the Black–Scholes model for a single asset having price S_t given by the equation

$$dS_t = r_t S_t dt + \sigma S_t dW_t, \quad t \in [0, T],$$

with deterministic $r_t \geq 0$.

Prove that for the price of an American call option, we have the equality

$$\sup_{\tau \in \mathcal{T}_{t,T}} \mathbb{E}\Big(e^{-\int_t^\tau r_s ds}(S_\tau - K)^+ | \mathcal{F}_t\Big) = \mathbb{E}\Big(e^{-\int_t^T r_s ds}(S_T - K)^+ | \mathcal{F}_t\Big).$$

That equality shows that the price of the American call on an asset that does not pay dividends is equal to the price of the corresponding European call.

Hint: Define $\tilde{S}_t = \exp\Big(-\int_0^t r_s ds\Big) S_t$ and prove that

$$\mathbb{E}\bigg(\Big(\tilde{S}_T - Ke^{-\int_0^T r_s ds}\Big)^+ \Big| \mathcal{F}_\tau\bigg) \geq \Big(\tilde{S}_\tau - Ke^{-\int_0^\tau r_s ds}\Big)^+.$$

Exercise 8.2. Prove that in the Black–Scholes model, the price of the American put in the model with risk-free interest rate $r = 0$ is equal to the price of the European put.

Exercise 8.3. Consider the Black–Scholes model with constant interest rate r, volatility σ, and dividend rate q. The prices of American call and put options are given by the expressions

$$C(t, x; K, r, q) = \sup_{\tau \in \mathcal{T}_{0,T-t}} \mathbb{E} e^{-r\tau}\Big(xe^{(r-q-\sigma^2/2)\tau + \sigma W_\tau} - K\Big)^+,$$

$$P(t, x; K, r, q) = \sup_{\tau \in \mathcal{T}_{0,T-t}} \mathbb{E} e^{-r\tau}\Big(K - xe^{(r-q-\sigma^2/2)\tau + \sigma W_\tau}\Big)^+,$$

where $x = S_t$.

Prove that

$$C(t, x; K, r, q) = P(t, K; x, q, r) = xP(t, K/x; 1, q, r).$$

Exercise 8.4. Let $P(t,x)$ be the price of an American put option in the Black–Scholes model

$$P(t,x) = \sup_{\tau \in \mathcal{T}_{0,T-t}} \mathbb{E}e^{-r\tau}\left(K - xe^{(r-\sigma^2/2)\tau+\sigma W_\tau}\right)^+,$$

where x is the asset price at time t.

(a) Prove that for every $t \in [0,T]$, and $x, y \geq 0$

$$|P(t,x) - P(t,y)| \leq |x-y|.$$

(b) Prove that there exists a constant $C > 0$ such that, for every $x \geq 0$ and $t, s \in [0,T]$,

$$|P(t,x) - P(s,x)| \leq C\left|\sqrt{T-t} - \sqrt{T-s}\right|.$$

Exercise 8.5. Prove Theorem 8.5 in discrete time. Consider a probability space $(\Omega, \mathcal{F}, \mathbb{P})$ with discrete filtration $\mathbb{F} = (\mathcal{F}_n)_{n=0}^N$. Let $\mathcal{T}_{n,N}$ be the set of all stopping times with values in $\{n, n+1, \ldots, N\}$. Let $Z = (Z_n)_{n=0}^N$ be an adapted sequence of integrable random variables. The Snell envelope of Z is the sequence $U = (U_n)_{n=0}^N$ defined by

$$U_n = \operatorname*{ess\,sup}_{\tau \in \mathcal{T}_{n,N}} \mathbb{E}(Z_\tau | \mathcal{F}_n), \quad 0 \leq n \leq N.$$

A stopping time $\hat{\tau} \in \mathcal{T}_{0,N}$ is optimal if $\mathbb{E}(Z_{\hat{\tau}}) = \sup_{\tau \in \mathcal{T}_{0,N}} \mathbb{E}(Z_\tau)$. Prove that a stopping time $\hat{\tau} \in \mathcal{T}_{0,N}$ is optimal if and only if the following conditions hold:

(1) $U_{\hat{\tau}} = Z_{\hat{\tau}}$ a.s.,
(2) $U_n^{\hat{\tau}} = U_{\hat{\tau} \wedge n}$, $0 \leq n \leq N$, is a martingale.

(a) Take for granted the discrete version of Theorem 8.2. Prove that for $\tau \in \mathcal{T}_{n,N}$

$$\mathbb{E}(Z_\tau | \mathcal{F}_n) \leq \max\big(Z_n, \mathbb{E}(U_{n+1} | \mathcal{F}_n)\big).$$

Prove that if $\hat{\tau}$ fulfills conditions (1) and (2), then $\mathbb{E}(Z_{\hat{\tau}} | \mathcal{F}_0) = U_0$. Conclude that $\hat{\tau}$ is optimal.

(b) Assume now that $\hat{\tau}$ is optimal. Note that $\mathbb{E}(Z_{\hat{\tau}}) = \mathbb{E}(U_0)$. Show that the supermartingality of U implies $\mathbb{E}(Z_{\hat{\tau}} | \mathcal{F}_0) \leq \mathbb{E}(U_{\hat{\tau}} | \mathcal{F}_0) \leq U_0$. Conclude that $Z_{\hat{\tau}} = U_{\hat{\tau}}$ and $U^{\hat{\tau}}$ is a martingale.

Exercise 8.6. Consider the function $V(t,x)$ defined by equation (8.2). Prove that if $g(t,x)$ is Lipschitz continuous with respect to $x \in \mathbb{R}^d$ uniformly in $t \in [0,T]$, then the same property holds for $V(t,x)$.
Hint: Observe that $X_T^{t,x}$ is a Lipschitz continuous function of x.

Exercise 8.7. Consider a Markov chain $(X_n)_{n=0}^N$ with values in $\mathbb{R}^d$. Let f be a random variable in $L^2(\mathbb{R}^d, \mu_{n+1})$, where μ_n is the probability measure generated by X_n. Define

$$(Tf)(x) = \mathbb{E}\big(f(X_{n+1})|X_n = x\big), \quad x \in \mathbb{R}^d.$$

Prove the estimate

$$\|Tf\|_{L^2(\mu_n)} \leq \|f\|_{L^2(\mu_{n+1})}.$$

Hint: Use the Jensen inequality.

Exercise 8.8. Consider the continuation function U_n of Section 8.2

$$U_n = \max\big(Z_n, \mathbb{E}(U_{n+1}|X_n)\big)$$

and denote $H_k = \mathbb{E}(U_{k+1}|X_k)$. Approximate U_k, as in the algorithm, by projecting on a finite-dimensional space and applying a Monte Carlo simulation. Let $\hat{U}_k$ denote the estimator of U_k obtained by these approximations and $\hat{H}_k$ the estimator of H_k. Suppose that $\hat{H}_k$ is an unbiased estimator such that $\mathbb{E}(\hat{H}_k|X_k) = H_k$. Prove that $\mathbb{E}(\hat{U}_k|X_k) \geq U_k$.

Conclude from this inequality that even for an unbiased estimate of the conditional expectation, the algorithm leads to upwardly biased estimates of the continuation function, which can lead to upwardly biased price estimates.

Exercise 8.9. Tsitsiklis and van Roy [90] proposed to compute the prices of American options by directly applying regression methods to the approximate continuation function $U_n = \max\big(g(t_n, X_n), \mathbb{E}(U_{n+1}|X_n)\big)$ defined on an M-dimensional space $\mathcal{H}_n$ with a basis $(e_m^n)_{m=1}^M$. For L independent paths X_n^k, $k = 1, \ldots, L$, define

$$U_N^k = Z_N^k = g(t_N, X_N^k).$$

Then for every $n = N-1, \ldots, 0$ compute

$$\hat{\alpha}^n = \arg\min_{a \in \mathbb{R}^M} \sum_{k=1}^{L} \left(U_{n+1}^k - \sum_{m=1}^{M} a_m e_m^n(X_n^k) \right)^2,$$

and define

$$U_n^k = \max\left(g(t_n, X_n^k), \sum_{m=1}^{M} \hat{\alpha}_m^n e_m^n(X_n^k) \right).$$

Finally, obtain the approximation of the Snell envelope at $t_0 = 0$

$$\mathbb{E}(U_0) = \frac{1}{L}\sum_{k=1}^{L} U_0^k = \frac{1}{L}\sum_{k=1}^{L} \max\left(g(t_0, X_0^k), \sum_{m=1}^{M} \hat{\alpha}_m^0 e_m^0(X_0^k) \right).$$

Prove that this algorithm approximates the price of an American option.

Exercise 8.10. Simulate the value of an American put option with a control variate. Design the Longstaff–Schwartz algorithm that, together with the price of the American option, computes the price of the European option with the same parameters. Let the simulation be performed on L independent paths. Denote by V_0^k the price of the American option on path k and by P_0^k the simulated price of the European option. Compute the control variate estimator

$$V_0^{cv} = \frac{1}{L}\sum_{k=1}^{L} (V_0^k - (P_0^k - P_{BS})),$$

where P_{BS} is the price of the European put option computed by the Black–Scholes formula.

Compute the price of the put option with parameters: initial stock price $S_0 = 90$, risk-free interest rate $r = 5\%$, volatility $\sigma = 30\%$, strike $K = 100$, and time to maturity $T = 0.5$ year.

Compare the variance of V_0^{cv} with the variance of the standard Longstaff–Schwartz estimator

$$V_0 = \frac{1}{L}\sum_{k=1}^{L} V_0^k.$$

Exercise 8.11. Consider the Heston stochastic volatility model

$$dS_t = rS_t dt + \sqrt{v_t} S_t dW_t^S,$$
$$dv_t = \kappa(\theta - v_t)dt + \nu\sqrt{v_t} dW_t^v,$$

with correlation ρ between Wiener processes W_t^S and W_t^v.

Compute the price of the American call option in the Heston model with parameters: initial stock price $S_0 = 50$, risk-free interest rate $r = 5\%$, volatility of volatility $\nu = 50\%$, mean variance $\theta = 4\%$, $\kappa = 2$, correlation $\rho = 0.5$, strike $K = 45$, time to maturity $T = 0.25$ year. Use the Euler-Maruyama scheme for the first equation (for stock) and the Milstein scheme for the second equation (for volatility). In these computations, take $L = 100000$ paths and $N = 100$ time steps on the trajectory of the Brownian motion.

Exercise 8.12. Let $Z = (Z_t)_{t\in[0,T]}$ be a nonnegative, right-continuous, regular process (cf. Definition 8.1) such that $\mathbb{E}\left(\sup_{t\in[0,T]} Z_t\right) < \infty$ and $\mathcal{M}$ the set of all right-continuous martingales $B = (B_t)_{t\in[0,T]}$ with $B_0 = 0$.

(a) Let $B \in \mathcal{M}$. Observe that for any stopping time $\tau \in \mathcal{T}_{0,T}$

$$\mathbb{E}(Z_\tau) = \mathbb{E}(Z_\tau - B_\tau) \le \mathbb{E}\left(\sup_{s\in[0,T]} (Z_s - B_s)\right).$$

Conclude that the following inequality holds

$$\sup_{\tau\in\mathcal{T}_{0,T}} \mathbb{E}(Z_\tau) \le \inf_{B\in\mathcal{M}} \mathbb{E}\left(\sup_{s\in[0,T]} (Z_s - B_s)\right).$$

(b) Let U be the Snell envelope of Z. Then U admits the Doob–Meyer decomposition

$$U_t = M_t - A_t,$$

where M is the martingale part of U and A is an increasing process starting at zero. Define $\tilde{M} = M - U_0$. Then $\tilde{M} \in \mathcal{M}$ and the Doob–Meyer decomposition of U reads

$$U_t = U_0 + \tilde{M}_t - A_t.$$

Obtain the inequality $U_0 \geq Z_t - \tilde{M}_t$. From this inequality prove that

$$\sup_{\tau \in \mathcal{T}_{0,T}} \mathbb{E}(Z_\tau) = \mathbb{E}(U_0) \geq \inf_{B \in \mathcal{M}} \mathbb{E}\left(\sup_{s \in [0,T]} (Z_s - B_s) \right).$$

From the above inequalities, conclude that

$$\sup_{\tau \in \mathcal{T}_{0,T}} \mathbb{E}(Z_\tau) = \inf_{B \in \mathcal{M}} \mathbb{E}\left(\sup_{s \in [0,T]} (Z_s - B_s) \right).$$

Exercise 8.13. The Longstaff–Schwartz algorithm (but also the algorithm of Tsitsiklis and van Roy) gives the lower bound of the price of an American option. To obtain the upper bound of the price, Rogers [76] proposed to use the formula of Problem 8.12

$$V_0 = \tilde{V}_0 = \inf_{B \in \mathcal{M}} \mathbb{E}\left(\sup_{s \in [0,T]} (\tilde{Z}_s - B_s) \right),$$

and approximate the minimal martingale B in this formula by a martingale sufficiently close to the minimal. In this formula, V_0 is the option price at $t = 0$, Z_t is the option payoff, and $\tilde{Z}$ denotes the discounted value of Z. There are many constructions of a suitable approximation of the minimal martingale. Below, the construction by Wang and Caflisch [91] is described. Let the price S_t of a single asset in the Black–Scholes model be given by the equation

$$dS_t = rS_t dt + \sigma S_t dW_t.$$

(a) Since $\tilde{V}_t \equiv \tilde{V}(t, S_t)$ is the Snell envelop of the option payoff $\tilde{Z}_t$, then $\tilde{V}_t$, as a supermartingale, has the Doob–Meyer decomposition $\tilde{V}_t = M_t - A_t$, where M_t is a martingale and A_t is an increasing process. Prove that

$$A_t = -\int_0^t e^{-r\tau}\left(\frac{\partial V}{\partial \tau} + \frac{1}{2}\sigma^2 S^2 \frac{\partial^2 V}{\partial S^2} + rS\frac{\partial V}{\partial S} - rV \right) d\tau,$$

$$M_t = V_0 + \int_0^t e^{-r\tau}\sigma S \frac{\partial V}{\partial S} dW_\tau.$$

(b) Let

$$\mathcal{C} = \{(t, S_t) \colon V_t > Z_t\}$$

be the *continuation* region, and

$$\mathcal{S} = \{(t, S_t) \colon V_t = Z_t\},$$

the *stopping* region.
Prove that

$$M_t = M_s - \tilde{V}_s + \tilde{V}_t, \quad \text{for } (\tau, S_\tau) \in \mathcal{C}, \quad s \le \tau \le t,$$

$$M_t = M_s + \int_s^t e^{-r\tau} \sigma S \frac{\partial Z}{\partial S} dW_\tau, \quad \text{for } (\tau, S_\tau) \in \mathcal{S}, \quad s \le \tau \le t,$$

and $\sup_{t \in [0,T]} \big(\tilde{Z}_t - M_t\big)$ is attained for $(t, S_t) \in \mathcal{S}$.
The above equalities suggest how to construct the martingale $\tilde{M}_t$ in the continuation and stopping regions. In addition, the search for the supremum can be limited to the stopping region.

(c) Design an algorithm to compute the upper bound of an American option. Following the construction of the Longstaff–Schwartz algorithm, divide the time interval $[0, T]$ into N subintervals $0 = t_0 < t_1 < \cdots < t_N = T$ and simulate L sample paths on these subintervals.
Step 1. During the forward pass, compute the asset prices S_n^k.
Step 2. During the backward pass, compute the option prices V_n^k and retain $\hat{F}_{n,k}^M$ obtained during these computations.
Step 3. In the consecutive forward pass, compute the value of the martingale $\tilde{M}_t$. The procedure is as follows: in each time step n, and on each sample path k, compare the value $\hat{F}_{n,k}^M$ with the payoff $Z_{\tau_n}^k$. In the continuation region as the increment $\delta M^k = M_{t_{n+1}}^k - M_{t_n}^k$ take the increment of the option price $\delta \tilde{V}^k = \tilde{V}_{t_{n+1}}^k - \tilde{V}_{t_n}^k$, in the stopping region use the Euler–Maruyama scheme to approximate the integral

$$\int_{t_n}^{t_{n+1}} e^{-r\tau} \sigma S \frac{\partial Z}{\partial S} dW_\tau.$$

Tracking the difference $(\tilde{Z}_t^k - M_t^k)$ in these computations, obtain its maximum on each path $\text{MAX}^k = \max_{1 \le n \le N} (\tilde{Z}_{t_n}^k - M_{t_n}^k)$.

Estimate the upper bound of the option price as an average over the maxima of each path

$$V_0 = Z_0 + \frac{1}{L}\sum_{k=1}^{L} \mathrm{MAX}^k.$$

(d) Compute the lower and upper bounds of the American put option with parameters: initial stock price $S_0 = 40$, risk-free interest rate $r = 4.88\%$, volatility $\sigma = 20\%$, strike $K = 40, 45$, and time to maturity $T = 1$, 4, and 7 months.

Exercise 8.14. Consider the American *perpetual* put option, which is the American option for maturity time T tending to infinity. In the Black–Scholes model, the price of this option is given by the expression

$$V_\infty(S) = \sup_{\tau \in \mathcal{T}_{0,\infty}} \mathbb{E}\Big(e^{-r\tau} g\Big(S e^{(r-\sigma^2/2)\tau + \sigma W_\tau}\Big)\Big), \quad g(x) = (K - x)^+.$$

Prove that the price of the American perpetual option is given by the formula

$$V_\infty(S) = \begin{cases} (K - S), & \text{for } S \le S^*, \\ (K - S^*)\left(\frac{S}{S^*}\right)^{-\gamma}, & \text{for } S > S^*, \end{cases}$$

where $S^* = K\gamma/(1+\gamma)$ and $\gamma = 2r/\sigma^2$.
Hint: V_∞ as a time-independent function fulfills the stationary Black–Scholes equation

$$\frac{1}{2}\sigma^2 S^2 \frac{\partial^2 V_\infty}{\partial S^2} + rS\frac{\partial V_\infty}{\partial S} - rV_\infty = 0.$$

Under the substitution $x = \ln(S)$, the equation is reduced to a second-order linear ordinary differential equation that can be solved by standard methods.

Exercise 8.15. (Front fixing method [67]). Consider the partial differential equation for the price of an American put option in the

Black–Scholes model

$$\frac{\partial V}{\partial t} + \frac{1}{2}\sigma^2 S^2 \frac{\partial^2 V}{\partial S^2} + rS\frac{\partial V}{\partial S} - rV = 0, \quad S > B(t), t \in [0,T],$$
$$V(T,S) = (K-S)^+, \quad S \geq 0,$$
$$\frac{\partial V(t,B(t))}{\partial S} = -1, \quad t \in [0,T],$$
$$\lim_{S\to\infty} V(t,S) = 0, \quad t \in [0,T],$$
$$V(t,B(t)) = K - B(t), \quad t \in [0,T],$$
$$B(T) = K.$$

$B(t)$ is the *free boundary*, a curve on which an early exercise of the option occurs.

Introducing the Landau transform

$$x = \frac{S}{B(t)},$$

change the problem in a domain with moving boundary $S = B(t)$ to a problem in a fixed domain

$$\frac{\partial V}{\partial t} + \frac{1}{2}\sigma^2 x^2 \frac{\partial^2 V}{\partial x^2} + x\left(r - \frac{B'(t)}{B(t)}\right)\frac{\partial V}{\partial x} - rV = 0,$$
$$x \in (1,\infty), \quad t \in [0,T],$$
$$V(T,x) = 0, \quad x \geq 1,$$
$$\frac{\partial V(t,1)}{\partial x} = -B(t), \quad t \in [0,T],$$
$$\lim_{x\to\infty} V(t,x) = 0, \quad t \in [0,T],$$
$$V(t,1) = K - B(t), \quad t \in [0,T],$$
$$B(T) = K.$$

This transformation gives a differential equation in a fixed interval (no free boundary) but with two unknowns, namely option price V and free boundary $B(t)$.

(a) Set up a finite-difference scheme (use θ-scheme) to solve the above initial-boundary value problem. Let t_n, $n = 0, \ldots, N$, denote the nodes of the time approximation. Denote by V^n the vector approximating $V(t,x)$ and B^n the approximation of $B(t)$ at time level t_n. Derive the finite difference approximation of the above problem. Show that the approximation has the form

$$F(V^n, B^n) \equiv A(B^n)V^n - f(B^n) = 0,$$

where $A(B^n)$ is a tridiagonal matrix and $f(\cdot)$ is a vector with components $f_k(B^n)$, $k = 1, \ldots, M$, where M is the number of intervals in the discretization in the x-direction (remember to change the unbounded interval $(1, \infty)$ into a bounded interval $(1, x_{max})$). Compute matrix A and vector f.

(b) Compute the price of an American put solving equation $F(V^n, B^n) = 0$, for $n = N-1, \ldots, 0$, by Newton's iterative scheme using parameters: initial stock price $S_0 = 90$, risk-free interest rate $r = 5\%$, volatility $\sigma = 30\%$, strike $K = 100$, and time to maturity $T = 0.5$ year.

Exercise 8.16 (Brennan–Schwartz algorithm). The Brennan–Schwartz algorithm [12] is an algorithm that works for variational inequalities in finite-dimensional spaces. The algorithm is a modification of the Gaussian elimination algorithm and is based on the *LU* factorization of tridiagonal matrices.

Consider the following finite-dimensional variational inequality

$$Au \geq f,$$
$$u \geq g,$$
$$(Au - f, g - u) = 0.$$

Assume that A is a tridiagonal matrix

$$A = \begin{pmatrix} b_1 & c_1 & 0 & \ldots & 0 \\ a_2 & b_2 & c_2 & \ldots & 0 \\ 0 & \ddots & \ddots & \ddots & 0 \\ \vdots & \ddots & a_{m-1} & b_{m-1} & c_{m-1} \\ 0 & \ldots & 0 & a_m & b_m \end{pmatrix}.$$

The Brennan–Schwartz algorithm works as follows: if A is a tridiagonal matrix with $c_k = 0$ for $k = 1, \dots, m-1$, and $b_k > 0$ for $k = 1, \dots, m$, then the above variational inequality possesses a unique solution for all $f, g \in \mathbb{R}^m$. This solution is given by the expressions:

$$\begin{aligned} u_1 &= \max(g_1, f_1/b_1), \\ u_k &= \max(g_k, (f_k - a_k u_{k-1})/b_k), \quad k = 2, \dots, m. \end{aligned}$$

(a) Prove the validity of the described solution of the variational inequality.
(b) Prove that if matrix A is coercive, i.e., $(Au, u) \geq C|u|^2$ with $C > 0$, then the transformation

$$\begin{aligned} \hat{b}_m &= b_m, \\ \hat{b}_k = b_k - \big(c_k/\hat{b}_{k+1}\big)a_{k+1}, &\quad k = m-1, \dots, 1, \\ \hat{c}_k = 0, &\quad k = m-1, \dots, 1, \\ \hat{a}_k = a_k, &\quad k = m, \dots, 2, \end{aligned}$$

transforms matrix A into matrix $\hat{A}$ with all $\hat{b}_k > 0$ and all $\hat{c}_k = 0$.

Exercise 8.17. Consider an American put option in the Black–Scholes model. Applying transformations $\tau = T - t$, $x = \log S$, $u(\tau, x) = V(T - t, e^x)$ obtain the variational inequality

$$\begin{gathered} \frac{\partial u}{\partial \tau} - \frac{1}{2}\sigma^2 \frac{\partial^2 u}{\partial x^2} - b\frac{\partial u}{\partial x} + ru \geq 0, \\ u \geq g, \\ \left(\frac{\partial u}{\partial \tau} - \frac{1}{2}\sigma^2 \frac{\partial^2 u}{\partial x^2} - b\frac{\partial u}{\partial x} + ru\right)(g - u) = 0, \\ u(0) = g, \end{gathered}$$

where $b = (r - \sigma^2/2)$.

Apply the Brennan–Schwartz algorithm with the finite difference implicit Euler scheme to compute the price of the American put option with parameters: initial stock price $S_0 = 100$, risk-free interest rate $r = 3\%$, volatility $\sigma = 30\%$, strike $K = 90$, and time to maturity $T = 0.5$ year.

Exercise 8.18 (Primal-dual active set algorithm). To solve a discrete variational inequality, one must solve on each time step the linear problem (8.28)

$$QX \geq G,$$
$$X \geq \Phi,$$
$$(QX - G, X - \Phi) = 0.$$

Instead of reformulating this problem as the system (8.29), one can introduce a vector $\Lambda \in \mathbb{R}^{M+1}$ to obtain

$$QX - \Lambda = G,$$
$$X \geq \Phi, \quad \Lambda \geq 0,$$
$$(\Lambda, X - \Phi) = 0.$$

The above linear problem can be solved by the *primal-dual active set algorithm* [9] for matrices Q that are P-matrices (let us recall that a matrix A is the P-matrix if all its principal minors are positive). The problem is then solved by an iterative method with a regularized equation for vector Λ

$$QX - \Lambda = G,$$
$$\Lambda = \max\bigl(0, \Lambda + c(\Phi - X)\bigr),$$

where the function max is applied componentwise and $c > 0$.

With the sets

$$\mathcal{I}^- = \{i\colon \Lambda_i + c(\Phi - X)_i \leq 0\}, \quad \mathcal{I}^+ = \{i\colon \Lambda_i + c(\Phi - X)_i > 0\}$$

the primal-dual active set algorithm reads:

Step 1. Initialize Λ^0 and $X^0 \geq \Phi$. Choose the stopping criterion $\eta > 0$. Set $k = 0$.

Step 2. Set $\mathcal{I}_k^- = \{i\colon \Lambda_i^k + c(\Phi - X^k)_i \leq 0\}$ and $\mathcal{I}_k^+ = \{i\colon \Lambda_i^k + c(\Phi - X^k)_i > 0\}$.

Step 3. Solve

$$QX^{k+1} - \Lambda^{k+1} = G,$$
$$X^{k+1} = \Phi \quad \text{on } \mathcal{I}_k^+, \quad \Lambda^{k+1} = 0 \quad \text{on } \mathcal{I}_k^-.$$

Step 4. If $\|X^{k+1} - X^k\| < \eta$ **stop**; else next k.

Compute by the active set algorithm the price of the American vanilla put option with parameters: risk-free interest rate $r = 10\%$, volatility $\sigma = 30\%$, strike $K = 100$, and time to maturity $T = 1$ year. Compute the price of the option for the initial stock price S_0 taking values in all mesh points in the range $[50, 150]$, and find the approximate values of the free boundary $B(t)$.

Exercise 8.19. Consider the variational formulation for the American put price in the Black–Scholes model

$$\frac{\partial u}{\partial \tau} - \frac{1}{2}\sigma^2 \frac{\partial^2 u}{\partial x^2} - b\frac{\partial u}{\partial x} + ru \geq 0,$$

$$u \geq g,$$

$$\left(\frac{\partial u}{\partial \tau} - \frac{1}{2}\sigma^2 \frac{\partial^2 u}{\partial x^2} - b\frac{\partial u}{\partial x} + ru\right)(g - u) = 0,$$

$$u(0) = g,$$

where $\tau = T - t$, $x = \log S$, $b = (r - \sigma^2/2)$, and $g(x) = (K - e^x)^+$.

Confine the problem to a bounded domain $x \in [-R, R]$. Introduce a partition of the interval $[-R, R]$ into subintervals $K_j = (x_{j-1}, x_j)$, $1 \leq j \leq M$, such that $-R = x_0 < x_1 < \cdots < x_M = R$. If the size of the interval K_j is h_j, set $h = \max_j h_j$. Define the discrete space V_h as the space spanned by linear hat functions

$$V_h = \{v_h \in X_h^1\colon\ v_h(-R) = g(-R), v_h(R) = g(R)\}.$$

Denote by $u_h(\tau, x)$ the solution of the above variational inequality in space V_h. Expanding $u_h = \sum_{i=1}^{M_r} w_i(\tau)\phi_i(x)$ in a basis $\{\phi_i\}_{i=1}^{M_r}$ of V_h, where M_r is the dimension of V_h, reduce the problem to the search for a vector $W(\tau) = (w_1(\tau), \ldots, w_{M_r}(\tau))$. Apply the implicit Euler scheme in time to obtain the discrete linear complementarity problem for vectors W^n, $n = 0, \ldots, N$, which are a discrete approximation of $W(\tau)$

$$W^n \geq g_h, \quad n = 1, \ldots, N,$$

$$E_h(W^{n+1} - W^n) + \delta t A_h W^n \geq 0,$$

$$(g_h - W^{n+1})(E_h(W^{n+1} - W^n) + \delta t A_h W^n) = 0,$$

$$W^0 = g_h,$$

where E_h and A_h are the mass and stiffness matrices, respectively.

Reformulate the above complementarity problem as a linear problem suitable for the projected SOR algorithm

$$QX \geq G,$$
$$X \geq \Phi,$$
$$(QX - G, X - \Phi) = 0.$$

Solve the linear system with the PSOR algorithm to obtain the price of the American put option with parameters: risk-free interest rate $r = 10\%$, volatility $\sigma = 30\%$, strike $K = 100$, and time to maturity $T = 1$ year. Take the integration domain $[-R, R]$ with $R = 200$. Compute the option price for the initial stock price, taking values at the mesh points x_j in the range $[-50, 50]$.

Exercise 8.20. The floating strike lookback put option is an option with the payoff

$$g(t, S_t) = M_t - S_t, \quad \text{where } M_t = \max_{0 \leq \tau \leq t} S_\tau.$$

The price of this option $V = V(t, S, M)$ depends not only on time t and stock price S but also on the maximum M. The variational problem for American floating lookback options is usually formulated after similarity reduction. After defining the variables

$$x = \frac{M}{S}, \quad V(t, S, M) = SW(t, x)$$

the variational problem reads

$$\left(\frac{\partial W}{\partial t} + \frac{1}{2}\sigma^2 x^2 \frac{\partial^2 W}{\partial x^2} - rx\frac{\partial W}{\partial x}\right)(W - x + 1) = 0, \quad x > 1, \quad t \in [0, T),$$
$$\frac{\partial W}{\partial t} + \frac{1}{2}\sigma^2 x^2 \frac{\partial^2 W}{\partial x^2} - rx\frac{\partial W}{\partial x} \leq 0, \quad x > 1, \quad t \in [0, T),$$
$$W(t, x) \geq x - 1, \quad x > 1, \quad t \in [0, T),$$
$$W(T, x) = x - 1, \quad x > 1,$$
$$\frac{\partial W(t, 1)}{\partial x} = 0, \quad t \in [0, T].$$

Solve the above variational inequality by the penalty method. Compute the price of the American floating put lookback option with parameters: initial stock price $S_0 = 50$, risk-free interest rate $r = 6\%$, volatility $\sigma = 40\%$, and time to maturity $T = 1$ year.

Exercise 8.21. Consider an American vanilla put with parameters: initial stock price $S_0 = 100$, risk-free interest rate $r = 5\%$, strike $K = 90$, dividend rate $q = 1.75\%$, volatility $\sigma = 30\%$, and time to maturity $T = 1$ year.

Compute the free boundary of this option. Consider different numerical methods: PSOR, penalty, Brennan–Schwartz, and front fixing. Choose the method that, in your opinion, seems to be the most efficient.

References

[1] Y. Achdou and O. Pironneau. *Computational Methods for Option Pricing*, Society for Industrial and Applied Mathematics (SIAM), Philadelphia, PA, 2005.

[2] L. Andersen and J. Andreasen. Volatility skews and extensions of the Libor market model, *Appl. Math. Finance*, **7** (2000), 1–32.

[3] S. Asmussen and P. W. Glynn. *Stochastic Simulation: Algorithms and Analysis*, Springer, New York, 2007.

[4] R. W. Bailey. Polar generation of random variates with the t-distribution, *Math. Comp.*, **62** (1994), 779–781.

[5] V. Bally and D. Talay. The distribution of the Euler scheme for stochastic differential equations: I. Convergence rate of the distribution function, *Probab. Theory Relat. Fields*, **104** (1996), 43–60.

[6] S. Barle and N. Cakici. Growing a smiling tree, *J. Fin. Engin.* **7** (1998), 127–146.

[7] J. D. Beasley and S. G. Springer. The percentage points of the normal distribution, *Appl. Stat. J. Roy. St. C*, **26** (1977), 118–121.

[8] A. Bensoussan and J. L. Lions. *Applications of Variational Inequalities in Stochastic Control*, North-Holland, Amsterdam, 1982.

[9] M. Bergounioux, K. Ito, and K. Kunisch. Primal-dual strategy for constrained optimal control problems, *SIAM J. Control Optim.*, **37** (1999), 1176–1194.

[10] J. F. Bonnans. *Numerical Analysis of Partial Differential Equations Arising in Finance*, Lecture notes, available on the web page of the author, 2018.

[11] P. Boyle. Options: A Monte Carlo approach, *J. Financ. Econ.*, **4** (1977), 323–338.

[12] M. J. Brennan and E. S. Schwartz. The valuation of the American put option, *J. Finance*, **32** (1977), 449–462.

[13] H. Brézis. Inéquations variationnelles paraboliques, Séminaire Jean Leray (1971), exp. No. 7, pp. 1–10.

[14] M. Broadie and J. Detemple. American option valuation: New bounds, approximations, and a comparison of existing methods, *Rev. Financ. Stud.*, **9** (1996), 1211–1250.

[15] R. C. H. Cheng. The generation of gamma variables with non-integral shape parameter, *Applied Statistics*, **26** (1977), 71–76.

[16] E. Clément, D. Lamberton, and P. Protter. An analysis of the Longstaff-Schwartz algorithm for American option pricing, *Financ. Stoch.*, **6** (2002), 449–471.

[17] R. Courant, K. Friedrichs, and H. Lewy. Über die partiellen Differenzengleichungen der mathematischen Physik, *Math. Ann.*, **100**(1), (1928), 32–74; English translation: On the partial difference equations of mathematical physics, *IBM J.*, **11** (1967), 215–234.

[18] J. C. Cox, S. A. Ross, and M. Rubinstein. Option pricing: A simplified approach, *J. Financ. Econ.*, **7** (1979), 229–263.

[19] C.W. Cryer. The solution of a quadratic programming problem using systematic overrelaxation, *SIAM J. Control*, **9** (1971), 385–392.

[20] S. Dekel and D. Leviatan. The Bramble–Hilbert lemma for convex domains, *SIAM J. Math. Anal.*, **35**(5) (2004), 1203–1212.

[21] E. Derman and I. Kani. Riding on a smile, *Risk*, **7**(2) (1994), 32–39.

[22] J. Dick and F. Pillichshammer. *Digital Nets and Sequences*, Cambridge University Press, 2010.

[23] D. J. Duffy. *Finite Difference Methods in Financial Engineering*, John Wiley & Sons, Chichester, 2006.

[24] E. Eberlein and J. Kallsen. *Mathematical Finance*, Springer Switzerland, 2019.

[25] D. Egloff. Monte Carlo algorithms for optimal stopping and statistical learning, *Ann. Appl. Probab.*, **15** (2005), 1396–1432.

[26] R. J. Elliott and P. E. Kopp. *Mathematics of Financial Markets*, Springer Finance, New York, 1999.

[27] N. El Karoui. Les aspects probabilistes du contrôle stochastique, in *Lecture Notes in Mathematics* Vol. 876, Springer, New York, 1981, pp. 72–238.

[28] N. El Karoui, C. Kapoudjian, E. Pardoux, S. Peng, and M. C. Quenez. Reflected solutions of backward SDE's, and related obstacle problems for PDE's, *Ann. Probab.*, **25** (1997), 702–737.

[29] L. C. Evans. *Partial Differential Equations*, American Mathematical Society, Providence, RI, 1998.

[30] A. Fog. Pseudo-random number generators for vector processors and multicore processors, *J. Modern Applied Statistical Methods*, **14**(1) (2015), 308–334.

[31] P. A. Forsyth and K. R. Vetzal. Quadratic convergence for valuing American options using a penalty method, *SIAM J. Sci. Comput.*, **23** (2002), 2095–2122.

[32] A. Friedman. *Stochastic Differential Equations and Applications*, Vol. 1, Academic Press, New York, 1975.

[33] J. E. Gentle. *Random Number Generation and Monte Carlo Methods*, Springer, New York, 2005.

[34] P. Glasserman. *Monte Carlo Methods in Financial Engineering*, Springer, New York, 2004.

[35] R. Glowinski, J.-L. Lions and R. Trémollières. *Analyse numérique des inéquations variationnelles*, Dunod, Paris, 1976.

[36] J. H. Halton. On the efficiency of certain quasi-random sequences of points in evaluating multi-dimensional integrals, *Numer. Math.*, **2** (1960), 84–90.

[37] D. J. Higham. Nine ways to implement the binomial method for option valuation in MATLAB, *SIAM Rev.*, **44** (2002), 661–677.

[38] N. Hilber, O. Reichmann, C. Schwab and C. Winter. *Computational Methods for Quantitative Finance*, Springer, Berlin, 2013.

[39] A. Hirsa. *Computational Methods in Finance*, CRC Press, Taylor & Francis Group, Boca Raton, 2013.

[40] J. Hull. *Options, Futures, and Other Derivatives*, Pearson, New Jersey, 11th edition, 2022.

[41] J. Hull and A. White. Numerical procedures for implementing term structure models I: Single-factor models, *J. Derivatives*, **2**(1) (Fall 1994) 7–16.

[42] P. Jäckel. *Monte-Carlo Methods in Finance*, Wiley Finance Series, John Wiley & Sons, Chichester, 2002.

[43] P. Jaillet, D. Lamberton, and B. Lapeyre. Variational inequalities and the pricing of American options, *Acta Appl. Math.*, **21** (1990), 263–289.

[44] R. Jarrow and A. Rudd. *Option Pricing*, Richard D. Irwin, Homewood, Ill., 1983.

[45] M. Jeanblanc, M. Yor and M. Chesney. *Mathematical Methods for Financial Markets*, Springer, London, 2009.

[46] S. Joe and F. Y. Kuo. Constructing Sobol' sequences with better two-dimensional projections. *SIAM J. Sci. Comput.*, **30** (2008), 2635–2654.

[47] B. Kamrad and P. Ritchken. Multinomial approximating models for options with k-state variables, *Manage. Sci.*, **37**(12) (1991), 1640–1652.

[48] I. Karatzas and S. E. Shreve. *Brownian Motion and Stochastic Calculus*, Springer, New York, second edition, 1991.

[49] I. Karatzas and S. Shreve. *Methods of Mathematical Finance*, Springer-Verlag, New York, 1998.

[50] A. G. Z. Kemna and A. C. F Vorst. A pricing method for options based on average asset values, *J. Banking Finan.*, **14** (1990), 113–129.

[51] P. E. Kloeden and E. Platen. *Numerical Solution of Stochastic Differential Equations*, Springer, New York, 1992.

[52] A. Kohatsu-Higa and M. Montero. Malliavin calculus in finance, in S. T. Rachev (Eds.), *Handbook of Computational and Numerical Methods in Finance*, Birkhäuser, Boston, 2004, pp. 111–174.

[53] N. V. Krylov. *Introduction to the Theory of Diffusion Processes*, American Mathematical Society, Providence, RI, 1995.

[54] H. Kunita. *Stochastic Differential Equations and Stochastic Flows of Diffeomorphisms* in *Lecture Notes in Mathematics* Vol. 1097, Springer, Berlin, 1984, pp. 143–303.

[55] D. Lamberton and B. Lapeyre. *Introduction to Stochastic Calculus Applied to Finance*, Chapman & Hall/CRC, Boca Raton, second edition, 2008.

[56] P. L'Ecuyer. Efficient and portable combined random number generators, *Commun. ACM*, **31** (1988), 742–749.

[57] P. L'Ecuyer and R. Simard. TestU01: A C library for empirical testing of random number generators, *ACM Trans. Math. Softw.*, **33**(4) (August 2007), Article 22.

[58] M. G. Larson and F. Bengzon. *The Finite Element Method: Theory, Implementation, and Practice*, Springer, Berlin, 2013.

[59] S. Larsson and V. Thomée. *Partial Differential Equations with Numerical Methods*, Springer, Berlin, 2009.

[60] F. A. Longstaff and E. S. Schwartz. Valuing American options by simulation: a simple least-squares approach, *Rev. Financ. Stud.*, **14** (2001), 113–147.

[61] G. Marsaglia. Random numbers fall mainly in the planes, *Proc. Nat. Acad. Sci. USA*, **61** (1968), 23–28.

[62] G. Marsaglia. Xorshift RNGs, *J. Stat. Soft.*, **8**(14) (2003), 1–6.

[63] M. Matsumoto and T. Nishimura. Mersenne twister: A 623-dimensionally equidistributed uniform pseudo-random number generator, *ACM Trans. Model. Comput. Simul.*, **8**(1) (1998), 3–30.

[64] B. Moro. The full monte, *Risk*, **8**(2) (1995), 57–58.

[65] K. W. Morton and D. F. Mayers. *Numerical Solution of Partial Differential Equations*, Cambridge University Press, 2005.

[66] H. R. Neave. On using the Box–Muller transformation with multiplicative congruential pseudo-random number generators, *Appl. Stat. J. Roy. St. C*, **22** (1973), 92–97.

[67] B. F. Nielson, O. Skavhaug, and A. Tvelto. Penalty and front-fixing methods for the numerical solution of American option problems, *J. Comp. Finan.*, **5**(4) (2002), 69–97.

[68] B. Øksendal and K. Reikvam. Viscosity solutions of optimal stopping problems, *Stochastics Stochastics Rep.*, **62** (1998), 285–301.

[69] B. Øksendal. *Stochastic Differential Equations: An Introduction with Applications*, Springer-Verlag, Heidelberg, New York, 2003.

[70] G. Pagès. *Numerical Probability: An Introduction with Applications to Finance*, Springer, 2018.

[71] A. Palczewski. Partial Schauder estimates for unbounded solutions of the Kolmogorov equation, *J. Elliptic Parabol. Equ.*, (2025), in press.

[72] F. Panneton, P. L'Ecuyer, and M. Matsumoto. Improved long-period generators based on linear recurrences modulo 2, *ACM Trans. Math. Softw.*, **32**(1) (2006), 1–16.

[73] A. Pascucci. *PDE and Martingale Methods in Option Pricing*, Springer, 2011.

[74] A. Quarteroni. *Numerical Models for Differential Problems*, Springer Italia, second edition, 2014.

[75] A. Quarteroni and A. Valli. *Numerical Approximation of Partial Differential Equations*, Springer, Berlin, 1994.

[76] L. C. G. Rogers. Monte Carlo valuation of American options, *Math. Finance*, **12** (2002), 271–286.

[77] M. Saito and M. Matsumoto. SIMD-oriented fast Mersenne twister: a 128-Bit pseudorandom number generator, in A. Keller, S. Heinrich, and H. Niederreiter (Eds.), *Monte Carlo and Quasi-Monte Carlo Methods 2006*, New York, Springer, 2008, pp. 607–622.

[78] M. Schroder. Computing the constant elasticity of variance option pricing formula, *J. Finance*, **44**(1) (1989), 211–219.

[79] R. Seydel. *Tools for Computational Finance*, Springer, London, sixth edition, 2017.

[80] W. T. Shaw, T. Luu and N. Brickman. Quantile mechanics II: Changes of variables in Monte Carlo methods and GPU-optimized normal quantiles, http://arxiv.org/abs/0901.0638v5 (ver. October 23, 2018).

[81] A. N. Shiryaev. *Essentials of Stochastic Finance: Facts, Models, Theory*, World Scientific, Singapore, 2003.

[82] S. Shreve. *Stochastic Calculus for Finance II: Continuous-time Models*, Springer-Verlag, New York, 2004.

[83] I. M. Sobol. On the distribution of points in a cube and the approximate evaluation of integrals, *USSR Comp. Math. Math. Phys.*, **7** (1967), 86–112.

[84] L. Stentoft. Convergence of the least squares Monte Carlo approach to American option valuation, *Manage. Sci.*, **50**(9) (2004), 1193–1203.

[85] J. C. Strikwerda. *Finite Difference Schemes and Partial Differential Equations*, Society for Industrial and Applied Mathematics (SIAM), Philadelphia, PA, 2004.

[86] D. Talay and L. Tubaro. Expansion of the global error for numerical schemes solving stochastic differential equations. *Stoch. Anal. Appl.*, **8** (1990), 94–120.
[87] J. W. Thomas. *Numerical Partial Differential Equations: Finite Difference Methods*, Springer, Berlin, 1995.
[88] V. Thomée. *Galerkin Finite Element Methods for Parabolic Problems*, Springer, Berlin, second edition, 2006.
[89] Y. Tian. A flexible binomial option pricing model, *J. Fut. Market*, **19** (1999), 817–843.
[90] J. N. Tsitsiklis and B. Van Roy. Regression methods for pricing complex American-style options, *IEEE Trans. Neural Net.*, **12**(4) (2001), 694–703.
[91] Y. Wang and R.E. Caflisch. Martingales and upper bounds for American-style options, *Comm. Math. Sci.*, **13**(3) (2015), 695–705.
[92] D. Zanger. Convergence of a least-squares Monte Carlo algorithm for bounded approximating sets, *Appl. Math. Finance*, **16** (2009), 123–150.
[93] D. Zanger. Quantitative error estimates for a least-squares Monte Carlo algorithm for American option pricing, *Financ. Stoch.*, **17** (2013), 503–534.
[94] X. L. Zhang. Numerical analysis of American option pricing in a jump-diffusion model, *Math. Oper. Res.*, **22** (1997), 668–690.

Index

F

G

H

I

J

K

L

S

T

U

V

W

X

Z